S0-ACK-602

CARL A. RUDISILL LIBRARY
LENOIR-RHYNE COLLEGE

# ACROSS THE WIDE MISSOURI

Oh, Shennydore, I long to hear you.
Away, you rolling river!
Oh, Shennydore, I can't get near you.
Away, away, I'm bound away
Across the wide Missouri.

'Tis seven long years since first I seed 'ee.
Away, you rolling river!
'Tis seven long years since first I seed 'ee.
Away, away, I'm bound away
Across the wide Missouri.

Oh, Shennydore, I love your daughter.
Away, you rolling river!
I'll take her across the yellow water.
Away, away, I'm bound away
Across the wide Missouri.

*Books by Bernard DeVoto*

THE CROOKED MILE

THE CHARIOT OF FIRE

THE HOUSE OF SUN-GOES-DOWN

MARK TWAIN'S AMERICA

WE ACCEPT WITH PLEASURE

FORAYS AND REBUTTALS

MINORITY REPORT

MARK TWAIN AT WORK

THE YEAR OF DECISION

LITERARY FALLACY

MOUNTAIN TIME

ACROSS THE WIDE MISSOURI

# ACROSS THE WIDE MISSOURI

*by*

BERNARD DeVOTO

*Illustrated with Paintings by*

ALFRED JACOB MILLER,

CHARLES BODMER *and* GEORGE CATLIN

*With an Account of the Discovery of the Miller Collection by*

MAE REED PORTER

AMERICAN LEGACY PRESS • NEW YORK

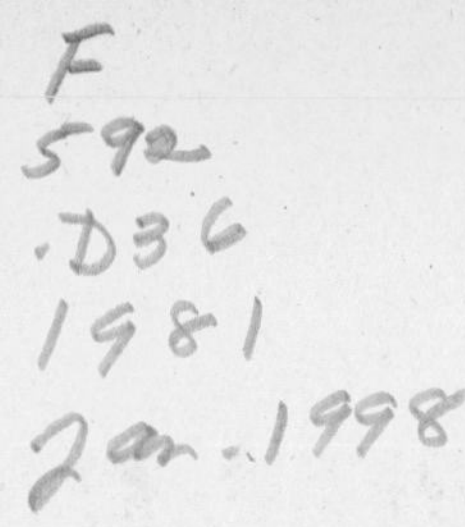



This edition is published by American Legacy Press,
distributed by Crown Publishers, Inc.,
by arrangement with Houghton Mifflin Company.
h g f e d c b a
Manufactured in the United States of America

American Legacy Press is a trademark of Crown Publishers, Inc.

Library of Congress Cataloging in Publication Data
De Voto, Bernard Augustine, 1897-1955.
Across the wide Missouri.

Reprint. Originally published: Boston: Houghton Mifflin, 1947.
Bibliography: p. 454.
Includes index.
1. Fur trade—West (U.S.) 2. West (U.S.)—History—To 1848. 3. West (U.S.)—Description and travel—To 1848. 4. Miller, Alfred Jacob, 1810-1874—Art Collections. I. Miller, Alfred Jacob, 1810-1874. II. Title.
F592.D36 1981 978'.02 81-10987
ISBN 0-517-10266-8 AACR2

TO

*Garrett Mattingly*

Dear Mat:

The ethics of literary reticence restrain me from printing on my title page, 'In collaboration with Garrett Mattingly's ideas.' Instead I print your name here to acknowledge the conversion of your property, for if anything in my text rises above information, I have taken it from you. And not only to acknowledge that the historian of Renaissance England has been working in the Rocky Mountains for a long time, teaching me most of what I know, but for other reasons too: because we look at men and events and the experiences of life without parallax, because it has been our good fortune to dismay the same minds, and because we have been friends since Noah's boyhood. So here is some more of the West, and in your tolerance it may be history.

Yours,

Benny

# ACKNOWLEDGMENTS

MY GREATEST DEBT in connection with this book is to Mae Reed Porter, the initiator and tireless forwarder of the complicated enterprise from which it has resulted, and to those who with her have granted me permission to reproduce the paintings of Alfred Jacob Miller: L. Vernon Miller, Alfred J. Miller, Lloyd O. Miller, Mrs. Joseph Whyte, and the Walters Art Gallery, all of Baltimore, the Boston Athenaeum, the New York Public Library, and the United States National Museum.

Much of my work has been done in museums. I have spent many days in the collections of the American Museum of Natural History and the Peabody Museum of Harvard University, and for information, guidance, criticism, and advice I am especially indebted to Dr. Bella Weisner of the former and Mr. Donald Scott, Dr. Joseph O. Brew, Mrs. Helen Whiting, and Miss Constance Ashenden of the latter. My debt to the National Museum arises less from Indian material than from its collection of Catlin paintings and from the advice and information patiently given me by Dr. Robert A. Elder, Jr., in person and by correspondence. I also owe a special debt to Mrs. Pierce Butler, curator of the Ayer Collection, and Mr. Stanley Pargellis, Librarian, of the Newberry Library of Chicago, and to Mr. Charles Nagel, lately of the City Art Museum of St. Louis, but now Director of the Brooklyn Art Museum. I should like to thank by name many officials and attendants of many art museums in the eastern half of the United States who patiently assisted an inquiry which some of them certainly considered absurd, but we were always nameless to each other.

Among librarians Mrs. Brenda Gieseker of the Missouri Historical Society and Miss Carolyn Jakeman of the Houghton

Library at Harvard have suffered most repeatedly from my ignorance, but have suffered cheerfully and worked with unfailing ingenuity at the task of reducing it. Everything in my text that is based on material in the Missouri Historical Society comes from inquiries made for me or photostats or microfilms sent to me by Mrs. Gieseker, who has guided me through far more material than is referred to. Miss Jakeman was called upon to follow leads for me or to suggest leads to me two or three times a week for eighteen months. My thanks to both her and Mrs. Gieseker carries the postscript that I have begun work on another book that will involve them in research.

I am indebted further to officers and attendants of the following libraries: the Henry E. Huntington Library, and especially Dixon Wecter, Robert G. Cleland, and Haydée Noya; the Minnesota Historical Society, and especially Mrs. Ilse Levi; the New York Public Library; the Boston Athenaeum; the New York Historical Society; the Bancroft Library; Yale University Library; the Wisconsin Historical Society; the Massachusetts Historical Society; the American Antiquarian Society.

Quotations from the Fort Union Letter Book, the letters of William Drummond Stewart, and a ledger of the American Fur Company and other manuscripts, specifically cited by footnote, are by permission of the Missouri Historical Society. Quotations from the journal of Mary Walker are by permission of the Henry E. Huntington Library.

Certain specific debts must be acknowledged by name. Dr. Robert Taft of the University of Kansas performed spectacular rescue work on my manuscript in the last quarter of the eleventh hour, saving me from spectacular errors in my discussion of early illustrators of the West and supplying me with information to take their place. Dr. Robert G. Cleland of the Huntington Library, with similar generosity, has operated on my Chapter VI, but he must be absolved from all responsibility for what I say in my own person when I trespass on his territory, the California aspects of the fur trade. Dr. J. Hall Pleasants of Baltimore and Dr. Macgill James of the National Gallery turned over to me their laboriously acquired notes on Miller and advised me in the difficult job of chasing down a few minutiae they had missed. Dr. James is the rediscoverer of Miller, the author of the first modern accounts of him and his pictures (which are the basis of everything since written), the curator who first mounted a Miller exhibition, and in general the blazer of trails and the discoverer of nuggets. I have also had much more than casual help from Henry Nash Smith and Donald McKay Frost. In the republic of learning it is an honor to be the almsman of such men.

Anyone who works in Americana and does not owe a sizable debt to the wisest head of them all, Charles P. Everitt, knows less than he might and has missed more than he ought. This is to thank him for good talk, invaluable information, assistance of many kinds, some of it perhaps best left unspecified, and the faith in the job undertaken that is the most important service anyone can give a writer. I hope to drink a horn of Taos Lightning to him at exactly 11 A.M. on the day this book is published and many a horn with him thereafter.

It is impossible to list all those who have given me help or information or put me in the way of acquiring it, but I should like to thank: Robert Henry Aldrich, Anne Barrett, Mary B. Brazier, Elaine Breed, Clarence S. Brigham, Paul Brooks, Lyman Butterfield, Roger Butterfield, R. Carlyle Buley, Charles L. Camp, Carvel Collins, Elmer Davis, H. L. Davis, Walt L. Dutton, Ira N. Gabrielson, Perry W. Jenkins, Frederick Merk, Perry Miller, Samuel E. Morison, Theodore Morrison, Henry Reck, Marian Roman, Anna Wells Rutledge, Arthur M. Schlesinger, Jr., Claude Simpson, Martha Stiles, Parian Temple, Lovell Thompson, Ann Williams.

The Index, which is incomparably better than any I could have made myself, is by Mrs. Marguerite Reed.

# PREFACE

THIS BOOK deals with the Rocky Mountain fur trade during the years of its climax and decline. I have not tried to write a comprehensive history even of those years. Since 1902 when General Hiram M. Chittenden published *The American Fur Trade of the Far West*, which remains the most valuable single book about the trade and the only general history of it, a staggering amount of new material has come to light and a great deal of scholarly work has been done on it. It is past time for someone to synthesize all this material and write a modern history. But no such synthesis is attempted here.

Instead I have tried to describe the mountain fur trade as a business and as a way of life: what its characteristic experiences were, what conditions governed them, how it helped to shape our heritage, what its relation was to the western expansion of the United States, most of all how the mountain men lived. And it is my privilege to illustrate my text with pictures of great historical importance. These are watercolors by a heretofore neglected painter, Alfred Jacob Miller of Baltimore. They are the only paintings of Rocky Mountain trappers actually made on the spot and the first paintings ever made of the Rocky Mountains, the scenery along the trail to Oregon, and the Westernmost Plains Indians. Most of them are here published for the first time.

That the book takes the particular form it does is due to an accidental combination of circumstance.

Some years ago Mrs. Clyde Porter of Kansas City became interested in the then almost unknown paintings of Miller. Realizing their unique importance, she determined to rescue Miller from obscurity and to secure for him the place in our history to which he is entitled. She began to lecture about him to historical and artistic bodies and she undertook to get his paintings published. For several years she suffered repeated disappointments. Publishers were operating under war conditions and so were unable to get paper of the quality and in the amount required, and they were unwilling to assume the very heavy financial burden imposed by color processes. In spite of discouragements that would have broken a less resolute purpose, she persevered until Houghton Mifflin Company undertook the present venture. Which is where I enter.

As a historian (riding on the commuter's local) I have interested myself in the growth among the American people of the feeling that they were properly a single nation between the two oceans: in the development of what I have called the continental mind. It is an austere labor and I have long sought relaxation from it by reading the annals of the mountain fur trade. For some time I have had in mind writing a book which might entertain the general reader with stories from those annals and at the same time focus and clarify for him some ideas about the trade. There are many monographs and specialized treatments of the trade. There are a number of popular syntheses of them, but too many of these lack both depth and accuracy and few seem aware that the fur trade was connected with anything else. When Houghton Mifflin Company invited me to write a book on the fur trade and proposed to illustrate it with Miller's pictures, I suggested one which would indicate the larger outline of the trade, fill in the outline with enough details to make it intelligible to a contemporary reader, and relate the parts to one another and especially to westward expansion as a whole. I shall have succeeded if the reader gets from the book a sense of time hurrying on while between the Missouri and the Pacific a thousand or so men of no moment whatever are living an exciting and singularly uncertain life, hurrying one era of our history to a close, and thereby making possible another one, one which began with the almost seismic enlargement of our boundaries and consciousness of which I have written elsewhere.

In the scholarship of Western history there remain many small and some large gaps. A number of the small ones I have filled in: some matters that were previously in question are settled by this text. In dealing with certain other hiatuses, however, I have had to follow authority in places where authority is open to question. The most important of these concern Bonneville, who needs exhaustive investigation by a qualified scholar.

I have specifically indicated in the text or by a note every instance in which I rest on second-hand knowledge. All factual statements not so marked rest on original sources, compared, appraised, and reconciled as well as I know how. All detailed accounts of events are from the stories of eyewitnesses. All descriptions are also first-hand, most of them supported by my own acquaintance with the country: the landscape of the fur trade has changed little in a hundred and ten years.

The nature of the enterprise has made Alfred Miller's patron, Sir William Drummond Stewart, the unifying force in the book so far as it has one. Not much all told can be found out about him; he left exceedingly little record of his seven years in the West. I point out, however, that the same is true of almost everyone else who took part in the mountain trade. The biographies of even the mountain men who were nationally spotlighted, Kit Carson for instance, or Tom Fitzpatrick, or Jim Bridger, necessarily rest on a thin basis of fact which must be amplified by the critical but still precarious deduction that puts the heaviest strain on a historian. But though Stewart's own record of his years in the Far West is meager and though the largest part of it is contained in footnotes to one of his novels, the records of the trade are tolerably complete in regard to the various parties he is known to have accompanied and the principal events in which he participated. Happily he saw all the important aspects of the trade during the six years of his first wandering in the West.

In addition to those six years I have treated the events of the year before Stewart first went west. The narrative runs from 1832 through 1838.

It has seemed best to treat separately the question of Miller's place in history. An appendix brings him into relation with Catlin, Bodmer, and the artistic conventions of his period. He enters the text itself only as an actor in the narrative or as the illustrator of it.

I have tried to maintain a decent uniformity in the spelling of names, especially place names and surnames. There is something of a guerrilla warfare among Western historians and antiquarians over spellings and I expect the usual denunciations from owners in fee simple of ingenious systems or of inspirations denied me. Since many of those who took part in the mountain trade were illiterate and practically all those who could write were spellers of uncommon versatility and enthusiasm, these disputes seem to me pointless. Few trappers were certain how to spell their own names or those of their companions or those of the landmarks they guided by; fewer still cared. So prominent a partisan as Andrew Drips signed his name in two ways and is carried on the books of the American Fur Company under both spellings. Etienne Provost is also Provot and Proveau in the literature and Provo on the map of Utah. Pierre Papin and Jean Richard are recorded in at least four spellings each, but that is a moderate variability: I have counted eleven different spellings of Bordeau, the bourgeois of Fort Laramie who entertained Francis Parkman. It seems to me that where accuracy is impossible consistency counts most. I use the official government spellings of place names except in a few instances where the government itself is not consistent and a few others where I think that my version has some historical value.

If anyone reads this book who has read earlier works of mine in which Indians figure, he will observe that herein I have emancipated myself from a pedantry of my betters. I was brought up to respect learned men and few scholars impress me so profoundly as the ethnologists. So heretofore, mutely enduring the discomfort natural to a literary man, I have used the spellings of Indian plurals that their guild oaths impose. It seems that when you bring Indian tribal names into English from the mother tongue, the plural has the same form as the singular. The ethnologist's medicine has commanded him in a vision to stand on those plurals, even when they are clearly English words, and neither logic nor a decent sensitiveness to style will move him to violate the sacred teaching. Up to now I have followed his precept, forcing myself to write not only 'twenty-one Arapaho' but also 'thirty-eight Crow' and even, God help us, 'one hundred and two Blackfoot.' But at last I have encountered an ethnologist who is willing to defy the rules committee, and one is all I need. 'There is no more sense,' George E. Hyde writes, 'in writing "seven Oglala" than in writing "seven Spaniard" or "seven western state." ' Check. I intend to write 'Blackfeet' from now on.

BERNARD DEVOTO

CAMBRIDGE, MASSACHUSETTS
*March 1, 1946.*

# FOREWORD

by Mae Reed Porter

Twenty-five years ago, when we lived in the little town of Glasgow, our house sat high on a hill overlooking the Missouri River. It was one of the chief delights of the family to sit on the pillared, honeysuckle-vined porch just watching the water. Occasionally a show boat tied up at the foot of the hill and sometimes there were shrill whistles from the government snag boats that took our imaginations back to the steamboat days when Glasgow was a river town of importance — even a challenge to St. Louis.

Several retired steamboat pilots, who told great tales of the glories and the tragedies of their period, still lived in the town, and when I realized that Lewis and Clark had, in 1804, passed our hill, I read their journal to see how it had looked to them. I found they had camped on the prairie across the river on Sunday, June 10; that so great a wind was blowing they remained for two days and had shot a buck and a bear. They reported our hill covered with a tangle of wild grapevines and trees.

Farther along in the journal I found that they spent the winter in the Dakota Mandan Country and on April 4, 1805, they were packing boxes of articles to be sent back to President Jefferson. These boxes contained stuffed antelope, a buffalo robe representing a battle fought in the neighborhood six years before, implements of Indian warfare, an ear of Mandan corn, plants, insects, and several cases of live things including a burrowing squirrel, a prairie hen, and four magpies.

Some years later I learned that Thomas Jefferson had the collection in his home at Monticello and that at his death it had been sent to a Peale Museum. I was determined to visit this museum and see what might remain of the collection.

In 1935, my chance came when my daughter and I visited the Peale Museum in Baltimore. Here we were disappointed to learn that the Lewis and Clark collection had been housed in the Philadelphia Peale Museum and that the building had burned years ago.

As we turned to go, Miss Margery Whyte, the secretary, said: 'If you are interested in Western history I have something in storage I might show to you.'

She brought out a pasteboard carton and placed it on a table. 'This is a collection of spot sketches on loan with us,' she said. 'They were painted by a young Baltimore artist, Alfred Miller, in 1837–38, while on an expedition into the West with a Sir William Drummond Stewart. We had an exhibition of them here a few years ago and if you will pick out a number, I will put some of them out again.'

We removed the newspaper covering from the top of the box and, filled with curiosity, began to lift out the contents — unmounted watercolor sketches one hundred years old and as fresh in color as the day they were painted. As we drew out one after another, we were impressed by their beauty and the story they told. They were of many sizes, and each one had been labeled by the artist with tiny penciled notes; 'make larger,' 'dust,' and so on. Miss Whyte explained that the sketches were made hastily, as the party traveled along, to be used as patterns for huge oil paintings that Sir William wished to place on the walls of his castle in Perthshire, Scotland.

Highly disgusted with life as a second son of one of the most ancient families of Great Britain, he had come to America in 1832 as plain Captain Stewart, but during his almost four years in the far West his status was to change, with the death of his brother Sir George. Not knowing that the Baronetcy waited, Stewart turned again west, this time with the artist Miller who was to provide him with reminders of the wild and romantic life he had found there.

Miss Whyte said that, after a summer of on-the-spot sketching that resulted in three hundred pictures, Miller had worked many months in Scotland at the castle, on the oils for which the sketches were preliminary drawings. When he had completed his commission, he laid the small sketches aside in his Baltimore studio, and on his death in 1874 they came into the possession of his brother's children and then to their descendants.

In the cardboard box before us lay a hundred of these sketches, and as we looked through them to find the best, I began to realize that we were seeing a collection unique in America, for after all in 1838 there were few artists willing to face the Indians. Catlin and Bodmer had both painted Indian life — one from 1832 to 1839, the other in 1833 and 1834, but they had little of Miller's artistic talent.

We returned to Missouri, but could not forget those sketches. A year later my husband went to see them and was immediately a convert to the idea that they should be in the Midwest, in the vicinity of Independence, where Sir William and his artist had outfitted before they started out across the Kansas plains.

Suddenly I knew that I simply had to own the hundred Miller sketches I'd seen in that box, and without delay I wrote to their owners asking for a chance to buy the collection. The figure named was possible. I took a plane for Washington, and studying them again, I was delighted by the many details that had escaped me the first time I saw them. I brought the collection back to Missouri where Mr. Paul Gardner, director of our Nelson Gallery of Art, realizing its importance to this section of the country, placed it on display in the Gallery.

Then there began for me several years of research. As the story connected with the sketches began to take form, I found the most valued assistance, as I returned again and again to Baltimore, in the facts concerning Miller's life given me by Mr. MacGill James, then Director of the Peale Museum. He had inherited his interest in Miller and some of his oil paintings, from his father, and had several years before arranged a showing of the watercolor sketches in the museum, giving them their first introduction to the present-day public.

Even our curiosity concerning the Miller oil paintings that had hung on the castle walls was satisfied. Mr. Wright Howes, dealer in rare books, in Chicago had purchased a number of the oils in Edinburgh for Mr. E. D. Graff of Winnetka and I had the pleasure of seeing them hanging in his house. Then, when lecturing in Oklahoma, I had had the thrill of placing one of my small sketches beside its eight-foot copy in the Philbrook Art Museum in Tulsa. It seemed odd that the tiny watercolor depicting a buffalo surround, that had last been with the large oil in 1840 in Murthly Castle, should in 1940 meet its replica again in the Philbrook Gallery. Mr. Vernon Miller, who possessed the original notes to the Indian sketches in which the artist had set down anecdotes and recollections, contributed the most important data of all when he let me study the artist's own picture by picture journal.

With this first-hand information it seemed the logical thing to do something definite toward presenting both pictures and story to the public, so the hundred sketches went off to a photographer to be made into kodachrome slides and the material became a lecture entitled, 'The West That Was.' But this procedure could reach only a few, so the idea of a book that might preserve and present these interesting sketches and the adventurous story to a large public began to develop. Then came Pearl Harbor and with it the fear that the American public would not buy expensive books and that dyes might not be available for making the reproductions. A year of waiting followed, and when a great upsweep in the sale of books on American history brought proof that in war we were turning to a real appreciation of our own country and the story of how she came to be, publication of our material seemed feasible. *Fortune* magazine, hearing of the collection, decided to print ten pages of the sketches in color in its January, 1944, issue.

Shortly after this I was fortunate in meeting Bernard DeVoto, who has long been an authority on the development of the West. He was tremendously interested in the sketches, and I am very happy that my collection with its attendant research material has made its contribution to this lively account of the Mountain Fur Trade.

# CONTENTS

# ILLUSTRATIONS

# DRAMATIS PERSONAE

PRINCIPAL PARTICIPANTS IN THE MOUNTAIN FUR TRADE DURING THE PERIOD OF THIS BOOK

THE AMERICAN FUR COMPANY, usually referred to as 'The Company.' This is the trust, and when the book opens it is trying to take over the mountain trade. Organized by John Jacob Astor, its active head is Ramsay Crooks, but the Western operations with which the text deals are under the direction of Pierre Chouteau, Jr., of St. Louis. His principal field director is Kenneth McKenzie, 'the King of the Missouri.' Before the book ends, Astor has sold out and the Company's Western Department and Upper Missouri Outfit have been taken over by the Chouteau interests as Pratte, Chouteau and Company.

Principal Company men who appear in the narrative:

Lucien Fontenelle
Andrew Drips
Henry Vanderburgh
Kenneth McKenzie
David D. Mitchell
Francis Chardon
Alexander Harvey
Alexander Culbertson
James P. Beckwourth, a mulatto and a Crow war chief, formerly an Ashley man
Samuel Tulloch
Jacob Halsey
Etienne Provost, a former Ashley man

THE ROCKY MOUNTAIN FUR COMPANY. The 'Opposition,' that

is, the principal objective of the Company's attack. In lineal descent from the Ashley interests, it is with its predecessors the greatest name in the mountains. Before the period of this book it had opened up the mountain trade, pioneered in exploration and discovery beyond any others in the history of the West, clashed with the Hudson's Bay Company, and gathered the great harvest of fur that aroused the Company's cupidity. The line began in 1822 and 1823 under the leadership of William H. Ashley, and most of the master mountain men are first seen as his employees. Ashley sold out to (Jedediah) Smith, (William) Sublette, and (David) Jackson. This firm in turn sold out to the Rocky Mountain Fur Company, whose proprietors were Jim Bridger, Milton Sublette, Tom Fitzpatrick, Henry Fraeb, and John Baptiste Gervais.

Principal RMF Company men in the narrative:

Jim Bridger (Old Gabe; the Blanket Chief)
Tom Fitzpatrick (White Head; Broken Hand)
Joe Meek
Louis Vasquez (Old Vaskiss)
Moses ('Black') Harris, also in turn a free trapper, a Sublette and Campbell man, and a Company man
Kit Carson, also a free trapper
Milton Sublette
Henry Fraeb
Doc Newell
Edmund Christy
'Markhead'

SUBLETTE and CAMPBELL, WILLIAM SUBLETTE (CUT FACE, LEFT HAND), and ROBERT CAMPBELL proprietors. A carrying and outfitting firm for the RMF Company and principal opposition to the American Fur Company on the Missouri during the period of this narrative. Both proprietors were originally lieutenants of Ashley.

The principal employee who appears in the narrative is Charles Larpenteur, later a Company man.

THE HUDSON'S BAY COMPANY. The chartered British monopoly, which before the narrative opens had merged with the most effective and most deadly opposition it had ever had, the Northwest Company.

Principal Hudson's Bay Company men in the narrative:

Dr. John McLoughlin, the overlord, the resident emperor at Fort Vancouver

Francis Ermatinger
Tom McKay
Michel Laframboise
Alexander McLeod
Courtney W. Walker, also briefly a Wyeth man and a 'lay assistant' to missionaries
Francis Payette

BENJAMIN LOUIS EULALIE DE BONNEVILLE. An independent and interloper, trying to break into the mountain trade. Captain, 7th Infantry, U.S.A. Perhaps on military business also.

Principal Bonneville men in the narrative:
Joseph Reddeford Walker, a Santa Fe trader and a thirty-third degree mountain man.
Michel Sylvestre Cerré, of the St. Louis fur aristocracy, a veteran of the Missouri River trade
Zenas Leonard

NATHANIEL JARVIS WYETH, ice dealer, inventor, and speculator of Cambridge, Massachusetts, trying to get a foothold in the mountain trade.

Principal Wyeth men in the narrative:
John Wyeth, cousin of Nat Wyeth
Osborne Russell, later of the RMF Company, still later of the Company
Joseph Thing
Joseph Gale

MISCELLANY: Gant (or Gantt) and Blackwell, a small independent firm; William and Alexander Sinclair, free trappers; Dr. Benjamin Harrison, on tour; Captain William Drummond Stewart of the British Army, his hunter Antoine Clement, and his painter Alfred Jacob Miller.

# «I»

# THE PRAIRIE TRAVELER (1833)

TO THE AMERICAN PIONEER as far west as Illinois and Missouri, the word 'prairie' meant a place without trees but with a soil so rich that planting it might be, as the Big Bear of Arkansas said it was, dangerous. The pioneer followed the Missouri River across the state named for it, and all the way the land was lush and fecund. At the western border of the state the Missouri turned north — and the word 'prairie' began to mean 'desert.' From here on the river was the boundary between God's country and the Great American Desert.

Something of this change may have been due to another word, 'savanna.' It was a word of poetry and power. A savanna was of the mind only, of the mind's edge, of fantasy. It suggested meadows in sunlight, groves beside streams, something lovely and rich and distant. While the pioneer was still in the piedmont, savannas were what you would see from the Cumberland Mountains when you looked down into a country still mostly fable, Kentucky. The Spanish sailors with bearded lips found savannas in Florida as long as that province too remained fable. The trouble was that Florida and Kentucky came out of fable, came out of it diminished by fact, and the savannas moved on west. There were savannas wherever you hadn't been along the Mississippi.

Savannas, that is, belonged with the spectral Kentucky, the land we hadn't come to yet, the fantasy, the American Lyonesse. And beyond the Mississippi they stretched to the Pacific Ocean, with grass as high as your shoulders and the air perfumed with the blossoms of exotic trees. It was known, however, that on the way across them you would reach the Stony Mountains. Sometimes they were called the Shining Mountains. (*La montagne dont la pierre luit jour et nuit.*) They were five miles high, a single ridge rising from the grass. It might be that they could never be crossed — but no matter, there were savannas all the way, the richest land in the world.

But not when we reached the Missouri River. Here savannas died of shock and steppes took their place. Meriwether Lewis and William Clark came back from the unmapped country in 1806. They had found marvels there but few of the marvels they might have been expected to find, not the Lost Tribes of Israel nor the Welsh Indians, not one mammoth, not even the mountain of salt that was to be a hundred and eighty miles long. But they had crossed a dry country, and that made an impression, as the fact that they had also crossed the Stony Mountains did not. They used the word 'desert' sparingly, but the word 'treeless' was everywhere in their journals all the way to the Continental Divide and it did not disappear entirely till they came hurtling through the Cascade Mountains in a dugout. They called many places barren and frequently noted that the soil seemed sterile. The book Nicholas Biddle made from their journals was out in 1814.

Zebulon Pike's book had been published in 1810. Pike had found the West a desert everywhere. He mentioned Africa; that meant the Sahara with the wind heaving sand up like the groundswell in mid-ocean. By the time Major Stephen Long's creative writer Edwin James got a book out, 1823, a lot of people were finding out at first hand what the West was like, but they did not write books. Major Long and Doctor James said it was sterile, the land of the cormorant and bittern. Nomads could live there but no one else could: there was no timber and but little water, the soil was poisoned, there was just cactus, artemisia, and sand. It was a country the fire had passed over.

Besides Africa James mentioned Siberia, and even before him, in 1817, a literary person who had traveled with John Jacob Astor's westering fur-hunters had introduced Siberia and for good measure had added Palestine and Tartary. Tartary made the best run: the West was steppes. A prairie would be a desert from now on. The western border of Missouri was fixed in 1820 and it separated the country of the pioneer from Tartary. The Great American Desert had been born.

Since before 1800 dugouts and pirogues had been bringing furs to St. Louis from the northern reaches of the Great American Desert. Through the eighteen-twenties keelboats brought them down from there and, beginning with 1831, steamboats. The overland trade with Santa Fe got started in 1822, though a good many people had gone down the historic trail and come back by it in the preceding years. The first pack trains from the Platte were home in 1825. In January, 1825, the Senator from New Jersey told his colleagues that the whole area from Council Bluffs to the Rockies, and from the Sabine River to Canada, was 'almost wholly unfit for cultivation and of course uninhabitable by a people depending upon agriculture for subsistence. . . . The whole of this region seems peculiarly adapted as a range for buffaloes, wild goats, and other wild game.'

By the time we deal with in this book, several hundred men were crossing the Great American Desert every year and its commerce had been incorporated in world trade. No matter: it was still uninhabitable, the soil would not grow crops, there was no grass domestic cattle could eat. Thus Washington Irving, who had never been there, in the late eighteen-thirties. Thus even Josiah Gregg, who had been there and loved it, in 1844. That last year was the one following the Great Migration, and in 1844 the editor of the *Christian Advocate*, whose church had had a mission in Oregon for ten years, thought that Botany Bay would be more favorable for emigration. In the same year Daniel Webster most certainly did not make a speech that has been attributed to him ever since: 'What do we want with the vast, worthless area, this region of savages and wild beasts, of deserts, of shifting sands, and whirlwinds of dust, of cactus and prairie dogs? To what use could we ever hope to put these great deserts or these endless mountain ranges, impenetrable and covered to their base with eternal snow? . . . I will never vote one cent from the public treasury to place the Pacific coast one inch nearer to Boston than it now is.' Mr. Webster has been libeled, he never made that speech — but the point is that the speech was so common in and out of Congress that any expansionist could believe he had. And John Charles Frémont, who crossed the wasteland in 1842, came back to say that maybe a grazing society could inhabit parts of it, but not many nor large parts, and the rest was steppes. Next year he changed his mind and began to render his principal service to American history by shrinking the great desert inward toward its center. Nevertheless, the West was the steppes of Tartary down to the California gold rush and on past that till the Union Pacific began to haul eastward melons that had been grown in its heart.

Geographers did not read the newspapers. By the early

eighteen-thirties the little home-town weeklies had printed enough letters and diaries by young men who had hunted beaver in the desert to locate all the landmarks east of the Rockies and all those in Oregon, if anyone had wanted to triangulate them. Only Albert Gallatin did. The War Department had enough information in its files to correct the maps, but didn't. Congressman John Floyd of Virginia, whose cousin had gone West with Lewis and Clark and died on the way, and Senators Linn and Benton of Missouri and a few other politicians did what the geographers and the army did not: they read the home-town papers and talked with the people who had been there. They knew how the West was arranged; the map-makers did not.

For the boys and girls who would go West, and their parents in whose minds the expansion of the United States to the Pacific was an increasing urgency, were studying maps whose information was grotesque. David H. Burr's *Universal Atlas* was published in 1836, the year when Narcissa Whitman went to Oregon. Its 'North America' has the Continental Divide where it ought to be, but this turns out to be pure chance: there is just one range of mountains, though it forks at about the site of Denver and sends one splendid branch kiting across the plains toward Kansas. There are no other mountains at all, not even the Cascades or the Sierra. Mr. Burr's 'Oregon Territory' takes its Columbia River system from William Clark's map and so gets it right. It does better by the Rockies than his 'North America,' making them multiple ranges at about 46° N., where they are multiple. But it centers them at about Boise and moves them as a formation well into the state of Oregon, say four hundred miles.

Mr. H. S. Tanner had published his *New American Atlas* ten years before, in 1826, but its maps remained current down to the eighteen-forties. Mr. Tanner also had a bulge in the single chain of the Rockies — and thus, like Burr, was better than many geographers who came after him — but he liked that bulge a little too much. At Denver the mountains are eight hundred miles wide, or halfway through Nevada. Mr. Tanner also gets the course of the Platte River about right and even gives it two branches, which is a notable advance over his predecessors and one which many of his successors thought too radical. But he lets the Snake River rise a hundred miles straight south of the sources of the North Platte and fifty miles east of the sources of the South Platte. His Colorado River rises somewhere in east-central Utah and if you were to follow his map a day's ride straight east from there you would reach the Rio Grande.

Tanner's and Burr's bulge at about the Bitterroot Mountains and Tanner's not-often-imitated Platte were about the only advances over William Clark that had been made by the time we deal with. In fact, apart from Clark's map, they were about the only advances over A. Arrowsmith and L. Lewis, *A New and Elegant General Atlas*, an English work published the year when Lewis and Clark started up the Missouri. Clark's map of 1810 had the Missouri, Columbia, and Yellowstone Rivers exactly right, and also the mountains which Clark had crossed. But those who took over his rivers remained skeptical about his mountains. Down to the eighteen-forties, with or without a bulge, the Rockies are usually a single chain and usually two hundred miles or more out of place. As for the interior West, the most dependable maps showed it as blank white paper; the others made it dreamland and were lots of fun.

The American fantasy needed no maps, however, and it was clear that once you got across Tartary you would reach the place where Kentucky came true at last. In that fantasy Lyonesse and Tarshish have always lain on the far side of the hill west of our town. That hill was now the Rocky Mountains and beyond them were the lost and waiting lands. The song said there was one more river to cross. It was the great River of the West and once you crossed it the land would be so rich that you could hardly plant your crops in safety. The imagined tide of that river rolling through Mr. Bryant's continuous woods made Oregon, not California, the Pacific Lyonesse. All you had to do was to cross the steppes. You would not meet the great Achilles whom we knew but you might meet the Welsh Indians. Brigham Young was still looking for them in 1854 and expected to find them in the red rock desert southeastward from his capital city. George Catlin had actually found them in 1832. Naturally enough, on the Missouri River.

Meanwhile, in 1833 on any street corner of St. Louis you could ask a bystander how to get to Lyonesse and be told. Several hundred men left the Missouri frontier every spring for Santa Fe, the Yellowstone, South Pass, the Green, the Columbia. They did not resemble Achilles, but they were prepared to meet several hundred others on the day appointed and at the place assigned, and did not care if the geographers had moved it a full ten degrees. They went about the blank spaces of the map like men going to the barn. The Great American Desert was their back yard.

They are our characters. It will be well to follow them with a remark of Garrett Mattingly's in mind. American history, Mr. Mattingly has said, is history in transition from an Atlantic to a Pacific phase.

* * *

The *Christian Advocate and Journal* was published for the edification of Methodist families. It would not be expected to affect the processes of history. But its Number 27 of Volume VII, published at New York on March 1, 1833, set free an energy that changed the alignment of empires in the Western world.

The contents of that issue, though elevating, are dull, except the item which secured the vast area called Oregon to the United States. This is a letter to the editor dated February 18 and signed 'G. P. D.' Its author was a wealthy merchant of New York City named Disoway, a pious and churchly man given to good works. He was particularly interested in the labors of Christian missionaries to save the souls and improve the condition of the Indians, in so much that he became secretary of his church's Board of Foreign Missions. He appears to have had some part, doubtless by contributing money, in the Methodist mission to the Wyandots of Ohio. These were the remnants of the once great Huron nation of Canada, who had moved to the country of the Shawnees and Delawares when the Iroquois all but annihilated their people in the seventeenth century. Since then they had been undergoing the slower extinction of the oncoming white settlements, which was now to be accelerated. The white man was making his ultimate blue-sky proposal: he was going to move the cis-Mississippi tribes west of the river, call the land from there on the Indian Country, and secure the Indians in their lands there forever.

This grandiose scheme had been negotiated for some years, but as it turned out the Wyandots were not to be moved until 1842. But they had sent a committee West to spy out the land, the summer before Mr. Disoway wrote to the *Christian Advocate*. One member of the exploring party was William Walker, a Christianized Wyandot halfbreed who had been well educated. (So well that, in reporting the proposed tribal lands unsuitable, he repeated the mistake of a generation of farmers from the Old Northwest and decided that the Iowa prairies were not arable.) When he got back to Ohio he wrote to his friend Mr. Disoway, and Mr. Disoway copied his letter verbatim in his own.

Mr. Walker describes his western journey and in detail the

lands intended for his people. But like his white friend he was more interested in eternal things and he soon forgot the prairies in order to recount an incident that had wrung his pious heart. On reaching St. Louis, he had called on William Clark, the famous companion of Meriwether Lewis in the first American overland expedition to the Pacific and now Superintendent of Indian Affairs. Every visitor to St. Louis called on Clark, but he seldom had a story so enthralling as the one he now told William Walker. There were at his house, so Walker reports him as having said, three chiefs of the Flathead tribe from the far Northwest, who had made the long journey from their country on a pathetic errand. There had been four of them but one had died, and in fact the remaining three were now grievously sick. Thereupon Walker, so he told Mr. Disoway, stepped 'into the adjoining room' and altered the course of history.

The Wyandot Walker had heard of the Flatheads but had never seen any of them. Now, he said, he found them small but symmetrically formed — and with pointed, not flattened, heads. Here he drew a sketch, which Mr. Disoway copied for the *Christian Advocate*. It showed the forehead slanting back from the eyebrows in a smooth, straight line so that it came to a point at the crown. (Consulting local authorities, Mr. Disoway told his readers that the heads were bandaged in infancy — 'the infant presents a frightful appearance, its little keen black eyes being forced out to an unnatural degree' — but the process was so gradual that it caused 'scarcely any pain.' Nevertheless this monstrous deformation of 'the human face Divine' is a reminder of the darkness in which the Indians live. It is a greater reproach to Christians because, as Mr. Disoway's correspondent makes clear, these particular heathen are seeking a light.)

And why had the Flatheads made their long journey 'on foot' from their country west of the Continental Divide, beyond the Bitterroot Mountains? That was the burden of Walker's letter, and of Mr. Disoway's. The Flatheads, Walker said, though they practiced deformation, were a naturally moral and religious people. Recently they had met a white man of a different kind from the godless trappers who were the only white men they had previously known. This one was a religious man and he had told the Flatheads that their 'mode of worshiping the Supreme Being was radically wrong and . . . it was displeasing to Him.' This was distressing news to a moral tribe but their instructor gave them leave to hope. White men, he said, knew the right way to worship the Great Spirit. Moreover, 'they had a book containing directions how to conduct themselves in order to enjoy His favor and hold converse with Him, and with this guide no one need go astray but everyone . . . could enjoy in this life His favor and after death would be received into the country where the Great Spirit resides.'

Thereupon, Walker said, the Flatheads determined to inquire into the right way and set their feet upon it. So they had sent four 'chiefs' to St. Louis, to consult with Clark, the most notable white man they knew of and a friend to Indians. And when they reached St. Louis the Red-Headed Chief told them they had indeed heard aright, and instructed them in the history of man from 'creation down to the advent of the Savior,' expounded the Decalogue and the meaning of redemption, and in short outlined Christian salvation. Walker added that another of the 'chiefs' died in St. Louis, but the remaining two turned homeward. He had some doubt whether they might not have died on the way. If they had, 'peace be to their manes! They died inquirers after the truth.'

Thus William Walker, a Christian Wyandot whose head echoed with the phrases of evangelical exhortation, to G. P. Disoway who, after repeating his letter, himself exhorted the readers of the *Christian Advocate*:

> The story has scarcely a parallel in history. What a touching theme does it form for the imagination and pen of a Montgomery, a Mrs. Hemans, or our own fair Sigourney. With what intense concern will men of God whose souls are fired with holy zeal for the salvation of their fellow beings read their history! . . . No apostle of Christ has yet had the courage to penetrate into their moral darkness. . . . Let the Church awake from her slumbers and go forth in her strength to the salvation of those wandering sons of our native forests. . . . What can be more worthy of our high estimation than to befriend our species and those efforts that are making to release immortal spirits from the chains of error and superstition. . . .

That did it. At once the religious press was on fire. 'It was a Macedonian cry of "Come over and help us,"' one writer says. 'It stirred the Church as it has seldom been stirred into activity.' It reminded a correspondent of the *Christian Advocate* that a mission-minded Methodist bishop had foreseen just such a need and had sworn, 'We will not cease until we shall have planted the standard of Christianity high on the summit of the

Stony Mountains,' where by a little license the Flatheads might be said to live. The Church must take the light to those seeking minds! And to stimulate the enlistment of missionaries, which would appear to have needed no additional stimulation, one of the godly improved on William Walker by inventing a supposed oration of the Flatheads.

It is a happy circumstance of history that Indians have always spoken the fashionable rhetoric of the period, whether a Donne-like imagery in Massasoit's time, the periods and balances of Doctor Johnson in Logan's time, or the McGuffey eloquence now attributed to the Flatheads. 'I come to you over the trail of many moons from the setting sun,' the spokesman is reported:

> You were friends of my fathers, who have all gone the long way. I came with an eye partly open for my people who sit in darkness. I go back with both eyes closed. How can I go blind to my blind people? I made my way to you with strong arms through many enemies and strange lands that I might carry back much to them. I go back with both arms broken and empty. Two fathers came with us; they were braves of many winters and many wars. We leave them asleep here by your great waters and wigwams. They were tired in many moons and their moccasins wore out.
>
> My people sent me to get the White Man's Book of Heaven. You took me to where you allow your women to dance, and the book was not there. You took me to where they worship the Great Spirit with candles and the book was not there. You showed me images of the good spirits and the picture of the good land beyond, but the book was not among them to tell us the way. I am going back the long and sad trail to my people in the dark land. You make my feet heavy with gifts and my moccasins will grow old carrying them, yet the book is not among them. When I tell my poor blind people, after one more snow, in the big council, that I did not bring the book, no word will be spoken by our old men or by our young braves. One by one they will rise up and go out in silence. My people will die in darkness and they will go a long path to other hunting grounds. No white man will go with them, and no White Man's Book to make the way plain. I have no more words.

The ways of Providence had led the Flatheads safely past the shoals of papacy and no Protestant could fail to respond. So it was settled. Oregon would now be American. The American Fur Company, Mr. Astor's trust, would get powerful help in its efforts to drive the only remaining foreign competition, the Hudson's Bay Company, from American soil. But also the

American Fur Company's system would be gravely impaired by the missionaries and emigrants who followed them westward.

And all because William Walker, piously lying for the greater glory of Methodism, drawing the head of an Indian he had never seen, had made it rise to a point, quite contrary to the facts.

* * *

For probably the Macedonian cry would have gone unheeded if the seeking Indians had not seemed so barbarous; the deformed head did the job. Whereas William Walker had not seen the Indians about whom he wrote with such pathos — the survivors had been gone from St. Louis for some months when he got there. Moreover, the Flatheads did not flatten, point, or in any other way deform their heads, which were quite normal. Walker's drawing corresponded to some hearsay he had picked up which described certain aristocrats among the Chinook Indians, a by then debased tribe who lived near the mouth of the Columbia River and were not interested in the white man's religion. Finally, though a Flathead did reach St. Louis with the party Walker was talking about, his three companions were Nez Perces and it was their tribe who had instigated the journey. Allowance may be made for the ideals of evangelical journalism.

As our text will show, the Flatheads were superior Indians. In the first third of the nineteenth century they were living in the place previously mentioned, Montana west of the Continental Divide. They were the principal group or tribe of a people who called themselves the Salish, meaning 'the people' — most Indians speak of themselves as the people, the right people, the best people, or the great people. However, in the sign language, the Esperanto of the plains, they were designated by pressing both hands, with the fingertips extended and touching, across the head just above the forehead. The origin of the sign is lost beyond recovery, but inevitably it was translated Têtes plattes, or Flatheads.

They had been pushed westward over the divide by the most teutonic of Plains Indians, the ferocious Blackfeet, whom, however, they were willing to fight at any time and frequently defeated. They lived in a root country and so were not solely dependent on the buffalo, and their culture incorporated many elements from the Northwest tribes. Nevertheless, they were horse Indians, buffalo Indians, and therefore, for purposes of this book, Plains Indians. They got along with their neighbors better than most tribes and were uniformly friendly to white men. The whites in turn liked them and professed to find their behavior, honor, honesty, and morality unusually good. White men contrive to maintain decorum when passing moral judgments on Indians.

Westward from the Flathead country, along the Snake, Salmon, and Clearwater Rivers where they flow through Idaho, lived a larger tribe, the most populous of several closely related ones, whom American and British trappers found even more agreeable and progressive. These Indians also had a horse and buffalo economy, though they dug the plentiful edible roots of their country, traveled to the annual salmon runs in addition, and were still more strongly influenced by the Northwest culture. Linguistically they belonged to what ethnologists call the Penutian family, whereas their neighbors the Flatheads were a detached fragment of the Algonkin family, the bulk of whose tribes lived in the East. Ethnologists use the name which the Flatheads bestowed on them, the Shahaptan, of uncertain meaning but perhaps a designation of the country they lived in. But the whites called them Nez Perces, again in rendition of the digital sign that designated them.[1] This in turn came from their former custom of piercing the septum of the nose so that ornaments could be worn there, a custom almost completely obsolete by the time we deal with.

The intertribal trade of the Indians was amazingly complex. Long before the Flatheads or Nez Perces met any white men in person they were occasionally getting manufactured goods, beads or pieces of cloth or bits of iron — brought up the Columbia from tribe to tribe before 1800, brought overland in the same way from the mid-Canada posts of the Northwest Company or the Hudson's Bay Company earlier still, perhaps much earlier. Sometimes, even, a bridle or a blanket had come all the way from the Comanches who had stolen it out of Mexico. When Lewis and Clark came among these people, they inspired a permanent loyalty to the Americans. In 1812 the pioneers of Mr. Astor's great Columbia venture reached the Nez Perces. The Northwest Company took over his establishment when war broke out. From then on these Canadians (the great rivals of the Hudson's Bay Company, with which they merged in 1821) sent traders to them. In 1818 they built a permanent post at the mouth of the Walla Walla River, naming it Fort Nez Percé for the principal tribe it served. Even earlier, but as part of the same effort to get at the interior West from the Pacific coast, they had built 'Saleesh House' on Clark's Fork, among the Flatheads. In 1824 the Hudson's Bay monopoly was challenged by the appearance at the latter of American traders under the great Jedediah Smith. Since then the Americans had been among them every year, had absorbed a large part of the Nez Perce and Flathead trade, and had succeeded in attracting portions of both tribes to the annual rendezvous, which had come to be a trading fair.

The first step in the white man's exploitation of the Indian, and it was the inevitably fatal step, was to raise his standard of living. From the moment when the Indians first encountered manufactured goods they became increasingly dependent on them. Everything in their way of life now pivoted on the acquisition of goods. And that is what was behind the long journey of the Nez Perces and Flatheads that opened the sluices of Mr. Disoway's eloquence.

The basis of the mountain fur trade was beaver. The Northwestern tribes had hunted the beaver but did not know how to trap it. So the Hudson's Bay Company had imported some of the mongrel, debased Caughnawaga Iroquois from Quebec to teach them trapping. Together with drunkenness these had learned a species of Christianity, and when some of them cut their debts to the Company by running away and joining the Flatheads, their religious practices were novelties that aroused the interest of their new brothers. The Iroquois explained their understanding of Christian medicine. The Nez Perces were getting similar instruction about the same time or a little later. In 1825 George Simpson, the overlord of the Hudson's Bay Company, took to the Red River (of Canada) headquarters a couple of boys from the Spokanes, who were neighbors of the Nez Perces and poor relations of the Flatheads — and from time to time others followed them. One of these educated youths, known as Spokane Garry, came back to his people a celebrity. He could read and write — accomplishments among the most powerful of the white man's medicine — he had other strange civilized skills, he could teach them to his tribe, and he could expound Christianity as it appeared to him. He was an experiment by the British monopoly, which frequently tended to favor educating the Indians — or some Indians — and made additional experiments. Moreover, vague parodies of Christianity had traveled up the Columbia. And, let us not forget, as early as 1817 at least, Hall Kelley had wanted to make Christians of the Indians in these parts.

What gradually dawned on the Nez Perces who initiated the famous journey to St. Louis was that they too could learn something of the white man's medicine, perhaps much more than this. 'Medicine' is best thought of as 'power,' and in the Indian's metaphysics power was an attribute of every creature, object, and operation, if only you could find out how to use it; a subsidiary meaning of 'mystery' is almost inseparable from 'power.' The Nez Perces understood that white medicine centered, as Indian medicine did, in religion. When they decided to ask for instruction in religion, they wanted to increase their power. They wanted, that is, to increase their magical control of nature in order to acquire objects which the white man possessed or knew how to make: guns and powder and other weapons most of all, tools, needles, beads, blankets, cloth, garments, alcohol, mirrors, and all the other goods of civilization. They wanted to acquire an advanced economy by means of the thaumaturgy which they thought made it work. They were altogether uninterested in Christian spirituality, morality, or salvation: they were satisfied with what they had.

The decision to act was first made by a particular band of Nez Perces who in 1831 delegated four of their number to go to St. Louis, whence goods came, and find out what could be done. One of these withdrew from the mission, feeling himself too old to make the trip. Every summer most bands of Nez Perces joined to make a buffalo hunt east of the mountains and usually the Flatheads went with them for mutual defense against the Blackfeet. The proposed quest was applauded by the tribe at large, and another Nez Perce joined the party. The Flatheads liked the idea, too, and three of them enlisted for the trip. Normally they would have traveled with a fur company caravan returning to St. Louis from the rendezvous, but in 1831 the plans of all fur companies went awry and a summer rendezvous was not held. Some years later Lucien Fontenelle of the American Fur Company told Marcus Whitman that the Indians traveled with him. If so, they got to St. Louis earlier than the October 1 that is usually given as the approximate date of their arrival.[2]

The muggy heat of the lowlands sickened the Indians. Two of the Flatheads and one Nez Perce gave up and turned back toward the mountains. The remaining four reached St. Louis, a Flathead named Man of the Morning, a distinguished Nez Perce named Black Eagle, and two young men of his tribe named No Horns on His Head and Rabbit-Skin Leggings.

In St. Louis you could pick up someone capable of speaking nearly any Indian language of the West, North, or Southwest, but there was no one who could speak Flathead or Nez Perce. Even the Red-Headed Chief, William Clark, the friend of Indians and a legendary hero of these tribes, could converse with them only in signs. They could make no eloquent speeches about the Book of Heaven or the blindness of their people — they could make no speeches at all. But they did manage to make Clark and others understand what they wanted — Clark better than most, doubtless, though even he would think in terms of religious instruction primarily. Whereas no one could help them very much, for they wanted amulets, incantations, and instruction in magic. So they lingered on in St. Louis, doubtless bewildered and distressed, in an obscurity that cannot be dissipated now. They must have found Indians whose language they could speak a little, and certainly there were many Indians and whites with whom they could talk in signs. It may be that they found mountain men who knew their country, who would give them ceremonious feasts, humble enough at best. No doubt they toured the city as all Indian visitors did, impressed and contemptuous by turns, superstitious, confused, arrogant, scared. They probably heard something of the trouble gathering to the northward which would precipitate the Black Hawk War next spring, and though St. Louis was tolerant of Indians they may have been under some suspicion because of it.

Black Eagle, the Nez Perce war chief, died on October 31, but first Father Saulinier baptized him into the faith whose medicine he had come in search of and then buried him in the Catholic cemetery. Man of the Morning, the Flathead, died soon afterward; Father Rous baptized him and gave him Extreme Unction, and he too was buried in the Catholic cemetery. The braves had given their lives in the service of their people, in a far country. The two young Nez Perces who were left, No Horns on His Head and Rabbit-Skin Leggings, must have been still more profoundly troubled in that country now. No one knows what they did there or when they went away, if they did leave the city. The Right Reverend Joseph Rosati, Bishop of St. Louis, who wrote the first known account of them, fourteen months before Disoway's letter appeared in the *Christian Advocate*, said they were gone by the end of 1831. But George Catlin met them on the steamboat *Yellowstone*, which he boarded for its second upriver voyage in late March of 1832. He did not get their story from them or from anyone else at the time, though he later heard it and played it up. But the *Yellowstone* stopped at Fort Pierre, built that year (Pierre, South Dakota), and the Sioux there gave a feast for them as visitors of note, and dressed them in magnificent deerskins and Sioux ornaments. So Catlin painted them in their new finery, and, not distinguishing between the tribes, called them 'Flatheads or Nez Perces.'[3]

The *Yellowstone* steamed on up the river, but only one of the seekers lived to tell his people what had happened, for No Horns on His Head died somewhere near the mouth of the Yellowstone River. Rabbit-Skin Leggings went on till he found a band of Nez Perces hunting east of the mountains. Then on his way homeward he was killed by Blackfeet. That was the autumn of 1832.

He would have told his people a long, fascinating, but in the end depressing story with more of marvels in it than of magic. He could tell them only that the white men had sympathized, had promised, and had done nothing — for no one had done anything by the time Rabbit-Skin Leggings left St. Louis. Still, something in his report was optimistic, for Nez Perces and Flatheads showed up at the next summer rendezvous and were expecting a journeyman white thaumaturge. They were a year too early. In the meantime Disoway's letter had lit a holy fire and in the following year, 1834, the Indians saw their first magician. He did not linger but went on past them and became a real-estate operator. But others followed him — more selfless and in the end more deadly.[4]

* * *

In 1833 St. Louis had a population of something over seven thousand and its steamboat age was beginning to roar toward the flush times. The town was mistress of the western waters, had been long before there were steamboats, when the traffic of those waters was by keelboat, flatboat, pirogue, and mackinaw. It was a river town, but if it was Huck Finn's town it was also Mike Fink's, who was not only a keelboatman but a fur-hunter. The rivers had made it more cosmopolitan than other places in America. It looked eastward to Pittsburgh and beyond, southward to New Orleans and the Gulf, northeastward to the Great Lakes and the St. Lawrence, and northward as far as boats of any kind could go. Here, more plentifully than anywhere else, the continental mind was showing itself.

But 'St. Louis — mixture of French & American character — French billiard room — market-place where some are speaking

French, some English,' Washington Irving had jotted in his notebook last September, putting up at the Union Hotel and going out at once to check impressions against what he knew of Europe and New York. For of all the rivers that were destiny to St. Louis, those that flowed from the wilderness counted most, the French had pioneered them, and the town polarized innumerable energies from the eastward in order to direct them west. Here was the headland from which the nation overlooked the West. The Ohio and the lower Mississippi were important, but the upper Mississippi meant more and the Missouri most of all. The Indians and trappers and voyageurs who brought a barbaric color to the cobbled streets were of the West, and an old and rich aristocracy, dating back long before Mr. Jefferson's Purchase, were borne on their shoulders. The Chouteaus, Bertholds, Prattes, Cérrés, Cabannés, and the like ruled the city by birthright, they got their wealth from the West, and they had led their own parties West to bring it back.

The wharves of the steamboat age multiplied along the river. Just above them, on a flat bench sometimes flooded by the June rise, stood the warehouses where the goods carried by the steamboats were stored for distribution and transshipment. Most conspicuous of all buildings on this bench, however, were large structures of gray and yellow stone which always smelled to heaven. These were the warehouses of the fur companies, the core of the town's economy. Here from all the northern and western rivers the pelts for which the trappers risked and lost their lives came down, and hence they went out to New York, Montreal, London, Leipsic, Lyons, St. Petersburg, Canton, Athens, Constantinople — to all the world. Some of the companies went back to a time when St. Louis was a Spanish town, some of them beyond that to the poignant, dimming days when it was the farthest outpost of Louis XVI — and even then was thrusting up Chouteaus. Almost from the beginning the dugouts had moved up the Mississippi and Missouri to the Indian country, after furs. In 1833 there were few businesses in St. Louis that did not somehow impinge on the fur trade. And John Jacob Astor had some kind of tie-up with most companies in the fur trade and was the principal force to be taken into account by all the rest.

Three and a half weeks after the *Christian Advocate* published Mr. Disoway's letter, on the morning of March 24, 1833, the steamboat *Paragon*, from the Ohio River, docked at St. Louis. Among the passengers who streamed down her gangplank was a thin, worn man of fifty, excitable, choleric, with a gift of invective. He spoke English by main force, through an unleavened Prussian accent, and the effect was not made more intelligible by the fact that years of military service and geographical exploration had cost him his teeth. He was traveling as Baron Braunsberg but he was Maximilian, Prince of Wied-Neuwied. He had with him the young Swiss artist, Charles Bodmer, and a servant whose improbable name, Dreidoppel, could hardly have been bettered among the Indians whom the Prince intended to visit. For he was in St. Louis to begin a scientific journey to the Indian country.

Maximilian had fought in the Prussian army against Napoleon, had been a prisoner of war, had fought again, had been promoted major-general and decorated with the Iron Cross, had ridden at the head of his division when the Allies entered Paris. This distinguished military career had been forced on him against his will by Napoleon's world war. For the Prince wanted a career in science and, after his patriotic obligations were discharged, embarked on one. He spent two years in Brazil, exploring its wilderness, studying the natives and the flora and fauna, and making a large natural-history collection which he took back to Wied. A book embodying his studies was published in 1820; like the one he was to write about the Indians it was accompanied by an atlas of illustrations. It won him a distinguished reputation and he prepared to engage in a similar study of North America. In the great spring morning of nineteenth-century science a man did not have to be a specialist and Maximilian had something of Humboldt's versatility, being a botanist, a zoologist, a geologist, a meteorologist and climatologist, something of a paleontologist, but mostly what we would today call an ethnologist. He wanted to use all his tools in a study of the West, but mainly he wanted to compare the Western Indians with the Indians he had studied in South America.

He had reached the United States on July 4, 1832, and after a brief tour of the seaboard had gone to New Harmony, Indiana. Not the embers of the extinguished communism attracted him there, but a group of accomplished scientists, at the head of them Charles Laseur and the great Thomas Say with whom Maximilian had long corresponded. He fell ill at New Harmony and, as the great cholera epidemic of 1832 came down the Ohio, panic running ahead of it, he decided to spend the winter there. He did so, enjoying the learned conversation of his colleagues and studying their libraries in preparation for his trip. Now at the end of March, 1833, he was in St. Louis.

Maximilian tasted the strangeness of this continental town, marveled at the Negroes, saw his first Western Indians, delivered his letters of introduction to the principal citizens, met William Clark, and solicited everyone's advice about his western journey. A deputation of Sauks and Foxes (there was only a clan distinction between the tribes) arrived in town. They were from the wiser bands, the ones that had refused to join Black Hawk in his gallant gamble of last year — when he had led his followers back to the tribal lands east of the Mississippi, made a soldier of Abraham Lincoln, caused the decimation of Winfield Scott's command by cholera, and eventually suffered defeat and capture. They had come, under the government-appointed and pacifist chief Keokuk, to ask Clark and General Atkinson to deal gently with Black Hawk. Clark invited Maximilian to a conference with them at his house and then took him and them by steamboat to Jefferson Barracks, south of the town, where Black Hawk was imprisoned. (He had been taken there the previous September. A few days later Washington Irving saw him there, and, most likely, Catlin painted his portrait about the same time. Keokuk need not have been troubled: the government intended to take the defeated warrior on what amounted to a triumphant procession through the East, doubtless to show that, however tough the Seminoles might be, there were some Indians whom the militia could lick.) Thus Maximilian got his first experience of one of the deadliest weapons the Indians had, their oratory.

It is clear that another guest on this trip to Jefferson Barracks was a globe-trotting Scottish sportsman, a half-pay army captain, who, like Maximilian, was a veteran of the Napoleonic wars, was making his first visit to St. Louis, and wanted to travel to the West. For Maximilian had met Captain William Drummond Stewart of Grandtully and for a time there was talk of their traveling together.

Stewart was an interesting man and one whom it would do to take along. He was in his thirty-seventh year. He was the brother of Sir John Archibald Stewart, eighteenth of Grandtully and sixth baronet, and was next in succession to him. At seventeen he had been appointed cornet in the Sixth Dragoon Guards. He saw service the next year and received a lieutenancy in the Fifteenth (The King's) Hussars. He went through the Hundred Days with his regiment and fought at Waterloo. He was promoted captain in 1820 and a year later was placed on half-pay when his battalion of the Hussars was mustered out. All that can be said certainly of the intervening twelve years since his retirement is that he was frequently at his seat, Murthly Castle, and that he traveled much as a sportsman and hunter.[5]

Beaked nose, black hair, and luxuriant mustache are cursive symbols for Stewart in Miller's sketches, where he is always mounted on a white horse. The mustache has been trimmed in the portrait (Plate LXXVI), the nose is modified, and there is an adequate suggestion of the romanticism and impetuosity that were prominent in his character. We have only one description of him and that is by William H. Gray, who traveled West with him in 1836, the year before Miller's portrait. Gray was a Presbyterian cabinet-maker who accompanied the Spaldings and Whitmans as a lay member of the mission to the Nez Perces. Devout sponsors recorded that he had an 'ardent piety' and 'a strong desire to do good,' that he was 'a thorough friend of Temperance (teetotal)' and 'all other benevolent efforts for reforming the world.' At this distance benevolence seems to have characterized very few of the missionaries and Gray not at all. The courage of all of them was conspicuous, but most of them were smug and unbearably self-righteous, besides carrying the period's evangelical sense of sin and superiority, which was as much dyspepsia as spirituality. In Gray the vocational self-righteousness reached a maximum; there are not above five persons in his book for whom he has a good word. And in the presence of Stewart he remembered not only that he was teetotal but that perfidious Britain was corrupt and an aristocracy.

Gray had heard that Stewart spent his winters in New Orleans, 'with the Southern bloods,' which was at least true in that Stewart had visited the town, and that his bankers had refused to pay his overdrafts and had advised him to travel to the mountains, 'during which time he could only spend what he had with him,' which is suggested nowhere else. Gray 'did not learn whether he was of the first, second, third, or fourth grade in the scale of English nobility' — no Old Homestead democrat would risk contamination by such decadence — and did not bother to get his name right, calling him 'Sir William Drummond, K.B.' Stewart was not yet a Sir and, since he was not a lawyer, if the man of God meant K.C.B., he was conferring an honor that neither George III, George IV, William IV, nor Victoria ever got round to. That year Stewart had a companion, 'a young English blood,' and they were not of the elect. 'Occasionally they would give chase to that swiftest of mountain animals, the antelope, which in most cases, especially when the grass was short, leave them in the distance, when Sir William and his companion would come charging back to the train, swearing the antelope could outrun a streak of lightning, and offering to bet a thousand pounds that if he had one of his English 'orses he would catch 'em.' A profane swearer, therefore, and a gambler, and it offended the missionary that 'the English nobleman, as a matter of course, was treated with great respect by all in the caravan; while in the presence of the ladies he assumed quite a dignified carriage, being a man (excuse me, your honor), a lord of the British realm.' British good manners and American servility exasperated Gray, who continues:

> He was about five feet nine inches high. His face had become thin from the free use of New Orleans brandy, rendering his nose rather prominent, showing indications of internal heat in bright red spots, and inclining a little to the rum blossom, that would make its appearance from the sting of a mosquito or sand-fly, which to his lordship was quite annoying. Though his lordship was somewhat advanced in age [he was then a few months short of forty] and according to his own account had traveled extensively in the oriental countries, he did not show in his conversation extensive mental improvement; his general conversation and appearance was that of a man with strong prejudices and equally strong appetites, which he had freely indulged, with only pecuniary restraint.

Teetotalism and rural York State democracy could not love an aristocrat. Stewart's education was no more than adequate to his station, but he wrote better prose than Gray, was the first man Gray had met who could speak a foreign language, had read history or poetry, or had traveled in strange lands, and certainly he was pleasanter company. A strain of Byronism that glints in Stewart's few known letters is a strong color in his two novels, which are wooden and absurd but dwell repeatedly on mysterious longings and melancholies, romantic passions, unhappiness and frustration, an urgent but never quite focused unrest. This moody dissatisfaction had made a wanderer of him, and the wilderness, its solitudes as well as its hazards, its beauty as well as its sternness, came closest to allaying it. He found the Yankees friendly, coming to admire their country as well as themselves. Like many another foreign man of feeling of the period, vaguely aware of strong social ferments about him, he thought that the Yankees might work out the best answer and he deeply admired the democracy of the frontier. He had traveled much before he came to the United States, he spent six straight years in the West and came back for another summer in 1843, and much of his later life was spent in travel. It seems likely that all this wandering classifies him in a type not uncommon after the Napoleonic wars, after all wars — men to whom campaigning and battle had been a climactic experience, giving them a sense of reality and function surpassing anything peace had to offer, convincing them that in extremity they had been most truly themselves, and leaving them to spend the rest of their lives looking for an experience, any kind of experience, that for even a moment would restore that lost splendor. Stewart came closest to finding it in the Far West. Eventually he would take an artist there to provide him with enduring reminders.

Maximilian had had a predecessor in these parts, for Prince Paul of Württemberg had twice traveled up the Missouri, to Council Bluffs and again as far as Fort Pierre. Furthermore, at Fort Union he was to meet an English gentleman, here under some kind of cloud and working in the trade. But Stewart appears to have been the first wealthy British sportsman who found the West a splendid playground. He thus founded a long line. The second one, the Honorable Charles Augustus Murray, who was to write a book about his travels and, like Stewart, was to try his hand at Western fiction, came two years later, in 1835, but traveled only the prairie edges of the West. In addition to sport and the search for his lost magnificence, Stewart may have had another motive for his adventure. He may have been in part on the King's business.[6]

* * *

The Prussian scientist and the Scottish sportsman had come to St. Louis because they wanted to travel to the West. Though we deal here with men to whom such a journey was routine, to America at large it was still a tremendous ambition and a tremendous undertaking. The national government itself had not ventured into the Far West since the time of Lewis and Clark, Long, and Pike — three pioneering expeditions inspired by Jefferson, one of them abortive. The journey was quite beyond individual enterprise, though a surprising number of visionaries, romantics, and crackpots at least began it. To go West at all in 1833 you had to go by means and under the protection of furtraders. As it turned out, Maximilian went with the trust and Stewart with the Opposition — with surviving and still very active representatives of the most expert opposition the trust had met in the United States, the opposition which this year it was at last beginning to defeat, too late. Maximilian reports rather odd advice from those whom he consulted. They told him that if he went overland, 'I shall not be able to observe any Indians . . . for if you happen to meet with them you must fight them, and therefore cannot become well acquainted with them, and secondly it is extremely difficult, nay impossible, to make considerable collections of natural history on such a journey.' This was nonsense on both counts. All overland expeditions by fur companies met hundreds of Indians, were in part made for the purpose of meeting and trading with them, and got along with them amiably enough. In fact, no overland fur caravan in full strength ever had to fight any Indians. Moreover, several sizable natural-history collections had already been made on overland trips and Townsend and Nuttall would make another one next year; some of them were as extensive as Maximilian's, which was destined to be lost to fire and the Missouri River in the end. It may be that the gentlemen of the American Fur Company coveted the prestige of royal associations and lied a little.

At any rate, Maximilian went up the Missouri, along the original pathway to the West, the one opened by Lewis and Clark, the one the fur trade had followed to the mountains till the hostile northern Indians closed the Missouri and forced it to take another route. And Stewart took that other route thus forced on the trade, the overland route that became the Oregon Trail and had been pioneered by William Ashley's memorable brigades. He traveled it with the annual caravan of Sublette & Campbell, who were Ashley's lineal successors and who were taking goods to some of the pioneers that had blazed the trail.

Here were the two principal energies in the mountain trade, the two principal ways of conducting it, and the two principal routes to it. The sequel will show how the methods were approaching each other, how even now distinctions could hardly be made that once had been clear and sharp. But we may note at the beginning that the American Fur Company had employed the traditional methods, and conservatively, up to recently. It used the water routes to transport its goods and bring back its furs, and two years back had immensely improved transportation by introducing a steamboat to the upper Missouri, in place of the keelboats that had to be sailed, poled, and cordelled sometimes for nine months up those untractable waters. It maintained fixed posts for the Indian trade and it depended more on Indian than on white trappers, though it had had to use the latter increasingly as it moved upon the territory of its stubborn and expert competitors. It traded in all furs — and even feathers, meat, grease, and tallow too — and by 1833 buffalo robes had already become a bigger annual value for its Upper Missouri Outfit than beaver was.

In order to reach the interior West, the last untouched fur country in the United States, William Ashley had revolutionized the trade when the Arikaras and Blackfeet forced him away from the Missouri. His successors — we are concerned with the Rocky Mountain Fur Company, who trapped fur, and Sublette & Campbell, who supplied them — retained the methods he had pioneered. They used land transportation, taking out goods and bringing back furs by pack train up the valley of the Platte River and through South Pass. They had maintained no fixed posts, though as a measure of competitive retaliation Sublette & Campbell intended to establish one this summer. Trade with the Indians was subsidiary; the mountain men (pre-eminence in that great title belongs to Ashley's men) trapped their own furs on the spot and traded with Indians only in chance encounters or at the annual rendezvous. This meant that they traveled over the entire West in small parties as success or failure in the hunt might take them, coming together in the summer at a designated place, whither the carrying company had arranged to bring the year's goods. It meant also that though they would take such fine furs as chance might put in their way — marten, otter, mink, silver fox — they were almost exclusively beaver hunters and were interested in buffalo robes only for their personal use. But by 1833, as has been said above, these distinctions were breaking down.

On Wednesday, April 10, the American Fur Company steamboat *Yellowstone* backed out of her slip into the Mississippi, crossed to the Illinois shore to take on wood, then headed upstream and turned into the Missouri. This was her third trip, a small tough boat built to specifications for the trade. Maximilian was on her. So, as a courtesy to him, was Pierre Chouteau, Jr., the active head of the great St. Louis firm which Astor had amalgamated in his trust — he got off at St. Charles the next day. So presently was 'the King of the Missouri,' Kenneth McKenzie, the hard-driving boss of another rival firm that had fought Astor to a finish and had to be taken into the trust almost on McKenzie's terms. He was the head of the Upper Missouri Outfit, a principal division of the Company which had to be called in to help the Western Outfit when it proved unable to lick the Opposition. McKenzie's job was, in Chouteau's words, '*écraser toute opposition*.' He was returning to his headquarters, Fort Union, to direct that destruction. There were other key figures aboard the *Yellowstone*. A corporation like the Company could use inside information about the activities of its competitors, strict enforcement of government regulations against them, a liberal construction of those regulations in its own behalf, and a dependable means of circumventing the government's plain intent to deal justly with the Indians and equably among traders. On the highest level it had such men as Thomas Hart Benton, who readily abandoned the equalitarian principles of the Jacksonian revolution when interests in fur were threatened, and Daniel Webster, whose notes and whose friends' notes the Company held.[7] But it was even more useful to have official representatives on the spot and the most valuable were the Indian agents. The *Yellowstone* was taking two of these upriver. One was John Dougherty, agent to the Pawnees, a sagacious and upright man but with leanings toward the Opposition; he would be watched and he might be converted. The other was John F. A. Sanford, agent to the Mandans, who for seven years now had used his office as a tactical headquarters of the Company and only last year had acquired another tie to it by marrying a Chouteau. The Opposition had tried repeatedly to get him fired and next year would succeed, whereupon he would become publicly an official of the Company. Formal history knows him as the owner of Dred Scott and the defendant in the great case. On this trip he was, as usual, distributing the government's annuity to the Mandans in such a way as to represent the goods as a benevolent gift from the Company to its neighbors at Fort Clark.

The *Yellowstone* carried the government goods and the bulk of the Company's annual supplies for its upriver posts. The usual complement of roustabouts were aboard and as well some pork-eaters, novices, for the posts and a handful of the upper class, trappers and traders going back to the job. Even in this first stretch taking a steamboat up the Missouri was one of the most precarious undertakings in the history of navigation. What any pilot might have learned about the river on his last trip, or even yesterday, was of no use to him today. The *Yellowstone* dodged snags and floating logs, got stranded on new or old sandbars whence she had to be pulled off by the whole company tugging at hawsers, was lightered by attending keelboats over unforeseen shallows, charged noisily into rapids that swept her back downstream out of control. The riotous rain and wind storms of the season flung her about. Floating trees pierced her hull at waterline; trees on the banks crushed her rails and sometimes penetrated her cabins. . . . To such an obbligato the royal naturalist went about his job. He made notes on the scenery and its geological indications, on the amazing flora, on the wild life, on the Indians who were met and entertained as the boat snorted slowly up the river. He and Bodmer explored the banks when she was held up or when she was moored for the night — no one tried to navigate the Missouri after dark. Remains of old trading posts became more common and one day a dugout coming downstream hailed them. Here was Lucien Fontenelle, the Company's most accomplished brigade-leader, one of the three who had taken it into the mountains to meet the Opposition on their own preserve. Since he was going to the mountains again this summer, was to take the Company caravan west from Fort Pierre, he came aboard.

The next day, twenty-four days out of St. Louis, they passed the mouth of the Platte and reached Bellevue. As an independent, Fontenelle had had a trading post here, but it belonged to the Company now and Major Dougherty's agency was near-by. The site, now a suburb of Omaha, had been important in the trade since the earliest upriver ventures. Here, a few miles downstream at the mouth of the Platte, and a few miles upstream at Council Bluffs,[8] a dozen or more now extinct fur companies had built posts for the Pawnee, Omaha, Oto, Ponca, and Iowa trade. And here Maximilian made his first close study of Indians, the Omahas. Ethnologists regard them as the most typical Plains tribe because their culture shared elements with practically all the others and because they had the most completely developed ceremonial system. They were so devoted to ceremonies, in fact, that they lost their fighting heart and they are a melancholy people in history. Someone was always raiding the Omahas, stealing their horses and women and goods, and scalping their warriors — who, however, had the most affecting death songs. They contributed much to the prosperity of their neighbors, especially the Pawnees and the Sioux, and they came to be habitual wailers — in so much that Brigham Young, who usually treated Indians with kindness, lost his patience and flogged some of them into silence. But they could look back on one great leader who had shown them what magnificence was like. This was a chief named Blackbird, as tough an Indian as ever lived, whose medicine included skill in the administration of poisons.

Here the country began to change, and the *Yellowstone* struggled on between bluffs, through even more dangerous shoals and rapids. They caught up with the *Assiniboin*, the Company's other steamboat, which was halted near the mouth of James River to await a rise that would enable her to proceed. She was new this year, was captained by another Company partner, Bernard Pratte, Jr., would presently take Maximilian aboard, and was not to have a long life. Beyond the Running Water or Niobrara they heard that the always treacherous Arikaras, the most hostile Indians this side of the Blackfeet, had been making trouble all winter and had killed, among others, the already legendary Hugh Glass. (It was true; the Arikaras had finally got apprehensive of government retribution for years of murder and robbery, were beginning to range southward toward the Platte, and would presently visit their friends the Pawnees, to keep away from soldiers.) One day the first antelope were seen and the next day the first buffalo. The *Assiniboin*, overtaking them and falling behind by turns, got news from upriver that not only the Arikaras but the Blackfeet were on the prod. So maybe the Company's fragile truce with them, the only one the Blackfeet had ever observed with Americans, was at an end.

Now they began to see signs of the Sioux, the most populous of Plains tribes, the Western equivalent of the Iroquois. On May 25, forty-six days out of St. Louis, they reached the government agency and Maximilian could study these vigorous, predatory people — he first saw the Yankton branch. He made notes on their physique and appearance, their artifacts, their customs; Bodmer sketched everything and made formal portraits. Four days later the *Yellowstone* reached Fort Pierre, built last year on the west bank of the Missouri three miles above the mouth of Teton River to replace Fort Tecumseh. It was the Company's post for the Sioux trade, one of the most important of all posts. The fort ran up its flag and fired its antique small cannon; the engagés rushed out firing their rifles. The *Yellowstone* answered in kind and nosed up to the rudimentary wharf. Indians and traders swarmed aboard, the level land was dotted with tipis, dogs snarled and fought by battalion, innumerable horses were grazing within sight, there were even milch cows, and here came the halfbreed Dorion, whose grandfather had briefly served Lewis and Clark, whose father the Astorians had made famous, and whose brother was to excite the admiration of Francis Parkman. Maximilian had reached his first objective.

* * *

Meanwhile, Captain Stewart had taken the overland trail, leaving St. Louis (probably) on April 13, three days after Maximilian. He probably traveled to Lexington or beyond by steamboat; most travelers did. He had met both William Sublette and Robert Campbell in St. Louis and was to join their caravan. The fantastic editor, politician, and soldier of fortune, J. Watson Webb, in his introduction to Stewart's first novel, remarking parenthetically that he was the best man in the country for a traveler touring the West to consult, says that he had given Stewart letters of introduction to General Atkinson of the Army and to William Ashley. It is seldom necessary to believe what Mr. Webb says, and all his statements about Ashley with at least half of those about Stewart are flatly wrong. However, by one means or another, Stewart had been led to travel with the Opposition. William Sublette, senior partner in the carrying firm, was to become an intimate friend of his. The Indians called him Cut Face or Left Hand; he was the oldest of five brothers who were in the mountain trade. His brother Milton was currently a partner in the Rocky Mountain Fur Company, to which Campbell was taking the summer caravan.

Sublette and Campbell were original Ashley men; they were tested experts in the mountains and had made sizable stakes in the trade, the last of that pioneering company who ever did so. Campbell had first joined the Ashley expeditions for his health's sake: he was tubercular. Cured, he became one of the best brigade-leaders — they were usually called partisans — and had now entered into partnership with Sublette; eventually he became a wealthy merchant and leading citizen of St. Louis. Sublette had been Ashley's most useful business lieutenant, as Jedediah Smith was his most distinguished partisan, and was only less distinguished than Smith in the field. He was a man of force and decision, a born commander, a shrewd business man, fitted by both knowledge and courage for the trade he was in.

He and Campbell had learned the moral of the fur business too well to occupy themselves with the actual trapping after the first great clean-up in a virgin country had been made — after many competitors, large and small, began to follow the Ashley trails to the Ashley country and to use the Ashley methods there. Sublette, with Jed Smith and Dave Jackson, bought out Ashley when he retired. For several years they carried the Ashley system more widely still through the mountains and on to California and the Columbia, Sublette in charge of the business, Jackson in charge of the trapping, and Smith mostly exploring new areas. They did a very large business indeed, but Ashley, who was banking for them, got a sizable share of the profits. This taught an unmistakable lesson and when Smith was killed by Comanches, in a southern venture that was intended to take the firm into the Santa Fe trade, Sublette and Jackson sold out to five of their leading partisans — Milton Sublette, John Baptiste Gervais, Henry Fraeb, the great Fitzpatrick, and the great Bridger. This firm was the only one properly called the Rocky Mountain Fur Company, though the title is loosely applied to all of Ashley's successors down to the triumph of the American Fur Company. Now Sublette and Campbell were in the carrying trade. They were purveyors and bankers to the RMF Company, whose anticipated profits would flow straight into their pockets. . . . The fur trade was not a business for softies.

Here the reader should work out on the map the orientation of the upper valley of Green River beyond South Pass and the Wind River Mountains, Fort Union on the Missouri at the mouth of the Yellowstone River, and the Platte River eastward from about the place where the Sweetwater joins it from South Pass. The upper valley of Green River may be thought of as the center from which the mountain trade was conducted. From Fort Union, toward the upper end of the traditional water route to the mountains, in the country of the Assiniboins and near the Blackfeet, the American Fur Company was directing its efforts to crush all opposition. In retaliation, Sublette and Campbell intended this summer to establish a rival post a mile or two from Fort Union, and William Sublette was taking goods for it up the Missouri by keelboat. Campbell was taking a pack train with goods for the RMF Company up the Platte route. Stewart joined his party.

So far as can be learned, Stewart kept no journal. No letters describing his adventures in any detail have come down to us. His two romantic novels contain much authentic background material, which will be cited, but they are nowhere history. This trip of 1833, however, can be followed to the rendezvous and beyond in the memoirs of another man who was making his first trip to the mountains with Campbell's train. This was

Charles Larpenteur, twenty-five years old, born in France but brought as a child to Baltimore. He wandered to St. Louis where he went to work for one of the O'Fallons and so naturally acquired a hunger for the West. He was now out to gratify it, though both an official of the American Fur Company and Robert Campbell had told him the fur trade was no life for a man of refinement. When he insisted, Campbell had signed him on for eighteen months at sixteen dollars a month. This made him a first-year man, a greenhorn, in the slang of the trade a pork-eater — and he was off to a trade which he never managed to get out of. He was a man of misfortune; his star was unfavorable. Charles Larpenteur never got the breaks.[9]

From Larpenteur we learn that another gentleman idler traveled with the party, Benjamin Harrison, a physician and the son of William Henry Harrison. Larpenteur says that he made the trip 'with a view to break him of drinking whiskey,' though the mountain trade was an odd choice for such a cure. His nephew, who, like his father, was to be President of the United States, told Doctor Coues that he was wild and adventurous, probably a sufficient explanation of his presence here, and Nathaniel Wyeth, who met him in the mountains, judged him unreliable if not actively dishonest. But his medical knowledge was useful and as a man of education and a restless disposition he would be companionable to Stewart. There was also 'Mr. Edmund Christy of St. Louis'; whether or not he was the Christy who figures in the annals of several fur companies is not clear, but he was taking a seven-thousand-dollar flyer with the RMF Company. Campbell was also taking to the mountains an Arapaho boy who had been in school in St. Louis and whose strange, affecting story someone should tell in full. Tom Fitzpatrick had found him lost and starving in the southwestern plains two years before, had called him Friday and informally adopted him, and had sent him East for some education. Now he was returning to his foster father and his country, a divided soul, an Indian who had learned to feel the emotions of a white man.

The caravan was Sublette & Campbell as jobbers and carriers. Its job was to get the goods to the rendezvous and to bring the year's fur catch back — to deliver goods, sell them, and buy furs. No wagons went with it, though Bill Sublette had taken some as far as the Wind River Mountains (just east of the Continental Divide) three years before, Bonneville had taken some through South Pass (over the Divide) to Green River in 1832, and it had been supposed ever since the return of Robert Stuart in 1813 that they could go all or most of the way to the Columbia. Campbell had about forty men whose chief duty was to manage an average of three laden mules apiece. They would come back with him from the rendezvous and though they were necessarily skilled workers, most of them must be seen as a somewhat lower caste, not winterers, not trappers, not mountain men. Campbell's lieutenant was his clerk, Johnesse in Coues's spelling, but his reliance would be an old companion in the great days, Louis Vasquez, the 'old Vaskiss' of the literature, an Ashley man, all rawhide and mountain wisdom, later to be Jim Bridger's partner. Besides the mules they had a sizable remuda of horses, twenty sheep which would give them meat as far as the buffalo country, and two bulls and three cows which were to be driven to the rendezvous and then on to the mouth of the Yellowstone, where they were to be the basis of a herd at the new post Sublette was to build there.

Three packs of goods, two hundred and fifty to three hundred pounds per mule, a little more for horses, twenty to forty tons all told. The amount was considerable but also it was stringently limited. The RMF Company, to which they were consigned, was composed of old friends and dear companions, but that did not count in business hours. When it sent goods to its upriver posts, the American Fur Company marked them up one hundred percent as a first charge before the field partners were to begin figuring a profit. Sublette & Campbell would charge the RMF Company a considerably higher mark-up than that, and were counting on its being increased by the differential (sometimes fifty percent) between mountain and St. Louis prices for the beaver in which it would be paid. In turn the RMF Company would double and redouble prices when it distributed the goods to either mountain men or Indians. When the mountain man was the ultimate consumer, he would pay, in beaver, prices which were seldom less than a thousand percent above St. Louis costs for only the most expensive items and which for many items ran up to two thousand percent. Only the best trappers, and they only when advantageously placed for bargaining, could clear their annual indebtedness for outfits and have something left. Few (except the 'free trappers') ever got out of debt, fewer still took a stake back East with them, none ever made a competence. But the operating companies seldom made a profit, either. The purveyors and bankers, who were usually the same firm (and, when not, usually had Astor or a

Chouteau or a Pratte somewhere in the background), had them where the hair was short. The mountain trade meant bankruptcy for most of those who engaged in it, though it meant enormous profits for a few — profits great enough to cover the appalling loss, waste, and overhead and still produce millionaires. It was the overlords who became the millionaires.

Well, what goods? Sublette & Campbell, for the RMF Company, were purveying supplies for the actual operations in the field. That meant primarily trapping and only secondarily trading with the Indians. There were certain basic necessities: powder and lead, traps, horses, mules; tobacco, bought at a few cents and sold at a dollar a pound; liquor, which was straight alcohol, bought at ten or fifteen cents a gallon and sold at a dollar or two or four dollars a pint, after being diluted fifty or seventy-five percent. Other staple necessities were shirts, coats, greatcoats, breeches, and blankets; such personal hardware as knives, hatchets, flints and steel, small tools. A few small luxuries, such as coffee and sugar, which homeless men would buy at rendezvous for a dollar and a half and on up to four dollars a pound. Beyond such things, free trappers in small groups and company trappers in larger groups would require limited quantities of goods for presents to and casual trade with the Indians. These were the same goods that the company as a firm traded at rendezvous. Powder, lead, tobacco, and alcohol first of all, with flints and repair parts for rifles and smoothbores. Then every kind of hardware that could be profitably transported, beginning with knives, hatchets, hatchet-tomahawks manufactured for the trade (manufactured war-clubs were also trade goods), files, fish-hooks, and the simple all-purpose awl (at sixty or seventy-five cents a gross, St. Louis) which the Indians used as needle, punch, augur, marlinspike, lancet, scalpel, and patent pocket tool-kit, and for which they would be charged up to a dollar in trade. (Or it might cost them nothing — next to tobacco it was the commonest present.) Next, blankets and various garments, and finally the beads, mirrors, bells, turkey or cock feathers, vermilion and other paints, and miscellaneous cheap novelties that were the luxury goods of the trade.

Larger quantities and a greater variety of goods were moving up the river in Bill Sublette's keelboat and the steamboats *Yellowstone* and *Assiniboin.* Take an actual invoice covering goods that presumably traveled with Maximilian on the *Yellowstone* and were consigned to Fontenelle and Drips at Fort Pierre, for the caravan which the former was to take to the mountains.[10] Certain indispensable items are not on this invoice, which in value covers about a fourth of an average shipment. Other invoices would cover the rest of it, and doubtless some of the goods he took West were drawn from the Fort Pierre storehouse. The reader must remember that Fontenelle's pack train was only a part, in fact the smallest part, of the Upper Missouri Outfit's equipment for 1833.

The prices quoted are a little hard to understand: they are well above the current wholesale quotations of this month at St. Louis, but they have not been advanced the full one hundred percent that was customary. The invoice totals $4297.62, and includes some goods not properly chargeable against Fontenelle and Drips, some firm and a few personal supplies, and some firearms that must have been left at Fort Pierre.

The Company is sending its field partisan 100 strings of large blue beads, three-fourths pound per string; 140 pounds all told of medium quality beads, red, blue, and white; 225 pounds of chalk-white beads at 37½ cents per pound, and 390 assorted strings of beads, 23 to 40 cents per three-fourths pound. Thirty-five pairs of one-point Mackinaw blankets ($2.67), 40 pairs three-and-a-half point, in blue, green, and scarlet (averaging about $9.50 per pair), and 75 pairs, and 9 half-pair three-point in the same colors plus white (from $5.89 to $9.45). It will take a lower profit on blankets than on most items: they will sell by the half-pair at from $16 to $20. It is sending a variety of cloths too diversified to list here, common cloths, stroudings, plaids, fancy calicos, flannels, worth close to $700 on the books, perhaps three thousand yards in all, destined to sell at about a thousand percent advance. Fifteen 'scarlet chief's coats,' whose usefulness we will encounter farther on, at $7.16 and 51 at $7.72 (chargeable to Entertainment, Overhead, or Goodwill), 29 'capotes' made of Mackinaw blanketing at $6.98 ($20 to $25 in the mountains), a dozen woolen caps, cock and 'foxtail' feathers. Half a long ton of rifle balls (thirty-two to the pound, six cents a pound here, about a dollar in the mountains), 1048 musket and 36 rifle flints and a few 'horse-pistol flints' which might be patent fire-lighters; about 300 shirts, cotton, calico, and linen; 4 gross of garters; 6 pairs children's bootees and 8 pairs misses' white stockings (doubtless for the squaws of partisans); 150 Northwest guns — that is, short smoothbore muskets made specially for this trade — 100 dozen 'common scalpers' and 55 dozen more expensive knives for murder with style, and 50 dozen oval fire steels.

The ledger page ends here. It had not yet got round to liquor, tobacco, and gunpowder.

A force that involved empires must be noted. Most of these goods were foreign, which explains an ambivalence in the politics of Mr. Astor, Mr. Ramsay Crooks, and the St. Louis magnates — as well as in Thomas Hart Benton, their loyal representative. Massachusetts and Connecticut, Pennsylvania and New Jersey were dizzily accelerating the industrial revolution in the United States but we were still behind. The Indian trade, which is to say the fur trade, had been at the very base of the struggle for Canada that lasted through two centuries, and a fundamental reason for the British victory was the ability of English manufacturers to produce both better and cheaper goods for the Indians — who were expert judges of quality. That ability still gave the Hudson's Bay Company a formidable advantage in Oregon — Astor had negotiated an understanding with it along the Great Lakes — and the American protective tariff increased it. Blankets were English or French, cloth was English, French, or Flemish, beads came from Milan or Trieste. The best hardware was English, though here we were rapidly overcoming our handicaps. No rifles made in Europe which sold at competitive prices were anywhere near so good as the American product — though fine rifles were infinitely better than ours — but the Indians seldom wanted rifles at this period. Traps, when not made by hand at about fifteen dollars each St. Louis, came from Manchester, and it would be nearly twenty years before the Oneida Community could achieve quantity production. Dupont's gunpowder was inferior to both English and French and which of these was better was a serial argument at campfires. . . . So that in his goods as well as his markets the mountain man was deeply involved with world energies.

* * *

Campbell mustered his party at Lexington, Missouri, which was farther east than the usual jumping-off places, Franklin, Independence, and eventually Westport. Here on May 12, 1833, Bill Sublette's thirty rivermen shouldered the long cordelle and started tugging his keelboat up the Missouri toward the mouth of the Yellowstone and, with wretched hangovers from a farewell spree, the overland party headed west.

Stewart, an army man, would fit into the life at once. The pack train traveled in a close approximation of military discipline.

It made camp in late afternoon and struck it at sunrise precisely as the King's Hussars would have done. The personnel were subject to the command of officers and noncoms, under severe penalty. They were formed into messes which ate together and rotated at the routine jobs. There were herd guards, horse guards, and, as soon as the settlements were left behind, night camp guards as well. (Though there was seldom danger of Indian attack, an attempt might be made to steal the horses any time.) There was no novelty to an old cavalryman in the willfulness of mules trying to buck off their packs, rolling with them, and suddenly bolting for the settlements and inspiring all loose horses to follow. Stewart had seen all this before and it is clear that he was a useful unpaid brigadier to Campbell. Everyone who mentions him through the next six years says that he was an accomplished partisan.

But though the world traveler was acquainted with wide horizons, from now on everything about the countryside was new and strange. They were on the route which Ashley's men had established and along which the United States was to follow its western star. (Oregon began at the Continental Divide, that is, halfway through Wyoming, and from the western end of the pass that crossed the Divide you could see the tips of Mexican mountains.) They headed westward into Kansas, then turned northwest, crossing innumerable creeks and such rivers as the Kansas and the Big Blue. Beyond that the Little Blue, which brought them to Nebraska, and on to the Coasts of the Nebraska, the valley of the Platte. This was prairie country, lush with grass that would be belly-high on your horse, or higher, by June. In May it was spongy from violent rains, in long stretches little better than a bog. The rains struck suddenly and disastrously, drowning you out of your blankets, interspersed with snow flurries or showers of hailstones as big as a fist, driven by gales that blew your possessions over the prairie and froze your bones. Continuous deafening thunder might last for hours at a time. It stampeded the stock, by day scattering packs for five miles perhaps, by night scattering horses and mules even farther — and every one had to be searched for till it was found. Every creek was a river, every river a sound, and every brook a morass — and across these a hundred and fifty horses and mules, with sheep and the cows, had to be cursed, beaten, and sometimes pulled by ropes. They squealed, snorted, bolted, bit, kicked, and got mired down. The prairies were beautiful with flowers, waving grasses, and the song of birds — all carefully noted in Stewart's novels — but not during the spring rains.

# THE LOOK OF THE WEST IN THE 1830's

Up to the establishment of freight and stagecoach lines in the 1850's there were two standard ways of getting to the interior West, by boat up the Missouri and by an overland trail that followed the course of the Platte and its northern fork. (Another route which branched northwestward from the Santa Fe Trail in Colorado was seldom used.) Their landscapes were sharply unlike but they had in common the quality of strangeness. The entire West was strange to the American eye. To the men with whom this book deals it was commonplace but to any other Americans going west in the 1830's or seeing such pictures as those reproduced here the land was not so much a foreign country as a different planet. Nothing that the American people had known prepared them for it intellectually or emotionally.

Bodmer took the Missouri route and all his landscapes reproduced in this section are of the stretch between the mouth of the Yellowstone and that of the Marias. They show a country eroded to unearthly shapes, a country for which three American languages have found the same term: mauvaises terres, malpais, badlands.

The Miller landscapes of this group are on or near the route of the most momentous roadway in American history, the one that came to be called the Oregon Trail. It is the route of the Western migration, though we do not see it here west of Green River. The arrangement of the pictures is, so far as is practicable, the sequence in which one going west would see their subjects.

Except for Plates XIV, XV, and XVI, which George Catlin had anticipated by a year, all these pictures are the first ever made of their subjects.

*Courtesy of The Walters Art Gallery*

PLATE I

## CHIMNEY ROCK *Alfred Jacob Miller*

The Platte was also known as the Nebraska (from a Sioux word meaning shallow) and its valley was poetically referred to as the Coasts of the Nebraska. As one traveled up that valley the grade inclined gently but steadily upward, the country grew drier, and the plains changed to a transition land that would merge with the mountains. About five hundred and fifty miles out of Independence a group of fragmented hills, buttes, and mesas signalized that the transition was beginning. Chimney Rock or The Chimney, a column of core rock whose softer covering had been worn away, was among the first of these nightmare formations. It was a landmark to all travelers of the Platte route.

*Courtesy of Mrs. Clyde Porter*

PLATE II

SCOTT'S BLUFF *Alfred Jacob Miller*

Forty miles west of Chimney Rock the fragmented hills have drawn together into ridges and ranges. These spurs and headlands have resisted the erosion that leveled out the country to the eastward. Geologically they are the tough core of what had been the dumping ground of the Rocky Mountains, and at Scott's Bluff they reach a height of eight hundred feet above the Platte, which flows near its base in a long curve. The trail usually clung close to the river as far as this formation; here it plunged through the hills by various routes, each one representing a vain hope of easier going. This also is a nightmare country and its shapes strained the imagery of travelers, who spoke of medieval cities, the landscape of the moon, and the countries of mythology.

Sioux Reconnoitering *Alfred Jacob Miller*

The landscape here is the Platte route anywhere between the forks and Chimney Rock or at intervals thereafter to Fort Laramie. Until 1834 any Sioux met here would probably have been on the warpath.

PLATE III

*Courtesy of The Walters Art Gallery*

*Courtesy of Mr. L. Vernon Miller*

PLATE IV

MOVEMENT OF THE CARAVAN — MIRAGE ON THE PRAIRIE

*Alfred Jacob Miller*

A memorable picture: a moment of the march caught perfectly, even to the flickering of a mirage in the distance. The train contains both wagons (whose military intervals will not be maintained long) and pack animals. In the right-hand corner hunters are preparing to ride off for buffalo. A returning hunter has laden his lead-horse with butchered meat. The scene is east of Fort Laramie and the low hills that stretch from left to right mark the Coasts of the Nebraska.

*Courtesy of Mrs. Clyde Porter*

PLATE V

A SURROUND *Alfred Jacob Miller*

A generalized but authentic study of a tribal hunt. It is somewhat overcrowded in the middle distance, for a herd so large as this one would probably be more dispersed.

PLATE VI CARAVAN ON THE PLATTE *Alfred Jacob Miller*

*Courtesy of Mrs. Clyde Porter*

Goods are being ferried by bull boat; horses will be swum across.

*Courtesy of Mrs. Clyde Porter*

PLATE VII

SCENE NEAR FORT LARAMIE *Alfred Jacob Miller*

Laramie Fork, at a very low stage, is in the foreground. The Platte, out of sight here, runs approximately parallel with the hills in the right background, about a mile from the fort. The high summit is Laramie Peak. Compare this site with that of Fort Union in Plate XVI.

PLATE VIII FORT LARAMIE *Alfred Jacob Miller*

*Courtesy of Mrs. Clyde Porter*

With an Oglala village camped for trade.

PLATE IX

*Courtesy of Mr. L. Vernon Miller*

INTERIOR OF FORT LARAMIE *Alfred Jacob Miller*

The presence of Indians in the quadrangle is unorthodox. This and the preceding picture are historical documents of primary importance.

## Independence Rock *Alfred Jacob Miller*

Fort Laramie was about six hundred and sixty-five miles from Independence. Beyond it the trail, still following the valley of the North Platte, headed northwest and then made a sweeping curve southwest — all this through chaotic, tortuous country that grew increasingly arid and eventually became a rock desert. Where the Platte turned due south the trail left it and made for the Sweetwater, which comes down from the Wind River Mountains on the Continental Divide. One hundred and seventy-one trail miles beyond Fort Laramie came the most famous landmark east of South Pass, the turtleback of reddish gray stone called Independence Rock, whose southeast face is shown in Miller's picture. Miller exaggerates its height a little; it rises one hundred and fifty-five feet above the Sweetwater. It was the Inscription Rock of the Oregon Trail. Many travelers carved their names on it; though many have been weathered away, some remain.

PLATE X

*Courtesy of The Walters Art Gallery*

*Courtesy of The Walters Art Gallery*

PLATE XI — DEVIL'S GATE — *Alfred Jacob Miller*

Five miles upstream from Independence Rock, the Sweetwater cuts this narrow gate, four hundred feet deep, through the ridge.

PLATE XII

*Courtesy of Mrs. Clyde Porter*

## Crossing the River by Moonlight *Alfred Jacob Miller*

It is unlikely that our artist saw a night crossing.

Indian Procession in Honor of Sir William Drummond Stewart *Alfred Jacob Miller*

*Courtesy of Mr. L. Vernon Miller*

PLATE XIII

See Chapter XII.

PLATE XIV

INTERIOR OF A MANDAN HUT *Charles Bodmer*

The Mandans and their neighbors on the upper Missouri, the Minnetarees and the Arikaras, lived in permanent huts of timber and earth, each large enough to lodge several families. Both artistically and ethnologically Bodmer's picture is one of the best ever made of Indian life.

*Courtesy of The New York Public Library*

CONFLUENCE OF THE YELLOWSTONE AND THE MISSOURI

*Charles Bodmer*

PLATE XV

*Courtesy of The Boston Athenaeum*

*Courtesy of The Boston Athenaeum*

PLATE XVI

View of Fort Union; the Assiniboins Breaking up Their Camp *Charles Bodmer*

PLATE XVII

HERD OF BUFFALOES ON THE UPPER MISSOURI

*Charles Bodmer*

*Courtesy of The Boston Athenaeum*

PLATE XVIII

THE WHITE CASTLES ON THE UPPER MISSOURI

*Charles Bodmer*

*Courtesy of The Boston Athenaeum*

Both this and Plate XV show typical scenes in the Missouri badlands between Fort Union and Fort McKenzie.

*Courtesy of The Boston Athenaeum*

PLATE XIX

## View of the Rocky Mountains *Charles Bodmer*

Since Maximilian and Bodmer never got more than a few miles beyond Fort McKenzie, near the junction of Marias River and the Missouri, Bodmer's title is inexact. No range actually a part of the Rocky Mountains can be seen from this vicinity. The peaks on the horizon must belong to either the Little Rockies or the Highwood Mountains, more likely the former. Both are detached ranges.

You took it. Since there was always a possibility of Indian trouble, daily drenchings and stampedes could be shrugged off with an oath. The officers' mess still had delicacies laid in at St. Louis and liquor to get warm on. The men had exhausted their coffee long since; there were bacon and ship's biscuit, some mutton if the boss hadn't eaten it all, and the knowledge that eventually you would meet buffalo. For some time the only Indians would be handfuls of tamed beggars and thieves. Our travelers were west of the Otos and Omahas, whom the river voyage passed. Along the lower Platte, which they reached two weeks out from Lexington, they would encounter the Pawnees. These were still a formidable people in 1833, brainy Indians, a match for any of their enemies, wide-ranging, expert thieves, liars, and extortioners. (This from the point of view of the whites; theirs will be stated later.) They were square in the path of the advancing empire, however, and it did not need many years to debauch them till they were the loudmouths and skulkers of the Oregon Trail. Later still they had a sort of renaissance when their hereditary war with the Sioux, perhaps the most continuous of Indian enmities, made them brilliant auxiliaries of the United States Army — and permitted us to destroy two tribes in one righteous cause. In the period here dealt with they must be accounted a superior Plains tribe. They would not attack a caravan that was in full strength — Indian war figured percentages — but you must watch your step.

Campbell's party reached the Platte well to the east of the forks, took the South Platte at the forks, and presently crossed to the North Platte. For a hundred miles the country had been gradually changing. The rains all but ceased, there was no more tall grass, drinkable water was becoming scarcer, the long upward inclination of the land had become apparent. The Platte was a thin mud that flowed sluggishly through innumerable islands of cottonwood and willow and might be a mile or more wide. It was the first of Western rivers to beget the standard quips — it was a mile wide and an inch deep and it flowed uphill, it was water you had to chew, it was good drinking if you threw it out and filled the cup with whiskey. Quicksands were added to the day's hazards; Miller's sketch is typical but can only imply the quaking and screaming of mules, who were intuitive about quicksands, and the bellowing of Campbell's bulls.

This was the country called the high plains, and though it would be the high plains for hundreds of miles, still it was by insensible stages making toward the mountains. Our travelers probably reached the North Platte at Ash Hollow. The plains had already set up undulant swells, and soon there began to be detached fragments of geologically ancient hills. They were scattered without pattern and so eroded by the unceasing wind that they worked on imaginations already oppressed by sun and distance. They grew larger and began to have names, Court House Rock, Jail Rock, Ship Rock, Chimney Rock, presently Scott's Bluffs.[11] By now the valley was fragmented by innumerable gullies, ravines, and even canyons; they were more easily crossed by pack train than they would be by emigrant wagons, but the comparative is not worth much and whichever route a pack train took through them always proved to be the wrong one. By now, however, in fact only a couple of days up the Platte, life had greatly improved. Captain Stewart, who had probably learned to cook over dry camel dung, was now cooking over buffalo chips. Gladly, for there was buffalo meat to cook.

Stewart may have had many motives for coming to the United States, but probably foremost among them was a desire to experience what seems to have been the finest of all sports on this continent, perhaps the finest sport hunters have enjoyed anywhere. Every variety of big game, from elephants to grizzlies, has its own devotees, but everyone who ever hunted buffalo on horseback in the West (except the skeptical Richard Dodge) found it the consummation of the sportsman's life. This was not because the buffalo was cunning or crafty, for it was the stupidest of mammals, nor because it was hard to come by, for it existed in far greater masses than any other large animal on earth, nor because it was dangerous in itself. What gave the hunt an emotion equivalent to ecstasy was the excitement, the speed, the thundering noise, the awe-inspiring bulk of the huge animal in motion, the fury of its death, and the implicit danger of the chase. Since for forty years this was a notable and unique American experience, we may pause to describe the sportsman's way of hunting buffalo.

Stewart first saw buffalo in late May along the Platte east of the forks, a usual time and place for fur caravans to meet them. This was calf-time, and so the cows, at other seasons incomparably the best meat, would be poor and stringy. The greenhorn had envisioned enormous herds whose passing shook the earth and whose bellowing made sleep impossible at night, but such herds would not form till the mating or 'running' season, well past midsummer. Before that season the buffalo would be encountered in small bands — from twenty or thirty up to a hundred or so — more or less cohesive, moving toward water or feeding on the short grama which was the most nutritious of all grasses. There might be many bands near together, mounting up to several thousand all told; or, even in what would be considered good buffalo country, a day's travel might reveal only two or three. The calves would be light in color, sandy red or even yellow; packs of wolves and coyotes would be trailing them but the bulls would be on guard. Yearlings would be darker and 'spike bulls,' the four-year-olds whose horns had smooth, clean points, would begin to show the colors of maturity. There was much individual variation, but a typical bull would shade from a bright blond at the forequarters and hump to dark brown or even black at the hindquarters and under the belly. At calf-time the thick woolly hair would be shedding toward the near-nudity of midsummer and the resulting patchiness would make a full-grown bull look even more ferocious and demoniac than a greenhorn's fantasy had painted him. Such a bull, say eight or ten years old, would weigh just short of a ton, seventeen hundred or eighteen hundred pounds. He would stand six feet at the shoulders. From muzzle to rump he might be ten feet long.

Sighting a bunch, the hunter tightened his saddle girth and verified the charge and priming of his weapons. He tried to get as close as possible, approaching upwind. Grazing buffalo could be stalked within certain bowshot — fifty to a hundred yards — by careful Indians or whites, crawling up draws, pushing a sagebrush ahead like military snipers, or even, as in a celebrated print of Catlin's, wearing wolfskins. If a successful approach were made, such a hunter might kill half the bunch, even with firearms, before the survivors showed any curiosity about what was going on. There was no such placidity, however, if the ungainly beasts caught the man-scent or saw any rapid or unusual movement. The sportsman hoped to ride undiscovered within three hundred yards but seldom did. Usually he was half a mile away when first one and then the whole bunch broke into a run, quartering downwind to keep the scent and yet escape from it. That was what the sportsman had come for: he began the chase.

Any tolerably good horse could overtake the fastest buffalo, but had to go full gallop to do so and sometimes had to gallop four or five miles, which was what broke horses down. This first wild run — most exhilarating in early morning when the thin air was electric in your lungs — was headlong over unknown ground which might have buffalo wallows or small gullies or sizable ravines in it and was certain to be pitted by innumerable burrows of gophers and prairie dogs. A fall might mean a broken leg for the horse, broken bones or concussion or death for the rider. In Frémont's report Kit Carson, as expert a hunter as ever lived, is first seen in action picking himself up from such a fall: 'though considerably hurt he had the good fortune to break no bones.' But long before the hunter overtook the buffalo he was, in Frémont's words, 'sensible to nothing else.' His heart was pounding in time with the horse's hoofs, he was straining forward in his saddle, and he was shouting at the top of his voice.

The buffalo were making by instinct for country too broken for a horse to follow, deep ravines or wooded coulees. If they were overtaken, the hunter's excitement became delirium. 'I could see nothing but a cloud of dust,' Francis Parkman wrote. 'In a moment I was in the midst of the cloud, half suffocated by the dust and stunned by the trampling of the flying herd; but I was drunk with the chase and cared for nothing but the buffalo.' There were buffalo all round, enormous in the murk, butting at the horse or trying to gore it (impossible if it kept its feet, of course), sometimes charging at it. Their hoofs flung dirt and clods into the hunter's eyes; his ears roared with a confusion of noises. There was no seeing what was ahead, but he had to select a victim, and at any season but calf-time the victim had to be a cow, a young one for preference. A trained buffalo horse, guided entirely by the pressure of the rider's thighs, sidestepped the sidelong charges and dodged the direct ones, coming up behind the right shoulder. When Indians coursed buffalo they used a lance or an arrow; one arrow was enough if properly placed and it was frequently driven clear through the beast so that it slid along the plain on the other side. The white man used his rifle and reloaded it on the dead run, pounding the buttplate on the saddle to seat the bullet which normally had to be rammed home. If he succeeded in that doubtful operation — pouring powder haphazardly from his horn, perhaps in a double or triple charge, and spitting into the muzzle a ball he had been carrying in his mouth — he was ready for another kill. If not, he used his pistols, less effectively. No matter: by now he was a madman and had to keep galloping, yelling, firing, till his horse was spent, his powder gone, or the bunch of buffalo dispersed as stragglers. Suddenly there was silence again. Far away other half-dozens were galloping ahead of other hunters, whose rifles might spout smoke as their companion looked up. Here and there over the plain was the fallen carcass of a buffalo, here and there a wounded beast sinking to its knees. Consciousness came back. The horse was snorting for breath and bathed with foam. 'I myself,' Parkman says, 'felt as if drenched in warm water.'

Meanwhile, if your horse had stumbled in a prairie dog hole or lost its footing in a ravine, you would have been gored and trampled.

'No animal,' Frederick Ruxton wrote, 'requires so much killing as the buffalo.' This was not quite true even of American animals, since the grizzly bear was harder to kill, but it was true enough. Ruxton goes on:

> Unless shot through the lungs or spine they invariably escape; and even when thus mortally wounded, or even struck through the very heart, they will frequently run a considerable distance before falling to the ground, particularly if they see the hunter after the wound is given. If, however, he keeps himself concealed after firing, the animal will remain still, if it does not immediately fall. It is a most painful sight to witness the dying struggles of the huge beast. The buffalo invariably evinces the greatest repugnance to lie down when mortally wounded, apparently conscious that, when once touching mother earth, there is no hope left him. A bull, shot through the heart or lungs, with blood streaming from his mouth, and protruding tongue, his eyes rolling, bloodshot, and glazed with death, braces himself on his legs, swaying from side to side, stamps impatiently at his growing weakness, or lifts his rugged and matted head and helplessly bellows out his conscious impotence. To the last, however, he endeavors to stand upright and plants his limbs farther apart, but to no purpose. As the body rolls like a ship at sea, his head slowly turns from side to side, looking about, as it were, for the unseen and treacherous enemy who has brought him, the lord of the plains, to such a pass. Gouts of purple blood spurt from his mouth and nostrils, and gradually the failing limbs refuse longer to support the ponderous carcass; more heavily rolls the body from side to side until suddenly, for a brief instant, it becomes rigid and still; a convulsive tremor seizes it and, with a low, sobbing gasp, the huge animal falls over on his side, the limbs extended stark and stiff, and the mountain of flesh without life or motion.
>
> The first attempts of a 'greenhorn' to kill a buffalo are invariably unsuccessful. He sees before him a mass of flesh, nearly five feet in depth from the top of the hump to the brisket, and consequently imagines that by planting his ball midway between

> these points, it must surely reach the vitals. Nothing, however, is more erroneous than the impression; for to 'throw a buffalo in his tracks,' which is the phrase for making a clean shot, he must be struck but a few inches above the brisket, behind the shoulder, where alone, unless the spine be divided, a death-shot will reach the vitals. I once shot a bull, the ball passing directly through the very center of the heart and tearing a hole sufficiently large to insert the finger, which ran upwards of half a mile before it fell, and yet the ball had passed completely through the animal, cutting its heart almost in two. I also saw eighteen shots, the half of them muskets, deliberately fired into an old bull at six paces, and some of them passing through the body, the poor animal standing the whole time and making feeble attempts to charge. The nineteenth shot, with the muzzle touching his body, brought him to the ground. The head of the buffalo bull is so thickly covered with coarse matted hair that a ball fired at half a dozen paces will not penetrate the skull through the shaggy frontlock. I have frequently attempted this with a rifle carrying twenty-five balls to the pound, but never once succeeded.[12]

And now the ecstasy of the chase over, there was a different ecstasy to come, for buffalo meat was the greatest of foods. Butchering for meat was done as in Miller's sketch (Plate LVII). That is, the carcass was propped on the belly, with the knees bent or with the legs stretched out.[13] The tongue was taken first — and was always taken as a trophy, as proof of the kill, even when a tough old bull quite unfit for eating had been killed. Then the butcher made an incision along the spine and cut away the skin down one side, using it as a table for his meats. What cuts he took depended on how plentiful the buffalo were. He always took the 'boss,' a small hump on the back of the neck, the hump itself, and the 'hump ribs,' which were the prolongations of vertebrae that supported it; then the 'fleece,' which was the flesh between the spine and the ribs, and the three-inch layer of fat that covered it, the 'side ribs,' and the lower 'belly fat' that was considered one of the greatest delicacies. He would probably take the liver too and such portions of the intestines as his tastes suggested. Then he would butcher out a thigh bone and use it to crack such other bones as might provide the best marrow. Francis Chardon, a celebrated factor of the American Fur Company, listed as specially choice 'the nuts' — the earliest Rocky Mountain oysters, therefore. But when buffalo were scarce all the meat was eaten. Nor are the books right when they reproach white hunters alone for reckless waste of meat, for the Indians were just as wasteful when it was plentiful and took only the cuts they liked most.

(There were special, empirical skills even in butchering. 'Ti-ya!' exclaims Old Bill Williams in Ruxton's *Life in the Far West*, 'do 'ee hyar, now, you darned greenhorn, do 'ee spile fat cow like that whar you was raised? Them doin's won't shine in this crowd, boy, do 'ee hyar, darn you? What! butcher meat across the grain! why whar'll the blood be goin' to, you precious Spaniard? [More likely, you damned greaser.] Down the grain, I say, and let your flaps be long or out the juice'll run slick — do 'ee hyar now?')

There were few delicate feeders in the mountains. The Indians preferred their meat high and kept the surplus till it began to rot. The river tribes liked the green, putrid flesh of buffalo drowned while crossing the ice and hauled ashore weeks later, 'so ripe, so tender, that very little boiling is required.' They ate the kidneys raw, but the delight of an Indian gourmet was to eat his way down a ten-foot length of raw, warm, perhaps still quivering gut — in one snapshot by an appalled white the gourmet squeezes out the gut's contents just ahead of his teeth. Guts or *boudins* were delicious to the white palate too, but they were first lightly seared above the fire. 'I once saw two Canadians,' Ruxton says, 'commence at either end of such a coil of grease, the mass lying between them on a dirty apishemore [saddle pad] like the coil of a huge snake. As yard after yard glided glibly down their throats, and the serpent on the saddle-cloth was dwindling from an anaconda to a moderate-sized rattlesnake, it became a great point with each of the feasters to hurry his operation, so as to gain a march upon his neighbor and improve the opportunity by swallowing more than his just proportion; each at the same time exhorting the other, whatever he did, to feed fair and every now and then, overcome by the unblushing attempts of his partner to bolt a vigorous mouthful, would suddenly jerk back his head, drawing out at the same moment, by the retreating motion, several yards of *boudin* from his neighbor's stomach (for the greasy viand required no mastication and was bolted whole) and, snapping up the ravished portions, greedily swallowed them.' The white man would eat the liver raw as soon as it was taken; he seasoned it with the gall or sometimes with gunpowder. But the feast was still to come.

'Meat's meat,' the trapper said, and he ate what meat was at hand, from his own moccasins, parfleche, and lariats, in 'starvin' times,' on through the wide variety of mountain game, of which some tidbits were memorable to gastronomes — boiled beaver tail, 'panther,' and as an acquired taste young Oglala puppy. But when coming out from the States you shot your first fat cow, or when after finding no buffalo for some weeks you reached them at last, you touched the very summit of delight. Nor can there be any doubt that buffalo meat, an indescribably rich, tender, fiberless, and gamey beef, was the greatest meat man has ever fed on. The mountain man boiled some cuts, notably the hump, and seared or sautéed others, but mostly he cooked them by slow roast, skewered on his ramrod or, as in Miller's sketch, on a stick. Every man to his own fire (unless messes, each with its own cook, had been appointed) and no man with more tableware than his belt-knife — gravy, juices, and blood running down his face, forearms, and shirt. He wolfed the meat and never reached repletion. Eight pounds a day was standard ration for Hudson's Bay Company employees, but when meat was plentiful a man might eat eight pounds for dinner, then wake a few hours later, build up the fire, and eat as much more. All chroniclers agree that no stomach rebelled and no appetite ever palled. Moreover, to the greases that stained the mountaineer's garments were added the marrow scooped from bones and the melted fat that was gulped by the pint. Kidney fat could be drunk without limit; one was more moderate with the tastier but oily belly fat, which might be automatically regurgitated if taken in quantity, although such a rejection interrupted no one's gourmandizing very long.

There will be occasion farther on to describe Indian methods of hunting the buffalo, the making of dried meat and pemmican, and the additional uses the buffalo served. It seems proper to point out here that buffalo meat was a complete diet. The modern experiments of Stefansson have shown why. Parts of it were eaten raw and abundant fat was eaten with the lean. The Indians who lived along the Missouri cultivated corn and squashes and their immediate neighbors sometimes got their produce in trade; those who lived near the Continental Divide and on the inner edge of the Great Basin regularly ate a variety of roots; all tribes knew many edible plants on which to fall back in starving times. But most of the Plains tribes lived exclusively on meat, and so except for two or three weeks a year did the mountain men. At rendezvous and at the beginning of the trip West there would be coffee, sugar, hardtack, and bacon, usually nothing more and these in sternly limited quantities. For the rest there was only meat and this meant primarily buffalo meat, fresh, dried, or made into pemmican. No hardier people ever lived. There was no scurvy; in fact, nothing is rarer in the literature than mention of a sick trapper. Almost daily immersion in the glacial water of mountain streams eventually stiffened their joints, but otherwise a trapper sick enough to be mentioned has a hangover or 'the venereals,' which he got from a squaw who had got them from one of his predecessors. One illness was attributed to the diet: greenhorns making their first acquaintance with buffalo were supposed to get dysentery. Larpenteur speaks of 'mal de vache,' others mention the same phenomenon, and there is some modern evidence that a shift to a meat diet may temporarily produce it. The chances are, however, that the facts which Larpenteur noted should be explained with a reference to another shift which occurred at about the same stage of the western journey. The travelers were now frequently drinking alkali-impregnated water, which is to say more or less concentrated solutions of Epsom or Glauber's salts, or of both.

This, then, is the mountain epicure's moment of climax. Hump and boss boil in a kettle, cracked marrow bones sizzle by the fire, there are as many ribs to roast as a man may want. Crosslegged on the ground, using only their Green River knives,[14] the trappers eat their way through six or ten pounds of fat cow. Wellbeing overspreads them; fat cow is an intoxicant only less persuasive than the alcohol which they will not taste again till the next rendezvous — unless the partisan has brought a couple of curved tin kegs for Indian customers and on some noteworthy occasion can be induced to broach one. Camp is pitched near some watercourse, a small creek or a rushing mountain river, with firewood and grass at hand. If there has been no Indian sign and if there is no reason to apprehend Indians, the fire will be built up when the meal is over. Here is the winesap air of the high places, the clear green sky of evening fading to a dark that brings the stars within arm's length, the cottonwoods along the creek rustling in the wind. The smell of meat has brought the wolves and coyotes almost to the circle of firelight. They skulk just beyond it; sometimes a spurt of flame will turn their eyes to gold; they howl and attack one another, and farther out in the dark the howls of their relatives diminish over the plains. In running season there will be the bellowing of the bulls. Horses and mules crop the bunch grass at the end of their lariats or browse on leaves along the creek. The firelight flares and fades in the wind's rhythm on the faces of men in whose minds are the vistas and the annals of the entire West.

It is the time of fulfillment, the fullness of time, the moment lived for itself alone. The mountain men were a tough race, as many selective breeds of Americans have had to be; their courage, skill, and mastery of the conditions of their chosen life were absolute or they would not have been here. Nor would they have been here if they had not responded to the loveliness of the country and found in their way of life something precious beyond safety, gain, comfort, and family life. Besides the specific attributes of that way of life and its country, it is fair to point out an extremity, perhaps the maximum, of American individualism and gusto. Moreover, solitude had given them a surpassing gift of friendship and simple survival proved the sharpness of their wits. There were few books and few trappers were given to reading what there were: talk was everything. In this hour of function there was the talk of friends and equals.

'Mind the time we took Pawnee topknots away to the Platte?' Louy Simonds asks Long Hatcher in Garrard's book.[15] And Hatcher says, 'Wagh! ef we didn't, an' give an ogwh-ogwh longside of thar darned screechin', I'm a niggur. This child doesn't let an Injun count a coup on his cavyard always. They come mighty nigh rubbin' me out tother side of Spanish Peaks -- woke up in the mornin' jist afore day, the devils yellin' like mad. I grabs my knife, keels one [turns him keel upward], an' made for timber, with four of thar cussed arrows in my meatbag. The 'Paches took my beaver — five pack of the prettiest in the mountains — an' two mules, but my traps was hid in the creek. Sez I, hyar's a gone coon if they keep my gun, so I follers thar trail an' at night crawls into camp, an' socks my big knife up to the Green River, first dig. I takes tother Injun by the har and makes meat of him *too*. *Maybe* thar wasn't coups counted an' a big dance on hand [even] ef I was alone. I got old bull-thrower [his rifle], made medicine over him, an' no darned niggur [Indian] kin draw bead with him since.'

The Americans, and especially the Americans who live in the open, have always been storytellers — one need recall only the rivermen, the lumberjacks, the cowmen, or in fact the loafers round any stove at a rural crossroads — but there have been no stories beyond those told by the map-minded breakers of trails, hunters of beaver, and exterminators of Indians. (Long Hatcher, a few pages past the casual anecdote of slaughter just quoted, will tell one of the great folk tales of our literature, his adventures in hell following a jug of Taos Lightning.) Most of their yarning has been lost to history, but it was a chronicle of every watercourse, peak, park, and gulch in a million square miles, a chronicle of chance happening suddenly and expectation reversed, of violent action, violent danger, violent mirth, of Indians whose thought was not commensurate with white thinking and therefore inexhaustibly fascinating, a fantasy of mythological beavers or grizzlies, of Welsh Indians or Munchies or the Fair God, of supernatural beings and spectral visitants and startling medicine and heroes who were cousin to Paul Bunyan. It was a shop talk, trapping, hunting, trailing, fighting Indians, escaping from Indians, the lore of animals and plants, and always the lay of the land and old fields revisited and new fields to be found, water and starvation and trickery and feasts. How Long Hatcher had lifted those Apache scalps. How one who was with us last year was eviscerated by a grizzly or gutshot by a Blackfoot. How Old Gabe outsmarted a Blackfoot war party, or Tom Fitzpatrick lay in his crevice while the Gros Ventres looked for him, or a Delaware, one of the Ishmaels of the West, had taunted the Arikaras who were killing him piecemeal. How one's partner had wandered into a canyon quite unknown even to these masters of geography, how another had stolen the daughter of a Sioux medicine man or a Taos rancher, how a third had forted up behind his slaughtered horse and held off fifty Comanches. How we came into Taos or the Pueblo of Los Angeles and the willing women there and the brandy we drank and the horses we stole.

Till at last the fire sank. The mountain man rolled up in his robe or blanket on his apishemore, loaded rifle beside him, and knife and pistols within reach, and might lie awhile listening to the wind and water and the coyotes. He might wake a few hours later, kick fuel on the embers, and roast another half-dozen ribs, eating alone while his companions slept and the horses pawed at the end of their pickets. Then sleep again till a grayness ran with the wind across the sky, in the shuddering cold of a mountain dawn someone was shouting 'Leve! Leve!' and it was time for breakfast on buffalo meat and the day's hazard of hunt or trail. . . . It was a good life.

Stewart found in it the best lenitive for whatever unrest had started him on his wanderings. Before reaching rendezvous he had certainly mastered the techniques of plains traveling, had found the hunting of buffalo (and of antelope, bighorn, elk, and bear, all to be met with in unbelievable numbers) beyond a sportsman's fantasy, and had let the West put its wish on him. He was to come back to it every year till his brother died and he had to assume, not willingly, if his novels tell the truth, the dignities of a baronet. It was a good life for those fitted to it. To be a mountain man you had to be something of a savage but you had to be something of a hero too, and Stewart came into the respect of men who were not easily moved to respect. In so much that presently he too was embodied in this nightly legend.

It is a fictional campfire that Frederick Ruxton describes and Killbuck, the old trapper who introduces his novel, is a fictional character, but both Ruxton and Killbuck are faithfully repeating true talk already old. 'Thar was the camp,' Killbuck says, at the campfire in North Park, along the sources of the South Platte, a few minutes before the Arapahos strike, 'and they was going to put out next morning, and the last as come out of Independence was that ar Englishman. He had a nor-west [Northwest Company blanketing] capote on, and a two-shoot gun rifled. Well, them English are darned fools; they can't fix a rifle anyways; but that one did shoot *some*; leastwise *he* made it throw plum-center. He made the buffler come, *he* did, and fout well at Pawnee Fork too. What was his name? All the boys called him Cap'en and he got his fixings from old Chouteau; but what he wanted out thar in the mountains, I never jest rightly know'd. He was no trader, nor a trapper, and flung his dollars right smart. Thar was old grit in him too, and a hair of the black b'ar at that. They say he took the bark off the Shians when he cleared out of the village with old Beaver Tail's squaw. He'd been on Yaller Stone afore that: Leclerc know'd him in the Blackfoot, and up in the Chippeway country; and he had the best powder as ever I flashed through life, and his gun was handsome, that's a fact.' [16]

Thus a case-hardened trapper, speaking of an admitted equal. Stewart's sovereigns omitted giving the veteran of Waterloo a reward for valor or achievement. There was no need of them when mountain men would freely say that there was a hair of the black bear in him.

# « II »

# THE BRASS KNUCKLES (1832)

THE PACK TRAIN of Sublette & Campbell with which Stewart went West in the spring of 1833 was heading for the upper valley of Green River, west of the Continental Divide. That valley was the very heart of the mountain fur country, and the rendezvous to which the pack train was taking goods had been appointed there for the summer of 1833. The rendezvous was the annual season of supply, trade, and saturnalia at which the brigades which had spent the year in the mountains outfitted afresh and turned over their pelts for transportation to the States. The system of maintaining roving brigades of trappers in the mountains and supplying them annually had been invented by William Ashley, though the Hudson's Bay Company had sent out brigades which ranged widely, traded with the Indians, did some trapping, and then returned to a fixed base. Ashley's successors, first Smith, Jackson & Sublette, then the Rocky Mountain Fur Company, had maintained the rendezvous system.

These three companies, the masters of the mountain trade, had opened up this whole area and for a few years had enjoyed a monopoly there. But the rich returns from the virgin field inevitably attracted others to the mountains. Various small companies were formed to exploit the field. We must pay particular attention to two experiments, those of Captain Bonneville and Nathaniel J. Wyeth. Finally, the fur trust, the American Fur Company, firmly based on its fixed posts on the Missouri River, had set out to take over the mountain field entirely. As the Sublette & Campbell train traveled toward the rendezvous of 1833, an American Fur Company train under Lucien Fontenelle was also traveling toward it from Fort Pierre. The Company had also sent a caravan to the preceding rendezvous, that of 1832.

These two years, 1832 and 1833, saw the climax of intercompany competition in the mountains. Since the events of the later year cannot be understood apart from those of the earlier one, we must interrupt our narrative short of the Continental Divide in 1833 and go back to cut the earlier trail.

First, however, let us take note of a class of mountain men who were annually becoming more numerous and more important to the trade, the 'free trappers.' They were trappers who went it alone, in small groups of co-equals or under the direction of the most knowing. They were of two castes, those who took an outfit on credit from one or another fur company and contracted to sell their furs to that company alone — Joe Meek called these 'skin trappers' — and those who regarded themselves as the élite, who traded cash in skins for goods and traded with whom they would for such prices as they could force. Both classes trapped wherever their judgment directed, without dictation or control by the fur companies. By 1833 there may have been several hundred free trappers in the mountains — it is impossible to determine how many. Their trade was exceedingly important to the companies, and the competition between the trust and the Opposition was in very great part an effort to dominate it.

Any free trapper who survived very long was on the evidence of that fact alone a graduate mountain man. Some of them were Ashley alumni or had learned their trade from his successors. (Among such in 1833 was a small party under Moses, or 'Black,' Harris, a notable expert whom we shall meet repeatedly.) Others represented the fragmentation of small fur companies, wildcatters drawn to the mountain trade by Ashley's profits which looked a good deal easier than they were. Through the eighteen-thirties almost all such efforts failed: they were insufficiently financed, they could not find enough good brigade-leaders, they could not compete, and they went bankrupt or else reorganized in the hope of being bought out for their nuisance value. Another group of free trappers represented an independent invasion of the mountains from the south, mainly from New Mexico and especially from Taos. They had been in the field for some years now. They trapped Colorado and the eastern and sometimes the northern portions of Utah and had sporadically visited southern Nevada, looping up from the few beaver streams in

Arizona. They had also reached California from the south, though traffic in stolen horses was to be a bigger business than beaver there. They were making the Colorado mountains their principal domain, and the RMF Company was trapping there only sporadically. North Park, Middle Park, and South Park or Bayou Salade were their favorite stamping grounds, together with the Arkansas, the South Platte, their tributaries, a few streams that fell into the Green near Brown's Hole and south of it, the Grand, the Gunnison, and the creeks that came down from the Front Range. Bent's Fort, built in 1832 for the Santa Fe carrying trade and the trade with the Arapahos and southern Cheyennes, came to be their principal headquarters. But the West was their back yard and many of them always showed up at the mountain rendezvous.

* * *

The events of 1832, the year before Stewart went West, are complex. The only clear way through them will be to follow separate parties to their meeting at the summer rendezvous, as we must also do when we come back to the summer of 1833. The reader is urged to work out the geography on Doctor Raiz's map.

The site of the rendezvous of 1832 was to be Pierre's Hole, a wild and romantically beautiful valley at the western foot of the Three Tetons. At the eastern foot of those peaks is Jackson's Hole: the trail between the two valleys crosses the range by way of Teton Pass, from whose summit the sudden falling-away of the world eastward makes one of the great vistas of the continent. Pierre's Hole, called Teton Basin nowadays, is in Teton County, Idaho. The south fork of Teton River flows out of it to the north, to reach the Snake a good many miles away. A range of lesser mountains called the Big Holes forms its western and southwestern wall. Between them and a range called the Palisades a gap opens, through which the waters beyond the southern end of the Hole reach the Snake southwestward, by a much more direct route than the Teton River takes. In fur-trade days a trail which reached the Snake from Green River branched to Pierre's Hole by way of this gap, and there was another trail midway between it and the one that crossed Teton Pass.

There are no adjectives adequate to express the beauty and sublimity of this, the Jackson's Hole–Teton Hole–Snake River country. The Idaho side of the mountains is greener and more timbered than the Wyoming side; both have a confused geography. The Snake is a noble and various river, nowhere lovelier than in the stretch from the lower end of its first great canyon till it comes entirely out of the mountains and tumbles over a ledge in the center of the modern town of Idaho Falls. Every inch of land and stream in these parts was intimately known to the mountain men; they had trapped it since Ashley's time, in fact since the wandering Astorians and Andrew Henry ten years before him. All the companies had left their names on peaks and rivers. Pierre's Hole was named for a Hudson's Bay Iroquois, Jackson's Hole for the partner of Bill Sublette and Jed Smith, a lake and a principal fork of the Snake for Henry himself, Hoback River for one of the Astorians, and the Snake, in the name used by the trappers, for Meriwether Lewis.

* * *

Captain Benjamin Louis Eulalie de Bonneville of the Seventh Infantry, U.S.A., was the son of a fugitive from Napoleon's wrath. He and his mother had been given safe-conduct to America by the semi-official sanction of Tom Paine. Graduating from West Point in 1815, he was presently assigned to frontier duty. He became a skilled prairie traveler and in the Indian Country and at St. Louis acquired an interest in the fur trade that eventually led him to enter it. His principal backer was Alfred Seton, one of the original Astorians. This clearly intimates that John Jacob Astor was also involved. In fact, it was while writing *Astoria* and at Astor's country seat that Washington Irving met Bonneville — and no one need be surprised to find the multimillionaire backing a competitor of his American Fur Company, for that is the way the fur trade worked. In the spring of 1832, Bonneville, taking two years' leave from the Army, raised and equipped a company for the mountains. One of his principal lieutenants, Michael Silvestre Cerré, was experienced in both the Santa Fe trade and the fur trade of the upper Missouri. The other was Joseph Reddeford Walker, though the full name prettifies Joe Walker, a hickory knot, one of the best and one of the toughest. Not too much is known about him before his association with Bonneville, but he also had been in the Santa Fe trade, had ranged the prairies, and was already a graduate mountain man. Miller's picture (Plate LXXXI), is no portrait but it gives the idea.

Cerré and Walker picked up at St. Louis and Independence a typical group of trappers and camp-swampers, Creole and

Canadian Frenchmen and American frontiersmen. They had to pay higher wages than the companies did because they were newcomers: master trappers could get a sizable bonus for signing on. They got some first-rate men, but the average was not high, for the companies had taken their pick first.

Bonneville was making a radical and intelligent experiment: he was testing a belief held by many but controverted by others, that wagons could be taken over the Divide and on to the Columbia. Bill Sublette had taken some to the Popo Agie — that is, to the eastern foot of the Wind River Range — in the summer of 1830, but was not disposed to try again. Wheeled transportation would be a considerable improvement if it proved feasible. A given number of men would need many fewer animals to transport the same amount of goods and the overhead would be reduced. Furthermore, much labor and vexation would be saved, since wagons need not be unloaded every night as mules and horses had to be. In the twenty wagons that composed his train, Bonneville was able to transport at least twice as large a stock of goods as we have seen Campbell carrying in 1833, in fact, enough to supply his anticipated trade for two full years. (His wagons were smaller than the sacred white-tops of the emigration and much smaller than the great freighters that traveled the smoother stretches of the Santa Fe Trail.) By the time he reached Laramie Fork, he was experiencing the cussedness that was to try the souls of innumerable emigrants: the high dry air shrank spokes and hubs and felloes, tires fell off and had to be first put back with wedges and later shortened by the blacksmith, wagon boxes started to come apart, something was always warping loose. And from here on he ran into the time drag — gullies, canyons, hillsides, and cliffs slowed him up. Like the emigrants he had to stop and corduroy the soft spots, build the half-roads called dugouts, or let wagons down slopes by cable. At rivers that could not be forded he had to take off the wheels and make bull-boats of the wagon boxes, sheathing them in hides so that they could be ferried across. Whenever possible the wheels were taken off and left overnight in creeks, to swell them. Thus, he fell behind the travel time of the pack trains. But the experiment was nevertheless an obvious success.

We have seen Campbell and Stewart on the earlier stretches of the Platte route, the most memorable of all American trails, the trail to Oregon. Bonneville traveled it to Green River and most of our characters will go West by it.

Not far west of Scott's Bluff the trail, still on the south bank of the North Platte, reached Laramie Fork. Storage reservoirs reduce the stream to a trickle or quite dry it up in the summer nowadays, but when the annual caravans reached it it was usually too deep and swift to be forded. The junction of the Laramie and the Platte was a historic crossroads: it was a key to the geography of the West. Westward the buffalo trails had led the Indians and eventually the mountain men to South Pass and the streams that fell into the Colorado and the Columbia. Another trail stretched south and north, the immemorial Indian highway east of the mountains, to the country of the Arapahos and Southern Cheyennes, and eventually Taos and Santa Fe, and to the Northern Cheyennes, the Crows, and eventually the Missouri River. Laramie Fork, brawling out of the Laramie Mountains to the westward, here crossed a wide plain, and Laramie Plain was anybody's country. It swarmed with buffalo and many tribes came to hunt them, but you were most likely to meet Arapahos, Crows, or the remnant Snakes who still lived east of the Divide. Presently we shall see the Oglala Sioux moving in to make it their country.

Beyond Laramie Fork the country began to pitch and heave, though it was gentle compared to what lay beyond the Divide. Collectively these ranges of low, rounded, carved-up mountains were called the Black Hills — black because of the cedar that grew on them — though that name now designates larger ranges in South Dakota. The trail hugged the Platte in what are now Converse and Natrona Counties of Wyoming, a desert of gullies, knife-edges, sage, greasewood, and alkali, increasingly steep, covered with flowers in June, relieved by small sweet creeks flowing among cottonwoods if you knew how to find them. Big Spring, Horse Shoe Creek, La Bonte Creek (on which Francis Parkman, griped by the same dysentery that hit everyone with the first alkali water, was to feel himself in danger of dying), Wagonhound Creek, Deer Creek, were some of the names to be remembered, all testifying to the price of water. In fact it was the accessibility of water that had determined this route. The trail kept looping back to the Platte and presently crossed it. This was the place which the emigrants would call the Upper Crossing, near the oil town of Casper, Wyoming, today.

Here the trail, which had trended either northwest or west for hundreds of miles, bore southwestward and then south. Fewer creeks were entering the Platte, they were smaller, they were called Poison Spider Creek or Poison Creek or had 'Stinking' or 'Bitter' or 'Bad' in their names because of the alkali. The creeks came out of the worst desert so far, raw-colored rocks wept by dust-storms. The only now-celebrated name hereabout is Red Buttes, a contorted rock formation painted a dozen different shades of crimson, carmine, and vermilion. Near here the trail left the Platte and crossed to the Sweetwater, a smaller stream. Its name, from l'Eau Sucrée, signalized not refreshment after alkali but an occasion when a mule, whose packs included the party's sugar, fell into it. Almost at once Independence Rock was in sight, a large turtleback rising almost out of the river. Our Plate X shows it admirably, and its base is now heavily buttressed by bronze placques set up in memory of travelers who reached it gladly in a weary land. It was the Inscription Rock of these parts, though there were also lesser ones. From the beginning those who passed this way liked to chisel their names in it, partly as an assertion of identity in a wilderness unimaginably large, partly the itch of American fingers at any blank space. Someone had even carved Jim Bridger's name there — Jim himself could not.

Independence Rock was not quite what Charles Larpenteur called it, 'the commencement of the Rocky Mountains.' But for several days mountains had always been in sight from the trail — the Rattlesnake Range to the northwest, rounded and low like the Laramies, and in an almost solid line to the south the Green, Ferris, and Seming Ranges. Five miles beyond the rock the Sweetwater breaks through a four-hundred-foot ledge by way of the narrow vertical canyon called Devil's Gate. (Our Plate XI.) The trail detoured it and reached the river again farther on. And now, far off, one could see what had only been glimpsed before, the true Rockies, the main range, the blue and purple snowcapped Wind River Mountains. Next year, 1833, Captain Bonneville was to make the first reported ascent of them, though Astor's, Henry's, and Ashley's men had been climbing them every year since 1811. The Captain estimated their height at beyond twenty-five thousand feet, almost doubling the reality. The next army man to visit them, Frémont, climbed a higher peak, correcting the error, named the peak after himself, and claimed to be the first white man to reach the top.

The Sweetwater flowed down from these immensities, and a pack train would travel on the average six days making toward the broad plateau at their southern end, their blue-misted tips always in sight. At that southern extremity they dwindle away in a double handful of rounded hills, and just at the foot of these hills the trail crossed the Continental Divide, by way of the historic portal, South Pass. It is a sagebrush plain about twenty miles wide, a saddle between the Wind River Mountains and a typical badlands farther south called the Antelope Hills. It was the gate through which the United States would reach its empire, but no one could tell just where the parting of the waters actually lay. There was a twelve-mile stretch between the sources of the Sweetwater, which flows into the Platte and so into the Gulf of Mexico, and Pacific Spring whence the conventional leaf, if only there were leaves here, could eventually reach the Gulf of California. Somewhere along that twelve-mile stretch, you crossed from the United States to Oregon. Mexico was in sight to the southwest.

Two or three days more, across a sagebrush flat hideous with sun and wind and alkali, broken by the gathering creeks called Little Sandy and Big Sandy, brought you to the great river which the trappers called the Siskadee. They were phonetically rendering a Crow word that means 'sage hen.' It was the Rio Colorado of the Spaniards, the river which Americans have called the Green. It was the heart of the fur country, we have said, and Bonneville was to establish that it was also something more.

* * *

Nothing of importance happened to Bonneville's party on the way out: the usual buffalo hunts and Indian alarms, the usual dysenteries, and as the altitudes increased the usual outbreak of 'mountain fever' — adjustment to thinner air, variously marked by headaches or vomiting or nervousness and depression. Near Laramie Fork a war party of Crows, who were out to avenge some of their kin killed by the Cheyennes, charged down on them whooping and firing. The Captain, an experienced frontier officer, prepared to fight, but this was just a greeting by Indians who were nearly always friendly to the whites. The Crows, who must be discussed in detail later, were in some ways the most notable and in many ways the most interesting of Plains tribes. This band proved exceedingly, in fact suffocatingly, friendly; they could hardly be pried away from their new white friends, whom they embraced repeatedly, uttering soft sighs of affection. When they left, Bonneville's men found that they had lifted all loose personal belongings. Theft was the Crow honor and up on the Big Horn, at its new post, the American Fur Company was beginning to pay them to harass the Opposition.

Bonneville crossed the Divide on July 24, 1832, and headed for Green River. Two days later a column of dust behind them to the east was taken for another and larger party of Indians — it was believed, correctly, that Blackfeet were in the vicinity — but proved to be Lucien Fontenelle's American Fur Company caravan making for the rendezvous at Pierre's Hole. He was bringing it from Fort Union, where the goods had been taken by steamboat up the Missouri, and the long, difficult route from Fort Union had already lost him the race with Sublette & Campbell to the rendezvous. Fontenelle exchanged the uproarious courtesies of the trail with Bonneville and hurried on toward the Green. Bonneville followed and the two parties camped together for the night. When Fontenelle set out the next day he took with him some of the best men Bonneville had, a small band of Delaware Indians whom he had promised inflation wages, four hundred dollars each for the fall hunt alone. (A good annual wage for a master trapper, and the American Fur Company would lose money on the deal — temporarily.) It was a lesson in mountain ethics and Bonneville absorbed it, at once sending out some scouts (doubtless headed by Joe Walker) to intercept a group of free trappers on whose trade Fontenelle was counting and to offer them goods in a buyer's market. His backers' losses began right here.

(The Delawares were the only Indians the mountain men ever thought of as companions in their trade. They were always in small bands and any group of whites who could get a band to join them were lucky. In 1832 they had no home in the West, though two years later a reservation was to be set aside for them in Kansas and various tribal remnants gradually came to occupy it. The Delawares had once been a great people. They were the Leni-Lenape of your schoolbooks, near relatives of Mr. Cooper's Mohicans. Pennsylvania and Delaware, with parts of New York and New Jersey, were their country — a famous council fire burned near the Germantown Cricket Club — and one of their great men was Tammany. But in the eighteenth century the Prussian Indians, the Iroquois, defeated them badly in the last of many wars, and with Prussian arrogance inflicted on them the direst of Indian insults, forbidding them to be a tribe or to call themselves men. Too many historians have accepted the Iroquois designation, the Petticoat Indians, and have supposed the Delawares were soft: an error of astronomical size. The survivors began to range westward. Located in Ohio, they again fought valorous wars but mostly against the advancing whites, so that again they were dismembered. Some joined the Miamis, the Piankishaws, and the Shawnees, and others crossed the Mississippi and set up for themselves. It was from these last that the Delawares who were mountain men descended. They mastered the plains culture and its survival skills, becoming expert horsemen, horse thieves, buffalo hunters, beaver hunters. They ranged from Texas to the Three Forks of the Missouri and beyond. They signed no peace with any Plains tribe and would gladly oblige any with a fight at any time. Their courage was absolute, even in the manifestations of courage as the white man understood it, and the selection of survival had given them extraordinary intelligence. They became mountain men by themselves, Frémont and others were to make them soldiers, and the Army was to find them better military auxiliaries than even the Pawnees and the Cheyennes. The point that distinguished a Delaware from other Indians was that you could depend on him.)

While Fontenelle hurried on slantwise toward the rendezvous, Bonneville went on to the Green and up it till he came to Horse Creek. Here he paused to recruit his horses and to build a log trading post. It was in the angle between the two streams, about three hundred yards back from Green River and five miles north of the mouth of Horse Creek, which, however, was only about two miles away to the southwest. Straight to the east, across the vast sagebrush plain, stood up the great truncated mesa that would be called Frémont Peak — miles away. The Bear River Mountains were in sight to the west. And Bonneville's log stockade and the country he built it in must have particular notice.

* * *

The United States government, reversing geology, exploration, history, and Spanish and American tradition, has decided that the Green River is not the Colorado. It is longer than the Grand River, which the government says is the Colorado, it flows more water, and before it joins the Grand develops the characteristics which the Colorado maintains to the lower end of the Grand Canyon. But the Grand rises in and is mostly enclosed by the State of Colorado, whereas the Green merely touches a corner of it. There had to be some belated logic for the name wished on a sovereign state against the hoarse protests of its inhabitants, however, and so the Grand is the Colorado.

Sublette County, Wyoming, is named for the five brothers

of whom the oldest was Robert Campbell's partner. Many of its streams and settlements and many of those in the counties that border it were named for Bill Sublette's friends, employees, and competitors. Its northern end is a jumble of mountain ranges, running every which way with no logic beyond the contortions of a world in labor. Two of them make a V which opens to the west. The little streams that flow down their sides join others that flow out of small lakes, and presently the meeting waters are Green River. These sources lie on the western slopes and at the western foot of the Wind River Mountains. Climb eastward to the ridge, go down a quarter of a mile, and you reach brooks that join Wind River, which flows to the southeast, turns north as the Big Horn River, and eventually enters the Yellowstone River half its length distant from the Wind River Mountains. Standing on that ridge above the head of Green River, you are seventy miles — along the high, saurian spine that stretches southeast — from the head of the Sweetwater River, which flows into the Platte and so joins the Missouri twelve hundred miles below the mouth of the Yellowstone. You are less than forty miles from the place, almost due north, where another gigantic accident of configuration starts the Yellowstone itself flowing northwestward to Yellowstone Lake, from which it emerges to make its long traverse of Montana. (As it leaves the area now called Yellowstone Park, it is not far from the Madison, one of the three forks which become the Missouri.) Moreover, after the brooks on the western slope of the Wind River Mountains have become the Green and flowed some ten miles down their westering V, a rolling range comes out of the north to turn the river straight south. From its eastern to its western base this range is barely ten miles wide at its narrowest and not more than twice that wide anywhere — and down its western slope the brooks flow to the Grosventre and the Hoback, and so to the Snake, and so eventually to the Columbia. For fifty miles the Colorado system is seldom far from the Columbia system, for a hundred miles not far from the Missouri system.

After the Green turns southward, already showing the color that gave it its name, its valley begins to widen. Eastward are the Wind River Mountains, whose crest forms the Continental Divide; usually they are in sight from the Green, though frequently hidden to the hips or even the shoulders by sporadic hills. Westward is a less lofty, less heavily timbered, less articulated system of ranges, whose fragments have separate names.

The valley is thirty, forty, fifty, eventually seventy miles or more wide, mostly a sagebrush plain, treeless except where the cottonwood, the West's lifegiver, marks the watercourses, or settlers have planted shade trees. It is a sterile country to most eyes, for no beauties except that of space come down out of the mountains. The first fifty miles of this, the Upper Valley of the Green, were the nerve center of the mountain trade. The river is enlarged by a succession of creeks from the east, the largest of them New Fork (which Captain Stewart was to make the scene of much heartache and confusion in his novels) and by many more creeks from the west. The southern end of the Upper Valley is walled off from an interior basin to the east by a range of hills, and when they end, the river swings to the southeast, a large and rapid stream now and full of trout. About twenty-five miles farther on the Big Sandy joins it, bringing the waters of the Little Sandy from South Pass, and a further stretch of about the same length brings it to the present town of Green River, Wyoming. Here it turns south, plunges into the mountains, becomes the river of John Wesley Powell, and runs through a series of spectacular canyons for hundreds of miles.

Horse Creek flows into the Green less than halfway down the Upper Valley. Its name is supposed to commemorate the theft of a horse from Tom Fitzpatrick. In fur trade days the delta between the streams (now irrigated ranch land) had plenty of pasturage and the groves along them supplied firewood and timber. And here at the beginning of August, 1832, a Captain of the United States Army built a trading post. Mountain men christened it 'Fort Nonsense'; one of them explains that the severe winters hereabout would make it uninhabitable. (Well, you could move to lower country for the winter: Bonneville did.) So it came down in the literature, most of it written by Bonneville's business rivals, as Fort Nonsense and Bonneville's Folly. Historians have perpetuated both names, explaining that this was a poor place to practice the fur trade, though it was the exact center of the richest remaining treasury of furs. The historians are wrong; there was nothing nonsensical in the location of Fort Bonneville.

Its owner took an ignominious licking from his competitors, who were always willing to suspend hostilities long enough to gang up on him. He did not know how to meet their methods but he was no fool. Partisans who had grown up in the trade managed their caravans no better than he, not a single man under his personal command lost his life, he made and commissioned important explorations, and he drew the first map of the interior West (at least the first one to be published) that had its principal geographical features in something like the actual arrangement. But there is something more.

One can hardly believe that in the late autumn of 1831 the Army, under the Secretary of War, would grant a two-year leave of absence to an officer who was going to Oregon without considering what he might accomplish there and briefing him accordingly. It is also suggestive that he was financed by an Astor man, a member of the primordial Columbia venture that had been urged and assisted by President Jefferson, the father of American geopolitics. Finally when Bonneville overstayed his leave (he applied for an extension in due form but the request miscarried), he was dismissed the service — only to be reinstated by the commander-in-chief, Andrew Jackson. It has been suggested that Old Hickory, as stern a disciplinarian as the Army had ever had, was expressing his admiration of Bonneville's map. But even an admiration for maps would hardly have justified a full pardon for a grave military offense.

Since 1827 the agreement by which Great Britain and the United States jointly traded in Oregon had carried a cancellation clause operative at one year's notice. The Hudson's Bay Company, one of those private monopolies which gave an appearance of inadvertence to the expansion of the British Empire, had a base on the Columbia and was dominating the trade along its affluents. From that base it was working eastward, into and across the mountains. The Rocky Mountain Fur Company had been fighting the British monopoly since 1825 and now the fur trust had joined the battle. The letters of Western traders, the reports of Indian agents, half the press of the United States, and the speeches of all Western Senators and Representatives were clamoring about the British threat to Oregon. So here was an army officer trapping furs in the international area, but not many furs.

Bonneville's letters to his commanding officers discuss the problems which military invasion of Oregon would involve. One glance at the map is enough to show that the site of Bonneville's Folly was the strategic center of the mountain area. This site would cover any expedition moving into Oregon from the States. It would block any expedition moving out of the Columbia region toward the routes or hunting grounds of the American fur companies. It held the western approach to South Pass. It covered all the routes to Pierre's Hole, the Snake River,

Great Salt Lake, and the interior basin. It also covered the Humboldt River route to California, part of which had been blazed by the Hudson's Bay Company and down the entire length of which Bonneville dispatched Joe Walker. It may have been Fort Nonsense to the companies that bribed Bonneville's trappers away from him, debauched the Indians he tried to trade with, and with the old hand's deftness frustrated a newcomer to the mountains. But it made sense to the War Department.

And on its site a year after it was built Captain Benjamin Bonneville of the Seventh Infantry, U.S.A., entertained Captain William Drummond Stewart of the King's Hussars.

* * *

While Bonneville paused to build his fort, Lucien Fontenelle moved on to the maze of mountains south of Jackson's Hole through which Hoback River flows to the Snake. Here a large body of Indians suddenly appeared, a whole village with squaws and children, horses and dogs and horse herds and travois. They were Blackfeet. That is to say, they were the Atsina or Gros Ventres of the Prairies, a tribe unrelated by blood or language to the three tribes of the Blackfeet but so closely associated with them that everybody called them Blackfeet. They were coming east along the trail which Fontenelle was about to take and coming from the vicinity of the Pierre's Hole rendezvous toward which he was traveling. Their hearts were visibly bad, the mood that made Indians most dangerous, and they seemed to be preparing to attack. Since you must always consider the Blackfeet hostile and must bear in mind that they might not hesitate to take on even a caravan in full strength, Fontenelle forted up at once. But the experience that had made the Gros Ventres' hearts bad had also temporarily taught them caution: they were fresh from a severe licking, they were lucky to be here at all.

So they declared a prairie truce and smoked with Fontenelle, who sent an express to Bonneville to put him on guard. They did not tell Fontenelle about their defeat, though he certainly guessed what had happened. Some of them wanted to see Bonneville's party, whose trail their scouts had cut long since — they wanted presents and with luck maybe they could get some scalps, which would help after a defeat. Fontenelle sent fifteen of them to Bonneville, in the care of one of the Delawares he had bribed away. A couple of Bonneville's Crow friends had come to pay him another visit. The Crows were implacable enemies of the Blackfeet, the only enemies who stood them off successfully, and his guests pointed out to Bonneville that fortune was offering him an opportunity which it would be scandalous folly to refuse — here were fifteen scalps at practically no risk. He could not see it their way and entertained the Gros Ventres with the ceremony required. Neither the fifteen nor various of their kinsmen who dropped in as the village moved on again got away with so much as a single horse. Bonneville, whom the Indians were beginning to call Bald Head, knew his way around.

* * *

Bonneville and the American Fur Company's westward caravan are now accounted for in relation to the Pierre's Hole rendezvous of 1832. We turn to a different species of fur trader, a man whose presence here shows how diverse and intricate the trade was becoming and how near the United States was to the combustion that would burn up the trade. He was Nathaniel Jarvis Wyeth from the pleasant rural village of Cambridge, Massachusetts. Before he started West in 1832 he had been in the business of selling ice from Fresh Pond, on whose shore he lived and where he invented ingenious machines to harvest his crop.

Wyeth was a typical Yankee business man of the period, a type which had spread American commerce all over the world. The originals had everything their contemporary successors lack: enterprise, ingenuity, versatility in innovation, guts, willingness to run risks for a profit, even long risks. Such qualities had bred up a race of merchant millionaires which Wyeth intended to join, and a fellow townsman of his, Hall Jackson Kelley, had turned his attention to Oregon.

Kelley's mind was incoherent with all the Western energies that become coherent during the years we treat here: trade, colonization, patriotic expansion, the conversion of the Indians. Long ago he had fallen in love with Oregon at a distance of three thousand miles. (Lewis and Clark, other travelers, and the sea captains told him it was fair.) He had spent most of his adult life propagandizing it to his neighbors and then the nation as an earthly paradise, a source of infinite riches, and a holy cause. He demonstrates how mixed history's velocities can be, for though he seems star-crazed, if not mad, there was nothing whatever wrong with his schemes except that they were premature — by no more than fifteen years. (The mad prophets of the West from John Ledyard on up to yesterday were only minds that ran a little faster than the clock.) By 1831, when Nathaniel Wyeth joined him, he had organized the Oregon Colonization Society, a joint-stock scheme whose basic purpose was to take emigrants to the northwest Canaan. The long dream was intended to take on flesh in 1832: a group of colonists and crusaders was to start for Oregon under Kelley. Not quite: 1832 was five minutes early. Wyeth withdrew and went it alone but took four of Kelley's converts with him. The next year also no one would enlist for holy Oregon: very well, Kelley would go anyway. He started for Oregon. By way of Mexico — and alone.

But the Cambridge ice-dealer who started in 1832 was not walking under the moon. He had been looking at Oregon with a business man's eye and had discovered a rich opening for his particular breed. During the American Revolution James Cook, the great English navigator, had sailed up the western coast of North America as far as Bering Strait — and had opened a new, golden trade for Great Britain. That trade (and the promise of empire) pivoted on the most valuable of all furs, the sea otter. Immediately the war ended, Americans pressed to enter it. . . . The Far West, the first faint stirrings of the continental mind, begin where you please — the rapids of Lachine, the flashing line of unidentified mountains which the Vérendryes saw at the western horizon, a river which the Indians told Robert Rogers or Jonathan Carver flowed into the stinking water and which one or the other of them called Ouragan. But one of James Cook's crew was a Connecticut Yankee named John Ledyard and when he met the American minister to France he found that Thomas Jefferson also had been thinking of the Pacific coast. Jefferson, in fact, had thought of it long before Ledyard and had once wanted to send George Rogers Clark across the unknown land that lay between, and eventually he did send Clark's brother William and Meriwether Lewis, to discover the river Ouragan from the east. But the sea otter were even more in Jefferson's far-ranging mind than the River of the West.

By 1787 the *Lady Washington* and the *Columbia* could be sent to the northwest coast in a reasonable expectation that they could outsmart the British in the otter trade. Even before the *Columbia* sailed across the bar into the river which thenceforth bore her name (July 20, 1793), she had established the triangular Northwest trade which made many Boston merchants rich and whose base was the sea otter. Thereafter Boston merchants, who were sea captains too till they had sons old enough to take their places on the quarterdeck, steadily forced back the Russians, whose monopoly the trade had been originally, and outsailed and outtraded the British till they won a virtual monopoly in turn. By 1832 their window panes were turning violet on Beacon Hill and the sea otter trade was all but dead, but a rich trade in other skins with the coastal Indians still flourished, constituting one leg of the triangle. We have touched this trade in Chapter I: it was from vessels along this coast that goods traveled toward the Flatheads.

Nathaniel Wyeth sat down to learn all that could be learned in Cambridge, Massachusetts, about the fur trade. (And a resolute lack of interest in the rude and distant region where it was conducted, which made his study difficult, has been bequeathed through generations of Cambridge librarians down to today.) He learned much and turned his mind to inventing the combinations, short-cuts, and turnovers by which his species had come to dominate American business.

He saw that a formidable burden to the companies which took the trade goods to the mountains was the appalling expense of transporting them overland. He arrived at the solution that John Jacob Astor had invented twenty years before, sea transport, and he assumed that Astor's failure had been due to the War of 1812, the treachery of his employees (but surely treachery had gone out of the mountain trade by now), and the consequently favorable position of the Northwest Company which later merged with the Hudson's Bay. But the coastal trade also paid an excessive overhead: vessels trading there, like those in the California hide trade, had to cruise the coast for months at a time, up to two years. Think of the interest, think of the insurance, think of the wages and keep of the crews. Well, then, send out your goods by sea and so cut down the freightage, wages, and findings, and avoid the great risk of loss of land transport. But also establish a series of fixed posts in the beaver country and down the Columbia, where goods could be stored and furs collected. So that when your ship arrived to discharge her cargo, your trade goods, she could get her homeward lading, your furs, at once. Wyeth understood that the Hudson's Bay Company, succeeding the Northwesters, had established a system something like the one he proposed. But in Cambridge he could not find out how well developed it was, nor how solid a financial basis it had, nor how completely it dominated the region of the upper Columbia. Besides, the Yankees could always skin the British, having a talent for cutting corners and finding many inventions.

One invention, he thought, was already at hand. In April, 1831, the brig *Owyhee*, which had been sent out in the Northwest trade, made Boston Harbor with a cargo that included not only furs but also fifty-three barrels of salted Columbia River salmon. They sold for fourteen dollars a barrel, and a few months later the brig *Sultana* cleared for the Columbia with a thousand empty barrels aboard. Salmon alone, then, could cover the entire expense of your sea voyage. Wyeth believed that he could find or invent other profitable sidelines. So he would realize his capital, raise as much more as he could (from relatives and business friends), and go to Oregon. He was prepared to try his hand at anything, but he counted on entering the mountain fur trade.

Through the fall and winter of 1831 he was furiously busy. Tobacco — it was a basic article in the trade and why not cut down the overhead by growing it in Oregon? So he tries to get an experienced tobacco grower to join the company he is forming and, not getting one, writes repeatedly for information about its culture and buys seed to take with him. A similar spate of letters goes to Maine fishermen (some of his backers lived in Maine), for they know about Atlantic salmon and can tell him what the fish's habits are and how it can be pickled and smoked. Maybe the government will subsidize his trip in the interest of exploration or of opposing the British. Edward Everett, representing Middlesex County in Congress, is besought to do what he can and by all means to gather information for Wyeth and get official permission for him to enter the Indian Country. Since he will be a newcomer, he had better, during his first year, trade mainly in staples, traps, powder, and guns (guns were hardly a staple), and so he buys forty dozen traps, 'such as used by Mr. Astor,' and what American firm makes guns like the Northwest fusees? He acquires a knowledge of Western geography, though he makes gross errors about the routes of travel. He fills his head with the history and statistics of the mountain trade — but, because he must use the wretched Western material of Cambridge libraries, he makes fundamental mistakes. Music will help on the overland march, he decides, and so he orders ten bugles and directs his companions (an enlisted company) to master them.

Essentially Wyeth's plan was sound and on paper it looked foolproof. But Nat Wyeth lived in Cambridge, and in Cambridge the world has always seemed simpler, more high-minded, and more amenable to reason than it proves to be when one goes out to mingle with the children of darkness. He was a learned innocent, as rank a greenhorn as ever tried the trade. He was like a novelist of passion about to encounter a passionate woman. He had no idea how complexly organized the mountain trade was nor how great a margin must be allowed for the incalculable variants of chance and immediate circumstance. He had no accurate idea of how many persons were competing in it this very year. He had far from enough capital to stay in business. There was no one to tell him the realistic details of trading with the Indians or to inform him that though the companies were cutting each other's throats they automatically helped each other cut the throat of any serious newcomer.

Sending most of his goods round the Horn by ship, he gathered his company of enthusiasts, speculators, and young adventurers, twenty-four all told.[1] They included his brother Jacob, a physician (two other brothers took a financial flyer in his venture), and an eighteen-year-old cousin of his, John B. Wyeth. (He soon wished he had left the boy in the East. John Wyeth came down with disillusionment, turned back from Pierre's Hole, and, when he got home, wrote, with the assistance of the famous Doctor Benjamin Waterhouse of Cambridge, a lively and exceedingly malicious book about his trip. A book 'of little lies told for gain,' Nat Wyeth called it. It contains one of the best contemporary descriptions of the cholera epidemic in New Orleans, but its account of Nat Wyeth is so distorted that it has caused some historians to underrate his intelligence.) These volunteers were to obey Wyeth absolutely and, after he had taken out the manager's share, were to divide the prospective profits equally. He clad them in a grotesque uniform and preposterously bought bayonets for their rifles. He took them to an island in Boston Harbor for a period of conditioning and military drill, then sailed with them to Baltimore and from there went to St. Louis and thence to Independence. (None of them had learned to throw a pack hitch.) All that distance he paid retail freight on his outfit, his traps and bugles, blacksmith and surgical instruments, a stock of trade goods, and one of the most amazing tenderfoot inventions ever intended for the West. This was a boat on wheels — thirteen feet long, four feet wide, 'of a shape partly of a canoe and partly of a gondola,' and joined by expert cabinet work since it could not be caulked because of the Western sun. In fact, he had three of them: the Cambridge logician had worked it out that this was the way to obviate the known trouble of crossing plains and mountain rivers. The Harvard boys lined up to jeer these contrivances as they rolled down Garden Street and called them 'amphibiums,' but Cousin John preferred a less learned title and settled for 'Nat-wyethium.' At St. Louis someone told the innocent some facts of plains travel and he sold his ducks for half what they had cost to build.

John Wyeth says that the party would never have reached 'the American Alps' if it had not been for Bill Sublette, and for once is telling the truth without adornment. Nat Wyeth was a man who never had to be told anything more than once and he learned mountain craft in a single crossing, being a journeyman by the time he reached Pierre's Hole and an old hand when he got to the Columbia — but he could not have taken his first company to the mountains unsupervised. He met Sublette at Independence, where Bill and Campbell had their caravan ready to start West with this year's goods for the RMF Company. A glance sufficed to convince Sublette that here was no threat to business and the hospitality of the plains prevailed at once. He took Wyeth's party under his protection and taught them their business. (Three faint-hearts, or realists, dropped out at Independence and three more turned back from the Platte.)

They traveled steadily under Sublette's expert direction and went through the routine experiences: storms, stampedes, alkali, buffalo, the mishaps of the trail. John Wyeth has pages of lofty derision for his cousin's obstinacy and mistakes, but Nat's journal proves that John was lying in some contexts and he probably was in others. (Why shouldn't a man who had committed himself be rigid in control? Nothing is more dangerous than the amateur on a lark.) Mountain fever got most of them and made their physician, Jacob Wyeth, seriously ill. Below Laramie Fork Tom Fitzpatrick came riding furiously out of the west. The RMF Company and many free trappers were gathered at Pierre's Hole, he reported. But so were the damned interlopers, the American Fur Company under Vanderburgh and Drips, and they were expecting Fontenelle with a convoy of goods. Fontenelle would be coming hell-for-leather to hog the trade. Hurry, then, hurry — and Fitz turned back alone to carry word that Sublette and Campbell were at hand, and to hold the Indians and free trappers in line. But before he started back, the caravan met a party of nineteen forlorn and hungry trappers. They had come West a year before as part of another hopeful St. Louis venture, the Gant and Blackwell partnership which aspired to a cut of the mountain profits. Now they supposed the firm was bankrupt, as it was more or less, and they were hungry. Fitz bought their furs from the leader, one Stephens, at what may be described as both mountain and starving prices. Then he rode westward, taking a spare horse. Presently he met some Gros Ventres, of the same gang that Fontenelle would meet later, in July. (This was the middle of June.)

Sublette hurried after him, but on this leg of the trip you could not hurry pack animals very much. Wyeth's horses were in bad shape and the ghastly going along the upper Platte and the Sweetwater had disenchanted his greenhorns, who now told him what they had been privately confessing to one another, that they had had enough of a fool's errand. He gave them leave to go back if they wanted to, which had its irony as they started through South Pass. They reached Green River waters and grizzlies and plentiful buffalo. On the evening of July 2 they were visited by some of Drips' men, either a party sent out from Pierre's Hole to meet Fontenelle or a trapping party who had not yet reached the rendezvous. Camped some miles away, they came on the invariable errand, to see new faces, to hear news of the States up to a year old, to exchange words with fellow craftsmen, and to eat and smoke with their kind. An hour or so after they went home, toward midnight, the Sublette–Wyeth camp was attacked by Gros Ventres.

The same village we have already mentioned twice. They were on their way home from a visit of several years with their Arapaho relatives in Colorado to the country they shared with their allies the Blackfeet. . . . The name Gros Ventres meant that no one could fill them up, the Arapahos called them Beggars, and most tribes designated them by terms of similar significance. . . . Like the Blackfeet with whom they lived they were always on the prod, and they were fools enough to charge this camp though not fools enough to press the charge home. They halted fifty yards away and poured a lot of fusee balls into camp in the dark. They gathered in five of Sublette's horses, one belonging to a free trapper who had joined up, and four of Wyeth's, then slipped away into the night. Nobody was hurt and the horses had been left loose because they were broken down. It was not much of a skirmish.

The train plodded on by the middle of the three trails described above, reached the Snake, crossed it, and on July 8 came into Pierre's Hole. Sublette was bringing about sixty men with him, Wyeth's party now numbered eighteen, there were nineteen (or twenty-two) in the Gant and Blackwell outfit, and thirteen free trappers under Alexander Sinclair had fallen in with Sublette soon after the night battle. Drips had about a hundred American Fur Company men on the spot and his partner Vanderburgh was gathering up other detachments to bring them in. About a hundred and twenty lodges of Nez Perces and Flatheads were camped here and more were on the way, probably with some hope of hearing of Rabbit-Skin Leggings and his companions or even meeting their magician. (Allow seven or eight Indians to a lodge.) Fraeb and Milton Sublette had brought in their brigades of the RMF Company and joined them with Fitzpatrick's. The other two partners, Bridger and Gervais, were known to be on their way to the rendezvous. But Tom Fitzpatrick, who had galloped ahead from the Sweetwater to bring word that Sublette was on the way, was nowhere about. He had not come in; the camp supposed he had stayed with Sublette. And there were Blackfeet about.

Other small groups of free trappers kept arriving at the Pierre's Hole rendezvous from all over the West, especially from the Colorado Rockies. (Kit Carson, who was already the most notable of those who frequented that country, did not show up this year.) Other Indians besides the Flatheads and Nez Perces were coming in too, mostly Snakes and Bannocks. There remains to account for the trust and the Opposition.

* * *

The effort of the American Fur Company to extend its monopoly to the mountains had been going on indirectly since 1828 and directly since 1830. It was begun by the Western Outfit, to whose aid the Upper Missouri Outfit was presently summoned. There is no need to describe these two great branches of the Company; their cores were the two most powerful rivals it had had to amalgamate in order to corner the Missouri River trade. (The Company, remember, was national in scope and international in its dealing. The enormous trade of the upper Mississippi, the Great Lakes, and their contributory waters was only one part of its empire and the Missouri trade was only another part.) Astor, now making millions in New York real estate, no longer gave much personal attention to the Company —

though at this moment he was anticipating the collapse of the fur trade and was preparing to get out in time to let his associates hold the bag while he continued to make money as their banker. (His son William and more especially the great Ramsay Crooks were running the fur trust.) The amalgamation of the two formidable Missouri outfits had attached to the Company the men who had caused it most trouble in these parts, Pierre Chouteau, Jr., and Kenneth McKenzie. Chouteau, who had the highest rank in the St. Louis feudal system, and who doubtless scorned Astor as an inconceivably inferior parvenu, had precisely the same kind of intelligence and talents, the genius of management and combination. He was a financier and had the empire-building mind, hard, brilliant, daring, speculative, ruthless. McKenzie was the McLoughlin of the trust, that is to say, the greatest field executive it had. Both were of the type which the nineteenth century was breeding plentifully in American business. They were a prophecy of all the trusts to come.

As early as 1827 McKenzie had sent an agent, Samuel Tulloch, to the mountains. He investigated the efforts of the Hudson's Bay Company to get a foothold in the mountains from its Columbia River base, and traveled the Three Forks and Yellowstone country with Robert Campbell of the Opposition, McKenzie's target. But it was too early to press the invasion and Chouteau held the impatient McKenzie back till they had made their river base secure. They gathered in the best traders from the shattered opposition on the Missouri. Then they started building posts — for they had decided that fixed bases were superior to the rendezvous system. Fort Union, which was first called Fort Floyd, was built in 1829 at a site of paramount importance, the mouth of the Yellowstone. Here he could trade with the Assiniboins, in whose country it was, and might seduce their allies the Crees, who were Hudson's Bay Company customers. And from here he could invade the mountains by two routes, the Missouri itself and the Yellowstone.

The next year McKenzie did the clearly impossible: he established a trade with the Blackfeet. These Vandals of the West traded with the British companies for the guns and hardware that supported their vocational terrorism, but would not let even the British trap in their country. They had repeatedly refused to trade with the Americans, murdering them at sight and hunting down all who entered their country.[2] No one could keep RMF Company trappers out of any country they proposed to trap, but they had lost many outfits, men, and beaver skins to the Blackfeet and now approached them only in strong force. But in 1830 McKenzie sent into the Blackfoot country one of his most knowing lieutenants, Jacob Berger, who had long traded among them for the British. Berger brought back a village of Blackfeet to Fort Union. The next year McKenzie sent another of his best men, James Kipp, to build a trading post deep in the Blackfoot country — near the mouth of Marias River — Fort Piegan. A year later the post was replaced by Fort McKenzie, a few miles away.

That same year a grandiloquent document was drawn up at Fort Union. It bound the Assiniboins and more notably the Blackfeet, 'lords of the soil from the banks of the great waters unto the tops of the mountains,' to make a peace with the American Fur Company 'so long as the water runs or the grass grows.' It was ratified according to 'the due mystical signs enjoined by the great medicine lodges,' which was staggering nonsense. To help out, McKenzie had some medals struck so that the Blackfeet would believe that the American Fur Company was the agent and strong right arm of the author of all medals, their Father in Washington. Finally, in 1832, the year of the Pierre's Hole rendezvous, he completed his system of bridgeheads by sending his Samuel Tulloch to build Fort Cass, where the Big Horn empties into the Yellowstone, deep in the country of the Crows — who had been good friends and customers of the RMF Company. Probably Tulloch had already been working on the Crows who lifted Bonneville's knives and possibles.

The Company now had a system of fixed posts among tribes which never before had found goods so easily available. And, incorporating the system of the Opposition, McKenzie had already sent brigades into the heart of the Opposition's country, the mountains. His partisans were Joseph Robidou, of a numerous family that had practically dug the Missouri, Lucien Fontenelle, Andrew Drips, and Henry Vanderburgh. They were river traders, who must now learn the mountain craft by following the Opposition brigades. In 1830 — the year when Smith, Sublette & Jackson sold out to the RMF Company — Drips and Robidou and Fontenelle followed them through their most private preserve, the Utah–Idaho–western Wyoming field, Cache Valley, Bear Lake, Salt Lake Valley, Ogden's Hole, Bear River Valley, the Snake, Ham's Fork. They ran into a fight between the RMF Company and the Hudson's Bay Company which, invigorated by its great McLoughlin, was trying to take over the field from the northwest. The RMF Company won the fight handily through its superior knowledge of the country and its much more liberal hand with goods and alcohol. This educated the newcomers fast, for they too lost skins and trappers, though mere bystanders. That same year Vanderburgh was following other RMF Company partners across parts of Wyoming and along the fringes of the Blackfoot country. Both he and his rivals had to fight Blackfeet, who found it difficult to identify an ally so far from Fort Union. If the Company's guns were killing the Company's employees, never mind.

The year was a laborious but enlightening education in geography, in competition, in bribery and deception and the hijacking of furs. Lessons continued through 1831. The newcomers dogged Opposition brigades across Idaho, into the Flathead country west of the Divide in Montana, down to the Beaverhead, along the Jefferson. They did not get many furs but they made friends of the Flatheads and the Nez Perces. They could strike out for themselves sometimes now and were pouring out the Company's resources regardless. Goods were cheaper in the mountains in 1831 than they had ever been before and wages were higher. The power of wealth began to tell. They could keep up this kind of infighting much longer than the RMF Company, whose contemptuous confidence was yielding to alarm as the summer of 1832 spun toward the rendezvous.[3]

Drips went to St. Louis with Fontenelle in the summer of 1831 (this was the brigade with which the Flathead mission traveled) and tried to bring back a small consignment of desperately needed goods. He did not make it and was forced to winter east of the Divide. Vanderburgh's brigade wintered in Cache Valley, Drips' in the Salmon River Valley of Idaho, near a large camp of the RMF Company. It was a tough winter. Blackfeet far from home kept shooting their horses. Bridger and Fitzpatrick made successful deals for their trappers and furs. Some of their men and more of their Flatheads were murdered by Blackfeet on forays. And they got a foretaste of what was to come when a Hudson's Bay Company factor, who was camped at the Beaverhead, sent them an express. The Blackfeet, he said, had been taunting him and his Pend d'Oreille companions with news that the King of the Missouri had built a fort on the Marias and was outfitting their people with many guns and much powder. Pretty soon McKenzie would make the Blackfeet irresistible. Then they intended to start down this way in force. They were going to exterminate the Flatheads and all other Indians in these parts. After that they would drive all white men out of the mountains.

When the time arrived for the spring hunt, the Company tactics remained the same: follow the Opposition. The Opposition got away from the Salmon River Valley before the Company was ready, so Drips' brigade moved south through Idaho to find their partisan. There were Blackfeet about, Blackfeet proper, not the Gros Ventres who were beginning to take the trail homeward from the Arapahos. Many horses disappeared, several men were killed, and when they joined Vanderburgh they found that he had suffered similar losses. The combined parties moved off in search of RMF Company brigades but met Drips first. He was bringing the greatly needed supplies and for two or three days they had a big drunk, somewhat marred by a sleet storm.

On Willow Creek in the Idaho lava fields they caught up with a RMF Company brigade at last. It was led by Old Gabe, Jim Bridger, the mountain craft personified, and it had made a superbly successful spring hunt, as Vanderburgh's men assuredly had not. But now he had some goods to spare and more were coming with Fontenelle, so he sent out emissaries to see if he could capture the Flathead trade. His express reached the Flatheads — at the angle in the Beaverhead Mountains on the Idaho-Montana border — three days too late to witness a battle. The Blackfeet had begun their campaign of extermination but the Flatheads had declined to be exterminated. They had driven off a large war party and were dancing round sixteen scalps. They promised to come in and make a trade after they had finished telling their supernaturals about their victory.

Vanderburgh was by now too cagey to let Bridger shake him off. Old Gabe's men trapped the Idaho and Utah streams till beaver fur thinned for the summer, and up every brawling mountain creek where they set their traps there presently came a party of Company men to float their sticks in the same water. Drips' St. Louis goods lasted long enough to snatch some free trappers' pelts from Bridger's grasp and to buy a few of his men. (Applied observation: Fitzpatrick and Bridger with the Hudson's Bay Company last year.) Another RMF Company brigade came in, Milton Sublette's, which had wintered in Ogden's Hole (Utah) and had made its spring hunt on the Bear. Milton Sublette, a partner and a brother of William, was not with it. He had got into a brawl with a Bannock war chief and been stabbed.[4] Joe Meek, now a veteran mountain man twenty-two years old, stayed behind to comfort his last hours and close his eyes. But Milton took a lot of killing and after six weeks was as good as new. He and Joe rode off to find their brigade. Near the Green they met a village of Snakes and for some reason these usually friendly Indians had their backs up. They were going to kill Sublette and Meek, but a war chief who had enough coups to defy public opinion got their killing postponed and that night helped them to escape. Snake women were held to be the prettiest of all squaws and this chief had a nubile daughter, whose name Joe Meek renders Umentucken Tukutsey Undewatsey and translates the Mountain Lamb. She made an understandable impression on the two. After the rendezvous, Milton took his brigade into country where this band might be found, found them, and married the Mountain Lamb. Two years later, Sublette going home, Meek married her, too.

Now, however, they had to find their brigade and in fact had to follow it all the way to Pierre's Hole. All the winterers had reached it and were waiting for the pack trains from the East: Fitzpatrick, Bridger, Gervais, Fraeb, Milton Sublette; Vanderburgh and Drips; the Flatheads, the Nez Perces, and odd lots of other tribes; various free trappers. Tents and tipis spread along the creeks. Large herds of horses and mules grazed the plain. Every day or so another little group came in, from as far away as the Three Forks, or South Park, or Brown's Hole. They had the winter's histories to exchange, the absent and the killed to account for, fellowship to renew. The spring catch was ready to be pressed into bales of about eighty skins each, roughly a hundred pounds. Everyone was mending buckskins, if he had or could hire no squaw to do it for him, repairing his arms and traps, and always yearning for the alcohol that the trains would bring. The rendezvous was ripe for climax. It had been a big year for everyone except the American Fur Company, which was still learning. The RM Company had sixty thousand dollars in beaver.[5] But they would lose the free trappers' trade, if Fontenelle should get there first.

The RMF Company partners had now to acknowledge that their dominion over the interior West had been broken. The trust had come closer than anyone else to mastering their methods, could probably outbid them only a few days hence, and could probably not be shaken off thereafter. Facing the hard facts, they did the previously unthinkable: they offered to divide the mountains with their rivals, each company to keep to its own half. Vanderburgh and Drips said no. They did not yet know geography well enough to insist on a fair division. They needed to learn still more mountain craft by watching its masters at work. Besides, they were sitting pretty: they had the resources of a trust to call on. Everything was going as McKenzie had foreseen and presently they would bankrupt the Opposition.

Fight it out, then. The RMF Company sent two men to hurry up Bill Sublette. (They missed him, got intercepted and robbed by Crows, and had to make their way back to Pierre's Hole on foot.) A day or two later Tom Fitzpatrick galloped off alone to do the urging in person. Vanderburgh and Drips sent out a similar party to put the gad to Fontenelle, then another one. Both rode out beyond where he should have been by now, but neither found him. One of the parties appears to have camped with Bonneville to wait for Fontenelle. The other one saw Sublette and took back to rendezvous the news that the RMF Company was in the lead. Halfway through the morning of July 8, under its canopy of dust, bridles jingling, mules braying, a hundred rifles rousing the entire encampment to answer in kind, Sublette's pack train, with Wyeth's malcontents and the late increments, came up Pierre's Hole from the south.[6]

* * *

Sublette was here first and the RMF Company would get the bulk of the trade, hold its own trappers, and buy a sizable number of its rivals'. But Sublette was expecting to find Fitzpatrick here, whereas everyone had supposed that they would come in together. So the celebration that had begun the moment Sublette's train came in, and went into crescendo as soon as the curved tin kegs of alcohol could be got off the mules, was dampened by the universal conclusion that a great man of the mountains had been killed. Search parties went out at once but only perfunctorily, for everyone knew that the country he had had to cross was full of Blackfeet — had they not shot up Sublette's camp? (One group of searchers later claimed to have seen from afar a band of Blackfeet holding a horse race and recognized Fitzpatrick's horse among the entries, but this may be doubted.[7]) But late that afternoon, emaciated, barefoot and all but naked, his body scratched and bruised, starving, almost out of his mind, Tom came into camp.[8]

What had happened to Fitzpatrick may be taken as a typical mischance, one of the accidents that were the daily risks of every mountain man. For it must never be forgotten that the country was more hostile than the Indians and that a momentary inattention or a little bad luck could press the trigger that made its hostility aggressive. Fitzpatrick was as expert a mountain man as ever lived: he was at the head of his profession. He was taking a long and calculated and justified chance when he rode out alone from Bill Sublette's train on the Sweetwater. And the major risk thus calculated he in fact passed successfully. It was what happened after he escaped the Indians that nearly cost him his life — and would have cost the life of anyone less expert.

Riding one horse and leading the other by turns, he pushed both as hard as was safe, traveling much by night, picking with care the places where it was safe to stop and sleep for a few hours. (Thickets where the horses could be hidden and grazed while he slept, at the head of small draws preferably, with the ways of escape carefully noted.) He came through South Pass to the creeks called Sandy and quartered toward the Green. He would reach it near the mouth of Cottonwood or that of Horse Creek, where Fontenelle and Bonneville would camp about three weeks later. From here he plunged into the mountains. And ran square into one of the migrating villages of Gros Ventres.

He was in a small valley hemmed in by peaks when he and the Indians discovered each other. Any Indians he might meet in these parts would jump a single white man and Tom recognized these as Blackfeet. They boiled round him. He abandoned his led horse, clapped his spurs to the one he was riding, and made straight overland — which is to say, up one draw, over to another, through brush, across rimrock, making for the ridge in hope of finding some conjunction of valleys where a short lead would enable him to give them the slip. No horse could stand such going very long and presently he had to streak straight up a mountainside on foot. The ride, of course, had carried him far from the course he had been following.

His pursuers found his horse and redoubled their yells — there were ceremonial outcries for such a triumph. By that time Tom had hidden in a crevice between rocks, at whose entrance he was able to heap stones and brush. The Indians swarmed like angered ants, crawling from rock to rock, loping across short open spaces, throwing themselves flat. Invocation of the supernaturals would be begun at once, for this was war. Medicine men would perform their rituals of gesticulation and sacrifice and would chant their prayers. Some of the young braves would stop to paint themselves, others would sing songs which their medicines had revealed to make them invulnerable. Some would put on the skins or feathers revealed in dreams, efficacious for the accomplishment of great deeds. Others would sprinkle themselves with the Indian equivalents of goopher dust. Many would recite the coups they had counted — a preliminary to nearly everything in an Indian's daily life. Otter skin, magpie feathers, eagle bone, prairie dog dung — everyone would have some private charm. But, whatever the liturgical rationale, the empirical job of rooting out the victim would go on.

It went on all day long. Many times some of the Indians came within a few yards of Tom's hiding place. Several times they all withdrew down the mountainside, then rallied and propitiated their gods and came back. Late at night Tom crawled out, took a sight by the stars, worked out which way was least likely to take him toward the Gros Ventre camp — and found he had figured wrong. He walked into the tethered horses and pitched tipis. He went back to his hole and lay there all the next day, with Indians nosing all round him — beagles or terriers who were willing to suspend the business of an entire village as long as need be to take one white scalp. The second night he tried again, fetched a wide compass round the camp, and headed into the mountains. When day came he hid in a thicket, saw his Gros Ventres again and that night got entirely away. From here on he trusted himself to travel by day. But, reaching the Snake, he made a small raft to get his rifle, powder, shot-pouch, and possibles across, and the swift current broke it up.[9] He was now without the tools of survival, having only his belt knife to live by. A man like Fitzpatrick was never lost for very long, not for longer than it took to find a landmark in a country whose landmarks he knew by heart. (As soon as any ridge permitted him to see the nipples of the Tetons he would be all right.) In fact, he made straight across a chaos of gulches he had never traveled, far from a trail, on a true bearing for Pierre's Hole. But he had to travel mountains on a diet of such buds and roots as he could find. Day by day his strength decreased. On the fifth day he found part of a buffalo carcass which the wolves had left. His flint and steel had gone with his rifle, so Zenas Leonard has him say that he made fire with sticks, though certainly he ate his carrion raw. His moccasins wore out; he cut up his broadbrim hat and bound strips of it round his feet. Every day he made a shorter distance, but he kept to his true bearing while he could still walk. He was on a beeline for camp when his companions found him.

* * *

Bill Sublette, then, brought his goods to rendezvous on July 8, 1832, and Fitzpatrick came in the same day. The RMF Company settled its year's accounts with its own trappers and began to get back any surplus pay in outfits for the next year and in the watered alcohol that promptly went on sale. The first days of any rendezvous were a magnificent debauch. In this period of renewed fellowship, good food, abundant liquor, and the presence of women the mountain men released the fantasies and longings of the year. They were men with the bark on and their diversions, which need not be touched on at the moment, were male. It was quite a time. It was also a good time for the companies. While a man had any credit left, while there was liquor for himself and the boys, while a few beads or a yard of cloth or a couple of hawking bells would enrapture any Indian woman or buy her from her proprietor, what trapper gave a damn about the relative value of the beaver plews he had taken last spring?

While the fusillades and the warwhoops echoed back from the hills, while the Indians did their tribal stunts for pay, while the trappers brawled and retched, the companies cleaned up. The RMF Company partners signed up a pleasing number of Vanderburgh's men, paying them spot cash in goods and contracting to pay them ruinously high wages for the year ahead. They and Sublette & Campbell got the entire free trapper trade this year. Six dollars a plew — dollars in goods at from five hundred to two thousand percent St. Louis. They bought pemmican from the Indians, the famous concentrated food of which you tried to keep a supply against thin times to come. They traded their worn-down horses with a knife or an awl or a handful of gunpowder for boot. They bought several hundred fresh horses for but little more — at an average of ten dollars St. Louis. The Nez Perces had learned selective breeding, which was beyond the comprehension of most tribes, and had developed a distinctive stock called the Pelouse horse, the 'Appaloosa' of a later date. (Their neighbors, the Cayuses, furnished the generic Western word for horse.) It had a spotted or sometimes a white rump and was the best Indian horse. The Nez Perces supplied it to their neighbors, who traded it across the plains, and drove large herds to rendezvous for barter.

Also they had artifacts to sell, especially moccasins and buckskins. The mountain man would likely outfit himself with expensive heavy shirts, breeches, and capotes of wool, but these would not last long in his business and he needed buckskin breeches and leggings to fall back on. He comes down in our iconography clad in this buckskin uniform, a native American costume always handsome in dry weather (though black where pageantry makes it tan) whose fringe and natural folds especially recommend it to sculptors. But the uniform signified that he had ripped his store clothes to pieces, for buckskins, though tough and so ideal for brush country, were uncomfortable. The best-smoked of them would turn rain for a good many hours (a Mackinaw blanket was as waterproof as a Navaho rug), but in the end even the best would get watersoaked and clammy, shrink painfully, and hang baggily when they dried.

Cutthroat competition did not impair the mountain fellowship. The employees of rival companies got drunk with great noise, the partners a little more formally. There were ceremonious dinners, with Vanderburgh and Jim Bridger and Bill Sublette toasting one another and exchanging news, reminiscences, and lies. Under the peaks, fifteen hundred miles from home, you were mountaineers together and your heart brimmed with affection for a fellow initiate at the moment when you were meditating the best way to bankrupt him. The RMF Company had won another round but the crisis remained. Fontenelle was on his way here with a rich train, and all the goods in it would buy furs or favor that should have gone to the partners. Moreover, the fragments of small companies and the bands of free trappers present at this rendezvous showed how seriously others were cutting up the partners' private domain. Finally here was Wyeth who was going to establish another company, and back somewhere to the eastward was Bonneville who already had established one and had Astor money behind him.

There were the most serious consultations by night in the partners' tents, among themselves and with Bill Sublette and Robert Campbell, who had them by the throat but would deal with them more favorably than anyone else would. The tactics of the trust could be charted: Vanderburgh and Drips would follow the partners' brigades, learn more about the country and the craft, and eventually with unlimited banking expect to crowd them out. What could the partners do? Nothing but fight. They had some artillery.

The decision was to send brigades under Fraeb and Milton

Sublette to the south and southwest, both to the Humboldt, whence the former would turn east to the Utah and Colorado streams and the latter swing in a loop through central Idaho to the Salmon River and neighboring streams. Bridger and Fitzpatrick would go east to the Yellowstone River, then quarter back to the Three Forks of the Missouri and so eventually to the Salmon. It is not clear where Gervais was to trap but one guesses the upper Green, for this fall hunt was obviously designed to sweep all the richest beaver streams in the mountains and all but the Green are accounted for.

Meanwhile there had been final rebellion in Wyeth's camp of greenhorns. Half his party, eleven men in all, had had enough desert, rain, snow, sandstorms, alkali water, bad food, and constant exhaustion. They had recovered their health in this pleasant valley below the Grand Teton, but they could see no future in the adventure business. The seceders included Wyeth's brother, the surgeon, and his flip young cousin John. They would go back to the States with Sublette and Campbell.

Not Nat Wyeth. He now understood how naïve his Cambridge notions had been. But if he had been schooled in realism at the hands of realists, he had also seen that his basic plan was sound. The mountain fur trade, now that he had seen its rendezvous, was quite as irrational economically as it had seemed beside Fresh Pond and offered as promising an opportunity to an organizing talent. Nat Wyeth would go on to the Columbia, for which he had originally set out. On the way there and after reaching it he would fill in the remaining details at first hand, especially the trapping. He bought pemmican and Indian goods, replenished his supplies, traded his horses for fresh ones, and was ready to move. But he was still in country that had Blackfeet in it as well. So instead of moving north out of Pierre's Hole, the shortest way to the lower Snake, he added his small party to Milton Sublette's. Sublette would head for the Snake southwestward and would travel it as far as Raft River or thereabout, whence he would strike for the Humboldt. By that time Wyeth would be beyond all likelihood of Blackfeet and could take his small group in comparative safety by the established route to the Columbia.

# « III »

# MASSACRE: SPORT AND BUSINESS (1832)

FRAEB AND MILTON SUBLETTE were ready to go to work first and would travel together to the Humboldt. Wyeth and his faithful remnant would go with them to be safe from the Blackfeet. So would Sinclair's band of free trappers and a couple of smaller groups. On July 17 they started out, moving south down the valley of Pierre's Hole, intending to strike southwest for the Snake River.

About the middle of July there comes into the air of the high places a golden emptiness, a washed look infinitely beautiful but melancholy with a premonition of fall. The early light seems detached from its source; till midmorning the highest slopes are touched with a powder-blue mist, which will intensify and come lower as the brief summer of the peaks runs out. The silver of aspen leaves turns brighter and the cottonwoods begin to be flecked with gold. Above the timberline dwarf oakbrush flies a flag of scarlet which will march down the mountainsides with the gold from now on. The light in the canyons has come through lavender gauze and the woods seem darker, more deserted, more given up to solitude.

Less than a hundred all told, the train made six or eight miles on July 17, probably getting altogether out of Pierre's Hole. They camped for the night in a valley with a stream in it, groves here and there, the mountainsides close to the creek. Shortly after they got started the next morning there appeared over the crest of a hill farther down the valley two files of horsemen. Sinclair's party, in the lead, stopped short. Sublette, Fraeb, and Wyeth came up to them and stopped. No party in such numbers was expected but might this be Fontenelle far off his course? Milton Sublette had a spyglass. No, not whites — Indians. They had a Union Jack (lately captured from John Work's Hudson's Bay brigade) and they must be the Blackfeet who had been in these parts for several weeks. The trappers threw the packs off their mules for breastworks and led mules and horses back into some timber. They sent a couple of men galloping off to tell the companies at rendezvous what was afoot. The Indians began to slant cautiously down the hillside, where the creek ran round its foot. As the files came over the crest the whites could see that this was a village — there were horse and dog travois, horse herds, women.[1]

They were one of the Gros Ventre villages who had been coming up the Green for a couple of weeks, who had shot up Sublette's camp, chased Tom Fitzpatrick, and picked off a number of wandering trappers along the southern edge of Wyoming. They were not Blackfeet but the Atsina, a detached fragment of the Arapahos who had moved into the Blackfoot country and worked out an alliance with its Tartars, speaking their language as fluently as their own, adopting their ceremonies and their feuds. The Blackfeet called them 'the gut people,' the Arapahos called them 'the beggars' or 'spongers,' and both felt superior to them. They had just completed a three years' visit with the latter in Colorado and were on the way home. That they had crossed the Divide here and were heading north on the western side meant that they were steering clear of Crows and, probably, that they thought they would get a shot at some Flatheads.

At something less than a mile the adversaries secured their positions and watched each other. Both needed time, the whites to let their rendezvous companions come up, the Indians to complete the full religious preparation for an attack in force. It was to gain time that a war chief rode out from the tribe toward the trappers. (War chief: any brave who had counted enough coups to entitle him to lead a war party on his own.) He was wearing a scarlet blanket and carrying a tribal medicine pipe. This last, to the accompaniment of ritual chants, had been taken from the bundle in which it was kept with a variety of holy objects, rattles, skulls, feathers, claws, skins, paints, bundles of herbs and tobacco. The bear skin, elk skin, and bird skins that protected it had been unwrapped to further prayers and posturings. The trappers would recognize it: a thick squat bowl (of greenish soapstone since these were Blackfeet) and a long flat wooden stem festooned with braids of multicolored cloth, dyed feathers, and other symbolical objects all liturgically important. Displaying it thus was a peace-pledge, a solemn declaration that for the time being the Indians would observe a truce. Good stuff if you could get away with it, but Blackfeet or Gros Ventres could not get away with it in the presence of these veterans and the chief was a fool to try. Sublette, Fraeb, and Sinclair knew that Blackfoot truces were one-way only.

In Sublette's party was a halfbreed named Antoine Godin. Two years ago the Blackfeet had killed his father, Thyery Godin, some seventy-five miles from here on Big Lost River, which for a time was called Godin's River in commemoration of the murder. Antoine rode out to meet the medicine pipe and a Flathead brave rode with him — a member of a tribe who had had to fight Blackfeet since the beginning of time, who could remember when they had had to fight them with stone-tipped arrows and sharpened sticks against Northwest Company muskets, who this year were under notification that the Blackfeet intended to exterminate them. The two made their plans as they rode. They came up to the chief, who brandished his symbol of peace and held out his right hand. Godin grabbed it — and had his man. 'Shoot!' he said and the Flathead shot. They took the scalp and galloped back, waving it and the scarlet blanket.[2]

The tenderfoot John Wyeth, who was coming up with the reinforcements from Pierre's Hole when this occurred, was horrified by the breach of faith. 'This was *Joab* with a vengeance — *art thou in health, my brother?*' he writes. But it was the right way to treat Blackfeet.

The Indians did not break off at once, as any tribe not in the Blackfoot tradition would have done the moment a sacred ritual failed them. They boiled and screamed, ran out a little to taunt the whites, anointed their bodies with various invulnerabilities, and stripped off the covers of their war shields which also promised they could not be hurt. Some squaws and children disappeared up the mountainside, others hurried pack animals around a bend in the valley, still others helped their men fort up. For the Indians would let the whites do the attacking. They withdrew into a grove of willows and cottonwoods, outside a loop in the creek and with the mountain beyond it. There, out of sight, they piled up a breastwork of fallen trees and their squaws dug foxholes behind it.

The whites closed up to distant rifle shot. Not caring to rush that grove, they contented themselves with firing into it at long range. There were upwards of a hundred Indians in there, perhaps two hundred. Bill Sublette found them thus irresolute when he came galloping up from the rendezvous with a hundred or two hundred trappers riding hard behind him and four or five hundred Flatheads and Nez Perces yelling behind them. Bill raged at the trappers for dawdling and at once supplied what the situation needed, a leader. He sent Wyeth's greenhorns back out of the way and bade them keep behind their packs and look after the wounded but let Nat Wyeth himself join the assault wave. He exhorted perhaps sixty volunteers, white and red, to follow him. He gave the Indians one flank and the whites the other. He and his partner Campbell made verbal wills, each instructing the other to carry out their provisions. Then he led his rangers into the willow grove.

They got shot up right there. The Indians in foxholes under their bottom log poured it in and most of the rangers' casualties occurred at the first fire. That stopped them and they too got behind logs, as Bill should have made them do to begin with. For a couple of hours they shot it out, the mountain men so seriously depleting their lead that they had to come back the next day and dig it out of the trees. They picked off occasional Indians and some of them got picked off in turn. 'The idea of a barbed arrow sticking in a man's body, as we had observed it in the deer and other animals,' says young John Wyeth, here watching the kind of Indian fight he had read about at Cambridge, 'was appalling to us all, and it is no wonder that some of our men recoiled from it.'

Sinclair was in the outer line, a good hard man who could not travel far on foot because he had lost some toes. He was shot, fatally as it turned out, and Campbell carried him out of the woods, then came back. One of Fraeb's men pushed a log ahead of him almost to the breastwork; it was hit several times but he got to an enfilading tree. One who had primed himself with liquor got clear up to the logs, climbed to the top, peered over, and came tumbling down with two bullets through his head. At some time in this stage of the battle Bill Sublette was shot through the upper arm. They propped him up behind a tree and he went on giving orders. The Flathead and Nez Perce auxiliaries were able to work halfway round their flank before the creek stopped them but here they were in a crossfire from their allies and some of them got shot.

It was a slow business — and a noisy one. Besides the gunfire there were the yells, howls, and ululations of the Indians on both sides. Custom required them to taunt and deride one another in their own languages and such others as they knew. You shouted that your enemy was a boy, a squaw, a homosexual, or that hares or other timid animals were in his ancestry, that he and his tribe ate dung or carrion and could not fight — and so on. If you needled him into rushing out where you could get a shot at him, so much to the good; if not, you could win a round on abuse alone. By late afternoon, with some five whites and as many Indian allies killed, Sublette's men had worked close to the logs. The Gros Ventres were not showing themselves but hugging their foxholes and waiting for a charge. There was no profit in charging. Sublette ordered some of his command to start piling wood and brush against the fort: he would burn them out. They got a sizable pile built but the Flatheads and Nez Perces protested: the cornered Blackfeet could not get away and they had many possessions which it would not do to burn. Voted down. The whites got ready to start their bonfire.

Inside the logs some of the Gros Ventres began to sing their death songs. These were not a preparation for the hereafter but a final magic to prevent death — another promise of invulnerability, revealed in dreams, reserved for the worst emergency. But one of them tried another taunt. He shouted that they knew they were licked and would meet death like the heroes they were but they knew also that they would soon be avenged. For, he said, several hundred lodges of their people were close behind. (That was more or less true.) They would come up soon and rub the victors out. Whether he spoke bad Blackfoot or worse Flathead, whoever translated him understood this as a declaration that hundreds of Blackfeet were at this moment murdering those left at the rendezvous, stealing the horses, and plundering the camp. The news spread among men who had the frenzy of battle on them. Some cool heads must have known better, but others, probably among the hundred-odd more circumspect who formed the reserve outside the woods, galloped off back to camp. Others followed them, stampeded by this new excitement, till only a handful were left to watch the fort. These sanely withdrew to the edge of the grove. A couple of hours later some of their friends came back shamefaced, having found everything serene at camp. But it was now too late to do anything, for you did not fight forted up Indians at night by choice. They bivouacked and mounted guard but the Gros Ventres stole away in the darkness, taking their wounded and some of their dead.

The next morning the whites rushed in on what Nat Wyeth

called a 'scene of disgusting butchery.' They found a wounded white man in the brush and took him out on a litter but he died. One of the white dead had been 'mutilated in a shocking manner,' which usually means that his genitals had been cut off. (To insult him in the spirit world, to give the mutilator greater power in this one, and to obtain material for religious ceremonies.) There were twenty or thirty dead horses and nine dead Gros Ventres behind the logs. Other Indian corpses were scattered down the creek and through the woods. The Indians later admitted that twenty-six had been killed, which indicates a good many more. There was a squaw with a broken leg who begged the mountain men to kill her. They declined but the Flatheads obliged, sinking a hatchet in her brain. The Flatheads and Nez Perces got their spoils, too, for the fleeing Gros Ventres had scattered tipis, robes, pelts, household equipment, and medicine bundles for some miles down the valley. A herd of forty-two horses was found intact where the squaws had hidden it. 'The din of arms,' Wyeth says, 'was now changed into the noise of the vulture [the buzzard, rather] and the howling of masterless dogs.' All told five whites and seven of their Indian allies had been killed, six whites and seven Indians wounded.[3]

They buried their dead behind the Gros Ventre stockade, where the ground was so trampled that graves would not be visible and so the bodies would not be dug up and scalped. The Flatheads scalped the dead Gros Ventres, among them, some say, several children. Then everyone went back to Pierre's Hole for a few days of alert waiting. The Gros Ventres were known to have been visiting the Arapahos and since this village had been on the way home, then very likely the war chief had been telling the truth and the rest of the tribe might be somewhere near. The homeward-bound Doctor Wyeth bound up Bill Sublette's wound and did what he could for the others — medicine could not do much in the mountains. The Indians performed their ceremonies of lamentation and victory. Around their fires the mountain men analyzed the engagement and began to create its folklore. Many of them had had the usual lucky escapes, including Henry Fraeb, who had had a lock of hair shot off. Also while he was fighting in the grove, back at Pierre's Hole his squaw had given birth to a son.

No more Gros Ventres showed up. Sublette and Campbell postponed their departure to let Bill's wound heal. But Stephens, the former Gant & Blackwell partisan who had sold his furs to Fitzpatrick on the Laramie, now decided that he had been gypped — he was right — and after an angry quarrel determined to go back and raise the cache regardless. He got four unattached trappers to go along and three of Wyeth's malcontents started with them, too eager to get the mountains behind them to wait for the strong Sublette & Campbell train.[4] It was foolhardy and a mistake. Three days later five of them were back, Stephens with a wound that soon proved fatal. The other two were dead and scalped in Jackson's Hole, just over the pass, where the Gros Ventres had got this measure of revenge. One of the dead was a Wyeth man, George More of Boston, the first fatality of that cloudy vision beside Fresh Pond.

But it was not the Gros Ventres' year. They picked up some of their tribe on the way through the mountains and were honing for action when they came upon Fontenelle and Bonneville, as we have seen. But they had used up most of their powder in the battle and the camps were too strong and too alert. They moved on — and they were going home east of the mountains after all. So they got into Absaroka, the Crow country, and a band of their toughest enemies cut them to pieces. It was the best fiesta the Crows had had in years — women, children, horses, war chiefs, boys, old men, and such personal belongings as were left. The Crows were accustomed to say that the Blackfeet were brave but too dumb to fight well, and these had been well shot up already. The Crows weighed down their horses with spoils, blackened their faces, and went home to dance round the scalps. Such Gros Ventres as escaped straggled on to their own country. They had to tell the Blackfeet, already smoldering because they had not exterminated the Flatheads, what had happened — and thus laid up trouble for the fur brigades that were heading north.

On the way back to the States, Sublette and Campbell made a detour to avoid the main body of the Gros Ventres but instead ran into them. They had had word of their relatives' defeat: they painted their faces and talked mean. But they knew Cut Face, wisely settled for twenty-five pounds of tobacco, and moved on. So did Sublette, taking the year's great catch of furs, the last bonanza catch in these parts. On the frontier he met a famous man who was making a tour of the prairies en route eventually to Fort Gibson. Washington Irving was traveling with a government commission which was to inspect the Indian Country that had been set aside for the dispossessed tribes. He would presently write two notable books about the breed whom he now met in the field.

'Their long cavalcade,' he wrote, 'stretched in single file for nearly half a mile. Sublette still wore his arm in a sling. The mountaineers in their rude hunting dresses, armed with rifles and roughly mounted and leading their pack horses down a hill of the forest, looked like banditti returning with plunder. On the top of some of the packs were perched several halfbreed children, perfect little imps, with wild black eyes glaring from among elf-locks. These, I was told, were children of the trappers: pledges of love from their squaw spouses in the wilderness.'

* * *

Back in the mountains the brigades took up the fall hunt. Milton Sublette led his small outfit to the Humboldt River. He seems to have arranged his marriage with the Mountain Lamb on this trip but their honeymoon was not propitious. For they found no buffalo along the Idaho–Utah–Nevada border and came into starving times. They ate such mules as they could spare and were glad to imitate the despised Diggers by baking messes of the black crickets of the country. (The crickets that were to come down by the billion on the Mormons' first crop and produce the miracle of the seagulls.) Joe Meek remembered that he had had another dish forced on him here. 'I have held my hands in an ant hill until they were covered with ants,' he said, 'then greedily licked them off.' They tried blood from living mules too, but Milton headed toward the eastern slope of the Cascades, where they got trout and eventually game. This was farther west than the plan had called for him to go, country which the Hudson's Bay Company had pretty well trapped out. (The monopoly's policy was to conserve beaver and trap it scientifically with an eye to the future — but Oregon was jointly occupied and the Crown might lose it.) Sublette's men took what plews they could, then turned back to central and eastern Idaho, trapping streams which they had worked last spring. Here an express arrived from Fitzpatrick and Bridger east of the mountains, saying that they had not been able to lose the trust.

The two partisans had moved on schedule from the rendezvous to the Yellowstone River, along it and its tributaries, and up to the Three Forks of the Missouri. They got started well before Vanderburgh and Drips, who had to go looking for Fontenelle till they found him on the Green. They re-outfitted and replenished their stock of trade goods, sent a trading party to the Flatheads, and hurried on to find the RMF Company. They kept finding them, losing them, finding them again, in the small parties that trapped the creeks or in the brigades that coalesced to move on to new country. Fitzpatrick and Bridger would slip over a divide and head somewhere else but the pursuers would soon pick up their camp sites and hurry on. Both sides trapped as much as they could but by now both were less interested in furs than in each other.

Most of this chase was conducted in the mountains north of Yellowstone Park, those to the west of it east of the Salmon River, and those that form the adjacent Idaho–Montana boundary. Finally Bridger and Fitzpatrick had had enough. They headed east. They were going to get out of the mountains, away from furs. Also they were going to enter the Blackfoot country and let Nature take charge. Vanderburgh and Drips pounded after them, on short rations because those ahead got the game.

Pick them up in the valley of the Big Hole River in Beaverhead County (southwestern) Montana, near the town of Gibbons and the site of the battle which the general it was named for was to lose to Chief Joseph of the Nez Perces. Bridger and Fitzpatrick led them northward down that valley, then over a maze of mountains northeast to the Deer Lodge plains (at Anaconda). Ominously, they here met a war party of Snakes, who had stolen some horses from the Blackfeet and succeeded in killing a squaw and a child. Down this valley, along Clark's Fork, twisting north, northwest, and west, almost to Missoula — and so almost to Hell Gate, which got its name because it was the place where buffalo-hunting Flatheads emerged from their mountains into Blackfoot country. (This was the Buffalo Road, the route followed by the transmontane Indians when they came east to find the herds.) There were excellent beaver streams here and so the RMF Company had turned away from them, northeastward up the Blackfoot River, over the Continental Divide and through a maze of mountains, and so down to the Dearborn River and the plains. Somewhere along the Dearborn, which empties into the Missouri above Great Falls, they caught up with Bridger and Fitzpatrick again. In the heart of the Blackfoot country.

The partners had had thin going too but they had brought their rivals down into the plains where they would trap no beaver. With a straight face they announced that they were going to the Three Forks, where there were still no beaver. Once this had been rich fur country. Drips headed there too and took most of the American Fur Company's men, but presently, he got the idea, let the partners go their own way at last, and turned back toward the mountains by way of the Madison River, that great trout stream. Vanderburgh had gone no farther than the Missouri and had already headed his smaller party back toward beaver. They came over the mountains and struck the Jefferson River north of the famous Beaverhead Rock of Lewis and Clark, being then only one range away from the Big Hole Valley whence Bridger and Fitzpatrick had decoyed them more than three weeks before. It was late September and a heavy snowfall added to their frustration. But they found buffalo and beaver. They followed up Ruby River, which Lewis and Clark had named the Philanthropy, trapping as they went. They crossed the divide to the Madison and here met the RMF Company again, this time by chance. After Drips turned back, the partners had trapped the Gallatin before crossing to Madison. They would go up it to the Divide and were able to get a lead because Vanderburgh had to wait for his small trapping parties to come in. When they did he started back toward the Jefferson, overland, hoping to take a short cut to his rivals.

There had lately been some Indian sign and it could have been made only by Blackfeet. Now — it was October 14 — a hunter found a buffalo cow that had been abandoned half-butchered, and that too must mean Blackfeet. The trappers wanted this investigated before breaking up to trap the stream. So Vanderburgh took a half-dozen men and started out. They found a fire still burning, another butchered cow, the trail of a small party. Farther on was a grove of trees and if there were Indians about they would be there. But on the way to it the scouts had to cross a small gully, and as they did so about a hundred Blackfeet (or so it seemed to Warren Ferris, Vanderburgh's clerk) rose up and shot at them from both sides. Vanderburgh was killed, a Canadian trapper was killed, Ferris was wounded, and he and the other survivors succeeded in riding out of range and back to camp.

This was near Alder Gulch, whose gold would first make Montana known to the world at large. And the RMF Company had succeeded in at least part of its design. It had got rid of one of the American Fur Company's field generals. But you could not intimidate the American Fur Company, whose executives lived in St. Louis and New York.

The Blackfeet stripped the flesh from Vanderburgh's bones and threw them in the river. His party, after a panic which the old hands quelled, found temporary refuge with a band of Flatheads big enough to be safe from Blackfeet. Presently they made their way west to the Beaverhead and Horse Prairie, within reach of the Continental Divide beyond which they had arranged to winter. They had cached some goods here on the way out and found Drips' party waiting for them. The Blackfeet had shot up his camp and stolen some of his horses. Some of Bonneville's hunters came in and they too had had a brush with Blackfeet. So had one of Bonneville's larger parties under Joe Walker, who passed by soon afterward. And an express arrived from the RMF Company saying that they had succored one of Drips' trapping groups, which had had one man killed and several wounded by Blackfeet.

The Blackfeet were working hard to make good their one-year plan and rid the mountains of white men. They put their mark on Jim Bridger too at just this time. He and Fitzpatrick, too wise to travel Blackfoot country in small groups, felt safe enough when they met a large band of Piegans, one of the three Blackfoot tribes. The Indians could count too and so their hearts were good. They sent out a brave with a medicine pipe as their neighbors had done at Pierre's Hole, and Bridger, the Blanket Chief, rode out to meet him. Just as the brave held out his hand, Jim thought he saw something suspicious among the clustered Indians, fifty yards away. He cocked his rifle. The Indian seized the barrel and turned it earthward as Jim fired, then wrenched it from his hands and clubbed him with it. Peace broke up in a double volley and a prolonged skirmish, both parties hugging the rocks. At dark the Piegans got away. The mountain men had rubbed out nine of them, paying three lives of their own and a few horses. Besides getting a cracked skull, Bridger had two arrows in his shoulder. His companions were able to pull one of them out but had to cut the shaft of the other and leave the head.

Another band of Piegans whom Bridger met soon afterward told him that their hearts had turned good permanently. The King of the Missouri had told them to display a white flag whenever they sighted white men, then go in and trade like Christians. They were going to act on this advice, they said, but let Jim watch out for the Bloods, another Blackfoot tribe. Yet when he sighted some Bloods and his men began to shoot, they too flew a white rag, came in to trade, and said they had decided to love the white brother and hereafter would murder only the Snakes. Damnedest thing that Jim had ever heard of in the Blackfoot country. But it didn't mean a thing.

That about finished the season. The companies had ruined each other's fall hunt, had thrown their resources to the winds, and had got involved in unnecessary, fatal Indian fighting. Business over till spring, the RMF Company came up to Horse Prairie and everyone was as friendly as your Cousin Joe. Together the rivals moved over the mountains into Idaho, to the Salmon River and down it to the Snake. Here they would spend the winter near enough each other to enjoy friendly intercourse, feasts, mutual hunts for meat, and an occasional piracy of each other's men. It was near the place where Bonneville had decided to winter and so they could continue their expert operations on him.

# « IV »

# PAUL BUNYAN'S FAIR (1833)

TRUST, OPPOSITION, AND BONNEVILLE wintered along the Idaho streams, within visiting range — a few days' travel. It was a severe winter, Flatheads and Nez Perces came in big groups to visit their white friends, and as a result all the companies had to move several times. (Bonneville's was in four divisions, each of the others in two.) A number of small parties got snowbound and had to eat their moccasins. Several solitary stragglers died of exposure. There were Blackfeet everywhere. They were still trying to make good their promise to exterminate the decadent demoplutocrats west of the Divide. They got off to a bad start in November, when a sizable war party [1] tried to blitz an encampment of Snakes and Bannocks on Godin's River. (Big Lost River, central Idaho, northeast of the Sawtooth Mountains.) They misjudged its size and some two hundred lodges erupted enemies at their first charge. Thereupon they exhibited the stupidity which the Crows alleged against them: they panicked and hid in a willow grove downwind. The Snakes and Bannocks set fire to it and happily rode down the Blackfeet thus flushed. Forty braves and five squaws left their hair, against eight Snakes. One of the eight, however, was a personage of note called the Horn Chief.

His medicine had promised him that metal would not kill him, an immunity that made him formidable in war. When the Blackfeet shot him through the heart, therefore, the Snakes knew that the bullet had been made of horn. And this ambiguity would be intelligible to Captain Stewart when he heard about it. His ancestral barony contained Birnam Wood, which had fulfilled a similar augury by coming to Dunsinane.

Losses made the Blackfeet mad. In brutal weather they hung about the various camps, driving off horses and lifting the scalps of stragglers, ranging from the Salmon to the Bear and crisscrossing the Pierre's Hole country where their allies had been shot up. The Nez Perce villages that were neighboring with Bonneville suffered heavily. He kept advising them to guard their herds, and a renegade Blackfoot who had taken citizenship with them exhorted them to get out and fight a war, but the Nez Perces trusted for security to snow and the high ridges. So their wealth kept diminishing and every week or so more squaws had to hack off some fingers. Unknown to Bonneville, one of his subdivisions wintering to the southward lost several men in a pitched fight with Blackfeet and had several more dry-gulched. As spring came on, the Blackfeet found the RMF Company moving toward a new camp on the Portneuf (Pocatello, Idaho) and harassed them for a month or so.[2]

When the canyons began to open up the Blackfeet remembered that it was the Flatheads they had promised to exterminate. (A medicine animal would have spoken to a priest in a dream or a bird would have come hedgehopping through a village uttering reminders.) Their brittle, weathervane minds fumed with contrition and they made off for the Flathead country. At the Horse Prairie (eastward from Lemhi Pass, Montana) the task force met some thirty Flatheads and shot it out with them. It was a bad day for the Flatheads, all but one of whom were killed. But they got enough in return to wet down the spirit of conquest. The Blackfeet had used up most of the ammunition they had got from the King of the Missouri, in so much that some of them were rumored to be using stones for bullets. They had had a fine winter, had struck enough coups to enhance their narratives, had left their scalps all over Idaho, and were showing an unfavorable balance. Even Blackfeet could count costs. They decided that the transmontane Indians took more exterminating than the glory was worth, and turned homeward to mourn their slain for a season and get more lead and powder from Kenneth McKenzie. They met enough trapping parties on the way, especially Bonneville's, to keep their hand in.

It had been a bad winter for Bonneville, whose parties had suffered heavy losses in lives and equipment. As the snow melted he traveled about outfitting them and getting them started on the spring hunt. He had impressed the Nez Perces but they had lost so many horses that he could not buy all he needed. When he started for the Malade River [3] he met RMF Company brigades under Gervais and Milton Sublette heading the same way. The veterans had learned where he intended to make his hunt — on the affluents of the Snake as far as the Boise and beyond — and intended to strip the country under the newcomer's nose. They did so — they had the savvy — and Bonneville's parties had to range farther northward, down the Snake, where the Hudson's Bay Company had the country well secured. The bands of Nez Perces, Flatheads, and Pend d'Oreilles whom Bonneville met loved him deeply, they told the neighbors that Bald Head had a generous heart, and he thought for a while that he might undercut the British. But though the Indians might love him and his presents, they knew that the monopoly would outstay all speculators. The shadow of its district superintendent was on them when Bonneville spread out his goods: they admired the exhibition but would not trade. The factor (probably Francis Payette) had not received his seasonal stock yet but held his Indians in control and began to work on some of Bonneville's trappers. Bonneville turned back to the mountains.

When he came down to the Green River rendezvous he had completed his first year in the West. He had twenty-two and a half packs of beaver, about twenty-three hundred pounds or eighteen hundred pelts. Eighteen hundred prime pelts would normally have been worth about ten thousand dollars but the price of beaver was declining and Bonneville's take for the year amounted to about eight thousand dollars St. Louis.[4] Since he had used up more of his trade goods than he had allotted for the first year, had lost many horses, had depleted his outfit, and had had men and furs hijacked by his rivals, he was already close to bankruptcy when he reached the rendezvous. Then he learned that the most promising of his ventures had come to nothing. The party he had sent to winter among the Crows and trap Powder River and the Yellowstone were destitute. His Crow friends had pillaged them. Tulloch of the American Fur Company, who was doubtless directing the Crows, got his trappers drunk and bought their furs for chickenfeed, in alcohol at that. And in the spring the Arikaras got their horses. It was a disastrous year.

But there were some certified mountain men in that party. When two of the Arikaras came into camp to smoke while their pals cut the lariats, they tied them up. Then they tried to exchange their prisoners for the horses. The thieves offered even up, one horse for one prisoner, then raised the bid a little, but ended by valuing wealth above kinship, drove off the herd, sang a mourning song for those about to die, and took to the trail. The mountain men built up the fire and threw the prisoners on it.

Skirmishing on the big time continued. Drips of the trust and Fitzpatrick of the Opposition visited each other during the winter and probably tried to argue and lie each other into some sort of terms. The RMF Company scattered its parties widely through Idaho, Montana, Wyoming, and Utah on a far-ranging hunt, one of the most expert ever made. Drips, now sole field commander since the death of Vanderburgh, could not keep pace with any considerable part of it. But he and his subordinates had learned fast and he had bought RMF Company trappers and overbid for free trappers in quantities that told heavily. He confined his hunt to country which his men had learned the hard way, the Idaho and Montana streams that descend from the Continental Divide. He sent small parties to the eastern Flathead villages, where they made a good trade. He had about nineteen thousand dollars worth of beaver when he came down into the upper valley of the Green to pitch his camp at the Opposition's rendezvous.

Considering the reckless prices Drips had paid (sometimes $9 a pound St. Louis for furs that would bring $3.50 on the market) and the losses in goods he had taken when Bridger and Fitzpatrick led him and Vanderburgh on their cross-country chase, the trust was by no means breaking even on its investment. But it did not need to. It was out, as Pierre Chouteau, Jr., directed McKenzie, '*écraser toute opposition.*' It intended to take over the mountains exactly as it had taken over the Missouri. 'You are under no restraint with regard to prices, but to get the trade even if the returns you make should not pay the first cost of the goods,' a Company executive wrote to a Missouri factor a year or so later — in words that expressed the policy for the mountains as well. 'You are well aware that this is the object of the Company and their positive instructions.' Coming down to rendezvous, Drips could feel satisfied that, in three years of western penetration of which only one had been full scale, the Company was within sight of its objective. His nineteen thousand dollars might represent a loss but the Company intended to get it back.

From the point of view of the Opposition partners, however, that nineteen thousand dollars was RMF Company money.

At least it was in beaver from RMF Company territory. When Nat Wyeth reached rendezvous four of the partners' brigades were in, with a total catch which Wyeth estimated at only six thousand dollars more valuable than the trust's.[5] One partner and an affiliated venture were still to be heard from, perhaps eight thousand dollars more. The margin of profit for the year, therefore, depended on the trade at rendezvous. Again fragments of small fur companies, Indians, and free trappers from all over the mountains would gather there, near Bonneville's Folly, and all of them, especially the free trappers, would have furs. That was why the race between Campbell and Fontenelle, bringing the year's goods from the States, was so important. Whoever got there first would get the trade. Fontenelle had got himself reprimanded for losing the race last year and was taking a shorter route this time — from Fort Pierre. At St. Louis Pierre Chouteau wrote morosely to Mr. Astor that somehow the Company always seemed to lose the race. It lost again.

The partners sent out Henry Fraeb and two privates to explain to Campbell that the case was urgent — perhaps also to make sure that Sublette & Campbell had not doublecrossed their friends and customers. They reached him just after he had ferried his goods across Laramie Fork. He had to wait several days while Fraeb made a circle to bring in some free trappers from the Laramies and Medicine Bows and it was in this pause that Captain Stewart got a chance to dispatch a she-grizzly with his heavy rifle after the party had poured some fifty balls into her. Presently a man of greater stature in the trade arrived, Tom Fitzpatrick himself, riding out of the west on the same errand that had brought him close to death last year. From then on it was drive all the way. On July 5, 1833, Campbell halted his caravan on the Green a few miles above Horse Creek, within sight of Fort Bonneville. Fontenelle came in three days later.

* * *

Thus Captain Stewart reached his first mountain rendezvous — and in the climactic year. It was great day in the morning when the train got in. As soon as from the highest hill they could see its column of dust above the plain the boys mounted and charged down. Stewart could have heard no such gunfire since Waterloo and probably had never heard such yelling. The United States had come to Oregon and several hundred Americans would get their first news of home in a year, some of them

# ON THE TRAIL

Like any other occupation the mountain fur trade had its routines, its typical sights and sounds, its daily problems, its emergencies, its satisfactions and relaxations. We present some of them in this section. Pictures by Catlin and Bodmer are included to represent the life at fixed trading posts on the Missouri. Most of these pictures, however, are by Miller and portray prairie travel and the daily life of an overland brigade. Nothing comparable to them has ever been published before, for Miller was the only painter who ever traveled with such a brigade. (The Canadian Paul Kane comes ten years later and portrays a different era, a different locale, and a different organization of life.) His sketches are both news and history. They provide a visual documentation that heretofore has been wholly lacking.

*Courtesy of Mr. L. Vernon Miller*

PLATE XX

## MEDICINE CIRCLES NEAR THE PLATTE *Alfred Jacob Miller*

Miller here sketches a subject that both Catlin and Bodmer had used before him. Modern ethnologists profess to be uncertain what purpose these circles of buffalo skulls (which sometimes included skulls of men or wolves as well) were meant to serve. The mountain men, however, understood that the Indians made them in order to draw herds of buffalo to the vicinity. This simple homeopathic magic accords with the principles of the buffalo dances which all Plains tribes had. The mountain men probably got the information from the Indians themselves, and there seems no reason to believe that they were wrong.

*Courtesy of Mr. Lloyd O. Miller*

PLATE XXI

## Caravan Starting at Sunrise *Alfred Jacob Miller*

The Indians in the foreground are Delawares, hunters for the American Fur Company. The camp's breakfast is over; the horse herd has been brought in and the teams have been hitched. The caravan is forming. Out of sight scouts and outriders will already be on the march and hunters will already have set out to find buffalo.

*Courtesy of Mrs. Clyde Porter*

PLATE XXII

BULL BOATING ON THE PLATTE *Alfred Jacob Miller*

Observe the amount of freight that could be carried by a boat made of only a few buffalo hides and drawing only a few inches of water.

PLATE XXIII LANDING THE CHARETTES *Alfred Jacob Miller*

Such steep ascents following small river fords would be an enduring plague of the emigrant trains.

*Courtesy of Mrs. Clyde Porter*

*Courtesy of Mrs. Clyde Porter*

FIRE ON THE PRAIRIE *Alfred Jacob Miller* PLATE XXIV

The villain was the man who let the cook fire spread.

PLATE XXV

WILD HORSES OF THE SWEETWATER *Alfred Jacob Miller*

Broomtails, not Hollywood or Zane Grey barbs.

*Courtesy of Mr. Alfred J. Miller, grandnephew of the artist*

## Buffalo Dance of the Mandan Indians *Charles Bodmer*

A moment of total savagery in a dance which was a fundamental ceremony as both religion and economics. The dance was intended to attract the buffalo in large herds but more especially to insure success for the hunt. It involved many symbolisms, including a sacrificial meal and the propitiation of the buffalo bulls by awarding to the old men who represented them the young wives of the hunters. The painting on the

bodies of the dancers and their shields, the staves and other objects they carry, all the paraphernalia of the dance have symbolical meanings. The ceremony lasted several hours and had an accompaniment of chants, pipes, and drums and a constant caterwauling.

Maximilian's text indicates that Bodmer was not able to sketch the dance when it occurred, so that the picture is a reconstruction, and that the one he actually saw was by the Minnetarees, not the Mandans.

*Courtesy of The Boston Athenaeum*

PLATE XXVI

*Courtesy of Mrs. Clyde Porter*

PLATE XXVII

SNAKE INDIAN COUNCIL *Alfred Jacob Miller*

PLATE XXVIII

THE BEAR DANCE *George Catlin*

*Courtesy of The Boston Athenaeum*

*Courtesy of Mrs. Clyde Porter*

PLATE XXIX

LAKE — WIND RIVER CHAIN OF MOUNTAINS

*Alfred Jacob Miller*

INDIAN GIRLS SWIMMING *Alfred Jacob Miller*

PLATE XXX

*Courtesy of The Walters Art Gallery*

Courtesy of Mrs. Clyde Porter

PLATE XXXI

BREAKING TRAIL TO ESCAPE INDIANS *Alfred Jacob Miller*

Miller's note says that one of these is Black Harris.

*Courtesy of Mrs. Clyde Porter*

PLATE XXXII

MULE EQUIPMENT *Alfred Jacob Miller*

A mere sketch but valuable for its detail. The empty pack saddle is Indian-made or else has been extemporized along the trail.

PLATE XXXIII

## Camp Along Green River *Alfred Jacob Miller*

This is the Snake camp at the rendezvous of 1837, some miles from the Company camp. The tipis pitched in the plain are probably there for purposes of composition. Those in the foreground are in the proper

*Courtesy of Mrs. Clyde Porter*

place, along the edge of a grove. The activity on the plain is typical, especially the constant movement of horses. The man with his back to us in the central foreground is probably Captain Stewart.

*Courtesy of The Walters Art Gallery*

PLATE XXXIV

NOONDAY REST *Alfred Jacob Miller*

Miller should have used the idiom of the trail and called this a 'nooning.' When circumstances permitted, the midday rest lasted several hours, through the hottest sun. Teams have been unhitched, packs taken off and piled. Horses and mules graze the short grass. Following dinner everyone 'shades up' — seeking whatever shade may be at hand, perhaps only that of a cart or a clump of sagebrush Miller's note complains that he has to stay awake and sketch the sleepers.

*Courtesy of Mrs. Clyde Porter*

PLATE XXXV

SHOSHONE CROSSING A RIVER *Alfred Jacob Miller*

The large village of Snakes at the rendezvous of 1837 supplied Miller with many subjects. His notes speak of this one as 'a quiet evening scene, with Snake Indians looking for a good fording place on their way to the camp from a hunting excursion.' He thought them 'more friendly, social, and hospitable' than other tribes. This means that he did not associate much with the Nez Perces and Flatheads and that Captain Stewart had prejudiced him against the Crows.

Courtesy of Mrs. Clyde Porter

PLATE XXXVI

EMBROIDERING THE WAR COSTUME *Alfred Jacob Miller*

The family seamstress is posed picturesquely, but the warbonnet (which Miller always calls a cap or a helmet) should not be on the ground.

*Courtesy of Mrs. Clyde Porter*

PLATE XXXVII

## A Trapper in his Solitary Camp *Alfred Jacob Miller*

The equipment is transcribed exactly, but the trapper would probably have staked out his mule before cleaning his rifle or putting his buffalo ribs to roast.

PLATE XXXVIII

Courtesy of Mrs. Clyde Porter

MIGRATION OF SNAKE INDIANS *Alfred Jacob Miller*

Certain later copies of this remarkable picture call the Indians Pawnees, but the landscape is too far west and they probably are Snakes.

*Courtesy of The Boston Athenaeum*

FORT MCKENZIE,
WITH THE COMBAT OF 28TH AUGUST, 1833

*Charles Bodmer*

PLATE XXXIX

This is the surprise attack by Assiniboins on a Blackfoot village that is described in Chapter VI. As a study of Indian war Bodmer's picture has never been surpassed.

*Courtesy of Mrs. Clyde Porter*

PLATE XL

TRAPPERS ENCAMPMENT—LAKE SCENE *Alfred Jacob Miller*

The mountains in the background are the Wind River Range. The lake is recognizable as Lake Damala or De Amalia, now called New Fork Lake and according to legend once called Stewart's Lake. This is its western shore. Camp has been pitched at the edge of a grove of quaking asps.

*Courtesy of Mrs. Clyde Porter*

PLATE XLI

THE BLACK HILLS, OREGON *Alfred Jacob Miller*

The Black Hills, so called because of the scrub cedar that grows profusely on them, were the ranges of buttes and minor mountains in what is now southeastern Wyoming. Such small valleys as this one, watered by streams and therefore choked with vegetation, broke the barrenness of country that was elsewhere desert. In our period these streams made it a great beaver country.

## Removing the Saddles *Alfred Jacob Miller*

A very casual sketch, but it has caught one of the most typical moments on the trail. When the horses have fully expressed their satisfaction on being relieved of their packs, they will be herded out to graze until twilight, then brought back and staked out as in our next plate, which the figure in the right foreground is anticipating.

PLATE XLII

*Courtesy of Mrs. Clyde Porter*

*Courtesy of Mrs. Clyde Porter*

PLATE XLIII

## Picketing Horses *Alfred Jacob Miller*

'The horses have been driven in,' Miller's note reads, 'and each man runs towards them as they come, secures his own horse, catches him by the lariat . . . and leads him to a good bed of grass where a picket is driven and here he is secured for the night, the lariat permitting him to graze to the extent of a circle twenty-five feet in diameter.' It is somewhat inaccurate to speak of a 'bed of grass' here, since the horses will be grazing the scant, sparse, but nutritious bunch grass of the high plains. The camp site has been selected earlier by the daily outriders, who have considered the availability of water as well as grass.

PLATE XLIV

TRAPPER RELATING AN ADVENTURE *Alfred Jacob Miller*

*Courtesy of Mrs. Clyde Porter*

Many of the symbols are in this picture. One may add the sound of the creek, the wind in the cottonwoods, the solo and chorus effects of prairie wolves, the movement of picketed horses, and the oncoming of the stars.

PLATE XLV

## Trappers and Voyageurs at their Meal of Buffalo Hump Rib *Alfred Jacob Miller*

Another set of symbols and an exact registration of details. Ribs of fat cow are roasting at the fire. The mess still has coffee, the greatest comfort on the trail. The central figure has his rifle at hand. Note the fringes on arms and legs of buckskin garments. They are not only decoration; the whangs will serve to repair nearly anything.

*Courtesy of Mrs. Clyde Porter*

*Courtesy of Mrs. Clyde Porter*

PLATE XLVI

GROUP OF TRAPPERS AND INDIANS *Alfred Jacob Miller*

A little later. The yarning has begun.

PLATE XLVII

SETTING TRAPS FOR BEAVER *Alfred Jacob Miller*

*Courtesy of Mrs. Clyde Porter*

The international trade in beaver fur rested on this operation. See Chapter VII.

*Courtesy of Mr. Lloyd O. Miller*

PLATE XLVIII

TRAPPERS STARTING FOR THE HUNT *Alfred Jacob Miller*

The end of rendezvous is the beginning of the beaver trail.

in two or three years. There were newspapers only two months old. For a few there were letters, for everyone there was talk with men who had read papers through the winter and spring and had lived in daily touch with the trivia of civilization — had seen children on their way to school, heard the whistles of steamboats on rivers, drunk milk from a farm cool-room, slept on feather beds. The West now learned, for example, that Jackson had vetoed the recharter of the Second Bank of the United States, that the democracy had returned him to the White House with a landslide vote, that South Carolina had declared the new tariff nullified within its borders only to have Old Hickory bare his teeth and settle that question for a generation, that a business recession had been setting in when Campbell left the settlements. From Congress down to the death of a parent or a fanning bee in one's home town.

The mountain men had gathered for their annual release. It came at five dollars a pint and upwards in what was called whiskey but was raw alcohol thinned with Green River water, thinned progressively so that the company's profit mounted with every round. An officer of either the British or the American Army was professionally acquainted with what Irving calls saturnalia but Horse Creek was able to instruct both Bonneville and Stewart. It was, Irving says, 'a rich treat for the worthy captain [Bonneville] to see the "chivalry" of the various encampments engaged in contests of skill at running, jumping, wrestling, shooting with the rifle, and running horses. And then their rough hunters' feasting and carousals. They drank together, they sang, they laughed, they whooped; they tried to outbrag and outlie each other in stories of their adventures and achievements. Here the free trappers were in all their glory; they considered themselves the "cocks of the walk" and always carried the highest crests. Now and then familiarity was pushed too far and would effervesce into a brawl and a "rough and tumble" fight but it all ended in cordial reconciliation and maudlin endearment.'

Stewart's impressions left a modest deposit in literature. About sixty pages of his second novel, *Edward Warren*, are set at this rendezvous of 1833.[6] Everyone is getting repetitiously drunk, guns pop constantly, an eye-gouging brawl breaks out every so often, but there are more careful observations as well. 'I found Spanish, English, French, Snake, and Crow,' the star-crossed hero notes, and he might have added Kanakas, Irish, Bannocks, Nez Perces, and Flatheads to the melting pot. A

Swiss sings 'the wild songs of his mountain land.' A guitar is produced and there is a good moment when Edward Warren delights the mountain men with 'Meet me by moonlight alone.' He sees trappers and Indians gambling at the 'stick' or 'hand' game, which could cost you your pile as fast as any game the white men knew. They were 'seated in a circle and chaunting the air which accompanies their game. A small piece of carved bone, often taken from the body of a fox [rather, from the femur of a deer, smoothed, carved, and painted], was held by the gambler, who joining his closed fists together one above the other, could thus pass it into either, he then separated them and threw his arms wide apart, singing and jerking his body up and down, and again bringing his hands together, and changing or pretending to change the bone, the gamblers choosing only when the hands were held wide apart. If the guess is right, the guesser pulls away his pile with that of the bone holder, previously arranged beside it. If inclined, a new bet is made.' And so on, an accurate description of the galloping dominoes that all the Plains tribes used.

Indians were drunkards of gambling. They usually played the hand game with teams or sides of half a dozen or more. They had incantations and rituals to deceive their opponents by magic as well as skill. The whites played it as individuals, making it a variation of craps with elaborate fadings and parlays. An Indian who had lost at it might have a bad heart and be dangerous for a while but none took thought of the morrow. Edward Warren describes 'a young squaw of the Utaw tribe, who had lost everything of her dress down to a scanty shirt' and was 'wistfully looking on, her small hands clasped and her beautifully formed limbs crossed one over the other; she never took her eyes off the ring, in which her whole desires seemed to be concentrated. My companion [Kit Carson, but actually he did not come to rendezvous in 1833] threw the beads he had won at her beautiful feet and with an almost imperceptible look of thanks for the gift she flung them down again to be risked in the chances of the game.'

Single men in the mountains easily admired the small hands, beautiful feet, and beautifully formed limbs of squaws when the villages arrived at the rendezvous. Snake girls were adjudged the best looking in the mountains.[7] In the few years between puberty and formal marriage an Indian girl might be strikingly beautiful. Moreover the girls of the Plains tribes were more fastidious in personal cleanliness than most American women of the period, especially the women of the frontier, and they were cannier with such feminine accessories as perfumes and adornments. But they needed only to be females when the trappers came to rendezvous from fifty weeks of bachelor life. No Plains squaws, except possibly the Cheyennes, were chaste by white standards. Their affections were spontaneous or the attention of a mountain man was flattery enough to activate them. Besides, it was hospitable to sleep with a white man, of your own initiative or at a husband's or father's suggestion. This was civility, but, beyond it, prostitution was an integral part of Indian economy. The handful of beads, the yard or two of cloth, the awls or bells or gartering which the trapper paid for a pleasant night may seem trivial. But they were wealth to a squaw and a fantastically generous remuneration for what any young buck of her village might exact of her gratis if he encountered her in the underbrush. Traffic in the charm of wives or daughters was also good business for the master of the lodge, and he brought his women to rendezvous as he brought the furs he had taken, for trade.

The business paid the companies well too, for the bells and beads and gartering were sold to men too urgent to haggle over the price. By night the cottonwoods along the creeks and the tents of the trappers were like the tourist camps outside of town today. And on page 275 of *Edward Warren* a footnote in which Stewart speaks in his own person suggests that the veteran of barracks and campaigns found at Horse Creek the diversion of any soldier reaching a new town.

There were, of course, more permanent relations than these rendezvous amours. Edward Warren remarks that 'the best looking of the young squaws . . . came over in groups to wonder at the riches of the white man, as well as to tempt him to dispense them, and many happy matrimonial connections were formed by means of a dower of glittering beads and scarlet cloth.' Mostly it was the upper class, the free trappers, who could afford a 'matrimonial connection' but one was desirable from the point of view alike of the companies, the trapper, and the woman. The conspicuous waste which Veblen finds a basic motive in the acquisitive society and the urge that no damned squaw was going to outshine my wife led the boys to buy everything they had beaver plews to afford. The mountain man's squaw in beads, feathers, bells, fringes, garters, mirrors, bangles, rings, and what-not is a human Christmas tree in the literature, and all this 'foofuraw' — frippery, decoration — had to be paid for at mountain prices. The squaw who got a white husband was in luck. She acquired wealth that would have been far beyond her reach otherwise and she was treated by even the most degraded white man with a consideration foreign to Indian folkways. Her husband might lodgepole her to keep her tongue in order. Some kicking and cuffing might be a routine way of maintaining balance in the relationship. On occasion she might be knocked out with the butt end of a hatchet — Jim Beckwourth recounts the approval of his Blackfoot father-in-law when he asserted male supremacy in just that way. But at worst, and even if she were discarded next year, she had raised her status, married into an élite, and acquired a higher culture.

Her husband was lucky too. Besides the solaces of the flesh, the comfort of a bedfellow in the wilderness, the human normality of a focus for domestic emotions — besides this, he got a helpmeet with an unparalleled education in marital partnership. His squaw dressed his furs for the market, made his robes and moccasins and shirts and breeches, raised and struck his tent or tipi and kept the inside of it clean and orderly, took care of his professional equipment, managed his horses and mules, skinned his meat, carried firewood and water — and brought up their daughters to do likewise. A woman's voice rang pleasantly after so many baritones. If her religious practices sometimes got in your way, nevertheless she was without ambiguities or neuroses. She was habitually gay, she talked agreeably if too much, she had wit and an exceedingly earthy humor. (Her jokes would curl a missionary's hair at forty rods.) She had memorized innumerable serial stories — of mystery, adventure, the supernatural. She sang well and was fertile in the invention of amusements. She made a home of your lodge, with its swept floor and meat forever on the fire, and it was not a bad home to come back to after a day on the beaver trail.[8]

The trouble was that when you married an Indian you made an Indian marriage. A woman was property and you had to buy her at a price based on the customer's ability to pay. Moreover, you married her family, which was seldom smaller than the band she belonged to. Cousins of a distant degree might come to live with you for long periods, and all the folks were glad to see you by platoons when your trails crossed. All had a lien on your possessions and all had constantly to receive evidence of your family affection. Your Indian relatives were as expensive as your annual jubilation at the rendezvous.

Without offending public opinion you could divorce your

wife as casually as you married her. You told her to go home and she went. If you felt a little at fault, both she and her father were glad to get a small settlement in goods. And since this was Indian law, you could have as many wives as you could afford and manage; polygamy, a rich man's privilege, had labor value. It could be emotional insurance too. Ruxton's hero La Bonte, whose name is historical though his adventures in the book have been synthesized, reflects when one of his two wives is kidnaped: 'Here's the beauty of having two wiping sticks to your rifle; if one breaks while ramming down a ball there's still hickory left to supply its space.' Farther on, however, his companion Killbuck makes an emotional trial balance and decides that on the whole he has lost. 'For twenty year I packed a squaw along. Not one but many. First I had a Blackfoot — the darnedest slut as ever cried for fofarrow. I lodgepoled her on Colter's Creek and made her quit. My buffalo hoss and as good as four packs of beaver I gave for old Bull Tail's daughter [320 skins, 400 pounds, about $2000 at the time he must have bought her; and he was being gypped, for $50 St. Louis in goods would have bought the daughter of an emperor]. He was head chief of the Ricaree [Arikaras] and came nicely round me. Thar wasn't enough scarlet cloth nor beads nor vermilion in Sublette's packs for her. Traps wouldn't buy her all the fofarrow she wanted; and in two years I'd sold her for one of Jake Hawkins' guns — the very one I hold in my hands. [$40 St. Louis but a good deal more in the mountains.] Then I tried the Sioux, the Shian, and a Digger from the other side, who made the best moccasin as ever I wore. [She must have been a Snake or a Bannock; he wouldn't have taken a Digger.] She was the best of all and was rubbed out by the Yutas in the Bayou Salade. Bad was the best, and after she was gone under I tried no more. . . . Red blood won't shine any ways you fix it.'

Cards, the hand game, drinking, brawling, an attempt at lynching, a couple of casual shootings engage the interest of Edward Warren, Stewart's surrogate, in the first days of this rendezvous. But the Indians most of all, and not their amatory freedoms but their sheer spectacle. They were natural showmen, flagrant exhibitionists, and in the amusement business for pay. A village approaching rendezvous was both a circus parade and the three-ring afternoon performance. Warren describes the Snakes' approach across the plain — squaws adorned with 'the most costly jewels of the land,' buckskins shining with white clay, 'housings and horse gear' in loud scarlet, horses of all colors and 'painted palfreys,' young bucks making their mounts gallop and curvet. Then the lodges were pitched and the older squaws boiled across the plain for water and fodder. The herds were turned out to graze. A traffic of visiting and bargaining, drinking, flirting, gaming was set up at once. Later there would be races, field sports, mock battles, an endless rehearsal for applause and cash of the skills the Indian practiced vocationally. Skills, incidentally, at which the trappers usually excelled them.

* * *

But if the rendezvous was Paul Bunyan's fair, it was nevertheless a business proposition. Like all fairs it made money from the concessions. The companies set up their booths and the abundance of goods stimulated the mountain men as Main Street's saloon, haberdashery, and hardware store work on harvest hands with their pay in their pockets. Watering down the alcohol sold to both trappers and Indians, the companies did nothing to restrain the Saturday night debauch. It was sagacious to keep the sales clerk sober, however, since liquor might soften him too with fellowship. So our Charles Larpenteur found himself promoted. He was a uniqueness in the mountains, a teetotaler. 'There was not a sober man to be found in camp but myself,' he says. 'So Mr. Fitzpatrick asked me if I would try my hand at clerking. . . . There were great quarrels and fights outside but I must say the men were very civil to me.'

The trapper had obligations to his women, to the brotherhood, and to professional pride. He dressed himself in this year's store clothes, the gaudiest for preference, and hung his casual or semi-permanent squaw with gewgaws. He staggered about toasting the boys till he vomited or passed out or got himself shot at or beaten up. (Last year at Pierre's Hole some of the boys baptized good old Pete with alcohol, practically by immersion since they poured a kettle of it over him. Then it was droll to snatch an ember from the fire and ignite him.) He came to, pulled his pals or sometimes his bourgeois from behind the sagebrush where sleep had overtaken them, and went to it again. Finally he would have to remember that he needed an outfit for the coming year: powder, lead, tobacco, minor hardware, traps if he were on his own, stuff for Indian presents and trade, a new capote for winter, a horse or two.

All this on his annual wages if he was a hired hand, or on

the skins he had taken since last summer (with his name or mark on them) if he were a free trapper. There are no quotations of mountain prices for 1833 but Zenas Leonard's note of the year before will do. He paid ten dollars a yard for coarse cloth and twenty dollars for fine cloth; domestic calicoes had cost about fourteen cents and French calicoes twenty to thirty-five cents at St. Louis, stroudings and flannels fifty to ninety cents, some very fancy stuff up to a dollar-ten. We have seen that diluted alcohol was at least five dollars a pint; two dollars a pound was standard for the luxuries of rendezvous, coffee, sugar, spices, pepper. On June 7, 1833, St. Louis wholesale prices current were: coffee, fifteen cents; domestic sugar, nine and ten cents; Havana sugar, twelve and thirteen cents. The St. Louis price of common alcohol does not appear but it would have been something over half of the thirty cents a gallon that whiskey brought. Leonard quotes two dollars a pound, mountain, for tea but must have been wrong for it cost more than half that at St. Louis. Two dollars a pound was standard for flour that had cost just over two cents at St. Louis, for six-cent lead, and for seven-cent domestic gunpowder. (French and English powder, which were more desired, had a duty on them in spite of Old Hickory's brain trust.) Osborne Russell estimates a flat two thousand percent over-all advance on St. Louis prices, and computations made here and there through the eighteen-thirties show that the mark-up was greater as often as it was less than that. The companies got an even bigger return from the Indian trade.

The summer of 1833, however, was as close to a buyer's market as the trappers ever got. The triangular competition, American Fur Company, RMF Company, and Bonneville, ran next year's wages up for hired hands and kept a floor under beaver for the élite. The RMF Company partners had to pay as high as fifteen hundred dollars for master mountain men to keep them from the trust, and as we have seen, had sometimes to pay as much as nine dollars a pound for beaver. The traditional price was four dollars a pound and an average pelt weighed a pound and a half, which gave the standard 'six dollars a plew, prime.' The determination of 'prime' usually left room for fenagling, but not this year. 'Kittens' and late spring furs were worth less, summer furs much less. (The coming of Sublette and Campbell to the mouth of the Missouri was having the same effect on prices and wages there, and McKenzie was bombarding his subordinates with commands to get the business no matter what it cost.)

We have observed that at St. Louis the price of beaver fell to $3.50 before the returning caravans got home. That was the little cloud that would grow. John Jacob Astor was preparing to get out of the business that had made his fortune, and ten years later the American Fur Company, which had bankrupted so many competitors, would itself be bankrupt. Since the seventeenth century beaver had been the basis of the fur trade. It was the basis because a quality unique to beaver underhair made it the best of all furs for felting. Now, at the moment when the trust was taking over the mountain field and likewise accelerating its exhaustion, the world market was beginning to break. The industrial revolution had produced machinery that made good felt from other, cheaper stocks, and silk hats were displacing beaver hats, which had been a world fashion for centuries. The price of beaver was due to rise again in the eighteen forties. But by that time the big companies were living on buffalo robes and other trade, and the beaver which the small companies took from the still exhausted West went into coats and other apparel.

* * *

When Stewart reached the rendezvous with Campbell's train, the RMF Company had set up its brigade camps near the mouth of Horse Creek. Cursing Fontenelle, the American Fur Company brigades were camped a mile or so away. Bonneville was at his fort on the Green, less than five miles away.[9] The large remudas of the companies and the larger herds of the Indians exhausted the forage. At some time during the three weeks of the actual rendezvous the two larger companies moved camp to get to better grass. (Perhaps they moved twice: the statements are ambiguous.) They went twelve miles down the Green and crossed it to New Fork, thus bringing Stewart to the edge of the country that was to be his Eden. The places he would return to every summer and the landscapes through which the sad romantics of his novels would wander lay upstream from the mouth of New Fork. New Fork Lake whence the river flows, half a dozen other large lakes named Fremont, Half Moon, Boulder, and the like, dozens of smaller lakes on the western slopes of the Wind River Mountains, such peaks as Glover, Pyramid, Mount Baldy, and Mount Bonneville — this is the Stewart Country. Today it is included in the Bridger National Forest.

After camp moved, the mountain life revealed a new hazard.

Let Edward Warren describe it. He is returning to camp by night along a narrow trail: 'There was light enough to distinguish a gaunt white wolf of unusual size in my way, who did not seem inclined to yield the path. My horse snorted and jumped aside. There was something terrible in the look of that wolf — the haggard eye and the hanging jaw — the indifference with which it approached in a narrow path alone — not to attack but not to yield; the lurid glare of the eye was never turned toward me but it passed slouching on.'

Edward Warren is a character in fiction and meets this wolf as an incident of the plot. Actually Stewart was in command of Campbell's night guard at the RMF Company camp when a rabid wolf made the second of two nocturnal visits there. Larpenteur, a member of the guard, heard the wolf amidst the terrified herd. He says he would have shot it but Stewart forbade on the ground that it was dangerous to shoot in camp.[10]

Wyeth says that three men were bitten at the RMF Company camp and nine at the trust's camp, then four miles away on the Green. At least one Indian was bitten, as well, and one of the bulls which Campbell had driven from Lexington for the post Sublette was building on the Missouri. Both camps were twice in a panic, though it was modified by the condition of those who still had the price of a drink. Joe Meek, twenty-three years old and a veteran of four years in the mountains, had a reputation to maintain and was full to the bung. So full that Stewart remonstrated with him: a man so drunk would have been bitten if the rabid wolf had chanced to come this way. Meek agreed that there was that danger, he might have been bitten; but on the other hand, he might have cured the wolf.

Several of the victims developed rabies and died in paroxysms before the camp broke up. Several others were stricken on the trail and wandered off into the mountains to die. Campbell's bull died on the way to the Yellowstone. Several inexplicable deaths of mountain men during the next two years were attributed to this visitation. The campfires had a new legend.

Larpenteur says that one of the RMF Company victims was named George Holmes: he 'was badly bitten on the right ear and face.' Then, on the way to the Yellowstone, Holmes 'now and then asked me if I thought he would go mad; although thinking within myself he would, being so badly bitten, I did all I could to make him believe otherwise. When he said to me, "Larpenteur, don't you hear the bull — he is going mad — I am getting scared," I do believe I felt worse than he did, and scarcely knew how to answer him.' Separating from him, Larpenteur later learned that Holmes had developed a phobia of crossing small streams, 'so that they had to cover him over with a blanket to get him across.' Fontenelle left two men to watch over him but they abandoned him and when Fontenelle sent back for him, the searchers were able to find only his clothes — he had wandered away naked and was never found.

The story has a flaw in it: how had this RMF Company man got with Fontenelle's party? It appears otherwise in *Edward Warren* in one of the footnotes where Stewart speaks straightforwardly about himself, not his hero. Here he says that he and George Holmes shared a 'bower of birch and willow' but on the night of the wolf's visit he had asked Holmes to sleep elsewhere — Stewart was expecting a girl. At the uproar caused by one of the wolf's appearances ('confused sounds, shouts, and the discharge of firearms, as well as the deep roar of a bull, such as he emits in terror or in rage') Stewart belted on his blanket and rushed out. 'Poor Holmes was seated on the ground, the side of his head and his ear bleeding and torn; a mad wolf was ravaging the camp. We did not get her, she had other lives to sacrifice elsewhere. Poor Holmes changed from that hour, instead of alertness and joy, melancholy and despondency grew upon him day by day, and though I stood beside him in another night, when we were but a small party in the hands of the Crow Indians and when neither of us thought to see another sun,[11] I felt I was linked in a death struggle with one, who whatever he might do to help a friend, considered his own fate as sealed. That day at noon he had quarreled with the camp leader for calling him "Beauty," a nickname by which he was known, from his blithe and sunny smile. Next day the eye was wan and the smile was gone. In November, a melancholy and wasted form set out with Dr. Harrison, the son of the general, and Major [Black] Harris in search of the stone which is believed to be the talisman for the cure of hydrophobia and his bones were left, we could never learn exactly where, on the branch of some stream and the bough of some tree, where I would have willingly made a pilgrimage to render the last tribute of regret and contrast the living memory with the dead remains. There never has quitted my breast a reproachful remorse for the part I played him on that sad night.'

* * *

Meanwhile the strategy of next year's business was being

worked out. Nat Wyeth came in with the two loyal followers who were left him and with a halfbreed Flathead boy named Baptiste and a twenty-year-old Nez Perce. He was taking them to the States and providence had given the Nez Perce a somewhat deformed head. Wyeth had traveled from Flathead House almost to the rendezvous with a Hudson's Bay party under Francis Ermatinger, and Ermatinger's presence in these parts was notification that the British monopoly was going to become as aggressive in the mountains as the American trust.

Wyeth had revised his ideas. When he reached the Columbia he had learned that the brig which had been carrying his goods had gone down at sea. That bankrupted his venture and only two of his diminished company remained with him. He would have to start all over — but he thought he could make it go next time. He had traveled the mountains with the RMF Company and gone on to Fort Vancouver (where he spent the winter) with the Hudson's Bay Company. He had seen the best men in the trade doing their jobs and he had applied a business man's intelligence to the system on the spot. It still seemed to him a bad system. His greenhorn notions out of Cambridge were dissipated and he had paid high for the knowledge that had displaced them. But he would reorganize and come back to the mountains.

Before leaving the Columbia he tried to make an arrangement with the Hudson's Bay Company. Wasted effort. The British would make terms when they had to, as with Astor on the Great Lakes, but in Oregon they did not have to. That idea coming to nothing, the indicated move was to form a combination against the big American companies. While Wyeth was traveling toward the rendezvous he met one of Bonneville's parties and sent the Captain a letter proposing that they merge their interest. On the upper Snake he met Bonneville himself. They traveled toward the Green together for a while and appear to have reached an agreement. Wyeth canceled his plan to go to the States and prepared to lead one of the new partnership's brigades to California. Bonneville, apparently, was to stay in the mountains, perhaps to work the lower Snake and upper Columbia country in accordance with Wyeth's letter.

A merger of these interests would have required some rapid refinancing back east but it was a promising idea. Together Wyeth and Bonneville would have had a better chance of withstanding the tactics used against them. Moreover, both had proved their fitness to lead field operations and Wyeth was an organizer and business strategist of unusual ability. The partnership would have begun, however, with a misconception, for it was succumbing to the golden fantasy of California. No part of California west of the Sierra divide and south of the San Joaquin valley was good fur country. Even in such fur country as there was, the resources and the elaborate system of the Hudson's Bay Company were required to turn a profit — if indeed the Hudson's Bay Company, which had been working the field for eight years, did show an over-all profit there.

But the partnership was abandoned almost as soon as it was formed. (Chittenden suggests that Bonneville may have been appalled by Wyeth's energy and afraid of being engulfed by it.) Wyeth went on to the Green ahead of Bonneville, resuming his original plan. Having learned wisdom, he wrote his brother not to let anyone in the fur trade know how his affairs stood. Then he wrote to Ermatinger, sizing up the rendezvous. The discipline and efficiency of the big American companies, he said, could not be surpassed. The Opposition was answering the trust's invasion of the mountains by invading the Missouri field and Wyeth wished 'good luck to their quarrels.' He added that Ermatinger 'would have been Robbed of your goods and your Beaver if you had come here,' though as he pointed out the rendezvous was west of the Divide and the Hudson's Bay Company had as much right as the Americans to be there. For 'there is here a great majority of Scoundrels. I should much doubt the personal safety of anyone from your side of the house.'

One had to get along with the scoundrels, however. Campbell was going on to the Big Horn and the Yellowstone, to meet his partner Bill Sublette at the new post, and would take the RMF Company's furs by that route. (Instead of down the Platte.) Wyeth decided to go with him — to see another part of the fur country and to examine the trust's system of fixed posts.

He drummed up some business too. Traveling west last summer after the battle of Pierre's Hole, he had struck up a friendship with Milton Sublette, one of the RMF Company partners. They met again at rendezvous. Presently the RMF Company contracted with Wyeth to bring out part of next summer's goods, to the amount of three thousand dollars. This arrangement further diversified his business by putting him into the carrying trade. Perhaps he could transport goods and furs for the small independents, perhaps he could do odd-lot jobs for the big companies, thus further increasing his discounts and decreasing his overhead. He and the partners posted forfeits for non-performance of contract, and Milton Sublette decided to travel to the settlements with his new agent. They had laid up trouble for themselves.

Bonneville decided to send his furs East by the route Campbell was taking. Since they would thus get protection through hostile country, he would not have to detach so large a party to guard them. Campbell would build bull-boats when he reached the Big Horn; Bonneville directed his bourgeois, Michel Cerré, to do the same and to travel within reach of him. Bonneville prepared to escort Cerré to the Big Horn but to keep out of touch with Fitzpatrick (who would escort Campbell), since he intended to get the jump on him in the field which they both expected to trap during the fall.

But Bonneville was going to make a speculation as well: he was sending a party to California. This venture remains ambiguous. Fontenelle wrote from the rendezvous to his big boss McKenzie that Bonneville was paying common hands up to a thousand dollars a year — as the local agent of McKenzie's policy Fontenelle was one reason why he had to — although he knew he would have to 'pay them with wind.' McKenzie's big boss, Pierre Chouteau, Jr., in turn wrote to Astor (who may have found the news more depressing than Chouteau supposed) that 'Bonneville, out of all his grand expedition will have only enough to pay the wages of his men,' and even that was probably an overestimate. In view of all this, sound business policy would have required Bonneville to concentrate his men, not disperse them, personally lead them through country known to be rich in furs, and diligently supervise them while they worked.

Probably he had decided to shoot the moon. One coup might make him solvent — and he was not the first by well over a century to be taken in by Cibola's continuous performance west of the Sierra. He knew that the Hudson's Bay Company had been sending annual expeditions to California — the Humboldt was called Ogden's River from one of their partisans. He knew that the one sent last winter had been larger than ever and since it had not got back yet did not know how disappointing the hunt had been. Besides, the adventures of any trappers in a far country always got a lordly magnification at the campfires. The same generosity had gilded the invasion of California from the south. Ewing Young, who had a great name in the Taos trade, had already led two trapping expeditions there from

New Mexico, the second one just last year, and had made a killing there. He returned to Taos rich in furs — most of them, however, not from California — and in profits from trade, both legal and piratical. The mountain telegraph that carried news of Young's success did nothing to minimize it. In short, there have always been persuasive reasons why you are sure to make a killing in California.

Nor may we forget that Bonneville was in the Army. There was certainly a political purpose in the Hudson's Bay Company's systematic cultivation of that field and an eye had better be kept on the British Empire. Americans were moving in from the south, the trade in hides was growing steadily, deserters from the hide ships were slowly building up an American colony, the uproarious Mexican-Californian politics were in their customary ferment, Congressmen went on annexing the golden shore in set speeches every so often — and it would be a good idea to find out something about California. The government itself had no information whatever about the overland routes and the land they crossed later than the return of Jedediah Smith in 1828, and beyond what Smith had reported it had no information at all. Mountain knowledge stopped with the Humboldt, Great Salt Lake, and such streams as the Taos men had trapped. One reason why Bonneville sent an expedition to California may have been that the Secretary of War ordered him to.

He selected his best man, Joe Walker, to lead the expedition. Walker had no trouble getting recruits. 'I was anxious to go to the coast of the Pacific,' says Zenas Leonard, of the bankrupt Gant and Blackwell outfit — and who wasn't? The campfire legends that came down from Jed Smith's expedition had been enhanced by an occasional stray who had been there with McKay or McLeod or Ogden, and Ewing Young's adventures had added a new sheen. California was an attraction to any mountain man merely as new country. But there were added señoritas, aguardiente in casks big as a beaver press, padres who stuffed you with beef from uncountable herds and soaked you in wine from mission vineyards, horses to be driven back by the hundred, summertime all through the winter, Indians so tame you need never mount guard, and again señoritas. Señoritas as willing and lovely as those in Taos, protected by mere greasers, with a weakness for desperadoes in buckskin. In a word, Wagh! Walker filled up his complement at once and about twenty free trappers decided to go along with him and take a whirl at the Sierra and the señoritas. Naturally, one of them was Joe Meek.

A slight measure of intelligence had been forced on the companies. The RMF Company could go on trying to lose its rivals in the gulches, getting them shot up by Indians, and thus keeping large parties of its own men from their jobs — or it could admit that the trust was here to stay. Fontenelle and Drips were not eager to lose more money, though they could if they must, nor to chase another mirage into the Blackfoot country, though they knew more now than they had known last year. They did the intelligent thing: they agreed to divide the country. The American Fur Company would hunt this coming year in the Flathead country, the Teton country, the valley of Great Salt Lake, and along the Snake and the Salmon — west of the mountains, where the British monopoly was infiltrating. The RMF Company would take the Green, the Yellowstone, and the Three Forks. The division was realistic but it was an admission by the partners that the trust could not be stopped. The rest would be just a matter of time.

The camps at New Fork began to break up during the last week of July. The Indian tipis came down and the long files of travois that carried them began to slant westward and northward over the hills. Hangovers cured, the trappers got their outfits ready: trap springs and gun flints renewed, possible sacks refilled, powder and lead and trade goods packed, a new horse, and all that drinking, gambling, and whoring just something to yarn about at the night fire.

The free trappers moved toward their hunting grounds, which were always secret and were sometimes determined by their private medicine or by paid consultation with an Indian medicine man. By next year's rendezvous, which was set for Ham's Fork, fifty miles southwest from New Fork, their trade would carry them to the Columbia, the Pacific coast, the Virgin and perhaps the Gila, the South Platte, the Arkansas, the Missouri, the Grand, the Canadian, the Rio Grande — and the thousand creeks that fed them. Among those now leaving New Fork were a good many whom their companions would report gutshot and gone under, mere wolf meat, when the lodge should be tiled at Ham's Fork next July.

Walker took his California legion down the Green and westward to the Bear, which he would follow to Great Salt Lake. Fontenelle also headed for Great Salt Lake. Drips took his brigade up the Green and into the mountains, making for the

Snake. Gervais set out for 'the Digger country,' which probably meant south and southwest of Brown's Hole, since the true Digger country had been closed to him by the agreement. The pack trains of the other RMF partners turned eastward for South Pass. Once through it, Fraeb would start for the Colorado fields of the Front Range, which the partners had revisited last year after ignoring them for a space. The others would turn north toward the Big Horn, the Yellowstone, Powder River, and the Three Forks. The most sagacious of them, Fitzpatrick, would see Campbell safely embarked down the Big Horn and then head straight for the Crow country to meet another invasion by the trust. Nat Wyeth went with Fitzpatrick. So did Doctor Harrison and Captain Stewart. They were going to see another aspect of the mountain trade and get a new slant on the Plains Indians.

# « V »

# ABSAROKA (1833)

It was back to the expert movement of the pack train, saddle leather creaking, sun and dust and fractious mules, the pungency of buffalo chips at the cook fire. They were heading through South Pass for the Popo Agie. Wind River comes down out of the mountains to meet it, makes a sharp turn to the north, and is the Big Horn from there on.

During the second day out, a Mr. Worthington, who is otherwise unidentified,[1] was chasing a buffalo when his horse threw him. The bull charged before he could get up but missed him by a good yard, turned and charged again — Worthington was up and running by this time — and again missed him. The second miss gave the victim a chance to kill the bull with a single shot and they discovered what he owed his life to. The bull was blind in one eye and good fortune had had Worthington on his blind side: saved by the laws of optics and three feet. A few days later Wyeth writes, 'Capt. Stewart had some sport with a [grizzly] bear near our camp in the willows which he wounded but did not kill. He represented him as large as a mule.' That same day Nat Wyeth's sagacity lapsed. Hearing that another grizzly, bigger than a mule maybe, had been located in a thicket, he turned greenhorn momentarily: he fired a pistol into the thicket and then started throwing stones, to bring Old Ephraim out. Ephraim came out — charging. Wyeth shot him but might as well have thrown another stone for he shot him through the body, where a grizzly could stand a volley from a company of dragoons. 'I ran as fast I could,' Wyeth says. So did Campbell and Milton Sublette, who were near-by. Their companions succeeded in killing the silver-tip with four more shots. Two days later Wyeth met still another grizzly, the biggest so far, but failed to kill it.

One of these impromptu hunts seems to have supplied details for Edward Warren's first meeting with a grizzly, which is told at length in the novel. Stewart endows his hero with emotions which he had certainly experienced himself and tells the story rather better and with fewer fantastic additions than usual. Then in his own person he inserts a footnote which, though he sets the incident in the Black Hills, may confess a mortification of this time. At sight of a grizzly:

> The cry was no sooner raised than every disposable hand was off: one hunter, better mounted than the rest, made for the opposite side of the stream and did not pull up until at its head, where there was a bushy thicket; there he awaited the bear, while the whole course below rung with the challenges of the eager troop. It was not long before the bear was heard by the solitary hunter (who was a greenhorn), he then got a sight of him through the bushes, put up his rifle, which snapped; it was a Manton which never missed fire; there was not even a cap on it, it had been washed the night before and never reloaded. The bear heard the snap but saw nothing and hesitating to face an unseen foe turned back; the hunter jumped down to load; the pursuers were coming on and the ball was home when the horse broke away from the slight hold and bounded off; the bear was again tearing up through the bushes. A [percussion] cap was yet to be adjusted, the animal was within ten feet when he received the ball in his cheek, which ranged through the whole length of his body as he was mounting an acclivity; he rolled back into the bushes, tearing them up with his teeth and roaring. The field came up and knowing what was the matter, each took a hasty aim. Twelve men fired, only one hit, and that was a cook.

This is an authentic picture of the excitement and confusion that a grizzly always produced in a party armed with guns which could kill one only by hitting him in the brain. Stewart must have been the greenhorn and the anecdote is an admission of unpardonable carelessness, carrying an unloaded gun.[2]

Doctor Harrison was widening his scientific experience. The Popo Agie touches oil country and there was a famous 'spring,' a slow ooze of oil through the shale. Its scent carried five or six miles and the mountain men liked to set fire to the shallow basin where the stuff collected (forty or fifty gallons a day) and watch the black smoke billow. They called it tar and, having heard that its Pennsylvania equivalent was medicinal, carried jars of it to rub into their arthritic joints. This spring was southwest of the present Lander but they knew others like it elsewhere, especially northward from the upper Platte. Doctor Harrison doubtless speculated about it with the intelligent natural philosophy that was so much more common among the educated before it grew into natural science. Immediately afterward he had to practice traumatic surgery.

Jim Bridger had sent a party ahead to look for a strayed trapper and to take some beaver along the Popo Agie. One of them made the mistake that a small party must not allow to be made: he fell asleep on night guard. Some Snakes, probably fresh from the rendezvous, had seen the party and determined to make the conventional pass at its horses. If the sentry had been alert he would have been able to detect them in time, a shot or two would have stopped them, and the affair would have passed off as routine and no feelings hurt. But when the horses woke him, warning him that Indians were at hand,[3] it was too late. Larpenteur says that the Snakes had 'caps made of bushes,' meaning they were using the usual camouflage. One of them shot the guard practically pointblank. 'The ball [this is Wyeth speaking] entered the head outside of the eye and breaking the cheek bone, passing downward, and lodged behind the ear in the neck.' For good measure another Snake shot an arrow six inches into his shoulder. In the uproar the Snakes got the horses, seven all told. When the combined parties came up Doctor Harrison removed both musket ball and arrowhead from the temporarily inconvenienced trapper — his name was Thompson — and made the inconvenience even slighter.

For a moment we touch the enchantment of American history. Following the night attack one of the party, Wyeth says, 'pursued them on foot but wet his gun in crossing a stream and only snapped twice,' and Wyeth says his name was Charbonneau. This may have been — Doctor Grace Hebard is convinced it was — Baptiste, the child born to the young Sacajawea during the winter which the great captains of the West spent at the Mandan villages. Meriwether Lewis eased his mother's labor by giving her some crushed rattlesnake rattles in a little water. William Clark called him Pomp and fell in love with him, as indeed he may be said to have done with Sacajawea, a beautiful girl, one of the most remarkable women in our history, a Snake squaw who had the tenderness of any white man's poem.[4] Clark dandled and tickled and spoiled him all the way across the continent and back, then had him brought to St.

Louis to be educated. He and perhaps his mother too lived there for some years and Baptiste learned French and English, ciphering and Roman history. If Doctor Hebard is right, he presently learned more. For in 1823 Prince Paul of Württemberg left the shade of Hamlet's university and came wandering up the Missouri, the first royal visitor to these parts, met Baptiste, and presently took him back to Europe. There, Doctor Hebard's narrative shows, he stayed for six years, a member of the royal household, and received a classical education and a princely training in the etiquette of courts. If so, he was by far the best educated and most polished gentleman whom Stewart met in the mountains (with a reservation for Lucien Fontenelle). He and his half-brother flicker through the mountain literature from here on. In 1843, on the last of Stewart's western journeys which will not be described in this book, Stewart hired him to drive a cart.[5]

On the way to the Big Horn (at the end of its tremendous canyon) they met Bonneville, who had been secretly sending his trapping parties west. Everyone now traveled down the river till it was out of the mountains and they could make their bull boats. Cerré, who was to transport Bonneville's furs, for some reason felt that he needed three. Campbell made two for a much larger cargo and intended to abandon them at the mouth of the Yellowstone, where he would transfer his furs to Bill Sublette's keelboat. Wyeth needed only one — and had it ready first. In fact, the ex-greenhorn had been wiping the eyes of his instructors rather often of late: he was now a graduate mountain man. His boat was made of three skins, tough ones, from elderly bulls. He says it was eighteen feet long, five and a half wide, sharp (he means narrowing) at both ends, with a round bottom and a draft of about eighteen inches. That is at least a foot more draft than it could have had but makes it the type shown in our Plate XXII, which illustrates the lading it could take. Wyeth's was less than half filled by his remaining furs (mostly taken last fall, a few during the winter, a few more in the spring), some buffalo robes he had got by trade, his two assistants and two Indians, himself and Milton Sublette. Such a boat was serviceable; in our contemporary slang it was functional. Wyeth says that his leaked a little; this would mean that a seam was imperfectly pitched or had parted where it was stretched across the willow or popple frame. A bull-boat must be taken out of the water and thoroughly sun-dried every so often or it would get waterlogged, and one long trip usually finished it, but its flexibility made it stauncher than any other craft in the rapid, shallow, snag-filled rivers of the high plains. The small half-oranges of the Mandans and other river tribes were longer-lived, being used for short hauls only.

There was a final round of farewells and healths, in so much that reaching some rapids three miles after embarking, neither Wyeth nor Milton Sublette felt up to the job. 'Too much liquor to proceed,' Wyeth says, 'therefore stopped.' Tom Fitzpatrick's brigade, with Stewart and Harrison, headed toward the Crow country, where we will pick them up in a moment. After seeing Cerré started downriver, Bonneville turned west to overtake his detachments and begin the fall hunt. Campbell, who was personally taking his furs downstream by bull-boat, sent his horses, cows, and remaining bull overland with a small party headed by Vasquez.

This last group was the first to observe a marked change in the attitude of the Crow Indians. The friendship of the Crows was sometimes exigent but it had always been genuine and especially warm toward RMF Company men. When Vasquez' party, which included Charles Larpenteur, met a band of Crows they were so friendly that they insisted on trading the whites out of most of their belongings. They made it clear that it was trade or else, and Larpenteur mourned his new blankets and his twenty-dollar sky-blue capote. The young bucks frequently tried to get tough in this way when they came upon a small party of white men, but ordinarily the head man would have ordered them to behave and would have his police club them away if they delayed. This chief decided that he loved his white brothers so much that they ought to be overjoyed to trade on the young bucks' terms. Then the Vasquez party met a full third of the Crow nation under the famous A-ra-poo-ash [6] or Rotten Belly. He was a mighty warrior, a great rain-maker, a gifted visionary, unquestionably first among the Crows. The upper part of his shield was blackened to represent a storm cloud and carried the head and claws of Thunderbird, whom he had seen in a vision while a boy. The great man really was a friend to the whites and so it was significant when he took Vasquez and his men into his own lodge: he was protecting them from his young men. He advised them to wait so that he could also protect them from a band of Blackfeet who were on their way here on a preposterous, a mendacious errand, to make peace with the Crows. Neither party would mean to keep the peace but each would hope it could kid the other into doing so for a while. The gesture shows that the year's losses had a little sobered the Blackfeet and that Rotten Belly had kept posted and knew they would be happy to meet RMF Company men in small force. His guests stayed till the peacemakers came in and Charles Larpenteur was not yet completely alkalied, being somewhat bothered by the Crow women. They were, he said, particularly fond of white men, 'rather too much so to preserve their honor.'

The Blackfeet had run into Bonneville and fought a perfunctory skirmish with him. More significant was the fact that on his way back to the mountains he was being stalked by bands of Indians who were obviously watching for a good chance. Some Snakes whom he met told him that these skulkers were Crows. Bonneville hurried out of Absaroka, the Crow country. He got clear of Crows for the time being but before long he was to suffer from their new foreign policy.

Meanwhile, without realizing it, the river voyagers, who were also meeting rudeness, had reached the source of the trouble when their boats came out of the Big Horn into the Yellowstone and pulled up on the bank at Fort Cass. 'We were treated with little or no ceremony by Mr. Tullock [*sic*] whom we found in charge,' Wyeth says, 'which I attributed to sickness on his part, well knowing that a sick man is never disposed to be civil to others.' But Samuel Tulloch was not sick, he was only serving the interests of the American Fur Company, for whom he had built this trading post in Absaroka last year. He was currently directing at least two Company agents who had been hired to live in Crow villages and move with them when they moved. Directing them, for example, in the procurement of just such trouble as Vasquez had experienced. The Company intended to attach the Crows as a satellite and friendly power.

Tulloch did do a little trading with his guests. Before the party started down the Yellowstone some Gros Ventres came to Fort Cass. Wyeth recognized the tribe he had fought at Pierre's Hole a year ago and says that they too wanted some peace with the Crows. They were not going to get it: instead they lost their scalps. The Blackfoot peace commissioners had already taken some Crow scalps on their way home.

They took to the Yellowstone, here a nobly beautiful river, and floated past the Rosebud, the Tongue, Powder River. The fifth day out from Fort Cass they reached the junction of the Yellowstone and the Missouri and poled their boats four or five miles up the latter to the American Fur Company's greatest post, Fort Union, with its hundred-odd engagés, their wives and children, and the shifting miscellany of Indians. Kenneth McKenzie was much more suave than his subordinate Tulloch, and had as his adjutant James Archdale Hamilton Palmer, a cultivated English gentleman who for reasons not on record had taken service with the Company and dropped the Palmer from his name. These two cosmopolites lived on the scale proper to McKenzie, the King or Emperor of the Missouri, and would cut Opposition throats with decent ceremony. Their royal guest Maximilian was not in residence at the moment — he had gone far up the Missouri to Fort McKenzie — but they would have no smaller hospitality for the Opposition than for a prince.

It is an amusing spectacle. Here was the major Opposition in person, Campbell, who would spend the winter at the post his partner Bill Sublette was at this moment building less than four miles away — where the Company and its subsidized Indians would pulverize him, but not till he had scared them and cost them much more than it was comfortable to pay. Here was Milton Sublette, whose partners had procured the death of McKenzie's old subordinate and companion, Henry Vanderburgh. Here were Cerré, the representative of a rival who would take some more extinguishing, and Wyeth who intended to go into the business. Company or Opposition, they would have committed such mayhem as chance might have offered in the field; so they had a good time at Fort Union. The King and his gentleman assistant regularly supplied themselves with brandies and vintage wines; there were quantities of smuggled liquor and, if that should fail, the produce of a still which McKenzie had just set up. The post's herd provided fresh milk, butter, and cheese — none of which the wayfarers had tasted since they left the States. There were white breads, half a dozen kinds of wild fruit, corn from the Mandans, game of every sort, and beef and fowl and mutton as well. There were Indian and halfbreed girls on call, though the Indians were likely to be Assiniboins who were not highly regarded for cleanliness or charm. There was a serial field day of hunts, horse races, cockfights, the hand game, lacrosse, the pageantry of Indian bands coming in to trade. At least fifty engagés were always in residence at the fort and as many more constantly coming and going, and all had adventure stories to tell round the evening fire. The factors dressed formally, clad their Indian wives in the latest fashions St. Louis had had word of from New York and abroad (with a good painted buffalo robe or Mackinaw blanket to set them off), and furnished their apartments with prints and luxury goods. They were worldly gentlemen, good talkers, of quick minds and a rich past. Wyeth says he particularly liked Mr. Hamilton and everyone acknowledged the charm of the King. They ran a good drawing room in the Assiniboin country.

But not when you got round to business.[7] When the travelers got ready to move on Cerré and Wyeth tried to buy some goods and some alcohol to trade down the river. It is hard to see why they wanted them, for they could expect little opportunity to trade and in fact got little, and knew they would have to pay mountain prices for whatever they might buy. In any event, they were outraged by the prices McKenzie charged them for trade goods and by his refusal to sell them any alcohol at all. So when Wyeth reached Fort Leavenworth on his downriver voyage he reported to the commandant that the American Fur Company was operating a still at Fort Union. Even if he had not been angered by McKenzie's refusal such a report was his duty as a public-spirited citizen. Also the hardest blow he could strike at a rival firm.

Everybody who traded in the Indian Country did so by government permission and on government license, both revokable. It had always been illegal to give, sell, or trade liquor to the Indians. Since July, 1832, it had also been illegal to take liquor into the Indian Country. But from the earliest days on it had always been altogether impossible to conduct the Indian trade without liquor. The Jesuits who first tried to prevent French traders from using it found that their own agents in the trade could not get furs without it. The Hudson's Bay Company had always had an idealistic desire to keep liquor from its Indians — when they got drunk they killed expensively trained traders — and had always supplied it whenever rival traders came into its territory, which was every year. No Dutch or American traders had ever tried to do without it: the Indian trade was based on getting the customers drunk, preferably before they began to bargain. The national government repeatedly prohibited liquor. But that was in Washington: government officials in the field used the prohibition to exact bribes from traders.

The position of the American Fur Company was clear. Its size and resources enabled it to use liquor and to buy officials on a scale which no competitor could afford. On the other hand its size and permanency made it much more vulnerable when the agitation of its competitors put the heat on the inspecting authorities. If he was forced to, an inspector could always find liquor on a keelboat or a steamboat, whereas a small trader could slip past him with enough liquor to make trouble for the Company in any given place. Both trust and Opposition advertised their own purity and denounced the other's crimes, and everyone bought inspectors when necessary. (A common device was to get permission for a party to take up to twenty gallons per capita for medicinal purposes on the summer trip to the mountains.) Both made so much noise, the Opposition through its Representative in Congress, General Ashley, and the liquor traffic got so scandalous that in 1832 the government forbade the importation into the Indian Country of the liquor whose use there was already forbidden. General William Clark promptly sanctioned the Company to take along fourteen hundred gallons of medicinal alcohol to ward off chills and fever. The Army, however, confiscated the whole stock. Clark had also permitted a small trader to take two hundred and fifty gallons into the dry area — and he got away from the Army. That would not do; so in the absence of enforcing agents the Company seized and ironed him at Bellevue and confiscated his liquor. It should have killed him too, for he hurried to St. Louis, publicized the assault and robbery, and brought suit. The Company had gone a bit too far, not even its Benton or its Webster could help it now, and for a time it looked as if the trust was going to be moved out of the Missouri and mountain trade altogether.

It did not run to that, though the victim collected nearly ten thousand dollars from McKenzie's outfit. But clearly both smuggling and bribery had to ease off for a while since too many people would be watching too closely. And the most effective opposition the Company had ever had, Sublette & Campbell, was establishing itself only four miles from the Company's biggest post. If the partners managed to get liquor to their new fort, as they certainly would, and if the Company could not get liquor, as the limelight made likely, there could be only one answer. McKenzie acted on it without hesitation: he bought corn from the agricultural Mandans and set up a still. His cut-throat methods would eventually have taken care of Sublette & Campbell anyway but the still shortened the process.

Nevertheless, Wyeth's report at Fort Leavenworth begot another rumor, forced an investigation, and required the Company to do some frantic lying and doubtless equally frantic bribing. And it brought the King of the Missouri downriver for more than a year. He was a good man to have out of the Indian Country and away from Fort Union while the wind was blowing.

This, however, was still in the future when Wyeth stepped into his bull boat and started down the Missouri, leaving one of his two remaining charter members at the mouth of the Yellowstone. He lost Milton Sublette when they reached the post that William Sublette was building, Milton deciding to wait there till the keelboat went down. That left Wyeth no one who had ever navigated the most violent river in the United States. But, he said, 'I can go downstream.' He did so, with sufficiently exciting adventures which are outside our concern. And from St. Louis he went home to Cambridge to prepare next summer's business.

* * *

It was August 15 or 16 when Tom Fitzpatrick started overland from the Big Horn to find the Crows. Jim Bridger's brigade traveled with him but for how long is not clear; they were not on hand when trouble broke out.

Fitzpatrick said he was looking for the Crows in order to get permission to make his fall hunt in their country. Actually he intended to meet the trust head on and do what he could with high prices for fur to undermine its new Fort Cass. Nevertheless, though his phraseology was intended for use on the floor of Congress by General Ashley, it was not wholly inaccurate. It was customary to pay a moderate lagniappe to Indians whom you might meet when trapping in country they had a recognized claim to, and the custom had a special validity with the Crows.

For the Crows had a rudimentary idea of conservation. They did not want Absaroka trapped out, and since they had a strong social discipline they could make their intentions more or less good. More striking still, they appear to have forsworn alcohol fairly successfully for a considerable period. At least they repeatedly said they would not touch it and there is testimony from a good many independent sources that a lot of them did not touch it — and there is no such testimony in regard to any other Plains Indians.

The Plains tribes varied widely in culture, customs, intelligence, and personality. Because the Sioux were the biggest and therefore the most powerful tribe and because from early in the Civil War on to the death of Crazy Horse they raised so much hell that they were constantly in the headlines, they are established in our accumulation of readymade ideas as the outstanding Indians of the West. The mountain men did not think so; in their empirical respect the Crows, the Cheyennes, and the Arapahos outranked the Sioux. A modern student knows that he cannot avoid using a white man's measuring rod but he tends to agree with the mountain men at least in regard to the Crows and the Cheyennes.

The Crows were big Indians, on the average the tallest on the plains. They were strikingly handsome, the women less so than the men by white standards. They wore their hair as long as possible and worked switches into it till sometimes it had an extreme length of ten or twelve feet, though folded back in heavy queues. They had the largest and best tipis and were the best-dressed of all tribes. Their women were superb tanners, tailors, embroiderers, and decorators, so that they did a big business with other tribes in shirts, leggings, and robes. In fact, the best Sioux warbonnets (which mean every kind of Indian in American iconography) were made by the Crows — as the best Sioux bows were made by the Nez Perces. The Crows were also weapon-makers to the neighbors they fought with, and the Blackfeet in particular liked their war shields.

The Crows fought the United States Army only once and that was a small skirmish; they made little trouble for the white man and next to the Nez Perces and Flatheads were the best friends of trappers. On the other hand, they fought all Indians. They never had an ally and made only one truce: with the Sioux, for a single year.[8] They thought of the Sioux as their principal enemies and when Sublette & Campbell brought the Oglalas to the Platte in 1834 and so upset the balance of power in the mountains forever, a pressure began which by about 1860 forced the Crows back as far as Powder River. They could not hold against the sheer weight of numbers but even this half conquest of Absaroka cost the Sioux dear, since the Crows were forever raiding them. More spectacular is the fact that they put a limit to the southward expansion of the Blackfeet, probably getting more Blackfoot scalps than any other tribe contrived to. But they would take on anyone and they raided everywhere. Primarily for horses. In envy and humility their neighbors paid them the supreme tribute: they said that the Crows were the best horse-thieves. The number of Comanche horses in their herds supported the judgment; it was a good thief who could steal horses from the Comanches. Moreover, as far away as the Crees there was a corollary: it was hardest to steal horses from the Crows.

It was a partnership of Cooper and McGuffey that established in the American conventions the idea that Indians were unemotional, dour, and silent. Nothing could be sillier. They were the most excitable of people, as emotional as Sicilians. When tribal councils, religious ceremonies, or the code for appearances before the white audience required gravity or impassivity they could lay it on like the German General Staff. Ordinarily, however, they jabbered like children and the McGuffey silent Indian is just an Indian who has not learned English. In a race of marathon talkers the Crows were unsurpassed conversationalists, orators, debaters, diplomats, and storytellers. Their humor was close to the white man's, free-flowing and low — their version of Old Man Coyote, the Plains Eulenspiegel, is the most obscene of all. They were tireless practical jokers too, with a college boy's relish for applied violence and embarrassment.

Their morals were nothing much. By white standards their women were the loosest of all squaws, which is something of a superlative. They did not punish adultery and Crow marriage may be described as a serial taking and putting-away: a veteran husband might wear hashmarks on his shirt signifying that he had made briefly happy as many as eighteen wives. In a word, the Crows, men and women, married and unmarried alike, thought continence no precious jewel. They had a Plains reputation for pederasty but this appears to have been a libel. There were a good many 'berdashes' among them, homosexuals who dressed and lived as squaws (though many were warriors) and who had full dignity in public estimation since they were supposed to be obeying instructions given them in vision by their medicines. But there were berdashes in all tribes.[9]

* * *

These were the people in whose country Fitzpatrick intended to make his fall hunt and whose trade he hoped to regain for the RMF Company while his ally Campbell forced up the price of beaver at Fort Union. He was entitled, by the record, to count on their amiability. But McKenzie had had his Fort Cass and his Samuel Tulloch at the mouth of the Big Horn for a year now. Besides that, he had at least two resident agents living permanently with the Crows, traveling with their villages, and keeping a stock of goods on hand. One of them was named Winter, the other was the fabulous Jim Beckwourth, an Ashley man (thus an old friend of Fitzpatrick's), a mulatto, one of the hardest specimens in the mountains, for some years past an adopted Crow and a war chief. Tulloch, Winter, and Beckwourth had the usual instructions from McKenzie: get the beaver. They were to make permanent Company customers of the Crows by whatever means, and we have already seen them in action.

Fitzpatrick is moving through Sheridan County, Wyoming, and Big Horn and Rosebud Counties, Montana, a country of hills and badlands and low ranges of mountains full of small creeks. It was the heart of Absaroka, the Crow lands, populous with buffalo, rich in beaver. His thirty-odd men broke up into groups of three or four and went out for a couple of days at a time to trap the creeks, so that Stewart now got instruction in the basic operation of the fur trade. The skins were cleaned and stretched by the trappers' squaws or the camp-swampers of the main party, then marked 'RMF Co' on the flesh side. The route took them across the Little Big Horn well below the place where George Armstrong Custer's private blend of egotism and stupidity would get the Seventh Cavalry massacred on June 25, 1876, across a low divide beyond which the creeks fall into the Rosebud, across the Rosebud, and on to the valley of Tongue River. It is a desolate country to modern eyes but it was full of game and when the Crows talked about it they paraphrased the frontier humorist who allowed that heaven must be a Kentuck of a place. The magnificent Big Horn Valley was its Heart.

On September 5, three weeks out from the Big Horn, the brigade met a village of Crows. The only first-hand accounts, two letters by Fitzpatrick (one unpublished), do not tell in detail what happened. But instead of reattaching the Crows to their old friends, Tom Fitzpatrick began to pay for having procured the murder of a trust bourgeois last fall: the Crows were now working for the trust. He pitched camp, left it in charge of Stewart (which shows that the veteran of Waterloo had proved his capacity to command mountain men) and rode over to pay a visit of ceremony to the village chief, three miles away. Unquestionably he got to work at once to overbid the trust, and the chief was delighted to meet his old friend Broken Hand. Meanwhile some of the chief's constituents repaid the visit, calling on Broken Hand's camp which was in charge of a Scotch captain who had had no real experience with Indians.

No one knows just how it was done. But the Crows would express the most effusive affection, and Stewart, besides knowing that they had always been friendly to the RMF Company, had unquestionably been instructed to strain amiability to the limit in order to warm their hearts to trade. The Crows would be full of good stories, would fling their blankets round the shoulders of their old friends, would create a tumult of laughter and back-slapping and pantomime to illustrate their victories of the last year. If Stewart had his guards keep their rifles at the ready, as certainly he must have done, the Crows would be wounded by such suspicion and would demand that the white brother heal the hurt by manifesting his trust in them. Of his own innocence or under instruction to give the Crows as much lee-way as they might demand, Stewart fell for this ancient dodge or one like it. Suddenly the knives, clubs, bows, and guns were out, and a Crow was attached to everything of value. All Indians who succeeded to this extent promptly went hostile and dared the victims to do something about it, hoping that they would: it took the greatest hardihood to withstand their taunts. When Fitzpatrick got back from buttering the head purchasing agent, he found that he had nothing left, nothing at all. The customers had taken all his horses, all his goods, his whole outfit of guns, powder, traps, blankets, other trade goods, and on down to Stewart's watch.

Neither Fitzpatrick nor any other RMF partner blamed Stewart, so he was not to blame. He behaved 'with great spirit,' Irving says, basing his account on Campbell, who got the story as straight as anyone could, and probably also on some of the eyewitnesses who had reported to Campbell. Joe Meek, who heard all the talk, says the same.[10] It was a case of complete surprise by means of trickery and against such odds fighting would have been silly. Stewart had about twenty-five men, all probably disarmed; there would have been at least four times as many Crows, armed to the teeth.

No man in the West handled Indians better than Tom Fitz-patrick. In a state of mind that may be imagined he rode back to the village chief and demanded the restitution of his outfit. The proof of his skill is that he got a little of it back, some horses and a few traps, he says, plus some rifles and a little powder, but no furs and none of his trade goods. Rage could do him no good and might get his whole party wiped out. So, biting the bullet, he turned west again to get out of Absaroka fast, catch up with Jim Bridger, and rearm and re-equip his men. The Crows hated to see a good horse go and had been persuaded against their better judgment to restore Fitz's. Irving remarks that they were 'anxious to wipe off so foul a stigma on the reputation of the Crow nation.' So before Fitzpatrick got out of the country he lost some horses again. Later on when he met Bonneville west of the Divide he learned that some of Bald Head's parties also had been stripped by the Crows.[11]

Fitzpatrick wrote to Ashley accusing the trust of having directed the robbery and said that a Company agent was present when it was made. That agent was probably Jim Beckwourth and there can be no doubt that Fitzpatrick was right: this was an incident in the planned destruction of the RMF Company and a counter to Sublette's lead in building a post near Fort Union. 'This has been a severe blow to Sublette and Campbell,' McKenzie wrote to his factor at Fort McKenzie. 'And although on their first start here [Fort Union] they made great show and grand promises to the Indians and although among the men nothing was talked about except the new company, they live now at the sign of "The case is altered."' Tulloch forwarded to Fort Union forty-three beaver pelts with the RMF Company's mark on them and apparently asked whether anything was to be done about them. Why, yes, McKenzie wrote him, if Mr. Fitzpatrick should show up at Fort Union, McKenzie would be willing to sell him the skins for the price of the goods traded for them to the Indians at Fort Cass, plus an equitable fee for freightage to Fort Union and for taking care of them. He was in the trading business and as willing to deal with Mr. Fitzpatrick as with anyone else, 'if I get my price. I make this proposal as a favor, not as a matter of right, for I consider the Indians entitled to trade any beaver in their possession to me or to any other trader.'

Unaware of the trouble Wyeth had laid up for him and the Company, the King of the Missouri was riding high. He had cleaned out one Opposition brigade, robbing it of the first fruits of its fall hunt, its entire stock of trade goods, and most of its outfit. He had neutralized the threat of Sublette & Campbell's new post by convincing Indians and free trappers of the vicinity that the Opposition could not win. He had turned the Crows loose in their country and the Blackfeet in theirs and beyond its borders. A damned good job of work.[12]

* * *

In the mountains the robbery was promptly — and properly —

ascribed to Jim Beckwourth, the mulatto chief of the Crows who was being carried on the trust's payroll at eight hundred dollars a year — he says three thousand a year. Jim already had a reputation as a tough hombre, a daredevil, a thug, and a liar, and a man eminent among mountain men for such qualities is not likely to have them questioned now. In the early eighteen-fifties, a wandering journalist found Jim in California, beginning to be old, his mountain days behind him, and ghosted his reminiscences. The result, *The Life and Adventures of James P. Beckwourth*, is one of the gaudiest books in our literature and may well be the goriest: at least more Indians are killed in it than in any other book known to this student. Various writers have appraised it variously but, apart from yarns in which Jim unnecessarily quadruples his own daring, it is in the main trustworthy and is sometimes an indispensable witness to the events it deals with. But among several slanders which Jim thought it desirable to refute was the accusation that he had instigated the attack on Fitzpatrick. The fantastic yarn he tells in rebuttal is sufficient evidence that those who accused him had the goods on him.[13]

Wherever Jim was, he found himself the most important personage at hand. So here; he says that he built Fort Cass at McKenzie's prayerful solicitation, directed Tulloch and Winter as his subordinates, watched over many other white engagés, conducted a large trade, and several times saved the fort and the Company's investment and the lives of the garrison from the Blackfeet. At the time of the Fitzpatrick affair, he goes on, the Crows had recently had many fights with the Blackfeet and the Cheyennes — in all of which Jim had slain his usual hecatombs, saved the nation's honor, and increased its wealth. (With his virginal she-warrior, the Pine Leaf, performing equal prodigies at his side.) But while Jim, the Red Fish, the Bloody Arm, the Enemy of Horses — while Jim was taking a day off from war, a party of twenty-three young Crows set out to find some Cheyennes. They found some. Fitzpatrick's party was with them and, in order to drum up business with the Cheyennes and 'for the sport of killing Indians,' helped them wipe out the entire Crow war party. In fact, one of Fitz's men shot the war chief who was fighting almost as well as Jim would have done. This with further details that add artistic verisimilitude to Pooh-Bah's narrative — and are a little hard to understand in that Jim says that no member of that war party survived the fight.

All this is pure invention but it provides the motivation. Presently in camp on the Big Horn (it was really Tongue River) Jim gets word that Fitzpatrick is near-by and wants to see him. Jim is too busy, and too dignified as well, having lately become (he says) co-head of the Crows, together with the celebrated Long Hair, in succession to the equally famous Rotten Belly (whose death Jim dates incorrectly). So he sends for Fitz, summoning him to the village. Fitz arrives with Doctor Harrison, several other gentlemen of leisure, and 'a Captain Stuart [*sic*], an English officer who had figured conspicuously, as I was informed, under the Iron Duke.' Jim observes that some of his people are eyeing the horses of the visitors and so, ever the punctilious host, he details some camp police to guard them. But it turns out that the Crows weren't thinking of stealing the horses: they had recognized some that the war party had taken when it left camp.

Next morning, the yarn goes on, Jim learns that his outraged people, after working themselves up with dances and mourning all night, have set out after Fitzpatrick. At once Jim jumps on a horse, which he runs so hard that it drops dead just as our hero comes on the scene, and summons the members of his secret military fraternity to accompany him. They reach the ambush prepared for Fitzpatrick, 'six or seven miles' away, just in time to save the lives of the whites at considerable risk to Jim's.

Here Stewart enters the drama. There was only one hope, Jim says, of getting them back to the village alive — for him and his fraternity brothers to take them up on their own horses, thus appearing to make prisoners of them for disposition later on. Everybody was exceedingly glad for this reprieve, everybody but Stewart:

> 'No,' said he, 'I will get on behind no d—d rascal; and any man that will live with such wretches is a d—d rascal.'
>
> 'I thank you for the compliment,' I returned, 'but I have no time to attend to it here.'
>
> 'Captain Stuart,' said Charles A. Wharfield, afterward colonel in the United States Army [unidentified: presumably Jim is making him out a RMF Company man], 'that's very unbecoming language to use at such a time.'
>
> 'Come, come, boys,' interposed Dr. Harrison, 'let us not be bandying words here. We will return with them, whether for better or worse.'

Following this Emerson Bennett dialogue, Jim's story says, he took the Fitzpatrick party back to the village and had his fraternity guard them against the vengeance of the Crows. Be sure that they were terrified. Be sure that Jim was noble. Straining his authority as co-monarch, he had the village searched for the goods stolen from them. He got back everything except five horses and some scarlet and blue cloth which had already been torn up for use.

> I was informed subsequently that the Englishman, as soon as he approached me, cocked his gun, intending to shoot me. It was well for him as well as his party that he altered his mind, for if he had harmed me there would not have been a piece of him left the size of a five-penny bit. I was doing all that lay in my power to save the lives of the party from a parcel of ferocious and exasperated savages; his life depended by the slightest thread over the yawning abyss of death; the slightest misadventure would have proved fatal. At that moment he insulted me in the grossest manner. The language that he addressed to me extorted a look of contempt from me but I had not time for anger.

Jim's ghost wrote elegant prose. Jim goes on to admit that he has been foully accused of instigating this 'fiendish plot,' and to deny the libel. Also he has 'been informed that Captain Stuart offered one thousand dollars to a certain individual to take my life.' Here Jim is remembering something that may actually have occurred, though he has substituted himself for another character in the leading rôle, as he frequently did.[14] Jim hurries past this, however, to describe an even more astonishing offer. He says that a 'fine iron gray' horse of Stewart's was among the five that he had been able to recover. Stewart thought highly of it and had been half distracted by its loss. Fitzpatrick told him that his only chance to get it back was to propitiate Beckwourth.

> Accordingly he visited me and said, '*Mr.* Beckwourth (he mistered me that time), 'can you get my horse for me?'
>
> I replied, 'Captain Stuart, I am a poor man in the service of the American Fur Company, to sell their goods and receive the peltry of these Indians. The Indian who has your horse is my best customer, he has a great many relatives and a host of friends, whose trade I shall surely lose if I attempt to take the horse from him. Should the agent hear of it I should be discharged at once and, of course, lose my salary.'
>
> 'Well,' said he, 'if the company discharges you for that, I pledge you my word that I will give you six thousand dollars for ten years.'

Sixty thousand dollars was high for a buffalo horse. But following this humiliation of the haughty, Stewart got back his horse and finally the Bloody Arm, co-chief of the Crows, led his friend Fitzpatrick and the remainder of the rescued safely out of camp and guarded them for fifteen miles on their way. But Fitzpatrick did not take his advice to keep going; instead, he foolishly made camp. So 'within an hour after his delay almost all his horses were taken by the Indians, not leaving him enough to pack his goods.' With this last statement Jim gets back within rifle-shot of the record.[15]

Beckwourth's story is, of course, preposterous. The circumstances of the attack on Fitzpatrick were quite otherwise and Beckwourth's supporting detail can be proved false. But that Jim would bother to defend himself so elaborately against an accusation which after all was only one of a hundred, and that he would invent a story which failed for a dozen pages to display him killing scores of enemies with the odds against him, amount to a confession. Furthermore, the particularity of what he says about Stewart suggests that Stewart may indeed have damned him for a rascal and defied him to his face. If he did, he was extremely injudicious in the circumstances — in any circumstances that involved a man whom Francis Parkman called 'a ruffian of the first stamp, bloody and treacherous, without honor or honesty.' No doubt the pressure was great on a man whose quarterings included 'an imperial crown within a double tressure, flowered and counter-flowered with fleur-de-lis' and who was here robbed by Indians under the command of a runaway slave. Maybe he even cocked a rifle at Jim as Jim says he did, though probably he had no rifle to cock, and certainly if he had, some cooler mountain man would have tackled him from behind. At any rate, he got under the old-bull hide of Jim Beckwourth as few ever did. So much so that Jim remembered the insult for eighteen years and then like many a writer before him avenged it in fiction.

Stewart also got a novelist's compensation. In *Altowan* and *Edward Warren* the Crows are always villains, sneaks, and cowards. They take repeated maulings at the author's hand and he makes their enemies the Blackfeet the noblest redskins of the plains.

## « VI »

# THE THEME OF WONDER (1833-1834)

SHORTLY AFTER THIS Stewart disappears into one of the hiatuses of the literature of the fur trade. Fitzpatrick had met Bridger and refitted his men sometime before October 26, when Bonneville found him in camp on Ham's Fork. (A tributary of Black's Fork, which is a tributary of Green River, in southwestern Wyoming, eighty-odd miles south and somewhat to the west of Horse Creek, where the rendezvous had been held.) Whether Bridger's brigade was with him is not clear. He was still there on November 13 when he wrote the previously mentioned letter to Ashley, which Harrison was to take to the States almost at once. In spite of the trust's land piracy he had made a good hunt: with two of his parties still to be heard from he had twenty-five packs of beaver. He notes that Bonneville, two weeks before, had had a pack and a half. He may have spent the winter thereabout: it was good country. No one knows where Bridger's outfit wintered. They may have been together and Stewart may have been with them. Or he may have been with either of them separately; the slight evidence could even be interpreted to mean that he wintered with Fraeb or Gervais. Or he may have gone back to the States, though this is very unlikely.

There is a strong presumption that he spent the winter of 1833–1834 in the mountains, and it is assumed here that he spent it with Bridger's brigade, whether he shifted outfits when Fitzpatrick met it or the two brigades combined. This was the only winter that Stewart spent in the field and justifies a chapter on that aspect of mountain life. But it will be expedient first to return to some of our other characters.

Back then to the Baron Braunsberg, Prince Maximilian, whom we last saw, part way through Chapter I, arriving on the *Yellowstone* at Fort Pierre, the American Fur Company post among the Sioux. (Pierre, South Dakota.) That was May 29, 1833. Among the *Yellowstone's* passengers was Kenneth McKenzie, bound to Fort Union to direct the tactics which we have seen applied in the field. There was also Lucien Fontenelle, preparing to start west with the caravan which we saw lose the overland race to Campbell. What follows here was of course concurrent with Stewart's trip west, the rendezvous, and the rest of our 1833 narrative so far.

The *Yellowstone* took on a lading of furs and robes — the winter and spring trade — and turned back to St. Louis. After a week of the Sioux, the first Plains Indians he had had a chance to study in detail, Maximilian went aboard the Company's other steamboat, the *Assiniboin.* McKenzie was with him still (and of course his artist Bodmer and his hunter and servant Dreidoppel) and on June 5 the upriver voyage began. Navigating the Missouri was no easier above Fort Clark than below it. In fact, the June rise which made lightering less common also made piloting more difficult and increased the hazard of floating logs and caving banks. But the fifty-year-old scientist was now beginning to reap his harvest. Not only was the country beautiful — the vegetation-choked bottom-land of the Missouri, in the midst of barrens — but for a botanist, a zoölogist, and especially for an ethnologist, it was wonderland. Maximilian's day was spent in a species of scholarly exhilaration while Bodmer sketched, Dreidoppel hunted specimens, and Indians of fascinating new tribes politely hunted specimens too, if only of prairie grass. On the fourteenth day the *Assiniboin* reached Fort Clark (roughly sixty miles above Bismarck, North Dakota) and the Mandan Indians, who had been known to the whites longer than any other Indians of the Far West, since the Vérendryes, in fact.[2] George Catlin had spent part of the preceding summer there; Maximilian was to spend the coming winter there. He met and made notes on some of the Mandans who figure in Catlin's book, and Bodmer sketched some of Catlin's sitters.

This is not the place to discuss the Mandans, who were very interesting Indians and had been friendly with the white men for nearly a century; so friendly that the frequency of lighter skins and blue eyes had convinced Catlin that they were the Welsh Indians. There had been a succession of trading posts here and at their now abandoned villages, farther downstream. In charge of Fort Clark was James Kipp, one of the trust's most effective partisans, who was Catlin's authority for much of what he said about the Mandans. He was currently assisted by Alexander Harvey whom Maximilian had already met, one of the best roving traders and as notorious a desperado almost as Jim Beckwourth. And Maximilian also touched the fringes of enchantment, for here was Toussaint Charbonneau, geologically old, the companion of Lewis and Clark and the widower of Sacajawea. All the West and all its Indians, three generations of chiefs and traders, had engrossed on his mind an incomparable pageant. He had come to these parts early in the last decade of the eighteenth century and, if with no spectacular success and not too much praise from a catalogue of employers, he had been working for fur companies, the United States Army, and the government ever since. Long ago he had developed a distaste for his own race. He was an Indian now, a good one, and lived with his people, not at the fort. He was as bent as a scrub cedar on a bluff, his face was as seamed as a claybank, but he was more sagacious than his overlords — in fact, he saved Maximilian from robbery — and could travel river or prairie forever, winter or summer. No one knows how old he was; the guess that he was seventy-five this summer is conservative. Five years after Maximilian's passing, a fourteen-year-old Assinboin girl who had been captured by his Arikara neighbors roused a spring fret in the blood of this man of many wives. Francis Chardon, Kipp's successor at Fort Clark, sold her to him and wrote in his journal:

> the young Men of the Fort and two *rees* [Arikaras] gave to the Old Man a splendid Chàrivèree, the Drums, pans, Kittles &c Beating; guns fireing &c. The old gentleman gave a feast to the Men, and a glass of grog — and went to bed with his young wife with the intention of doing his best.

Maximilian had little time to study the river tribes, their domed earth huts, or the parade of their daily life, but he filled his notebook and worked Bodmer more than union hours. The Fort was a village square for neighboring downriver Arikaras and upriver Minnetarees as well as the Mandans. A party of Crows, close relatives of the Minnetarees, were on hand as well. They were a delight to the scientist, who praised their physiques and artifacts, their aristocratic bearing, their mastery of the savage way of life. Among them was Rotten Belly, whom we have met, then the principal chief of the Crow nation, and the chief who would succeed him when the Gros Ventres killed him next year. This last was the celebrated Long Hair, whose name certifies that he had carried one Crow fashion to a tribal championship.

After a twenty-four-hour stop the *Assiniboin* resumed her voyage on June 19. She had taken on a couple of Blackfeet, which shows how technology had increased the safety of plains travel. On a peace or trading mission, the Blackfeet would have had to bring an army with them to this vicinity if it had not been for the steamboat, an innovation only two years old. Bodmer painted one but the other refused on the ground that this was dangerous medicine and would get him killed; but it was he who got killed, at Fort Union. The boat went on through a continuous circus performance of the river tribes, straightened out into a long, westering, still more dangerous stretch of the Missouri, survived a series of violent storms, and came near blowing up when fire broke out and was extinguished just short of the year's shipment of gunpowder. She reached Fort Union, the largest of the river posts, on June 24. This was six days from Fort Clark and Maximilian was seventy-five days out of St. Louis.

In about a third of the time a keelboat journey would have required, Maximilian had had about eighteen hundred miles of river travel.[3] A glance at the map will show how far he had come into the greater West. In the usage of the fur trade he reached 'the mountains' at Fort Union, though uniformities of custom and experience should bring Fort Clark and perhaps Fort Pierre into the mountains too. His arrival at Fort Union on June 24 should be correlated with the westward journey of Stewart and Campbell. On June 24 they were still east of Laramie Fork; they would cross the Divide on July 2 and reach the rendezvous on July 8.

Fort Union was in the country of the Assiniboins, rowdy Indians of the Dakota stock and therefore relatives of the Sioux, with a long record as bad actors. Crees from Canada frequented the place too. Maximilian had come far enough to study any aspect of the Plains culture he might want to, and the life of this great post, with its hundred or more engagés, its resident halfbreeds, and the constant arrival and departure of Indians and white traders, could have supplied material for years of study. (This was big business. The post kept on hand close to a hundred thousand dollars worth of trade goods,

St. Louis.) But Maximilian wanted to go still farther and see more. So McKenzie, who stayed here and took over the management from his assistant, Hamilton, arranged to send him on to the Company's farthest and most dangerous post, Fort McKenzie in the Blackfoot country. D. D. Mitchell, the factor of that post (Kipp had built it) was going to take this year's goods there by keelboat, and Alexander Culbertson, who was soon to succeed him, was going along.

Maximilian's book comes alive at Fort Union but we have not time for its narrative. Here in the upper Missouri he got a reminder of his young manhood. A large village of Assiniboins arrived and as they came across the flat in their stately, spectacular formation, dressed in their best robes, squaws driving the travois and yelling at the dogs, warriors on parade with feathers and paint and medicine symbols, they started to sing a 'song consisting of many abrupt, broken tones like those of the warwhoop.' Close to three hundred of them were singing it, a wild bass chorus with falsetto grace-notes echoing back from the hills, and Maximilian had heard its like before — 'the song we heard in the years 1813 and 1814 from the Russian soldiers,' in Napoleon's time. He hardly slept for making notes and hardly allowed Bodmer to sleep. But the keelboat *Flora* came down the Yellowstone from Fort Cass with furs that Samuel Tulloch had dispatched. Mitchell loaded her with his goods. He and Culbertson, Maximilian and Bodmer and Dreidoppel, and a boat's complement of forty-seven started up the Missouri on July 6. Stewart and Campbell had reached Horse Creek.

Twenty-six men shouldered the cordelle that morning. Traveling by keelboat was somewhat safer than by steamboat, though hardly enough to soothe the timid, but it was far less comfortable. Maximilian and Mitchell had bunks in the small cabin but the *Flora* leaked and nothing could have kept the rain out — it was driven in by winds of hurricane strength which repeatedly had the boat out of control. With a keelboat you used the sail when possible, poled in that agonizing march down the catwalk when the river was shallow enough and not too swift, but mostly pulled the lumpish craft with up to several hundred yards of hawser. The cordellers waded through shallows and waist-deep mud, tramped the crumbling edge of claybanks, hung by their eyebrows to slopes of rock, snarled the rope on snags or trees or boulders, stumbled, fell, rolled, and cursed their ways upstream in as grinding a labor as men have ever done anywhere. The prince had to lend a hand only in emergency, so he climbed hills, clawed his way through underbrush, or made excursions into the country all day long, shooting buffalo and bears and bighorn and rattlesnakes, weighting the boat down with specimens animal, vegetable, and mineral, cursing Dreidoppel, clambering everywhere, seeing everything. A man of his age stood a fair chance of dropping dead but Maximilian of Wied-Neuwied could take it.

He was, Culbertson says,[4] fond of his pipe, and his favorite wear was 'a white slouch hat, a black velvet coat rather rusty from long service, and the greasiest pair of trousers that ever encased princely legs.' This was badlands country and most of Bodmer's best landscapes were done here, but though Maximilian records his satisfaction in having the nightmares of erosion put on canvas, apparently Bodmer could not work hard enough. He and Dreidoppel, Culbertson goes on:

> seemed gifted to a high degree with the faculty of putting their princely employer into a frequent passion, till there is hardly a bluff or a valley on the whole upper Missouri that has not repeated in an angry tone, and with a strong Teutonic accent, the names of Boadmer and Tritripel [*sic*].

For more than a month they toiled upstream, past the mouth of Milk River, the Musselshell, and finally the Marias. Six miles beyond the last they came on August 9, thirty-four days out from Fort Union, to the end of their passage. (Rendezvous had broken up. Stewart, Campbell, Bonneville, and Wyeth were on their way to the Big Horn.) Fort McKenzie was only a few miles downstream from where Fort Benton would ultimately be built, and Fort Benton, itself only a few miles from the great falls of the Missouri, would be the head of steam navigation. When Maximilian got there the fort's complement was twenty-seven engagés; their squaws, children, and in-laws brought the census to fifty-three. Fifty-three people represented the American Fur Company's penetration of the Blackfoot country, precariously carrying on a trade that reached through its customers and their vocational murder far west of the Divide, to the country of the Flatheads and Nez Perces and Pend d'Oreilles and Kutenais, southwestward to Great Salt Lake and the Utes and Snakes, southward to the Crows, and to all itinerant white men in between. They were carrying on this trade in constant danger of being killed by their customers.

There were Blackfeet at Fort McKenzie throughout Maximilian's stay there, camped immediately in front of it or a few miles away. For these Junkers who would not keep the peace with anyone else could not keep it among themselves when they were in any considerable numbers, and it was necessary to maintain an insulating distance between villages. All three tribes of the Blackfeet (the Siksika) were here in force, the Blackfeet who gave their name to the others, the Bloods (Kainah), and the Piegans. Their confederates the Gros Ventres, who had had such a melancholy summer and fall last year, also showed up in force.[5]

They were a surly race. One student confesses his feeling of anticlimax when, knowing them in history as the free-wheeling terrors of the West, he first saw their reservation descendants and noted a facial expression he had seen on no other Indians. Many of them had the turned-down mouths, hollow cheeks, and bitter-taste grimace of veteran evangelical deacons; they looked like holy Baptists and it turned out that some of them were. And yet, *mutatis mutandis*, this may mean a continuation of their inter-tribal dislike of one another. The Blackfeet proper were capricious: no one could predict their attitude an hour in advance. The Piegans were a little more genial; they were the ones who had listened to McKenzie's emissaries, begun the trade, and kept it going. The Bloods were the most Teutonic of all. Nobody liked them, including their friends. They were the first to take offense, the first to break a truce, the first to murder. They did all three while Maximilian was at Fort McKenzie.

He was learning how the fur trade was conducted at a fixed post, and it was radically different from the life of a roving brigade. If there was more comfort here, the dyer's hand had to be more constantly subdued to what it worked in. If the danger from Indians was more intermittent, it was also more acute, for they came in whole villages, not in the usually small bands that roamed the hunting country. You multiplied by fifty the strain and vigilance of a casual meeting with Indians and repeated the exercise week by week. Maximilian was able to observe the work of experts, Berger, who was the interpreter and had mastered Blackfoot psychology, Culbertson, who was to run this post till it was given up, and especially David Dawson Mitchell, who was as distinguished a master of his specialty as Tom Fitzpatrick was of his. Mitchell was a great man in the trade. He had risen to this eminence in the American Fur Company by proved merit. Presently he was to tire of the fur trade and leave it; in order to bring him back the Company had to make him a partner. Later he was an Indian agent, then a celebrated cavalry leader in the Mexican War,[6] finally Superintendent of Indian Affairs. A man who directed the Blackfoot trade possessed an extremity of courage; one who survived the job had an extremity of skill.

The economy of the post had to go on, regardless: hunting, to supply the garrison with meat (subject to ambush by the customers), herding the horses day and night (with the customers obligated by Indian honor to steal as many of them as they could), blacksmithing, boatmaking, tanning and curing and pressing furs, dispatching and receiving trading parties, keeping the fort in repair and preparing it for winter. So did the economy of the Indian villages that were camped here or near-by. Maximilian watched the preparation of furs, the making of pemmican, the constant tailoring and dressmaking of the squaws. (He observed that scores of them had their noses cut off; the Blackfeet had different moral standards than the Crows and this was the way they punished adultery.) The handicrafts of the polished-stone age were going on all round him and he filled a lot of notebooks. The Blackfeet were not so good at them as some Plains tribes and had to keep interrupting their warfare so that they could trade, especially with their inveterate enemies the Crows, for bonnets and decorated robes and clothes and weapons and parfleches and utensils. Their ceremonies were without end: dances to bring the buffalo or to propitiate some supernatural who had indicated his displeasure, seasonal observances that had to be made at the appointed time, private magic at the dictates of private medicines, individual quests for game or vision or feathers or goopher dust that required the co-operation of neighbors, fraternity rites, lodge meetings, supplications for aphrodisiacs, commemoration of the heroes. Town criers were always summoning emergency assemblies to meet special situations and the normal death rate was always adding mourning shrieks to the bedlam and amputated fingers to the general bloodiness. Someone was always yelling and clattering rattles to scare diseases out of the sick. The beauty of Indian music, whether vocal or instrumental, is somewhat esoteric to such white men as do not live in Santa Fe, and Maximilian's ears suffered from an energetic, lethally monotonous caterwauling that nothing could shut off. Day or night there was no escape from the drums, the thump of moccasined feet, and the singing that was just 'hi-ya' in Indian scales. Observation of other tribes had made Maximilian a sophisticate; the jugglery of the Blackfoot medicine men, he found, was not up to Broadway.[7]

The villages were here on business and the trade went on in the customary ways at set times. All such posts as Fort McKenzie consisted of square or rectangular stockades, of which at least two walls, if not more, were cabins or sheds: living quarters, warehouses, storehouses, workshops. (See Fort Laramie in Miller's close-up, Plate VIII.) The main entrance was a gate opening on a corridor whose walls were such structures. Another gate closed the interior end of this corridor and prevented access to the interior quadrangle. In the walls of the corridor, windows (capable of being barred and secured) usually opened from a warehouse. You admitted Indians to the quadrangle only in small groups and only when you knew them well and had them covered; you almost never admitted them to a storehouse, unless there was some pressing need to awe them with your wealth and then only in still smaller groups. When trade began you first closed the interior gate so that no one could get beyond it. Then you admitted to this dead-end corridor as many of the clamoring customers as you thought the circumstances warranted and shut out the rest by closing the exterior gate. Then you traded, working either at the storehouse windows or in a small showroom where goods were displayed, and working with the manner of a sales agent who has had ecclesiastical training, but also with a number of armed guards posted.

The job of Mitchell and his subordinates was precarious and infinitely delicate. The trader had to know in what order to give presents to chiefs and what amount would prevent suspicion of niggardliness without suggesting that he was afraid. He had to know how long to haggle, where to set his cellar and ceiling prices, when to give in with an appearance of generosity, when to break off bargaining with a show of scorn or indignation. He had to know when to be insulted and when to have a hide that would turn insult and threat. Most of all he had to know when to use liquor, when to discover that he had none left, whom to give it to, whom to deny it at any risk, how much to give a particular customer, when it was best to put laudanum in the alcohol and suppress a nascent fight with Mickey Finns.

The Indians were Teutonic, none more Prussian than the Blackfeet. Their overbearing arrogance, their military pride and ceremonialism, the fastidiously sensitive brutality of their honor, the childlike fondness for goosestepping in magnificent uniforms of a stone-age mentality prolonged into the nineteenth century had an intensity hard to realize today. When a new village arrived to trade, the braves put on their most overpowering lodge garments, medicine bundles, and real and symbolical weapons, caparisoned their horses with feathers and bells and ribbons, painted their chests and faces with ashes and blue earth and yellow-moss pigment and vermilion (from the Company, ten dollars a pound), and then staged parades and drills strikingly like Homecoming Day at a military prep school. Thereafter Mitchell had to inflate their pride by making the *grossgeneralstab* more gorgeous still. Here is where the 'chiefs' coats,' lieutenant-generals' uniforms, and grand exalted nabobs' costumes which we saw shipped up the river got in their work. It was the style-show opening. Mitchell dressed them in frogged and epauletted uniforms with buttons the size of paperweights and gold lace as thick as any that Winfield Scott, himself no bush-league George Patton, wore when calling on an ambassador. There were stripes down the trousers. There were shakoes and pompoms. The chiefs looked like a minstrel-show cakewalk in heaven and they shoved out their chests and strutted, counting their coups competitively. They sighed and applauded like a congregation of Follies girls at a Mainbocher private showing. Then Mitchell hung the Company's medals round their necks. He was the local sales manager of a private corporation but the medals suggested, and he said, that he was representing the White Father.

It was wonderful. Also it was dangerous stuff. You might be quite right in giving Bull's Tail the most gorgeous outfit on the ground that he represented the highest tribal dignity or had brought most trade to the Company this year. But you might thereby wound Thunder in the Hills, who not only had a simple lust for gold lace but might feel that his achievement in bashing in the heads of three Flathead squaws in a single afternoon entitled him to it. When you wounded the Thunder's feelings you also offended his band, whose pride suffered with his. An Indian with hurt feelings was dangerous. Thunder might go back to his lodge, mark off an altar in the dust, burn some sweet grass on it, and start singing to his scalping knife. His gang might then go after you — or after Bull's Tail and his gang. Before Maximilian's eyes the award of a field marshal's uniform to a Blackfoot chief — who, Mitchell explained to the others, had been the Company's best friend this year and should be an example to them if they wanted to be field marshals — put the Bloods on the prod. Presently they killed the nephew of the Blackfoot chief. Threats, pony-riding, war songs followed. The Blackfeet were going to wipe out the Bloods; the Bloods were going to teach the Blackfeet humility. Settling such extempore wars was a routine part of a factor's job. Mitchell got the Blackfoot village to move some miles away (their trade being finished) till their hearts were better. Presently they were back again.

Individual trading was just as explosive. A Blood killed one of the fort's engagés in the showroom, in a dispute over prices. He was a Company employee, of course, and presumably life meant something to him. But the trade had just begun and what the hell, business is business. The Bloods said it was an unfortunate accident and Mitchell passed it off as one. A group of Bloods tunneled into a storehouse and got some wealth for nothing before they were discovered. Another band arrived, looked over the market, and announced they didn't like the current quotation on beaver. Time to drive foreigners and their cartels out: if the market was being artificially supported they would exterminate the Americans and go back to trading with the Hudson's Bay Company up north. Mitchell recognized this as Blackfoot pressure, routine business practice in this area of international trade, and was not impressed by the war paint and medicine songs. All this time he was translating blankets and turkey feathers and hawking bells for personal adornment, and powder and balls and scalping knives for a monopoly of the Flathead trade, into beaver and other furs and buffalo robes. Maximilian studied it with the absorption of the detached observer. He was everywhere, making his notes, and Bodmer was everywhere illustrating them.

On the evening of August 28 about twenty-five lodges were set up outside the fort. Upwards of a hundred and fifty Piegans, then, a band that had probably come in that day, had a fine time on American Fur Company alcohol with the dancing, singing, coup-counting, and ritualistic bragadoccio it inspired. They killed a regiment of enemies in pantomime and fell asleep. At dawn the next morning one of the post's hunters charged into Maximilian's room shouting '*Levez-vous, il faut nous battre!*' The former major general was going to see some Indian war. In his scientific eagerness he poured an additional charge into his already charged rifle. When he reached one of the corner blockhouses and fired it through a porthole at the melée, it kicked him back against the rear wall, whence he caromed off to roll on the floor.[8]

If this was extempore war it was nevertheless full-scale, and full-scale Indian war was uncommon, for the Indians did not like to practice it. Indians were warriors by profession but they made war for glory and for wealth. Preferably they traveled in small bands by stealth, tried to surprise an enemy who was in small force, made a single pass at him to get his horses, his equipment, and his scalp, to count their coups, and to get away. If the pass succeeded, fine; if it did not, they got out as fast as possible — better luck next time. An Indian calculated odds; if they did not seem greatly in his favor he waited till they got to be. The typical encounter with mountain men was a rush for the horses after an expert crawl right up to the herd, or the cornering of a small party of trappers by a whole band of Indians in exceedingly favorable circumstances, or best of all the ambushing of a single individual. Even in exceedingly favorable circumstances the Indians frequently failed to attack. Repeatedly two trappers held off bands of Indians till they had had enough and went away; sometimes a single trapper did. He could always take at least one Indian to hell with him and it might be as many as three if he had pistols. There was no percentage.

(The technique? Two trappers surrounded in open country took care always to have one rifle loaded. A solitary trapper simply kept his loaded rifle aimed at his surrounders without firing it. A good shot could count on a kill at a hundred yards — not with certainty at a longer range. Call seventy-five yards certain range for an Indian bow or not much more than fifty for a smoothbore musket. The Indian's job was to get the trapper's rifle discharged at him at something over a hundred yards, then run in to his own effective range and shoot before the trapper could reload. He had from twenty to thirty seconds in which to cover thirty or forty yards.) [9]

Some six hundred Assiniboins and Crees had caught the Blackfeet drunk and asleep. Indians, as we have said, were vocational fighters but also they were savages and they always lost their heads momentarily when surprised. Besides, these were Blackfeet and, as the Crows said, dumb. When Maximilian got to where he could see, their tipis had been cut to pieces, a lot of their women and children had been shot, and they were choking the corridor to the post which Culbertson had opened to them. At the onslaught they had run in circles and had tried to pick up some of their property before getting into the fort. So the Assiniboins had a field day. One of them grabbed Culbertson, who was trying to break the jam at the gate, and pulled him aside, killing the Piegan he was shoving in and yelling, 'Get out of my way, I'm after Blackfeet.' He wanted to make clear that this was not an attack on whites.

Mitchell had supposed it was and had lined up his engagés along the stockade to repel the charge. Most of them had privately sold their regular issue of powder to the Blackfeet and had to wait for a new issue from the magazine. Mitchell also issued it to his customers, who were making louder battle noises than the royal veteran of a world war had ever heard. A fighting Indian is a shrieking Indian and to the yells of the warriors in action were added the incantations of priests and of other warriors invoking their medicines before fighting, the wailing of already mourning squaws, and the ministrations of physicians who practiced traumatic surgery by means of songs and rattles. Dogs and horses in the quadrangle and the running about of miscellaneous Indians also helped out. The Assiniboins had pretty well cleaned out the encampment at their charge and accomplished little more after Culbertson got the gate closed. (This is the moment of Bodmer's magnificent picture, Plate XVI.) They shot one white man in the foot and wounded a horse and a dog. One of the engagés had killed an Assiniboin at eighty-six paces. The attackers presently withdrew some three hundred yards.[10]

Mitchell ordered cease fire as soon as he was sure that his fort was not the objective. (Though the Assiniboins traded at Fort Union, after all they were Company customers.) Some of the engagés had the frenzy of battle on them, however, and went out with the Blackfeet when they pulled themselves together. Remembering science again, Maximilian went with them to get the skull of the dead Assiniboin. The corpse had been scalped and the Blackfeet were shooting at it and their squaws beating it with clubs, paying special attention to the genitals. Blackfeet from the distant camps now began to arrive at the gallop. Nobody could have been more eager for war and glory, but they had broken down their horses on the way and could not catch up with the enemy, who were withdrawing. The first ethnologist of the Blackfeet admired their regalia and the innumerable objects which their medicines had directed them to wear for invulnerability in battle.[11] He observed their 'shouting, singing, and uttering their warwhoop' with the eye of a tactician. He also observed that of the fire-eaters who stormed into the fort for ammunition and the haranguing that was an indispensable preliminary to battle, a good many chose not to go out again and fight Assiniboins. A lot of them satiated their battle lust by shooting up the solitary dead enemy, who was 'now so pierced and burnt as scarcely to retain any semblance of the human form.'

One of the chiefs reproached Mitchell for holding back his men, called the whites cowards for not helping their unhappy friends, and threatened to break off McKenzie's treaty. (One of his colleagues, however, was lamenting that he did not have a piece of that medicine paper, for it would surely make him invulnerable.) The customer is always right and so Mitchell formed an American Fur Company detachment of light dragoons and led it off to the hills where, at extreme range, the Blackfoot and Assiniboin armies were now futilely belching at each other. He spent several hours there and succeeded in getting some action out of the Blackfeet but not much. He had a horse shot under him, so did Culbertson, they and their men did some damage, and the Assiniboins slowly fell back several miles to a grove beside the Marias River, whence they kept charging out at the Blackfeet whenever they saw a good chance. They were now outnumbered but had the Blackfeet cooled off, and after a morning of exposing his men while the Blackfoot deities advised discretion Mitchell came back to the fort. It was his turn to talk about cowardice. The battle lasted all day on these terms. The Assiniboins had used most of their powder by nightfall and moved away to the Bear Paw Mountains. The Blackfeet followed them at a judicious distance and next morning claimed to have killed another one. Score: perhaps six Assiniboins and forty Blackfeet killed, a good many more of at least the latter wounded.[12] Women and children count full value.

Some Blackfeet now loved the American Fur Company devotedly because Mitchell had fought for them. Others were hurt by his taunts and the usual alibi lodge was convened. Some tried to propitiate Mitchell, some the supernaturals who had obviously been angered. Maximilian, the major general, ascribed some part of the licking they had taken to their habit of firing their muskets without aiming them. He also criticized their sanitation. 'They never wash or cleanse the wounds, and the coagulated blood was still on them on the second day.' They let the wounded children lie on the ground, exposed to the burning-glass sun, till they died. And they killed some of their wounded by howling at them, jerking them about, and sounding bells and rattles in their ears to expel the demons. He helped Mitchell's men treat some of the wounded somewhat more sensibly and no doubt was gratified by one chief's assurance that the reason no Assiniboin had been able to hit him was the medicine invoked when Bodmer painted his picture the day before the battle. But on the whole Indian war had more interest for the ethnologist than for the military critic.

He stayed on through another uproar of Blackfoot customers quarreling with one another, threatening the Company, and practically laying siege to Fort McKenzie. For a while it looked as if Mitchell would have to massacre some of them if they delayed massacring one another, and he did have to send his horses away. This and the stories of Blackfoot wars with the Crows and the rumor that the Assiniboins were coming back were all data to Maximilian. But it was the first week of September, the ground was white with frost at daybreak, the crows and ducks and geese were flying south, and the music of locusts had begun. Time to be moving. He had hoped to spend the winter in the mountains but Mitchell would not assume responsibility for royalty in the Blackfoot country. There was nothing to do but to go back downriver. Mitchell had a mackinaw boat made for him and assigned him an experienced voyageur and a crew of three. He filled it with specimens of flora, fauna, and Blackfoot culture, said good-bye to Mitchell and Culbertson, and started down the Missouri on September 14.[13] He spent a month at Fort Union continuing his studies, enjoying the conversation of McKenzie and Hamilton, and paying frequent visits to the master mountain man, Robert Campbell, at his Opposition post. Then on October 20 he went on to Fort Clark, the Mandan post under James Kipp. Here he spent the winter and did his most valuable work for American ethnology. But this narrative can follow him no farther. He was a good man.

Meanwhile the Bonneville brigade under Joe Walker and its associated free trappers, whom we saw leaving the Green River rendezvous for California at the end of July, had been living myth, fable, and saga all together. About sixty of them had started for the coasts of illusion.[14] Some of them had previously traveled the country between the Snake and the Humboldt with Milton Sublette. They spoke of the Humboldt (which is the name Frémont gave it) as Ogden's River, after Peter Skene Ogden of the Hudson's Bay Company, who had named it Mary's River. They had the mountain man's accurate hearsay knowledge of that part of the trip. They had a similar but dustier knowledge of Jedediah Smith's trips across the Salt Desert, up and down California, and back. They knew how Ewing Young had traveled by the southern route and what he had found on the golden shore. That was enough knowledge for mountain men and there was no better partisan than Joe Walker. But do not, because it was blithe and careless, underrate the courage required for this plunge into country which none of them had ever seen, which few white men had ever seen, large parts of which no one had seen, and across which they would have to blaze their trail.

They went to Great Salt Lake, probably by the familiar route down Bear River, killed buffalo and dried sixty pounds of meat apiece. Then they turned their faces into the west wind and followed them. They must either have gone to Bear Lake and taken a line toward the Humboldt from there or else moved straight west from the north end of Great Salt Lake, say by way of the Raft River Mountains. For they missed the Great Salt Desert which Jedediah Smith had traveled, the worst of all American wasteland.[15]

Soon after reaching the Humboldt they began to experience an annoyance that was to give them a bad name in history. There were few beaver in those parts, since the Hudson's Bay Company had cleaned out the originally sparse stock, and they needed what they could get, as well for food as to pay their way. The traps they set disappeared so regularly that soon they had to give up trapping. (Traps were usually not company equipment; they belonged to the trapper and cost him from ten to twenty dollars, St. Louis.) Metal-covetous Diggers were getting them and presently these pint-size, degraded Indians began to skulk along the route. Individually, in the open, and with your eyes on them, Diggers were the most harmless of living creatures. They were such Indians as could exist in this desert: living without shelter or in sagebrush huts, feeding on whatever was at hand, the carp and suckers of alkali-tinctured streams, sunflower seeds and the bulbs and roots of desert plants, piñon nuts, grasshoppers and black crickets and the grubs of seasonal flies that breed in alkali pools. They had few clothes and such as they had were mainly made of woven grass — though Leonard saw some who had amassed some beaver and one who was wearing a beaver robe.[16] Many of them, in fact, had no way of making fire and had to do without it for long periods. They had only the most rudimentary artifacts. In most respects they were quite unlike the tribes from which they had degenerated and which had crowded them out of competition. Mark Twain, describing himself as a worshiper of Cooper Indians, said that the Diggers nauseated him, called them 'treacherous, filthy, and repulsive,' and decided that they and the Australian bushmen must have descended from 'the selfsame gorilla or kangaroo or Norway rat.' Everybody found them repulsive — and noisome, tick-ridden, and lousy as well. Why not? Theirs was the most miserable life lived in North America since the ice retreated.[17]

But if the Diggers were contemptible individually and in the open, they were dangerous in numbers and by night. Walker was parading before them the wealth of Ophir and Cathay: dogs and two hundred-odd horses and mules that could be eaten, besides the incredible, the intoxicating equipment of the white man. The dispossessed beheld riches and the starving bounty. They swarmed by the hundred and if he had let them come near his camp, he and his party would have been massacred. Also, if the Diggers had got their horses they would have starved. He had to keep them away. He had his men kill ducks and riddle targets before their eyes, to show what his armament could do. No use; in hundreds they kept insisting on coming in. So Walker loosed his men on them and had thirty or forty of them killed. It is hard to see what else he could have done. Some of his men who had killed no Indians before enjoyed this cheap victory and that is repulsive. But it does not diminish the fact that Walker's action was necessary. It worked; the Diggers now kept their distance.

The massacre occurred near Humboldt Sink. Walker led his men to Carson Lake and on to the Sierra. He now faced what is, historically, the worst passage in our westering. The going had been hard ever since Great Salt Lake; here it became shocking. No one need say more than that these mountain men required over three weeks to force the Sierra. It is equally significant that some of the pork-eaters despaired on the way and wanted to turn back. They were soon silenced: Joe Walker was in command. Broken-down horses died and were eaten; others had to be killed for food. Walker had come up by way of the lake now named for him and he finally found a practicable way down to the headwaters of Merced River.[18] Much of this passage was in the geography of fable and it rose to a climax when he led his men to the edge of a chasm from the dark side of the moon: they were the first white men who ever saw the Yosemite. Also he laid down in his brain and nerves a deposit of recognition, reference, and savvy that later on was to save two emigrant parties directly and innumerable ones by indirection. Joe Walker was preparing the future of his countrymen.

History was winding another coil round the national core as this gang of sixty mountain men, half starved as all travelers of the Sierra would be for a long time to come, came down from the October snow-blocked gulches of the high sierra to the climate of the Happy Isles. Another bead had been added to a lengthening string, and the westering energy of the American people had caught up with Jedediah Smith. The boys had acorns to eat now, the giant acorns harvested by the somewhat more developed Diggers who lived here and whom Joe did not slaughter. They went down to lower slopes where the great woods were full of deer and bear, so they could feed like mountain men again and like mountain men lament that there were no buffalo. Then they reached the great valley of the San Joaquin, partly civilized Indians who spoke the word 'Spanish' and pointed west, herds of branded horses, and finally an acceptable substitute for buffalo, the fat longhorns of California that had developed so differently from the scrubs of the Texas chapparal. Then on the night before the great shower of Leonids by which so many events of this year can be dated, they heard a strange noise. It startled them for they could not identify it, though some thought it might be the California earthquakes that had already got Paradise libelled. But Joe Walker knew what it was. He had led his men within sound of the Pacific.

They followed the San Joaquin to San Francisco Bay the next morning, November 13, 1833, and had reached the end of the West. Thinking it time to find some Mexicans, they struck southeastward to the lower arm of the bay, followed its eastern shore, and finally crossed to the open beach. And here they closed the circle and brought together the two nationalizing energies of the West. For a ship was anchored offshore, it sent its boats when they waved a blanket, and Joe Walker's overland adventurers were rowed out to the California trader *Lagoda*, Captain Bradshaw, out of Boston.

Bradshaw broached a keg of California brandy and he and his ship's company feasted their bearded countrymen, who feasted them turn and turn about for some days. Presently Bradshaw sailed away, promising to meet them at Monterey, that sleepy, delightful handful of mud hovels whose literary charm has lasted to our day. After they had made some moccasins and breeches they too started out for Monterey. But on the way there they reached the fifteenth California mission, the largest and perhaps the most celebrated, San Juan Bautista. Here were great farms and orchards and vineyards, workships and wells and flower gardens, a high altar of old redwood, Indian carving and Mexican painted saints, olive presses and storehouses of wine and brandy, and Franciscan friars who were more pleased to have these guests than a feeling for history would have justified. Why go farther? They settled down to spend the winter in this summer isle.

We know little about that winter. But we know what California life was at this time, which is the period of cloudy dream and slow decay, with the practically independent province in its waning afternoon, the shadow coming on as the little cliques formed and such omens as Ewing Young and Joe Walker appeared out of the east. If not for the mission Indians (whose lot may be too easily pitied), it was for white men one of the most delightful ways of life the world has ever known. These Californians were a feckless, indolent people: their habitat permitted them to be. None except the Indian peons worked hard, they contrived not to exhaust themselves, and few others had to work at all. They lived outdoors and on horseback. The goodness of the earth and the fruits thereof were theirs for the taking, could be taken without effort, and could never be exhausted. Almost uncountable herds of horses and cattle increased geometrically with only the most casual supervision. One of the first lessons Walker's men learned was that persons who had taken their horses — always punishable with death on the American frontier — had not stolen them. There were horses for everyone: take what you want.

They helped their new friends break horses (in a manner of speaking), butcher cattle for the hide and tallow trade, ride after and slaughter some absconding Indians. They joined the continuous fiestas and competed with their hosts, easily beating them at marksmanship and taking an equally offhand beating at every form of horsemanship. They found a native sport to their taste, baiting bears with bulls from the ranchos. They ate the simple, highly spiced fare (mostly beef and beans) of the commonalty and the banquets of the Franciscans. The California women, Joe Meek says, 'were well formed, with languishing eyes and soft voice.' It was Taos all over again but increased and with a more complaisant public opinion, for the California climate diminished the prudery of even Mexican husbands.

One of these girls embellishes the chapter which Frederick

Ruxton gives to a raid on California by mountain men, including Joe Walker, in his novel which is nine-tenths history. (*Life in the Far West*, already quoted several times.) She is Juanita, 'a stout wench from Sonora, of Mexican blood, hardly as dark as the other women who surrounded her, and with a drop or two of the old Spanish blood struggling with the darker Indian tint to color her plump cheeks. An *enagua* (a short petticoat) of red serge was confined round her waist by a gay band ornamented with beads, and a chemisette covered the upper part of the body, permitting, however, a prodigal display of her charms.' Juanita has seen Americanos in Sonora and is not alarmed when word comes that fourteen mountain men have invaded California in force: 'They're fine fellows, very tall, and as white as the snow of the sierras. Let them come, say I.' Her anticipation is justified and she rides back over the Sierra with Ned Wooton, being duly married to him by Fray Augustin of the mission. As for her sisters, Ruxton says with a straight face that no mountain man ever offended the modesty of a woman but adds that the pressure of time might occasionally require them to lasso a California beauty 'should the obdurate parents refuse consent to an immediate union.' By the record, the beauty herself seldom refused.

Ruxton makes a charming story of his raid, which has elements of Ewing Young's and other invasions and is set not at San Juan but at San Fernando Rey de España, the seventeenth mission, near Burbank. He has the already mentioned Fray Augustin with a household of Mexican and halfbreed nieces and nephews, an ancient hidalgo named Don Antonio Velez Trueba, and a representative selection of friars, Indians, and villagers. His raiders include the historical LaBonté and Markhead as well as Joe Walker and his semi-historical hero Killbuck. Much of his action, including the massacre of Diggers, is from Walker's journey and he tells an incident of the Sierra starvation, a story that is rumor in the annals. According to this yarn some Indians who had declared a prairie truce with Joe Walker got compensation for his annual reduction of their tribe by giving him a feast which included a meat course that was unidentifiable till it turned out to be one of his companions, lately killed. Alfred Jacob Miller, who in 1837 painted Joe with one of his seasonal squaws (see Plate LXXXI), was among a sizable number who heard that Joe was the protagonist of this vomitory tale.[19] (Miller sagaciously refrained from asking him if it were true.) Ruxton gets a great deal of charm into his account of the raid, and his pictures of the alarmed Californians and of the mountain men sitting cross-legged on the mission floor are exact. ('Wagh!' says Killbuck, refusing a chair, 'this coon ain't hamshot anyhow and don't want such fixin's, he don't.') Once the respective honors of invaded and invaders have been satisfied, they all turn to and drink the mission wines and brandies served them by 'the houris of Paradise' till Mexico and the United States are enraptured with each other. Walker takes over the mission before he passes out and orders Fray Augustin and the Don hobbled lest they recover first. Next day he and his men select some four hundred of the best horses and drive them off toward the mountains. Fray Augustin is 'glad to get rid of such unscrupulous guests,' but Don Antonio is 'loth to part with his boon companions' and invites them to visit his ancestral estate when they go to Spain.[20]

Ruxton's historical models stayed on at San Juan till the middle of January, when various reasons, the jealousy of husbands no doubt among them, made it wise to move camp farther from the villages till late spring should open the passes. Meanwhile Walker had taken a couple of his men to Monterey, called on the authorities there, and had another rousing party with Captain Bradshaw. The Governor, who understood the needs of his province, offered Joe a tract of forty-nine square miles, Joe to choose the location, if he would settle permanently in California and bring in fifty mechanics. Joe declined, though he was, Leonard says, 'well pleased with the country.' No doubt he could quickly make a fortune there but 'his love for the laws of the United States and his hatred for those of the Spanish Government' urged him away — he must have been sober at some Fourth of July celebration. But some of his men thought otherwise. In the Santa Clara Valley and at Monterey it was easy to remember the temperature of mountain streams, the prices the companies asked for liquor and tobacco, the desert of the Red Buttes and similar stretches where you would have to eat your moccasins if the buffalo chanced to be elsewhere, and Blackfeet who had not been missionized screaming at daybreak and lodging an arrow in your pardner's throat. Besides being mountain men some of them were such mechanics as the Californians wanted, 'carpenters, hatters, &c.' While drinking the mission wines and singing with Juanita to guitars they had picked up easy cash as practicing handy men. 'A rough table (more like a bench) consisting of rough hewn boards nailed together will cost 8 and 10 dollars. A pair of similar made bedsteads the same.' Two of them had made a windmill which brought them a hundred and ten dollars or the equivalent.

So George Nidever and five others decided that beaver wouldn't shine. They wanted to stay on in this soft spring, this recurrent fandango. They added themselves to the gradual increment of Americans and Englishmen who supplied a catalyst for the plans of the War Department and the visions of John Charles Frémont. There were a few retired mountain men here already, strays from Ewing Young's and the Hudson's Bay Company brigades, perhaps from unrecorded ventures out of Taos too. Like deserters from the hide ships they were doing well for themselves and they set a model for Walker's six deserters: put on sombreros and velvet breeches, learn to use a lasso, and marry into the cattle aristocracy.

Walker was going back more or less by the trail he had blazed. Some of the free trappers who had come with him wanted to see more of the world — naturally one of them was Joe Meek. So they headed south and detoured round the mountains to the Colorado River: the route of Ewing Young, of the California-Sonora and California-Mexico City communications, and in part of the Old Spanish Trail. They followed the Colorado to Bill Williams Fork. (Mohave County, Arizona.) Here they were astonished to meet Fraeb's brigade which had come this far after wintering in the Green River country. Both parties (if the story is true: no one but Joe Meek has ever testified to it) had made fantastically long and laborious journeys even for mountain men. Meek signed up with his old employers but, he says, refused to help them when they perpetrated an atrocious massacre of the peaceful, civilized Hopis. Then with Kit Carson and others he crossed the Sangre de Cristo Mountains and ranged out into the plains east of the Front Range. In the course of this trip Joe's party had the daylong battle with the Comanches which Kit Carson's autobiography also describes. After winning it, they moved toward Green River, taking in Middle Park and South Park and moving on to Bear River before heading toward the rendezvous of 1834. A scrutiny of the map will show that Joe Meek had seen some territory in the last year.

Joe Walker took his band back over the Sierra.[21] He had traded part or all of his meager beaver catch to the padres and had three hundred and fifteen horses, forty-seven beef cattle, forty dogs (K Ration), and a replenished stock of powder. Also plenty of mission brandy. He tried to find easier going than his westward crossing had revealed and, heading south of his outward bound trail, struck the headwaters of Kern Rivers and found the pass across the divide that has borne his name ever since. This was indeed an easier crossing, though in part because the snows had receded. But the desert east of the mountains was no softer than it had been farther north. The stock began to die of thirst and the men drank their blood as they did so. The dogs 'would approach the men, look them right in the face with the countenances of a distracted person, and . . . would commence a piteous and lamentable howl, drop down, and expire.' But Joe got his men through and angled toward his old trail along the Humboldt. The Diggers came swarming again, again Joe did his utmost to keep them away without bloodshed, and again he had to turn his men loose. They 'fell on the Indians in the wildest and most ferocious manner,' Leonard says, rode them down, killed and scalped fourteen, and thereafter were left alone.

Thereafter too it was a commonplace story, the traverse of a desert by expert travelers. It was July 14 when at last they rejoined Bonneville on Bear River. The boys scattered among the campfires to begin their yarns about the sunken Lyonesse they had seen. And Joe Walker had to tell his commander that the experiment in shooting the moon had failed altogether. No beaver; his backers' money lost. Bald Head was not cheered. He was so bitter about Joe Walker that Washington Irving, seeing him through Bonneville's eyes, never realized that Joe had performed offhand one of the prodigies of Western history.

Also he had increased the potential that a few years later would be called Manifest Destiny.

# « VII »

# THE WINTER LODGE

IT WAS BAD TO TELL the tales in summer, old Red Water informed Francis Parkman, up in the Laramie Mountains of Wyoming where Whirlwind's village of Oglala Sioux had made their hunting camp. If he should sit down to tell stories before the frost began, the young men going out on war parties would be killed. But one afternoon while the skirt of the lodge was turned up to catch the breeze and the camp slept in still heat, the old man fell to remembering the first time he had ever seen white people.

It was when he was a boy. He and three or four others set out to hunt beaver. But he was by himself when he found a beaver house. He wanted to see what it was like and so he had to dive down to the tunnel entrance under the water and then crawl a long way till he came out under the dome. It was dark and close and little Red Water was tired. He slept or fainted. When he woke in the darkness again he could hear the voices of his companions far away, singing a death song — a death song for him. But also he could dimly see a man and two women sitting at the edge of a forest pool.[1] They were white people and their paleness frightened him. So with great difficulty he made his way out to daylight again. He went straight to the place above that pool of water. He beat a hole in the ground with his war club and sat down to watch it. Soon the nose of an old male beaver appeared in the hole. Red Water dragged him out, and two female beavers came up through the hole and he took them too.

The beaver were the white people he had seen. And Red Water knew that this was right. For, he remarked to Parkman, beavers and the whites were the wisest people on earth: they must be the same species.

In the Indian bestiary all animals were wise and had supernatural powers but the beaver was always among the most sagacious. The religious rituals for taking him were very complicated. The wilderness mind of the white trappers might also call on magic to assist the hunt when it was going badly, and not a few regularly invoked amulets or incantations when they set their traps. They too knew that the beaver was very wise — and their job was to outthink him.

Part of the trapper's skill was to know the habits of beaver, to recognize likely sign, and to decide the right places to set his traps. A brigade making a hunt broke up into small parties which normally worked by themselves for several days at a time, splitting further into twos and threes for the actual trapping. They worked the streams and we must think of them mostly in mountain meadows or similar flats where the streams were slow enough to be dammed. Late in the afternoon, 'between sunset and dark' was the usual time to set traps. In some secrecy. For, says Osborne Russell, one of our best annalists, 'it was not good policy for a trapper to let too many know where he intended to set his traps' — plews were valuable. Normally they worked upstream, because sign of other trappers or of Indians might come downstream and because the country grew safer as you moved higher. With the incessant cognition of electronics, the trapper's mind was receiving and recording impressions all the time. He hunted beaver, read the country, recorded his route, watched for hostiles, and planned for all eventualities — in a simultaneous sentience.

The beaver had built his house of small branches, with a five-inch plastering of mud for roof and outer walls, on the edge of the pool his dam had created. It was perhaps six feet high and twice as broad. In the middle of the earth floor was such a pool as young Red Water had seen. There were in fact two such pools, sometimes more than two; they were the exits of the tunnels which had been dug down through the earth to the stream bed above the dam. There, weighted down with mud and water-logged snags, was the winter hoard of saplings and branches whose bark was the beaver's food. Before the Indians learned to use traps they were accustomed to hunt by blocking these tunnels, chopping through the roof of the house, and then digging out the beaver.

The white man set his traps at the natural runways of the

beaver, just inside the water where a path came down from the bank or the dam or where the slide entered the pool. That was when he expected to take the beaver on its lawful occasions. Mostly, however, he baited the traps and set them in places favorable for attracting the beaver and for drowning him when caught. The bait was a musky secretion taken from the beaver's preputial glands. It was used straight or doctored with other odorous substances in whose efficacy the trapper believed. He called it 'medicine,' 'castoreum,' or the like and carried it in a plugged horn bottle at his belt. (It perfumed him, vocationally.) Selecting the proper place for his trap, he set it in water of the proper depth and drove a stout, dry 'trap pole' through the ring at the end of the five-foot steel chain into the bank or bed of the stream. This was to keep the beaver from dragging the trap (which weighed at least five pounds) out on the ground and into the air, for if he did so he would escape by gnawing off the paw by which he had been caught. He was killed, that is, by drowning. Sometimes his struggles unmoored the trap but too late; in that event the pole or a separate 'float stick' that had been attached would show where the carcass was. When every other preparation had been made, the trapper smeared a little of the pungent castoreum on a twig or willow which he arched just above the surface directly over the trap's trigger. The scent attracted the beaver — a dog owner will think of his pet's behavior when there is a bitch in heat in the same block — and when he approached the bait stick he was caught by the foot.

All this was subject to infinite variations, the adaptation to circumstance that is a large part of skill. It was all conducted in the water too, for the man scent had to be eliminated. The trapper waded into the stream at a sufficient distance from the selected place, carrying the already set trap, and after he had sited and baited it he waded a sufficient distance before leaving the stream. He splashed water over his own trail and took many other precautions.

Normally the traps were raised at sunrise or before, in the dimness that was both most dangerous and most secure. A full-grown beaver weighs thirty to sixty pounds and the pelt a pound and a half or two pounds when finally prepared. The catch was usually skinned on the spot and the trapper, whose line was five or six traps, took the pelt and the medicine glands back to camp. (Camp was never in the same place two nights straight.) He usually took the tail too for it was considered a delicacy when charred in the fire to remove the horny skin and then boiled

At camp the pelt had to be rough-cured. The flesh side was scraped free of tissue and sinew and then the hide was stretched on a frame of willow like an embroidery hoop and given the sun for a day or two. When it was dry it was folded with the fur inside and marked with the trapper's or the company's symbol. When 'packs' were made they were pressed into compact bales of about a hundred pounds at the posts by machines made for the purpose or at rendezvous by rigged-up contraptions of logs and stones.

All this was work for the swampers or camp-tenders in company brigades. The free trapper had to prepare his plews himself unless he had a wife or there was a village of Indians at hand where he could hire a squaw. Care of the catch from here on was, like everything else in mountain life, an individual responsibility. It involved keeping the pelts dry, drying them promptly if they got wet, and perpetually safeguarding them on the trail. At lower altitudes they had to be periodically beaten and aired but there were no moths in the mountains.

Trapping was complicated by high water during the spring hunt, which produced the best furs. Spring or fall it was conducted in the water of mountain streams, and the mountain man's occupational disease was rheumatism. His joints creaked and he will be seen at dawn limbering his legs and arms at the fire. The water got colder as the days shortened and the blue of canyon shadows deepened. Before the end of September there would be a dust of snow in the basins and mountain meadows. The brigades moved down to the bench lands and on toward the plains. Ice formed along the edges of even the swiftest streams and trapping would seldom last anywhere later than early November. Time to think of wintering.

* * *

Skill develops from controlled, corrected repetitions of an act for which one has some knack. Skill is a product of experience and criticism and intelligence. Analysis cannot much transcend those truisms. Between the amateur and the professional, between the duffer and the expert, between the novice and the veteran there is a difference not only in degree but in kind. The skillful man is, within the function of his skill, a different integration, a different nervous and muscular and psychological organization. He has specialized responses of great intricacy. His associative faculties have patterns of screening, acceptance and rejection, analysis and sifting, evaluation and selective adjustment much too complex for conscious direction. Yet as the patterns of appraisal and adjustment exert their automatic and perhaps metabolic energy, they are accompanied by a conscious process fully as complex. A tennis player or a watchmaker or an airplane pilot is an automatism but he is also criticism and wisdom.

It is hardly too much to say that a mountain man's life was skill. He not only worked in the wilderness, he also lived there and he did so from sun to sun by the exercise of total skill. It was probably as intricate a skill as any ever developed by any way of working or living anywhere. Certainly it was the most complex of the wilderness crafts practiced on this continent. The mountains, the aridity, the distances, and the climates imposed severities far greater than those laid on forest-runners, rivermen, or any other of our symbolic pioneers. Mountain craft developed out of the crafts which earlier pioneers had acquired and, like its predecessors, incorporated Indian crafts, but it had a unique integration of its own. It had specific crafts, technologies, theorems and rationales and rules of thumb, codes of operating procedure — but it was a pattern of total behavior.

Treatises could be written on the specific details; we lack space even for generalizations. Why do you follow the ridges into or out of unfamiliar country? What do you do for a companion who has collapsed from want of water while crossing a desert? How do you get meat when you find yourself without gunpowder in a country barren of game? What tribe of Indians made this trail, how many were in the band, what errand were they on, were they going to or coming back from it, how far from home were they, were their horses laden, how many horses did they have and why, how many squaws accompanied them, what mood were they in? Also, how old is the trail, where are those Indians now, and what does the product of these answers require of you? Prodigies of such sign-reading are recorded by impressed greenhorns, travelers, and army men, and the exercise of critical reference and deduction which they exhibit would seem prodigious if it were not routine. But reading formal sign, however impressive to Doctor Watson or Captain Frémont, is less impressive than the interpretation of observed circumstances too minute to be called sign. A branch floats down a stream — is this natural, or the work of animals, or of Indians or trappers? Another branch or a bush or even a pebble is out of place — why? On the limits of the plain, blurred by heat mirage, or against the gloom of distant cottonwoods, or across an angle of sky between branches or where hill and mountain meet, there is a tenth of a second of what may have been movement — did men or animals make it, and, if animals, why? Buffalo are moving downwind, an elk is in an unlikely place or posture, too many magpies are hollering, a wolf's howl is off key — what does it mean?

Such minutiae could be extended indefinitely. As the trapper's mind is dealing with them, it is simultaneously performing a still more complex judgment on the countryside, the route across it, and the weather. It is recording the immediate details in relation to the remembered and the forecast. A ten-mile traverse is in relation to a goal a hundred miles, or five hundred miles, away: there are economies of time, effort, comfort, and horseflesh on any of which success or even survival may depend. Modify the reading further, in relation to season, to Indians, to what has happened. Modify it again in relation to stream flow, storms past, storms indicated. Again in relation to the meat supply. To the state of the grass. To the equipment on hand. . . . You are two thousand miles from depots of supply and from help in time of trouble.

All this (with much more) is a continuous reference and checking along the margin or in the background of the trapper's consciousness while he practices his crafts as hunter, wrangler, furrier, freighter, tanner, cordwainer, smith, gunmaker, dowser, merchant. The result is a high-level integration of faculties. The mountain man had mastered his conditions — how well is apparent as soon as soldiers, goldseekers, or emigrants come into his country and suffer where he has lived comfortably and die where he has been in no danger. He had no faculties or intelligence that the soldier or the goldseeker lacked; he had none that you and I lack. He had only skill. A skill so effective that, living in an Indian country, he made a more successful adaptation to it than the Indian — and this without reference to his superior material equipment. There was no craft and no skill at which the mountain man did not come to excel the Indian. He saw, smelled, and heard just as far and no farther. But there is something after all in the laborious accretion that convolutes the forebrain and increases the cultural heritage, for he made more of it.

* * *

As the snow — and the game — came farther down the mountainsides, the trappers prepared for winter. Free trappers were welcome at the fixed posts, which would receive them up to the limit of accommodations and extend their courtesies to the overflow who had to camp near-by. This had the merits of readily available supplies, a basic store of food in bitter weather, co-operation in hunting meat, and variegated companionship. It had disadvantages too; large horse herds were an even harder problem than small ones, large meat hunts required long expeditions, and the winter of the plains where the posts were located was more severe than that of the mountain basins. As the years passed trappers set up winter posts of their own. Jim Beckwourth built one at what is now Pueblo, Colorado, there came to be others in or near the Front Range, and a species of institutional wintering developed at them.[2]

The commoner practice of free trappers and the invariable custom of the company brigades, however, was to winter in the mountains. This necessitated finding a favorable campsite. It must have as mild weather as possible, plenty of wood and forage, and abundant game. The answer was some sheltered valley head in the lee of prevailing winds, with wooded streams, a south slope so that the snow would blow away from the suncured bunch grass, preferably with wintering buffalo and with forested mountainsides where other game would be found. We have seen Bonneville, the RMF Company, and the American Fur Company wintering in such valleys along the Salmon and Bear River and in Cache Valley (Utah). Brown's Hole came to attract small parties and South Park became a kind of winter paradise — both are in Colorado. Jim Bridger eventually built his trading post on Black's Fork, the southwestern corner of Wyoming, in a basin where he had wintered with the RMF Company. Such valleys, which were frequently intervales, had gentler weather than the higher altitudes and the lower plains. Habitués of Sun Valley will understand why.

Cottonwoods or evergreen groves would shelter the stock during storms. The trappers built cabins or lived in tipis, for tipis were admirable winter dwellings. (They were admirable dwellings at any season.) These were sited with regard to sun and wind and water and might have accessory structures for storage. Bands or even villages of friendly Indians — Nez Perces, Flatheads, Snakes — were encouraged to winter with the whites or near-by. They and their horses increased the problems of supply but they were interesting neighbors, they were valuable for defense, and their women could be hired to do most of the winter work.

Much of this had to do with tailoring. We have seen that

the mountain man preferred wool clothing when he could get it but probably he had little that was still serviceable when winter came. If he had worn skin breeches, he had stagged them at the knees and sewn on legs of blanketing which would not shrink intolerably when they dried. But now he or his wife or his customs tailor would have to make entire outfits, moccasins, leggings, breeches, shirts, caps, mittens, robes. Many skins, dressed free of hair, were used regularly: doe, buck, antelope, bighorn, elk, even rabbit skin. Each had its specific uses, advantages, and drawbacks. Robes, either with or without the hair, were made from many of the same skins and from such others as beaver (very expensive, of course), wolf, or even rockchuck. Buffalo hides had innumerable uses. The hides obtained in summer and fall hunts were tanned for tipis, bags, the carryalls called parfleches,[3] containers of many kinds, rawhide in all its forms. But the robes used for winter wear, for bedclothes and bed covering, and for winter moccasins, were made of hides taken in the winter, when the hair was thickest. Moccasins were also made of many other skins, for many purposes, in many patterns. For winter they might be fur-lined like those just mentioned, or, if not, might be stuffed with loose hair or even leaves or sagebrush bark. Women's moccasins were more likely than men's to have knee-length leggings sewed to them. For both sexes the elaborately quilted or beaded moccasins displayed by museums were ceremonial or Sunday-best shoes rather than daily wear. The ordinary work shoe was made in quantity, for it was not a durable article. Trappers, who preferred to buy them but frequently had to make their own, did a large traffic in them with the squaws at a few cents per pair. Those of the Plains tribes usually had parfleche soles, for the unsoled ones of the forest tribes would not turn cactus.[4]

For moccasins and the leggings which both Indians and trappers wore, usually to the hip, the best material was last year's tipi. New lodges were made annually — with much ceremony, by squaws who had ritualistic training and collected fees — and the skins of the old ones were saved for clothing. They had had a year's smoking from the daily fire and so dried smooth and without stretching. The squaws kept a stock of rolled skins of all kinds which had been tanned when taken. (Winter was the best time for tanning since cold and lack of sunlight would lengthen the process.)[5]

Stormbound days and long evenings made it the best time for dressmaking too, and your wife and those of your Indian neighbors were forever busy with their rolled skins, awls, and sinews. (The various animal sinews, especially those of the buffalo, were the Indian's thread. Splitting them for size was a task of exquisite skill. Those taken from different parts of the body had different properties which gave them specific uses.) They made your garments, their own, and a surplus for trade. The squaws had been trained in sewing from early childhood and any museum will show the fineness of their work. This was also a time for embroidery and decoration. Beads, porcupine quills, various bird quills, grasses, paints, ermine tails, fringes of other fine furs, small animal and bird bones, bits of metal, bells, braided hair, various fleeces and feathers — such materials filled the squaw's workbasket which she had repacked at every move throughout the year. She worked in traditions of art and craft that were old and very rigid. Religious rituals were part of her task; so were certain social obligations to older women who had either taught her skills or sold her the proprietary right to use them. Some specialized tasks or some steps in ordinary ones might be forbidden her; these she would have to have performed by women who had the right, with accompanying fees and feasts. But she was a skilled artisan and a happy one. She sang, chattered, made jokes, and marriage never looked better to a bachelor than when he saw a pardner's squaw sewing.

Winter was a preserving season for women and to some extent for trappers. For example, it was a good time to make pemmican, the best of all concentrated foods. The 'winter pemmican' of the literature, which is sometimes spoken of unfavorably, was made not in winter but following the fall hunt, when the weather was likely to be unsettled and thorough drying difficult, so that the product might turn sour. 'Summer pemmican,' the Grade A stuff, was made in late winter and early spring. The meat, almost but not quite exclusively buffalo meat, was first dried in the way always used by trappers and Indians whenever they had a surplus following a hunt. It was cut into slices and strips an inch or so thick, scored crisscross, and spread out on racks of cottonwood poles high enough to keep it from dogs, wolves, and vermin. Not so much the sun as the wind dried it and the process, which winter cold did not affect, took four or five days. It could be shortened to three days if during the first one a slow, smoky fire was maintained under the frame, and such smoking made the product sweeter and tastier. The result was the universal dried meat, jerky or *charqui*, of the literature, a first-rate food in itself. It was always carried by trapping parties.[6]

Pemmican, however, was in a class by itself. All the gristles and sinews that might be present in jerky were removed and the residue was pounded in a mortar or on a parfleche till it was pulverized. This powder was loosely packed in a parfleche bag, melted fat was poured over it, and the mouth of the bag was sewed up. Thus packed, pemmican would keep for years. It was a splendid high-energy food, a complete diet in itself. It was also a great treat (some cynics dissenting), incomparably richer and more flavorsome than jerky. It could be eaten uncooked or fried, roasted, or boiled, by itself or in combination with anything you had on hand. The luxury article was 'berry pemmican,' into which pulverized dried fruits of any available kind had been mixed, most often wild cherries with their stones.[7]

Fats were preserved separately. The boiled and refined 'tallow' that played an important part in the Canadian trade served all the uses of butter. Like pemmican, it was sewn up in bags of standard size and weight. The most abundant buffalo fat was that which lay along the back. When sun-dried it was a gourmet's delicacy. It was also slowly fire-dried, cut up into sticks, and wrapped, or it was dried after being boiled; in these forms it was a staple rather than a treat. Kidney fat, if not eaten raw, was dried in long slices or briefly boiled. Tribes which raised or bought corn used kidney fat in a favorite tidbit, softening it over the fire and then pounding it and the corn together in a mortar.

Squaws were good cooks and the Indian diet, which the wintering trapper took over entire when he had a wife or lived among Indians, was by no means so sparse or monotonous as the books say, if the camp was in good country. Its basis was the pot of meat which was always stewing over the fire in the middle of the lodge and a portion of which was set before every visitor as soon as he entered. (Indians had no fixed hours for meals; they and the trappers ate when they were hungry.) This was replenished with whatever fresh-killed meat came in. Roasted and boiled, baked in kettles or the ground, other meat dishes were standard. All were flavored with herbs, roots, leaves, and grasses which the squaws dried and whose properties they knew. The edible roots already mentioned were prepared in various ways. Roots, leaves, and buds that made good salads could be found under the snow.[8] In short, trappers and Indians lived high when food was abundant, and winter camps were pitched in places where it was expected to be abundant.

Protracted storms or the migration of game would produce

shortages. And hunting was a daily job. The boys ranged through the woods, hillsides, and plains, usually on snowshoes. If the snow was too soft or deep for horses, they had to carry their take on their backs. There were problems of keeping the surplus from wolves. If the meat could be hung in trees it was safe from them but not from animals that could climb. Russell tells of burying some under three feet of snow and burning gunpowder on top to add another deterrent to the man-scent, but it did not work. No device worked for very long.

Protecting the meat from large or small vermin was a constant problem, winter or summer, in camp or on the trail. From porcupines to grizzlies the entire fauna liked to have their meals killed for them, as the modern camper knows. The modern camper, however, seldom if ever is troubled by the most skillful of all thieves, the wolverine. This pest is not considered by modern students to have any extraordinary animal intelligence.[9] But they could not have convinced the mountain men. To them the 'carcajou' was literally demoniac: he had an infernal ancestry. He would even steal beavers from traps and he regularly made a bloody garbage of the winter trap line that was run for fine furs. No cache of meat was safe from him and he did not work on shares. Few ever saw him, so his supposed size varies in the annals. Our painter, Alfred Miller, who claims to have seen one, makes him the size of a St. Bernard dog, which is too big, and adds that his body was shaped like a panther.[10] Osborne Russell saw one at work. Russell had killed a couple of bighorns for meat. He took some cuts back to camp and hung the rest in a tree. Next morning he went back for it and found a wolverine at the foot of the tree. 'He had left nothing behind worth stopping for,' Russell says. 'All the traces of the sheep I could find were some tufts of hair scattered about the snow. I hunted around for some time but to no purpose. In the meantime the cautious thief was sitting on the snow at some distance, watching my movements as if he was confident I had no gun and could not find his meat and wished to aggravate me by his antics. He had made roads in every direction from the foot of the tree, dug holes in the snow in a hundred places, apparently to deceive me.'

Russell conceded that 'a wolverine had fooled a Yankee,' but halfbreeds and voyageurs had a different explanation: Ruxton reports them as believing that the carcajou was 'a cross between the devil and a bear.' Ruxton's companion in Colorado, a Canadian, said that he had once fought with one for upwards of two hours and had 'fired a pouchful of balls into the animal's body, which spat them out as fast as they were shot in.' Later when Ruxton drew a bead on one the Canuck shouted so loud that he missed; in fact, he missed with both barrels of his rifle, and his companion refused to let him waste more powder. If he had shot fifty balls, 'he not scare a damn.'

* * *

Some years before Miles Goodyear established a species of ranch on the eventual site of Ogden, Utah, Osborne Russell's small party of trappers wintered there with some halfbreeds and some Snakes for neighbors. A Canadian who had a Flathead wife invited the bachelor Russell to join his lodge and Russell was glad to do so, for the woman was a good housekeeper. He instances their Christmas dinner. They had stewed elk and boiled deer meat (not 'venison,' Russell says, calling that a greenhorn's word). The Flathead had hoarded some sugar, which was rare, and some flour, which if it was wheat flour and not a meal made of roots, was priceless. She made cakes and a pudding, tricking out the latter with a sauce of dried berries. There were six gallons of coffee with the sweetenin' boiled into it and 'tin cups and pans to drink out of, large chips or pieces of bark supplying the places of plates. On being ready, the butcher knives were drawn and the eating commenced at the word given by the landlady.' (Squaws would not eat till their men had finished.) Whites, breeds, and Snakes gorged themselves and fell to discussing 'the political affairs of the Rocky Mountains.' One Snake chief was losing his constituency and a brother would probably succeed him. This led to a critical discussion — by experts — of the fighting qualities of other Snakes, and on to their rivals among the neighboring Bannocks, Flatheads, Nez Perces, and Crows. This would introduce the stately autobiographies of the warriors here present. It was not only ritual but etiquette to recite your valorous deeds and the degrees and privileges they had earned for you. Dinner finished, the men smoked fraternally, then went out to celebrate the day by shooting at a mark.[11]

The trapper who had a wife was most enviable in winter. A woman kept a lodge as neat as any farm kitchen. With snow banked deep around the skirt of the lodge, heavy skins over the entrance, and curtains running round the entire circumference inside, it was easily heated and free of drafts. The floor had been packed hard. Bed springs were willow frames, mattresses were buffalo robes, and there were robes and blankets for bedclothes. There were backrests of rawhide thongs and screens that could be used against either heat or draft. All one's possessions had their proper places and the orderliness that determined them had the usual overlay of ritual. Any squaw had too many relatives and too many friends and they visited her too often, filling the lodge with gabble till its proprietor protested. When there was no company your wife chattered continuously. She talked while she was cleaning your rifle, cutting and sewing a shirt, rubbing a skin smooth. Some of her talk would have raised blisters on an oak. Much of it rose from the black and steamy ferment of savage fears. It was full of dreams, tribal gossip, legends of prescient animals or demons or heroes who lived before we came out of the earth, the ancients, signs and portents and warnings and ghosts and voices, traditional proverbs and aphorisms supposed to contain the world's wisdom, and wisecracks that had been handed down the ages and may have grown a little thin by now, especially when attributed to magpies or grasshoppers. Nevertheless, it was woman's talk — under the peaks by firelight with the winter wind outside.

The ease of the winter camp might be broken by marauders, by prolonged storms, by the need of moving if forage or game should be exhausted. We have seen various brigades shifting to other valleys in midwinter, and that or any other move that led out of the sheltered places risked disaster in mountain winter. To travel at all in snow was so nearly impossible for horses and mules that only necessity justified the risk. The crust gashed their legs; a few miles of floundering to their bellies broke them down; the storms that swirled out of the peaks killed whole herds. The winter journeys of the annals, from camp to camp or from camp to Indian village, were by snowshoe and long expresses were by snowshoe and dog-sled. It was not uncommon for a brigade wintering 'on the other side' to send a midwinter report or a requisition to St. Louis. Black Harris was one specialist in winter travel. Such a party would consist of no more than two or three (Bill Sublette and Joe Meek in one instance) and a sledge loaded with robes and pemmican. It would travel through December, January, and February, in the awful cold of the peaks and the more awful cold of the plains.

The stories of winter desperation, however, are not of such business trips but of hunters getting lost, snowblinded, blizzard-bound, and eventually without gunpowder. They wandered till they starved or a skulking Blackfoot lifted their hair, when their friends would find their wolf-cleaned bones in the ultimate canyon next spring. Or else the compass needle in their cerebellum steadied to a course, the will that a blizzard could not extinguish kept pulsing, and, feeding every fourth day on winter buds exposed by a gale or on the remnant intestines of a jackrabbit from which they had scared a wolf away, they kept on till at last they crawled to the edge of a grove where the day's work party was stripping cottonwood bark for the horses.

But come back to the rooftree. To what Russell called the Rocky Mountain College. He said that he had greatly benefited from its sessions. Joe Meek, who had left the States too hastily to learn to read, acquired the skill in winter lodges. Such books as there were had the value books have wherever men are lonely and were worn out just as they were in the forecastles of New Bedford whalers or the bivouacs of any army. Occasionally a diarist mentions a Shakespeare, Byron, Scott or other poet, a sentimental novel, a history, or even a Bible. (Russell mentions not only the Bible but 'Clark's commentary on it,' which must have produced serial arguments dealing with what the boys could remember of predestination, immersion, and the awareness of abounding grace.) Years later when a mountain man was a disreputable tolerated among the sacred castes of the United States Army because he could find wood and water where West Pointers would die for want of them, an officer related a further step in the literary education of Jim Bridger. Old Gabe had been disturbing the captain's sleep by waking in the night, eating, and then singing Injun by himself to a tin-pan accompaniment. The captain thought that if he could keep Jim awake later he would sleep later and, since Jim had not had Joe Meek's advantages, tried reading to him by the camp fire. The first experiment was not happy for Captain Humfreville picked *Hiawatha* and Jim Bridger's point of view toward Indians differed from Mr. Longfellow's. Jim's esthetic sense had been stirred, however, and he wanted to know what was the best book ever written. Humfreville voted for Shakespeare and Jim hurried off to the emigrant trail and questioned wagon trains till he found a copy of the plays. He bought it for a yoke of oxen worth one hundred and twenty-five dollars and hired the evenings of a literate youth to read it to him. 'The boy was a good reader and Bridger took great interest in the reading, listening most attentively for hours at a time. Occasionally he got the thread of the story so mixed that he would swear a blue streak, then compel the young man to stop, turn back, and reread a page or two till he could get the story straightened out.' The mind that had memorized a third of a continent absorbed blank verse easily enough and Jim developed a trick, which Huck Finn's Duke of Bilgewater would also use, of pouring it out again happily intermingled and begemmed with mountain oaths. But they came at last to *Richard III* and that put an end to literature, for Jim would hear no more about a man who, king or no, was mean enough to commit matricide.

Jim himself signalized a nobler literature of the Rocky Mountain College. He happened to encounter the right journalists and his name got attached to a folklore of winter nights that was his profession's rather than his. His then are the peetrified forests where peetrified birds sang peetrified songs, the eight-hour echo that was so useful since you could wind it up by shouting 'Time to get up' when you went to bed, the glass mountain which made so powerful a lens that you could see elk feeding twenty-five miles beyond it and was so transparent that its base was littered with birds which had beaten their brains out against its invisible cliffs, the peak that had been a mile-deep hole when Jim first came to these parts, innumerable miraculous leaps including one across a wide chasm which he could cross because the law of gravity was peetrified, the flight up a box canyon which ended with the pursuing Indians killing the narrator, a hundred or a thousand other yarns that have come down in the West and are useful to its novelists and radio stations today. Bits of this Never-Never country are strewn through most of the literature, with white Indians and fabulous animals and trips to hell and the passages of suspended reality that are Indian at base. There is enough of it, if properly pieced together, to add another continent to literature's geography of fable and someone should map it for us.

Still, it is not so much the anthropophagi and men whose heads do grow beneath their shoulders that one listens for in this firelight as Othello's other themes, antres vast and desarts idle, moving accidents by flood and field, hairbreadth 'scapes i' the imminent deadly breach, and being taken by the insolent foe. John Colter, Hugh Glass, Edward Rose, Jim Beckwourth. Jed Smith burying to their chins in desert sand two companions who would die unless he could get water to them. The Astorians' boats wrecked at Caldron Linn. Bonneville (in 1834) similarly wrecked in that lower canyon of the Snake which to this day has not been traveled from end to end. Or any chapter from any great man's memoirs, Bridger's or Carson's, Fontenelle's or Fitzpatrick's. Or any chapter from any mountain man's memoirs. Any story you want: men going mad like John Day, or wandering across half the world like Ezekiel Williams, or being marched in Spanish leg-irons like James Ohio Pattie, or navigating the canyons of the Green like Ashley. Murder, starvation, massacre, endurance, the will not to die. Or any other theme.

These were technicians of wilderness life. Their talk was shop-talk that took the prodigious at an easy stride, and the reminiscences of campaigners. The arts and crafts they practiced, the struggle with the wilderness, the war with Indians — these were their stories. Or with the sardonic edge. Take for one item the laughter when someone remembered any episode in the career of that gnarled grizzly-hunter Joe Meek. He was trapping a creek with one Stanberry, who was pint-size and therefore quick to take offense, when some remark raised the question which was the braver. The argument could have only one issue and they agreed to settle it the next day with Hawkens at thirty paces. But that evening while the boys were working out the procedure a wounded grizzly charged through camp, as dangerous as half a million volts, and stood at bay. As the boys scattered one of them shouted that here was a good chance for Joe and Stanberry to make their point to a useful end. Wagh! Both grabbed their rifles and charged the grizzly, which charged too. But before shooting it Joe beat it over the head with his wiping stick. That settled it, for nobody could be braver than a man who used a coup-stick on a grizzly.

Or that time when Joe climbed a tree to escape grizzlies but a pal did not and Joe sat on his limb yelling advice while the bears grunted and nuzzled round the pal in his roll of robes. Or the grizzly that treed Joe and two others, then wrestled each tree in turn trying to shake them down. Or the time Joe and his pardner Hawkins killed a grizzly on an island in a river, stripped, and swam to it and then were chased downstream by an only wounded and furiously swimming bear and, landing, had to run naked across the prairie while the boys split their sides. Or the time when Joe and Hawkins and Doughty and Claymore chased a grizzly into a cave and went in after it and found it was three grizzlies. Doughty stayed outside and shot them one by one as the boys ran them out, but he nearly missed for laughing — Daniel in the lions' den warn't shucks to Joe Meek.

And once Joe seen a she-grizzly and offered to go git her if Markhead would hold his horse. He got to a good forty-yard shot but the cap of his gun jist pooped. Old Joe he started to run for his horse but the boys was scairt and they didn't wait for him. The bar took off too and Joe he just got a new cap set when the bar froze on to his capote. Him and the bar wrastled with that thar capote and Joe he got the muzzle of his gun into the bar's mouth. But damn me if Old Betsy warnt double-triggered and Joe he'd been too busy to set her. So by the time he got the trigger set the bar she knocked the bar'l out her mouth and the ball hit her in the shoulder and only made her madder. Went on wrastlin' and no chanst to load the gun. Right hyar up comes her two cubs, as the bar knocks Joe's gun squar out of his hands, and she was so damn mad she started to box one of their ears. Joe he managed to git out his knife. He tried to git her behind the ear but she bats the knife out of his hand too and comes close to takin' one of his fingers with it. Joe was bleedin' now and the bar she still had him by the capote but the other cub runs in too and the old girl she takes time out to cuff him down. So that gives old Joe his chance and he grabs his hatchet from his belt and sinks it into her brain. That done it and Joe he come 'to the conclusion that he was satisfied with bar-fighting.'[12]

Joe Meek was a blithe soul; he was wont to set the table in a roar. Once when he was riding in to camp after a day's trapping, he thought he would give the boys some fun. So he kicked his horse into a gallop and began to yell 'Blackfeet!' which produced prompt action at camp. Sidesplitting. Funniest thing was, some Blackfeet happened to be crawling toward the horses at that moment and when Joe started yelling they thought he had seen them, and they had to show before they were ready to. The boys laughed and laughed.

* * *

We may transcribe a single page of the saga as a trade reminiscence round a winter fire, the time when Osborne Russell was camped with three others near the mouth of a small stream that flowed from the northeast[13] into Yellowstone Lake. (In Yellowstone Park.) He and a pal named White were alone in camp — the others were hunting meat — when they saw some Blackfeet making toward the horses. They dived into the pine forest — and into Blackfeet, who parted in front of their guns. White got an arrow in a hip. He pulled it out and kept going and at the next step Russell got one in the same place. A few yards farther on he got another one through the thigh, which brought him down momentarily, though he was able to hop fifty yards farther and, with White, get beyond some fallen logs.

The Blackfeet swarmed round, howling like prairie wolves, but missed their victims in the thicket. As they keened down a false scent, White and Russell hobbled to the lake, where they could hear the Indians plundering their camp. White's nerve failed and he began to mourn and fuss. Russell bawled him out: maybe White was going to die but Os could crawl till he found and shot an elk, which would give him food and shelter till his wound healed. (He said White was a rich man's son who had been raised a sissy.) They lay out for the night. Next morning White's scratch was almost healed but Russell's leg was so swollen that he could move only on some sticks which White cut for crutches. They moved off. The Blackfeet were still about and had to be detoured, but they met a Canadian who was of their party: a sack of salt was all that was left of camp. Russell washed his wounds with salt water and plastered them with 'beaver's oil and castoreum,' which helped. They moved as fast as Russell's crutches would permit and on the third day the Canadian, who was so badly scared that he would not range out of sight, killed a couple of ducks. It began to rain. (They had just the clothes in which they had been jumped and just the powder and balls that hung at their belts.) But that night they killed an elk. They fire-dried the meat in the rain. Next morning Russell abandoned his sticks and could carry his own rifle.

They made westward across Chicken Ridge and the Red Mountains to the eastern branch of Lewis Fork, where they camped by some hot springs and, the next day, crossed to Heart Lake.[14] Now, moving south, they killed and dried more elk and made moccasins. Early September at Jackson's lake is early November at lower altitudes and the Tetons, which they must now cross, wore an autumn cape of snow. They needed a full day to cross the Divide and camped in the boisterous winter winds of the peaks. The next day they got all the way to Henry's Fork (Fremont County, Idaho), which would have been good going for athletes, let alone a cripple. They gathered dry grass to sleep on and found that they had enough jerky left for only one meal. There was no game from here on. They made the Snake the next day — this too was fast travel — and crossed it below the forks. It was 'nearly swimming' deep and so cold that it 'caused me much suffering during the night.' But 'we were on our way at daybreak and traveled all day through the high sage and sand down Snake River. We stopped at dark, nearly worn out with fatigue, hunger, and want of sleep, as we had now traveled sixty-five miles [more than that, in fact] in two days without eating.' They were making for the nearest succor, which would be Fort Hall, ten miles or so from the present Pocatello. They got to within ten miles of it the next day and here Russell's bad leg cramped so hard that he could travel only a hundred yards at a stretch. But presently they met one of the fort's halfbreeds who gave them horses and they reached Fort Hall, 'sun about an hour high, being naked, hungry, wounded, sleepy, and fatigued.' Courtney Walker, factor for the Hudson's Bay Company, gave them fresh clothes and set out jerky, buttermilk, cakes, and tea. The tea, Russell says, kept him awake till midnight. And nine days later the fourth member of their original party arrived at Fort Hall safely enough, having made much the same journey alone.

Just any mountain men who had drawn the wrong card.[15]

Or, since this narrative has had little opportunity to present Indians in repose, we may listen to the wife of a wintering trapper. She may be a Minnetaree and her sisters are said to be expert housekeepers, pretty, uninhibited, without pruderies, ingenious at lovemaking, fond of it.[16] This winter night she has dressed with the circumstance proper to the wife of a free trapper. Her dress is of fine doeskin or mountain sheepskin, whitened or tanned *café au lait*. The skirt comes just below her knees and a short fringe with bells and occasional deer hoofs runs along its uneven hem line. A few tassels of rawhide are sewed to the skirt, and the patches of colored cloth they are affixed to, are outlined with beads. The dress is tightly girdled at the waist with a four-inch leather belt, intricately beaded with geometrical designs in blue, white, red, and green. The upper part of her dress has a few designs in paint and, if it is very special, a central rosette of colored quill-work. A deep, capelike yoke falls from the shoulders to make half-sleeves (since she is not a nursing mother the dress is sewed all the way up to the armpits and thus is form-fitting above the girdle) and this is the most richly embroidered part of her costume. Beads, split quills, bits of metal, fringe, perhaps some tufts of ermine or other fur, have been arranged in graceful patterns. Where the yoke ends, a *V* or a diamond or some similar device in beads or paint draws your eye toward her breasts. The costume suggests the dresses periodically ascribed to Balkan peasants except that it is leather and its embroidery glass. A light, hairless robe of elkskin may be thrown over her shoulder like a scarf and it is painted with symbolical designs. She is wearing beaded moccasins and knee-length leggings that come down over their tops if they are not sewed to them.

She may be sixteen or seventeen and her name is All Blossoms, though the Kentuckian who bought her calls her Sal or the equivalent of Toots. She has dressed her hair with a scented pomatum of her own making, brushed it (with a section of porcupine tail in a wooden handle) till it is glossy, parted it in the middle, and let it fall freely down her back and over her shoulders like a Vassar freshman the year this is written. She has reddened the parting with vermilion and, since she is a Minnetaree, may have brushed a little of the pigment through her hair. She has rouged her cheeks and the backs of her hands with red ochre. (She used a foundation cream before spreading the pigment with her fingers.) A tiny black beauty patch, a single circular dot, is tattooed in the center of her forehead, another on the bridge of her nose, another over each cheekbone. Her body and her garments have been scented with her kitchen-made perfumes — various dried herbs, dried flowers, sweet grass, horsemint, the needles of sweet pine, pulverized, perhaps blended, used as a sachet or worked up with castoreum or some other base. All Blossoms reclines on a bed of buffalo robes laid on a spring of willow sticks. She leans against a backrest of rawhide thongs, and another robe is thrown across her knees. She speaks English of a kind but her husband knows her native tongue and it is in Hidatsa that she tells him how the dance of the black bears came about, back in the beginning. She has heard the story many times among her people, told both by the tribal storytellers, one of whom may have owned it as a writer owns a copyright and got royalties for telling it, and by her father, her mother, and the garrulous aunt who lived with them. She tells it artfully and with enjoyment but also with a reverent awareness that she is performing a religious ritual.[17]

A Minnetaree broke a sacred object over his leg and so the leg swelled till he was helpless. When the village went on a hunt his four wives piled up some provisions for him and left him. He was alone and so he wept. But after a time the wife whom he did not love came back and helped him and carried water for him, saying, 'I want to live with you. If you die, I want to die also.'

There was so little food, however, that she had to search the abandoned earth lodges, like the Mandan hut in Bodmer's plate, for a few kernels of corn which mice had stored away. For four days while she was searching she heard a voice singing sacred songs but though she looked she could not see the singer. On the fourth day (four is the number with greatest power) she entered a lodge but though again she searched carefully for the singer (perhaps a cricket or an ant) she saw nothing except a rabbit snare of fiber-string that someone had left there. She wondered if the snare might have sung the songs and her husband thought that possible when she told him, so she brought it to the lodge. She also brought some buffalo hair, which her husband wove into snares for snowbirds. Then, because while gathering wood, she had seen something with long ears, he also made some additional rabbit snares.

The woman snared birds and rabbits and maybe they could survive the winter on such fare. But now when she went into the woods she began to see something big, with long ears and a white tail. So her husband made a deer-snare, telling her how to catch a deer by the neck. She caught one and killed and dragged it to the lodge rejoicing, for this made it certain that they would live through the winter. The next day she snared another deer, but on the third day besides snaring a deer she saw, on the far side of the Missouri, a man killing a buffalo bull. She crossed on the ice, thinking he would give her some meat, but he behaved rudely and would not speak. He threw a severed leg to each of the cardinal points, discarded the head, and then snowshoed away, dragging the carcass with him. The woman took the forelegs and head to the lodge and told her husband what had happened. He had been afraid that some enemy had taken her.

The next day the woman snared her fourth deer and saw a different man killing a buffalo bull across the river. This one did not behave rudely but gave her some meat. The third day it was the first man and again he was surly and again he scattered the legs to the cardinal points. On the fourth day it was the kind man and he gave her not only the legs but some intestines too. She took her meat home and told her husband that she wanted to follow these strange men. He agreed and made her some corn balls for food and filled his pipe and told her to take it with her. 'If I do not return within four nights,' she said, 'it will be a sign that I am dead.'

(So far the story has been only part dream. From here on it is wholly dream. But in All Blossom's mind there is no distinction between dream and history.)

While her husband wept, the woman followed the snowshoe-tracks to the northward. At last she came to a lodge on the edge of some timber — and it was an eagle-hunters' lodge, the men living in it had made ritual observances and were trapping eagles to get feathers for ceremonies. Meat was drying at the door and the woman was afraid, for these might be enemies. A voice inside spoke in her own language, telling a companion to get some firewood. The voice was using black-bear language and that was proper, for eagle-hunters impersonate black bears. But when they called her into the lodge they were not eagle-hunters, they were black bears.

They were sitting in a circle inside the lodge. Those on the left had their hair combed in the fashion of the surly man, those on the right in the fashion of the kind man. The woman sat down on the right side of the door and the bears on the left side began to shout and quarrel among themselves, each saying that she was going to be his wife. The bears on the right side said nothing till a servant had cooked a buffalo paunch and given it to the woman to eat. Then they told the bears on the left that if they had wanted her for a wife they should have been kind to her but they had been rude instead. 'It is we,' said the kind bears, who were the older ones, 'it is we who have called this woman to us here, not you. Our son down at the village is in great need and we want to help him. This woman is our granddaughter.' By that saying the kind bears adopted the woman.

Now she knew that the kind bears had called her here and she put her pipe in front of them, and her corn balls. They passed it twice down their line till it came to the first one again, who lit it and smoked and spoke derisively to the others, saying, together with other allusions, 'You say big words. You are always saying, "I can catch eagles no matter how high they fly in the sky. I can catch them with this snare down in the timber."' Then they all smoked, and they declined the corn balls till they reached the smallest one, who broke them up and distributed them.

After the ceremonial eating and smoking, the bears asked the woman when she was going home. Right now, she said, so they each gave her a little piece of dried meat. They gave her snowshoes too and told her to carry the meat on her back. But first, they said, they would teach her a ceremony which she in turn was to teach to her husband, a ceremony to be made in their name. So they instructed her in all the dances and songs of the black-bear ceremony till she knew them perfectly. When she started home the bears promised that they would come to the village four nights hence.

When the woman reached her lodge she heard her husband weeping and calling for her. 'I am here,' she said and her husband rejoiced. For 'I have been weeping, thinking enemies had killed you.' She took the pack of dried meat from her back and at once each piece in it became as large as the big piece from which it had been cut. Now the woman told her husband the story of her adventures. He was happy and told her to prepare a feast for the ceremony. 'Perhaps,' the woman said, 'the bears will doctor your leg.'

On the fourth night they came, in single file, the leader carrying a buffalo skull (a necessity for magic and especially for divination), and another one carrying a wooden pipe. They entered the lodge solemnly when the woman opened the door. She paid a buffalo robe for the skull, and another robe for each of the snares they brought, and another one for the pipe. For her husband was the son of the black bears. And the little man who had first lighted the pipe was really a bent-stick snare. But he became a man and lived with the other hunters in the eagle-hunters' lodge. And he told the woman's husband, his son, that he would doctor his leg. He put a bait of meat over the ankle and set a snare there. And a snake thrust its head out of the ankle and looked at the bait but jerked back inside again. Presently, however, the snake's head came out again and began to eat the bait. The bent-stick man caught it in his snare and with great difficulty pulled the snake out of the injured leg, which would be all right now.

'And that,' All Blossoms said, her face solemn in the firelight, 'that is how the black-bear dance came to my people. Only those who have the right to dance it and to keep the medicine bundle that goes with it (including the snares and the wooden pipe) can consecrate an eagle-hunt. And only those have the right who are descended from the black bears.'

# « VIII »

# TO MEN BENIGHTED (1834)

ON SATURDAY, August 16, 1834, the brig *Pilgrim* made out of Boston Harbor and began beating down the bay. A head wind forced her to anchor and it was not till midnight that a young man from Harvard College, proud of his duck trousers, his checked shirt, and the half-fathom of black ribbon over his left eye, was sent to the captain's cabin with word that the wind had hauled. Then, 'A-a-ll ha-a-nds; up anchor, a-ho-oy!' Richard Henry Dana bawled down the hatch with, he was afraid, less than an old hand's assurance. He was oppressed by his multifarious ignorance. The orders shouted through the night were strange but less strange than the actions they produced. Young Dana was frozen in bewilderment while the *Pilgrim* got under way. 'There is not so helpless and pitiable an object in the world as a landsman beginning a sailor's life,' he wrote. In this mood he entered on his great adventure.

The *Pilgrim* was in the hide trade. She would eventually make a shellbark of this college boy who had sailed before the mast because an attack of measles had impaired his eyesight. She was taking him to the California coast and many strange experiences — and spinning one more thread in the pattern of expanding history. Ahead of Dana were many rendezvous on the golden shore, with the test of manhood, with a lifelong dedication, and quite as unpredictably, with one of his professors. The movements of history are sums of private accident and private will. Here were a hide ship traveling the continent's perimeter, a college boy hoping to strengthen his vision so that he might have the honorable, cantankerous career of a Dana, and while the *Pilgrim* sailed for Cape Horn the curator of the Botanical Garden of Harvard College crossing the continent's diameter toward the same California beach.

In such items of personal intent history was setting out the chalk and plumb lines of a new age.

* * *

For while Joe Walker's men (some of whom Dana would meet) made fiesta in the California weather, while Captain Stewart hunted on snowshoes in the Green River country, while Maximilian measured the skulls of Mandans at Fort Clark, while the small and the great of the mountain fur trade waited out the winter of 1833–1834 — the new era that would make them all anachronisms showed a faint, premonitory stirring in the United States. New kinds of men were going West.

Now the holy zeal waked by the letter of the halfbreed Wyandot William Walker welled into action. The pathos of the Flatheads — seen as Chinooks with pyramidal heads — would be assuaged and the white man would bring them his Book of Heaven and save their souls. The Presbyterians and Congregationalists in their American Board of Commissioners for Foreign Missions made the earliest start, and only a series of mischances kept the Reverend Samuel Parker, an elderly divine of Middlefield, Massachusetts, from traveling to the Flatheads in 1834. But Mr. Parker reached the frontier too late to join a caravan west. (He went home but his companions stayed there and opened a mission to the Pawnees.) So the Methodists were first in the new mission field, Oregon and the Rocky Mountains. That was appropriate for it was their *Christian Advocate* that had sounded God's trumpet for the crusade. The instrument their Mission Board chose was a tall, slow, awkward, powerful evangelist then teaching a church school at Stanstead, Quebec, just over the line from Vermont whither his always pioneering forebears had moved from Massachusetts. The Reverend Jason Lee had had a late illumination and had come later still to his education in divinity. But he felt called to minister to the Indians and had asked the Canadian organization to send him West before the American organization chose him. When President Fisk, his old teacher, told him the election had fallen on him he accepted at once. 'I go as Paul went to Jerusalem,' he said, and chose his nephew Daniel Lee, almost as old as he, to make the journey with him.

Jason Lee is a hard man to make out and his great importance in American history is seamed with ambiguity. That is not because he had any of the malaises that rioted in the souls of so many missionaries to the Indians. He had experienced the earthquake of evangelical conversion but he appears, as Samuel Parker and Marcus Whitman also appear, never to have belonged to the twice-born. Manifest Destiny had selected a thorough extravert as the advance point of its religious expansion. No conviction that he was a miserable sinner depressed Jason Lee for a moment. His innumerable protestations of unworthiness were purely formal, as ritualistic as a Flathead's puff of smoke blown skyward, and he was much less likely to grovel before the wonder-working providences of God than to congratulate himself on the obvious fact that they had been worked for his support. He was, besides, hearty, adaptable, courageous, ingenious, ready. The motives of such a man are usually simple and should be easily read, but there are few decisive points in the career of Jason Lee where the inquirer can be sure why he acted as he did. He was often self-deceived and the energies of history certainly deceived him. Those deceptions stand between him and his interpreters today.

When the Methodists established the Mission to the Flathead Indians (in 1833) the Board estimated that many thousands of dollars would be needed to finance it. The Board appropriated three thousand dollars of its own funds and began a violent excitation of the already violently excited mission spirit among the faithful. And after Lee was ordained Missionary to the Flatheads he set out on a mission tour that carried him through New England, the Middle States, and the Ohio Valley. At its very beginning in November, 1833, one of the most striking manifestations of God's providence in a career singularly blessed by such beneficence, occurred in Boston. For Lee, who had just preached there, had tried unavailingly to find anyone who could tell him anything at all about the West whither the finger pointed — and now the Boston newspapers said that a citizen of Cambridge (a town which one of Lee's ancestors had helped to found) had returned from the Rocky Mountains. Lee hurried back to Boston to meet Captain Nathaniel Jarvis Wyeth. For anyone who came back alive from the West was, not unjustly, promoted captain in the public view.

Wyeth told Lee about the country he must travel, the Indians he would meet on the way, and the Flatheads whose missionary he was. (He said they were Deists, which might barely bring them within the understanding of Boston.) He appeared on the public platform with Lee and pleaded for mission funds. More still, he invited the missionary party to travel with the brigade which he was preparing to take west in 1834 and to ship their mission equipment in the brig which he had chartered for the Columbia River portion of his plan. But the greatest of Wyeth's contributions to the mission cause was the Indian boys he had brought to the States, the halfbreed Flathead boy and the Nez Perce young man who, as we have noticed, by another singular providence had been born with a head a little flatter than most.

With these exhibits before their eyes no congregation could hold out against Lee's exhortations. In all the suburbs of Boston and as far away as Andover the money rolled in, and Lee had found a device that would prove even more useful when he next saw civilization. In the opening months of 1834 he preached his way west with his nephew Daniel Lee but without the Indian youths. Wyeth was to jump off from near Independence and after the customary call on Clark in St. Louis the Lees got there on April 22. They had been joined at Cincinnati by Cyrus Shepard of Weston, Massachusetts, a godly young man who had been made a member of the mission. Shepard was not a minister, he was a layman, but he was no less sincere and no less dedicated for want of ordainment and he became the rock of the Oregon Mission. But at Independence Lee went looking for 'lay assistants,' or in unchurchly language, hired hands. In the hamlet of Richmond he picked up a couple of youngsters, Philip M. Edwards and Courtney M. Walker. They would help with the outfit and the small herd that Lee was taking west but, though they are described as of a modest sobriety, they had no interest in the salvation of Indians. Though Walker would for a while work for the Hudson's Bay Company, in him and Edwards, thus casually enlisting for a transcontinental trip, we may see the establishment of still another type that would reproduce itself in ever-increasing numbers. They just wanted to see Oregon.

* * *

Nat Wyeth must have had short nights since he got home. He was going to make his all-out effort to conquer a place in the mountain fur trade. More than that, in fact, for he could dominate its carrying business if his scheme worked. Back in Cambridge making order of the knowledge he had worked for and dearly bought in two years of the West, he was surer than ever that the scheme would work. It could hardly fail. If his salmon business paid for his ship round the Horn — and who could doubt that it would? — then he could cut the cost of transporting trade goods at least sixty per cent. Since this cost was the heaviest burden of the mountain trade, no competitor could stay in the ring with him. He had the business licked: it was automatic, a Q.E.D. His logic, the intensity of his conviction, and his obvious knowledge of the trade convinced the Yankee speculators. He formed a new company and got it capitalized for twenty thousand dollars, then for twice that. Not bad for a man who had lost his shirt. Wyeth was to get a quarter of the profits for managing the business and he took as much stock as he could raise money to buy.

His energy during the winter is oppressive. Cousin John's book of little lies about the failure of Nat's greenhorn expedition was out, having been written in great part by Doctor Waterhouse, who believed that Yankees ought to stay home and let Oregon slide. That had to be combated in the press and so did letters and lying rumors by other seceders from the first venture and by the father of one. The details of finance, purchase, transportation, and preparation had to be attended to. Trade goods, traps, plenty of alcohol, all the expedition's necessities had to be arranged for, from Baltimore and New York to Louisville and on to St. Louis. Letters went to outfitters at Independence for horses and mules. He learned how to determine longitude and latitude. Then to make sure he hired a Boston sea captain, Joseph Thing, as his adjutant and taking him west would make a sourdough of him in a pleasant reversal of Old Stormalong's career. He chartered the brig *May Dacre* and cleared her for the Columbia with goods and salmon-drying equipment and the missionaries' outfit. He corresponded with Bonneville's backers in an effort to get their carrying business. He made a similar try for the RMF Company, whose contract for three thousand dollars worth of goods was the one tangible asset his company had. (He pointed out that his sixty percent saving would not only secure them against the American Fur Company but would also cure the annoyance of small companies whose marginal existence added to the trade's chaos.) Milton Sublette, his friend and the author of his contract, came to Cambridge — ominously, he had a sore foot. Bill Sublette came to New York and had to be handled with extreme care, for fear of the double-cross. Moreover, Wyeth's vision got a sudden and spectacular enlargement when he made contact with a surviving brother of Jedediah Smith and began to work the Santa Fe trade into his plans. It would not cut into his fur and salmon business — might bolster it in fact. More important, it would simplify inventory, make for a more rapid turnover, reduce overhead, increase discounts, and provide off-season employment for men, horses, and mules. On paper Wyeth was approximating John Jacob Astor. The mid-century managerial mind was trying to organize another field.

On his way west he wrote a final memorandum to Captain Thing, who was closing up in Baltimore. One cause of desertions by engagés at the frontier had to be allowed for: Thing must provide 'some medicines for the clap and pox.' Then Wyeth was off down the Ohio, for St. Louis and Independence, to oversee the final preparations for his make-or-break commitment. Meanwhile history, which was using him in several ways to heighten the energies of its new age, had selected him to facilitate still another one. He was going to provide conveyance and protection for another species of the new men who were going West.

One of them, Thomas Nuttall, was no greenhorn but an innovator and pioneer with a distinguished reputation. An English printer, he had emigrated to the United States where he had learned mineralogy and mastered botany. As a young man, he had accompanied the Astorians as far up the Missouri as the Arikara villages, somewhat south of the Mandan villages. He and his fellow botanist John Bradbury, who was also on that expedition, were the first trained scientists who ever entered the American Far West — that was in 1811. The wonderland of unstudied plants had kept Nuttall in an intoxication just short of frenzy. The voyageurs of Hunt's party labored with him in vain, trying to tell him that he was risking not only his life but also Mr. Astor's money when he wandered off through prairies, thickets, and bottom land. But no Indians existed for Nuttall, there were no mischances, no interruptions or delays, no possibility of disaster or death, there was only the flora that no one had seen. So the voyageurs cursed him, decided that he was touched, and kept an eye on him when possible. He came down the river with Manuel Lisa, who had raced Hunt upstream under a cloud of unjustified suspicion. Eight years later he again made a scientific exploration beyond the frontier, the southwestern frontier this time, up the Red River and into the country of the Osages. Harvard made him curator of its Botanical Garden. He published an account of his southwestern tour and also botanical treatises of great importance. Then, his interests turning to the field of Wilson and Audubon, he mastered another science and won an entirely new fame as an ornithologist. He held the title of Lecturer on Botany and Zoology at Harvard when his friend Wyeth first went West and loyally gathered specimens for him.

He was forty-eight now but the chance to go all the way, to see the other side, dissolved his age in a new hope. God only knew what plants and birds there might be. He resigned his appointment and was off.

He had communicated his zeal to a correspondent and friend of his, a young Philadelphian named John Kirk Townsend, who was something of a physician and more of an ornithologist. Townsend, then twenty-five, got himself appointed a traveling representative of his town's two big foundations, the Academy of Natural Science and the American Philosophical Society. He was to serve them well, and American science at large, and American art and literature. Moreover, on his return he was to publish an account of his Western travels that remains one of the most interesting of such chronicles and is invaluable to history.[1]

Another thread in the pattern. Nuttall and Townsend are the first lengthening of the scientific radius. For the first time an effort is made to add exact observation and classification to the empirical knowledge of the Far West that had been heaped up by the mountain men and was almost wholly confined to them. A man just short of fifty and another man half his age, they were simply two individuals whose enthusiasm had found action in an exhilarating adventure. But, as with Jason Lee and his companions, a quintessential part of nineteenth-century America was going West with them. They were still another repository of Manifest Destiny and conductors of still another energy that has gone on operating up to now — and incidentally helped to form the continental nation and the continental mind.

Nuttall and Townsend reached St. Louis on March 24, 1834, found Wyeth there, and had him take them to an outfitter for buckskins, blanket capotes, and the hard wool hat that was the progenitor of the cowboy's Stetson. Untroubled by their amateur status they started five days later to walk across Missouri just to see what it was like. Frontiersmen, birds, plants, and animals delighted them in equal measure but they had got only as far as Boonville, twelve days out, when a steamboat coming up the Missouri proved to have Wyeth on it. They boarded her and on April 14 she brought them to the already raucous hamlet of Independence, the germ from which the Wild West was to grow. Here they bought horses and hired an experienced roustabout to wrangle them.

The scientists had a fortnight to ride about the prairies, accustom themselves to camp life, and study the mores of the frontier. During the winter Jackson County had risen against a sect of millennialists who had settled there under promise from the Lord God Jehovah that when Judgment Day arrived, as it would in a couple of years, the perfected society of heaven would be administered from Independence. (With the further stipulation that the lost Eden of Adam and Eve was not far away.) The 'Mormonites,' as Townsend called them, had been driven into the unsettled lands of Clay County but now there were reports that the banished were going to descend on their Zion and put the heretics to the sword. (It was true that back in Ohio Joseph Smith, who loved to brandish swords, had raised a posse that included angels as well as saints and was marching on Independence with a serialized apocalypse for accompaniment. But an outbreak of cholera, which was really a disguised providence, broke off the expedition.) Meanwhile Wyeth was reducing the chaos of any outfit about to start west — packing goods, forming his men into messes, shoeing horses and mules, hunting strays, turning back stampedes, quelling brawls, picking up loose ends. Townsend admired his expert government of the individualists who worked for him. The missionaries had not yet come in and Wyeth wrote his Boston bankers that 'if they preach much longer in the States they will loose their passage for I will not wait a minute for them.' Milton Sublette with a small party of twenty men, apparently mostly replacements for the RMF Company, came up and would travel with Wyeth. The missionaries reached Independence on April 22 — Townsend thought that the powerfully built Jason Lee looked competent to survive the wilderness. But they lost so much time buying their mission herd and hunting for opportunities to hold final feasts of holy love with the few Methodists on the frontier that Wyeth moved out on April 28 and let them worry for a day catching up with him.

* * *

April 28 was an early start. A light winter and a precocious spring had brought the grass at least two weeks earlier than usual. But there was an additional reason why Wyeth must make his jump-off as soon as he could. Even before he started, the business ethics of the mountain trade had begun to operate.

Last year Captain Stewart and Doctor Harrison had paid Sublette & Campbell 'about $500' covering transportation and findings. Since the RMF Company had been their principal hosts, Sublette & Campbell had credited that sum to the company. But now at Independence when the company, in the person of Milton Sublette, drew on Sublette & Campbell for its five hundred dollars, the firm would not honor his drafts. Bill Sublette had learned, apparently through Doctor Harrison's leakage, of the contract for goods which Milton had made with Wyeth. He refused to pay the drafts which he had authorized unless Milton would stay home. (Thus depriving Wyeth of expert help on his trip and of a principal to his contract.) Probably this was a subterfuge: he was simply making trouble. Bill and Milton were loving brothers but this was business and Wyeth sagaciously bought better horses than he had intended to for it was clear that he would have to race Sublette to the mountains. This ran his expenses up and the price of horses and mules was already higher than he had calculated in Cambridge. Including Bonneville and the trust, five full-sized outfits were already competing on the border.

Wyeth, then, started on April 28. He had about fifty men and about one hundred and forty horses and mules of his own, Milton Sublette with about twenty men and their remuda, and the five missionaries with their horses and milch cattle. He had beaten Bill Sublette to the start, a sizable achievement. But Bill, who was going to the rendezvous and from there to the fort at the mouth of the Yellowstone where by now his partner Campbell had taken a brutal licking from McKenzie, finished his preparations at leisure, confident that he could outmarch his competitor.[2] He was taking with him one of the greenest tenderfeet who ever left a record of their western adventures. This was a young Ohioan named William Marshall Anderson and though he wrote not only as a greenhorn but with the strained jocosity that passed for well-bred humor in that generation his diary provides a useful cross-check on the other narratives of 1834.[3]

Since all Western crossings resemble one another, we will follow no more in full detail. Wyeth's is better documented than most and its principal interest is the proof that adaptable, intelligent greenhorns like Townsend and Lee could become prairie travelers without much pain when they had skilful supervision. Wyeth soon demonstrated that he had mastered the partisan's job. It was just as well, for the 'bad foot' which had troubled Milton Sublette at Cambridge had by now become a crippled leg. Though Townsend diagnosed a fungus infection it would appear to have been much worse, perhaps osteomyelitis. Nine days in the saddle were all that Milton could stand and he turned back to the settlements, where the leg was amputated.[4] Wyeth took command of his party and drove on. Nuttall was an old hand before he started and Townsend soon became one. Captain Thing, the navigator on horseback, settled in too and the robust Lee, shepherding his mission and herding his cows at the rear of the long pack train, could be neither tired nor dismayed.

Lee held up his end. He took his regular trick on the night guard. He went out with the hunters, though his largest usefulness was in bringing back the kill. One night when the horses stampeded he took charge of the party that rode a day-long circle to bring them in. He liked the rough life and reported more pleasure in eating, in fact, in sheer sensual outdoor living, than he had ever known before. (Exactly on schedule he suffered an attack of 'diorhae.') No one who worked with such gusto in the daily chores would be thoroughly disliked and, besides, Lee did not have the Holy-Joe sanctimoniousness that made most of his successors odious. He got along with the untamed, though he was noting in his diary that they were the most abandoned men he had ever seen. They were 'complete infidels' and had no thought of the damnation laid up for them. Wyeth's occasionally issuing a ration of alcohol shocked the man of God for the crew naturally got drunk on it. 'Would to God that the time may come when its use shall be entirely abandoned except as a medicine,' he wrote in South Pass. We may pause for a moment and mourn, for this is the first known sigh of a prohibitionist in Oregon, Jason was no man to let it go at a sigh, and a wholly new emotion has appeared in the West.

Here in the wild country Lee's dutiful protestations of his shortcomings seem perfunctory and though there are occasional prayers for the success of his mission they are considerably less common than one would expect. But God kept the mission in mind: He would not suffer His servant to fail. It is God who finds the water at the end of a dry drive and it is God who sends a buffalo or an elk when meat runs out. The daily hazards of the trail are passed by a series of special providence with Jason Lee's address on them. And a lament that was to be constant with all the missionaries begins here, with Lee's indignation because Wyeth kept his train moving on the Sabbath. It was their idea that the partisans should halt and devote the day to hymns and meditation but except when God caused a delay for that very purpose no partisan ever saw it their way. Still, when Lee publicly offered thanks to Heaven for the dispensation that brought a herd of buffalo within range, he was within the approval of the mountain men. For that was exactly what the Indians did.

The daily life of a scientist on the trail did not need portents from heaven. Heaven was right here and an earthly blessing too, for Nuttall and Townsend were encountering new species every day. Since there was another ornithologist along, Nuttall mostly confined himself to botany, filling his bag with desert plants by day, sketching and annotating them by the evening fire. Townsend's shotgun filled his bag every day too. 'I think I never before saw so great a variety of birds within the same space,' he wrote on the way to Laramie Fork. 'All were beautiful and many of them quite new to me; and after we had spent an hour amongst them and my game bag was teeming with its precious freight, I was still loath to leave the place, lest I should not have procured specimens of the whole.' The regret was justified but he had reason to be content. The collections he and Nuttall made survived incredible mischances in the next few years and, in some part damaged, got safely to the States. Some of Townsend's specimens achieved immortality in the last part of Audubon's *Birds*, some of his notes got into the *Ornithological Biography*, and many of the Western plates in the *Quadrupeds* rest on him. Similarly with Nuttall: American botany got a permanent enlargement at his hands.

Respect them, for they are in our heritage. Townsend dreamed of a Western expedition all of whose members would be scientists — botanists, geologists, 'mamologists,' ornithologists, entomologists — for the secret riches of a million square miles would open to them. As the years passed the frontier of scientific knowledge, here humbly moving west, did indeed draw even with the other frontiers. Someone should tell the story of that laborious accumulation of known things down to its splendid chapters, the railroad surveys and the great postwar studies that finally coalesced in the Geological Survey and the Bureau of Ethnology — before academic science was in the field at all. But the rugged chapters come first with such men as these two and their successors in the next twenty years. Perhaps most honorably with lieutenants and captains of the United States Army who were sent west on the hopeless job of disciplining a hundred thousand Plains Indians with half-companies of incompetent cavalrymen, but who were not too depressed by the mission to study the fossils and the strata, the bench levels, the butterflies, the grasses and flowers and trees, the indexes of skulls, the structure of the sign language. They helped a people, who have never thought of them, to know a country and to live in it. They too were servants of the continental mind.

Townsend relished the experiences of a greenhorn and appreciated his frequent absurdity. He laughs with his mentors when, as a greenhorn invariably did, he chooses the toughest bull to shoot in a herd of buffalo that is full of fat cows. Lacking Lee's farm experience at butchering, he is consumed with admiration of the hunters' skill. He is stricken with guilt when the swift passing of some antelope stimulates his sporting impulses beyond control and he shoots a beautiful doe with 'large, soft, black, eyes,' though there is no present need of meat. 'I felt myself the meanest and most abhorrent thing in creation.' He delights in a young antelope that is caught by a hunter, fed milk from one of Lee's cows, and added to the party under the name Zip Coon.

Early in the trip Townsend came close to making a costly error. The caravan met a village of Pawnee Loups on a hunt and had to make the usual negotiations and pay the usual tax to pass, detouring the herd. Townsend was on early guard that night. Coming back from his tour to the tent which he and Nuttall shared with Wyeth and Thing, he was startled by 'a pair of eyes, wild and bright as a tiger, gleaming from a dark corner of the lodge and evidently directed upon me.' He thought a wolf had followed the scent of meat into the tent, raised his rifle, and put his finger to the trigger. 'With a loud "Wah!"' an Indian leaped up and seized the rifle barrel. Another appeared with an unsheathed knife. As they struggled Wyeth woke and settled matters, explaining to Townsend that these were guests and to the Pawnees that Townsend was not on the warpath. They all lay down again but Wyeth touched Townsend's shoulder and pointed to his own rifle clasped between his legs and to the knife and pistols on his chest. Townsend made his own armament ready but could get no sleep — especially since the Pawnees' eyes still glittered in the dark. Next morning, however, he and the brave he had almost assassinated exchanged knives — symbol of undying friendship — and his new friend put on an exhibition of archery for him that left him gasping.

There is a good scene, also described by Lee, when they go out on a hunting party headed by Wyeth's chief hunter Richardson, who looked to Townsend like Cooper's Hawkeye, and spend the day under the Plains sun without water. By the time they killed a buffalo Lee was for a long gallop to the Platte, miles away. But Richardson said that relief was now at hand: they had 'cider.' He opened the paunch 'from which gushed the green and gelatinous juices' and dipped out some of the last water that the bull had drunk. He offered his companions the first drink but, Lee says, 'it was too full of excrement to please my fancy' and the two said no. Richardson laughed and 'drank it to the dregs, smacking his lips and drawing a long breath after it with the satisfaction of a man taking his wine after dinner.' (Townsend speaking, of course.) Richardson had an alternative and invited Townsend to drink blood from the heart. He could resist no longer and did so 'until forced to stop for breath.' His blood-covered face made Lee roar with laughter. And when he got back to camp his first swallow of water made him vomit the blood. He says pensively that he never drank blood again.

All this was incidental to one of the fastest crossings on record. By forced marching and a couple of night drives Bill Sublette passed Wyeth on the thirteenth day out. He kept going at the fastest pace an expert partisan could set but was able to gain only twenty-four hours on Wyeth, who knew what Sublette was racing for and, to the admiration of Townsend, had the skill to stay on the track with him. By May 29 they had reached Chimney Rock and on the evening of June 1 they splashed across the ford of Laramie Fork and arrived at a sizable event in Western history.

* * *

For Bill Sublette, hurrying to spoil Wyeth's trade, had left thirteen of his thirty-five men here at the great cisalpine crossroads and they had begun to build a trading post. William Marshall Anderson, the engaging greenhorn with Sublette, claims to have brought a bottle of champagne this far and to have used it in a cornerstone ceremony. He says that Bill wanted to name the new post Fort Anderson after him and that he, a modest man, held out for Fort Sublette. The caravan's clerk, he says, horrified by the sight of his employer refusing a drink, solved the dilemma by proposing Fort William, which would honor both. Fort William it was, whoever named it, and it became Fort John when the American Fur Company took it over but neither name suited the mountain man's sense of fitness. It was Fort Laramie to the vulgar from the beginning and as Fort Laramie it comes down in history, of which it saw God's plenty.

It was square on the crossroads, the north and south Indian trail that was older than any record, and the road toward South Pass which with Lee's coming it is at last right to call the Oregon Trail. (The road of Robert Stuart but more especially of Wil-

# THE HUNT

Trappers and Indians had to live off the country. Both lived primarily on buffalo meat and both preferred it to any other game. Hunting buffalo was a daily job when there were herds at hand, and meat was dried and sometimes made into pemmican against the times when they would not be at hand. There were, however, many other staples, even many other delicacies. You took what you could get and in the desert or on the upper slopes days might pass without your getting anything. The buffalo were always on the move, other game made unpredictable migrations, especially in the fall, and some country simply had no game.

Brigandage and warfare were conditions of Indian society and skill at both was the dominant social ideal. Except for occasional truces and a very few traditional alliances all Plains tribes were hostile to one another. The transmontane Indians got along among themselves much better but when they came to the buffalo country they had to assume that any tribes they might meet there would be hostile. The mountain men had to make a similar assumption but had to act on it much less. In large parties they were usually safe from any tribe except the Blackfeet, though when they met a large party of any Plains tribe they had to be on guard against a possible explosion. In small parties trappers were not safe from any Indians east of the mountains except usually the Crows — and their property was not safe from the Crows.

*Courtesy of Mrs. Joseph Whyte, niece of the artist*

PLATE XLIX

## INDIANS TESTING THEIR BOWS *Alfred Jacob Miller*

This is not so much a test as a contest and vigorous betting is certainly going on. The Indians are probably Snakes, but the bow which the contestant is drawing may have come from the Nez Perces. It is made of horn (backed with sinew) and has a double curve, a powerful model and one which the expert Nez Perce artisans made in quantity for the trade. Miller says that a favorite distance was thirty or forty yards and that good shooting required you to hit a two-inch bull's-eye at that distance. A good marksman, however, could shoot such a bow just as accurately at twice that distance and could kill with it at considerably longer range.

*Courtesy of Mr. L. Vernon Miller*

PLATE L

## Herd of Antelope *Alfred Jacob Miller*

An antelope was a 'cabri' (kid) to a voyageur and a 'goat' to an American trapper. The fastest of all Western game animals, antelopes could easily outrun a horse. They were found in greater quantities than any other game except the buffalo, in herds as large as the one Miller pictures here or larger. Indians sometimes chased a herd into an inclosure like those made for trapping wild horses or coursed it with relays of horses after stationing sentinels to drive it into a roughly circular path.

*Courtesy of Mrs. Joseph Whyte, niece of the artist*

PLATE LI

## Crow Indians Attacking Buffalo with Lances

*Alfred Jacob Miller*

This was the most difficult way of killing a buffalo and probably the most dangerous too. It required great skill and a trained horse. Preferably you would put an arrow into the buffalo before trying to dispatch it with a lance.

*Courtesy of Mrs. Clyde Porter*

PLATE LII APPROACHING THE BUFFALO *Alfred Jacob Miller*

PLATE LIII LASSOING WILD HORSES *Alfred Jacob Miller*

*Courtesy of Mr. L. Vernon Miller*

Courtesy of Mr. L. Vernon Miller

STRIKING BACK *Alfred Jacob Miller* PLATE LIV

INDIAN FEMALE RUNNING A BULL BUFFALO PLATE LV

*Alfred Jacob Miller* Courtesy of Mrs. Clyde Porter

PLATE LVI

NIGHT SCENE — BUFFALO ON THE PLATTE

*Alfred Jacob Miller*

*Courtesy of Mrs. Clyde Porter*

The Platte is widening toward its traditional appearance east of the forks. There is plenty of warrant for a night crossing by buffalo.

*Courtesy of Mrs. Clyde Porter*

PLATE LVII TAKING THE HUMP RIB *Alfred Jacob Miller*

The classical position for butchering.

PLATE LVIII BUFFALO CHASE *Alfred Jacob Miller*

In the Catlin convention. Observe the correct approach from the right side.

*Courtesy of Mrs. Clyde Porter*

*Courtesy of The Walters Art Gallery*

YELL OF TRIUMPH *Alfred Jacob Miller* PLATE LIX

Demonstrating that the convention of your boyhood was sound.

HUNTING BUFFALO *Alfred Jacob Miller* PLATE LX

A primitive method of hunting, driving them over a cliff, which Miller never saw.

*Courtesy of The Walters Art Gallery*

PLATE LXI

A Surround *Alfred Jacob Miller*

*Courtesy of Mrs. Clyde Porter*

An authentic study — all the details stand up under minute examination. Note the charging bull in the lower right-hand corner.

BUFFALO CHASE *George Catlin* PLATE LXII

*Courtesy of The Boston Athenaeum*

*Courtesy of Mrs. Clyde Porter*

PLATE LXIII

## Running Fight, Sioux and Crows *Alfred Jacob Miller*

Miller's war pictures are authentic but not eyewitness. He obviously listened carefully to the stories he heard, for he accurately represents the mounted warfare of the Plains. The most synthetic of his pictures is Plate LXVI, which he worked over a good many times in order to get a composition that suited him.

STAMPEDE BY BLACKFEET *Alfred Jacob Miller*

This is a typical night rush on the horses, the commonest kind of skirmish between Indians and trappers. The Blackfeet are making the utmost possible noise in order to frighten the herd, not to confuse the trappers.

PLATE LXIV

*Courtesy of Mrs. Clyde Porter*

*Courtesy of Mr. Lloyd O. Miller*

PLATE LXV BEATING A RETREAT *Alfred Jacob Miller*

PLATE LXVI WAR PATH *Alfred Jacob Miller*

*Courtesy of Mr. Alfred J. Miller, grandnephew of the artist*

liam Ashley's men.) Here, with a desert to the east and a worse one to the west, and grueling travel in both directions, here there were rich grass, cottonwood groves, clear water, and Laramie Peak in the sunset to suggest the mountains that lay ahead. Emigrant trains invariably halted here as if coming to an oasis. Goldseekers who lived to reach Fort Laramie knew that one hazard was behind them, for the cholera never crossed this meridian. It would draw all wandering trappers, all Indians who came to the Laramie plain to hunt or en route anywhere east of the mountains, the Oglala Sioux, and finally the United States Army who would take over the post and try to keep a third of the West peaceful from this site.

Sublette was thus creating history out of what seemed to him a simple move in opposing the fur trust. He took to the trail again, traveling still faster because he had left part of his goods behind for his new post. That night Wyeth came up and camped beside the first logs that had been laid. Two or three free trappers who had been traveling with him turned off toward the Laramie Mountains. They moved Townsend to amazement by their nonchalance and made Lee scornful of the fainthearts in the East who had advised against his mission. 'Yea, they run greater risks for a few beaver skins then we do to save souls, and yet some who call themselves Christians, tell it not in Gath, would have persuaded us to abandon our enterprise because of the danger which attended it.' This was another Sabbath and though it had been spent profanely he was glad of the holy day and remembered the weary time before he could hear from home. So would many thousands more at Fort Laramie.

* * *

From his arrival at Independence on, Wyeth had understood what Sublette was trying to do. The day Sublette passed him on the trail he sent an express ahead to find Tom Fitzpatrick, announcing that he was on the way with the goods contracted for and that, through Dr. Harrison's venality, Sublette & Campbell knew of the arrangements that had been made and where they were to rendezvous. He also announced that his plan for water transport had gone through and would enable him to supply next year's good at an attractive reduction. A month later he sent another express from the Sweetwater, urgently soliciting Fitzpatrick not to contract with Sublette for either goods or carriage. He hurried on through South Pass. On June 17 he rode ahead looking for Fitzpatrick. The next day he found him twelve miles up the Green from the mouth of the Sandy. Bill Sublette, getting there first, had exerted his leverage and Milton Sublette was thirteen hundred miles away. Fitzpatrick on behalf of the RMF Company repudiated the contract.

The intricate, self-adjusting combination that Wyeth had formed was wrecked. The first, the vital year of the Columbia Fishing and Trading Company was smashed irretrievably. Wyeth was too good a business man and too robust a mind to let the shock paralyze him and his letters from the rendezvous to his principals and his friends are resolute. He immediately began to devise expedients and calculate new combinations to save as much as might be. Neither Fitzpatrick nor Sublette had intended to create a threat, they supposed they were destroying one, but they had made Nat Wyeth a dangerous man. Meanwhile, there was nothing to do but to see whether he could get any business at the annual fair. He and the defaulting Fitzpatrick moved straight west to Ham's Fork, where the rest of the RMF Company and the American Fur Company were in camp, together with the usual miscellany and the usual Indians.

Here Captain Stewart comes out of the wings again. Presumably he had been with Jim Bridger's brigade which had wintered near the site of the rendezvous [5] and had then moved south through Colorado east of the Front Range. We can only speculate that Bridger had started in that direction, that Fraeb or Gervais or both joined him somewhere along the way, and that with one or the other of them Stewart traveled to Taos and thence to the Gila. The footnote in *Edward Warren* already quoted ties him up with Stephen Louis Lee, who had branched into the fur trade from the Santa Fe trade and had some kind of connection with Bent and St. Vrain. Kit Carson was also with Lee and their party had wintered at a fort lately built by Joseph Robidou somewhere up the Uintah River before it flows into the Green. (Uintah County, Utah, upriver from Ouray.) Lee was in Taos that spring and Carson left him to join Fitzpatrick, who had first taught him mountain craft.

There are a few accounts of what happened in the mountains this spring and such as there are contradict one another and are vague at best. Clearly, however, this is when Stewart first met Carson, who appears in person as a character in his novels and who contributes some adventures to his heroes besides. He would have heard of two of Kit's feats of the past winter, a long solitary pursuit of an Indian who had got away with the horses, and the treeing by two grizzlies that Kit always remembered as the most precarious moment in a life lived always on a knife-edge.[6] Almost certainly Stewart met some of the roistering free trappers who were coming home from California by the southern route, Joe Meek among them. Possibly he was with the group who massacred the Hopis so brutally, possibly with the group from which Meek and Carson and a few others rode out to the terrific daylong battle with Comanches already alluded to. It was one of the great battles of the literature, with forty-two Comanches killed before the chiefs broke off, the trappers uninjured, and a seventy-five-mile journey on foot afterward before they reached water.

And to this spring belongs an incident that became a legend in this West. The Reverend Samuel Parker heard about it a year later, they were still telling the story thirteen years later, and the literature contains half a dozen allusions to it in between, but of direct evidence we have only the footnote in *Edward Warren* already cited to establish Stewart's presence in the mountains. That footnote covers the better part of two pages and follows the introduction of the novel's hero to one 'Mark Head,' who is said by his companion to be 'the best and most reckless trapper of these parts except one.' (No guess hazarded here about that one superior: it was a reckless superlative.) This is the Markhead who briefly appears in a number of chronicles and is something of a major figure in Joe Meek's reminiscences, where he is jovial, reckless to an extreme, and ready to cap any of Meek's deviltries. He is introduced as a character in Ruxton's *Life in the Far West*, as a companion of LaBonté and Killbuck, of Meek and Bill Williams, and of the free trappers who accompanied Walker to California. In *Adventures in Mexico* Ruxton calls him 'one of the most daring and successful trappers' and says that he was killed in the Taos uprising of 1847. Meek told Mrs. Victor that he was a Shawnee but this is unlikely since everyone else speaks of him as white.

In his long footnote Stewart says that Markhead 'was considered one of the most successful beaver hunters of the West; though rather under the usual scale of intellect, he had contrived to get through difficulties and dangers such as had checked or baffled men who considered themselves as possessing more intelligence and experience than himself.' Stewart then goes on to tell his story, which is set in the mountains somewhere near Taos. In the party was a young Iowa named Marshall who 'had become so lazy and disobedient that Bridger and Fitzpatrick had discharged him and he was (without an animal) obliged to follow the camp on foot.' Taking pity on him, Stewart hired him and outfitted him but eventually had to threaten to fire him for general worthlessness. That night the Iowa ran off with 'a favorite rifle, my best running horse (Otholoho) and another.' Stewart mourned the rifle but as a sporting man he could not bear to lose the horse. It was, he says, 'the swiftest in the West, beat the Snake nation and would, had there not been unfair play on the part of the man who took charge of him the night before the race, have beaten all the horses of the whites.' (We catch a glimpse of the sports at rendezvous.) Enraged, Stewart denounced the Iowa and said 'I'd give five hundred dollars for his scalp.'

Markhead took him seriously. Stewart organized several small parties to chase the Iowa and Markhead and a Mexican actually found him — running buffalo on his fine new race-horse. 'Mark thought there might be some technical difficulty about the reward if he did not bring the scalp, or he was afraid of the Spaniard [Mexican] joining the other. Marshall was putting the cord to rights as he was about to mount, when Mark shot him dead under the horse's neck. In the evening, between us and the sun, the loiterers of the camp saw two men leading two horses making their way towards camp, and on a rifle was displayed the scalp of the horse-thief. This was a little more than I looked for and I tore the bloody trophy from the gun and flung it away.' The legend says, however, that he paid the bounty.

And alas, Stewart adds, next year the Blackfeet got the horse.

Apparently the brigade or brigades that Stewart was with moved to rendezvous west of the Front Range, through the Colorado parks. At any rate, Stewart comes into full view again on Ham's Fork. Townsend says that another Englishman was also at rendezvous, one Ashworth, otherwise unidentified. Though some historians have assumed that he was or had been traveling with Stewart, it is clear that they had not met before.

Wyeth, aided by early grass and good weather, had made the crossing from Independence to Green River in fifty-one days, remarkably fast time, though Bill Sublette had beaten it by either three or four days. It was a good year for traveling fast but Cerré, bringing Bonneville's goods, was several days behind Wyeth (at Ham's Fork he had still not reached his own rendezvous) and the American Fur Company later still. There are about a dozen eyewitness accounts of the Ham's Fork rendezvous of 1834, and they show the first faint setting-in of the trade depression. These were not the high and far-off days of 1832 or 1833, still less the fabulous gatherings of the late eighteen-twenties when the unrivalled Ashley men, the cocks of the mountains, the champions of champions, had roared and swaggered in a land which no one but them could claim.

Townsend was sick with a violent fever following exposure and lying in his tent was tortured by 'the hiccoughing jargon of drunken traders, the *sacré* and *foutre* of Frenchmen run wild, and the swearing and screaming of our own men.' Not to mention the halfbreeds and Indians, 'their obstreperous mirth, their whooping and howling and quarreling . . . dashing into and through our camp, yelling like fiends, the barking and baying of savage wolf-dogs, and the incessant cracking of rifles and carbines.' The missionaries were infinitely more depressed. Here were the sins that kill, infidelity and gambling and drunkenness and fornication — and nothing whatever to be done about them except to close one's eyes when possible and groan unto the Lord. Jason Lee longed with a full heart to preach a sermon, for there were hundreds of white men to listen, but had the sense not to propose one. 'My God, my God, is there nothing that will have any effect on them?' he prayed in his diary. He heard some Indians singing something that had a faintly Christian rhythm, but they went out from the ceremony, built a fire, and began a war-dance. That was hard to take, though Lee confessed it was interesting too, but he was shocked by some trappers who joined in. The wicked were like the troubled sea and salvation was far from them.

But he bore himself with dignity when the wicked threatened. Wyeth took him aside and told him that some of the RMF Company trappers, learning that gospel sharks were on the trail, had been threatening to give him hell (Lee's words) when they appeared. Unquestionably there had been resentment as well as laughter at the news, for the mountain men wanted no spoil-sports in their domain and nobody who might carry the threat of permanent settlement. Wyeth advised Lee to be on his guard, to avoid every appearance of offense, and to show no timidity if molested. He added that if the missionaries were molested they could depend on him to protect them by whatever means might prove necessary, however severe — and meant what he said. Lee replied that he 'feared no man and apprehended no danger from them when sober and when drunk we would endeavor to keep out of their way.' Let us, he added, seek them out right now. So with Wyeth he went to the RMF Company camp, a mile or so away, where Bill Sublette had them to dinner and treated Lee with suave courtesy. All that is wrong with the story is Lee's notion that it was Bill or some other partisan who had made the threat. Sublette assured him that he would keep his men in hand. 'How easy,' Lee mused, 'for the Lord to disconcert the most malicious and deep laid plans of the devil.' Not only the Lord had an eye on Lee.

Townsend, a young man now a full two months in barracks, was impressed by the available loveliness of the Nez Perce maidens, who were got up in their finest doeskins. So was Sublette's greenhorn, Anderson, though he was startled if not shocked to find that the ladies rode horses astride. Here was one who was superbly dressed and was riding a horse equally gleaming with metal and beads but 'her proud head was turbaned with a most filthy and disgusting clout.' Still, Anderson loved the whole uproarious show. There was always something happening along this midway and there was always spectacle. One day a grizzly charged through camp, scattering everyone. Little Chief, a Flathead dignitary, ran for his weapons and killed it, giving the hide and claws to Anderson. Little Chief had adopted him as a brother because Sublette had revealed that he was a nephew by marriage of William Clark, whom the old man had met twenty years ago.

Another day there was a sudden uproar and the camp erupted. A buffalo bull came charging through but instead of being scared everyone was laughing, firing guns into the air, and yelling encouragement. For behind the buffalo came a Nez Perce named Bull Head, whom the boys called Kentuck. Last night he had promised Sublette to entertain his guest and now he was making good — yelling 'Hokahey!' and driving the bull ahead of him. Great stuff and the mountain men cheered Bull Head and the bull till they had had enough, when they filled the beast with arrows and rifle balls and let his carcass float off down the Green. Anderson mentions another Nez Perce, one who had been with Bill Sublette at the battle of Pierre's Hole and like him had been wounded there. He and Bill slapped each other's backs and noisily remembered their glory, then went off to have a drink and damn the Blackfeet.[7]

Anderson's statement that there were fifteen hundred Indians at the rendezvous is something of an exaggeration. He was misled by their swarming at the liquor tents and show counters 'like flies on a sugar barrel or niggers at a corn shucking.' They bartered skins, robes, horses, and women, replenishing their outfits and filling their skins with alcohol. They chattered in all their languages (including Chinook, the pidgin-Indian of the Northwest) and mingled with the halfbreeds of all tribes and their dear friends the Yankees, Canucks, Mexicans, and Kanakas. They chased buffalo across the sun-hazy flat. They were always herding their horses to fresh grass, bringing lodgepoles from the hills, departing on the sudden senseless whims of all Indians, snarling themselves in howling dogs, making orations. Then one day the whole camp moved farther on to find untouched grass and the picture got impressed on Anderson's memory. 'It was an unbroken line of human beings constantly changing route and elevation. At one and the same time it was ascending and descending eminences; at one and the same time swaying both to right and the left to avoid obstacles or overcome difficulties — the little front point, by some inscrutable power of resistless magnetism, seeming to drag the whole mass after it at will.' The greenhorn stood gasping while the long snake glided through the sun, travois scarring the ground, babies staring from their mothers' backs, old squaws cursing the dogs, braves swaggering with archepiscopal dignity, and the wind ruffling the feathers of their lances. It reminded Anderson of the pilgrims on their winding way in Bishop Heber's hymn.

* * *

End of a long splendor. The American Fur Company has no chronicler in the literature of this rendezvous, which is too bad. Back in the States its organizer, whose prescience never failed when money was on the line, had read the future accurately and on the first of June, 1834, had unloaded. (The mountain and Missouri business went to Pratte, Chouteau, and Company, the rest of the great trust to Ramsay Crooks and his associates.) Astor had made his millions and would let others hold the bag while he took a safe profit banking for them. But here on Ham's Fork the campaign begun by Pierre Chouteau, Jr., and Kenneth McKenzie came to its intended triumph. The Opposition folded. The Rocky Mountain Fur Company went under.

Wholly ruthless price-cutting, wholly ruthless trade-practices, incitation of Indians, subsidization of pinprick rivals, bribery, piracy, and miscellaneous corruption — all of which the RMF Company also employed so far as its smaller resources permitted — had done the job. For three years the mountain trade had grown steadily more murderous and more chaotic and now the partners could compete no longer. The era that had begun with Ashley's superb invasion of the interior West ended right here, and those who signed its epitaph were, still short of middle age, men who had come with Ashley or as his advance guard to the then untouched mountains. The RMF Company dissolved. Tom Fitzpatrick and Jim Bridger, dealing Milton Sublette in by proxy, formed a new company and bought out Fraeb for hardly twenty-five hundred dollars in goods and outfit and Gervais for little more than fifteen hundred.[8]

The five ex-partners were masters of a specialty. They had grown up to it, hammering out their mastery on the spot. They were Ashley men, the truest mountain men, the explorers of the interior West, its first exploiters, the instructors of all others. There was no other calling for them — as there was no other calling for any but a handful of their trappers. After a few further trapping ventures Gervais went to Oregon and seems to have settled there. Milton Sublette, though he rode West again with a rubber leg, died of his mysterious ailment at Fort Laramie in 1836. Fraeb stayed on in the mountains, joining the growing number of small independents who worked thin tailings more efficiently than the trust could, and was sometimes in the trust's employ. He was killed by Sioux in 1841 after a famous fight. As for the best of them all, Fitzpatrick and Bridger, the American Fur Company had been able to develop no partisan who could quite equal them and, like all victorious corporations after a merger, was eager to sign them up.

It did so a year later. In fact, it got a rope on them this year. The new partnership had had enough of Bill Sublette and Robert Campbell, its carriers and bankers. They had come West with Jim and Tom under Ashley in the great dawn, when the West lay open to men of strong hearts, and had shared with them the desperation and the glory of the heroic years. But one reason why the RMF Company had been gutshot and the principal reason why Sublette and Campbell were now rich men — one with aspirations to Congress, the other with a name for hospitality in St. Louis as lordly as any Chouteau — was that they knew where the money was and did not let an old companionship come in between. They went on and though the texts usually say that they took their quietus from the trust next year, they were still grievously troubling it with their know-how, skullduggery, and subsidized independents as late as 1837. But they would take no profit from the new firm, which called itself Fitzpatrick, Sublette, and Bridger. The partners contracted with Fontenelle to sell their next year's furs to the trust.

Wyeth saw that the gentlemen who had cut his throat had also cut their own. He knew the moral, for it fitted him. Writing Milton Sublette from Ham's Fork, he absolved his friend of complicity in the deal that had ruined him. Both Milton and Fitzpatrick had meant to buy his goods when they contracted for them, he acknowledged, but Milton's brother had bribed Fitzpatrick to run out on the bargain. 'Now, Milton, business is over between us,' he wrote, 'but you will find that you [the new company] have only bound yourself over to receive your supplies at such price as may be inflicted and that all you will ever make in the country will go to pay for your goods.' That was the economy of the mountain trade in a single sentence and Wyeth added a summary that was exactly true, 'You will be kept as you have been, a mere slave to catch beaver for others.'

The rage that ran in Nathaniel Wyeth was no less intense because it was contained. He had to save what he could, and if other days, then other expedients. Just over the next range to the west were the advancing outriders of an organization far more powerful than the late RMF Company or even the Western Department of the trust, a century and a half old, infinitely wise and crafty, ruthless, a miniature empire, the Governor and Company of Adventurers of England trading into Hudson's Bay. At one of the stormy conferences between the defaulting partners and Nat Wyeth, Joe Meek heard him say, 'Gentlemen, I will roll a stone into your garden that you will never be able to get out.' He went straightway from Ham's Fork and did just that.

* * *

The Little Chief who had liked Anderson was a great man among the Flatheads. He was tall or short, fat or lean, old or middle-aged, depending on whose diary you are reading,[9] but there is no doubt that he was a jovial soul, a wise leader, a distinguished and very tough warrior, and one of the best performing equestrians in the whole Rocky Mountain circus. (He is usually Insula or a variant spelling in the literature, but sometimes Red Feather, and Michael to Father DeSmet.) He was here with a large delegation of his people and a larger contingent of Nez Perces had accompanied him on the same errand — to see whether the white men in St. Louis had answered the Macedonian cry and sent a thaumaturge to teach the petitioners the religion that would make them rich, powerful, and happy. Three years ago they had sent their committee to the Red Headed Chief, William Clark, the four resolutes of whom each one had lost his life on the mission. Each year they had come to rendezvous in the hope that Clark had kept his promise. Now at last their priest had come, the Reverend Jason Lee, and had brought four assistant medicine men and a sizable outfit, all duly dispatched by the fervor of many thousand Christians and paid for by their contributions.

But, the Flatheads and Nez Perces learned, no sale.

There is exceedingly little mention of his intended parishioners in Lee's diary. He says they shook hands with him and welcomed him. He is pleased to hear some of them holding what he takes to be religious services (they were — Indian faintly tinged with Catholicism) while the depraved trappers drink themselves stiff. And that is absolutely all. He does not even visit their camp and when as he prepares to move on they ask him if he intends to come back, well, 'We told them we could not say positively now.' There is little more in the verbose letters which he sent to his superiors and underwriters — who after all had ordained and commissioned him to save Flathead souls. There is, however, the remark that 'it is easier converting a tribe of Indians at a missionary meeting than in the wilderness.' A glance had made it clear that the Flatheads were not going to be Methodists.

Jason Lee never satisfactorily explained to anyone why, on reaching the people whom his God had directed him to serve, he did not hesitate even momentarily but passed by on the other side. The explanations which lay and religious historians have supplied vary too greatly to be reconciled and none are convincing. He was simply a carrier of the *Zeitgeist.* Here in 1834 it can almost be seen running in his veins. By another three years it spoke with his voice.

Something must be allowed for the valley of Ham's Fork. It was a celestial place to mountain men, sheltered, rich with grass and running water and cottonwoods. But to Eastern eyes it was a desert — hideous with untimbered peaks, the parched earth cracking open, sagebrush and greasewood stretching for miles under a sun that tortured eyes and brain, empty of all that meant farmland to the American memory, lapped round by a million square miles of wilderness where no association of home could be called up. Black crickets crawled in its dust. Rattlesnakes baked at its sagebrush roots. The wind that was never still blew alkali dust into your eyes and throat. It was a repulsive country — how would a civilized man live in it?

Moreover, Lee was an evangelical Protestant missionary.

There was booming across the United States a conflagration of zeal for the salvation of souls in distant lands. Twice-born, bigoted, selfless, altogether ineducable men and women were taking Christ, the Bible, the goods of the industrial revolution, and calicoes to cover the nakedness of the heathen, to three-quarters of the globe. Fiji, Melanesia, New Guinea, Sierra Leone, Nigeria, Liberia, the Congo, Kenya, the Sandwich Islands, Madagascar, India, China — wherever there were heathen so lost in darkness that they knew neither the gospel nor underdrawers, there at this very moment the riptide was running. No one will ever tell in full the heroism or the stupidity of the foreign missions, the holiness-saturated devotion of the missionaries or their invincible foolishness. There were only two agencies for the extension of civilization on a large scale, armies and missions, and in the light of history the primitives who drew the armies were much the better off. The missionary was a man glad to submerge self in a holy cause but, except in a minority so small it does not count, his dedication locked him away from reality so completely that at this distance he seems crazed if not crazy. The heathen were not people to him: they were souls.

Without hesitation Jason Lee would have suffered death for his God, his church, or his mission. That is not in question. Before he answered the call, in the long nights of doubt and agony and prayer, seeking for the sign that was at last given him, there was leached away everything that may be called selfishness. But it was altogether impossible for him to desire to do for Indians anything except what the prayers and sacrifices of many devoted people sent him out to do: to bring their souls to Christ. It was altogether impossible for him, in Stanstead, Quebec — or anywhere — to form a realization that the heathen souls were inclosed in an envelope of personality, which in turn had been born of a savage culture. When such a man met the Indians at last they might move him to compassion or even to despair. But also they moved him to overwhelming, overmastering disgust.

Four years after this brief stop at Ham's Fork, Lee visited the mission which his Presbyterian colleagues, or competitors, had founded in the country to which he had originally been sent. There he wrote a letter to his nephew Daniel at their mission on the Willamette. He has a careful, sparse praise for the Presbyterians and a qualified pleasure in such progress as they could show. But as he speaks of the converts a casual clause illuminates this entire chapter of American history as if by lightning. 'The truth is they are *Indians*,' Lee says and underscores the noun. In that revelation is the sum of effort, failure and consummate folly.

He met the Flatheads and Nez Perces at Ham's Fork. There is no way of knowing whether disgust or despair moved him chiefly, there is no way of knowing how conscious he was of the instantaneous discharge of his mind's potential. But the cerebellum and the spinal cord knew. You could not make Christians of Indians. First you had to make white men of them.

And of course Jason Lee was right. The story of civilizing the Indian is only a story of degrading him. The massacre of the Whitmans and all the failures of godly men who were twice-born, as Lee was not, proved only what the carrier of the time-spirit had known instantly on being confronted by the Indians who had stretched out their hands in supplication. First they must be white men. So he wasted no time. On his way here he had learned enough to know that you could not make them white men in such country as this. Therefore he went straight to a place where he thought the experiment had a chance to succeed. To the western side of the Cascades, the magnificent valley with its rivers and rainfall, its rich soil and its waterpower, its promise of the farms and villages and neighborliness in which his personal culture had been formed. To Indians whom forty years of lay effort had already made into white men about as much as was possible, which is to say they were degenerate, debauched, diseased, despairing, and about to die. There he would set up his mission and serve God by making farmers, carpenters, herdsmen, users of soap, teetotalers, hymn-singers, monogamists, and newspaper-readers of whatsoever Indians he might find there. This, he realized, would be at best a small fraction of the universal hopes that had sent him West. But it would be a beginning and at least there was some hope, as assuredly there was no hope at all in the mountains, that it might succeed. That it could succeed only by means of the greatest cruelty men can inflict on other men, only by breaking down the culture that made them men — this mattered not at all, it was the end in view. Thus Lee's decision at Ham's Fork.

The importance of this decision to the United States will not escape attention. Mr. Arthur M. Schlesinger, Jr., has persuasively argued that the fires of revived religion which marked the eighteen-thirties served the propertied interests as backfires against the radical democracy that was crowding them hard. Well, the missions which the revival sent to foreign lands served those interests in a different way — and other interests too. Shall we instance the opening of China to American goods or

Herman Melville's observations on expansion in the Marquesas? Shall we remember by what steps the Pearl of the Orient became American? The land, Mr. MacLeish has said, was waiting for its westward people. Certainly its people were at this moment ceasing to wait for the westward land. The mountain fur trade had made it known, opened it up, blazed the trails, located the water and the grass, named the rivers, triangulated the peaks, learned how to traverse the Great American Desert. There remained only for this knowledge to be disseminated. The ore was now being mined out of which the wagon tires, the trace-chains, and the plowshares would be forged. For the westward people it would be expedient to have the British Empire stopped in Oregon . . . and to have the Indians made into white men at the loss of their power. The time-spirit, it has been remarked, ran in Jason Lee's veins so clearly that it can be seen throbbing in his pulse. History has no accidents: Jason Lee and Hall J. Kelley, the prophet of Oregon colonization and the first American known to have proposed that the Indians of the Northwest coast be christianized, reached Oregon in a dead heat. Thereafter Jason Lee, in a devotion of spirit which cannot be questioned for a moment, served Christian salvation in ways indistinguishable from the promotion of real estate. The Missionary to the Flatheads labored to build the City of God as a colonizer of the Willamette Valley.

He was, that is, like the mountain men and Nathaniel Wyeth, an instrument of the national will. It was Jason Lee who, on July 4, 1834, at Ham's Fork, Wyoming, directed his assistants to pack up the outfit and prepare, not to travel with the Flatheads to Montana, but to go on to the Columbia with Wyeth. It was Jason Lee who gave the orders but it was Manifest Destiny that cast the vote.

* * *

They started out on July 4 but the wicked staggered as they went, for Wyeth gave them their due in raw alcohol. They scandalized Lee with their 'fighting frolic' and made our scientists dive for foxholes when they fired a salute to liberty. Captain William Drummond Stewart with his fine horses and his camp-swampers joined the caravan. He was going to go all the way — finish his traverse and meet some fellow-countrymen. He met one when the party reached Bear River on its second day out, Thomas McKay, one of the Hudson's Bay Company's most experienced brigade leaders and a stepson of its great McLaughlin, the overlord of Oregon. Wyeth's new plans included him and his outfit.

The party had begun the leg of the Oregon Trail that would be a steady crescendo of disaster when the wagon trains began to travel it. The scientists were charmed by Soda Springs, always a blessed oasis to the emigrants, and doubtless Stewart enjoyed the chase when a grizzly charged the pack train, though he must also have been humiliated when Richardson had to kill it. Zip Coon, the baby antelope, had to be shot when it broke a leg. The boys tried to fill its place with a grizzly cub, which snapped and scratched, and a couple of buffalo calves which butted everyone, with particular attention to Townsend. They sighted a Blackfoot scout and McKay, who was traveling this leg with them, was enraged when he got away without being winged. This was a hilly desert country increasingly blackened by outcrops of lava but the little streams were choked with trout fairly barking to be caught. On one of them they met Captain Bonneville, U.S.A. He had made his spring hunt as far as the Hudson's Bay Company's Fort Walla Walla, but the Company's Indians held to their best interest and the Company's factor, Pambrun, would sell him no goods. Just a few days back on Bear River he had met his returning California expedition under Walker and had learned that his great speculation had failed. He was a busted sucker and he knew it, but he had to play out his string. He was making another invasion of the British monopoly, heading for the Columbia, and was entertaining a casually encountered Hudson's Bay brigade when Wyeth and Stewart rode up to make a call.

Entertaining the brigade with a view to mountain trade: if he got the (unnamed) factor stewed, maybe he could steal some business. He had some honey and he had some alcohol; he mixed them and got to work. Irving says it was the desire to treat with the Britisher, but Townsend says it was the meagerness of the supply that made him dour about meeting his friends. He had to exercise the trail's hospitality in alleviation of the trail's thirst, however, and Stewart and Wyeth were good men at a treat. They drank the keg dry and rolled back to camp through a rosy desert.

Wyeth and McKay, traveling near each other, left Bonneville behind. Presently they reached the Snake River, that splendid water. Here somewhere in its bottom lands and on the edge of the Portneuf, a small affluent, Wyeth fixed on a site.[10] He went into camp. Here in what was still a no man's land between the British and American fur companies, within easy reach of tribes that traded with both, he was going to build a post. He named it Fort Hall after one of his backers. Its establishment was another sign of change. According to promise he was rolling a stone into the garden of those who had defeated him. It was going to stay there.

Under Richardson a small hunting party went out to scour the country and make meat, for presently they would be where game was hard to get. For some reason Stewart did not join it but Townsend did and had a rough but exciting time, much beset by grizzlies. Everybody had narrow escapes from them, they shot many, and at night there were grizzly stories by connoisseurs. The yarns fascinated Townsend and he heard plenty of Indian stories too. The campfire works its magic in his journal and here is a halfbreed who has been shot through the neck by a hunter while he was wearing elkskin and antlers hunting elk. Here is a mountain man actually weeping as he remembers a fight with Comanches long ago when a pal was killed. And the time when Richardson killed his horse and forted up behind it against three Indians, killing two of them because he had a pistol in reserve when they jumped him and riding a captured horse triumphantly away from the survivor. . . . They made their meat, mostly bear meat, and went back to Fort Hall. Its builders had been living on bear meat and Professor Nuttall, grown gaunt on the diet, was sighing for buffalo or, by a miracle, beef. McKay had come up and gone into camp.

Hazard of the trail. On the way back one of the hunters started to reload his rifle, which he had just discharged. He didn't wipe it and a piece of smouldering patch was in the barrel, so that when he poured the powder in he was showered with flame. His face was all one blister and there was not much that one could do for burns in the wilderness. This sort of thing must have happened scores of times.

At the fort Jason Lee had overexerted himself on a lesser hunting trip and fallen ill. He read the Bible and Mrs. Judson's pious meditations and, he thought, profited from them. But now that which he had greatly wished was vouchsafed him. On Sunday, July 27, 1834, in the Snake River bottoms, McKay asked him to preach. 'A respectable number' of Wyeth's men, perhaps the professed infidel Wyeth himself, certainly Stewart and the scientists, and most of McKay's Indians, halfbreeds, and Canucks (who understood English with some hiatuses), gathered in a grove to listen to the man of God who, now that his chance was come, found his voice weak and his own interest strangely lukewarm. He braced himself and told his congregation that they could not be partakers of the Lord's table and the table of devils. They must not seek wealth for themselves but every man another's wealth. (A better description of their lives than he knew.) If any offered sacrifices to idols, let him not partake. For the earth was the Lord's and the fullness thereof. Whether ye eat or drink or whatsoever ye do, do all to the glory of God.

Thus Paul to the Corinthians — and the tall, broad-shouldered zealot in the poplar grove within sound of flowing water could have combed his Bible through without finding a text less intelligible to the congregation. But there it was and the gospel had at last been preached in Oregon. (The histories say for the first time but one doubts if it was even the first sermon in interior Oregon, or even the first Protestant sermon.) Three-thirty in the afternoon and Wyeth's men listened gravely because they had come to like the big evangelist and McKay's Chinooks and Cayuses because this was talk to a supernatural. They must have disconcerted Lee by kneeling and rising when he did, for that was popish. Then they went away and held their own Sabbath. Toward sunset it led to a horse-race and one of the riders, a Canadian named Kanseau or Casseau, was thrown and rolled on. They carried him to McKay's tent where the gentlemen were dining. He was cupped and bled but he died the next morning. So Fort Hall got its first grave and Lee read the Ninetieth Psalm and First Corinthians fifteenth over it, the Canadians sang a Latin, popish requiem, and his squaw had her people perform their rites. 'At least he was well buried,' Wyeth wrote that night.

On July 30 McKay and the missionaries and Stewart started for the Columbia. Wyeth lingered six days more, long enough to finish the bastions of Fort Hall and dedicate it with what he calls 'a bale of liquor.' Townsend, no Puritan, says it was the worst debauch he ever saw, calls the camp 'besotted,' and says that the mountain men were 'tiger-like.' 'We had gouging, biting, fisticuffing; some even fired guns and pistols at each other, but these weapons were mostly harmless in the unsteady hands which employed them.' But the fort was wet down and the American flag, made of 'bleached sheeting, a little red flannel, and a few blue patches,' raised over it. So Wyeth detached twelve men to run it and took to the trail.

The record is scant from here on and there would be no point in the details anyway, for Stewart and the missionaries are moving out of the locale in which this narrative is set. The country is desolate or dreadful or spectacular by turns or all together, but always hard and growing steadily harder. It would be pleasant to know what impact the Snake River chasms, the lava, the bald peaks, the writhen landscape made on our romantic nobleman as his horse picked its way along the route thousands of our emigrants were to take. He never gives this country more than an allusion in his fiction, but it was new and that in itself was a charm for the romantic soul. He was, Lee's diary shows, companionable with the missionaries. (He was, of course, a Catholic though at this time not a communicating one.) The series of cascades and rapids beyond Twin Falls would impress him more than they did the missionaries, who were having hard going with their cattle while Stewart hunted and explored.

They camped for a week at the place later called Three Island Ford, to recruit the stock. Here McKay's expeditionary wife died. Next morning he took another one. But first he called in her family and announced that he was not going to pay for her, since white men did not buy their women. He was just being thrifty, but the missionaries approved, for this raised the status of marriage. Moreover, when the family curiously agreed, that was proof that they were eager to acquire white ways. Presently McKay gave the missionaries some provisions, which was another special providence, and told them they must go on from here alone. For he said he was going to stay here till spring, trapping and trading. So he was, but also he was going to trump Wyeth's ace. He went to the mouth of Boise River and built the trading post thereafter called Fort Boisé. It was the nearest the Hudson's Bay Company had yet advanced to the heart of the mountain trade and it did what it was meant to do, it undercut Fort Hall.

Lee's diary, our sole source for Stewart's movements at this time, shows no awareness that he and his Scotch friend were doing anything unusual when with three companions and a few Indians they went on alone till they caught up with a party McKay had sent ahead. There is hardly a suggestion of the strain they suffered, though as they left the Snake, crossed the first range, came down into the Grande Ronde, and moved on to the western Blues they were on a stretch where the emigrant trains began to founder. Perhaps Lee was buoyed up by his 'holy and thrice blessed' privilege of halting for the Sabbath. Following one of these days of praise, however, he read Byron's 'Sardanapalus,' which he unquestionably got from Stewart. He did not think it would better the heart or mend the life and its author was an infidel or at least 'a total stranger to all vital experimental religion.'

There was a series of special providences when Cayuse Indians gave the missionaries food and a Walla Walla gave them three horses. The Lord had softened the savage heart and in return Lee treated the chief's daughter for a headache. Bonneville passed near them and Lee and Stewart rode over to dine with him, apparently on a teetotal basis. All this had used up the month of August and it was September 2 when missionaries, Stewart, and the cattle came to Mr. Pambrun at the Hudson's Bay Company's Fort Walla Walla, where the river it was named for flows into the Columbia. They had at last reached the River of the West and Stewart was in the great American fief of his country. We learn here that he had a sad allergy. There was only fish to eat and he could not eat it, so he killed a horse. Three days later Wyeth and the scientists came up. They met one another as old friends long separated.

The rest of the journey was not in the idiom they had all learned so straitly: it was by water. Pambrun took the missionaries' cattle, giving them an order for replacement at Fort Vancouver, and manned a boat for them and another one for Stewart. After a day or two by land Wyeth also took to boats and from here on they were always meeting one another, seasick and tossed about by rough water and rougher storms. They came through the great gorge of the Columbia, were swept onward, portaged the Cascades, and on September 16 reached journey's end, the Hudson's Bay Company capital, Fort Vancouver, a few miles up the Columbia from the mouth of the Willamette — and on the north bank to be on British soil if Oregon should be divided logically.

Here Wyeth learned for certain that his enterprise had crashed altogether (he had had a rumor before). His ship the *May Dacre* had been struck by lightning and had spent three months refitting at Valparaiso. So she had missed the salmon season. All three supporting legs of his elaborate scheme had broken. He was now just a man with a fort which the Hudson's Bay Company would isolate, a stock of goods which it would buy at its own valuation, and a company of engagés whose pay would be hard to raise.

It is not only thanksgiving at safely reaching the end of the trail that suddenly brings Lee's diary to life. Here were sawmills, a great farm, orchards, herds, flocks. In short, improved real estate. In short, something which the Missionary to the Flatheads instantly recognized as more important than the salvation of Flathead souls — loathsome with sin and heresy and damned to the eternal burning. 'O Lord, do thou direct us in the choice of a location,' he prays. Quite superfluously. Even an infidel could guess that the Lord was going to direct His servants to locate right here.

It is expedient to leave them here, dining with the great McLoughlin at the nerve-center of his empire, beside the blue and rapid river, with the great cone of Mount Hood to the eastward. Presently it would develop that the Lord wanted His promoters to drive a stake in the fabulously rich soil of the Willamette Valley, within reach of its best water power, where they might start teaching tamed Indians to spell out texts, sing hymns, and improve farmland. Wyeth got busy at the hopeless job of saving something from the wreck and we will meet him next summer. (Part of the wreckage was a salt kettle intended for his salmon-drying which, abandoned later on, became at the hands of Ewing Young the first liquor still in Oregon and thereby the basis of Jason Lee's temperance society, also a first.) Townsend, whose Pacific passage had been pure delight, signed on with McLoughlin as a surgeon and began to collect anthropological specimens. Nuttall lingered too in a new suburb of the naturalist's heaven and will be seen again.

And on October 27, 1834, a sick man was carried across the Columbia to Fort Vancouver and a great and crazy vision reached its wretched end. Memorials to Congress, letters to the press, mass meetings, pamphlets, resolutions, prospectuses had got Hall Jackson Kelley exactly nothing. His American Society for Encouraging the Settlement of Oregon Territory had ended up as just himself. He had not even had the time-sense to sign up with Nat Wyeth, who briefly belonged to it and might have saved it. Its collapse left him nothing but his dream and so a year and a half ago he had started — alone except for the dream — to Oregon. He went by way of New Orleans, Vera Cruz, La Paz, and finally San Diego. In California he succeeded in getting nine converts to the dream and finally another one who was worth more than all the rest, the Ewing Young who had twice taken mountain men from New Mexico to the golden shore. They moved northward and Kelley caught malaria and might have died of it if the annual Hudson's Bay brigade had not found and cared for him. The brigade leader, Michel La Framboise, brought him on to Vancouver.

Kelley had reached dream's end. So McLoughlin, the King of Oregon, refused him the gentlemen's table and holed him up in a little shack. The governor of California had sent word that these were horse thieves, as some of them were, though not Ewing Young. The King did not yet understand that the United States had arrived in the persons of Wyeth, the scientists, and the missionaries, but he knew that Kelley would mean the end of Great Britain on this coast if given his head. Even if he had not been accused of consorting with thieves Kelley could not have eaten with the gentlemen.

As for Stewart, all that is known is that he stayed on here and hereabout till spring floods moved down the Columbia and it was time to start for the mountains.

« IX »

# PARABLE OF THE SAMARITAN (1835)

STEWART, WYETH, and the missionaries reached Fort Vancouver at mid-September, 1834. Three weeks later Wyeth gave Stewart letters of introduction to his brothers in New England and Baltimore, so the wandering Scot had already decided to return to the States in 1835. The travelers then dispersed on their various businesses. With the energy of a man who would not admit defeat, Wyeth ranged everywhere, building a fort on Sauvie Island at the mouth of the Willamette, coursing the country to see what could be done, trying to make something of the now hopeless plan to dry salmon, sending out trapping parties under the nose of the Hudson's Bay Company. Nothing would go right for him. Even the venture at Fort Hall was cracking. It was the right place for a trading post, even with the British monopoly at Fort Boisé, and its bourgeois and garrison appear to have made no serious mistakes. Simply, Wyeth was misfortune's stepchild and news came of repeated losses and discouragement. When one of his sweeping circles took him back toward Fort Hall to see what he could do about it, some Kanakas whom he had hired away from the Hudson's Bay Company deserted with their outfits — and that was typical. Indians he hired stole his horses; he was afraid his men would raise his caches. His journal is a monotonous account of rain, snow, wind, turbulent rivers, exhaustion, ill health, and dogged effort. But in December he filled his ship with lumber and sent her to the Sandwich Islands. Townsend, the young naturalist, sailed on her, had a pleasant and active winter, and was aboard when she came back in April, 1835, with cattle, sheep, and goats for Wyeth's island fort.

Listening to the inner voice, Jason Lee entered on his mission, a long way from Flathead Lake, and consecrated the Lord's house. It was built in the Willamette Valley, one of the great valleys of the world. When the missionaries reached French Prairie, so named because superannuated voyageurs of the Hudson's Bay Company had settled there and made farms, they recognized a leading. They began to fell trees, hew puncheons, and split clapboards. Indiana, Illinois, Wisconsin — beside hundreds of creeks thousands of movers were doing just the same, a brotherhood of axe and adze and frow who supply an American symbol. The little cabin they built beside the Willamette sixty-odd miles up from its mouth was just any cabin in any clearing — except that it was raised in Oregon and the American empire would form round it like a pool. McLoughlin approved the decision from a tangle of conflicting values, desires, company policies, and blunders. He had them out of the mountains, he had them south of the Columbia, and if the end was foreseeable, why, he had new friends to talk to. He sold them seed and cattle and all the material and supplies they needed. They drove an American furrow in Oregon soil and began to think of starting a school and preaching to the Indians. Some Indian boys and girls came in and asked to stay — dirty, lousy, and so nearly naked that clothes had to be made for them at once. A special providence of God had given some of this handful of rice-Christians pointed heads, like those which William Walker had not seen. They were Chinooks: providence had furnished the mission some broken-spirited novices who would be docile. That attended to, Lee opened the solicitation of his Mission Board that was to last for years. Send us families, send us females, send us laymen — send us farmers, mechanics, workmen — send us machinery and plows and fruit trees and seed. Send us 'temporals' — we have enough divines. Send us colonizers, empire-builders, a population. This is the richest land in the world.

There was already an empire on the north bank of the Columbia, which the monopoly and the government believed would be British soil if the worst happened. Captain Stewart disappears there for the winter. Fort Vancouver, now Vancouver, Washington, was about a hundred and fifteen miles up from the mouth of the Columbia and some six miles east from where the many-mouthed, island-blocked Willamette flows into it from the south. It had been built in 1825, following the merger of the Northwest Company and the Hudson's Bay Company, and a great man had been put in charge of it.

Doctor John McLoughlin was a physician who had found the

life of a Northwest partisan more fascinating than medicine; physically a giant, an imperious man and an imperial mind, a despot and a statesman, a master of leadership and administration. And in Oregon he had shown what monopoly could do with the fur trade. The Hudson's Bay Company had the wisest of all systems — or what would have been the wisest if history had co-operated. It farmed the fur country practicing conservation, taking only a calculated percentage from a given field and then letting it lie fallow till the animal population had been restored. It maintained a steady market and a fixed price for furs, and so stabilized its economy. It established a hierarchy of organization and command but preserved the career open to talent. It enforced a military government on its employees. It extended the same rigid control to the Indians, managing them with the wily wisdom amassed in more than a century and a half, and governing them with a code of wilderness law the infraction of which invariably meant punishment. So much so that the name of the Company was justice to the Indian, and Hudson's Bay men in two and threes, or alone, could travel any of the Company's wilderness in safety. The Company's history in the Pacific Northwest is not a chronicle of solitary murder and impromptu war, the bloody history of the American fur trade, but the orderly record of the British imperial caste dealing wisely, sternly, and profitably with any set of natives.

That is, in places where the Company was a monopoly. It conserved the fur crop in its private fields but exhausted it as rapidly as anyone else where there was competition. It neither gave, traded, nor sold liquor to Indians so long as no other traders invaded its preserves; when they did, it had more and cheaper liquor than anyone else. Its chivalrousness seems courtly beside the rough trail hospitality of the Americans — and it fought competition more bloodily than they ever did. The American Fur Company's dealings with the Missouri or the mountain opposition were gentle and bush-league compared to the Hudson's Bay Company's century and a half of annihilating French, Canadian, and rival British enterprises. Its final competition with the Northwest Company, which made the best fight and usually won it, meant many years of theft, hijacking, ambush, and solitary murder more deliberate than anything the American companies ever saw, and rose to a small civil war with pitched battles — whereupon His Majesty's government had at last stepped in and forced peace and amalgamation. The Company, hiring the Northwest partisans who had outskilled its own, thereupon applied its peaceful system to Oregon. Back in the mountains it fought the Americans with the weapons the Americans used but west of the mountains it was the just, paternal despotism of a monopoly managed by experts and empire-builders. It could have run the Columbia country as a profitable fur farm forever if the democracy beyond the mountains had not skyrocketed into this orderly wilderness first mountain men, now Christian missionaries, and in another five years the nesters who had abandoned their forest clearings to the next wave.

But McLoughlin's ten years as resident king had made the Department of the Columbia as neat as a blueprint. He moved the headquarters from Astoria, which was near the mouth of the river, to Fort Vancouver not only to locate it on presumably permanent British soil but to get it into farming country and away from the coastal Indians. These tribes, whose culture differed greatly from that of the Plains tribes, had had thirty years of the coasting trade. Our history knows no bloodier or more depraved toughs than the sailors and sea-captains — American, British, Russian — who traded into the inlets and river mouths from the sea. The Indians were just as bloody and depraved; and the China trade, of which this business was a part, rested on a confused warfare. When the continent-girdling Northwest Company came down from the north to pirate Astor's business, its partisans had no choice but to continue the practices which the sailors had instituted. Historians who are fond of setting off a firm but kindly, just but peaceful British policy against the raw slaughter which the Americans used, ignore the record of the Northwest Company in Oregon. By the time it merged with the Hudson's Bay Company it had, at a considerable cost in the lives of its employees, reduced the Indian population fifty percent by means of murder, alcohol, and disease. It had broken the culture and morale of the coastal tribes and developed to an extreme their talents for theft, beggary, treachery, and murder.

McLoughlin had changed all that. Locating upriver among less debauched Indians, he had made Hudson's Bay Company subjects of them. For the most part they were well-behaved and scrupulous in keeping business contracts, and the life of a Company man was secure in Oregon. To be sure, he had had the help of an agent always powerful in the white man's burden. Long before Lewis and Clark got to the Columbia, venereal and other diseases brought by the ships had begun to cut down the Indian population. The slow, sure process was accelerated by the establishment of civilization at Vancouver. The mysterious epidemics that followed settlement everywhere in a new country here proved extraordinarily lethal to Indians. For ten years they raged among the river tribes. By 1835 the Indian population of Oregon west of the Blue Mountains had been reduced by at least three-quarters. A single generation had accomplished in Oregon results that would have required three generations in the East. This also was convenient for the emigration that was to come.

However, here was the King of Oregon, 'The White Eagle,' and here was his kingdom. He had developed a system that surpassed Nat Wyeth's most desirous dreams. The home farm at Fort Vancouver covered nearly two thousand acres. There and at lesser farms and at the holdings of retired voyageurs turned out to grass, McLoughlin raised enough cereals to supply a large part of his Department. The productivity of this soil was not lost on the Methodists, who also observed McLoughlin's occupation of water-power sites and began to covet them in the name of God and the American empire. He had herds of beef cattle, too, developed from California imports: promptly the future of Oregon as a cattle country came to the missionaries in a vision. He had sawmills, blacksmith shops, cooperage shops, shipyards, salt works, fisheries. He had Wyeth's sea transport, with an annual Company ship coming up the river, and the great, if all but endless, waterway communication through Canada to the Red River and on to Montreal. He had a series of trading posts — as far east as the Flathead country in the United States, along the northern rivers, and while New Caledonia remained part of his territories, almost as far north as Alaska. He had immediately followed Jedediah Smith's lead and sent annual caravans through southern Oregon to California, and we have seen his encroachment on the American fur country in the Rockies.

At Fort Vancouver Stewart found a mixture of aristocratic and barbaric splendor that would be perfectly familiar to a Scotch nobleman. The partners who came down the white water from the tremendous northern forests, where for months partisans and voyageurs alike experienced the full severity and squalor of wilderness life, stepped ashore into an ordered, ceremonious life as punctilious as a court. They dressed according to the requirements of their station — and their wives were the most expensively clad of all Indian women, with the Company ship bringing China silks and French laces and London busks to adorn the hips that would widen and the breasts that would sag increasingly every year. They dined in exact precedence and full ceremony. On the most delicate chinaware elk roasts and grizzly steaks were borne in state by halfbreed or Kanaka servants dressed in a kind of livery. Here were an Englishman's port and the toasts proper to gentlemen, though McLoughlin is supposed to have drunk but one glass a year (when the principal brigade set out) and is known to have permitted no drunkenness within his sight.

Stewart was a year too late to meet David Douglas, the great botanist whose name comes down to us in our most magnificent fir and in so many other species. But at such an outpost of the British Empire in the nineteenth century there were always scientists, scholars, and noblemen making their extemporized colonization and maintaining a nostalgic perfume of the court in a society of natives and halfbreeds. There were such at Vancouver, with a minister of the Establishment on the way, who proved intractable of native marriages and confirmed McLoughlin's preference for the American Methodists. There were the globetrotters of any outpost station and there were the local specialists: Tom McKay whom we have seen, John Work, Michel La Framboise, Black Douglas who would be McLoughlin's successor, Sam Black, Peter Skene Ogden. These and their wives and children; the miscellany of Canucks, halfbreeds, Indians, Kanakas, the traffic upriver from the sea, the traffic downriver from Canada, the traffic overland from the States and Mexico. And the superb spectacle when the canoe fleets landed or the pack trains departed — British spectacle, more ordered and more quiet than the American kind, with brighter colors and more seemly songs, with a touch of the durbar and many touches of His Majesty's Guards setting out for foreign service.

A microscopic but complex nucleus of civilization on the rim of the world, with the great North over one horizon and the great West, here made the East, over another, California to the south, China across the water. Forever England on the edge of forests whose trees rose a hundred feet or more to the first branch, on the bank of the River of the West rolling its tide westward to the ocean of Drake and Cook —but the ocean also of John Ledyard and Robert Gray. They were the Company of Adventurers of England Trading into Hudson's Bay, Prince Rupert's Company founded at Oxford thirty years before the seventeenth century ended, when the plague drove the court of Charles II out of London. From the lower end of Hudson's Bay they had moved northward to the Arctic and westward to the Pacific, summoning to their aid that other imperial instrument, His Majesty's Army. The Army had marched to the falls of the Ohio, to Mackinac, to Niagara, to Lake Champlain — to wherever. And between them the Company of Adventurers and the Lobster Backs had disposed of the French Empire in North America. The Lobster Backs, it is true, had lost the United States, but the Adventurers had kept Canada. The line from Fort Vancouver to the past is clearly traced.

At Ticonderoga on Lake Champlain today, in a fine museum, the tourist sees the wine bottles, the Limoges cups, the wig-curlers, the dueling pistols, the laced and epauletted and befrogged satins of the boys who drilled their gun crews and drank the King's health and gossiped of London plays and mistresses within those thick stone walls, and lost their scalps within a hundred yards of those same walls if they drank too many healths. So now the grandsons of their survivors, on the edge of greater forests, beside far more important waters. But, in 1835, not for long.

* * *

Presumably Stewart saw a large part of the Pacific outpost during the open, rainy winter, for he was not a man to sit still. But we are not sure of him till February 11, 1835. On that day Nat Wyeth, beating down the Columbia in a leaky dugout through rain and a gale that had driven the river at him in high walls, came to the Cascades. At that stretch of turbulent water he found Francis Ermatinger 'with a brigade of 3 boats taking up the outfit for the upper forts.' Stewart was with Ermatinger and so had got an early start for the mountains. Ermatinger's own post was Fort Walla Walla, where the small river of that name flows into the Columbia at the foot of a bold bluff, beyond which the gorge begins. Since February is no time to cross the mountains it is certain that he made a long stay at Fort Walla Walla, reasonably safe to guess that he visited the company's Spokane House farther to the north, less safe to guess that he may have gone on to Fort Colville or Fort Okanagan. At any rate by June 10 he and Ermatinger and a small party reached Fort Hall from the upcountry on their way to the rendezvous. Since Fort Hall is no more than a ten days' journey at most, they may have got there by June 20. They were much too early.

The site was Green River Valley again, at or near the mouth of Stewart's favorite New Fork. This would be the first rendezvous under the American Fur Company monopoly. Fitzpatrick, Sublette and Bridger, the partnership formed from the ruins of the RMF Company, were already under contract to the Company and would this summer dissolve their partnership and enter its employ directly. They had bought Fort Laramie from Sublette and Campbell, who sent an early caravan to stock it and then sold out. Its purchasers promptly turned it over to their new employers — and so there were in the mountains this year, besides the trust, only Wyeth, the bankrupt Bonneville and the free trappers. The latter came to the rendezvous in larger numbers and there were more Indians than ever before. There were Utes, a large delegation of Snakes, and many Flatheads and Nez Perces. The last were still hopeful. The priests who had come last year to teach them had hurried on. But this year maybe there would be others and maybe they would stay on with their petitioners.

Heretofore we have seen the caravans from the States reaching rendezvous in late June or early July. The clans gathered at a comparable time this year but the train was more than a month late. The tents had been pitched along New Fork, the racing and hunting and wondering what had happened had continued for a full five weeks when the Company's new employee, Tom Fitzpatrick, and not the expected Lucien Fontenelle, brought it in on August 12.

Fontenelle had brought it as far as Fort Laramie, his newly acquired mountain headquarters, and there had turned it over to his new partisan. He had left Liberty, across the river from Independence, on May 15, a little later than the average jump-off. Instead of making for the Platte by the usual route he took his train up the bank of the Missouri to Bellevue, which had been his own post before he joined the Company. The reason for the change appears to have been the increased development of and emphasis on Joseph Robidou's new post, which was eventually to become the city of St. Joseph. Bellevue was only a few miles from the mouth of the Platte and the route which Fontenelle thus took — to Plattsmouth and then up the river to where the old trail reached it near Grand Island — was to be an alternate route for caravans from now on and eventually a route for emigrant trains.

At Bellevue there was an inexplicable delay in getting the train ready. Then there was a further delay and when the impatient watchers on the Green finally met their companions they learned that there had come close to being no caravan at all this year. For while Fontenelle's men lingered at Bellevue they began to fall sick with Asiatic cholera.

This was the cholera's third year in the United States. And this, the first outbreak of cholera in North America, was part of the pandemic which began, so far as modern scholarship knows, in India in 1816. It was mankind's worst epidemic since the

Black Death; it may have been worse than the Black Death. It burned slowly in native India for seven years but reached the Ganges delta in 1826. In three more years it came to the Caspian Sea and by 1830 it was flaming across Russia and the Near East. The next year it was at Mecca, whence the pilgrims, dying by the thousand, carried it into the southern Mohammedan lands. 'The years 1831 and 1832 were terrible years throughout Europe. From the Caspian Sea the pestilence crossed by boat and caravan to the Black Sea and ascended the Danube into southern and central Europe . . . traveled along roads to the headwaters of the streams of the Baltic drainage area . . . it accompanied all human travel.' [1] England first felt it in the summer of 1831 and the next year it was all over the British Isles.

Wretched Irishmen packed in the holds of emigrant ships brought it to Canada early in 1832. They and their hosts died like flies. It traveled up the St. Lawrence and came to the United States down Lake Champlain and by canal boat to Albany. From Albany it traveled down the Hudson to New York, reaching the city in a dead heat with other cases that came directly across the Atlantic. Meanwhile it traveled westward by the Ohio River and the Erie Canal. (We noted that in the fall of 1832 Maximilian stopped at New Harmony in fear of cholera and perhaps acquired a light case.) It traveled down the Great Lakes and all but wiped out the unfortunate detachment of soldiers whom Winfield Scott was taking to subdue Black Hawk. That was the year when John Wyeth, coming back broke from his uncomfortable trip to the mountains, reached the panic-stricken city of New Orleans, hired out as a gravedigger at two dollars a day, helped fill excavations with the dead, and finally caught the disease himself but survived. New Orleans suffered dreadfully in 1832 but had another ghastly outbreak in 1833, and in that latter year Missouri, Kentucky, and in fact all the interior valley experienced the same horrors that the seaboard had seen the year before. (Hope of avoiding the cholera determined Captain Stewart's route to St. Louis.) That year saw the end of the American epidemic as such but the disease smouldered in many places, to break out viciously in some of them every year and eventually in 1849 to sweep much of the country again and to find an excellent forcing bed in the gold rush.[2]

In 1833 the disease went up the Missouri as far as Fort Union, though it lost some of its virulence on the way. Thereafter there were pockets of it along the Mississippi. One of these was St. Louis, where a few cases begot the usual terror every year. Barring an occasional steamboat case on the way to Independence, however, it got no farther west. But now, on June 10, 1835, at Bellevue the first victim in Fontenelle's party showed the familiar symptoms. The disease strikes like a thunderclap and sometimes runs its course in a few hours. Diarrhoea and vomiting are severe from the beginning and soon become violent. Prostration is complete. The severe fluid loss, which may produce blood loss as well, shrinks and wrinkles the patient's skin. His face grows hollow, his nose sharpens, he begins to turn blue. He is at an extreme of agony. In a few hours, or, at most, a few days, he dies or rounds the turn and begins to mend.

No one could mistake what was wrong with the first victim. This group of prairie travelers must have felt the frenzied dread that made the well as wretched as the sick. The caravan might never start for the mountains; many of them might die. So Lucien Fontenelle woke a greenhorn who was traveling with him. The greenhorn was a physician and in bad health at that, exhausted by travel, agonized by a chronic pain in his side for which he had lately bled himself — and he was a missionary. He had a companion, an elderly Yankee parson. Fontenelle's men had not taken kindly to the Christians who were following in the steps of Jason Lee. They had been offended like Wyeth's men of last year by the missionaries' dislike of traveling on the Sabbath, by their piety, by their gentility. And they had manifested their dislike — guffawing at the greenhorns' mistakes, cutting loose the raft which was to ferry their little outfit across the river, on one occasion rotten-egging the sick physician, and, at least so the elderly gentleman believed, plotting to murder both of them once they were well into the wilderness. Fontenelle, waking his greenhorn in the night to tell him that cholera had struck, must have been under a slight chagrin.

Nevertheless Doctor Marcus Whitman roused himself and got to work. For twelve days they had a vicious battle with the plague, new cases every day, one of them Fontenelle himself, and at least three deaths. Whitman saved the caravan — by his constant nursing of the sick it must have been, for the calomel he ladled into them could only have added another terror to cholera. But, dragged down by his own inflamed side, he would not be licked. He warmed them, fed them, comforted them, saw them through, got the camp moved to higher ground and cleaner surroundings — and suddenly they were all convalescing, the attack was over. Just to show that they had not been too humbled, some of the boys went out and murdered an Arikara halfbreed whom they had been meaning to get for some time. But from now on they would make no trouble for the missionaries.

* * *

The flood was running faster and had caught up two remarkable characters. The Reverend Samuel Parker, lately pastor at Middlefield, Massachusetts, but more recently a dominie at a girls' school in Ithaca, New York, had tried to answer the Flatheads' appeal last summer but had reached the frontier too late to join a caravan. Now he had made it and had brought with him a physician whose zeal he had roused during the winter. Samuel Parker was fifty-six years old and a scholar, a gentle, unworldly man of books, a dweller in parsonage studies, but he was going west by pack train as tranquilly as a man half his age would go by automobile today.

At fifty-six he was set in his ways, inelastic, of a certain dignity, and this may have caused some friction with the younger, more adaptable Whitman, who took to prairie travel with the enthusiasm many greenhorns found roused in them. At least when the waspish William Gray came to write his history, he said it did. Parker, Gray said, 'could not put up with the offhand, careless, and as he thought slovenly manner in which Dr. Whitman was inclined to travel.' He didn't like Whitman's eating with his knife, Gray says, and adds other bits of squeamishness. But though Whitman's journal contains an occasional impatience, though the two temporarily disagreed before parting, and though Whitman formally complained when Parker failed later on to abide by the arrangements then made, the chances are that Gray was seeing them both through his own bile. It colored most of what he looked at.

Parker was a Congregational divine, Whitman a Presbyterian 'missionary physician.' They were agents of the American Board of Commissioners for Foreign Missions, a joint Congregational-Presbyterian enterprise, which had sent them out to investigate the plea of the Flatheads and Nez Perces for religion. They are a more pleasing pair than the Lees of last year and much more pleasing to the modern mind than the depressed, guilt-ridden, dedicated souls whom the American Board began sending out the next year.

Samuel Parker may be permitted some crotchets in thanks for the cool, analytical intelligence he shows as he grapples with the West, the Indians, prairie travel, and all the stupendous novelty that might easily have overwhelmed so old and settled a man.

Throughout this period there is no more sagacious writing about the West than his *Journal of an Exploring Tour Beyond the Rocky Mountains.* Whitman wrote no books; the only writing that admits us to his mind is his letters to the American Board and other letters and the laconic entries in diaries that are fragmentary and much too brief. But in the first journey he is a man losing his private concerns in a great cause; from now on he is completely dedicated. From now on too he is a great man — and it is not the brutal tragedy he is heading toward, twelve years in the future, that gives him the dignity of destiny itself in the student's mind. Not the murdered mission at Waiilatpu but a life lived to the sole end it freely set itself. In a different way, in a way that is much more appealing, Whitman was as much an instrument of the time-spirit as Jason Lee.

There is a refreshing lack of evangelical self-reproach in both missionaries, only a couple of exclamations all told, and no special manifestations of God's providence. Far behind his schedule, Fontenelle laid the gad to his men. There were about sixty of them, about two hundred animals, and six wagons. These last were an innovation, or rather a revival, which strongly interested Whitman. For Parker had introduced him, and probably suggested his marriage, to a golden-haired, beautiful woman on the verge of spinsterhood, vivacious, more flirtatious than was proper to one so pious, a fine singer, who ever since girlhood had wanted to consume herself as a missionary to the heathen. All these attributes were laying up trouble for Narcissa Prentiss and the Oregon Mission. But she had promised to marry Whitman and had bedeviled the American Board till it authorized her to join the Western missions, the sooner the better, though, the Board hoped, as a married woman. That did not necessarily mean Oregon but if Fontenelle's wagons held up they would give Whitman leverage to make it mean Oregon. He kept an eye on them when he could, which was not often, for he had to manage the pack mules of the missionary outfit unassisted by Mr. Parker. Mr. Parker disengaged himself from chores, would not cook, would not make or break camp, and when the alkali dysentery prostrated Whitman on schedule, went off to dine with Fontenelle in scholarly abstraction.

Fontenelle was on the alert for Arikaras, the river pirates with chronically bad hearts who had taken to the prairies a year ago to avoid being impressed by the military sent to purify them a little. He did not meet them, for Colonel Dodge was taking his Dragoons west to impress all Indians who might hear of him, and the Arikaras were moving ahead of him up the South Platte, fast. Fontenelle did meet a large band of Pawnee Loups under one Bad Axe, who were making a hunt. They would not let the whites go on ahead lest they scare the buffalo away and insisted on traveling with them for a couple of days, Parker trying to instruct Bad Axe, whose countenance suggested that he wanted instruction, in the Christian mysteries. But they could converse only in signs, a language which Parker had not mastered — and 'which is far more unintelligible than I had anticipated.' The packers began to grumble for they did not like Pawnees and there would have been trouble but Fontenelle paid a toll and they were permitted to go through.

On the North Platte they found the buffalo in great and daily increasing abundance. Fat cow for everyone and sport for everyone but Mr. Parker. And sport for him, too, before long, for there came over this sedate man an urge he found it hard to reconcile 'with a good conscience.' He had never supposed that he would want to 'trifle with the life even of the most insignificant animal' but he was forced to admit that he wanted to chase a buffalo. He did so, brandishing an unfamiliar shooting iron and spurring his horse into a herd. Selecting a victim, he 'dismounted in order to take a more steady aim than I could otherwise have done.' He wounded his bull and, though he didn't know it, received a special manifestation of providence, for it did not charge. The boys gaped when he described his adventure, then instructed him: when you shoot buffler, stay on your horse.

On July 22 the party camped a couple of miles from Chimney Rock. Parker and Whitman rode over to inspect the famous column. A large herd of buffalo came stampeding toward them and by now they knew enough to recognize this as a bad sign. They hurried toward camp, whence Fontenelle was already sending a party to protect them from whoever might be driving the buffalo. But the whooping madmen who galloped out of the dust firing guns were not hostiles but some of Fitzpatrick's men who had come to see what had delayed the caravan and to find out what the news was since May, 1834. Two days later a similar alarm did mean Indians and Fontenelle had his men in battle order at once. Just out of rifleshot, however, the charging horses were set to running in circles and the guns were fired at nothing, both of which meant peace. Forty of the peaceful, dressed for a ball, came into camp and proved to be Oglala Sioux. Presently the caravan overtook a very large village of them, fully two thousand. They were Bull Bear's band, the greater part of the Oglala subdivision, and they were headed for Fort Laramie.

This was momentous: the Sioux were moving into Laramie Plain. It is said, on evidence not quite conclusive,[3] that they were moved to do so by an invitation of Sublette & Campbell's to migrate here, the preceding summer. The idea was to entice as many Company customers as possible from the established, very profitable Sioux post on the Missouri, Fort Pierre, and attach them to the Opposition's Fort Laramie. But Fort Laramie had passed to the Company a month or so before Parker and Whitman got there, so if the Opposition really were responsible for the Oglala migration they had merely redistributed some of the trust's trade. But there were Sioux on the Platte now and they would never abandon it. And this destroyed the structure of international relationships, producing a turbulence which was to last till the tribes were no longer capable of making war. Their inveterate enemies, the Pawnees, were now straight east of them, their inveterate enemies, the Crows, straight north. The reaches where Fontenelle met them were traditionally Cheyenne and Arapaho country. But the country just to the west — Laramie Plain, with its vast buffalo herds and its crossroads, the Laramie Mountains, the Medicine Bow mountains — had always been a kind of Kentucky or Rhineland. No tribe quite claimed it, no tribe dominated it, many tribes came there to hunt. Snakes and Bannocks from the west, Utes from the southwest, Cheyennes and Arapahos, Crows, Pawnees hunted buffalo here, raided one another, and made prairie truces so that they could trade. Now the Sioux, a populous, arrogant, and bellicose people, were going to try to establish a protectorate over it. In the service of orderly government and a peaceful condominium they warred here with nearly everyone for a generation.

The Reverend Mr. Parker found them well favored, well dressed, and clean, and makes the unexpected observation that their women were 'less pendulous' than other squaws he had seen. The caravan and the Oglalas moved on together and at evening, July 26, they reached Fort Laramie. Fontenelle gave his men a bust the next day and the missionaries had to watch a mass drunk. They expressed less disgust in their journals than Lee would have done but it was quite a day. At the end of it one brawler shot a colleague in the back and when it was clear that he had only half-killed him, went for another gun to finish the job — but was restrained. Fontenelle broached kegs for the Oglalas, too, to cultivate trade relations, so that Fort Laramie resounded. Having begun to dance, the Oglalas made a three-day job of it and ended with the holy ceremony that brought the buffalo to be killed. The hunters put on their masks and horns and costumes, the others with the squaws sang the sacred chants and beat the sacred tom-toms. And here Mr. Parker was outraged.

'I cannot say I was much amused to see how well they could imitate brute beasts, while ignorant of God and salvation. The impressive enquiry was constantly on my mind, what will become of their immortal spirits? Rational men imitating beasts and old gray-headed men marshaling the dance! and enlightened white men encouraging it by giving them intoxicating spirits as reward for their good performance.'

So, ignoring the confusion of tongues, he addressed several groups of them on the true nature of God and, going into his own medicine, sang, 'Watchman, tell us of the night.' The elderly voice rose in the heat-shimmering immensity of this summer desert:

Traveler, o'er yon mountain's height
See that glory-beaming star.
Watchman, does its beauteous ray
Aught of joy or hope foretell?
Traveler, yes: it brings the day,
Promised day of Israel.

The Sioux listened reverently; they held all religions sacred.

Men and animals rested at Fort Laramie for five days and then on August 1 Fontenelle said good-bye to the missionaries. They asked him for a statement of expense: passage and findings. 'If anyone is indebted it is myself,' he said, 'for you have saved my life and the lives of my men.' So Lucien Fontenelle shook hands with them, wished them well, and turned them over to Tom Fitzpatrick. . . . He is a shadowed man, this Fontenelle, and legends have gathered round his name. He was of noble French blood, some say of royal blood, and there had been a mysterious romance in his earlier life. High-born relatives of his lived in New Orleans and there is a story that he once called on a sister there after years of separation, and that she could not recognize in the grizzled, buckskinned thug the young courtier she had known. Also, a sister, the same one perhaps, is said to have made a western journey with him and the legend is that the present New Fork Lake in the Wind Rivers was named De Amalia or Damalia for her. Fontenelle is worth a biography but no one has written it yet.

The wagons left at the fort, Tom Fitzpatrick, now a Company partisan, took them down the last leg of the trip headlong —

Independence Rock, the Sweetwater, South Pass, and on August 12 the mouth of New Fork, where the impatient clans had been waiting for five weeks. While the jubilation broke out like a prairie thunder storm, the missionaries met such notables as Jim Bridger and Kit Carson, the Nez Perce and Flathead reception committees, and Captain Stewart of the British Army.

* * *

May we assume that enough has been said about release and debauch at the summer rendezvous? The trappers drank as many pints of alcohol as ever at five dollars a pint, sang as many songs, held as many horse races, bought as many squaws (more, maybe, since more were at hand), and rang as many echoes from the hills. Rendezvous was the mountain man's Christmas, county fair, harvest festival, and crowned-slave carnival of Saturn — this year as always.

Well, in the camp of Andrew Drips a big thug named Shunar or something similar began to feel his liquor. He had a record: he had beaten so many men into fear of him that others walked round him at a distance. Suddenly he went into his alligator phase and announced that he wanted some bones to crunch. Voyageurs, the French, were too easy game, he said, and Americans were panty-waists — 'he would take a switch and switch them.' (Kit Carson's amanuensis: it certainly had more hair on it than that.) He didn't want too much exercise today, so maybe an American would do. Or a Frenchman — Shunar was in no mood to quibble — or a Mexican or even a Dutchman. The point was, he had to have a man for lunch. He swelled round, making a noise. Noise as such would not offend mountain men but this kind was a trifle injudicious. The boys waited a moment to give one another room, for after all this was a big chunk of tough, but not for long. Kit Carson obliged, five-feet-four only but cougar all the way. He told Shunar that the camp was full of Americans who could beat hell out of him and that as the least of them he could, too. It is quite certain that the amanuensis is editing again when Kit goes on to report himself as saying 'that if he used such expressions any more I would rip his guts.'

Mr. Stanley Vestal has it on the authority of Arapaho tradition that there was more in Carson's picking up the gage than a simple feeling for the honor of the American wildcat. According to his story Kit, twenty-four and at the top of the free trappers, was sparking a girl in the Arapaho camp, a mile or so from the rendezvous. Shunar had tried to make her; failing that, he had stalked her by night and tried to rape her, failing again but only because he had to loosen his grip on her in order to cut her chastity-rope. Kit had found his courtship stopped short by the consequent antipathy of her brother to all white men, had asked the reason and been told. He was not only waving Old Glory, he was getting himself a wife.

He was a bad man to monkey with and it is sufficient proof of drunkenness that Shunar, instead of taking to the hills forthwith, got his rifle, mounted his horse, and began to utter the wolfcries of the professional killer, mountain style. Carson grabbed a pistol, leaped on his horse and rode up to the howling desperado. 'Our horses were touching,' Carson says; that was Shunar's mistake and he got no chance to make another one. He began to have a soberer thought when Carson asked him, *pro forma*, if he were the American whose bones were going to be crunched, and said no. They both shot at once, Shunar inadequately for Carson lost a lock of hair only. Kit got him in the gun hand, thus putting him out of commission, hurried back for another pistol, and finished the job.[4]

Thus the introduction to the American Board's representatives of a young man who was in the top rank of his profession. All who rose to distinction in that profession were necessarily fit instruments. We have seen a number of the masters: two Sublettes, Campbell, Harris, Drips, Fontenelle, Gervais, Berger, Fraeb, Joe Robidou, Joe Walker. Others who were just as distinguished as they have not been mentioned because they worked other portions of the mountains, mostly the Colorado Rockies, or because they happened not to cut the trail of this narrative. These are not diminished when it is pointed out that three men were a cut above them, quintessential mountain men, at the top of the craft. To mastery of mountain skill and of the complex job of leadership, and to wisdom in geography and the management of Indians, Tom Fitzpatrick, Jim Bridger, and Kit Carson added something else. They were born a little closer to the West, carried it more centrally in their minds and hearts, had the final superiority that is very slight but makes all the difference, and rightly come down in tradition as the senate of elders. It was chance that gave Bridger a greater celebrity than Fitzpatrick; he came to be eyes and brains for the Army at a time when newspapermen were coming west and could give national expression to local reputation, whereas Tom's culminating services were to departments of the government which had not yet hired press agents. And it was the luck of the draw that made Carson a greater national figure than Jim; he happened to go to work for a man who had genius for publicity, a wife with an equal genius for it, and a father-in-law who had the same genius and a national broadcasting-booth as well. John Charles Frémont let the nation know that it had a great man in greasy buckskins, and the spotlight of 1846, playing on Carson when it played on him, fixed the picture which publicity had sketched. These three — and it is sagacious not to rank or even differentiate them — are the mountain man as master craftsman, partisan, explorer, conqueror, and maker and bequeather of the West. They are important historically because they were the best of a trade group, small and shortlived, who had a maker's part in extending the national boundaries and the national consciousness to continental completion.

And Samuel Parker had a dim inkling of this. What he says about this commonplace shooting scrape in Green River Valley has the condemnation of an educated democrat who lived in the lawfully governed New England, where frontiers, Indians, border thugs, and the violence of all three had been forgotten. It also had the abhorrence of a Christian for the sin of Cain. But it is singularly moderate in tone and it is embodied in a passage which understands the life of the mountain men sympathetically and as justly as any ever written. Mr. Parker is shocked, rather less so by murder than by the blasphemy of trappers who sell packs of playing cards to the Indians as the white man's Bible and tell them that God will punish them with the flames of hell if they do not surrender their wives and daughters for the purpose aforesaid. But Mr. Parker is not stampeded. Here was one missionary who not only knew that the mountain life was hard and sore but could praise courage, loyalty, friendship, hospitality, and the unfrightened mind, and who could see that, in whatever mysterious ways, Providence was using the mountain man for no mean purpose.

Another spectator made other use of this mountain duel. Captain Stewart eventually became a novelist, an unbelievably bad one. A long account of a Green River rendezvous in *Edward Warren* has already been mentioned herein. It is by a good deal the best passage in either of Stewart's two novels. The rendezvous described is basically the one Stewart first saw, that of 1833, but he weaves into it recognizable details from others — and gets Kit and Shunar into it, and even himself.

An English traveler, a captain, complains to Old Bill Williams (the former Methodist circuit rider who gave up souls for beaver, became a celebrated mountain man, and was bequeathed to modern fiction by Frederick Ruxton) that he is spitting too often and too inaccurately. In America, the Reverend Bill replies, the white race is divided into two sexes — one spits and the other has no call to, 'and those who spit will not be stopped by any Englisher, and will go on to the end of the chapter.' This reminder of who won two wars occurs in a skin lodge where Tom Fitzpatrick is playing euchre with several men of whom one at least is historical, an associate of Joe Meek's named Cotton. Moreover, Edward Warren, who reports this conversation in which his creator figures, has been brought to this lodge by Kit Carson. Carson has just saved him from manhandling and possible death at the hands of Shunar and some tough companions.

Shunar's assault on Edward Warren is a sequel of an earlier brawl. There would be no point (even if it were possible) in untangling the hellish plots that have been practiced on Stewart's hero, in whose cruel treatment at the hands of his family the author's fantasy of his own family quarrels may perhaps supply some coloration. But on the way to the rendezvous Warren falls in with Fontenelle's caravan after tribulation. Joe Meek, one of his known companions named Phelps, Bill Williams, and various other historical mountain men are with Fontenelle or near-by. For reasons of plot and skullduggery Warren is invited to a feast and is there hazed by various parties, with particular reference to some horses which secondary villains have stolen from him but which he is accused of having stolen originally. He vehemently hurls the accusation back at the cads. Whereupon Shunar, who, like most of the characters in the novel is suddenly materialized on the scene without introduction or explanation — Shunar 'then said I was a liar, upon which I knocked him over and a struggle ensued.' During this struggle Warren gets a knife in the back but it is only a slight wound and Bill Williams snatches him away, saving his life. He and the caravan move on to the rendezvous. There he meets Etienne Provost, Insula or the Little Chief (identified as a Snake), Drips, various other actual people. The passage about the rabid wolves which has been quoted follows.

Later Warren is outside a 'shanty' when Shunar, 'naked to the waist' and exceedingly drunk, rushes out and aims a blow at him but misses. Warren is about to reply in kind when Kit Carson, also suddenly materialized out of nowhere gun in hand, tells Shunar (quite without relevance to this or any other passage) that he can have the young man tomorrow but he belongs to Kit tonight, and takes him up behind his horse. 'Whether this was taken for an evidence of fear by the bully of the camp, or that he now felt himself backed up by the gathering of the crowd it was difficult to say, but he made a rush as the horse moved and I barely missed getting into a regular fight. It was evident that no one there wished to seize [Carson's] horse or come in contact personally with the rider, who, replacing the pistol in his belt, sounded the shrill yell of the country and made his charger curvet through the mass which had surrounded us, who swore they would make us into small pieces when we should meet again.' The last threat by Shunar's pals has no part in the diabolical villainies of the plotters which soon land the hero with a rope round his neck. But the passage testifies to Carson's reputation and to Stewart's admiration of him. It goes on to describe Kit: he 'was of much shorter and slighter stature than myself; his head, without other covering than waving locks of light brown hair, was occasionally turned to me as he carolled some stanzas of the air of Bruce's March, then much the fashion among the American boys, and showed a pleasant and open countenance, with blue eyes.' [5]

There were less tense moments at rendezvous. We saw Jim Bridger get an arrow in his back in the fall of 1832, soon after the contrived massacre of Henry Vanderburgh. Doctor Harrison, who traveled with Old Gabe the following summer, appears not to have inspired confidence in his professional skill for the arrow remained. But Marcus Whitman was different. Bridger consulted him, the doctor proposed to operate and did so — before crowded bleachers of Indians and mountaineers. When the incision was made Whitman found that the three-inch, barbed iron arrowhead 'was hooked at the point striking a large bone and a cartilaginous substance had grown round it.' This involved extensive butchering out, which the bleachers would criticize with the vocabulary of the trail, but, Parker says, 'the Doctor pursued the operation with great self-possession and perseverance.' Whitman expressed surprise that Old Gabe had been able to go about his business with so large a foreign body in him but was speaking as a greenhorn. 'In the mountains, Doctor,' Jim told him, 'meat don't spoil.'

Whitman had made a lifelong friend. Also he had captured the admiration of the trappers. Another one who was carrying an arrowhead had it removed as soon as Jim was finished, then others who bore similar mementoes, and thereafter all the boys who needed repair jobs presented themselves. Hyar's a sawbones! So the medical mission began. It was to continue, extending across thousands of square miles, till the Cayuses ended it. Whitman had begun to weave his figure in the pattern of the future.

* * *

The colored ball must come to rest when the wheel stops spinning but there is no mathematical formula to predict where. Twenty miles from here and a year ago Jason Lee, Missionary to the Flatheads, seeing the same Indians that Whitman and Parker talked to now, had known at once that God directed him to go on to other fields for other purposes. The needle of our national destiny swung on its pivot and pointed in one direction when it came within the field of an impalpable lodestone. Now there was another of those moments that fascinate one who looks back, the moments of beginning, when the previously undetermined comes into law.

There were the usual banquets in state with Fitzpatrick and the other grandees. But also there were meetings with the Flatheads and Nez Perce grandees, who had now met their priest.

In May, 1806, Lewis and Clark, on the back trail, met the Nez Perces, who had made a most favorable impression on them last year and with whom they had left their horses over the winter. The Nez Perces saw that the whites were thin and worn and hungry, so the chief had a couple of horses driven up and killed for them. He said that they had lots of horses, more than they could use, and the white captains and their men could have as many of them to eat as they might need or want. 'This,' Meriwether Lewis wrote in his journal, 'is a much greater act of hospitality than we have witnessed from any nation or tribe since we have passed the Rocky mountains. in short be it spoken to their immortal honor it is the only act which deserves the appellation of hospitallity which we have witnessed in this quarter.' Clark found them 'much more clenly in their persons and habitations than any nation we have seen sence we left the Illinois.' And on leaving he summed them up. They 'are in general stout well formed active men. they have high noses and maney of them on the acqueline order with chearfull and agreeable countinances; their complexions are not remarkable . . . they appear to be cheerful but not gay, they are found of gambling and of their amusements which consists principally in shooting their arrows at a targit made of willow bark, and in rideing and exersiseing themselves on horseback, raceing &c. they are expirt marks men & good riders. they do not appear to be so much devoted to baubles as most of the nations we have met with, but seem anxious always to riceve articles of utility, such as knives, axes, Kittles, blankets & mockersons [and] awls. blue beeds however may form an exception to this remark; This article among all the nations of this country may be justly compared to gold and silver among civilized nations. They are generally well clothed in their stile. . . .' So every white man who ever wrote about the Nez Perces till it was time to steal their lands. They were superior Indians, they made no trouble, they liked and admired white men.

Their desire for instruction in the mysteries was genuine and paramount, as clean as the desire of these Christians to give them what they wanted. Both desires were simple and altogether hopeless. The heritage of nineteen hundred years of thought and practice was at the disposal of the Christians, proved accurate to the minutest subdivision of a mil scale. The first step, the step on which all subsequent ones depended, was to bring souls to God. Teach the Flatheads and Nez Perces God, Jesus, immortality, primordial guilt, the history of the Jewish monotheists, redemption, transfiguration and crucifixion and resurrection, the majestic poem in which western man has embodied his understanding of how his fate works out. Teach them baptism, repentance, the seeking, the knowledge of God's presence, the wish for oneness, the sacrament of God's body and blood, misericordia and magnanimity, the metaphor and symbolism in which western man has expressed his understanding of what life means. That was the step on which all others must be added.

The Indians receiving instruction were men of the age of polished stone. Their minds had a metabolism, a systole and diastole, circuits of afference and efference and affect, which had come down a long evolution quite incomparable to the aggregate which we whites have chosen to call the consciousness of western man. Their poems and metaphors and symbolisms, their myths of awe and wonder and man's aloneness and the immensity of the universe and the soul groping for meaning in the night watches — had no impress that came down from the herdsmen of Asia Minor through a long refinement to worshipers in fourteenth-century cathedrals and on to John Calvin, whose vicars were now on Green River. When they were told about Jesus they must think of Him as, say, one of the young men who for many tribes come up a vine through the hole in the earth and start looking, through the wars and sorceries of the world, for their father the sun. Grace abounding or the consciousness of God's presence, or sin, or contrition, or charity, or what you will, could reach them as idea only by reference to concepts which had been painfully integrated in the thinking of a different kind of man, a man whose intelligence had a different content and a different functioning, and at that a savage.

They tried, both Indians and whites. There they stood, the seekers and the bearers of truth. Marcus Whitman, this moment taking his first step down the path whose end he reached on November 29, 1847, has the full charge of irony implicit in the nature of men's relationships. We must not diminish it by forgetting in the intricacy of Christian thought that what these Indians wanted was the philosopher's stone, and that what they expected of it was guns and scalping knives and blankets and glass beads and metal tools.

Two highly ceremonious traditions met in the tent of the missionaries. The men of God for whose coming the young men had died four years ago were now here and the Flatheads and Nez Perces, their faith justified, made them welcome. A Flathead elder said that he was old and could not learn much, was deaf and could not hear much, but rejoiced to have lived to meet a man who was personally acquainted with supernaturals. A Nez Perce said that what the traders had told him about the true supernaturals had reached his ears but he had not been able to make it sink through to his inward parts: he would be taught and would obey according to his understanding but knew that he would make mistakes and asked pardon for them in advance. Insula, the Flathead dignitary, said that his heart had so rejoiced at news of the teachers' coming that he had ridden out for three days to meet them but had not cut their trail and had had his horse stolen by Crows. Now that he had heard the teachers speak, he added, he no longer grieved for the horse. It was an expert Indian who could steal a horse from Insula — and an impressive missionary who could reconcile him to the theft.

One question which the American Board had sent Parker and Whitman to answer was answered at once. The sincerity of these Indians' desire for religious instruction could not be doubted: the word given to the world by William Walker and the *Christian Advocate* was a true word. There was this difference between these two and the Methodists of last year, that they did not for a moment consider refusing the plea. They adjourned to talk it over and to get information from the mountain men. Here Captain Stewart proved most useful — and played a part in determining one of the channels of American history. He described the country where the Nez Perces and Flatheads lived;

he had traveled it last fall and this spring. He summarized the way of life of those tribes and of the Spokanes, Pend d'Oreilles, and Cayuses who were their neighbors. He went on to discuss the tribes beyond the Cascade Mountains — and if the missionaries had learned from the Indians that the Lees had abandoned them, it was Stewart who informed them that the Methodist mission had been established on the Willamette, that there would be neither support nor competition from the Methodists. He described the annual cismontane hunts of the Flatheads and Nez Perces, and the raids of the Blackfeet. He summarized the natural resources of the Nez Perce country: the salmon and the deer, the camas, the timber, the arable land. He had been especially impressed by the rich valley at the foot of the Blue Mountains, the Grande Ronde, and he commended it to his listeners as the best site for their mission station. They pumped him dry and checked his information by the masters of geography and ethnology who had brought them here.

Whitman was convinced and, as his journal shows, he was shocked by Lee's betrayal of his suppliants. There was a great urgency and it must be faced at once. If he and Parker carried out the plans made with the Board before they started West it would take two full years to fulfill the so-long-deferred hope of the Indians. For they would need the rest of this year to go on to the Nez Perce country and all of next year to return to the States, and not till 1837 could they come back with personnel and equipment for a mission establishment. They had been instructed to determine whether a mission were possible and desirable. That was settled — and Whitman could save a whole year if he were to go back to the States now and show the American Board that it was settled. But how could he leave his companion, elderly, Christian, and a greenhorn, to complete their joint inquiry in the wilderness alone? Whitman was caught in an agonizing dilemma. Parker solved it. If Whitman stayed and the two of them went on together, he said, they would not be safe unless they had divine protection. And if he had that it would make no difference that he was traveling alone.

After more discussion and prayer they decided it that way. They told the chiefs that their mission was assured, from where the sun now stands. Doctor Whitman would go back and return next year with teachers who would live among them. Mr. Parker would go on and look at their country. (They avoided talking over a similar project with the Utes and Snakes present at the rendezvous: Parker recognized their need of salvation but first things must come first.) The chiefs were jubilant and assigned a young Nez Perce to the assistance and personal supervision of Parker. He was the Bull's Head, who last year had entertained Bill Sublette by driving a buffalo through camp, and Parker hired to help him with the small outfit a voyageur named approximately Compo who could speak Nez Perce. Whitman found a Nez Perce boy who could speak a little English and got permission to take him East, so that they could master each other's language in the year to come. His name was rendered Tackitonitis; Whitman simplified it to Richard. Then a Nez Perce elder brought his son to Whitman and asked him to take the boy too and teach him religion on the way. Whitman demurred: two untutored savage adolescents would require a lot of management. But Parker would miss no chance to save a soul and asked him to accept the boy, Ais, commissioning him to inquire among his friends at Ithaca till he found a home for them for the winter.

Mr. Parker's tiny outfit would travel for a few days with Jim Bridger, who was taking a Company brigade to the northward and thence to the Yellowstone River country. Jim moved his men three miles from rendezvous on August 21 and camped for the final check-up. Whitman rode over to spend a last evening with his fellow-missionary. Next morning they 'sought the blessing and guidance of God' and said good-bye, each with the heaviest foreboding. Fitzpatrick needed another week to wind up the rendezvous. Then on August 27 he took the back trail to Fort Laramie, a late start after a late rendezvous. Whitman went with him. So did Stewart, who had now spent three summers and one winter in the mountains and a winter on the lower Columbia. He had traveled the West from St. Louis to Fort Vancouver, from Taos to the mouth of the Yellowstone, for to admire and for to see. As a British officer he had transposed military camp craft into prairie and mountain travel and taken part in a dozen skirmishes with the natives of this alien bush. As a British sportsman he had shot the big game of this new frontier, grizzlies and bighorn, antelopes and mountain goats, and above all buffalo. He was going back to civilization now but only for a while.[6]

* * *

With a tranquil heart Samuel Parker rode into the unknown. Besides Bridger's brigade, which was making for Jackson's Hole, most of the Flatheads traveled with him for a while. Like Lee before him he held divine service on the first Sabbath, at the mouth of a canyon with the tips of the Tetons in sight to the north. Old Gabe's men listened respectfully, Parker says, and 'I did not feel any disposition to upbraid them for their sins but endeavoured affectionately to show them that they are unfit for heaven and that they could not be happy in the employments of that holy place unless they should first experience a great moral change of heart by the grace of God.' It made strange hearing, hemmed round by the desert of late August, and maybe the strangeness was what made them attentive. But as he talked a band of buffalo came round the swell of a hill and Mr. Parker lost his congregation. There was fat cow for supper and the boys made such a feast of it that Parker, Joe Meek tells us, 'rebuked the sabbath-breakers quite severely.' Joe adds that he would have been wise not to enjoy the tenderloin so obviously himself for the boys were not trained in dialectics and could not distinguish between sins.

Still there is something fabulous and heroic in Samuel Parker's horseback ride, with Greek Testament and unfamiliar sidearms, through this mountain wilderness. His Indians treated him with exquisite consideration, bringing him wild berries and ranging widely to get him fresh meat. He climbed a minor peak and saw the ribs of the continent, coming back 'much gratified with what I had seen of the works of God' and dreaming of a time when plows would break this soil, the lowing herds put an end to silence, and altars to his God be set up here. On to Pierre's Hole where he heard the story of the famous battle — with much scorn for the barbarous white men and a very snooty footnote in his book about the inaccuracies of Washington Irving. Here Bridger, who was already sending out trapping parties, turned east toward the divide and left Parker alone with his Nez Perces and Flatheads. He liked them better the more he saw of them, had been instructing them in the elements of Christian belief (as well as might be by means of an interpreter) and was jubilant when an elder asked him to explain the sacrament of marriage to a number of his charges who had been practicing divorce. He did so and found his parishioners 'ready to practice instructions as soon as received.' All but two at once set up housekeeping again.

After each Bible class he would hear the Indians talking over the new doctrines up to a late hour. He records the speech of a chief who said he had 'been like a little child, uneasy, feeling about in the dark after something, not knowing what.' He taught them to kneel, too, and to pray. When a boy died he stood at the grave and explained the immortality of the soul — so eloquently that the chiefs woke him from sleep that night and desired further good talk about it. So in the happy, tragic illusion that he was bringing these loyal hearts to Christ he made his amazing way, on to the Salmon River, rejoicing in his singular fortune as an instrument of God and writing down observations on the countryside that remain among the most intelligent we have. Food had got short, there were no buffalo to be found, and Parker caught a dangerous cold — with Doctor Whitman far away. But the Indians nursed him carefully and when he prayed for buffalo a sizable herd appeared, which taught his companions far more than he could know about the efficacy of prayer.

Most of the Indians left to follow the herd. Parker's immediate friends and guardians stayed with him and though his health was not restored he methodically kept on, pressing always into the wilderness. He was still no better when, impatient with the slow progress of the village, he prevailed on a small party to hurry ahead. His strength was failing and he had lost much weight. Sometimes his courage sank as he thought of the enormous mountains still to be crossed. He wondered if he must die here with his mission unfulfilled and no Christian to pray beside his grave. He rebuked himself for doubting but found that he doubted still. Thus till the last half of September, the chasms of the Salmon River, the forest gloom of the Clearwater, and at last the Snake: the old man's will and faith sufficed and he began to mend. He was recovered when, on October 6, he reached Fort Walla Walla, the courtly Pambrun who commanded it, and a table spread in the wilderness. Bread, butter, sugar, milk — forgotten in the long traverse of the land. But there was an even greater wonder and Samuel Parker could rest his old bones in a chair.

The last valley by which he had reached this inn had pleased him beyond anything else he had seen — familiar species of trees, wild roses blooming in Indian summer, a land running over with fatness, he thought — and it might be the best place for the mission. Wrong by a few miles but no more than a few, and we could leave him here, the curious agent of what seemed God's will but had better be described as the rising intention of his countrymen. He had left Liberty on May 15; it was October 6 when he got to Fort Walla Walla; and on the eighth, having said good-bye to the remaining Nez Perces and paid off his driver and interpreter, he set off down the Columbia in a dugout with three Walla Wallas. At the Dalles he met a man known to him for great works and good ones too, Nat Wyeth, still trying — and failing — to make something of his problem in mathematical certainties. Wyeth had made notes on Chinook, the *lingua franca* of these parts, and copied them for Parker, who then set out in another dugout with other Indians.

After all he had endured the ghastly river trip seemed mild enough and on October 16 he stepped ashore at Fort Vancouver — Doctor McLoughlin with outstretched hand inviting him to share the governor's house this winter. It seemed the end of the journey to Samuel Parker and he noted that through all these months he had not truly suffered from the monotony of diet that was here so abundantly relieved, and that never once had he been forced to eat dog or horse. But it was not the end, for with only a day's rest he took to the river again, rowed by Kanakas this time and accompanied by the naturalist Townsend, whose conversation roused nostalgia for the world of learning he had left. He had another crowded month of it, to the mouth of the river and back again, seeing everyone and everything and coming at last to meet his fellow workers in the vineyard, the Lees. But he was with the family of a retired voyageur at the moment which makes his best exit from this narrative. The moment when, traveling up the Willamette, he came to the great falls. The Willamette, which flows through the entire history of Oregon, is a noble river, is the river whose myth supplied a great name, the Multnomah, and the plunge of those waters over their rock shelf roused many ideas in the mind of this tireless divine: the country fertile as any on earth, the water which had been rushing down this chute through all the generations of man but had never turned a wheel. Samuel Parker looked at his watch. 'It was two o'clock and all was still except the roar of the falling water. I called to recollection that in the year 1809 I stood by the falls of Genesee River and all was silence except the roar of the cataract. But it is not so now, for Rochester stands where I then stood.'

And it is not so now, for Oregon City stands where he then stood and Portland is twelve miles away.

* * *

Thus the new men and the intensifying energy. There was another aspect, too, in this summer of 1835, for the United States Army marched farther west than it had ever been before. The First Regiment of United States Dragoons, which in the summer of 1834 had been sent to the Wichita Mountains of Oklahoma and on to the Red River, was sent to the foot of the Colorado Rockies. Last year its mission had been to awe and pacify the Comanches, Kiowas, and other tribes who stole and murdered along the Santa Fe Trail, and to make peace among them. This year it was primarily to impress the pirates of the upper Missouri, the Arikaras, who, as has been noted, prudently abandoned their homes and took to the prairies. Three companies of Long Knives, about one hundred and twenty all told, were considered sufficient for the task. One of them was commanded by Lieutenant Lancaster P. Lupton who would presently leave the army to escape court-martial, enter the mountain trade, and establish a post in the country he was now seeing for the first time. John Gant, lately partner in the firm of Gant and Blackwell, was attached as guide. So was Big Fallon, as fantastic a mountain man as the trade ever produced, a giant who had preceded even the Ashley men into the mountains and had roamed the entire West ever since, though mostly in the southern reaches. By the end of another ten years he would be in California, in time to share the Bear Flag fantasy and play a leading rôle in the rescue of the Donner Party.

The Dragoons marched upriver from Fort Leavenworth to the mouth of the Platte at about the time Fontenelle left Liberty, but escaped the cholera. Thence, pausing to hold councils with every band of Indians they met and to indorse the Pax Americana which the government still supposed it could impose by good will on the entire West, they chased the Arikaras up the Coasts of the Nebraska. The Indians had no difficulty staying out of reach — the Army never did learn to march as expeditiously as any fur caravan — but yielded to curiosity and Colonel Dodge's assurance, carried to them by Gant, that war was not intended. The principal chiefs and prophets came in, accepted presents, and listened to Dodge's stately rebuke of their villainies. Lieutenant Kingsbury, who kept the regimental journal, noted that they were the wildest and most savage tribe of Western Indians, which was hardly true, though they were the most annoying, and that they were the best-looking Indians he had ever seen, a compliment no one else ever paid them. Dodge, a first-class fighting man and an old hand with Indians, could have had little belief in the moral platitudes he voiced to them and none in their promises of amendment. The Arikaras told him that they had repented and hereafter would lavish affection on any white man they might encounter. They posed statuesquely and rode away, with the cold deck in their sleeves.

That was on the lower South Platte. The Dragoons went on up the river almost to the foot of the Front Range, then took the worn trail that came down from Fort Laramie and followed it to the Arkansas. This was the country of the Arapahos and Dodge began to meet them when he got south of Fontaine Qui Bouille. There was a big powwow on the Arkansas, hundreds of Arapahos and a sprinkling of other tribes. With Pike's Peak behind them and the Spanish Peaks at their right hand, the Dragoons then headed homeward by way of Bent's Fort and the Santa Fe Trail. There were other Indians to talk to, notably a village of Southern Cheyennes, and a new species of mountain men drifted in for talk and store food, Mexicans, the dogged trappers of the southernmost Rockies who have had too little celebration. The Dragoons were back at Fort Leavenworth by the middle of September, after a trip that taught them a good deal about their profession but produced no spectacular events and few if any results. But the Army had been west now. Beginning with Frémont it would come again repeatedly, until it came to stay.

The summer saw practically the end of Bonneville's venture. The previous autumn he had made a second invasion of Hudson's Bay Company territory but, after a strenuous passage of the Blues, had found the poaching even more strenuous than before. The Company's Indians would not trade with him, the Company would not sell him supplies or even food, and he went back on short rations to the mountains. He had lost his fall hunt but the winter camp (in Bear River Valley) became proverbial among the trappers for abundant buffalo and high jinks. In the spring he learned that the brigade he had sent to hunt along the upper Arkansas (the Colorado Rockies) and winter there had not done so. It got the by now customary rough handling, first from Crows and then from Blackfeet. Bonneville's own spring hunt was a failure. Throughout the last year, in fact, ever since the return, empty-handed, of Walker's California brigade, Bonneville had seemed oppressed and at a loss — unable to plan a proper campaign or hold a lieutenant to his plans. His best trappers had been hired away from him or he had been forced to pay ruinous wages to keep them; others were deserting with furs and supplies. In July he outfitted a single brigade with his remaining goods and left it in the mountains, where word of it simply peters out, and took the rest of his party back to the States, a failure who had lost the investment of his backers. He had overstayed his original leave by almost two years and his application for extension, taken to Washington by Cerré, had got lost in a tangle of War Department red tape. So he found that he had been dismissed the service. He applied for reinstatement and presently received it by order of the President himself, Jackson going over the heads of the generals for reasons which can only be guessed but seem obvious.

Nat Wyeth's enterprise was running out. He had spent the spring and summer constantly on the move, from his post on the island at the mouth of the Willamette to Fort Hall and back and all about, but nothing had come of it. Deserting, massacred, drowning, his men melted away. The *May Dacre* came back from the Sandwich Islands safely enough but with no profit from his flyer in lumber. The ambitious salmon scheme produced only half a cargo plus a few barrels specially salted for his friends. Wyeth doubted the quality of the product since he had not been able to supervise the curing process — and had learned at a high cost that help was not, in this country, to be trusted. By September, with seventeen of his last year's party killed or dead of the Vancouver epidemic, he acknowledged that he was washed up. He had the ague himself and it gave him a moment of uncharacteristic depression. Beside the River of the West he remembered the mudflats of the Charles and boyhood expeditions in the gentler wilderness of Norton's Woods, writing to Uncle Jarvis in Baltimore that his business was scattered over half the deserts of the earth and he 'a powerless lump of matter in the extremity of mortal pain with little hope of surviving a day,' and in truth 'glad to go down with the sun.' Nat Wyeth, however, could not pity himself very long and even while voicing his melancholy was preparing to go home next summer and return to the ice business at Fresh Pond. But it would be a good idea to go by way of Santa Fe from the summer rendezvous, and to determine whether there was anything in his old notion of entering the New Mexican trade.

Wyeth still had a brigade in the mountains, based on his Fort Hall. It was led by an old RMF Company man named Joseph Gale. (A wisecrack of his has come down. When Doctor McLoughlin refused to sell him supplies at Vancouver he is supposed to have said that he had an uncle on the way to Oregon, who was rich enough to buy them all out and would. Doctor McLoughlin was impressed — and not enlightened when Gale said his uncle's name was Sam.) He was inept as a partisan and a species of ineffective despot. Osborne Russell, who was with him, records a series of small rebellions by the men and more or less disastrous mistakes by their commander. Bannocks and Blackfeet killed and robbed them and in the end the remnants had to join Jim Bridger's brigade, their entire effort lost.

It seems to have been a fair year with the mountain brigades of the American Fur Company but the approaching shadow could no longer be ignored. Beaver would not rise: the St. Louis price remained too low to pay a profit. This year for the first time the trade in buffalo robes at Fort Union was worth more than that in beaver. The same was already true at Fort Pierre and was becoming true at Fort Clark, and now that the Oglalas were moving to the upper Platte it would presently be true at Fort Laramie also. With the price of beaver down and the penalty of ruthless overtrapping now manifest in an increasing scarcity of plews, the Company could not much longer support the overhead of large mountain brigades. It would soon begin to concentrate on its fixed posts and on the trade in robes, letting the Indians do the hunting. The best bet in the mountains was such operators as Kit Carson, who this year led a small party, Joe Meek among them, through the familiar fields. They were frequently in touch with Bridger and joined him in the usual brushes with the Blackfeet, but they were on their own. Such parties were composed entirely of experts, their greater mobility allowed them to operate profitably on a smaller return in furs, and they needed no capital.

The Company took a bad loss in August when its steamboat the *Assiniboin* was wrecked and burned at the mouth of Heart River. Eleven hundred packs of robes (ten to the pack) were destroyed, Francis Chardon says, some beaver, and the miscellany of her cargo. With it were most of the specimens, zoölogical, botanical, and ethnological, that Maximilian had collected so sedulously. It was a severe loss and thereafter the Company preferred to hire its steamboating done for it.

Presently cholera appeared at Fort Clark, having lost much of its virulence on its way upriver. It seems not to have gone farther — at least Larpenteur at Fort Union does not mention it. Chardon caught it and so did his squaw. He treated it with 'salts,' laudanum, and camphor, which would hardly have sufficed at Liberty where Whitman treated Fontenelle's men. The epidemic went through the Mandans, whose trade Chardon conducted at Fort Clark, but not enough of them died to suit him. Few traders, perhaps none but the younger Alexander Henry, ever hated Indians with the unremitted zeal of Francis Chardon. His journal bristles with heartfelt cursing. Even as he records his minor case of cholera he notes that a party of Mandans, including the famous Four Bears, Catlin's Mah-toh-to-pa, Maximilian's Mato-Tope, had started for the Yankton Sioux to avenge a murder, and heartily hopes they will be successful — 'God send them Speed, it is perfectly imaterial how fieu of them return. I wish both parties a severe conflict and heavy losses.' He kept count of the rats killed at Fort Clark — from fifty to upwards of two hundred every month — and the inventory has a clear symbolism. His charges were, he said at about the same time 'without any exception (except the Crees) the meanest, dirtiest, worthless cowardly set of Dogs on the Missouri,' which, though it helps to correct George Catlin's exuberant Rousseauism, is violently absurd. Chardon preferred the Sioux a little, at least he took three wives from among them and notes in his summary of his first fourteen months at Fort Clark that he has killed '1056 House Rats and have Made a Fine Boy who I have named Andrew Jackson in Honour of the Old Gentleman.'

Chardon lived to see a satisfactory epidemic sweep through the Mandans.

## «X»

# THE MERIDIAN PASSAGE (1836)

SOUTH PASS, JULY 4, 1836. The annual pack train of the American Fur Company, commanded by Thomas Fitzpatrick; a considerable outfit, seventy-odd engagés, upwards of four hundred horses and mules. Fitzpatrick's adjutant is Black Harris, the specialist in solitary and winter travel. Harris rides at the end of the Company train to keep an eye on the technique of the march and to enforce trail discipline. A Company cart (a 'charette' as in Miller's drawings) is going through the Pass this year — and with it a light wagon which will presently establish itself in American history forever. At the head of the train Fitzpatrick is the familiar figure of the partisan, thin-faced, gaunt, eyes sweeping the land, Hawken rifle unslung and held across the saddle. He looks in fact like a Ranney painting of the next decade or a Tait lithograph of the following one. Beside him on a superb black horse rides his hawk-nosed, mustached friend of three years' standing now, Captain William Drummond Stewart. Stewart is making another trip to the mountains and has outfitted himself with two fast horses which he commissioned Bill Sublette to buy for him for the sole purpose of racing mountain men and Indians. He has two new Manton guns, imported by way of New Orleans, and he started West with so many luxuries that they required two light wagons, but the wagons have been left behind at Fort Laramie and pack mules substituted. The Captain has a companion this year, 'Mr. Sillem, a German gentleman' and his two blooded horses.[1]

We may assume that the train camped for the night of July 3 at the last tangential touch of the Sweetwater, in the greenery of its shallow gully where it comes down out of the hills, and we know that it camped for the night of July 4 at Pacific Spring or at the little Sandy. From camp to camp this was a tremendous day for any westering party — any party, that is, which had newcomers in it, for it was just a day's drive, and a dry one, to veterans. But it crossed the parting of the waters, the fundamental divide of the continent, and it marked the end of the United States. From water to water was twelve miles and somewhere in that stretch you left home behind and came to Oregon. Frémont, who had Kit Carson to help him, found the true height of land only with great difficulty and no doubt incorrectly, for he had no instruments sensitive enough to make sure. He estimated that the final rise where the continent parted and fell away on both sides was about equal 'to the ascent of the Capitol hill from the Avenue at Washington.' But it was enough for any traveler that somewhere in that twelve-mile stretch of dun and olive sagebrush he crossed the fundamental watershed and the frontier of fable. No one ever more momentously than some of those who crossed it with Fitzpatrick on Independence Day of 1836.

So large a train must stretch out for the better part of a mile. From that impalpable divide, looking southward for eight or ten miles across seemingly unbroken level of sage, one's gaze rested at last on a low ridge, a little greener than the aching plain, a fragmented prolongation of the Antelope Hills. Northward the sage stretched with the same illusion of smoothness for perhaps five miles, then hills thrust up, detached, rounded, mesalike, grouped in a formal composition and leading to the last peak of the Wind River range, a lesser peak but higher than the flat perspective of this empty air made it out to be, prowlike, abrupt, with a side falling away. At the utmost extent of one's vision southwestward, a slate-blue vagueness which seemed to float above the earth meant mountain peaks that were in neither the United States nor Oregon but Mexico. In this vast emptiness the sage and greasewood seemed level as a surveyor's bench but that was another illusion of thin air, for actually the plain undulated and thrust up sizable buttes. Actually also the baked, heat-quivering surface was not so dry as it seemed; there were gullies with snow water in them and even an occasional, incredible small patch of marsh.

The composition opened outward to the West, and westward into that widening vista Fitzpatrick's caravan plodded under the weight of sun, under the steel-white zenith, under the rippling canopy of brown and bitter dust. Eyes narrowed by the glare were red-rimmed with alkali. Alkali smelled too, like the vague nastiness of a chemistry laboratory, but not enough to overcome the reek of turpentine and resin from the hot sage — yet when the wind coming up from Green River drove the dust momentarily away, one's lungs took in a clean, electric air. Voices were microscopic in space, cursing the demoniac cussedness of mules. . . . Fitzpatrick and Stewart and the unexplained Sillem in the lead, an outrider or two on each flank, three-quarters of a mile of diabolism and dust, then the Company cart and Black Harris with a headful of trail cunning.

But behind Harris the momentous thing: a light four-wheeled wagon without springs, fourteen horses and six mules, fifteen head of beef and milch cattle — and the missionary party. The new missionary party that was a revolution. Marcus Whitman and the two Nez Perce boys who had gone East with him last year and a third one inexplicably found at Liberty. A dubious hired hand named (or spelled) Dulin and a nineteen-year-old youth named Miles Goodyear who was hellbent to be a mountain man — and soon made the grade. Also William H. Gray, a 'mechanic' of attested piety and proved malice whom the American Board had added to the party for no sound reason. Also the Reverend Henry Hart Spalding. Also, and here was the difference, Mr. Spalding's wife, Eliza, and the wife whom Marcus Whitman had married during the winter.

Fitzpatrick had sent the usual express to tell the clans that he was approaching the rendezvous, which was to be at Horse Creek again this year. So now, past midafternoon, above the crawling heat-mirage to the westward there was a flurry of moving dots, at the appearance of which the reflexes of Fitzpatrick, Harris, and Stewart were instantaneously activated. The figures running through illusion might be elk, which at a distance looked like horsemen, but they might be mountain Indians and hostile ones. Shouted commands from partisan and lieutenants; rifles slipped from the saddle loops and their priming renewed; the gaps closing; tranquil tension, eyes fixed on that motion in deceptive light. It resolved itself into men on horseback, about fifteen of them at a dead gallop. As the distance lessened they could be heard yelling — the piercing ululation of the war shout. They were Indians and white men mixed but Fitzpatrick saw a piece of shirting tied to one of the brandished gun-barrels and told his charges these were friends. Friends, however, who probably awed the women as much as any hostiles could have done and who at that moment fired a volley over the heads of the caravan. They galloped down its whole length, yelling, jumping their horses over clumps of sage, rolling round their necks, making them buck, spinning them in the zigzag of an Indian charge. Still at the gallop they came back the whole length of the caravan, which by now was firing its own guns in welcome. Nez Perces and trappers flung themselves to the ground and shook hands with their friends — but only for a moment. They had to gape at the most inconceivable sight ever seen here, the first white women who had come to the mountains.

Two of them. In heavy boots and swathed with yards of skirt. Riding sidesaddle. Eliza Spalding, tall, naturally thin and emaciated by travel and illness, dark-haired, sallow under her tan, frightened and appalled by the uproar of hospitality. And Narcissa Whitman who was neither frightened nor appalled — she was delighted. A smaller woman than Eliza but by no means emaciated, the period's ideal in womanly curves, blue-eyed, tanned now but memorably blond. Men always remembered her face and her red-gold hair. Men in fact remembered Narcissa, and though she was dedicated to God's service she was charged with a magnetism whose nature no one could mistake. The Nez Perces had never seen a white woman. Joe Meek and the three equally gnarled trappers who rode here with him had not seen one for years. They had their memories and their fantasies and Narcissa fulfilled them.

There are significant scenes in Western history but few so significant as this moment of uproar and wonder in a sagebrush sea. A Sioux chief is supposed to have once said that his people were not alarmed till they saw plows in the emigrant wagons and his remark has served innumerable chroniclers who may forget that the Sioux had no way of knowing what a plow was. A truer symbol for the chief would be these two women surrounded by Indians and men in buckskin, in Oregon, west of the Continental Divide.[2]

* * *

Whitman had married his Narcissa in February. The ambiguity of this full-blooded woman who had been deflected from marriage until what was for the period a late age, and who since childhood had longed to immolate herself converting the heathen, was manifested at her wedding — she wore black and dressed her whole family in black. Robed as the bride of death, then, Narcissa Prentiss stood up in the little church of Angelica, New York, and was married. (She had made herself some bright calico dresses, though, to gladden the eyes of the Nez Perces.) In black she sang with the choir and congregation a hymn by the Reverend Samuel F. Smith, the author of 'America.' She was a fine singer, she had a voice which, like her bearing, troubled men's hearts, and she sang the last stanza alone:

In the deserts let me labor,
On the mountains let me tell
How he died — the blessed Savior —
To redeem a world from hell!
Let me hasten
Far in heathen lands to dwell.[3]

A dramatist writing the tragedy of the Whitmans would open with the black-robed bride singing of longed-for deserts to a family whom she would never see again. But the lines of force had been laid down long before, and Marcus and Narcissa went straight from their wedding to the first intersection of those lines. They crossed at Cincinnati, where the Whitmans joined Henry H. Spalding and his wife Eliza. Spalding, originally commissioned by the American Board to the mission among the Osages, had proved to be the only ordained minister whom Whitman could secure for Oregon. He was in fact originally disqualified for that mission because the Board did not want to send to Oregon a man who had children and, in the fall of 1835, Eliza was pregnant. Fate saw to it that the child was stillborn, however, and as time shortened and one after another nominee to the mission declined or proved undesirable, it came to taking Spalding or else postponing the whole endeavor for another year.

The failure of the Oregon mission was implicit in the dream from which it sprang. But the tragedy is the more bitter in that the men and women who composed the mission, some of them heroic certainly, were under compulsion to make trouble for one another on the way to serving God. And in the soul of Henry Harmon Spalding, who proved to be the ablest of them all in the frustrate task of understanding Indians, two sores that would not heal secreted a poison that affected all his fellow missionaries from the beginning to the end. Spalding had been born out of wedlock. No doubt illegitimacy was what turned him to God's service but it did so with an omen of disaster. At best the evangelical Protestant ministry was surcharged with guilt. Add the guilt of bastardy, at least doubled since it was a mother's as well as a son's, and one might be, as Spalding assuredly was, harrowed by humiliation and intolerance. The perturbed spirit found no absolution for itself — and no charity for anyone else.

Spalding stretched the errant race on the rack that tortured him and saw much too clearly how far his companions fell short of pleasing God.

Moreover, during his early student days he had lived in the home town of Narcissa Prentiss and worshiped in the same church. The beautiful soprano, in whose eyes was peace and in whose body was disturbance, affected the insecure aspirant to the ministry as she affected many men. Spalding fell in love with her and she rejected him. Now, married in a true union of souls to the twice-born, guilt-ridden Eliza Hart, he was going to help establish the Oregon mission as a subordinate to Marcus Whitman, who had succeeded where he had failed. And he was privileged to travel west with the lost Narcissa on her honeymoon. Even before they reached the frontier Spalding undertook, for holiness' sake, to bring her and others to a realization of the evil in her character and to help her root it out so that God's grace might enter in.[4]

There were other dark omens at the beginning, too. On their way to St. Louis, traveling urgently because they were behind time, the missionaries overtook a party whom the American Board was sending to the Indian frontier and traveled on to Liberty with them. Benjamin Satterlee and his wife had been appointed to the two-year-old Pawnee mission. Traveling with them was Emeline Palmer (she had tutored one of Whitman's Nez Perce boys during the winter) on her way to marry the head of that mission, Samuel Allis.[5] Mrs. Satterlee was desperately ill, but Whitman decided that she could travel. They reached Liberty. Allis came down from Bellevue and Spalding married him to his Emeline. Just a week later the tubercular Mrs. Satterlee died. The little group of missionaries were just 'preparing to follow her lifeless remains to the graveyard, to commit it to its mother earth' (Eliza Spalding speaking) when the American Fur Company steamboat on which half of them were to have traveled to Bellevue came up the river. The funeral was broken off and they hurried to the wharf to hail the boat, but the captain refused to stop. They went back to the grave and finished the ceremony. But in a frenzy of unfinished preparations they must now all hurry overland, under threat of missing Tom Fitzpatrick. The Oregon mission came close to failing at the start but after three weeks of frantic travel to Bellevue and beyond it, they caught up with Fitzpatrick, well into the wilderness at the Loup Fork of the Platte. On that wild, amateurish dash Spalding was sick most of the time and Whitman was at the limit of exhaustion.

Whitman and the ragged stray they had picked up, Miles Goodyear, who wanted to apprentice himself to a mountain man, proved tough and skillful enough to get them there — but only just.

* * *

Eliza Spalding's diary is sporadic and consists mostly of her devotions. William Gray, the mechanic whom the American Board had sent as a lay asssitant, described the westward journey in his *History of Oregon*, with positively festering appreciation of his own indispensability to it. It is to be hoped, though we have no evidence except that a woman married him, that someone liked William Gray during his lifetime, for no one can like him in retrospect. In this part of his book his malicious envy has not yet become malignant but he found little to praise in the morals, skill, industry, intelligence, sincerity, or companionability of either the mountain men, the gentlemen travelers, or the missionaries. He had a high regard for the lay assistant — and it is clear that the lay assistant suffered an occasional guffaw, if no more, from the ungodly. But mostly one follows the trip in the letters and journal of Narcissa Whitman who, whether twisted into her sidesaddle or riding on the baggage in the springless wagon, contrived to enjoy the strange wonders of the West and the behavior of godless men. She even contrived to melt a particle of Gray's wintriness, for though he thought her unintelligent, scorned her as worldly and derelict in Christian duty and even flirtatious, he did admit, mingling lemon juice with the ink, that she was a lady.

It was midnight of May 27 when the missionaries caught up with Fitzpatrick. Stewart and his Mr. Sillem were with him, and their engagés and two wagons. With his known tastes, the evidence of his later trips, and the dislike of the teetotal Anglophobe William Gray, it may be assumed that the wagons contained an epicure's stock of potted foods, cheeses, sardines, preserved fruits, the various compressed or evaporated meats and vegetables which began to come on the market in this decade — and enough brandies, whiskeys, and vintage wines to allow for plenty of breakage en route. There could be nothing else the Captain would take in two wagons and this would seem to be the beginning of high life on the Oregon Trail. (Already there was precedent for it on the Santa Fe Trail.) Miles Goodyear could begin his apprenticeship and satisfy his long yearning at once, for Tom Fitzpatrick and Black Harris must have been high among those who had drawn him to the mountains. Miles was under only the retrospective calumny of William Gray, who had in fact hired him and admitted that he made a good hand as far as the Snake River. But after leaving the missionaries for Indians whom he considered more companionable he 'married a native woman (some say three),' and so made Gray suspect that he was a deserter from the army. Finally there was Milton Sublette, late partner of the RMF Company, late co-owner of Fort Laramie. We last saw him turning back to the settlements after a few days with Nat Wyeth in 1834. His leg had been amputated and a second operation had been performed on the stump; an invalid, riding in a two-mule cart, he was making a last visit to the country of his great days.

'I never was so contented and happy before. Neither have I enjoyed such health for years,' the bride writes to her sister from the forks of the Platte. The mysterious deflection had been amended, the withheld eagerness had been released, this was a well-married woman who was honeymooning up the Coasts of the Nebraska, and it must have been within a day or two of this letter that Narcissa conceived her child. While she was still east of her ultimate mission field at least, she lived deeply and with delight. Spectacle, work, companionship, men and pack animals, country, marriage — everything was fulfillment. The torture of a sidesaddle did not bother Narcissa but it was increasingly hard on Eliza Spalding, who rode more often in the light wagon. Narcissa sometimes rode with her and drove the team when she did so. Gray drove the heavy wagon, dispassionately appreciative of his skill and self-sacrifice from mile to mile. The Nez Perce boys — Richard Tackitonitis especially appealed to Narcissa; he called her 'Mother' and she loved to listen to his version of English — drove the herd. Its eventual purpose seemed less important than the comforts it provided on the way. For they milked four cows every day and so had cream and trail-made butter. They had bread too, as no one did in the Company train, for Narcissa baked it at the embers every evening. But she did not have to cook the meat, once they reached the buffalo, for Marcus took over. He had learned the art last summer and cooked each cut as the mountain cuisine required. Like the mountain men, Narcissa wanted no other course if there was fat cow. She says it disagreed with Eliza but the euphemisms in Eliza's diary suggest the usual experience on reaching alkali waters.

The two women are the first of so many thousand. The invincible domesticity of the American pioneer wife was beginning to operate on the rigors, the deficiencies, and especially the conventions of the trail. And Narcissa, the first of a great company, was bringing the amenities west. She would formally invite the gentry to tea. The table was ground cloth of India-rubber sheeting and the stately guests sat round it cross legged. (She says 'husband always provides my seat and in a way you would laugh to see us,' which would make Spalding dour and Gray contemptuous.) The anxiety of a hostess along the Platte would be to keep the blowing sand off the table and out of the 'tin basens' that were teacups. She had her own knife belted round her waist like a trapper and admits that forks were sharpened sticks. However, Fitzpatrick, Milton Sublette, Harris, Joshua Pilcher (more ancient in the trade than any of them and making the trip west as Indian Agent), Stewart, and Sillem would be courtly in the purple evening, and even Eliza's diary lacks the expected dislike of infidels. Narcissa frankly delighted in them, and at a guess in Harris most of all. He was a sunny liar like Jim Bridger, had been in these parts since Laramie Peak was a deep well, and his talk was of the Western universe.

('I've trapped on Platte and Arkansas and away up on Missoura and Yaller Stone,' Ruxton has Harris say to an imaginary woman in St. Louis, but why not to Narcissa? 'I've trapped on Columbia, on Lewis Fork [the Snake], and Green River; I've trapped, marm, on Grand River and the Heely; I've raised the hair of more than one Apach and made a Rapaho come afore now; I've trapped in heaven, in airth, and h—; and scalp my old head, marm, but I've seen a putrified forest.'

Thus the lead to Ruxton's version of Black Harris's or Jim Bridger's celebrated yarn. The winter following the great meteor shower Harris and his pals come suddenly out of deep snow into a summer valley, where in leafy trees above lush grass the birds are singing. In this miracle land Harris shoots a bird whose head goes on singing as it spins away from the body, but when he picks it up he finds that it is stone.

'"Hyar's damp powder and no fire to dry it," I says quite skeared.

'"Fire be dogged," says old Rube [Herring], "Hyar's a hos as'll make fire come."'

So Herring takes a cut at a cottonwood tree only to chip a large piece out of the axe blade, which scares them both. The horses are shaking with fright, too, and rightly for the grass they are trying to crop is stone. But young Sublette (probably Andrew or Solomon is intended) comes up, an educated man who apparently knows what is up when his hunting knife breaks off some brittle leaves, 'a-snappin' like Californy shells.'

'"What's all this, boy?" I asks.

'"Putrefactions," says he, looking smart, "putrefactions or I'm a niggur."'

Here the St. Louis hostess is distraught. 'La, Mister Harris, putrefactions! why, did the leaves and the trees and the grass smell badly?'

And Black Harris, 'Smell badly, marm! Would a skunk stink if he was froze to stone?') [6]

If not this yarn, which Fitz and Stewart would loyally applaud in its thousandth edition, then certainly many others from Harris's repertoire. Here then as sunset fades to the velvet night of the high plains and the sage smells sweet again with evening, here is a new face that may be seen with the firelight on it — Narcissa, crosslegged or on the knees of Marcus, the curly red-gold hair shaken by her laughter. It is hard to remember the pallid Eliza, whose decorum pleased William Gray; one sees Narcissa's liveliness between the gaunt Fitzpatrick and the scarred Harris,[7] with Captain Stewart and the equally courtly Pilcher laughing with her as they sprawl on their hips beside the fire. Our Byronic Scot, who appreciated the charms and graces of Blackfoot, Snake, and perhaps Cheyenne girls, made the heroines of his novels Italianate beauties with olive skins and 'lustrous, raven locks.' But he was certainly not immune to the blond loveliness that captivated everyone who ever wrote about Narcissa except the umbrageous Gray, and would be the less immune at such a fire against such a backdrop. The legendry of the West has even bestowed on him a regret proper to his own fiction. The story is set at the rendezvous of this year where, among old friends met again, Stewart was talking to Nat Wyeth who was on his way home at last. Wyeth is supposed to have asked him if he had ever regretted his exile from Scotland, and Stewart is supposed to have answered, 'Never, until I beheld the beautiful Mrs. Whitman. Why was one so fair born to an American judge? [Justice of the peace.] Why should she marry a missionary to the Indians of the far West, where her beauty and charm will not be appreciated? What would I not give to possess her love and be at home in Scotland?' [8]

History could mildly covet that romance and at least it is clear that Stewart's Christina could not greatly have stirred his longings in absentia. He had come to Yankeeland less than two years after marrying her and was able to separate himself from her charms for nearly seven years. But it is safe to reject the fantasy of Narcissa strolling with Stewart in Birnam Wood and laughing at his table, and think of the known chill of Henry Spalding, who, when the guests bowed over Narcissa's hand and returned to their own part of the forted circle, must retire to the tent of striped bed-ticking they had in common and watch his lost love lie down by the side of Marcus Whitman.

To the stretch along the middle Platte a footnote in *Edward Warren* ascribes an adventure with a grizzly. Stewart speaks of Whitman as 'a most excellent man, a curious divine, for he sometimes preached, and a most bold operator, for he without hesitation let out water from the chest with a pen-knife or cut out an arrowhead with a butcher's knife, which had been for years wandering about in Jim Bridger's back and hip, which I have in my pocket while I write.' [9] A grizzly is cornered in a clump of brush and Fitzpatrick proposes to leave him there till the greenhorns can come up. Whitman is in the lead when they come and his horse becomes unmanageable when it scents the bear. 'We were credibly informed afterwards that the doctor and his steed had a furious conflict for a moment, among the bushes; but all we of the hunt know of our own knowledge was, the doctor, though a large and powerful man, came upon the stage describing a parabolum over the intervening shrubs. The bear roared and charged — the doctor gathered himself up and ran — the bear passed me, almost lifeless with laughter, untouched; and the doctor never saw him, nor any other, till the day of his death.' (Presumably, 'nor any other' means that no one saw this particular bear again — the novelist's style is sometimes obscure.)

They had met the caravan on the Loup Fork on May 27 and Fitzpatrick had them at Fort Laramie by June 15, which is expert traveling. Here the women were able to hold their first wash day and the event was almost as memorable as the first chance to spend a Sabbath in devotions. They made a thorough job of it — and at the request of Fitzpatrick or Fontenelle, who was the bourgeois of the fort now, Henry Spalding preached to the engagés on the text of the Prodigal Son. Religious services in the West had got on an annual basis, for this was the third straight year, and there appeared to be some results. A trapper rejoiced in the ceremony and received 'with great joy and thankfulness' the Bible which Eliza Spalding gave him. The fur company now transferred its goods from wagons to pack mules but Whitman was determined to push his experiment farther. He left the heavy farm wagon at Fort Laramie but, in defiance of advice, resolved to take the light one with him. Since the going got much worse as the trail turned northwest to avoid the Laramie Mountains, he was doubling his labor — and it had seemed at maximum all along, for that the missionary outfit had kept up with Fitzpatrick was due to the everlasting energy of this man of will and sleeplessness. The Company decided that it was interested in the experiment and assigned a man to help him make it. The cart which bore the failing Milton Sublette went along, too.

Getting the wagon across the gullies and round the buttes of the red desert had Whitman coming into camp long after dark. The expert Fitzpatrick was making a record drive. They stopped at Independence Rock long enough to add to the desert register the names of Eliza Spalding and Narcissa Whitman, the first at the top of a new page. The frail, resolute Eliza began to show the strain now and had to ride in the wagon nearly all the time, though even a sidesaddle would seem easier on an invalid than the crunch and detonation of wheeled travel up the continental plane. Her resolution had also to contend with the calomel and bleeding of Whitman's heroic medicine. So they came on July 4 to the Divide and the gunfire of Joe Meek and his associate horribles. Two days later Fitzpatrick brought them to Horse Creek and the full-scale mountain welcome to which Meek's noise had been only the prelude.

* * *

The Nez Perce had a thaumaturge at last — in the end he turned out to be Spalding, not Whitman — and they made him welcome. The squaws had learned from the whites that women were to be greeted with a kiss, so Eliza and Narcissa were smothered with salutations. The Nez Perces were here in force, so were the Flatheads; there were Bannocks, too, and a whole village of Snakes. They swarmed round the white squaws in relays, touching their hair, fingering their dresses, inspecting their outfit and possessions — all with the sewing-circle volubility of Indians. It was just as well that the women had not mastered the language, for the critical comments of Indians are not inhibited. They were, however, getting to work on it. Gray says that Eliza began to make a Nez Perce vocabulary at Horse Creek. He adds that the Indians preferred her to Narcissa who, he says, forgetting that she had been exchanging lessons with Richard all the way West, was too busy flirting with dazzled and savage mountain men to pay much attention to her charges. Her offense consisted of undervaluing William Gray.

The Indians decided to make it old home week in honor of the white women. All four tribes joined in a wild west show, rodeo, and frontier day. They put on their ceremonial costumes — Gray notes that the warriors were nearly naked and, with preposterous inaccuracy, that some 'native belles' were chiefly dressed in beads — and opened the performance with a grand parade. 'Captain Stewart, an English nobleman, and Major Pilcher waited on the mission ladies and politely informed them of the object of the display; they assured them there would be no danger or harm and remained at their tents while the cavalcade passed.' It passed, galloping and curvetting, with medicines fluttering from lances, with musketry, with the gorgeous swagger of Indians on display, with the uproar of Indians having a good time. It was much better than anything Bill Cody would ever direct. It delighted not only Narcissa but Captain Stewart as well, in so much that next year he would procure a repeat performance and have Alfred Miller paint it.

The literature says little about this rendezvous though such annalists as Joe Meek and Osborne Russell and Kit Carson were there. Meek describes the trappers as bashful, as odd an adjective for mountain men as the thesaurus could produce, and says they 'contented themselves with promenading before her tent.' (It is unnecessary to identify the reference of 'her.') But Joe is spotlighting his own act: the adventurer monopolizing the beauty, sprawled like a younger Ulysses on a buffalo robe while he relates the serial of his daring and misfortune but changing pace sometimes to play for a deeper impression with a wish to give up 'bar fighting and Injun fighting' and take up the pastoral, rewarding life of a farmer in the Willamette Valley. He was impressed in turn, for later on he turned over his daughter to Narcissa to be educated. He succeeded in vindicating the urbanity of the Rocky Mountain trapper — Narcissa rejoices in the number who come asking for tracts and Bibles and suggesting that they had, for the moment anyway, 'leisure for reflection and study.' She thinks she could have disposed of enough to load 'one or two animals' and feels that 'a missionary might do good in this field.' If the missionary were Narcissa, yes; but one wonders what the boys did with the pious literature thus begged from the blonde.

We are indebted to the shock of William Gray for some useful portraits. In his *History of Oregon* (not a happy title for the contents) Meek appears as 'a tall man, with long black hair, smooth face, dark eyes (inclining to turn his head a little to one side, as much as to say "I can tell you about it"), a harum-scarum, don't care sort of man, full of "life and fun in the mountains" as he expressed it.' He was, Gray unnecessarily adds, fond of telling yarns; Gray spoils one that is told in Mrs. Victor's book. He says that Meek had a halfbreed son just beginning to talk and had conscientiously taught him 'to say "God d—n you," doubtless considering this prayer the most important one' for use hereabouts.

A Kentuckian whom this narrative cannot identify is 'Major' in Gray's narrative, 'a man of medium height, black hair, black whiskers, dark-brown eyes, and very dark complexion.' His companion whom Gray calls 'the Doctor' is Doc Newell, one of Joe Meek's closest buddies. He joins the catalogue of those whom Gray cannot bring himself to approve. Doc later worked for the Hudson's Bay Company (Meek's undependable memory, in fact, has him working for it in 1836) and the British taint damned him in that Anglophobe mind. One trapper does soften Gray a little by accepting and even offering to pay for a Bible, though the man had asked for 'books,' that is, just reading matter. The rest, through a list of eight, are variously disparaged. Gray clearly had to take some ribbing at the rendezvous, maybe some pushing around.

He says otherwise — and his report of what the mountain men made of the missionaries may be quoted, with allowances. He says they liked Whitman 'on the whole,' which is as close as he could come to admitting the obvious fact that they had admitted him to full standing and fellowship, with all the perquisites. He says they thought that the 'stern, commanding' Narcissa (*sic*!) might eventually sour Marcus and considered her too educated and refined for the Indians. (Gray contrives to suggest that she condescended not only to the trappers but to Marcus as well.) 'As to Spalding, he is so green he will do to spread on a frog-pond; he may do to preach to Indians but mountain men would have to be fly-blown before he could come near them.' (Gray is befogged by mountain idiom as well as by his own emotions.) He says they thought Mrs. Spalding first-rate, wondered what she could see in her husband, believed she could do anything she might set her hand to, and 'didn't put on any frills' — which establishes that Narcissa had snubbed Mr. Gray up to some percent of his deserts.

And what did the wicked think of Gray? Even the wicked could not be withheld from admiring him. 'He is young yet, is not quite so green as Spalding; he seems inclined to learn a little; by the time he goes to the Columbia River and travels about more, he will know a good deal more than he does now. He may do well in his department if he "keeps his eye skinned." I suppose by this expression was meant a sharp lookout for swindlers, rogues, and thieves, to see that they do not lie, cheat, and steal, every opportunity they may have, or at least that you do not allow them to take your property under false pretences.' Gray adds, he was under compulsion to add, that they predicted the Hudson's Bay Company would ruin the missionary enterprise if the Indians did not.

Well, here comes the Hudson's Bay Company with a sizable outfit under the quarterbreed Tom McKay and his senior officer John McLeod, bringing the British trade all the way to the American rendezvous for the first time. And with them was Nat Wyeth, going home at last, his four years in the mountains having ended in complete failure. On the way here he had arranged to sell the stone which he had rolled into his rivals' garden. Though the deal was not concluded till next year, Fort Hall would be a Hudson's Bay post. (He retained his fort at the mouth of the Willamette, with the Methodist ex-missionary Walker in charge, but nothing came of it.) From here he was going to take the trail south from Fort Laramie to Bent's Fort and then travel the Santa Fe Trail eastward. This was to see whether he could find a place for himself in the commerce of the prairies, which he had begun to inquire about two years ago. It was a last inquiry into the business of the wilderness that had so fascinated his Yankee mind beside the gentle waters of Fresh Pond. But in the end the canyons, deserts, and peaks of wasteland had no place for Nat Wyeth. He went back to the ice business and prospered. Still, there were now mementoes of the interior desert in greater Boston. They made a fit addition to the scrimshaw of whalers, heathen gods from Polynesia, the art of China, and the miscellany on whatnots of junk and bibelots from all the seas. And in due time a young Federalist named Parkman, whom the West had also drawn within its magnetic field, appeared in Wyeth's office, asking advice.

To the consternation of the missionaries, Samuel Parker had not accompanied McLeod and McKay. According to his promise he had started for the rendezvous and had made an extraordinary river circuit, going as far north as Fort Colville and Fort Okanagan. He had renewed his acquaintance with the Nez Perces and preached to them again. He had talked with the Cayuses, the Pend d'Oreilles, the Walla Wallas, and the Spokanes. He had filled his notebook and his head with observations, suggestions, statistics. He did not put them down in the letter he sent on to rendezvous — Gray says, and was lying, because he was afraid they would alarm or somehow serve the Hudson's Bay Company, which presumably had no statistics about the country it had ruled for so long. But he did put them down in a book which served a larger purpose, since it became the first guide book for the Oregon emigration and remained one of the best.

Parker was ready to go on to the rendezvous but he dreaded that long trip on horseback — over the timbered and precipitous Oregon and Idaho mountains, across the lava desert, on to the Green and to South Pass and then all the weary way to St. Louis. Samuel Parker was a brave man and had an untroubled soul, but there were so many hills to lift up his heart unto and the desert of Isaiah was so wide! After all, he was fifty-seven years old. And when he reached Fort Walla Walla he learned that the Indians with whom he expected to travel intended to go to the rendezvous not by the trail — which he had traveled and which he had nerved himself to travel again — but slowly, hunting as they moved, along their own circuitous route. It had dangers that he knew not of: he did know that it moved down the spine of the continent. He thought of those mountains. He had had enough and no one will presume to blame him. He turned back down the Columbia, the route on which he need not ride a horse or climb a mountainside, and at Fort Vancouver McLoughlin applauded his good sense. He dropped down to the mouth of the great river — by Company steamboat and this is, remember, 1836 — and there gratefully took passage on the bark *Columbia* (named after a great ship but not to be mistaken for her) for the Sandwich Islands. There he waited five months till a ship cleared for home, and so he finished his circumnavigation by sea. It was May 17, 1837, when the lookout called 'Land ho!' That was Block Island but they could not make harbor and it was not till the next day that the *Phoenix* made up the Thames River and Samuel Parker, a faithful servant, came ashore at New London.

* * *

Let us take a moment for the Reverend Samuel Parker's conclusions about the Western missions for whose sake he had traveled the wilderness till his bones tired. He liked Indians — and thus separated himself from almost all the Protestant missionaries. That he did like them may be due to the fact that he spent only a year among them and spent that year not often out of touch with white men and such comforts as their culture could maintain in the desert. Whatever the explanation, he looked at

Indians favorably and free of reproach, with an understanding liberality that is altogether astonishing in a Congregational divine from Massachusetts. At the end of a year's observation and analysis he could not decide whether the Indians were going to be exterminated by the whites or allowed an evolution that might civilize them. He could see 'no reason existing in the nature of things or in their present condition' which implied the inability of Indians to receive civilization. Rather, he thought, 'a consistent and persevering attempt to raise a race of freemen' would be 'fraught with as much promise and encouragement as it was in earlier days to elevate our ancestors.' We must remember that he was thinking of the Indians he knew best, the agreeable, adaptable, friendly, and highly intelligent Nez Perces.

But, he said, it would have to be a gradual process and while it went on the Indians must be protected from white men. They should be protected from the white man's diseases — the venereal diseases, he chiefly meant — and from the alcohol that was a hundredfold more destructive. They must get what they had never had — and this is his wildest fantasy — they must get some elementary protection from the courts, some faint security in their basic rights to life and the possession of their land. Some kind of colonial status should be worked out for them. And so on — he saw as essential to their survival and progress a few elementary decencies, a small fraction of the axiomatic humanity that is supposed to underlie men's dealings with one another. But Parker knew quite well that he was romanticizing: these ideas were outside the culture, the mores and folkways, the ideology of a nation that had been working its way west for two centuries.

So he anticipated the worst. 'The wrongs inflicted upon this race of men' foretold the future and, he said, not the hundredth part of these wrongs had ever been told. In their country 'our border and refugee men' had no law for Indians except murder. He was thinking of the trappers and, in support, told two stories. One was from Wyeth's memorial to Congress, though it is also in Irving and in Parker's friend Townsend. Simple anecdote of a mountain man who shot an Indian not for stealing his traps but for looking as if he intended to steal them. The boys thought that one very funny and also the one about Stewart told earlier in this text, the offer of five hundred dollars for the scalp of the half-breed who stole his horse, fee claimed by Markhead. Thus Stewart, who had contributed much miscellaneous enlightenment to Samuel Parker, rounds out his service with some depressing evidence toward the future. Just specimens, Parker says. He had no great hope for the eventual civilization of the western Indians.

In the judgment of this narrative, Parker saw the country, the Indians, and the future of both as clearly as anyone who went West during the first half of the nineteenth century, understood them incomparably better than most, and in particular was so much more intelligent about them than the other missionaries that he is in a class by himself. He was wrong in only one important judgment. It was not the mountain men in whom the threat of destruction lay. It was in the emigrants who were soon to come down the trail, whose coming was so notably facilitated and in great part procured by the missionaries — not least by Parker himself.

* * *

About this time the Gros Ventres paid a debt. A band of them appeared on the Portneuf River, across from Fort Hall, whither the missionary party would presently take the trail. Among them was a renegade white man named Bird. He called to an engagé of the fort whom he saw on the far bank, asking him to come over and make a trade for some beaver. The engagé was that Antoine Godin whom, at the battle of Pierre's Hole in 1832, we saw riding out to kill and scalp the Gros Ventre war chief who was bringing the medicine pipe to propose an armistice.

Godin crossed the Portneuf and he and the customers sat down to smoke. When the pipe came round the circle to him the Gros Ventres shot him in the back. They lifted his scalp before he died. Then Bird carved the initials 'N J W,' for his employer, Wyeth, in his forehead and the party rode away, the account closed.

* * *

Parker had recommended the Grande Ronde and the Clearwater River, the Kooskooskee of Lewis and Clark, as mission sites. It is guessed here that he recommended them as well in the now lost letter delivered to Marcus Whitman at the rendezvous. The arrival of McLeod and McKay solved an anxiety of the missionaries: how to get on to the Nez Perce country, for they could not get there by themselves and it was not clear how much help their effusive parishioners could give. So Whitman and his company — and the wagon — moved over to the Hudson's Bay camp, a couple of miles away. He asked Fitzpatrick for his bill and Tom asked what his professional charges were. There were none, he said, and Fitzpatrick made the courtly answer. So Whitman had made himself respected and even beloved by a breed of men whose standards of manliness were high. He and his, he wrote, had received nothing but favors and kindness from Fitz and his men — and no wonder.

On July 18 McLeod took to the trail. The worst part of the journey lay ahead, the part that tried men's souls after the emigration began. There were not only the worst deserts, the highest and most precipitous mountains, the longest dry drives, the most dangerous river fords — there was also the cumulative strain. An increased tension between the Whitmans and the Spaldings did nothing to ease it. The cause is clear, the ferment in the soul of Henry Spalding. It is mostly allusion or less than allusion in the diaries and letters and records of the succeeding years, but clearly Whitman disliked Spalding by now, clearly he had abundant cause, and clearly Spalding could not suppress his tormented impulse to make Narcissa a better vessel for God's grace. Spalding was sick a good part of the time now, Eliza most of it. Even Narcissa's health faltered, though probably this means she was in a queasy period of her pregnancy. But also the desert was closing in on her consciousness at last. She was so far from home, the wilderness was so diminishing to personality, and the future was so inscrutable. From here on there is a lot more religion in her diary and correspondence than there had been before.

Whitman himself had long since been resolved into pure act. Marcus Whitman had a stocky and powerful body but it had been in part undermined by an undiagnosed ailment and his strength was chiefly will, not muscles. He entered this narrative in 1835 and in that year had twelve years still to live. One has no knowledge of anyone anywhere who worked harder or worked more constantly at the far edge of mortal resource than Marcus Whitman did during those twelve years. The judgment of an elegist that he was not the right kind of man by temperament or thought to deal with Indians was probably right. That increases rather than diminishes one's admiration of the polarized will that for twelve years kept him at his gigantic labor.

Now, west of Ham's Fork, we must see him not only surmounting the vexations and emergencies of the trail but also taking a wagon West as he had set out to do. He took it up gulches and mountainsides and slopes steep enough to be called cliffs, across quicksands and rimrock and lava knifeblades and sagebrush flats, through groves and swamps and forests and creeks and the Snake River. It could not be taken a day's travel west of the Green if past history counted but he took it. When Fort Hall was behind them an axle broke at last. That should have ended matters, for there was no wood that would serve for another one but it did not. One axle was left. So Whitman made a cart of his wagon and, throwing away still more of the outfit and so sketching another precedent for the emigration, drove on. But when they got to Fort Boisé either the description of the Blue Mountains that lay ahead discouraged him or else he decided that he had had all the additional, unnecessary fatigue that even he could support. He left it there and the thesis of wheeled travel to the Columbia had not been proved. Not quite.

'Feel sometime as if it was a long time to be traveling,' Narcissa wrote. She recalled a text: the heavens over her were brass and the earth iron under her feet. Under the feet of the cattle, too, and Marcus had, she says, to shoe some of them — rather, to shrink rawhide over them. McLeod was traveling Indian style — without making a noonday pause — and the women were not able to take their accustomed rest on an apishemore behind a robe rigged as a sun screen. But McLeod did what he could for them — Narcissa had conquered still another heart. Twenty miles below Salmon Falls Whitman reduced his cart still farther and resolved to jettison even more of their small outfit — if he had to make this trip again, he wrote, he would bring nothing whatever except clothing for the trail and equipment for the nightly camp. Nothing was left of the cart now but the running gear and he told Narcissa that she would have to leave in this desert the little trunk her sister had given her in York State, with its handful of feminine things. She brought herself to obey, crushed and appalled, but McLeod 'asked the privaledge' of packing it on one of her mules. He asked many similar privileges. He sent her various kinds of food — they were living on jerky for the most part and she could not love it; she dreamed of bread in her mother's kitchen, and an occasional hatful of berries or a trout taken from the Snake was a delirious treat. He got her tent set up before the slower missionary outfit plodded into camp. He cheered her along the way and yarned for her at the evening fire and went out to shoot ducks for her. As they neared Fort Walla Walla he rode ahead to bring her back a melon.

We may set down two descriptions of an incident, as a useful index to the reporting of news. Ten days west of rendezvous, Narcissa wrote:

> Mr. Gray was quite sick this morning & inclined to fall behind camp. Husband & myself thought it would not be prudent to leave him alone & rode with him about two hours & half, when he became very feeble & inclined to lie down. By this time we were so far behind camp that Husband thought it not prudent for me to remain with them any longer & sent me on to overtake them. Soon after Mr. Gray gave out entirely & Husband left him to come for the cart & return for him. I had overtaken an Indian & told him how sick he was, who went back met Husband & both returned to Mr. Gray. The Indian helped him on his horse got up behind him, supported him in his arms & in this manner rode slowly into camp.

Now William Gray:

> Two days before we reached Soda Springs one of the mission party became quite unwell and unable to sit upon his horse. He was left, at his own request, on a little stream, while the caravan passed on some six miles farther to camp. After remaining alone and resting some two hours, The Lawyer [this is 'Kentuck'] and an Indian companion of his came along, picked up the sick man, put him upon a strong horse, got up behind him, and held him on till they reached camp. Dr. Whitman gave him a prescription [enough calomel to cover a knife-blade, maybe?] which relieved him so that next day he was able to continue the journey with the camp. This transaction has always been a mystery to the writer. The place where the sick man was left was a beautiful stream and a good place for a camp for the whole caravan. The sick man was wholly unable to proceed; did not ask the caravan to stop and bury him, but simply informed them he could proceed no further; his strength was gone; they would leave him to die alone if they chose. A word from McLeod would have stopped the caravan. Should the mission party remain with him? He said: 'No; go on with the caravan and leave me, you will be compelled to seek your own safety in continuing with the caravan; I am but an individual, leave me to my fate.' He requested a cup that he might get some water from the stream, close to the side of which he wished them to place him. Dr. Whitman remained with him as long as was deemed safe for him, and passed on to overtake the caravan. The Lawyer and his companion came along two or three hours afterward, picked up the dying or dead man (for aught the caravan knew) and brought him into camp. My impression of this transaction has always been that McLeod wished to get rid of this young American, who was then in the service of the missionary party.

McLeod, of course, had no such wish and was merely leaving a man with a physical bellyache somewhat less sharp than his spiritual gripes to rest for a while — watched over by a physician and a good nurse — before coming ahead. The temptation to separate oneself from William Gray for an hour or so, however, would certainly be strong. And at that, there were those in the West who would have lived longer if Gray had died on Bear River.

Finally the Indians, who were afraid that these missionaries would decide to pass them by as the Lees had done, accepted their promise that they would not and took their own route home. The missionaries reached Fort Hall, Captain Thing, factor, on August 5. Two laborious weeks later they were at Fort Boisé, where the women could do their washing for the third time on the journey and where the cart was at last abandoned. The hardest stretch was still to come, the Blue Mountains at the end of it, the slopes and chasms where the emigration was to be wrecked repeatedly. The party had split up now, to accommodate to the slower travel of the cattle and probably also to secure some peace of mind, the Whitmans traveling ahead with McLeod. On August 29 Narcissa looked down into the distant valley of the Columbia and far to the west could see a great and breathless sight, the perfect cone of Mount Hood. On September 1 they reached Fort Walla Walla, with what thanksgiving may be imagined. Now McLeod could really entertain Narcissa — cushioned armchairs, salmon, pork, cabbage, turnips, potatoes, melons, beets, salt, tea, even bread and butter. Townsend and the handsome Pambrun were on hand to bow to the ladies. There was a private room with a bedstead. There were cattle, turkeys, pigeons, swine, goats. A cock flew to the palisade and crowed.

Here they might have stayed, for Whitman had decided that this vicinity was the right place for the mission. (Fort Walla Walla was the Hudson's Bay Company post for the Nez Perce trade.) But he had also decided that they must first go to Fort Vancouver and get what assistance in tools and equipment they could — it was bitterly clear that they could survive only by favor of the Hudson's Bay. So they did, traveling with Pambrun for McLeod and Townsend had gone ahead. The boat trip, dangerous and uncomfortable enough, was infinitely safer and more comfortable than what had gone before — though at one portage Narcissa found her clothes and person crawling with hundreds of fleas. They reached Vancouver on September 12, one hundred and eight days after catching up with Tom Fitzpatrick on the Loup Fork of the Platte. Now Narcissa had the great McLoughlin and a large population to enchant. And did so. And she wrote, 'I feel I have come to a father's house indeed, even in a strange land has the Lord raised up friends.'

This brief stay at Fort Vancouver is the last period of ease, safety, and a minimum of civilized decency that the Oregon Mission ever knew. Vancouver was a great station in glorious country, country superb with harvest when they reached it, but its opulence was less welcome than its society. Narcissa had a gift for happiness — it sustained her through eleven years that without it could hardly have been more than two or three — and here were children to teach (halfbreeds mostly and mostly to be taught hymns, building on the elementary instruction of Samuel Parker), and women to sew with in the intimate, unilateral society she would never know again. The halfbreed wives of McLoughlin, Douglas, and other factors were women of dignity and some culture, there were a couple of white women, and there was a miscellany of lives bound together. There was even one comic strain that was to run through the rowdy history of Oregon, for Jason Lee had founded his Temperance Society and Narcissa could rejoice. McLoughlin wanted her to teach his daughter, wanted her to spend the winter here, wanted her for the love of God to stay here till her child was born.

But no. Whitman, Spalding, and Gray went back up the river to find a mission site. They found two. One was twenty-five miles up the Walla Walla River from the Hudson's Bay Company post, with a fine stand of timber, good drainage, and indications of fertile soil. The Indians called it Waiilatpu and it was Whitman's choice. The time-spirit was heading up; far below consciousness he was thinking, no matter what he had thought up to now, less of the Indians he was to minister to than of the rising wave behind him, the empire that was to follow his trail. For what determined this site was its commanding importance to the trail that would arrive here from the East and lead hence for the West. It was not even in the country of the Nez Perces, who had started all this, who had sent their young men to St. Louis to ask for teachers.

Or at least, though the Nez Perces ranged here, the Cayuses lived nearer Waiilatpu than any Nez Perce band did. A tribe either related to the Nez Perces or so long their neighbors and allies that they had the same culture. A small tribe, its population thinned by immemorial war with the Snakes. The Cayuses had besought the missionaries to locate among them. When Whitman decided to, the concern of the Nez Perces was profound. Narcissa summarized their warning: 'They do not like to have us stop with the Cayouses. Say they do not have difficulty with the white men, as the Cayouses do & that we shall find it so.' In the end they found it so.

Whitman would probably have ignored his clear vision of the wave of empire combing toward the crest, would probably have located among the Nez Perces, if a solution had not been ready made and at hand — even obligatory. The journey had made one fact crystal clear: the Spaldings and the Whitmans could not live together. So the division was recognized and rationalized. The Nez Perces got their priest, Henry Harmon Spalding. In the heart of the Nez Perce country was the place where the Clearwater flows into the Snake, and Parker, who noted this as a desirable site, had probably recommended it in the letter he sent to rendezvous. The existence of Lewiston, Idaho, today demonstrates that Parker too had a feeling for what was to come. The Nez Perces, however, favored a valley ten miles up the Clearwater, Lapwai Valley. Voted. Spalding would establish there the mission to the Nez Perces that had been contemplated. And Whitman would drive his stake at the strategic Waiilatpu and was probably already thinking of other sites that might be occupied, as Tshimakain and Kamiah eventually were.

They had their Indians get to work raising the first crude structures and presently Spalding went downriver for the women. For the materials and supplies too — which McLoughlin provided. He was God's most valuable servant, it proved, and in the end the betrayer of his empire. Narcissa said good-bye to him and had the mercy of sharing a boat with McLeod while the Spaldings traveled in another one. This was November 3, 1836, and she stayed a while at Fort Walla Walla with the Pambruns — Mrs. Pambrun was another of those squaws of white men who had the strength of the earth and the pitying kindness of womanhood. Marcus Whitman soon had a chimney and a floor in his shack and on December 10 he brought Narcissa, now six months pregnant, to Waiilatpu, getting there after dark so that when he lifted the blanket that served as a door firelight from her hearth shone through. 'My heart truly leaped for joy.'

It begins here. Narcissa was twenty-nine on March 14, 1837, and that day Marcus Whitman, resident physician to twenty thousand square miles, delivered the first American white child born west of the Continental Divide, his daughter Alice Clarissa. He went on delivering children, white, red, and halfbreed, Eliza's daughter the following November and anyone's son or daughter within two weeks travel by horse or dugout. And by June of

1844 one Cayuse and twenty-one Nez Perces had been received into the First Church of Oregon, having satisfied Spalding and Whitman that they were Christians. That was its total Indian membership and it moved to the Willamette Valley after that day when an unconverted Cayuse threw Narcissa's thrice-wounded body into the mire and another one raised it by the red-gold hair and lashed her face with a pretty beaded whip.

This is not the place to relate the quarrels, frustrations, heart-break, aspiration, and magnanimity of the mission. Remember the dedication that went into it, so mistakenly conceived that there must somewhere be Milton's Lucifer to appreciate the irony of human hope, white or red. Remember the labor too.

On his pinnacle Lucifer may perhaps see that there was some way to make a bridge from the new stone age to nineteenth century Anglo-Saxon thought. But not in a few years. One need not climb to that pinnacle, however, to see those few years. During them there is a steadily narrowing gap on the western trail between the figure of Marcus Whitman in the 'leather pantaloons' which Doctor McLoughlin gave him and a company of white-tops, the first of the companies that would keep coming till Oregon came in. And till the Nez Perces were uprooted from their country, though they had bred up a chief whom the whites called Joseph and who, after a century, seems singularly kin to Marcus Whitman.

* * *

Toward the end of April, 1836, while the Whitmans were crossing Missouri toward their jump-off, the *Pilgrim* beat down the California coast from Monterey and dropped anchor in San Diego harbor. Richard Henry Dana had rounded the Horn in her two years before but he was with the *Alert* now, at San Diego. He was going home to Boston. There was thanksgiving in his heart — and yet he had not only proved himself a man in California, as he seems to have had a secret doubt he might not (a doubt like Francis Parkman's), but he had taken California and the sailors and the strange beauty and the life of hard-working, humble men into his love forever. Even as he rejoiced over the end of his exile his mind was playing a counterpoint of British man-o'-war's men singing chanteys at the capstan, of the high cliff he had descended to dislodge a stiff hide that was stuck there, of Kanakas talking by the evening fire, of fandangoes, and carved, painted saints. He was going home to write a great book. And all the rest of his life he would catch himself listening for the murmur of California surf and looking up to catch a glimpse of velvet breeches slashed to the knee.

There were some otter skins and several barrels of beaver pelts in the *Alert's* hold. Dana had seen an occasional stray mountain man who had settled here to marry a plump wench and live in fruitful ease beyond the reach of blizzards and Blackfeet. He had heard of a band of them — Young's or Walker's but the annals do not identify it — who had rendered mountain justice to a Californian who had murdered a resident American. The alcalde of Los Angeles would do nothing about the murder, so the mountain men, with the small handful of Americans and British in the vicinity, had taken over the town, set up a court, empaneled a jury, tried and sentenced the murderer, shot him in due form, and notified the local government that there had better be no protest. In a romantic land this had the texture of home and something of romance as well. Moreover, in the hide trade there was a certain humility, an inadequacy, when someone mentioned the Northwesters, the great Boston and Russian and British trade to the Columbia. That truly was 'romantic and mysterious, and if it takes the ship round the world by way of the Islands and China, it out-ranks them all.' So much so that as the *Alert*, homeward bound, was making a northing from Bermuda she tried a brag and suffered a humiliation when she spoke of the schooner *Solon*, out of Plymouth harbor with a cargo of vegetables that might halt an incipient outbreak of scurvy.

'The grave, slab-sided mate of the schooner leaned over the rail and spoke to the men in our boat. "Where are you from?" Joe answered up quick, "From the Nor'west coast." "What's your cargo?" This was a poser but Joe was ready with an equivoke. "Skins," said he. "Here and there a horn?" asked the mate.'

But on the San Diego beach one of the Pilgrim's mates told Dana that California was going to produce still another marvel, that the brig had brought down from Monterey 'a sort of oldish man' who came from Dana's college and spent all his time picking up flowers and shells and such truck and packing them in barrels. Dana racked his brains, wondering what itinerant Harvard man could be on the golden shore but his imagination could suggest no one. Then he saw an old gentleman with white hair, 'in a sailor's peajacket, with a wide straw hat, and barefoot, with his trousers rolled up to his knees picking up stones and shells.' Dana recognized the Lecturer on Botany and Zoology and would 'hardly have been more surprised to have seen the Old South steeple shoot up from the hide house.' He shook hands with Thomas Nuttall, who had crossed to Oregon, gone on to the Sandwich Islands, and come back to Monterey and thence here. Another wandering came to an end and Nuttall took passage to Boston on the *Alert*.

At the rendezvous of 1836 on Horse Creek we lose sight of Captain Stewart again and cannot pick him up till the end of the following winter. He went back to the States, almost certainly with Fitzpatrick. On the evidence of a few random hints in the literature and the content of his novels, it is assumed here that he absented himself from the rendezvous for a while and took his 'German gentleman' to his favorite country, the Wind River Mountains beyond the headwaters of New Fork. It is guessed that when the rendezvous broke up he may have joined his small outfit to Bridger's brigade for a week or so.[10]

The western slopes of the Wind River Mountains have many small lakes and a number of good-sized ones. Innumerable small creeks run through the evergreen forests, coalescing into streams large enough to be named. This country is the setting of Stewart's two romances. His exiled heroes and the dusky, mysterious girls, who appear to be Indians but are European beauties of high rank, wind endlessly in and out among these lakes, pursuing and being pursued, suffering capture, and risking incest. The noble Blackfeet travel this country under a romantic white chieftain, Altowan; so do the perpetually thievish Crows. A legend says that one of these lakes was once named Stewart but there is no historical record to bear it out and the Forest Service knows nothing of it.[11] Assuming that the lake which appears most often in Miller's sketches of next summer is the one in question, it can be identified as New Fork Lake, perhaps the third largest on the western slope, some miles north of Fremont Lake. It was once called DeAmalia and is the Damala of William H. Jackson's photographs. Doubletop Peak, close to twelve thousand feet high, rises to the eastward, and beyond Doubletop is a medley of ridges rising to the Divide and thrusting up the highest summits of the Wind Rivers, Gannet, Warren, Helen, Sacajawea, and Fremont.

There were fish and game here beyond the avarice of sportsmen, though certainly not buffalo in quantity. We may assume the tents of Stewart's party beside the blue water, on the edge of timber, the proud horses (which would have been ridden out at the rendezvous) in a picket line, a couple of hired swampers keeping camp and preparing the trophies for shipment. The heir of Murthly and Grandtully and Logiealmond would ride out for bear, elk, the cougar that made so deep an impression on him, antelope — contending with 'that great hunter,' Antoine Clement. But there would be use for his fowling-pieces as well as his rifles and he and Sillem would make a fine execution of the local grouse (sage and pine hens), quail, doves. Trout from the streams, too. Altogether it was a sportsman's idyll in late July, the crest of mountain summer. Then, if the guess is right, a week or two with Bridger's outfit before taking the trail to Fort Laramie and starting for the settlements with Fitzpatrick.

We must correct the record here. In Mrs. Victor's *River of the West* events of at least three different years are confused in Joe Meek's account of this fall of 1836 and the succeeding winter. Meek has Bridger wintering in the Powder River country, which is in part accurate, and says that Fontenelle's brigade wintered with them, which may be true but probably is not. He also says that Stewart joined the camp and that our artist Miller was with him: both statements altogether wrong. He goes on to say, 'About the first of January [1837] Fontenelle, with four men and Captain Stewart's party, left camp to go to St. Louis for supplies. At Fort Laramie Fontenelle committed suicide in a fit of *mania à potu* and his men returned to camp with the news.' This assertion, or rather the part of it that concerns the death of Fontenelle, has been universally repeated in modern studies. But Stewart could not have been in the mountains as late as January, as Chapter XII will show, and Fontenelle did not kill himself in January, 1837. He will appear in Chapter XII, the summer of 1837, and though he is a hard man to follow from then on, the Missouri Historical Society has a letter from him to P. A. Sarpy dated more than a year later, August 5, 1838, and it seems likely that he died sober at Bellevue in 1840.[12]

Bridger was playing a return engagement in the Blackfoot country and had the usual vicissitudes there. He took his brigade up the Green, over to Jackson's Hole, through Yellowstone Park, down the Yellowstone, overland to the Rosebud and then north. Meek appears to have been one of Carson's men this year and again they were usually in Bridger's vicinity. Meek says that a leftover band of Bonneville's also joined up. Presently the Blackfeet reacted and from then on through the winter there were the expected battles. Old Gabe, who liked to kill Blackfeet, seems to have had his most successful season. But there was an ominous scarcity of beaver. Osborne Russell speaks well of a winter camp on the Yellowstone but the penumbra was advancing over the mountain trade.

* * *

Certain moments in history are like a man waking at night and counting the strokes wrong when he hears a clock strike.

August 1, 1836. Two days' ride beyond Soda Springs, well into the Idaho desert, exhausted by the recent going, Narcissa Whitman wrote only a couple of lines in her journal; she had remembered that at home in Angelica, New York, this was Monthly Concert day and its 'sweet and sacred influence' helped her bear her weariness. Osborne Russell with sixteen other Bridger men was camped on the Yellowstone River, near the southern boundary of the Park, trapping the creeks and waiting for Bridger to come up. Jim himself was somewhere between there and the Green. If the assumption made earlier is justified Stewart would be saying good-bye to him for the winter or would have said it a couple of days earlier and headed toward Fort Laramie. Fitzpatrick was at the Fort.

And at Buffalo, New York, about five in the afternoon of August 1 the schooner *Wave* sailed for the Soo. She had been chartered by a general and carried about sixty members of his army. He had commissioned a major of artillery earlier that day, adding him to a staff that was to include five captains and two first lieutenants and two ensigns of artillery, a captain and a third lieutenant of Life Guards, and a commissary and assistant commissary. Bearded, mustachioed, his handsome face scarred by saber wounds, the General was a martial figure, and a tailor with imagination had made his uniform. And why not? He was the Liberator of the Indian Nations. He was Montezuma II. With his army, whose artillery had no guns, he was off to the Red River of the North, where among the métis and roughnecks of the Hudson's Bay Company he intended to enlist up to two hundred volunteers. Then he would continue the project that began at Buffalo on this first day of August. That project was the emancipation of New Mexico and the conquest of California.[13]

No one knows who James Dickson was; no one knows what became of him. It was guessed that he had been English once and he told a Scotch traveler at the Soo that he had lately been operating a gold mine at Fredericksburg, Virginia. Still he presented himself as a military man and is calling himself General when he first comes into notice. He had been to Mexico. He told the Scotch traveler that he had been waylaid there and suffered nineteen wounds, which suggests that scars on his face may not have been got in cavalry charges. If Mexico, then perhaps Texas, too. He may have joined one of the squads of extemporized light cavalry which for a couple of years had been having brushes with similar bands of Mexicans. (In the spring of 1836 they coalesced into that Texas Army which won a revolution and has more descendants in the direct line today than even the army of Northern Virginia.) In any event when he arrived in Washington, sometime during the winter of 1835–1836, he was using the electric potential of Texas, whose declaration of independence followed in March.

He said he was raising recruits for Texas Independence. He was handsome, acquaintances called him well-bred, on the record he was a talker of great power — and the country village of Washington, always vibrating with international intrigues of great or small voltage, was truly seething this winter. It was a time when no diplomat anywhere could possibly mistake the portent of Texas. (In the event it took eight years to get the Lone Star annexed but that was for reasons that could not be calculated or even felt in March, 1836; six months would have been a sound bet.) But as he wore his brilliant if not quite identifiable uniforms to the town's levees, he had his eye on an area even larger than Texas.

There must have been horrible oaths of secrecy, for at the very least James Dickson had the conspirational mind. (Except for one thing he would look, at this distance, like any of a line that was already three centuries old, the costumed conquerors-to-be anywhere in the Indies or the Antilles or south of Tampico who at any café table or under any palm tree were to lead their elephants and chariots to glory tomorrow afternoon. But somewhere in him, say in the cortex of the pineal gland, a crystal pick-up was fluttering with a signal that did not come from the past.) After those oaths he told his neophytes that he had been talking secretly to Indian chiefs. Among them, he said, were Cherokees. And that also was sagacious in Washington at that moment. For the policy of removing the Eastern Indians to the Western lands reserved to them in perpetuity (which, remember, sent the Wyandot William Walker out to look at the prairies) had, in December of 1835, got round to the remnants of the once great Cherokee nation, and they had signed a treaty of acceptance. See it in the most favorable light, see it as we like to see it now, forgetting the obscene frauds, and still this ultimate removal from the lands where De Soto had found their ancestors could not altogether delight the Cherokees. They might be in a mood. They were; and, Dickson confided to his hearers, the Cherokees were going to congregate, come summer, at a place convenient for his plans. So were other tribes of the frontier.

And then — conquest! With his halfbreeds from the Red River settlement, General Dickson would march on Santa Fe. Up the Missouri, that is, up the Yellowstone (up the Big Horn too, though he does not specify it), to 'the Southern pass.' This would bring them to the Mexican frontier, and the way thence to Santa Fe seems to have been known to him clearly enough. At Santa Fe he would wipe out the insignificant garrison, declare himself Montezuma II, General and Leader of the Liberating Army, and call on the New Mexico Indians to rise and strike off their chains. As Montezuma II he had printed manifestoes ready to set up in public squares. 'Accompanied by a great army of well-mounted soldiers [the manifestoes read in Doctor Nute's translation] with shields and with lances sent by God and by the Holy Mother of God, Mary most Holy, I, Montezuma II have come to succor and save my comrades in the lands of Mexico.' He came as the waters come in the rainy season. He came to destroy the slavery of Cortez. To take back the land from the whites, and the gold and silver mines, the wheat and corn. Raise the standard of revolt, raise the cry of 'War to the knife.' And so on, tantantara zing boom, and Abraham, Isaac, and Jacob mentioned at the end no less than Mary and Jesus. Montezuma II, the heir of Montezuma the Great and Montezuma the Second, was presumably high priest of Quetzalcoatl, the plumed serpent, and Huitzilopochtli, to whom prisoners of war must be sacrificed. But he cared no more for discordance in his religious underpinning than Joseph Smith did, who six years earlier had founded a church which also had a Mexican past.

With Santa Fe conquered, Montezuma proposed to plunder the whole province of New Mexico and then lead his army into the mountains of California. There he would wait for the Cherokees and their allies to join him. Together they would conquer California. Montezuma would reign over the golden shore, making it the sanctuary of Indians, an empire of Indians. It would make the proposed Indian Country of the American government a bush-league idea, mangy and poverty-stricken. It would be the final Indian nation. Montezuma would form a military government to rule over it but no white man could own an acre of it. . . . He intended to advertise to the customers that he would personally support each one of them for a year out of his personal take. (What is an echo by premonition?)

Presumably James Dickson loved Indians or thought he saw a profit in saying that he did. But he was also advertising his conquest to a different set of prospects. 'The blood-red flag is near our borders,' a gaudy poem of his announced in a Baltimore paper, and he notified Southerners in particular that a terrific uprising of the Indians was already on the march, with a 'banner of rapine' and a massacre flag.

Ocmulgee and Flint rivers pour forth your sons
  Montgomery! Mobile! be first in the field;
Louisiana! Missouri, come on at once
  And be to your country banner and shield.

And what was behind all this? In the context of April, 1836, General Dickson's sales-talk is suggestive:

The Comanche, the Pawnee, those Indian tribes
Bought over by Mexican munitions and bribes
Are once more preparing, roused from their lair,
To lay our frontier desolate, bare.

So the General promises his gallant prospects a war 'alas, too horrific, And peace be granted only on the Pacific,' and Mexico will regret her aggression. A lot of them are going to be killed — he judges that the Southern sentimentalists of the age of iron and roses will ask nothing better — but their souls, ascending with swiftest pinions will watch their comrades march on to more vast dominions.

The post-general-emperor a little flats his exordium:

Off in the stilly night
  On the far prairie
With the stars for our light
  The hymn of liberty
Shall be sounded yet.

But with liberty heaved in, the scheme would appear to have had everything.

It is a testimony to James Dickson's conversation that he had got some sixty Americans and Canadians to fall for this besotted nonsense. But it is a greater revelation of the time — of the stuff that had been cast into the pot to boil. Besotted nonsense, and yet on August 1, 1836, there were sixty men who, looking westward, didn't think it was. Moreover, the Hudson's Bay Company didn't think so, either. A lively concern traveled along its network when Montezuma talked of taking his army to the Red River settlement. The Company notified its home office and London in turn notified the War Office. It was the Company's opinion that Montezuma might not only find recruits among the métis, who God knows had but slender reasons to worship their rulers, and it was not altogether sure he could not work up enough force to add the Red River country to his empire.

A half-dozen of the General's principal converts, most of his officers, in fact, had a fur trade background. Most of them, too, were halfbreeds. One was a son of the Hudson's Bay Company's Doctor John McLoughlin, and another the son of the American Fur Company's Kenneth McKenzie. The latter's presence was one reason why the Hudson's Bay Company was skittish about this filibuster, for the King of the Missouri was among its most virulent enemies.

General Dickson had a coat of mail in his military baggage; in the outcome he found no use for it, but it lights up another eddy in his swirling mind. His great moment must have been the August afternoon when the expedition to liberate the Indians sailed from Buffalo, for the Army of Liberation mustered greater strength that day than it ever did again. Men of too small soul or insufficient bowels for the Conquest of Spanish America began to drop away, especially at Detroit. The Conqueror had talked too much; a cynical press had written him up; the Hudson's Bay Company had instituted inquiries. Moreover, some of the financing was shaky. So the sheriff of Detroit came aboard the *Wave* and clapped the army under bond on the charge of having killed some cattle. Conquest nearly got stalled but Dickson gave a draft for the alleged damage and though the major of his gunless artillery boiled with rage they did not have to fight. An American army officer, commanding a small fort near-by, vouched for their peaceful intentions and, diminishing, they got started again. They got to the Soo and at mid-September began a slow passage of the upper lakes. (The major of artillery was studying Spanish for the conquest to come.) It was mid-October when they reached the far end of Lake Superior and struck overland.

'Our expedition has caused much excitement here & our purpose has preceded us many hundred miles,' the artillery major wrote. It had preceded them, perhaps hopefully, in the American Fur Company's Northern Department at least, for it equipped the army with safe-conducts and alleged guides. So for two months, first by canoe and then by snowshoe, the dwindling Army of Liberation marched toward Santa Fe, but in the direction of the Hudson's Bay Company's Pembina. It went, that is, northwest across Minnesota — the St. Louis River, the Mississippi, Lake Winnebagoshish, Cass Lake, Red Lake. Prairie winter, Paul Bunyan's winter, roared down out of the north. Atrocious cold froze their hands and feet; snowstorms holed them up in drifts. Game was hard to find and only an occasional meeting with an Indian or a trapper kept them from starving. Just beyond Thief River (Minnesota) they really foundered, those who were left, for the Sioux guides who were supposed to be taking them to Pembina deserted and no one knew the way. The expeditionary force went to pieces. Some turned back. Dickson and a couple of others kept on. The major of artillery and a few more presently followed him but did not find him. Starving and beset by blizzards but occasionally helped out by Indians, they made Pembina, which proved to have no garrison. The major learned, however, that his general was surviving though 'frozen in a number of places' and by December 20 the Army of Liberation was reunited at Fort Garry. It now numbered twelve. The Hudson's Bay Company could relax; so could Santa Fe.

But not the General. He spent the winter at the Red River settlement but the dream would not fade. Sometime in March of 1837 he appeared at Fort Clark, the American Fur Company's Mandan post. Of his empire at least the dream and a spare sword were left him, for Francis Chardon, the fort's bourgeois and a man not remarkable for loving-kindness wrote in his journal March 21, 'Pleasant weather. I was Presented to day with a Sword from Mr. Dickson — the Liberator of all Indians.' Four days later, in a spring cold snap Dickson started out the way his star had led him from the beginning, up the Missouri. It was bad country and contained bad Indians but the Conquest had called for him to go to the Yellowstone and travel up it in the direction of South Pass. Chardon says, 'Mr. James Dickson, the Liberator of all Indians, started with Benture [a Company engagé] for Fort Union.' Thereafter silence except for Chardon's ambiguous entry of June 14, which does not clearly indicate what had happened but suggests that Dickson had gone an indefinite distance upriver and then turned back. At any rate, it was only a few miles above Fort Clark, that Touissant Charbonneau, old as Rameses but as active as ever, met him. Chardon's journal says, 'Charboneau arrived from the G. V. [Gros Ventres — the Minnetarees] — says that eight boats from Fort Union will be here tomorrow — left the Liberator the other side of the Little Village, as he is tired of walking, and has lain himself down to die.'

Here Montezuma II dissolves into the air and vanishes from history. He probably did not die to the northward of the Mandans or of a broken heart. But he never looked on Carcassonne, either.

Simply a grotesque. The scheme for the liberation of all Indians, the enlistment of gallant Southron youth, the utilization of the Texas revolution were items in one of the crackbrained dreams that occasionally relieve the tedium which is the antiquarian's daily job. General James Dickson was a zany blown up out of nowhere for no cause, of no relation or effect or meaning, and blown out beyond the horizon and still without cause.

And yet.

We are permitted to look ahead just ten years from that August afternoon of 1836 when the Army of Liberation set out from Buffalo. Ten years bring us to 1846, the year when the United States crystallized out a definable pattern of events from the solution into which this narrative has seen many ingredients filtered. On June 14, 1846, a gang of miscellaneous roughs, toughs, mountain men, visionaries, empire builders, and young men on holiday, a gang not greatly different from the Army of Liberation, came down on the hamlet of Sonoma and, after capturing a general in bed and getting jovially drunk on his brandy, announced that they had begun the conquest of California. At once, another gang much like it, a gang that had a liberal quota of mountain men headed by Kit Carson, joined them under the command of a general who is not altogether unlike Montezuma II — his name was Frémont. And on August 14, 1846, an expeditionary force of the United States Army rode into Santa Fe, formed in the plaza, and watched General Stephen Watts Kearny salute the American flag as it reached the top of the pole, and heard him announce the conquest of New Mexico.

Waking in the night, a crazy dream still pulsing in his mind, James Dickson had merely counted wrong when he heard the clock strike.

## « XI »

# THE CONQUEROR (1837)

James Dickson's decision to die beside the trail carried this narrative forward out of its proper chronology — and was quoted from the journal of Francis A. Chardon. Chardon commanded for the American Fur Company (actually, Pratte, Chouteau & Company) at the Mandan post, Fort Clark, on the west bank of the Missouri, eight miles below the mouth of Big Knife River. He was a curly wolf.

That June of 1837 seemed just like any other late spring month on the upper river. The Missouri was so low that Chardon wondered if the Company's annual steamboat would be able to come even this far. Both the Fort and the Mandans — a couple of miles downstream — had been running short of meat, so the appearance of buffalo in the vicinity was gratifying. There was a traffic of the post's traders coming and going. Those who had spent the winter among the Indians were bringing in the furs they had traded and the goods that were left, for the season was over. It was a wretched return. The whole resident trade among the Minnetarees was 630 robes and 180 pounds of beaver. The Mandans had made only 350 robes and 100 pounds of beaver. Must be the Indians' fault — in Chardon's view everything was their fault. He had a succession of Indian wives — the Sioux woman who bore him two beloved children had recently died — but he acutely disliked all Indians and hated his clients, the Mandans. Someone was always licking them, usually the Sioux, and that was fine with Chardon. The Yankton Sioux, whose village was nearest, had been raiding them a good deal and early in the month a chief took out a war-party in retaliation. They found a Yankton camp on the Cheyenne River (sixty miles away in South Dakota) and tried to make off with the horses, but were discovered. They hightailed for home. A group of five made it first, then thirteen, the last reporting that two had been killed and two wounded. The next day four more came in, and three days later the remaining twelve — they had been fourteen but two lost their scalps. All the others had thrown away their robes so that they could travel light, in moccasins and g-strings, but this last batch were, for Mandans, practically victors: they had killed a Sioux and taken three horses. The day before they arrived Chardon set down a gratification: 'An Old Mandan Cheif (The White Bear) died to day — regretted by None that Knew him, as for me, and Many More of the Fort, are glad of his disappearance.'

On June 17 Chardon started downriver with eight laden mackinaws that had arrived from Fort Union. He was hoping to meet the Company steamboat which would be bringing his two-year-old son Andrew Jackson, who had been sent to Fort Pierre along with the body of his mother. He did meet her the next day, the *St. Peter's*, Bernard Pratte, Jr., captain. That day, June 18, he traveled with her to within twenty miles of Fort Clark; she went on and unloaded the Fort's goods on June 19 and steamed upriver on the twentieth. 'All hands frolicking,' Chardon writes. But the *St. Peter's* had left death behind her.

The routine goes on for a while. Another Mandan war party comes back without Sioux scalps — brave warriors in time of peace, Chardon quotes Davy Crockett. Some Arikaras and Mandans join together and start out, hoping for a more prosperous war — 'may they never return is the only wish I can bestow on them.' Still another band of brave warriors comes back without glory. June ends and this month the Fort has killed 31 rats, which makes 1717 all told since Chardon took charge. He tries to get some Minnetarees to return the Company horses they have stolen. No deal. On the Glorious Fourth the officers drink 'a glass of good old Monongahela' to Old Hickory. The Arikaras come to dance for their trader; so do the Minnetarees. Meat is low again and the Mandans of the Little Village leave in force to find buffalo. Then on Friday, July 14, 'a young mandan died today of the Small Pox — several others has caught it — the Indians all being out Makeing Meat has saved several of them.'

That is the beginning — and that is what the *St. Peter's* had done when she stopped at Fort Clark. At some stage of her upriver journey smallpox had broken out.[1] Several cases were in the infectious stage at Fort Clark and though Chardon and his lieutenants tried to keep the Indians away from the boat, they could not. Six years later Chardon told John James Audubon that one of them stole a blanket from a dying member of the crew, and that though a reward for it was offered at once it could not be got back. He says nothing about this in his journal and the story of the stolen blanket has a quality of legend and reappears at Fort McKenzie and, in fact, nearly everywhere else. (There is nothing improbable in it: the smallpox virus is long-lived and infection from a blanket is thoroughly possible.) It may well be that some victims on the boat had recovered and that some others were in the incubation period — that the Indians were let aboard in good faith. However it started, it moved slowly for a while. Most of the Indians were off hunting at their summer villages but within two weeks it had appeared in all the camps. The Minnetarees were slow to catch it and the Arikaras still slower, but it blazed through the Mandans from the beginning.

They knew whom to blame. The first attempt to kill Chardon was made on July 28, when a young brave came looking for him but was caught in time. From then on the fort was practically under siege. The White Cow ordered Chardon to clear out and take his men with him. A young widower stood outside the Fort howling for revenge. Someone was always coming up to the palisades to bellow threats and then go away and sing his death song. Others stood on the domed roofs of the Mandan huts and wailed and threatened, their voices a thin curse from downriver. Moreover, it was clear to the Mandans not only that the whites had deliberately brought the disease, and not only that they had secret remedies for it which they refused to give the sufferers, but that they were magically protecting the Arikaras. The Arikaras thought so too for a while and when their neighbors sent a pipe and demanded help in wiping out Fort Clark, they said they would exterminate the Mandans if they touched a single white man. They sent word of their promise to Chardon, who prepared a hundred guns and half a ton of powder for them in case it should turn out that way.

The second chief of the Mandans was Four Bears, Catlin's Mah-to-toh-pa, Maximilian's Mato-topé. He was a remarkable Indian — even Chardon liked him. The tribe's ancient splendor survived in him; he was mighty in council and mightier in war, by far the greatest warrior of them all. He had led his people against all their enemies, the Assiniboins as far north as Red River, the Cheyennes as far west as the mountains, and always the Sioux. He had many coups — time after time he had enabled his people to wash the mourning paint from their faces. Catlin counts them in detail, embellishing them from his own stock of Rousseauian fantasies; in fact, Four Bears comes close to being the hero of Catlin's book. In Maximilian's book he has dignity, courtliness, pride; the scientist found him a very superior savage. He had always been a friend to the whites; he not only liked them (one of his daughters had married James Kipp) but understood the unique importance of the Mandan trade to the white economy and tried to make his people understand it. Not particularly approving of the business ethics they recommended to Indians, he had nevertheless tried to explain them to the Mandans. Now, as the tribe died round him, he got a better perspective.

Catlin says that 'this noble gentleman . . . to whom I became so much attached' saw his wives and children die, covered their bodies with robes, and though recuperating went out to a hilltop to starve. On his last day, 'he had just strength enough to creep back to the village, when he entered the horrid gloom of his own wigwam and laying his body alongside the group of his family, drew his robe over him and died.' But actually Four Bears had more iron in him than that. When he felt the fever come upon him he dressed in his most ceremonious garments. (Shirt of mountain sheepskin, quilled, bound with ermine skins, fringed with enemy scalps; deerskin leggings to the hip, quilled and fringed; quilled moccasins; warbonnet (from the Sioux); grizzly-claw necklace; parfleche shield with cover of skunk fur; bow of horn backed with sinew (from the Nez Perces), arrow case of cougar skin; tobacco case of otter, catlinite pipe with skins of woodpeckers; medicine sack of beaver; lance and war club. And the robe which Catlin himself had reproduced: Four Bears kills a Sioux chief, a Cheyenne, another one; Four Bears turns back a Sioux raid singlehanded; he creeps into the tipi of the Arikara who had killed his brother and murders the murderer; he duels with a Cheyenne — with Sioux — with Cheyennes — with Assiniboins.) Then he got on his horse and rode about the village singing sacred songs and trying to rouse his people for one last foray. This time he wanted the young men to wipe out Fort Clark. He could not raise his last war party and so he went up to the fort alone, unquestionably looking for Chardon. Missed him. He went back to the village and died. But first he managed to communicate his revised ideas to such of his people as survived to hear them. Here they are in Chardon's spelling, the day after Four Bears' dying speech:

My Friends one and all, Listen to what I have to say — Ever since I can remember, I have loved the Whites, I have lived With them ever since I was a Boy, and to the best of my Knowledge, I have never Wronged a White Man, on the Contrary, I have always Protected them from the insults of Others, Which they cannot deny. The 4 Bears never saw a White Man hungry, but what he gave him to eat, Drink, and a Buffaloe skin to sleep on, in time of Need. I was always ready to die for them, Which they cannot deny. I have done every thing that a red Skin could for. them, and how have they repaid it! With ingratitude! I have Never Called a White Man a Dog, but to day, I do Pronounce them to be a set of Black harted Dogs, they have deceived Me, them that I always considered as Brothers, has turned Out to be My Worst enemies. I have been in Many Battles, and often Wounded, but the Wounds of My enemies I exhalt in, but to day I am Wounded, and by Whom, by those same White Dogs that I have always Considered, and treated as Brothers. I do not fear *Death* my friends. You Know it, but to *die* with my face rotten, that even the Wolves will shrink with horror at seeing Me, and say to themselves, that is the 4 Bears the Friend of the Whites—

Listen well what I have to say, as it will be the last time you will hear Me. Think of your Wives, Children, Brothers, Sisters, Friends, and in fact all that you hold dear, are all Dead, or Dying, with their faces all rotten, caused by those dogs the whites, think of all that My friends, and rise all together and Not leave one of them alive. The 4 Bears will act his Part.

By now between ten and twenty Mandans were dying every day. And here was a young Arikara at the barred gate of the fort, waiting for Chardon. An engagé named Oliver went out to see if he could turn the Indian's mind toward peace — or presents. The Ree shot and killed him. Chardon and others, including the half-breed Garreau who was the fort's interpreter, boiled out in pursuit. The Indian stopped at the river bank and announced that he would die here. Garreau shot him and, drawing his knife, 'ripped his body open.' That night the Indian's mother came to the fort, asking to be killed. Garreau was about to oblige with a hatchet but they stopped him.

'Nothing but an occasional glass of grog keeps me alive,' Chardon wrote. To the terrors of siege and foreboding the actuality of the disease was now added. It ran through the garrison, Chardon himself got it (but lightly), and three died. Chardon sent his little Andrew Jackson with two men in a canoe to Fort Pierre. No use: the Sioux had been making use of the opportunity fortune had sent them — had been raiding the pest-stricken Mandans.

So there was smallpox at Fort Pierre by now and little Andrew Jackson Chardon died.

The wind brought a horrible stench from the village — and the death songs and the threats. An old Indian sleeping in the fort dreamed of a white bear — big medicine; his nightmare shouts brought the garrison out on general alert. There was always a new alert, three in a single day. Heavily armed, parties went out for wood or water, wondering if they would live to get back. One scared scout came flying back because he had seen two strange mounds of earth. Dugouts hurrying to shelter at the fort brought word that the Assiniboins had the disease now, the Blackfeet, the Minnetarees. The last had quarantined their village and were making threats. Most of them, however, were still at the summer village, which was untouched. So Chardon sent Charbonneau there with a present of tobacco, directing them to save themselves by staying there. The old man had to travel by night; he could never have made it in daylight. And no use, for there was too much intercourse between the villages and, besides, the Minnetarees wanted to save their corn: they came back and began to die. There was a new outbreak of rage and more threats. But the supernaturals now intervened on behalf of Chardon. He told Audubon that he was listening to the angry tirades of some chiefs one day when a dove (a wood-pigeon perhaps?) flew in through the door and perched on his arm. It was in flight from a hawk but the chiefs did not know that and when it flew away they asked what it meant. Chardon saw his chance. He said that friends of his had sent it to ask if it were true that the Mandans were going to kill him but that he had told it to report that there was nothing in the rumor, the Mandans were his friends. At least, after that medicine they would not kill him.

The structure of savage thought was being undermined. Empirical remedies for certain mild distempers had been hit upon in Indian practice but even these were magical, a few out of hundreds that happened to work. (On the whole the Indian pharmacopoeia was not much less scientific than that currently used by white physicians, Marcus Whitman, say.) Doctors or laymen had learned these remedies in dreams after fasts or rituals, and all treatment of disease was a religious jurisdiction. A victim of the smallpox had been attacked by evil spirits or had had evil power directed at him. The spirits had got into his body and must be exorcised; the power must be neutralized. Rigorous thinking about the universe had uncovered its laws; logic had then worked out the proper application of principles. There were specific songs, chants, dances, rituals for specific effects; there were also amulets, spells, magic ointments, holy waters. The proper song must be sung the proper number of times, at the right stage of the ceremony, with the correct accompanying ritual. When the desired effect was not produced, it was clear that the right ritual had not been used or that it had been used incorrectly. A new diagnosis was required, or perhaps a ritual of greater power was called for. This in general — but private revelation added an infinity of variations. Objects or substances associated with a practitioner's medicine could expel demons or neutralize evil powers. Fur of the totemic animal or feathers of a bird, grass from its den, wood from the kind of tree it had stood beside in the medicine dream. Or stones that looked like it or a dried bit of its dung. Or perhaps more rigorous rituals, more painful ordeals, more prolonged supplication might bring some better vision — 'Some of them,' Chardon says, 'have made dreams, that they talked to the Sun, others to the Moon, several articles has been sacrifised to them both.' And the priests rattled their gourds, beat their drums, howled, sang, danced — and the suffering died in uproar.

But the supernaturals revealed nothing. The victims continued to swell, break out with pox, ache, vomit, grow delirious, and die. So there came a point when the savage mind understood that it had misconceived the universe: its theory of reality would not hold. When the bases of thought are proved an error, nothing is left but frenzy. A teutonic death-lust overspread the Mandans. . . . Two sick braves debate the manliest way; one cuts his own throat, the other forces an arrow down his throat into his lungs. A brave shoots his wife, then disembowels himself. A newly widowed squaw kills her two children and hangs herself. A young man has his mother dig a grave, walks out to it with his father's help, and lies down in it. When the son of another one dies, he tells his wife that they ought to join the boy in the after-land; when she agrees he shoots her, reloads his gun, takes the muzzle in his mouth, and pulls the trigger with his toe. Many others take the same way out, many tomahawk their wives. 'They destroyed themselves,' Catlin says, 'with their knives, with their guns, and by dashing their brains out by leaping headforemost from a thirty-foot ledge of rocks in front of their village.' Many others drowned themselves, rushing into the river for relief from fever. . . . Chardon records several odd cures. One Mandan, distracted by the opening of his pox, rolled in the ashes of the fire; the treatment worked. Another rolled in a mud puddle and baked an inch-thick layer of adobe all over his body; when it came off it took the skin with it but the patient got well. And 'An Indian Vaccinated his child by cutting two small pieces of flesh out of his arms, and two on the belly — and then takeing a Scab from one that was getting well of the disease and rubbing it on the wounded part, three days after, it took effect and the child is perfectly well.'

Uncontrollable panic had some of the Indians rushing out to nowhere by day or under the moon. Sometimes a group who were still healthy would abandon their sick and move a few miles out on the prairie, not knowing that the virus traveled with them. But mostly the Mandans stayed in their villages and died. They could not bury the dead or even hold the appointed ceremonies for them. There were corpses in the huts, in the doorways, in the cornfields, naked or half-dressed or covered with blankets and a few possessions for the after-land set out beside them. The stench blown toward Fort Clark got worse. The Sioux kept coming to gather the corn and more scalps. Dog and wolves and rats fed on the dead.

By August 11 Chardon wrote that the Mandans were dying so fast he could not keep his statistics current. On September 2 he thought that the disease might be losing its virulence for some of those who caught it were recovering. Almost at once he had to change his mind, and the worst of the outbreak among the Minnetarees and Arikaras was still to come. On September 19 he estimated that at least eight hundred Mandans must be dead and was gratified by the wonder-working ways of providence: 'What a band of RASCALS has been used up.' A second wave traveled through his post but in October there was no danger of massacre and the garrison could go about its business unperturbed. Company traffic upriver, downriver, and among the tribes was resumed. Touissant Charbonneau, whom not even Time could kill, took to his circuit for information and, if possible, trade. But Indians and engagés were still dying of smallpox in December and again in January. Chardon's journal hardly seems normal till the February entry which records that he has sent an employee to the Arikaras 'to be cured of the Venereal.' There was some trade by March (1838) though the Arikaras were still dying and would presently move up to occupy the Mandan village by the Fort. When they did so they left forty old women to starve and Fort Clark might be said to be in full operation again when Chardon, stirred by some uncharacteristic humanity, went down and gave them a meal. One meal.

This was the second time smallpox had ravaged the Mandans, for it was an epidemic toward the end of the eighteenth century that had made them move from their old villages farther down-river and establish these near Knife River. The earlier epidemic had halved their population; this one killed much more than ninety per cent of them. The best estimate is that the tribe numbered about sixteen hundred in June, 1837. Few if any more than a hundred were alive six months later.[2] No tribal organization could be maintained; the survivors lived with the Minnetarees or the Arikaras from then on. There are no full-blooded Mandans today.

So ended a people whom most white men liked, though from the lesser Alexander Henry on there had been some who, like Chardon, abhorred them. They were the first of the Western Indians whom the white men knew as a tribe. (The elder Verendrye, who visited them in 1738–1739, had probably had predecessors.) They had always been friendly to white men. Lewis and Clark had spent a winter among them. So had many others, finding their manners agreeable, their living standard high since they had agriculture, their earth lodges comfortable, and their women ardent. They were not a predatory people; as Indians go, they were pacific and it was their stockades and fortifications rather than their valor that kept the Sioux from exterminating them. In fact, they suffered almost as much, over the years, from the Sioux and the Assiniboins as from the whites and their smallpox. But the whites did for them in the end. 'Them,' Chardon's report of Four Bears' speech runs, 'them that I always considered as Brothers has turned Out to be My Worst enemies.'

* * *

The *St. Peter's* made her fatal stop at Fort Clark June 19 and 20. The Company's Jacob Halsey, on his way to take command at Fort Union, was prostrated soon afterward. So was his half-breed wife, who gave birth to a daughter and died. Halsey was the only one recognizably infected when the boat reached Fort Union and he was quarantined. But his three-year-old son and a clerk developed the disease fifteen days later. A panic like the one that Fort Clark had witnessed broke out at once: justly, since twenty-seven of the garrison were eventually infected and four died, and since the local Indians were not Mandans but the much tougher Assiniboins. They were off hunting at the time but seven of their women were at the post. These were the greatest potential source of danger and the melancholy Charles Larpenteur, still at Fort Union, still a clerk and unfortunate, thought that they ought to be sent away at once. His advice was not taken. The Fort possessed a doctor book, a Family Medical Companion, which was studied under the imminence of death. It prescribed vaccination but there was no vaccine. (A couple of months later when the *St. Peter's* got back to St. Louis, the government would rush quantities of it to the Indian country — too late.) The decision, 'with a view to have it all over and everything cleaned up before any Indians should come in on their fall trade, which commenced early in September,' [3] was to inoculate. So smallpox matter was taken from Halsey's pustules and the seven squaws and ten other persons had 'Death put in their veins.' Larpenteur's phrase and he says that they were locked in a small room and that a week later 'there was such a stench in the fort that it could be smelt at the distance of 300 yards.' He says that he could not enter the room — his squaw was in it and was one of those who died — without holding a vial of camphor to his nose. Some, he says, went crazy and others 'were half eaten up by maggots.' [4] Larpenteur is understandably bitter but the management of Fort Union during the epidemic was more intelligent than that of Fort Clark. The sick were nursed carefully and taken out into the shadow of the palisade in late afternoon. No one was allowed near them except those who had been vaccinated or had had the disease. Chittenden denounces the inoculation as an unexampled brutality inflicted to preserve the Company's business. But inoculation had a century of frontier tradition behind it and offered the most promising solution to the exceedingly dangerous problem. Furthermore, it succeeded: only three of the seventeen died but the virus was the same as that which had killed fifteen out of every sixteen Mandans.[5]

Halsey and his lieutenants did their utmost to keep the Assiniboins away from the fort. Whenever a band approached, an interpreter was sent out to warn them away. Inevitably this aroused their suspicions: it must mean that the whites were stealing the annual bounty from their father in Washington or else were working some evil medicine against them. So the band would come in and set up their lodges in the accustomed place on the flat. Halsey says categorically that he permitted none to enter and supposes, as was good science at the time, that the air was infected for a half-mile around, about as far as the dreadful stench would reach. Larpenteur supplies the true explanation: four or five braves scaled the pickets of a horse-stockade and tried to run the herd out. They were discovered in time and got off with only two. Those two were the most valuable ones, however, and four of the garrison rode off in pursuit. They succeeded in talking the Indians out of the horses and brought them back. They were the most expensive horses the Assiniboins ever stole for one of the posse was infected, and now they had the smallpox.

From then on there was no confining it. Larpenteur says that one band whose chief beat on the locked door and demanded to be admitted were persuaded to depart by the sight of a convalescent boy 'whose face was still one solid scab,' but they probably visited some of their kin on the way. There were always Assiniboin lodges on the flat and so there were always dying Assiniboins in the ruins of Campbell's old fort, which Halsey set aside as a pest-house for them and where they were attended by their old women. Halsey appointed an undertaker, too, one Brazeau who carried out the dead every morning and dumped them in the bushes. 'On asking him "How many?" ' Larpenteur says, 'he would say "Only three, sir, but according to appearances in the hospital, I think I shall have a full load tomorrow." '

So Fort Union, like Fort Clark, was hideous with death and deafening with magical practice. And the Assiniboins, like the Mandans, stampeded in blind terror of their demons. They were not sedentary Indians, however, and every band who rode away from the fort in panic carried the disease to their neighbors. Thus the virus was loosed on the prairies. But though it traveled fast and far, there was nevertheless some safety in flight, for bands broke up into smaller bands and many of these escaped infection. Figures about the Assiniboins are wholly undependable. Halsey estimates that eight hundred of them died, which would be a small percentage considering the losses of other tribes. McKenzie says that they and the Crees lost seven thousand, which is certainly a large overestimate. Schoolcraft, who contradicts himself from volume to volume, omits figures but says that they 'were swept off by hundreds' and that 'whole villages' were 'nearly annihilated.' But they kept on coming to the fort and after the local epidemic had subsided trade was resumed. And resumed briskly. Fatalism was on the Assiniboins. They expected to die soon, they told Larpenteur, so why not a frolic before death came? He did a good business exchanging alcohol for robes and the few shots fired at him were just the usual exuberance of the customers, not payment for the smallpox. But the crabbed chief Left Hand burned his American flag and promised to avenge his deaths.

It was a more serious threat from the Assiniboins than it had been from the Mandans but nothing came of it except an increase in the routine horse-stealing. Writing his principals, Halsey is not disturbed by the threat. He is not, in fact, disturbed by the terrible disaster inflicted on the Indians — at his personal agency. What does trouble him is the money loss. He does not know whether Fort Union will cover its overhead this year. (It did.) The loss to the Company will be 'incalculable, as our most profitable Indians have died.' The future looks dubious. The great McKenzie had succeeded in attracting to this post a large part of the Canadian trade which the Hudson's Bay Company had previously monopolized, but now that may be lost. For 'all diseases introduced to the Indians by the whites must have a tendency to make them malicious.'

* * *

The disease soon reached Fort Cass, the Company's Crow post, but no Indians were there. The Crows were far out in Absaroka hunting, and, if evidence is needed that they were an intelligent people, consider that, hearing about the smallpox, they stayed there. Their historians had preserved the memory of an epidemic long ago, the one that had assailed the Mandans before Lewis and Clark met them or an even earlier one; one of their shrines was 'the Place of Skulls,' where two of their ancestors had chosen to jump off a cliff rather than die of smallpox. So no Crows died of it this year.[6]

Alexander Harvey, known as a robust character and soon to have a shining reputation as a desperado, was waiting at Fort Union when the *St. Peter's* got there. He had brought down the Fort McKenzie keelboat for the Blackfoot trade goods. He hurried back upriver with them, hoping to escape the infection, but one of his cordellers and an Indian girl developed it just as he reached the Judith River. Sending word to Fort McKenzie, Harvey properly stopped there. A large part of the Blackfoot nation was camped at the fort, five hundred lodges of Bloods and Piegans. The young but very able Alexander Culbertson did his best to explain the disease and warn his customers. No use: they had come in for the summer trade, they suspected that Culbertson was practicing a swindle on them, and their historians had not told them about smallpox. They told him that if he did not have the boat brought up they would go and get it. After further warnings, Culbertson agreed to order it on to the fort but he made a formal oration commanding them to remember what he had said and not to hold them responsible for what would surely happen. He sent an express to Harvey telling him to come on. Two of Harvey's crew died after he reached the fort but the Blackfeet were not impressed. They turned in their skins and robes — they had lately gone in for mass production of robes, as the Company had been urging them to do — for the summer's outfit. It included a heavy armament in guns and powder for the annual campaigns against Crows, Flatheads, and all comers but the Blackfeet were not going to widen their *Lebensraum* this year. They made a quick job of it: in five days their lodges were down and they were off to the mountains.

Nearly the whole garrison of Fort McKenzie, including Culbertson, caught the disease. There were twenty-seven deaths. The comparative resistance of whites and Indians is shown by the fact that all but one of them were squaws, wives of the engagés. The same ghastly scenes characterized this outbreak; at the height of it they could not bury the dead and had to throw them in the river.

And then all summer long not a single Indian came to Fort McKenzie. It was amazing though they must have understood. Early in the fall Culbertson set out to call on the customers — to find out what was wrong. He got deep into the Blackfoot lands before he saw anything at all. Then at the Three Forks he found a village. No sound came from it as he approached, there were no horses or dogs, no children, no uproar. Presently they smelled the stench and then 'hundreds of decaying forms of human beings, horses, and dogs lay scattered everywhere among the lodges.' (The animals had been killed either sacrificially or in the frenzy of the deathlust.) They found two old women alive, too weak to travel with those who had fled, crawling demented among the corpses. And out from the village, on the prairie, on toward the mountains, every so often the rotting body of a Blackfoot who had died as he fled from his angered gods.

So it was throughout the Blackfoot country. The Gros Ventres got off most easily, having been somewhat immunized by an epidemic in the southern plains in 1831 while they were visiting the Arapahos. The other three tribes, the Blackfeet proper, fared worse than anyone else except the Mandans. There is no way of knowing how badly they fared. Estimates vary from Halsey's seven hundred, certainly too small, through Culbertson's 'six thousand, or about two-thirds of their whole number,' too large and bad factoring, to Schoolcraft's characteristic eight thousand. No matter: all summer and into the fall along the rivers and across the high valleys of the Blackfoot country smallpox was doing more for pacification than the fur companies had ever been able to do. Hereafter that country would be open — though not safe.

* * *

Late in the fall of 1837, the Skidi Pawnees, one of the principal divisions of the nation, while out on the fall hunt met a band of Oglala Sioux. It was like Crows meeting Blackfeet: there was only one course to take. The Pawnees waded in, won a glorious victory, sent a satisfactory number of Oglalas to the spirit land, and took something over twenty women and children prisoners. (They would be adopted into the tribe: one of the usual ways of maintaining population.) It seemed sagacious to go home at once, however, for the Oglalas might come in force to wipe out their dishonor and propitiate their dead. The Skidis abandoned the hunt and so were on starvation rations throughout the winter. Moreover, some of their prisoners had smallpox.

The Pawnee nation, which ranged from the Loup Fork of the Platte to the Republican River, numbered ten thousand. (Granting the terms of any census of Indians.) Like the Gros Ventres they had been partially immunized by the epidemic of 1831–1832 but that meant ultimately that nearly every lodge would be mourning its children. There was a terrible execution among the young and from the Skidis the infection traveled to all the other subdivisions. Messrs. Dunbar and Allis, whom we have noted as founding the Pawnee mission, estimated next year that a quarter of the nation had died.

The Pawnees were friendly to few people but were friendliest to the white men — and for that fellowship eventually got the usual recompense in full. They were semi-sedentary, cultivated corn, and lived in huts just north of Quivira, the fabulous province of gold and pomp to which The Turk led Coronado from Cibola. Their close relatives the Wichitas were in fact the people of Quivira and they themselves were the people who Castañeda says lived in Harahey. They were among the most religious of Indians; if their ceremonies were not so elaborate as those of the Arapahos, they had a more intricate system of belief. Until lately they, or at least the Skidi band, had practiced human sacrifice — the only Plains Indians who did. The rite climaxed a ceremony of propitiation to their angriest deity, the Morning Star, and was performed as a last resort when he was punishing his people. The ritual was presented in the presence of the most sacred objects the tribe possessed, notably the medicine bundle.

(Nearly all Plains tribes had a similar or equivalent collection of most-sacred objects. They were skins and feathers and a scattering of other totemic material, all immensely symbolical.) The victim must be a captive and a virgin and she was offered to the Morning Star in a ritual suggestive of the Aztec sacrifice though unrelated to it. Twenty years before, however, a daring freethinker whose name Wissler renders Petalasharo had rescued a Comanche girl from the sacrifice; later he had intervened again, twice. At his urging the Skidis had given up the practice — or at least for some years had decided that the Morning Star was not sufficiently angry to require it.

Now as the children died and their parents wailed among the huts, the Skidis knew that they had sinned; they were no better than apostates. So they decreed a tribal penance and a restoration of the apostolic church. They had a Sioux virgin and, in April, 1838, after their desperate winter, it was getting along toward planting time when the Morning Star must be worshipped. The victim must be kept in ignorance of her fate but she must be treated with unvarying kindness, venerated as an instrument of the supernaturals, and fattened by constant feasting — always eating alone since if anyone were her host another taboo would require him to protect and defend her. An extended ritual began at the time appointed, fasting, dancing, prophesying, singing, with all the riot and ecstasy these must eventually develop. On the morning of the last day the virgin was sent about the village to ask for wood and sticks. The priests took such of them as were ritualistically proper and consecrated them. Two posts were erected on a platform; two crosspieces joined them and a slow fire was built between them. At dusk after purifying her and themselves for the last time, the priests stripped their offering naked, painted half her body black and the other half red, and suspended her by wrists and ankles between the posts, over the smoky fire. Many boys who had also been ceremonially purified then shot the stiff stalks of joint-grass into her breast and body, scores of them. The reeds penetrated only a little way; some of them caught fire and burned. All this was done with an intricate accompaniment of sacred chants and dances, all supervised by the medicine men since to err in the sacrifice would be to make the god angrier, and all bringing on the frenzy. The holy incense billowed with the smoke, the firelight rose and fell, fat dripped into it from the pierced body of the shrieking girl — till at last the ordinance was fulfilled and a priest shot an arrow into her heart. He and his assistants then cut out the heart and burned it, and cut the flesh from her bones and buried it in the cornfields or gave it to the tribal dogs. They left the skeleton hanging there on its frame and the Morning Star was appeased. . . . Thus the Skidi Pawnees, trying to eradicate evil from the world.[7]

* * *

The Commissioner of Indian Affairs reported that the epidemic first appeared among the Chickasaws, who infected their neighbors the Choctaws, and that 'by the early and diligent use of vaccine matter much was done in this quarter to arrest the ravages of the disorder.' He adds that the disease spread from the Chickasaws and Choctaws to 'the northwest.' This is as close to an official finding as we have and it is probably not correct. The Chickasaws and Choctaws may have had a smallpox epidemic in 1837 and it may have been stopped by vaccination, though one doubts the latter, but the epidemic that reached the Plains tribes did not originate with them. They were permanently located on the lands assigned them in the southern part of the Indian Country, in the part later called Indian Territory, now Oklahoma. But the Pawnees, who were nearer them than any other of the Missouri tribes, caught the infection last of all and caught it from the Sioux, who lived north of them. Moreover, the tribes between the Chickasaws and Missouri seem not to have had the disease at all and it did not travel overland to the mountains, as it must certainly have done if there had been any sizable outbreak among the Civilized Nations.

The Commissioner goes on to say that 'vaccine matter was sent by a gentleman who was traveling to the Columbia River region, with a request that he would endeavor to introduce it there,' and this statement has its oddity. Since no gentleman would be traveling to the Columbia in 1837 after news of the epidemic reached St. Louis, the Commissioner is saying that he took no measures to protect the Northwest Indians till the following year — and that he then sent out some vaccine hoping that someone would find some use for it. As for the tribes who were suffering from the disease, he sent 'a medical gentleman' who 'on this benevolent errand vaccinated about 3000 persons' and there is hope that 'much prevention was effected and good done.' This also, it would seem, in 1838. Secretary of War Poinsett's report shows that his Department ordered more and considerably stronger measures than were actually put into effect. Nothing, however, could have done much good.

The Commissioner says that of the six Missouri River tribes principally affected — the Mandans, Arikaras, Minnetarees, Sioux, Assiniboins, and Blackfeet — at least 17,200 died. It may be: this is as good an estimate as any other and no estimate could be even moderately accurate. There were no data. There was no census of the tribes. Their numbers were estimated on the basis of guesses by traders and Indian agents, which were serviceable but must be assigned a margin of error up to fifty per cent. (Unless made by one of a very few good agents, Pilcher, for instance.) And there was no way whatever of knowing how many Indians had the smallpox, how many died, how many recovered. The surviving Mandans could be counted and their sedentary neighbors could be interrogated. But as for the migratory tribes — next year the bands were obviously much smaller than they had been and beyond that everything was speculative. That is enough, however, to indicate the historically important fact: that the balance of the Missouri tribes had been permanently altered. The importance of that fact is what caused the grotesque overestimates of the fatalities that were made at the time. D. D. Mitchell, who should have known better, guessed that 150,000 Indians died of the smallpox — more than twice as many as the tribes that had the smallpox numbered. Mitchell was displaying the shock of the afflicted tribes and of the white traders. The figures are grotesque but the implication is not: the relationships of peoples in these parts would be different hereafter from what they had been up to now. So, as the agonized letters back and forth of Pratte-Chouteau's home office and its factors bear full witness, so would the fur trade.

We have seen international relationships permanently upset by the migration of the Oglala Sioux to Laramie Plain. The smallpox epidemic also changed the balances of power. Resultants of these and other forces would eventually come to national attention under such names as Crazy Horse, American Horse, Sitting Bull, Red Cloud, Gall, Tall Bull, Roman Nose, White Horse, Little Wolf, Dull Knife, Satanta, Chivington, and Custer.

There is no reason to go into the rumor and folklore created by the epidemic. Jim Beckwourth, who in his time got blamed for nearly everything that happened west of the Missouri, was blamed for this. In lodges among the tribes whom the Crows and their Enemy of Horses had devastated and in the camps of mountain men who did not love him, it was told that Jim had procured an infected blanket and sold it to the Blackfeet, the enemies of his adopted people. We have seen how the Blackfeet got the infection and have seen that same infected blanket turn up in two other contexts, attributed to two other villains, and in both cases wrongly. Jim Beckwourth was, if one wants to step outside the historical frame, what Francis Parkman called him on Beacon Hill, 'a ruffian of the first stamp, bloody and treacherous,' though that he was also 'without honor or honesty' is less clear. But he had nothing to do with the smallpox epidemic on the upper Missouri in 1837. The accusation was natural to Indians who understood none but a personal agency. It is less understandable among antiquarians of today, some of whom have repeated it and more of whom have based their treatment of the epidemic on ideas no more tenable.

For instance, the abuse heaped on the American Fur Company. This narrative will not be suspected of admiring the business ethics of the Company. But it must protest the tendency of twentieth-century historians to hold the eighteen-thirties in American history to ideas which the eighteen-thirties had never heard of, which they would not have understood, and which produce confusion or nonsense when imposed on them today.

It may be pointed out that the American Fur Company could take neither a quick nor a long-term profit from the death of seventeen thousand customers. Sound business judgment — and there was no better judgment than the Company's anywhere in the United States — would have sacrificed this year's trade, if necessary, to protect the future trade. The outrage of modern scholars shocked by the Company's cynical lust for profit is absurd in view of the fact that every responsible Company agent — Chardon, Halsey, Harvey, Culbertson — tried to sacrifice the 1837 trade. They failed to but they failed because of the state of human knowledge and the nature of the neolithic mind.

In the fifth decade of the twentieth century it is easy to say that the *St. Peter's* should have tied up somewhere till the smallpox aboard had burned out, or should have returned to St. Louis, and that meanwhile the Indians should have been kept away from her. Try to do it.

In 1837 the germ theory and the concept of immunization did not exist: Pasteur was ten years short of investigating even his silkworms. No one knew how smallpox was communicated. If the best physicians of America had been aboard the *St. Peter's* they would have done exactly what the Company agents did: they would have instructed the uninfected to avoid miasmas, to eat no foods that were held to alter the proportions of mythical bodily attributes, and on the first symptoms of any illness whatever to take strong physics and various magical substances. The best physicians knew empirically that it was best to isolate smallpox victims as soon as you knew what they were suffering from (long after they had become infectious); the Company agents had the same knowledge and acted on it. But no one had any understanding of the rationale of quarantine.

Suppose, however, that they had had the knowledge of every American today — except the million or so who belong to anti-vaccination, anti-vivisection, anti-research organizations and sometimes produce smallpox epidemics which differ from that which destroyed the Mandans only in that the rest of us have been vaccinated. Suppose, that is, that they had differed absolutely from the Americans of 1837 who would not themselves be quarantined — who had refused to be quarantined during the cholera epidemic of five years before which devastated half the United States and who in the presence of smallpox always acted very much as the Indians did. Suppose all this. Then just how were the Indians to be kept from the sources of infection, the steamboat and the trading posts? Neither the germ theory nor the theory of immunization nor the medical theories of 1837 could be put to them in concepts which they could understand. The neolithic mind had its own theories and had proved that they were sound. Quarantine the victims and the Indians would nevertheless sneak into the quarantined places — as in fact they did. Refuse to trade with them and they would contrive to steal the trade goods or force the agents to trade with them regardless — both of which they in fact did. Sometimes, though hardly on predictable occasions, an Indian would believe what a white man told him about the unknown. He would believe it as he understood it. But when an Indian was refused admission somewhere or when he was refused his customary trade or the delivery of his annuities, both the empirical and the theoretical knowledge of the neolithic mind told him he was being swindled and he would entertain no further hypothesis.

But the government should have halted trade and vaccinated the Indians? On the basis of what information, when two-way communication between St. Louis and Fort Clark required four months or more? With what authority, within what powers of government, with what public sanction, according to what thesis? And just how? Perhaps half the physicans in America, at best not a quarter of the population, believed in the efficacy of vaccination. Neither the War Department nor the Bureau of Indian

Affairs had authority to take such action — we have seen the Commissioner hoping to persuade some Indians by way of a private individual. Congress and a vociferous public would have attended to any officials who tried to coerce the Company, to coerce any white men whomsoever. As for compelling or persuading any great number of Indians to submit to the insertion of a certainly diabolical medicine in a scratch on their arms, consult the records first of religious missions and then of scientific foundations that have tried to deal with the neolithic mind all over the world. Including the rural white population of the southern United States in the twentieth century.

We have here a specimen of the *a posteriori* thinking that corrupts history, as no one knows better than the historian of frontier societies, who has to cut his trail through an undergrowth of twentieth century ideas projected backward, usually with indignation. Take, since it does not involve Indians, the notion that the westward-making American pioneer culpably, and to the eternal loss of posterity, destroyed the forests of the Middle West. It is a cornerstone of belief in every mind entitled to call itself liberal and it is taught in the very grade schools of the nation. Well, in the first place, the pioneer did no such thing. He cut down portions of the forests in order to get fields, thereby increasing the productivity of what remained. If the pioneers who made clearings for farms had been the only people who cut down trees, the forests of northern mid-America would probably be healthier today than when the frontier reached them and the problems of flood and erosion would be about what they were in 1800. (That is to say, pretty serious.) What leveled the forests was not the farmers but industry — the oil industry which wanted barrels, the railroad industry which wanted ties, and the lumber industry which wanted boards and planking.

Yet the personal responsibility of the farmers cannot be got out of popular American history, which continued to belabor them with ideas that began to seep into American thinking with the twentieth century. But, to accept those ideas and work with a virtual movement again, just what was A. Lincoln's father supposed to do? Was it on the whole desirable (even with regard to posterity) to settle Indiana? If so, how do you farm Indiana without first making clearings? (On the way to answering this question consult the nature of unforested Indiana land, the accepted frontier ideas about arable soils, and what agronomy knows now but did not know then.) If clearings were necessary, what principles or theorems were to guide Thomas Lincoln in selecting the site of a clearing and determining its extent? If a residue of indignation remains because Thomas Lincoln's neighbors burned the surplus trees they felled, whereas they should have been put to some economic use beyond potash and pearlash, name that use and specify how these wasters of their progeny's wealth were to get the logs to market. Other nagging questions remain. What were the differences between Indiana forests and European forests where conservation was practiced? What were the differences between European and frontier American conceptions of natural resources, private and community ownership, the public domain, the future? How, in terms of past time, would you have communicated your ideas to Tom Lincoln and his neighbors? How would you have applied them? How would you have enforced them?

Such questions are simple relatively to those which concern the meeting of civilized and neolithic cultures. And relatively to the trade in furs in the Rocky Mountains and the American northwest during the first half of the nineteenth century.

After more than two centuries during which Indian tribes had exterminated one another and the French and British empires had fought repeated wars incidentally to the fur trade, it became evident that the best way of conducting it was by means of a government-regulated monopoly. 'Best' means here with greatest justice to the Indians, with least bloodshed, with maximum economy, with maximum stability, and with most rational expectation of conserving furs for the future. That having been said, it must at once be rephrased: within the British political system the experience of the Hudson's Bay Company indicated that an intelligent, intelligently regulated monopoly was the best way of conducting the fur trade so long as it could be completely safeguarded from wildcat competition.

A government-regulated monopoly in the United States during the first half of the nineteenth century was not only impossible, it was inconceivable. Not even a system of government licensing and supervision would work. The ideas of government, politics, economics, business, and free will held by the people of the United States forbade.

Then the government should itself have conducted the trade? It tried to, and that also was too alien to the beliefs and experience of the American people to be tolerated. Business could get into the government easily enough, whether at the level of Congressman Ashley, Senator Benton, and Secretary Webster, or at that of the inspectors and Indian agents who were carried on private as well as public payrolls. But government could get into business only so far as the annual pork trade in Congress permitted: river and harbor improvements, postoffices, postroads, subsidies for canals and railroads — all except the first two of which meant money, not management. The situation would not change till enough people had different ideas and could make them manifest, which was not till after the mountain fur trade ended. In the period we deal with here neither the Indians nor honest business practices as we now conceive them lacked advocates. But there were not enough to produce an effect.

Bribery, the corruption of government agents, the debauch of red Americans, murder, theft, piracy, hijacking, the liquor traffic, private war, the employment of public force in private war, and other criminal practices characterized the Western fur trade. (As they had characterized the French, Canadian, and British fur trade.) They were deplorable. But they must be seen in relation to such facts as the West itself.

In the more than a million square miles where the fur trade ranged there was no permanent white population whatever. The area was wilderness and more than half of it did not belong to the United States. In the part that was not American neither government nor the public will could do anything at all; in the part that was American government was powerless to do anything more. No one phrased the active sentiments of the Americans in full but they may be summarized as: the western wilderness belongs to us, let's see what we can do with it, and let us have no government there except on terms which will help and not hinder us in achieving our ends as we see them. Moreover, the West was not only wilderness, it was vastness. It was too vast for government to exercise the police power. You cannot send a company of dragoons with a pack train of supplies from Fort Leavenworth, Kansas, to Lander, Wyoming, in pursuit of a man who has murdered an Indian or stolen a beaver plew. Nor can you guarantee from St. Louis the responsibility of a civil servant at Pierre, South Dakota, who has been bought by a fur company. The American Fur Company was only the first of those persons and corporations in the far West, as Judge Roy Bean was not the last, of whom it is historically true that they were the law west of the river. Before legal responsibility could be possible in the West, it was necessary to settle the West. That implied, besides many other things, the Oregon and California migrations, the gold rush and the development of the interior mining West, and the building of the Pacific Railroad. (During which time the mountain fur trade and a large part of the Indian question disappeared.) The West being settled, the application of legal forms to business, a rudimentary legal justice, and a rudimentary social justice could not be established till the settlers of the West so changed the sentiments they brought along as to desire them. That eventually happened, but those rudimentary decencies still could not be established until the West could forcibly exact them of the East. It took time. The development of the American social pattern had given the East a powerful money interest in preventing rudimentary legal and social decency from being established in the West.

This is to say that the history of the mountain fur trade is part of the history of the West. The West has always had to make up its law as it went along. It has always been both ahead of and behind statutory law as imported from the seats of power. It has always been exploited by absentee owners and managers under the sanction of imported law. And further, the Indians of the West had a twofold misfortune, which history has eventually got to deal with as twofold. They were, like all Indians, a neolithic people in conflict with a higher culture. But they were also Westerners. That means that they were the first victims of a developing system whose later and successive victims have been white. As such they must be seen in relation to the vastness of the unoccupied West, the developing industry, the growth of the nation's population, and the proliferation (in part implicit in part imposed) of a system of financial control which converted property, manipulated credit, and stripped the resources of the plundered province to the sole end of canalizing eastward whatever wealth the West might produce. None of this justified the murderous violence applied to them but a preliminary step toward the writing of history is to state that violence in relation to the less murderous violence that was a condition of white society in the West.

Historians of the West have not yet completed that preliminary step. This narrative calls attention to the fact that historical judgments must be peripheral or inane until the preliminaries of historical statement have been made, and now feels free to return to its job.

## «XII»

# A PAINTER ON THE TRAIL (1837)

We left Jim Bridger's American Fur Company brigade in camp for the winter of 1836–1837 somewhere in Absaroka, the Crow country. Meek says on Powder River and Russell says the Yellowstone, a few miles from the mouth of Clark's Fork.[1] Both may be right; the brigade may have wintered in two divisions. Both describe this as a winter of unusual comfort, and also as, in Meek's words, 'thoroughly demoralized.' For some reason Bridger was spending Company alcohol on his men, which meant big times in the mountains. And now the Crows abandoned whatever remained of their temperance policy. The chiefs came to pay calls of ceremony on Old Gabe and got drunk. Following up the innovation, he sent traders to their villages with alcohol instead of goods. The chiefs were methodical about it. They selected details from the camp police who must remain bone-dry, while their friends guzzled, and must protect the trader. Armament was checked at the door so far as possible, and then everyone who had robes or plews or moccasins or anything else that was negotiable came in and started drinking. 'Every form of drunkenness,' Meek says, 'from the simple stupid to the silly, the heroic, the insane, the beastly, the murderous displayed itself.' The Crows rolled about and vomited and fought and screamed and slept — so much so, Meek says with simple awe, that they shocked the mountain men. As they approached coma the trader kept increasing the proportion of water to alcohol, debasing the currency till a few teaspoonfuls would buy a robe. When the village sobered up there were more widows and orphans than there had been and everyone was broke. An impoverished Indian counted on making a stake by theft or war, so when his traders came back with the take Bridger moved camp.

At the end of January, bored with inaction, Osborne Russell took a half-dozen pals out to find buffalo and instead found himself opening the Blackfoot season. A Blackfoot winter-sports party, well down into Absaroka, chased them back to camp, pretty thoroughly shot up. The humiliation had to be avenged for the sake of both pride and trade relations, so a few days later they found another sports-party and chased it into some old log breastworks and cleaned it up. The exchange had cost the Blackfeet the equivalent of a rook. On Washington's Birthday, therefore, Bridger, from his observation tower, saw the distant plain swarming with them. He had the whole camp get to work forting up a big square with logs and brush, in a bend of the river at the foot of a bluff. Night guard was doubled. Russell had the nine-to-midnight trick. Winter in the Montana plains — windless, no bottom to the thermometer, the stars eight feet away, tree branches booming like gunfire. Russell would hardly expect attacking Blackfeet before the false dawn but any time was right for an attempt on the horses. He got neither. Instead the sky suddenly lighted up with a superb aurora. Blood-red, it rolled and writhed and zigzagged and faded in and out for two full hours. No attack in the morning either, so Bridger reconnoitered and found the Indians quiescent in a large camp a few miles away. When that night also was quiet Russell began 'to fear we should not have a fight after all our trouble.' In the morning an Indian scout chased a white scout back to camp with a bullet in his heel and then a thousand Blackfeet started to cross the ice toward camp. The boys (there were about sixty of them) got ready but the Blackfeet halted out of rifle range and the head chief came far enough forward to talk sign. He held out clasped hands, struck his left fist several times with his right palm, used both hands to describe the outline of a medicine pipe, and raised his extended right hand till it pointed up and out. 'Friendly — fill pipe — smoke — go away.' He turned his back on Bridger's camp and led his big village away in the direction of the Three Forks. The red aurora had been in the Blackfeet's half of the sky. They probably remembered it next July when the smallpox came.

Peace — when the odds were that big — was okay with Jim Bridger. But in the earlier skirmish the leader of his Delaware contingent, his name was Manhead, had been killed and Joe Meek was sore. You had to wipe out an adverse coup by striking one of your own. So he took a companion and skulked along the Blackfoot trail. That night the two of them crept into the camp, watched a group of gamblers playing the hand game for a while, then cut loose nine horses and went home with them, the debt settled. The campaign and the spring hunt moved off in step. The brigades broke up into trapping parties which combed the Big Horn, the Yellowstone, the Gallatin, Madison, and Jefferson, the tangle of mountains north of Yellowstone Park, the Park itself, Idaho west of the Divide. Kit Carson at the head of sixty men had a three-hour fight with Blackfeet and had to hightail in search of Bridger when his powder ran low. With the Delawares, Russell's small party got some more Blackfeet to help Manhead in the spirit world. Joe Meek's division ran into nest after nest of them, was always chasing or being chased, and had to trap beaver with one hand on their rifles all through the hunt. Meek had left Carson's employ and was back with the Company, teaming up with his rowdy friend Doc Newell. Late in the spring they stirred up a snappy little affair when they found a Blackfoot camp in a narrow draw. Joe, Doc Newell, and several others went into action at once, crawling along a bluff above the camp. The Indians reacted strongly, pinned them down, flanked them, got above them, and drove them into their own camp and surrounded it. Next day Bridger's main party appeared in time to help out. The battle spilled out of the besieged camp into the plain, which filled with galloping duels. Meek nearly went under when a Blackfoot came up while he was reloading but the brave strung his bow too tight, the arrow dropped, and Joe collected. 'Cotton' Mansfield got himself surrounded by shrieking Blackfeet and was heard to shout, 'Tell Old Gabe that Old Cotton is gone,' but he wasn't for some of the boys came up in time. Doc Newell toppled a brave from his saddle and leaped down from his own horse to collect the scalp. He was just slashing at it with his knife when the Indian rose up and sailed into him. Doc couldn't get his left hand free for the Indian had decorated his hair with some hardware that caught his fingers. They fought in a circle, their knives clashing, till Doc got home on the brave and could lift the scalp at his leisure.

(This is the fight which Joe Meek later claimed inspired a famous painting, 'The Trapper's Last Shot.' He says that John Mix Stanley was along and was so impressed by one tableau in which Joe figured that he immortalized it. But, as Note 4 of the Appendix (page 450) shows, Stanley did not go to the Far West until 1846, did not meet Meek till 1847, and did not paint 'The Trapper's Last Shot.')

Bridger's party soon put the Blackfeet to flight. Joe Meek almost managed to get a squaw who was unhorsed but her husband galloped by and she grabbed his horse's tail and was saved. A few days later during a prairie truce a brave came riding into camp with his wife and daughter. Considering the number of scalps his people had lately gathered, this was odd if not careless, and some of the boys wanted to penalize the folly. Joe and Kit Carson interfered and led the Indians safely out of camp. Joe, who was getting low on tobacco, demanded some as a fee. The Indian valued his safety at two chaws, paid them, and rode off.[2]

A typical spring hunt in the Blackfoot country — but not typical in the number of plews taken. The indications of the last two years were reinforced: the beaver country was nearly trapped out. As summer came on the parties worked southward, rendezvous having been set for Green River Valley again. Russell, coming by way of South Pass, reached the Green on June 10 and found a camp already assembled about half-way between the mouths of Horse Creek and New Fork. It was an unusually big camp and a mixed multitude — 'the whites were chiefly Americans and Canadian French, with some Dutch, Scotch, Irish, English, halfbreed and fullblood Indians of nearly every tribe in the Rocky Mountains.' The fair would be a Company monopoly again, which meant that Indians and free trappers would be thoroughly rooked. But they had to wait nearly a month for the pack train and Fitzpatrick. They made it a prolonged rodeo. Game was abundant. The squaws cured robes, made lodges, tailored and mended clothes, put up pemmican. The braves and the trappers hunted meat as it was needed and enjoyed their vacation. 'Some were gambling at cards, some playing the Indian game of hand, and others horse racing, while here and there there could be seen small groups collected under shady trees relating the events of the past year, all in good spirits and health, for sickness is a stranger seldom met with in these regions.'

The Nez Perces were mostly laboring to get their Henry Spalding established so their delegation this year was small, Russell says about a half-dozen. A village of Bannocks, sixty lodges, came up and camped three miles away. (The Bannocks were detached Shoshones who lived in southern Idaho, with permanently bad hearts and nothing that white men recognized as virtues.) They were coming for the annual trading fair with peace in their hearts and all the auspices favorable. But they had gathered in some horses and traps on their way here, from a small party of trappers on Bear River, and had blandly brought the take with them. When restitution was demanded, they said no. Several trappers and a couple of Nez Perces rode over to the Bannock camp, found its proprietors out making meat, and came back with the stolen horses. Outraged, thirty of the thieves galloped over to the white camp and demanded their booty. They didn't feel any real need to fight the white men they said, but they would be happy to reclaim the horses from the Nez Perces and let them make something of it if they wanted to. This was interesting and the mountain men turned out in a hurry. Most of the Bannocks sized up the band and started to leave in a mood of renewed peace, but one of them went on the prod and began to abuse his gang with the insults that would always make an Indian fight. We started out for these horses or some scalps — let's take what we came for. Jim Bridger had appeared and was holding by the bridle one of the horses in dispute. That simple fact should have made a pacifist of any man in the mountains, red or white, but the brave was believing his medicine. He reached for the bridle Jim was holding and at once permanently lost interest in horses. Twelve more of his band were killed before they could get away. The boys rode over to the Bannock village, plundered it, sent it hell-bent westward, and followed it, sniping, for three days. After they returned to camp a delegation of Bannocks came in and said they had the idea now — if they would be good Bannocks could they stay for the trade? They could and did.

* * *

During the winter of 1836–1837 the activity of two of the characters who have figured in this narrative notably enriched the American heritage. As we have seen, Thomas Nuttall was back in the States, with his freight of specimens. John Kirk Townsend who had originally gone west with him wasn't as yet; shortly after Narcissa Whitman met him on the Columbia, he sailed for the Sandwich Islands (November, 1836) but did not get back to Philadelphia till a year later. Bales of specimens he had collected, however, had been forwarded to his principals, the American Philosophical Society and the Philadelphia Academy of Natural Sciences. And during the year the great Audubon had returned to the United States from London, where his son was watching the slow production of *The Birds of America*. The great work had already been in the press for ten years and, as it turned out, had two years still to go. Originally it was to have consisted of eighty parts, four hundred plates, and of these Audubon had completed all but eighty-five when he sailed for America. He hoped to get more subscribers there but mostly he hoped to find some way of doing those remaining plates. Most of them had been allotted to species of the great unknown, the mountains and the Pacific coast. He was fifty-one, he never did have enough money to fund his labor properly, a financial panic in London was canceling many British subscriptions to the *Birds* (as Mr. Van Buren's panic of the next year would cancel American subscriptions), and there was probably no way that he could travel the West and make the studies and collections that his great scheme required.

Considering his record, there is no doubt that John James Audubon would have started west against the odds. And in fact seven years later, in 1843, when fortune was kinder, he did make a rewarding trip up the Missouri. (This was the year when Stewart revisited the coasts of illusion and for a while there was talk of their traveling together.) He got to Fort Union, lodged there for two months in the room which Maximilian and Bodmer had used for an identical purpose, and made an overland trip some distance up the Yellowstone. To this journey we owe his buffalo, the grizzlies, and other plates in *The Quadrupeds of America.*

But in 1836 he was spared the strain of travel and uncertainty and the pressure of haste. Six weeks after he arrived in the United States he read a description of Nuttall's and Townsend's specimens. He hurried to Philadelphia, found that the collection contained at least forty new species of birds, and began negotiating for them with the Academy of Natural Sciences. In Boston Nuttall promised him all his duplicates but Philadelphia proved more resistant. In the end he was permitted to buy about ninety of Townsend's skins and to sketch such others as he wanted. During the winter of 1836–1837 at Charleston, South Carolina, he made drawings of them, and about seventy eventually became plates in *The Birds of America.* This rich addition is the reason why the work contains some composite plates (contrary to Audubon's original intention) and why supplements carried it beyond the number of plates first announced.[3]

* * *

Mr. Alfred Jacob Miller was twenty-six years old and an artist, a Romantic painter who had had nearly two years of the brisk wind that was blowing through the studios of Paris and Rome. He had talked many nights away with Horace Vernet and his young men, at many cafés, in many ateliers. He had sat at the feet of Horace Greenough, had traveled to Rome with Nat

Willis (and been arrested at the frontier, where his copies of paintings in the Louvre had been mistaken for originals), had abjectly worshiped Thorvaldsen. He had discussed the beautiful with all the young men. And he had made an impression too: in Paris they called him 'the American Raphael.' Conceivably that was a title not difficult to earn in 1833.

America was something else. It was the early morning of our first national period when Miller got back to Baltimore in 1834 but a painter had to scratch hard and turn a penny where and as he could. He had to varnish ancestral portraits, copy in any style demanded, gild a frame, compose something prettily symbolic when the children's dog died. Baltimore was not too receptive of Miller's talent and in the fall of 1836 he went to New Orleans. He took a studio on Chartres Street and after some scrambling made a small place for himself in this old town of mixed cultures and an esthetic tradition.

In March or April of 1837 Miller had recently completed a large canvas, a painting of the city of Baltimore under the romantic haze of early evening, as seen distantly from Loudenslager's Hill. It was the haze that had interested him, the soft light tones of the sky above the 'kept down' base that had become obligatory in landscapes by young men. He had heard of a process called 'dry scrambling' — he wondered if it were not how Turner achieved his delightful obscurity — and decided to try it on the sky above Baltimore. (He meant 'scumbling.')

He was working on another canvas when a gentleman came into the studio, nodded to him, and began to examine the portraits and landscapes on the wall. Miller thought his visitor might be a Kentuckian, though to be sure no bowie knife was visible and one would be expected. The gentlemen 'had on a gray suit with a black stripe worked in the seam of his pantaloons and held himself straight as an arrow . . . he had a military air.' After gazing for some time at the view from Loudenslager's Hill, he said 'I like the management of that picture and the view.' Presently he went away — without buying anything. He was back a few days later to explain himself, giving Miller a card which introduced him as Captain William Drummond Stewart of the British Army. The captain explained that he had spent four years in the Far West and was preparing to go there again this summer. He wanted 'a competent artist to sketch the remarkable scenery and incidents' and offered Miller the job, telling him to call on John Crawford, the British consul, and to discuss the offer with his own friends.

The chance thus offered a young man of twenty-six was something like an offer today of a four or five months' tour of Asia and the South Pacific by Army plane. Miller did call on the consul, who assured him that Stewart was the rightful heir and good for the passage money, but he had probably accepted the offer the moment it was made. He would make the grand tour, he would go west.

Whether Stewart had spent the winter in New Orleans or had gone to the British islands as he had done the preceding year cannot be determined. New Orleans seems the likelier since this time he had brought his hunter, Antoine Clement, with him and even with the available half-alligator men Miller found that he 'was like a fish out of water.' Calling at Stewart's lodgings, Miller would find him playing cards with 'that wild child of the Prairie' to keep him occupied.

There appears to be not even one day-by-day journal of the caravan trip west in 1837, and as far as the rendezvous it must be described by inference — inference from the journals that describe the rendezvous, from slender fur company records and a line or two in the scant Stewart-Sublette correspondence, and from the notes which Miller wrote to identify and accompany his water-color sketches. These last make a frequently interesting, sometimes valuable document in Western history. There are one hundred and sixty-six notes in the manuscript that is nearest the original state. Some of these, however, have been revised in line with Miller's later reading of Ruxton and Frémont, and there is no way of knowing whether others may not have been revised in line with his reflections. Some allowance must be made for such revisions but it is not important. In the main Miller's 'Rough Draughts for Notes to Indian Sketches' is accepted here as eyewitness testimony.

Though in fact Stewart made another trip west in 1838 and then came back again in 1843 and made a fantastically luxurious one, it may be that he expected his 1837 venture to be his last. Possibly the strained situation which one deduces existed between him and his brother had eased somewhat, possibly he had learned that his brother was in bad health, possibly years or some unknown event made him face more resignedly the prospect of living with Christina. But he was taking a larger and more luxurious outfit than ever before, as if for a final splurge, and he wanted an artist to sketch the country so that he could paint it for Murthly Castle.

Antoine Clement was his head man. Three other engagés

named Louis, Auguste, and Pierre are named in Miller's notes, and a cook called Jean or John. A ledger of Pratte, Chouteau & Company at the Missouri Historical Society shows payments on behalf of Stewart to François Lajeunesse, and since one of them is for steamboat passage he was certainly Stewart's employee. (This is the François Kaskaskai Lajeunesse who with his brother Basil went west with Frémont. They had learned the mountain craft working out of Bent's Fort, and Basil, who was killed by the Modocs at Klamath Lake, was one of the Pathfinder's favorites.) We are therefore sure of five besides Miller and there must have been several more. Miller's allusions sometimes indicate a considerably larger party, though in any event not enough to account for the discrepancy between his figures of the Company caravan and those which Osborne Russell gives.[4] Stewart had taken two wagons west last year and would need at least two this year, if not three. He made a longer stay at the lakes, which implies a larger party. One guesses a minimum of eight besides Miller and Stewart himself, and explains Miller's contradictory notes as a failure to make clear that Stewart had been given certain executive duties by Fitzpatrick.

We are sure of the canned delicacies this time, for Miller mentions wine and porter and describes a trapper wolfing an entire box of sardines which Stewart had intended as *hors d'oeuvres*. He says that Stewart had three new rifles by Joseph Manton at forty guineas each, considerably less than would be expected. One of them which was turned over to Antoine must have been the heaviest so far taken to the West. It used balls that ran twelve to the pound.

Stewart, Miller, and Antoine Clement went from New Orleans to St. Louis, presumably in April. The town, as the great ganglion in the nervous system of the West, was rocking with financial upheaval. The bitterest money war in American history and the wildest speculation of the nineteenth century had precipitated the first national depression. The final Specie Circular, Andrew Jackson's broadside at the money trust, had gone into effect in August of 1836. Requiring hard-money payments for government lands, it had brought down the whole fantastic structure of speculation and with it the whole system of wildcat banking — that is to say, most of the American banking system and all the Western banks. Foreign investors had dumped their American securities, trade had all but halted, unemployment had spread across the country. It had been a bad winter for the United States, with bread riots in most cities and the unvarying gutlessness of financiers producing a mass despair not unlike the panic of the Mandans when the smallpox struck. It was a worse spring as Mr. Van Buren took office, specie disappeared, and doomsday seemed at hand. The letters of Pratte-Chouteau to the American Fur Company's office in the spring of 1837 have the United States on its deathbed. They were right in this, that the West was in the first of its bankruptcies. But if St. Louis was using merchants' script and bar slugs for money, it was still a boom town. The flood from the East kept rising. Illinois and Michigan and lower Wisconsin were filling up. The trade with Santa Fe was doubling, and this at least was in the silver dollars of Mexico which the wagon trains brought back. In short, the West was bankrupt and booming at the same time — and that would describe the West from here on. The pattern and mechanism for its exploitation by Eastern capital had been worked out, and if the price of beaver sagged lower, Pratte-Chouteau was sending its caravan west as usual. And doubtless William Sublette and Robert Campbell were finding good fishing in roily waters.

These last were gentleman bankers now; they went no more to the West but sent Bill's three young brothers. They were still the Opposition on the Missouri too and would not have been if there had not been money in it. Sublette's country-house was Stewart's headquarters and Campbell also was his friend. Possibly they envied him his eagerness to make the golden journey to Samarkand. There were long evenings at Sublette's place, where buffalo grazed in the paddock and Rocky Mountain bears were staked out with chains, and Miller heard stories of the great days. He ate the food of Samarkand there, too, for Bill Sublette every year commissioned his employees to bring him bags of pemmican and sides of jerky when they came back. He kept it on hand to serve ceremonially at his house and offer to old-timers who might drop in at his office. But Stewart would not see Bill's brother Milton again. He had not returned from last year's invalid journey west. We saw him turn back from the rendezvous to Fort Laramie, and there late in 1836 he died.[5]

The travelers also frequented the home of the town's greatest man, William Clark, the father of all Western adventure. That illimitable hospitality was nearing its close now; Clark had only fifteen months to live. And either here or at Independence a young man from St. Louis joined the party. Miller speaks of him as P——; he was a young blood with a stern father. P—— had backed too many cards and horses, had too much engaged himself with the town's pleasures, and so his parent 'dispatched him with us for a wholesome change of air.' It turned out to be a permanent change for the young man died in an accident, following rendezvous.

The Company was not jumping off from Bellevue as it had for two years but had reverted to the original practice of leaving from the vicinity of Independence.[6] Tom Fitzpatrick was in charge again and Black Harris was with him. They also had an ancient of days to share the command for Etienne Provost was along.[7] He was one of the elders of the West and was now reunited with Fitzpatrick who, like him, had been an original Ashley man. They had broken into the Great Basin practically at the same time. One or the other or both had been in the party that first traveled South Pass from the east.[8] Provost has sometimes been credited with the discovery of Great Salt Lake and certainly was within sight of it only a few weeks at most after Jim Bridger. That was only thirteen years before this summer, but in the time scale of the mountain trade it belonged to an earlier epoch. In the autumn of 1824 Provost's party came down Weber Canyon through the Wasatch Mountains (and had a notable fight at the canyon mouth) and Bridger's party crossed the range fifty miles farther north and came down into Cache Valley. Jim floated down the Bear River in a bull-boat to find out where it flowed and brought back word that it emptied into an arm of the Pacific Ocean. Thirteen years had sufficed to map the entire West in the minds of such men as the three first-comers who were now reunited. The width of those years may be measured by the fact that Tom Fitzpatrick, whose mind was a register of all that had ever happened in the mountains, was only thirty-eight. Beside him, Provost, who had been a trapper on the Missouri before Ashley entered the trade at all, was from geological time. He was fifty-five and, Miller says, 'With a corpus Round as a porpoise.'

Besides the Company there was also a band of free trappers, so from the beginning of the trip Miller had all varieties of mountain men to watch and could listen to the whole saga. The story of Hugh Glass and his grizzly went down in his notebooks — it is far from unique as a story of either bears or mountain courage but it has been lodged forever in our legends. At another campfire he heard a grizzly story about Markhead, probably pirated from Joe Meek. It had Markhead boasting that he could shine in any company and, to make good, following the beast into a thicket to kill it with a belt-axe and getting part of his scalp torn off.[9] That the potent symbol of the campfire made an impression on the artist is evident in his sketches and his notes. The boys tell him the folklore of the carcajou. With a straight face they describe the herb that immunizes Indians to rattlesnake bites. (Doctor Coues, a celebrated botanist, believed that one all his life, hoping to find a specimen sometime.) Black Harris describes his putrified forest and much else from the country of fable. The Canadian engagés dance to a jew's-harp. And Stewart contributes to this nightly serial. 'At other times,' Miller says, 'our leader would entertain them with his adventures in foreign lands, the curious cities and monuments of antiquity he had visited. It was edifying to see the patience with which he answered their simple questions as if they were matters of course and full of importance, all the while maintaining a gravity that was most amusing. It is not to be wondered at that he became immensely popular amongst them. No doubt all of the men would have followed him into any danger regardless of consequences. One of them told us that he (the Captain) had a "h'ar (hair) of the Grissly in him," meaning bulldog courage.' [10] Thus the veteran of Waterloo to the veterans of local wars, and Miller says that though he would describe his campaigns he said nothing about his part in them.

Only in Miller's notes, in fact, does Captain William Drummond Stewart figure in the literature of the fur trade at greater length than the casual journal entries that have been quoted. Miller brings him to life. He enforced military discipline on his party and served as a lieutenant of Fitzpatrick in the conduct of the Company train. He gave Miller a single privilege, that of hiring a substitute for night guard duty, but made him care for his own horses. If a member of the guard fell asleep he made him travel on foot all the next day, which was standard practice. The nightly camp must be made by the numbers, packs piled just so, horses watered according to the rulebook. He understood 'the management of unruly spirits,' Miller says, and describes a slugging match which broke out in camp. Stewart forbade anyone to interfere and one of the fighters got beaten up. Stewart sent for him. 'You have been fighting and are well whipped.' Yes. 'By Jove, I am heartily glad of it. No doubt you richly deserved it. I shall have no further trouble with you and am certain you will not boast of it. You can go.' He then summoned the strutting victor and told him that 'if he ever heard of his boasting in any matter of having whipped Louis, he would dismount him and make him walk for a week.' There were no more slugging matches.

Or he rides out ahead with Antoine when some Indians appear on the hills, and conducts a long inquiry with them in sign language to make sure they are friendly before he will let them approach the camp — rifle across his saddle, nerves alert, eyes searching, Old Bill Stewart the partisan, a long way from Birnam Wood. Or wrapped in a mackinaw blanket he upbraids Miller for being depressed by an unseasonable three-day rain, saying that his early training must have been faulty. Or he teaches Miller a lesson in mountain craft; this at Independence Rock, which Miller goes out to sketch when the camp is pitched near by. (Plate X.) 'Selecting the best site & setting to work being completely absorbed, about half an hour transpired when suddenly I found my head violently forced down & held in such a manner that it was impossible to turn right or left. An impression ran immediately through my mind that this was an Indian & that I was lost. In five minutés, however, the hands were removed. It was our Commander. He said, "Let this be a warning to you or else on some fine day you will be among the missing. You must have your eyes and wits about you." '

Miller describes him as a martinet, and one with a temper. There were two tempers in camp. Antoine Clement was a half-breed. . . . A fine artist of the Cattle Kingdom would eventually put that into words once and for all, of a fictional character named Charlie Bird. 'That Charlie Bird, he's half Cherokee and half white, and them's two bad breeds.' [11] . . . Miller rode out with Stewart and Antoine one morning to get on with his sketching. Stewart had given an order which had not been obeyed, and 'he would not tolerate any neglect.' He said so to Antoine, who in his turn would not suffer reproof. They blazed at each other. Miller points out that whereas Stewart could trace his ancestry to the Conqueror and the hunter would be considered well off if he knew who his parents were, the leveling process of the mountains put them 'on a perfect equality, well mounted, armed with Manton rifles, neither knowing what fear was.' He expected them to start shooting — and he was twelve miles from the caravan, he didn't know in what direction. It had about reached the shooting point when a band of buffalo came over the horizon. 'The ruling passion overtopped everything': Antoine and Stewart were off a gallop and Miller's nerves could unwind. Two fat cows stretched on the prairie, noble lord and noble savage rode back together.

The buffalo impressed our artist as they did all greenhorns. He sketched them in color and prose. He marveled at Antoine's skill, saying that he killed a hundred and twenty on the way to rendezvous and noting his morning spirits when he rode off toward the herd singing '*Mam'selle Marie, qui est bonne comme elle?*' or '*Dans mon pays je serais content.*' Miller repeats all the clichés of newcomers to the West. The prairie dogs share their burrows with rattlesnakes; rattlers crawl into his blanket or someone else's in the night cold. Thirst on the prairies is almost unendurable but discipline will not permit you to drink out of turn when you reach a river and pride of craft forbids you to carry water between rivers. On the baked horizon there is suddenly the blue shimmering of a lake with cool green trees beside it but the horses do not snort or even raise their ears and the train slogs onward in heat made manifest, for this is only a mirage. The cook (in one note Jean Anglais, in another an Englishman named John) tries his hand at hunting and gets lost. At nooning everyone crawls into what shade he can find, under a charette or in the fringe of sagebrush, and sleeps — except Miller who must stay awake and sketch the others. Several times a band of broomtails, the runty wild horses of the plains (promoted to tear-jerkers in our time), thunders by and makes our romantic gape with 'the beauty and symmetry of their forms' which didn't exist, and 'their wild spirited action, long sweeping manes and tails, variety of color, and fleetness of motion,' which did. (He sees some Indians, presumably Company Delawares, go after one band with lassos.)

The Indians fascinated him most. Twenty-five or thirty Delawares were with the caravan from the beginning. Soon after crossing the Kansas, on the way to the Platte, they reached the Pawnees — and in Miller's notes they have the character which the emigrants were to give them later on. They demanded tolls and tribute for permission to cross their country; they asserted, rightly enough, that they were the white man's friends; and they stole everything that was loose. Fitzpatrick and Stewart doubled their horse guards but the Pawnees went on hoping — 'from the tops of bluffs, behind rocks, and out of the long grass of the prairie they watched us and kept themselves posted.' Fitz was relieved when he got beyond them.

One morning a hunter came galloping back toward the train yelling 'Indians!' Another one followed him with word that there was a swarm of them and there would presently be some hair-lifting. Miller says that the pork-eaters who had been bravest at the campfire were scared stiff, whereas the veterans went on chawing tobacco — it was old stuff to them. (He confesses that he was as sensitive about his scalp 'as a Chinese about his long cue.') Fitzpatrick, Harris, Provost, and Stewart rode out to meet 'a piratical hoard of painted wretches coming down on us at top speed, armed to the teeth and riding round us in a menacing manner.' Pure form. The white chiefs sat down with the red ones, Miller joining the circle, and smoked to the sky, the earth, the cardinal points, and the preservation of American-Amerind friendship. The Indians demanded their prairie tribute, 'cloths, ammunition, knives, tobacco, blankets,' got it, and went their way, 'the trappers invoking *peculiar* blessings on their livers, hearts, and other interior organs.'

Miller does not say so but these were probably Oglala Sioux. At any rate some days to the eastward from Fort Laramie the caravan met a big band of Oglalas and traveled with them to the fort. A famous band too, for it was Bull Bear's. It could have been up to half the tribe (Miller's notes indicate a large party but not how large) for since Sublette & Campbell first induced them to leave the Missouri for the Platte more and more had migrated every year till almost all of them were here. They were divided into two loose federations, this one under Bull Bear, the other under that Smoke who as 'Old Smoke' appears so prominently in Parkman's *Oregon Trail*. The migration had upset not only the polity of Indian nations but the white economy as well. Lieutenant Lancaster P. Lupton who had come west with the Dragoons in 1835 had resigned his commission the next year and set up in the fur business on the South Platte, near the present town of Fort Lupton, Colorado. Since this was less than a hundred miles due south of the Company's big Fort Laramie and within easy reach of all the Indians who traded there, the Company was this year, 1837, subsidizing its periodic employee Peter Sarpy in partnership with its one-time rival Henry Fraeb. They were building a trading post, Fort Jackson, six miles away from Lupton's. Just to make sure, it was also backing one of the younger Sublettes, Andrew, and Louis Vasquez in still a third post only a few miles away. Since all these were in the area which Bent's Fort drew on, the powerful and sagacious Bent brothers promptly established a subsidiary of their own on the South Platte.

The Oglalas had moved within striking distance of the Pawnees, their immemorial enemies, and were constantly raiding them. They were also in an excellent position to raid the Crows, who were old enemies, and the Snakes, who were even older ones. They did so. But they had acquired two new enemies, this being country claimed by the Arapahos and the Cheyennes

# THE MEN -- AND THEIR WOMEN

'This child hates an American what hasn't seen Injuns skulped or doesn't know a Yute from a Shian mok'sin. Sometimes he thinks of makin' tracks for white settlement but when he gits to Bent's big lodge on the Arkansa and sees the bugheways, an' the fellers from the States, how they roll thar eyes at an Injun yell worse nor if a village of Camanches was on 'em, an' pick up a beaver trap to ask what it is — just shows whar the niggurs had thar brungin' up — this child says, "a little bacca ef it's a plew a plug, an' Dupont an' G'lena, a Green River or so," and he leaves for the Bayou Salade. Darn the white diggins while thar's buffler in the mountains.'

— Long Hatcher in Garrard's *Wah-To-Yah.*

'When you ride up to that camp, you ride a-whistlin' real loud and pleasant. That Charlie Bird, he's half Cherokee and half white, and them's two bad breeds.'

— Bill Doolin in Gene Rhodes's *The Trusty Knaves.*

Others again stood carelessly among the throng, with nothing to conceal the matchless symmetry of their forms, and I do not exaggerate when I say that only on the prairie and in the Vatican have I seen such faultless models of the human figure. See that warrior standing by the tree, towering six feet and a half in stature. Your eyes may trace the whole of his graceful and majestic height and discover no defect or blemish. With his free and noble attitude, with the bow in his hand and the quiver at his back, he might seem, but for his face, the Pythian Apollo himself.

— Francis Parkman, *The Oregon Trail.*

PLATE LXVII

*Courtesy of Mrs. Clyde Porter*

SELF-PORTRAIT *Alfred Jacob Miller*

This pencil sketch, drawn on the back of one of the water colors, shows Miller at about the age he was when he went West. Dignity or fashion came upon him as he grew older and a later self-portrait shows whiskers and a pointed beard.

*Courtesy of the United States National Museum*

PLATE LXVIII RABBIT-SKIN LEGGINGS *George Catlin*

The only member of the Nez Perce and Flathead mission in search of teachers who lived to return to his people.

*Courtesy of The Walters Art Gallery*

BEAR BULL *Alfred Jacob Miller* PLATE LXIX

Previously unknown, this is the only portrait of a very famous Indian, really named Bull Bear, the chief of the Oglala Sioux. See Chapter XII.

*Courtesy of The Boston Athenaeum*

PLATE LXX MATO-TOPE *Charles Bodmer*

Four Bears, the great man of the Mandans.

*Courtesy of The Boston Athenaeum*

PEHRISKA-RUHPA *Charles Bodmer* PLATE LXXI

One of the finest Indian pictures ever made. The Minnetaree war-chief is dressed in his costume for the dog dance described by Maximilian.

*Courtesy of Mrs. Joseph Whyte, niece of the artist*

PLATE LXXII

Louis, Rocky Mountain Trapper *Alfred Jacob Miller*

*Courtesy of Mrs. Clyde Porter*

PLATE LXXIII

MAKING PRESENTS TO SNAKE INDIANS *Alfred Jacob Miller*

PLATE LXXIV

JIM BRIDGER IN ARMOR AT GREEN RIVER

*Alfred Jacob Miller*

*Courtesy of The Walters Art Gallery*

Looking west across the Green River plains between New Fork and Horse Creek at the rendezvous of 1837.

*Courtesy of Mrs. Joseph Whyte, niece of the artist*

PLATE LXXV

## Jim Bridger in Armor Crossing a River

*Alfred Jacob Miller*

Either the conception or the portrayal of Old Gabe in casque and cuirass should speak for itself. Though not a portrait, this is the only approximation of one before Bridger's old age.

*Courtesy of Mr. L. Vernon Miller*

PLATE LXXVI

STEWART AND ANTOINE *Alfred Jacob Miller*

Stewart, more carelessly drawn, is also the principal figure in Plate LXXIII and may be identified in several earlier pictures by his beaked nose or the white horse on which Miller preferred to mount him, though Stewart himself says that his favorite horse was black.

*Courtesy of The Walters Art Gallery*

PLATE LXXVII ANTOINE CLEMENT *Alfred Jacob Miller*

'That great hunter,' later a retainer at Murthly Castle.

*Courtesy of Mrs. Clyde Porter*

BILL BURROWS *Alfred Jacob Miller* PLATE LXXVIII

A slight sketch which is valuable for the authenticity of its details.

*Courtesy of Mrs. Joseph Whyte, niece of the artist*

PLATE LXXIX

## TRAPPERS DANCING AROUND THE CAMPFIRE

*Alfred Jacob Miller*

The trappers' liking for this amusement delighted Indians and depressed missionaries. A fiddle was fine, an Indian drum would do, but musical accompaniment was not indispensable.

*Courtesy of Mrs. Clyde Porter*

PLATE LXXX

STRUGGLING THROUGH QUICKSAND *Alfred Jacob Miller*

Quicksands occurred along all the rivers of the plains and might be encountered in those of the mountains. They were a desperate and profanity-breeding annoyance, more so to wagon trains than to pack trains, but they were seldom dangerous. A horse or a mule could usually extricate itself and could always be pulled out. The melancholy of oxen sometimes led them to submit to the slow death, however, and a mired-down wagon drawn by three teams of oxen required enormous exertion by all hands. The stories of human deaths in quicksands along the Oregon Trail are folklore.

*Courtesy of Mrs. Joseph Whyte, niece of the artist*

PLATE LXXXI

BOURGEOIS WALKER AND HIS WIFE *Alfred Jacob Miller*

Bonneville's great partisan, the exterminator of Diggers, the entrepreneur in California horses, and the discoverer of the Yosemite.

— first-rate Plains Indians, fully as tough and intelligent as the Sioux if not so numerous. The Thirty Years' War got under way. And Bull Bear presided over it.

He was 'a great chief but something of a tyrant,' Mr. Hyde says with marked understatement, 'holding his turbulent followers in check by roaring at them and promptly putting a knife into any man who did not heed his orders. He had never paid for a wife, taking the girls that pleased his eye and letting their parents whistle for the customary payment. He would not endure a rival. . . .' [12] He was as tough an Indian as the Plains ever saw, insatiable in war, bringing death and glory wholesale to his people. Four years after Miller saw him and painted the only portrait of him (Plate LXIX) his furious temper got him into a scrape which allowed the resentment of some of his people to come to a head. A group of conspirators, including Old Smoke and a youth named Red Cloud who would later repeatedly show up the United States Army, resolved to get him. They did so and Mr. Hyde says that Red Cloud may have been the one who killed him. This is the murder which Parkman describes at length: he heard about it not far from where it happened. It produced a sort of civic anarchy and martial decline among the Oglalas for some years. That in turn had its effect on white history for it kept the Sioux too busy repelling enemies to be much bothered by the Oregon migration.

Miller says in a note to his portrait that 'the head of this grim chief shadows forth his character; fierce and impetuous in his passion, he recognized no law but his own will. . . . In calling his people to counsel, he would listen to them, state his own opinion and follow it. They would not dare to question his imperious will.' [13] The head chief was not the only one who impressed Miller; the Sioux were among the handsomest of Indians, tall, powerfully built, Roman-nosed, and they held the artist's imagination. 'They reminded us strongly of antique figures in Bronze & presented a wide & ample field for the sculptor. Nothing in Greek art can surpass the reality here.' He was exasperated by the failure of sculptors to come west and make use of such models, especially those sculptors who had made up Indians from their reading and imagination. 'Sculptors travel thousands of miles to study Greek statues in the Vatican but here at the foot of the Rocky Mountains are as fine forms stalking about with a natural grace (never taught by a dancing master) as ever the Greeks dreamed of in their happiest conceptions.' Moreover, the artists who are to make use of the Indians had better get out here soon for 'they are melting away like snow flakes in the sun.' The whole note reminds one of Francis Parkman's similar admiration of the Oglalas. Parkman also talked about Greek statues and quoted Benjamin West's exclamation on first seeing the Apollo Belvedere, 'By God, a Mohawk!'

Miller worked hard while he had the chance. Eight of his sketches are certainly Oglala; more may be. He repeated an experience which Catlin had often had: when he was painting one brave who was the complete image of the fighting man a delegation came to protest that since the sitter had no coups there was no reason to make his portrait. The splendor of the Oglala accoutrements delighted him, fine buckskin, ornamented shirts and skirts, tipis, most especially the warbonnet. Someone should have told him that though the Sioux squaws were indeed expert, the Sioux got their best costumes by trading with the Crows.

* * *

At Scott's Bluff Miller made one of his best sketches. Here at the edge of the Rattlesnake Hills he was seeing the plains beginning to break up, a strange landscape beginning to change into a stranger one. 'At a distance as we approached it the appearance was that of an immense fortification with bastions, towers, battlement[s] embrazures, scarps & counterscarps.' Hereabout they began to get additions to their diet. Stewart's fowling-piece was uncased on behalf of what Miller calls the Rocky Mountain pheasant — the sage grouse or sage hen of the West. He says that it is almost as large as a full-grown turkey, which is magnifying it, and adds that 'feeding principally on artemisia [sagebrush — the buds] gave a wild and rather bitter taste to the flesh,' which means that Stewart had not learned to take out the crop promptly. He finds that the jackrabbit tastes about like eastern rabbits but is three times as large, and says that a large tortoise (unidentifiable here) is as delicious as terrapin. Stewart and Antoine have been hunting bighorn and antelope too. Miller trustingly accepts the trappers' yarn about the sheep landing on their horns when they leap from cliffs, the more readily because he is surprised to find how large the horns are, noting that one specimen is three feet long and twenty inches in circumference at the base. He makes an inevitable observation: 'In ascending the rocks in herds, they gave notice of their locality by the loose stones that came rattling along the declivities.'

Miller does not date the arrival at Fort Laramie (he does not date anything) but five weeks or less from Independence would be right with Fitzpatrick at the throttle. There would be the usual gunfire when they came through the cottonwoods and saw the fort in the plain a couple of miles away. Stewart sent his Auguste ahead to get the 'blooded stallion' which he had brought out last year and had left here for the winter. (With, Miller says, strict orders that no one should ride him and that he was to be exercised at the end of a halter.) While the post's engagés took charge of the train, part of whose freight would remain here, and while they yipped and pounded the shoulders of the stateside crew, the officers went into the fort. Miller's eye caught '5 or 6 first class engravings, one of which was Richard and Saladin battling in the Holyland and from these immediately surmised that the Commander of the fort was a refined gentleman.' He found he was correct when Lucien Fontenelle hurried in.

Miller felt the release that all travelers felt here. The fort was oasis, hermitage, hostelry, coolness and greenness after a weary land. And Fontenelle had a consummate refreshment for his guests, crocks of milk.

And now Miller acquires primary importance for history. This was the original Fort Laramie which had been christened Fort William, as the Fort Laramie that succeeded it was christened Fort John. We saw its sill laid by Sublette's men in 1834. Miller reaches it in 1837. Three years later Lancaster P. Lupton, who already had a post on the South Platte, built another one on the North Platte about a mile and a half from Fort Laramie. This is the 'Fort Platte' of the literature, a commodious and strongly built establishment that later passed to another Opposition firm, Sybille, Adams, and Company, and later still to Pratte, Cabanne and Company, also in opposition. The building of Fort Platte stimulated the Company to rebuild Fort Laramie, whose timbers were beginning to decay. It did so in 1841, moving to a new site farther up Laramie Creek.[14] They built the new post of adobe. Miller's sketches therefore show the original fort at its original site. They are the only known pictures that do, though as a note points out Elliott Coues says that he has seen a sketch which he does not further identify. And Miller's notebook entries are an addition to the small number of first-hand descriptions.

He says that the fort 'is of a quadrangular form with block houses at diagonal corners to sweep the fronts in case of attack. Over the front entrance is a large block house in which is placed a cannon, the interior of the fort is about 150 feet square surrounded by small cabins whose roofs reach within 3 feet of the top of the palisades against which they abut. . . . The Indians have a mortal terror of the "big gun" which rests in the block house as they have had experience of its prowess and witnessed the havoc produced by its loud talk.' And again, 'There was a cannon or two sleeping in the towers over the two main entrances. . . . They are intended to keep the peace.' This is the only known statement that the cannon of the later fort had been mounted in the earlier one, and Miller's estimate of the interior dimensions shows that the Company had enlarged the post somewhat since taking it over. His pictures show the timber construction, a hitherto unknown outside stairway to the blockhouse over the main entrance, and the loopholes for the cannon. They suggest that the quadrangle had been completely filled out with buildings.[15]

In his distant view Miller has achieved some of the great emptiness of the plain. Too bad he lacked the next generation's management of Riviera light, for the desert sun above Laramie needs rendition. The memory of it must have been vivid for the landscapes of the next leg of the trail are among those he worked up most carefully in the Walters copies. When the Company took to the trail again — June 27 can be worked out from William Gray's diary — there was the Platte to cross in bullboats, then the southwestern detour across a desert of naked chromatic rock. The Sweetwater and Independence Rock next, and Miller notes some of the names carved on this sprawling tortoise, Bonneville, Sublette, Wyeth, Campbell, Sarpy, and Pilcher. There was also a Nelson, perhaps the one who convulsed Joe Meek by failing to shinny up a tree when a grizzly was after him. No true American could pass up the chance: they carved 'of the Nile' in the granite following the name. Devil's Gate, Cut Rock, and the Sweetwater dwindling toward the eastern entrance of South Pass. Miller made no sketch of the opening on Oregon, there is nothing to draw there but distance and hot sagebrush, but he had a moment of prophecy. 'The whizzing of steam on the "sweet water," the whirring of car wheels through the "South Pass," are a foregone conclusion.' Samuel Parker thought the same. But there is no railroad in South Pass to this day.

They came through the western portal. There 'as we proceeded quietly along our ears were saluted by sounds that raised the pulse immediately and to which we had become sensitively alive. It was a tremendous yell of a large body of men [say half a dozen] and we heard the clattering of their horses as they came down the valley. As soon, however, as we had a sight of them, we were relieved. It was a body of trappers who had heard of our approach and sallied forth to give us a greeting. This is done by a "feu de joie" of blank cartridge [wrong; no mountain man would ever spike his rifle] and a hearty shaking of hands among the merry fellows, for they found many of their comrades in our company, and when we encamped for the evening our Captain gave them a grand carouse in the shape of hump ribs, buffalo tongues, and mountain sheep. In addition to this, a metheglin made of honey and alcohol, potent and fiery, was concocted and circulated amongst them. The jovial fellows paid their respects to it again and again, sang their French songs, related their adventures

> Wherein they spoke of most disastrous chances
> Of moving accidents by flood, by field [*sic*] . . .

It was soon evident that they could not hold out, in short, one after another toppled over. The *conqueror* had it all his own way & overpowering sleep came to their relief.'

Thereafter on to the rendezvous, Green River between New Fork and Horse Creek.[16]

* * *

They put on a good show for Stewart and Miller at this, the thirteenth mountain rendezvous. Miller met as notables a good many of Stewart's friends, Drips, Kit Carson, Joe Walker, and especially Jim Bridger. Stewart had brought a present for Bridger, presumably sending to Murthly Castle for it. Miller describes it as a coat of mail and again as a suit of armor; it looks like casque and cuirass and greaves in his pictures. Whatever it was, the mountains had seen no queerer sight than Old Gabe costumed as Sir James and parading the Green River flat in armor. Presumably they told him about jousts and tourneys and cheered him when he tried, for that armor worked into the legends.[17]

The Hudson's Bay Company was on hand again under McLeod, and an increased number of free trappers, and some small companies. But it was an Indian year. The Bannocks who had had to be licked a couple of weeks ago had accepted probation and were back, behaving themselves. The handful of Nez Perces they had jumped were still here. William H. Gray who was on his way to the States, had a few Flatheads with him. Just before reaching the Green he had met and been scared by some Utes, who had passed up their chance to eradicate some vermin and had come on peaceably enough. A few Crows appeared, well out of their country. They impressed Gray as teetotalers — probably he saw them at the wrong time — but Miller admired their superb leather work and they traded him three scalps, presumably Sioux. One of them coveted a silver-mounted pipe-tomahawk that Stewart was wearing at his belt and when the Captain refused to trade it warned him to keep an eye on it. Stewart did so but the Crow got it. There were also some lodges of Arapahos, handsomely made and painted, and Miller correctly describes their moccasins. But the largest delegation was the Snakes who were here in force, at least half the three thousand whom Miller counts.

It was the Snakes who put on the formal parade which Miller pictures in our Plate XIII. Every year the visiting tribes staged various spectacles; they loved them and the whites would pay. This time the Snakes, coming up the day after the caravan did, made it a formal opening. About two hundred and fifty braves on their best horses — and they bought good ones from the Nez Perces — rode in full dress ahead of the village. Stately chiefs, caracoling horses, medicine men juggling as they rode, deep-voiced chants, warwhoops, muskets firing, arrows skittering across the plain. Sometimes a squad of young braves break into a gallop, angling away from the column in pursuit of an imaginary Sioux, hanging by their heels on the far side of their horses, shooting arrows under their necks. Other performers do all the tricks that are still called Cossack. Others leap to the ground and take imaginary scalps, then ride on singing the scalp song. Everything is orderly again when the procession nears the Company camp — column of files, lances and painted war shields at salute, the dignity of a Nazi sub-führer or a minstrel-show cake-walker swelling the noble chests and making the noble faces solemn. . . . And behind them the Snake village is strung out for well over a mile, dust from the scraping travois, from the horse herd which the boys are driving, from the interweaving horses of the squaws. Old men and women ride the travois atop the piled tipis and parfleches; so do young children. Stolid babies swathed to the chin in cradles stare out from their mothers' backs. The squaws who have to manage all this are shrill and profane. There is an incessant brawling of excited dogs. Reaching the river and its cottonwoods, the village breaks up into its components. Even noisier now, the squaws help one another put up the tipis. The horses are watered and herded across the plain. Braves first, then boys and girls, finally the hardworking squaws move off to gape at the white camp, inspect its gauds, begin to calculate what they will buy, steal what they can, and maybe get a slug or two of alcohol 'on the prairie.'

Miller saw it as a blend of Buffalo Bill and the Louvre. He called the annual release a saturnalia but had no reproof for it.[18] He says that some drunken Indians ran wild and that there was the usual number of fights. There were also the usual visits of ceremony, everyone calling formally on everyone else, Fontenelle and Bridger on McLeod, everyone on William Gray (who mentions two visits from Miller and a separate one from Stewart), and everyone on Captain Thing, Wyeth's former partisan at Fort Hall who was going home at last.[19] Such stately banquets, rich with fat cow and Company alcohol and Stewart's blander drinks, gave the Baltimore greenhorn the ritual of the West, the yarns gaudier every time the drinks passed. At such a feast he met Joe Walker and someone privately told him the story of Joe's eating the flesh of his own men. Because Walker had entertained him and because he decided that on the whole it would be judicious not to inquire about it, Miller didn't; he only indirectly mentioned it in his notes and did not clarify the passage till he wrote captions for the Walters copies of his pictures.

There were even statelier pleasures. He was invited to attend a Snake council called to discuss raising some hell with the Sioux. It was like a meeting of the grand lodge. 'Those of the listeners on foot were squatted on the ground, while horsemen dressed in picturesque colors were as motionless as the statue of the commendatore in the opera of Don Giovanni.' In the order of rank and employing the conventions of their most developed art, the war chiefs rose, qualified themselves by counting their coups, and declaimed. Miller missed the fine points in translation, of course, and could not have understood the reasons for grunts when the critical audience approved, but he took the show without being bored, as few could. Later one of the Indians invited him to a feast. He had sampled the full mountain cuisine but the idea of eating dog disgusted him. He could not affront the host, however, so sought advice from a mountain man. Easy enough: for a paper of vermilion to give his squaw the trapper would go with him. Indian hospitality recognized the institution of the vicar. Miller could be the honored guest and his hired hand would eat the puppy. (And maybe Mr. Miller is faking, for most of these tribes did not eat dog.)

The Snakes provided a full half of the scenes Miller was furiously sketching. A brave smoking in the shade of a tipi while his squaw labored. Another one absently fondling a dog. A squaw throwing a lariat on a horse that is trying to dodge her — and this may be the first portrayal of a craft that was to become a national admiration.[20] Other squaws riding in the races, free style, which were staged daily and which Indians and trappers alike bet on to the limit of their wealth. Other squaws just riding ('à la mode Turque,' the fascinated young man wrote), or just squaws, one swinging from a branch — and Miller would sell this one over and over in Baltimore — one swimming while a group of her friends looked on. As has been remarked, the Snake women had a reputation for comeliness. (Shocked but fascinated, William Gray was writing in his journal that the sinful trappers won and lost women by wager, that what was called marriage most assuredly was not marriage, that 'the buying and selling of Indian women is a common occurrence at this Rendezvous.') Miller liked the male Snakes on horseback, too, putting some down literally, composing pretty night and storm scenes for others. He sketched their encampments and their herds. He invented one chasing a Crow. He snapped them crowding round Stewart for presents. And he made fairly formal portraits of others, including one Red Elk who politely counted his coups while he sat for the artist and the Snake's Little Chief (not to be confused with the Flathead, Insula), who was 'in every sense superior to any Indian that we met with.' Little Chief, it appears, had reclaimed some stolen horses for Stewart during one of his earlier journeys and was most welcome at his camp.[21] He also counted his coups as a courtesy and went on to draw them. Miller's account is an excellent early description of Plains art.

> I noticed that all four legs of the horses were on one side. This arose from want of a knowledge of perspective. He also colored them with the stick end of the brush instead of the hair end, not probably having seen before an article of the kind. By a slight 'poetic license' the calves of the enemy were placed before the 'os tibia' instead of behind. Another thing noticeable was that his war horse, himself, and immense helmet [!] of feathers occupied the whole field. The enemy are diminutive creatures and he is spitting them like larks. Of course we are left to imagine that his aids and men are with him. Fifteen arrows above the enemy signified that [that] number had 'gone under' but Ma-Wo-Ma [Little Chief], like a prudent and crafty general, says nothing about his own loss.

He found romance to paint, too, though he seems to have misunderstood some of it. If a sketch called 'Indian Elopement'

(No. 123) is not made up, there was a runaway marriage at the rendezvous but it must have been a wife-stealing and not, as Miller thought, an intertribal love story. He also represents in 'Aricara (Female)' a mountain man as 'affianced' to a girl and giving her a dowry that he had to pay for with a pledge to the Company of three years' earnings. We may be sure that no trapper paid that much for a wife and that, if he paid anything, he did not platonically entrust her to her family when he started on his hunt. And then romantic passion struck in Miller's own tent, which he was sharing with the young man named P—— from St. Louis. One of the most toothsome wenches in camp was a Flathead girl who Miller says was 'one of the belles of the Rocky Mountains.' She could have been no more than fifteen or she would not have been desirable and probably not a belle. P—— fell for her but could make no time with her. She would accept his presents and flirt with him in the presence of the gang but would not stroll in the evening. It was mortifying, for P——'s way with white ladies was one of the reasons why his father had sent him west, and his companions grew ribald as his sustained pursuit went on failing. Then one day the whole camp roared for a free trapper struck his tent, packed his mules, and rode off toward the hills, taking the girl with him. When he got back to the settlements Miller made a pretty calendarlike picture of this (and later a huge oil for Murthly) and as 'The Trapper's Bride' it became a staple of his studio trade.

He had been sketching the routine of camp, too. A sudden storm leveled a lot of tents and this may have inspired his sentimental picture of two Indians riding in the rain. He saw at least one scalp dance, probably more, but for some reason did not sketch them. Two or three war pictures which are wholly fictitious may have been inspired by some rumors that circulated. The Hudson's Bay Company camp heard that the Snakes and Bannocks were going to attack it in force. That was unlikely, but McLeod, who trusted no Indians, got ready to repel raiders. Nothing happened. Presently the Snakes stole some horses from a Company trader and several others from the visiting Crows. The Company Delawares proposed to join the Crows and help get them back but that would have been bad for business and someone got the case settled out of court. Then a group of trappers who had started for the mountains came back in a hurry, having met some Blackfeet who, they claimed, numbered at least a hundred and twenty. Not even Blackfeet would raid a rendezvous but there was the usual excitement. Again nothing happened. Miller could hardly paint the scene but it probably inspired some of the action in *Edward Warren.*

* * *

After a while Stewart packed up his outfit and, with some guests from the brigades, headed toward his favorite camp ground on the headwaters of New Fork. Before this, however, William H. Gray, the lay missionary, had departed for the States and a predictable cravenness. . . . As may have been intimated here, Gray was not a lovable character. Few men or women could tolerate him long and he practiced the strictest economy in tolerating anyone. But he was being used by the vortex of forces that was preparing to give us the West and his eastern trip of 1837 was important. It also shows the rate at which those forces were accelerating. Remember that Gray and the Whitmans and the Spaldings had come west only last year.

Gray seems to have taken the Spalding side in the Whitman-Spalding disagreements of last summer, though he was later to take the other side. He went on with Spalding, helped him raise the first cabins of the Nez Perce mission at Lapwai, and spent part of the winter there. After a visit to Fort Vancouver, he started back to Lapwai in the early spring of 1837. (The up-river trip was fantastically difficult: if no one can take Gray to his heart, he enforces respect for his ability to accept hardship and apply the mountain crafts it taught him.) At the end of March, traveling with a Hudson's Bay Company party under Francis Ermatinger, he met Spalding near the present site of Spokane. Spalding had left his pregnant wife alone with the Nez Perces and was headed for the Hudson's Bay Company's Fort Colville.

This meeting was important. Spalding had found the Nez Perces responsive to his teaching — much more responsive than Whitman's Cayuses — and intelligent, eager, co-operative, so far as such words had meaning in mission work among Indians. Gray was dissatisfied — insubordinate and envious. The holy Presbyterian zeal that burned in him could not accept an inferior status. The talents of William Gray, objectively appraised, entitled him to be at least equal in importance to Whitman and Spalding, whom he had objectively appraised in his notes. He wanted a career adequate to his gifts: he wanted a mission of his own. Now he found himself with the greatly encouraged Spalding in the country of the Spokanes, a small tribe closely related to the Flatheads, who had no missionary but had wanted one from the beginning. They were also convenient to Waiilatpu, Lapwai, Fort Walla Walla, and Fort Colville. Moreover here was that 'Spokane Garry' who was mentioned in our first chapter. The Hudson's Bay Company had sent him while a boy to its Red River headquarters and his ability to read, write, and practice other white mysteries had been a powerful incentive in the first delegation to St. Louis. The two missionaries now saw him instructing his people — in a way — in the true religion. When they preached to the Spokanes they decided that he had excellently plowed the field. Moreover, Spokane Garry was growing potatoes, had a lot of them, and offered Spalding some for seed. The potatoes mightily impressed the missionaries: they proved that converted Indians would be farmers.

After only the briefest and most perfunctory consultation — Gray does not even mention invoking God's guidance — the missionaries decided that the hour must be seized. Gray would go to the States at once, call on the American Board (whom he violently shocked when he strode into the office) to raise and equip another mission, and bring it back to the Spokanes. The plan had everything: further support for the Oregon Church and independent command for William Gray. They conceived the plan between breaths, or at least between sermons, and acted at once. Spalding returned to Lapwai. Gray sent a letter to Whitman, still the titular and always the actual head of the mission, telling him what he was doing, which was generous and even condescending of him, and went on to Flathead House with Ermatinger, intending to go from there to the summer rendezvous and join a party for the settlements. Thus Spokane Garry, whom the British had educated, made his second contribution toward the enlargement of the United States.

Gray's writing is notable for spleen and vagueness: no one can tell from either his journal or his book just which Indians accompanied him. He uses 'Spokane' and 'Flathead' interchangeably which is not wholly unsound but maddens the student who tries to decide what happened.[22] The original plan was for him to take east 'three Natives of the three different tribes,' and this probably meant a Flathead, a Spokane, and a Nez Perce. But whether any of those who eventually started east with him from the rendezvous was a Spokane is beyond determination.

From Flathead House Gray and Ermatinger set out with the main tribe early in May, bound for the buffalo country. They had a month of leisurely travel while the Indians made meat and dug the bitterroot that was a staple of their economy. Ermatinger maneuvered small groups of trappers. Gray preached and sang to the Flatheads, taught them items of belief, and dressed wounds and prescribed for illnesses. (He coveted Whitman's right to add M.D. to his name.) They had a brush with some Blackfeet that did not amount to much. Then on May 31 they came down into the Big Hole basin, the northwestern part of Beaverhead County, Montana. There were Blackfeet everywhere. On June 1 some of Ermatinger's trappers got shot up and a Blackfoot band made a distant, futile attack on some Flatheads. The next day a band of Flatheads met a detachment, charged it, licked it, chased the survivors into the hills, and brought back five scalps.

The summer feud had opened favorably but Gray now had a tense two weeks. To begin with, he had to endure six days of a scalp dance. (His horror produces a valuable description but he could not relate this savage fervor to the odds on making Christians out of Indians.) The hills swarmed with Blackfeet, hundreds of them; there were daily and nightly alarms. He saw something few ever saw, a handful of Blackfeet losing their blood lust and coming in to beg protection and suggest a formal peace — the Huns of the Plains scared stiff. As the Flatheads moved on toward Deer Lodge Prairie, innumerable Blackfeet hung on their flanks, sent delegations in to smoke and discuss peace, and constantly threatened, swaggered, bullied, stole, and tried to work themselves up to a war which it proved they did not quite have the guts to make. The initial victory had counted heavily; for the moment, the Flatheads had the Blackfeet stopped. This wholesome attitude of mind and some expert management by Ermatinger maintained the truce, even when the main bodies of the two tribes passed right through each other on the march. In awe of the incredible, Gray even forgot that this might be a special providence.

When the tension was eased at last Gray, with some Indians and Ermatinger's little halfbreed son, left the tribe and the trappers on June 15 and crossed the Divide to the Salmon River. The little party moved southwest to Fort Hall, visited Captain Thing for a while, and resumed the march toward rendezvous. Not far from Horse Creek they caught up with the Hudson's Bay party under John McLeod, Narcissa Whitman's conquest of last summer. McLeod had letters for Gray from Spalding and Whitman bearing on his new mission and was chaperoning four Indians whom Spalding had selected to go with him. Gray speaks of them as Flatheads; some or all of them may have been Spokanes.

Here was something that Gray could get his teeth into. He could begin to bellyache about his superiors. He could begin to bellyache about McLeod — who charms one by replying to the usual complaint of missionaries, 'There is no Sabbath in this country.' And he could begin accusing his Indians of lack of respect. They conspired to disobey him, understand, and they failed to appreciate their good fortune in being selected to travel with Mr. Gray. He had them antagonized almost instantly.

He was also in a tearing hurry to get east. McLeod's camp and Andrew Drips' which came up moved on to the designated site, and Gray was harrying both partisans for advice on how to get started before the returning caravan should leave. (This was two weeks before Fitzpatrick got there.) Drips' advice was blunt: Don't try. Don't try, you damned fool. Everybody else said the same.

Gray was having a difficult time. He had had to watch the Flatheads do their scalp dance. Now some Delawares staged one of their own. Presently a small advance party of the Snakes arrived and put on another one. Moreover, there was some liquor at Drips' camp and therefore some debauchery. Also blasphemy accompanied by loud laughter. Also the horrid trade in female flesh. The only satisfaction Gray got was from the urbane Crows, who had manners and extended them to him. He wondered if the American Board should not open a Crow mission, the more so since they seemed to be temperance men. He got out his flute and played some hymns for them.

Black Harris arrived with the express and Gray began to worry him about getting started. Harris finally told him — probably to shut him up — that a Statesbound party might possibly be formed before Fitzpatrick led the caravan east. A mistake. It convinced Gray that the idea was feasible and that if necessary he could do it himself. When Fitzpatrick arrived, with Miller and Stewart and the rest, it developed that the return journey would not begin for at least three weeks. Three weeks of godlessness, the demon rum, profanity, blasphemy, and carnal sin. Not for Mr. Gray. He enjoyed the honor of formal calls from the partisans, the young painter, and the low-living Scotch captain, but there was sin all round him. He determined to form a party of his own and though every partisan at the rendezvous told him not to,[23] he did so. They started east on July 25.

It was Gray's private party and he had supplied it at the rendezvous with plenty of coffee, sugar, and flour besides dried meat and bitterroot. Its composition is not entirely clear. Apparently three white men started with him, one of whom, named Barrows, dropped out at Fort Laramie — Gray says he was lazy and fell behind but we should not rule out the possibility that he had grown bored with sanctimony. There were either five or six Indians.[24] One was a Nez Perce, one an Iroquois halfbreed, and the remaining three or four were Flatheads, all apparently but not certainly true Flatheads. Two of them — they were taking up the quest their people had begun six years before — were sons of a war chief named Grand Visage. The Big Face brought them to Gray, after Gray had so antagonized his own Flatheads and those whom Spalding had sent him that only one remained willing to make the trip, and solemnly entrusted them to him. He wanted his sons to learn about the white men and their religion, he said, and he did not want Gray to 'make fools of them by making them drunken and bad men when they returned.' Gray promised not to make them slaves to the liquor habit and the chief need not have worried. It was not drink but poltroonery and criminal folly they had to fear from William Gray.

They were off on July 25 and at once everyone was disrespectful to Mr. Gray but a cloud moving ahead of them was God's personal benignancy to him. The country and the Indians set snares for his feet in vain, since Providence went on before. On August 2 they reached Fort Laramie, where again the men who knew tried to dissuade him from going on — wait here till Fitzpatrick comes. One Woods who commanded in the absence of Fontenelle (and whom Osborne Russell considered a tightfisted miser) told Gray that the country ahead was full of Sioux and that their hearts were bad — any Indian hearts would be bad in the presence of so small a party. Just a couple of days ago, Woods said, they had killed a halfbreed at Chimney Rock. 'In my own mind,' Gray wrote, 'these circumstances have cleared our way of Indians, rendering it less dangerous for us.' The logic is eccentric but Gray found support for it in the fact that a Sioux brave who was staying at the fort asked him to dinner. Surely that proved it, and though his two remaining white companions and his Indians were 'fearful about proceeding,' William Gray in a condition of infallibility was a hard man to stop. He got them going down the Platte on August 4.

Past Scott's Bluff, Chimney Rock, the Court House. August 6 was the Sabbath but though Gray longed for the sanctuary of our God he had the sense to keep going. So on the morning of August 7 they approached Ash Hollow, where the emigrant trail was to reach the North Platte from the South Platte, where there would later be two big massacres and a handful of smaller ones. Let us now follow Gray's diary.

Seeing something that might be a buffalo, Big Eneas and another Indian rode ahead to investigate. It was not a buffalo, it was a Sioux. He began to ride round in a circle to call his pals, who came on the run. They ordered Gray and his party (by signs) to accompany them to their village. Woods had told Gray what to do in such a contingency and he refused, giving them some tobacco and ordering his party to go on. As it did so the Sioux tried to snatch a whip from Gray's Nez Perce. Gray gestured him to get going fast. The Sioux grabbed Gray's bridle to halt him but he broke away. He made himself a rear-guard till they reached the river. It is not clear why they had to ford the Platte here but they rode into it. At once the Sioux opened fire. Two of Gray's Flatheads rode back a little to cover the crossing. No use. Gray's horse was shot from under him. Heavily fired on, they got across but so did the Sioux, who chased them up a small bluff where they tried to fort up. Gray put down his rifle and walked forward for a parley. The Sioux kept on shooting, put a ball through his hat, and grazed his head with another one. 'I then concluded that blood and murder was the determination of our enemies and returned to where I had left my gun.' Another ball grazed his temple and some of the Sioux got close enough to run off half the horses. They got some of the packs too, and Gray hoped that this would satisfy them. It didn't.

It now developed that there was a white trader with the Sioux. While the little group hugged the ground and returned the fire, a voice hailed them in English from among the attackers. Gray says he was 'a Frenchman by the name of Joseph Papair.' [25] He wanted to know how many 'Frenchmen,' that is, white men, were in the party. Gray's Mr. Callaghan (his other white companion was named Grimm) told him there were three, whereupon Papair said that the whites must come in or be killed. They desired Papair to come forward and talk it over. He did so and the three whites met him half-way, their Indians holding back 'to await the event of our consultation.' Gray says that he explained who the Indians were and what they were doing here: going forth on God's business to the States. 'Papair said to us the Sioux were determined to kill them and we must not say anything about them or we would be killed; while we were talking, the Sioux passed us, rushed upon my Indians, and butchered them in a most horrible manner.'

After this murder the Sioux took Gray and his two companions to their village. He learned that the final rush had cost his captors three killed and that three or four more had been wounded earlier. (A sense of his valor grew on Gray and it was fifteen dead Sioux when he wrote his *History of Oregon.*) One of the dead was the son of the village chief, a stately man with warbonnet, medicine pipe, and a medal of Andrew Jackson. They painted the corpse for his spiritual journey, sang his death song, and adjourned to dance round the bloody scalps. Gray's own Indians thus furnished the trophies for the fifth scalp dance he had had to witness in six weeks.

The chief explained that he had no quarrel with his white brothers and turned them over to Papair, who in Gray's diary thus gets credit for saving their lives. The next day they were given some scrawny horses and a small outfit and escorted to the ford by some of the camp police. Very miserable, they took to the trail. Two weeks later they reached Council Bluffs where D. D. Mitchell was down from Fort Union (having been lucky enough to escape the smallpox) and Gray was sufficiently restored to the holy life to discuss a possible mission to the Blackfeet. A day later he met Dunbar and Allis of the Pawnee mission. He does not say so but they must have told him that Doctor Satterlee, whose wife had died in the mission party of last year, had this year been murdered by Indians. (Gray was later to say by trappers.) He went on to St. Louis and the East, and the last entry of his diary piously remarks that in his round trip of some ten thousand miles he has experienced 'the goodness of God in unnumbered ways.' [26]

Thus William Gray's journal, a document prepared for the American Board of Commissioners of Foreign Missions and written with them very clearly in mind. In some notes appended to it Gray tells the Board that the Flatheads are an estimable people, mild, cheerful, brave, frank, and generous in their treatment of the white man. They will share their last morsel with him and are ready to 'sacrifice their own life to preserve his.' Gray instances his own Indians: 'I could not prevail on them to leave me till they were butchered before my eyes, although at the commencement of the attack there was no prospect of their escaping death from the Sioux.'

Horse feathers. The mountain men, who had a code of conduct which they would not transgress, knew what had happened. Joe Meek, writing while Gray was still alive, heard the story otherwise, though his discreet amanuensis, Mrs. Victor, has him say that he could not believe what he had heard. The way Joe Meek had it was that Gray traded Indian lives for white ones. 'No doubt,' the Meek-Victor account says, 'the Sioux took advantage of some hesitation on his part.' Whoever supposes that Gray hesitated is entitled to. But the unbelievable rumor got to the mountains before Gray returned in 1838 and was believed. 'The mountain men, although they used their influence to restrain the vengeful feelings of the Flathead tribe, whispered amongst themselves that Gray had preferred his own life to that of his friends.' The old Flathead chief too, who had lost a son by the massacre [two sons according to Gray's account], was hardly able to check his impulsive desire for revenge; for he held Mr. Gray responsible for his son's life.' . . . The Flatheads never had any luck with Protestants.

There were witnesses who could hardly be impeached and those rumors were not born of a dream. The white trader Papair would tell what happened as it happened and this was precisely the kind of event about which the Sioux would be least moved to lie. That the rumor followed Gray from here on is suggestive evidence that something had been wrong in the behavior of this righteous man who was so eager to save the Indians from sin. It would have been better for the church and for all white men during the next twenty years of Oregon if he had adopted the ethics of the blasphemous mountain men which held that you must not desert a partner in a fight. There is also a text about him who loses his life. And another one which, however, would require a missionary to think more of his client than of his client's soul: '. . . hath no man than this.'

* * *

Stewart's guests on his trip to the Wind Rivers would be chosen from among the brigade officers, Bridger or Fitzpatrick, Drips or Fontenelle, Harris or Provost, but just who and how many they were cannot be told. Enough that they were friends of the trail and the mountains, willing to relax with some amateur hunting and some talk late at night over Stewart's cheeses, wines, brandy, and porter. Miller says that fifteen or twenty Indians who had a grudge against one of Stewart's engagés skulked the trail most of the way and adds that it was rough going. However, he appreciated the country at its end and almost all his lake pictures were made here, most of them at New Fork Lake. Everything was as 'fresh & beautiful as if just from the hands of the creator' and the tourist who could go into ecstasy at sight of Mont Blanc and a single Swiss lake had a glorious future ahead of him here. The railroad which he saw coming through South Pass would bring the tourist, and hotels which have not yet arisen by those waters would care for him. Like most Americans Mr. Miller was breathing expansionism unaware.

Miller's notes tell of 'noble trout' that 'were unsophisticated and bit immediately we placed the bait near their mouths in the clear water.' Stewart had lost his flies but didn't need them, being able to use hooks made on the spot of wire or pins. Miller specifies two special comforts — by no means the whole stock. He says that the captain had laden a mule with an 'anker,' a cask of about ten gallons, of brandy and one of port. Reaching the first lake, the party found a bed of wild mint and if Stewart had not been Americanized to juleps he had experts with him. 'We draw a partial veil over the proceedings. Gentlemen will mix their liquors. Wit came from heads not suspected of being troubled with it before and "All went merry as a marriage bell." On retiring they went to bed with candles [and] it was found advisable to let them lie under the first bush they happened to fall [into] with no fear of their stirring till morning. They needed no further opiate.'

A week or two, then, of the sportsman's ritualistic release from reality, in the western slope of the Wind River Mountains where the early autumn of the high places would be coming on. Sportsmen cannot usually verbalize their emotions. The amateur hunter's life, very old in Great Britain, was also old in the United States and these days are of the Frank Forester tradition. The gentleman idler refreshes himself with hardships of the primitive that satisfy deep urges — but already, even in the Rocky Mountains, the primitive had to be in some degree contrived. We may repeat an earlier observation, that even in the eighteen-thirties the mountains are serving a sophisticated purpose as they continue to do still — and this with Plains Indians in full vigor, the fur trade still flourishing, the missionaries in Oregon but three years, and the emigration not even begun. We may not venture to speak for the Scotch nobleman, a war veteran and a romantic, since he has not spoken for himself. But the solace he found in the Far West may be suggested by the motto which he printed in 1854 on the title page of his second novel. That motto reads: 'It is somewhere written, "There is something not unsimilar in point of freedom between the chimney-sweep who clings to the walls of his garden and the sailor who clings to his mast."'

They went back to rendezvous and it is certain that when the big camps broke up Stewart made another trip in the fur country. It is certain because several of Miller's sketches show the Tetons and parts of the itinerary are hinted in his notes. Joe Meek adds confirmation. Miller locates the party on Wind River and again, by inference, in the Crow country, that is, along the Yellowstone, Powder River, the Rosebud and thereabout. Meek has them also on the fringes of the Blackfoot country to the northward. If so, they were most probably with Bridger, though possibly with Fontenelle or even Drips. Meek, who may well be remembering all the way back to the attack on Fitzpatrick and Stewart in the fall of 1833, says that Stewart's party was attacked by Crows, that its horses were stolen, and that the ministrations of Doc Newell got them back. There is a vague allusion to something similar in one of the least satisfactory of Miller's notes. But the specific note that tells about a Crow attack on Stewart is appended to a copy of the huge oil painting which he later made for Murthly Castle. And though this note does not date the attack, the later note on the same picture made for the Walters Gallery proves that it is an imaginary rendition of the 1833 skirmish.

And here the record comes to a full stop. Stewart and Miller went back to the States, certainly with the Company caravan, which seems to have been commanded east of Fort Laramie by Drips. We first pick up Stewart again in October; he is at St. Louis and the chimney-sweep has begun to cling to the walls of his garden, the sailor to his mast. Stewart executes a power of attorney to one John Stewart of Marshall Place, Perth, Scotland, authorizing him to ask, demand, sue, and receive various sums owed him, especially a residual inheritance from his grandmother. His attorney is also to demand 'annuities coming from Sir John Drummond S. of Grandtully in Scotland.' [27] There is a legend, appropriate to these ancient Scottish houses, barbaric as Indian families and decadent as Venetians, that before coming to America Stewart had quarreled with his brother, the baronet, quarreled in the manner of Sir Walter Scott's fiction, beyond reconciliation. In Stewart's novels both heroes experience romantic cruelties at the hands of their families.

He was still in St. Louis on November 25 and the prison house had closed in still more. From the records of St. Louis Cathedral:

> On the 25th of Nov. 1837 we the undersigned Bishop of S. L. have baptised Wm. S. of Grandtully in Scotland, second son of Sir. Geo. and lady Catherine Drummond S. 40 years old [he was a month short of 42] who has returned to the faith of his illustrious

ancestors. The Godfather has been the Right Revd. Dr. Simon Bruté, Bishop of Vincennes.

Joseph, Bp. of St. Louis
Simon G. Bruté Bishop
J. N. Nicollet
Jos. H. Lutz — Prest. Sec.[28]

A week before this solemn reconciliation, the British consul at New Orleans wrote to Stewart. His eagerness to supply any amount of money may be a slight further indication that the sixth baronet's health was known to be failing. Crawford, the consul, says that Miller has lately arrived in New Orleans and looks vigorous. One Vernufft is in London on a business venture in which both Crawford and Stewart are his partners. Crawford is sorry to learn (from a letter of Stewart's that has not been found) that some importations which he sent to St. Louis have been damaged but trusts that the cask of wine will prove sound. There is some fever at New Orleans, yellow fever, no doubt, but the first frost has assured good health from now on and Stewart is urged to come downriver. Mr. Crawford's letter is entrusted to a Mr. Stiff, who is a good John Bull.

And that is all that can be learned about the younger son of the house of Stewart, Old Bill the mountain man, in 1837.

* * *

About this time Osborne Russell relieved himself of a grouch. With an Irishman named Allen, an Englishman named Granberry, and a lowly pork-eater named Conn, Russell made a fall hunt in the western part of Absaroka, on detachment from Fontenelle's brigade. A band of Long Hair's Crows tried to play a very funny joke on them by stealing their guns. They did not pull that joke off but sang war songs all night and next morning were discovered to have played an even more side-splitting joke by getting away with the horses and all the beaver plews so far taken. The trappers began the long pedestrian journey to the nearest succor, Fort Laramie. They met another band of Crows who were in a still more jovial mood, so playful that Allen addressed them formally: 'if you follow us or molest us we will besmear the ground with blood and guts of Crow Indians, and do not speak to me more, for I despise the odious jargon of your nation.' This misunderstanding of the loyal Crow nature desolated the visitors who, carefully addressing no more jargon to Allen, reproached Russell for monstrous unfriendliness. When Russell told them that their brothers had made off with all his possessions they were heartbroken, made lachrymose orations, and spoke somewhat irrelevantly of their long love for the Blanket Chief, Jim Bridger. Then these little friends of all the whites, perceiving that they had to deal with old hands, departed, bearing their sorrow with them.

The four trappers resumed their tramp through sleet and snow and a great scarcity of meat, up the Wind River and over to the Platte. Two weeks of it and they rejoiced when there was wood and were ecstatic when they found buffalo. When they reached Fort Laramie, Fontenelle, its commander, had not yet brought his brigade in. Russell, who was stiff and doubled up with rheumatism, could get no service from Fontenelle's exec, presumably Woods. The boys asked for robes and shirts. 'Blankets, shirts, or coats I have none, and Mr. Fontenelle has left no word when there will be any come up.' Well, some apishemores would do for the moment, they said, and were granted some patched and dirty ones.

> But necessity compelled me to take it, knowing at the same time there were more than 500 new robes in the warehouse which did not cost a pint of whisky each. But they were for the people in the U. S. and not for trappers. This was the 21st day of November, 1837. I never shall forget the time, place nor circumstance, but shall always pity the being who held imperial sway over a few sticks of wood, with five or six men to guard them. It was not his fault, for how should he depart from the way in which he had been brought up? And what is more, trappers have no right to meet with bad luck, for it is nothing more nor less than the result of bad management. This is the literal reasoning of bandbox and counter-hopping philosophers, consoling the unfortunate by enumerating and multiplying their faults, which are always the occasion of their misfortune and so clearly to be seen after the event has occurred. I would rather at any time take an emetic than to be compelled to listen to the advice of such predicting and freakish counsellors.

A few days later another of Fontenelle's trappers, one Biggs, came in. His small group was camped snugly fifteen miles away. He was outraged to find master mountain men treated so contemptuously. He proposed a revolt: let Russell and his companions come to the Biggs camp, outfit themselves from the Company supplies it contained, make meat for Biggs, and then they could all go off together on their own. Mr. Woods came to his senses abruptly and outfitted the Company's employees. They went off with Biggs but not in revolt and stayed at his camp in luxury till Fontenelle came back. Fontenelle had their outfit and plews, having replevied them by force from a former employee of Bonneville's to whom the Crows had traded them.

It worked out. But that a man like Russell could be so treated, and be forced to take it, is evidence enough that the great days were coming to an end. The Company would not have dared to refuse an outfit to a good trapper before this year. No Company bourgeois, however powerful or snooty, would have dreamed of refusing.

# « XIII »

# AWAY, YOU ROLLING RIVER (1838)

THIS NARRATIVE would be under reproach of niggardliness if it came into its final chapter without an expedition against the Blackfeet. It turns to the Napoleon of the Blackfoot wars, Jim Bridger, and his memorialist Osborne Russell. Jim's brigade spent the winter of 1837–1838 in the bottoms of the Powder River which, Russell says, supplies the 'fat of the land' this year, abundant dry grass and cottonwood bark for the horses and illimitable buffalo herds for the trappers. When spring came on the big party moved west through Absaroka, to the Tongue and on to the Little Big Horn and down to its meeting with the Big Horn. Significantly, there was so little beaver sign that Bridger hardly bothered to send out trapping parties. Country going to hell. There proved to be so few beaver anywhere hereabout that Jim turned away from the Crow lands and headed toward those of the Blackfeet.

Russell pauses to describe a mountain man's outfit and for the last time so may we:

> A trapper's equipment in such cases is generally one animal upon which is placed one or two epishemores, a riding saddle and bridle, a sack containing six beaver traps, a blanket with an extra pair of moccasins, his powder horn and bullet pouch with a belt to which is attached a butcher knife, a wooden box containing bait for beaver, a tobacco sack with a pipe and implements for making fire, with sometimes a hatchet fastened to the pommel of his saddle. His personal dress is a flannel or cotton shirt (if he is fortunate enough to obtain one, if not antelope skin answers the purpose of over and undershirt), a pair of leather breeches with blanket or smoked buffalo skin leggings, a coat

made of blanket or buffalo robe, a hat or cap of wool, buffalo or otter skin, his hose are pieces of blanket wrapped around his feet, which are covered with a pair of moccasins made of dressed deer, elk or buffalo skins, with his long hair falling loosely over his shoulders, completes his uniform. He then mounts and places his rifle before him on his saddle.

Toward the end of May, 1838, most of Bridger's trapping parties, loosely in touch with one another, were in the vicinity of the Three Forks of the Missouri. They had come to the very heart of the Blackfoot *Lebensraum* without meeting a single Blackfoot. Concentrating, to be on the safe side, they started up the Gallatin. They struck the trail of a village only three or four days old and presently understood why they had been able to trap in peace. On June 2, crossing to the Madison, they saw a solitary tipi pitched near the river bank. Approaching it, they found it occupied by nine Blackfeet, all dead from smallpox.

The village sign led up the Madison and the next day Bridger took his men away from the river, toward the mountains. The boys objected vociferously. The sign showed that this village couldn't be more than three times as large as our side — was Jim gittin' cautious? Okay. He looped back to the river, continued up it till he thought he was near enough the Blackfeet, and camped in the narrow gulch through which a tributary creek came down. The next morning they scouted out the village, three miles away, and prepared to open the season. Russell, deciding to sit out the overture, took a spy glass and climbed the highest near-by rock to watch. The commandos, fifteen volunteers, rode as near the village as possible behind the shelter of a ridge, dismounted, crept up to the crest, and started shooting into the tipis. They got in three or four rounds while the Blackfeet milled round, then, when they mounted and rode yelling toward the ridge, ran back to their own horses and headed for camp. The Blackfeet followed them but stopped about three hundred yards away, fanning out in a semicircle on a point of rock.

End of the first stage of any pitched battle with Indians, for at three hundred yards an Indian gun would not hit anything and a trapper's Hawken would hit what it was aimed at only by chance. The Blackfeet wasted ammunition letting go at the contemptuous whites, as Indians always did, and worked up their ferocity by the prescribed rituals. This stage lasted about two hours and ended when one of them shouted to the whites in the Flathead tongue 'that we were not men but women and had better dress ourselves as such [the fightingest of Indian taunts] for we had bantered them to fight and then crept into the rocks like women.' One of the trappers was an Iroquois, a survivor of the band which the Northwest Company had brought west more than fifteen years ago, and nobody could call an Iroquois a squaw in safety. He exhorted his white associates to wipe out the insult, stripped naked, and 'began to utter the shrill war cry of his nation.' A sense of history made Russell's party cheer 'the sound which had been the death warrant of so many whites during the old French war.' About twenty trappers were in reach of the Iroquois' eloquence and since about a hundred and fifty Blackfeet were concentrated on that rocky point, the odds were proper for Bridger men. These twenty followed the Iroquois on the run into the musket fire, up the ridge. At the top they cached for a minute or two to get their breath, then rose up and went to it. They chased the Blackfeet, killing a satisfactory number, down to their horses and on to the village. End of round three.

That was enough for honor and when the night passed without incident the Bridger Tenth would have been willing to adjourn the war and get back to business. But the Blackfeet had not satisfied their honor and had spent the dawn drawing up a cavalry skirmish line to head off the white camp. So while the greater part of the camp struck the tents and tranquilly packed the mules, the Iroquois irreconcilable collected about thirty volunteers, including Russell, and led them off at a trot through the brush. He brought them out in the flank of the skirmish line, thirty yards away but still hidden by the bushes. They could hear the Blackfeet talking while they watched Bridger's camp come down. The trappers tightened their saddle girths, took four or five rifle balls apiece in their mouths for quick loading, and waited till the Iroquois judged the right time had come. He 'sallied forth with a horrid yell and we followed.' Surprise always took the fight out of an Indian — it was this that gave the white man his biggest edge — and the Blackfeet simply quirted their horses and lit out. The boys chased them to just beyond rifleshot of the village and waited there for camp to finish packing and come up. When it did so they fell in at the rear and moved on with it. The year was off to a good start.

But it proved to be a different year. As they rode through this country they passed familiar battlefields where good men had gone under and had taken their quota of Blackfeet with them, but now Blackfeet were hard to find. They moved southwestward over the mountains and came to Henry Lake — in a cove of

Idaho directly west of Yellowstone Park. Here they found a Blackfoot village so small (fifteen lodges) that they could wipe it out without raising a sweat. They prepared to do so — but as they rode toward it, they 'met six of them coming to us unarmed, who invited us in the most humble and submissive manner to their village to smoke and trade.' Queer doin's for Blackfeet — which way did their stick float? They found out. 'We were ashamed,' Russell says, 'to think of fighting a few poor Indians, nearly dwindled to skeletons by the smallpox.' If mountain life was various enough to produce some Blackfeet who wanted peace, its versatility comprehended a group of trappers who were willing to spare some Blackfeet. They stopped and smoked, did some trading, and moved on.

That was mid-June. Bridger took his unmolested brigade through first-rate beaver country — Henry's Fork, the upper plains of the Snake, Pierre's Hole, Jackson's Hole. Here at the eastern foot of the Tetons Russell and one companion went out to take a final hunt — something tarnation wrong with beaver, nobody had taken many plews. They trapped the creeks that cut the tumbled mountains south of the Hole and then made for Green River Valley and the rendezvous. When last summer's fair broke up, this year's had been set for the vicinity of Horse Creek again. But when Russell got to Horse Creek there was not a single camp there nor any sign that one had been there. On the door of a crumbling log structure which had been a storehouse last year he found a paper with a message scrawled on it. It read, 'Come on to Popoasia: plenty of whiskey and white women.'

'Popoasia' was the Popo Agie River — that is, east of the Continental Divide. And this notice, posted at what had been the nerve-center of the mountain fur country, was another sign of the times. En route to rendezvous the American Fur Company caravan, led this year by Andrew Drips, had decided to change the meeting place and had sent an express ahead to post the notice. (Conceivably the decision had been made by Fontenelle at Fort Laramie or even at Company headquarters in St. Louis.) Hard times a-coming. This new site was nearer Fort Laramie, which meant a cut in the overhead to adjust to the diminished fur crop. And also it was in the United States, not the jointly occupied Oregon, and so maybe the Hudson's Bay Company would stay away. As Nat Wyeth had forecast, the lower costs of the British system were paying off.

Russell and his companion rode on desirously, east through South Pass and north across the foothills that hug the foot of the

Wind River Mountains to the Popo Agie and down that to where it meets the Wind River and the two become the Big Horn. (About the same route which we saw Bonneville, Wyeth, Campbell, and Fitzpatrick take to the Big Horn following the rendezvous of 1833.) Every other band of trappers, Company or free, that panted toward the delights of Horse Creek had to do the same. The advertisement was in good faith: when they reached the beautifully wooded flat in the angle between the rivers, there was Drips' annual caravan in camp, with the tents pitched in the customary formations, the trading booths set up, the horse herd smaller and the wagon park bigger than ever before, and earlier arrivals acting on a resolution to make this the most ecstatic rendezvous of them all. It was a sound determination for there was plenty of evidence that the new era of whose intimations everyone had been aware was now at hand.

Tom Fitzpatrick was not there this year; he cannot be located anywhere in 1838. The caravan had found Fontenelle in charge of Fort Laramie but he seems not to have come on with it. Most of the Mountain Register were there when Russell arrived, however, or got there soon afterward. The specialist in solitary travel, Black Harris, had come out with Drips and had been assigned his usual job as advance courier: presumably it was he who had posted the notice at Horse Creek. Joe Walker was here and had opened a line of business he would specialize in, driving California horses east to sell.[1] Captain Stewart was here with a luxurious outfit and possibly a friend. (The friend is named by no one.) There was a scattering of sojourners and vacationers, and there were two sons of William Clark.

The whiskey was as advertised — and so were the white women. Four of them, wives of some more missionaries, and besides their husbands the party included a bachelor named Rogers and a couple of hired hands. All four couples had honeymooned along the trail and at least two of these unions were marriages of convenience, or co-operation, for the expeditious management of God's work among the Indians. Cushing and Myra Eells appear to have got married in the ordinary course of nature; so do Asa Bowen Smith and his wife Sarah. Not Elkanah and Mary Walker. Mary, who was twenty-seven this year had long yearned to share the holiness of saving heathen souls. The American Board, however, had only limited uses for 'unmarried females': females were exposed to dreadful experiences and shocking sights in heathen lands and the Board liked them fortified by the wisdoms and tolerations of marriage. Mary had been told that a place might eventually be found for her as a teacher of mission children at some decorous station. But Providence intervened almost as soon as the Board mailed its letter. There came to the office a letter from the rawboned, powerful, devout, and paralyzingly diffident Elkanah Walker, who had lately been appointed a missionary to the Zulus. Preparing for his service, Mr. Walker had had to face a question of the most elementary realism. His letter reminded the Board that he was a bachelor and, though he confessed that the question was delicate, he was not a man to shrink when duty spoke and he fired it straight at his superiors: 'Is it advisable for me to go out without a companion?' Clearly it wasn't, and there must be a leading in the fact that Walker was at Bangor, Maine, and hardly a hundred miles away, at Baldwin, there was an unmarried female who was longing for the mission field. The Board undertook to do some holy procuring, notified Walker of what God had wrought, and prepared Mary for her opportunity to achieve bliss and consecration. It took the temperate Maine blood something less than forty-eight hours to arrive at betrothal but the preparations for marriage moved more slowly. Presently the Zulus were seen to be about as bellicose as the Indians and the Board canceled Walker's appointment because they were warring again. So he was available to be sent to Oregon when the Board decided that the request for reinforcements which William Gray so unexpectedly brought them should be granted. Engaged in April of 1837, Mary and Elkanah were not married till March, 1838. They shared the missionary concern for the Christian population of Oregon and Mary was pregnant long before she started west.

William Gray worked faster. He had come east to enlarge the mission and procure necessities for it, among which an helpmeet was high on the list. (He was satisfying an envy by taking a three-months course of medical lectures during the winter and called himself 'Doctor' till he got to Waiilatpu, where Marcus Whitman excised the title.) But either he had some small selectivity or, as seems more likely, it was hard to find a woman who could tolerate the prospect of Mr. Gray even for the love of God. But on February 19 he met Mary Augusta Dixon and on February 26 he married her, thus completing his personal outfit. . . . Both the Eells and the Smiths were married in March, presumably with some earthly affection entering in.

The presence of William Gray at the rendezvous was of immediate interest to the first sizable band of mountain men who got there. The missionaries were already appalled by alcoholic indulgence but they had no reason to suppose they would be molested. Then on the night of July 4 Myra Eells' journal recounts, 'We were awakened by the barking of dogs, soon we heard a rush of drunken men coming directly towards our tent. Mr. Eells got up immediately and went to the door of the tent; in a moment four men came swearing and blaspheming, inquiring for Mr. Gray and asked if Mr. Richardson [Wyeth's old hunter, whom the missionaries had hired to run their outfit] was at home. Mr. Eells answered their inquiries and said little else. They said they wished to settle accounts with Mr. Gray, then they should be off.'

The boys did not like the Christian ethics practiced by this man of God who would not fight for his companions, pupils, and parishioners, who in fact would trade their lives for his. They stood there damning him while Myra Eells and Mary Gray, frantic with terror, tried to get sufficiently dressed to crawl out under the canvas wall. William Gray was hidden somewhere in that tent and he was willing to fight for his own life, for he was loading the rifle which Cushing Eells had carried from the settlements to the Popo Agie without loading it. A signal manifestation of God's providence occurred, the most useful one ever vouchsafed to Gray: the upholders of a different ethics did not see him. If they had they would have completed the Sioux's work but they roared and swore for a space and then the liquor in them turned the other way. They began to sing, pressing the Reverend Mr. Eells to join them. Eells said he did not know their tunes and was telling no lie. They mellowed further, apologized for keeping him awake, and went away to torment a hired greenhorn who was sleeping near-by. 'We were,' Myra Eells says, 'constantly in fear lest they return.'

They did not return, at least not for that purpose, and the point of view finally prevailed that killing a missionary, or even inflicting traumatic baldness on him, would not be creditable to their profession. But though spared murder this little group of courageous, bemused, antagonistic, and quarrelsome Christians, making an agonizing journey toward a doomed mission, got as much mountain realism as it was in them to endure. (Eells was by a good deal the best of them but none had the quality of Whitman, Parker, or Lee, and especially there was no Narcissa.) Their nerves were still jangled by this atrocious scene when Bridger's brigade came roaring into camp. They and Drips' men embraced one another with hellish noise, then fifteen or twenty of them rushed to feed their eyes on white women, bringing a Blackfoot scalp and banging an Indian drum. The dog which Myra had innocently supposed would protect them from all harm lit out howling and swam across the Popo Agie. Old Gabe's men danced round their scalp for the admiration of the women and, Myra says, 'they looked like the emissaries of the Devil worshiping their own master.' The next night another dozen of them in full war paint came and danced for the white squaws again. They may have been a little ghastly, bearded as well as covered with vermilion and ochre, dressed in blackened buckskins, drunk, howling, and in song. Myra does not even try to describe 'the horrible scene they presented' but dismisses it with another reference to the devil and a patent longing for an exorcism. She does, however, provide an authentic detail, saying they were 'all rejoicing in the fate of the Blackfoots in consequence of the smallpox.'

* * *

These missionaries, the last whom the American Board sent to its Oregon Mission, are the most unmistakable intimation so far of the emigrants to come, but the forecast gets over the line into burlesque. They were especially like the emigrants in contentiousness. Only a hair divides a consciousness of grace from self-righteousness and from the Bible of all Protestant missionaries who went west the parables of the Pharisees appear to have been omitted. Here were four married couples and a spare bachelor, Cornelius Rogers — twenty-two years old, a volunteer, and by far the most genial of them all. No one could possibly have had a higher voltage of God's grace and they recharged every night and by day also whenever the train paused long enough for a prayer meeting. But the result was a superiority to one another at once sanctimonious and belligerent, and they quarreled their way from Westport to the Columbia mile by mile. For purposes of recrimination there was a rough division of couples, the Walkers and Grays against the Smiths and Eells, but this may have been merely a division by half-tents and in any event was subject to constant realignment, for all would quarrel with any and the allies fought each other when the enemy was not at hand. Ordinary human cussedness, which always chafed in the forced companionship of the trail, seemed all the more insupportable because it could be called unrighteousness, and the ordinary epithets of contention gave greater pleasure in that they were being used in God's service. The truth is that none of the married couples could more than endure any of the others, and

Mary Walker intimates that her husband became suddenly more conjugal when he was momentarily relieved of Smith's company. But she also thought that her husband was too much influenced by Asa Smith, too easily swayed by him, too subservient to him — and at the same time she was corrosively jealous of Sarah Smith, hating every word that Elkanah spoke to her.

'Mrs. Smith undertook to help Mr. W. correct me for dictating Mr. Gray. . . . I feel so tried with Mr. W. I know not what to do. He seems to think more of Mrs. Smith than of me. Spends a great deal more time in her society than in mine. . . . I feel cruelly neglected.' Thus the wife of Mr. W., who is sure she tries to do the best she can. A calf from their herd was bitten by a wolf and a general quarrel resulted, whether to kill and eat it or try to save it. It blew up to a tempest that raged from then on — and this is early May. 'Mr. S. & wife seemed much less inclined to make concessions. . . . It seems to me he is more out of the way than Gray.' And a week later, 'Mrs. Smith very much out with Mr. Gray. In a fret all the time. Mr. W. seems to feel quite as I do toward them. Hope we shall be enabled to treat them right. That they will see their error and reform. Fear I am not as plain with them as I ought to be.' Mary might have spared herself that reproach: they were all as plain with one another as the English tongue permits. And 'Mrs. S. tries my patience talking about Gray as she calls him all the time. I wish she could see how much like him only worse she gets.' But the next day Elkanah and Gray are in agreement and Mary thinks they are a strange company of missionaries but wonders secretly which of them is the most intolerable — and does not mean intolerant. And 'Mrs. Smith & Eells being unwilling to give away milk we divided and gave away part of ours. Think we shall enjoy what we have left as well as they.' And 'In the evening gave Mrs. Smith a small piece of my mind about milk matters, etc.' And 'Mr. Smith in the tent all day with his wife. Kept up a constant whispering much to my annoyance.'

And 'The uneasy fretful disposition of Mrs. Smith together with her incessant whispering are very unpleasant to me. Her husband is much of a hog at table as I have [remarked?] & he frequently treats me with what I [deem?] rudeness. There is about them what [looks?] a good deal like pure selfishness. — Mr. Eells is very [uninteresting?] and unsocial & his character the *I* eclipses the whole [horizon?]. Dr. Gray is exceedingly fractious. It is rather difficult getting along with him. He however treats my husband and me politely. More so perhaps than any others of the company. When Mrs. S. chances to hear her husband talked about it is sure to be nothing good. But with me it is the reverse. My husband [word illegible] to gain friends let him go where he will.' But Mary wished her Mr. W. might be more engaged in religion and she thought he ought to show more interest in the scenery.

This is merely any mile or any day. Like their predecessors these people inspire respect for dedication, however warped, and for courage. None of them appears to have been intelligent. Eells had the rectitude and angularity of the evangelical saint, enough of it to be morally impressive and not quite enough to seem diseased, and some of the others had character within the terms of a piety that is also repulsive bigotry, others did not. Eells and Walker have solid bulk in the history of Oregon, the former made almost monumental by his unyieldingness, but that bulk is more lay than ecclesiastical and much more ecclesiastical than religious. (The Christian church in Oregon was many things: among them a serial brawl.) Their personalities vary, from the clear-sighted, composed, and rather likable Myra Eells and the diffidently serious-minded Elkanah Walker, through mediocrity stiffened by smugness and egotism, to cravenness in the Smiths, to the unvarying repulsiveness of Gray. One has to scour them of Gray's spleen but decides that there is something in what he said.[2] Some may suffer injustice from history as the penalty of having kept no journals, and what seems mildly attractive in Myra Eells may be only the naturalness of her prose. But they were just any small, ardent, and neurotic lusters after heathen souls, of a type that became noisome across the seven seas, and they were altogether inconsiderable considering Whitman and Spalding. The American Board was not bright to send any of them west and it was mad to send them as a group.

Moreover, all of them except Gray were greenhorns and none had Whitman's and Jason Lee's ability to master travel skills and to adjust to novel situations. Gray was an accomplished traveler by now but nothing could cure him of stupidity, obstinacy, and arrogance and he made repeated mistakes as the result of all three. All earlier missionaries had been welcomed by the mountain men, if not at sight then soon afterward, but Andrew Drips took one look at this peripatetic slugging match for heavenly favor and asked them to travel by themselves. Gray insisted that it was impossible, it was impossible, and Drips relented. But the caravan disdained the greenhorns and the greenhorns abhorred the wicked. So, with ineptness, quarreling, the softness of greenhorns, and the guilt of saints, abetted by a summer that was late, cold, and rainy, they made about as uncomfortable a crossing as any on record. They traveled by day and camped at night with the masters of plains life, who took their ease in all weathers. But they were too stupid and too righteous to learn.

Like Narcissa and Eliza the women were casting the lines that emigrant wives were to follow — botanizing, collecting curious pebbles, gaping at the scenery, putting on their nightgowns and frantically scrubbing all their other clothes when they got a chance, growing used to buffalo chips for fuel, laboring to bake and roast and contrive variations on the staple diet. Thousands of wives to come find a voice when after a night in the rain the party reaches the Platte from the Blue and Myra Eells writes, 'I am so strongly reminded of bygone days that I cannot refrain from weeping.' From now on the Platte will be acquainted with women's tears. Mary Walker put it more forcibly a month later: 'I cried to think how comfortable father's hogs were.' The Pawnees, though they behaved unusually well, frightened the women and the fear of Indians, whose souls they were undertaking to save after all, was with them from then on. Everyone was exhausted all the time, the men from the management of the herd and awkwardness at prairie travel, the women mostly from side-saddles. (Gray has sensibly recommended buckskin 'drawers,' which was more than Narcissa and Eliza had been favored with, but no one had courage or sense enough to tell the girls to admit their legs and fork their horses.) They were sick in rotation and in groups — colds, rheumatisms, the unspecified 'fevers' which medicine of the time took note of and differentiated from the 'vapors' which most of them were. For one must see here symptoms that would be widespread and constant as soon as the greenhorns began to come in force. There are dreads and melancholies specific to the tenderfoot in the plains and mountains, a true neurosis, usually mild but sometimes severe, and in fact a neurosis that sometimes, with the right pressure or the right inner weakness, becomes a psychosis. It is the effect on the ego of loneliness in infinite space, emptiness, barrenness, and the inescapable sun.

And of course they were not far up the Platte when alkali dysentery hit them all. Mary Walker had it longest and most violently. It was not, however, as constant as self-righteousness, self-pity, and the bickering that came to be as much a consolation as a trial. Along with her diarrhoea Mary mentions as a striking phenomenon a day when 'Mr. W. gets along without quarreling.'

Perhaps the presence of Indian wives, ten or fifteen all told, in the Company caravan is responsible for the reticence of our diarists about the damned, though in any event little of the exterior world could have withstood the battling and the guilt. It is a sign of the times that some unidentified wayfarers, free trappers, no doubt, overtake them and join the caravan, and another one that they meet a party coming down the Platte. To the missionaries the latter was just a chance to send letters home but Myra Eells does identify one of the travelers as 'Mr. Renshaw'; he may be Jean Richard. Mary Walker mentions a gentleman, from the context apparently not Stewart, who had traveled a good deal and described Switzerland, Italy, and an illegible country, and told about dogs digging men out of the snow. At the very beginning of the trip Elkanah records a visit from Drips, Stewart, and Harris, who brought them a gift of pork (Mary separately saying, 'I thought Mr. S.[mith] acted rather hogish') and acknowledges that all these gentlemen treated them courteously. Thereafter there is practically no mention of the caravan, Drips, or Harris, and little more of Stewart. Gray could not stand a gentleman and especially a British gentleman, as we have seen, but the urbane Captain must have visited the missionaries and especially their wives more than the diaries say. Stewart's mules took fright and overturned his wagon on May 21. (That was the day when the Reverend Asa Smith let a cook fire get away from him and everyone spent the nooning putting it out.) Some of the delicacies he had certainly been sharing with them got spilled. It is the first mention Myra Eells has made of him since April 28, when she also noted the visit Elkanah mentions and added that she entertained them with biscuit and cheese.

So far none of them had said anything at all about the presence of a man who was a more vivid sign than all the others that the new age was hard at hand. The Delawares had been assigned a reservation at last, just beyond Westport, the new river town which was competing with Independence and would surpass it. A good many of the wanderers had begun to settle there and when Drips took his train into their lands there was waiting for him one who had made friends with the Delawares on two journeys down the Santa Fe Trail and had learned a little of their language. Both these ventures in the Santa Fe trade had been exceedingly small; they had done nothing to relieve the speculator's successive bankruptcies, and, in fact, he was sojourning among the Delawares as much to avoid creditors as for any other reason. He was thirty-five, a Swiss, an ex-draper, an ex-stationer, and a superb liar. Yet liar is an unjust word. He was headed, he was destined, for the West, for California — two provinces of fantasy — and among fantasts worthy of the provinces he was to become supreme. He was currently creating and elaborating a fantasy of immense personal solace: that he, a runaway debtor who had had to leave Europe secretly lest he be clapped in jail, who had had no experience of soldiering and had been too humbly born to be an officer, was a Captain 'formerly of the Royal Swiss Guards of Charles X of France.'

It is altogether certain that he had no idea why he was traveling, in complete ignorance of all that lay between and almost complete ignorance of what could be found there, toward California. He did not need to know. Vastness and empire swam in his mind, and for the West of immensity and illusion the hour was quickening. The hour and the place and the man approached one another. The ether vibrated, the impalpable began to be palpable, and as Captain John A. Sutter of the Royal Swiss Guards, Johann Augustus Sutter had started West.[3]

Considering that all the goods were now packed in carts or wagons — another sign of the times and of the struggle to reduce the overhead — Drips' time of thirty-eight days from Westport to Fort Laramie was not remarkable. The ladies felt the invariable relief at seeing houses once more, and Myra Eells' remark that the fort 'compares very well with the walls of the Connecticut State Prison' was meant as praise. They could be farm wives for a few days: wash their clothes and themselves, beat dust out of bedding, bake some bread that would satisfy their honor. Fontenelle and Woods were at the fort and made the usual call of ceremony, with Drips and the wives of all three. It may be that Gray, urged to an uncharacteristic charity by observing monogamous and semi-permanent marriage, did not tell the ladies that it was also unsolemnized. At any rate they received the unsanctified wives with kindness, gave a tea for them, and encouraged them to make repeated visits. Myra remarked that 'the children are quite white and can read a little.'

Gray had had enough wheeled travel beyond Fort Laramie two years ago and turned over to Drips and Fontenelle the wagon he had with great labor brought this far. That meant the more nagging if less strenuous labor of a pack train from here on. They traded some stock at the fort, wrote letters, brought the respite to an end, and moved on with Drips June 3, eight days after their arrival. And moved on brawling. A realignment had lately allied the Walkers and Smiths against the Grays and Eells, but Smith was nearly as great a strain on everyone as Gray and rendezvous brought bliss to Mary Walker when he resolved to build a brush lodge of his own. She wondered if the course he was pursuing might not cost him some misgiving but it would be sweet not to hear his tongue.[4]

* * *

There was wickedness at the rendezvous but there was great solace also: they had three Sabbaths straight beside these still waters and could leach away their guilt. On the first of them Elkanah Walker held morning service, to the intense gratification of the group, and with nine sightseers from the camp looking on. His text was an act of revenge he would never have consciously performed, 2 Peter III, 7: 'But the heavens and the earth which are now, by the same word are kept in store, reserved unto fire against the day of judgment and perdition of ungodly men.' Perhaps the sparseness of the congregation was what led Cushing Eells to choose for his text at afternoon service the psalmist's warning, 'If I regard iniquity in my heart, the Lord will not hear me.' Mary Walker filled out the day with Baxter's *Saint's Everlasting Rest.* A week later as many as forty of the damned came to hear Smith in the morning, 'many of whom would not understand what was said but they enjoyed the singing.' Since even Mary confessed that the heat made her languid, presumably there were fewer when Elkanah preached that afternoon. On the third Sunday the arrival of good news so excited Myra and Mary that neither says anything about divine service.

The ladies had set up their farmwife's kitchen. Once the laundry was done, they had a frenzy of cooking. They made puddings, mince pies (from fat cow, deer meat, elk, and bighorn), and since they were all Yankees a lot of doughnuts — fried in the alien fats of bear or buffalo. Also they made bread of the flour they had brought with them, yeast-risen bread, and this was the greatest marvel to mountain men, who began to find occupation near the missionary camp when perfumes out of boyhood drifted with the smoke through the willows by the river. Joe Meek was not a shy man, so it must have been the antagonism of Gray, who smelled sulphur in his vicinity, that restrained him. Joe had occasion to follow the missionaries' trail after rendezvous and at Bear River was tormented by the odor of baking bread. While he fought down an impulse to humble himself, one of the ladies gave an Indian a hot biscuit as a reward for singing a hymn. Joe could not sing hymns, so he collared the Indian in the bushes and ordered him to go back and sing another one. When piety was again rewarded Joe got the first taste of bread he had had in nine years.

While their husbands tinkered with the outfit, the ladies moved New England to the Popo Agie by setting up a sewing circle. Humble, frantically inquisitive squaws hung round them in platoons, touching them to see the blood move under this odd white skin, inspecting the mysterious articles in their personal outfit, fingering unheard-of things like brooches and hartshorns and pancake turners. The white squaws had odd but admirable equipment for dressmaking: thimbles, emery bags in the shape of strawberries, needles of many sizes but all small to Indian eyes, darning eggs, embroidery frames, threads of all sizes and colors, yarns, silk flosses. They could do no finer work with these tools than the red ladies did with awls and split sinews but they could work with stupefying ease and speed. So the squaws sighed and chattered and brought the ladies the bright cottons their husbands had been buying for them at the trading booths and the ladies made dresses for them, unquestionably longer in the skirt than Indian fashions prescribed. Myra mentions Mrs. Joe Walker and Mrs. Craig; Mary, Mrs. Roberson. (Craig was an old RMF Company man; there were numerous Robinsons.) Others in quantity are mentioned but not named. Myra, who sniffs at the mean quality of the cloth and is scandalized by its cost of two dollars a yard, says she made 'a gown for Mr. Jay,' but probably means for his squaw. But she also made one for Mr. Clark, who is not known to have had a wife here, and this suggests the dismaying effeminacy of a nightshirt in the mountains.

They all continued to be shocked by mountain society, whose ideals appeared to be precisely those of Indian society. But they received the formal visits of the partisans. Myra mentions Drips, Doc Newell, and Jim Bridger. Jim was not only satisfying the amenities when he called on them, he was trying to raise the status of Christians in his men's eyes. He felt an obligation to them because they were in the same business as Marcus Whitman, who three years ago had removed from his shoulder what Myra calls an Indian spear. There is no mention of Sutter or Stewart but both unquestionably entertained the ladies several times. Sutter would not fail to bring his fine manners to the tents in the willow grove and, stretched on buffalo robes, spin a vision of his military past and his imperial future. Stewart would certainly find the Snake and Arapaho girls comelier and more agreeable but had the obligations of a gentleman. The hawk nose and the curled mustache certainly did not warm the ladies beyond the correctness of a deaconess summoned to tea by the village atheist, and Stewart's wines, porters, brandies, and liqueurs would get no takers here, though his olives, potted meats, candies, and fruit pastes probably did. One assumes that both parties behaved with propriety and sought pleasanter company as soon as possible.

Then on Sunday July 8 a small, confident, and temperately uproarious outfit came in from the west. It was Francis Ermatinger with a Hudson's Bay Company party in territory unquestionably American, and let the trust make something of it if it wanted to. He began to sign up trappers who could see that the American Fur Company was not what it used to be. Also he had letters from Spalding and Whitman with news of the mission. And there were traveling with him not only the vague Mr. Ewing who had come west last year but also Philip Edwards and Jason Lee from the Methodist mission on the Willamette.

The salvation of the coast and river Indians had succeeded amazingly: the Methodist mission was a farming and stock-breeding business, an owner and claimant of water powers, and a land company so prosperous that the British had probably lost Oregon. There is kinship between Brigham Young and Jason Lee, the principal author of this wealth. Both understood the imperative necessity of building up God's kingdom on earth and giving the church militant an adequate base for its campaign against unrighteousness. Moreover, the Methodist Mission Board had been supplying Lee with both cash and assistants with a lavishness that made the American Board look miserly. The Willamette mission was now spacious in the possession of orchards, hayfields, staple crops, buildings, sawmills, beef herds, milch cattle, machinery, boats, temperance society, confiscated whiskey still, and real estate that was certain to rise. It also had some schools where a handful of children learned a form of English from pretty Biblical pictures which were somehow more proper than the Romish ones that horrified their distributors, and where another, less stable handful of adult rice-Christians sang hymns and cultivated the fields at wages that would strain no treasury of God's vicars. They were all from degenerate, disheartened tribes which, it was clear to everyone, would dwindle into extinction without causing any awkwardness. There was some heart-searching because the station Indians were obstinate, stupid, and obviously unable to value the sacrifices made on their behalf, but only in leisure moments after the day's empire-building. The Willamette witnessed none of the soul's agony that oppressed the missions on the Walla Walla and the Clearwater, suffering wholly different pains in the competition for markets. Jason Lee did not quite say that the dedication of Spalding and Whitman to an experiment noble in purpose but impossible in fact was damned nonsense, but he spent his life in an undeclared conviction that it must be.

He was the missionary as advance guard of empire. He intended to save such Indian souls as the mission's services might eventually reach after the local miserables had been cleaned up or pushed out — by transforming a migratory society to a sedentary one, shifting a hunting economy to agriculture, and thereafter erasing everything in the neolithic consciousness so that nineteenth-century white culture and the grace of God could flow across it like the color in a wash drawing. He saw the enormousness of this job and so he understood that its first requisite was a powerful, developed white society in Oregon. Natural piety shielded him from conceiving that this society might be British, and it must have been the time-spirit that forbade him to realize that any sizable society of whites meant the end of the Indians, whether damned or saved. Jason Lee was a particle, an exceedingly vigorous particle, from the core of the expansionist consciousness, an inflexible will swept into the field of the national will, an instrument of the gigantic forces that had sent him spinning out in advance of those to come like an asteroid moving on the edge of a planet's orbit.

When he meets his brothers in God on the Popo Agie in July, 1838, the potential of the domestic empire is stepped up before your eyes. The Mission Board had sent additional missionaries to the Willamette (by sea) in both 1836 and 1837. Among them were Anna Pittman, whom Lee married in July of 1837, and Doctor Elijah White, something of a William Gray but a bigger and more important man, therefore a greater trouble-maker and gear-stripper. Neither these recruits nor the impressive sums of money which the Board had sent to Oregon, however, were on the scale which Lee's imperial if not imperially phrased vision implied. He determined to go to the States and make the Mission Board, the Church at large, and the American people understand what saving the Oregon Indians and Oregon required. His colleagues approved, so he was off to demand more missionaries, more money, and especially more laymen. Give me farmers, mechanics, carpenters, laborers — give me the men to plant a colony in the new world.

Remembering the sensational effectiveness of the Indian boys whom Nat Wyeth had taken east, he equipped himself with two like them for the Sunday School circuit. One of these was a Chinook and had a pointed head — at last — so that the congregations who remembered William Walker's plea could see for themselves the necessity of hay barns and neat cattle on the Willamette. (In an ecstasy of semantic piety Lee always spoke of him as 'a real Flathead.') He was also accompanied by three sons of Tom McKay, who were to be sent to school.

And Lee did exactly what the gathering forces, now near eruption, required of him. Reaching the States, he began to evangelize the nation on behalf of Indian souls and Oregon real estate. Through more than a year he made repeated tours, New England, South, Midwest, Washington, New York — churches, missionary societies, Sunday schools, young people's societies, lay gatherings. He told them about the settlements of Hudson's Bay veterans whose looseness threatened Indian morals and who clouded Methodist titles to water power. He told them about Indian hunger and thirst for righteousness, which increased as the square of the distance, and about the crushing labor of the missions and the expectation in grain and lumber and cattle. He told them about the blasphemies and debaucheries of mountain men, the depth of the soil along the Willamette, the soft Oregon winter. And the Indian boys proved to have been an inspiration, a leading from on high. They were Indians, which is to say orators and actors and exhibitionists. They were in a strange country and so more easily even than other Indians were moved to melancholy, trance, and vision. They spoke a broken English which made more appealing the distortions of Christian idea they voiced and gave an added pathos to their tears. In a word they wowed the audiences to whom he exhibited them. Lee made them Christian evangelists who abhorred liquor and their memories of home made them real-estate promoters, and it did the cause no harm when one of them died. The devout were appalled by the darkness of the Oregon Indian and inspired by his longing for the light. Also the panic had ruined the farmers' market, a succession of bad crop years was beginning on the midwest frontier, and there were always malaria and prairie winters. The Oregon country had an evangelical radiance — and no one understated the promise it held out to a people who for two centuries had been looking for a better home to the west.

Lee sailed for Oregon again in October, 1839, going round the Horn with more missionaries and fewer laymen than he wanted, with opulent supplies and a guarantee of ample money for mission industry and real estate. But even before he sailed, in the spring of the year a wholly new kind of Oregon caravan had jumped off at the frontier as the direct result of his labor. The thing had started now.

But in the summer of 1838, on his way to the rendezvous, he stopped at both Waiilatpu and Lapwai, calling on Whitman and Spalding. They had had two years of labor even harder than his, more doubt and foreboding, much greater anxiety. Both of them now understood the infinity of labor and time that must stretch ahead of them if the great vision were to be fulfilled, and Whitman had begun to doubt that it would be. They were in a more arid country than the Willamette Valley, a country of much harsher winters, less productive, separated by hundreds of miles from any economic system or any society which could sustain them. (In fact, the white pioneer required well over a generation to bring this country in.) Now here was Lee fresh from a success astonishing even in terms of frontier booms and not satisfied with it, going east in the confident expectation of promoting a bigger enterprise. It stung. Also it begot a vision.

So with Whitman's collaboration Spalding wrote a letter to the American Board and Lee took it with him when he went on. The Oregon Mission might be made effective in the service of the dream, they said, if the Board would back it with some of the earnestness an investor brought to his kind of dream. They needed thirty ministers, thirty school teachers, ten doctors, ten machinists — all with wives. They needed several tons of iron and steel to be worked into tools and machinery. They needed cook stoves and parlor stoves. They needed a moderately plentiful supply of trade goods — including a hundred dozen scalping knives. Candle snuffers, cowbells, school books, hymn books, a flouring mill. . . . It was impossible, it was fantastic, it was foolish, and at least Whitman soon repented it. It was addressed to a charitable foundation whose income had been curtailed by the financial panic, a foundation furthermore which not only could not realize what Western Indians were but had all the heathen in the world to think of besides. Gray, reading the letter at rendezvous, understood this and wrote the Board saying that he did.

At the same time Gray's letter contained the truth which all missionaries had to face sooner or later: that it was wasted effort to preach Christianity to Indians who were not civilized. The first requisite was to make them agriculturists but no missionary saw that in the terms of the nineteenth century that was altogether impossible. The letter to the American Board must be seen in that light, and if Marcus Whitman, a giant working gigantically for an end forbidden, did not in April of 1838 consciously understand what his nerve-ends had already told him, he soon did. Greatly strengthening the Oregon Mission would not only have saved Whitman's life, it would have made Waiilatpu a better instrument for the service to which Whitman was to devote it. Failing reinforcement in men, supplies, and money, he had to assume an even greater labor and habitually perform the impossible, as he made his Christian mission the waystation that enabled the emigration to reach Oregon.

* * *

The missionaries started west with Ermatinger on July 12 and the rendezvous camps on the Popo Agie broke up on the twentieth. Between the rendezvous and St. Louis Captain Stewart again disappears from the record. Presumably he took his outfit along the trout streams and into the high meadows where game was thick, for the sportsman had come west to do just that. He may have pushed through South Pass and revisited the lake country on the western slope which was to color his reveries all his life. He may have made a last circuit with a party of trappers, renewed his acquaintance with the Crows, ridden with some of Bridger's men in search of the less bellicose Blackfeet. Certainly he took a final ecstasy in the buffalo chase and brought fat cows down at improbable ranges with his Manton and joined his warcry to Antoine Clement's at the kill. Whatever he did, it was a shorter tour than usual, for he was in St. Louis on September 28, if not before. On that date he wrote to John Crawford, the British consul at New Orleans.[5]

Then a few days before October 11, Mr. Crawford entrusted to a Mr. Osterlok who was going up the river a letter from Scotland forwarded to him by courtesy of a banking house. And on the eleventh he wrote to Stewart in his own person and inclosed another letter which carried the same news, this one from the Marquis of Breadalbane. It was important news: Sir John Archibald Stewart had died at Paris May 20, 1838, the day when his brother was crossing from the South fork to the North fork of the Platte. Captain Stewart was now Sir William, nineteenth of Grandtully and seventh baronet. And writing from New Orleans the consul expressed his satisfaction on the baronet's safe return from the wilds, for 'I think there must be some danger among the Indians.'

Sir William took his time. He was master of Murthly and Grandtully and Logiealmond now, not to mention Birnam Wood, and he would have to go home to settle his inheritance, begin adjudicating the disputes of cottagers, and resume a marriage that had made no claim on him since the spring of 1832. In fact, he would have to do a lot of things that called for no expertness with buffalo, Crows, or Shoshone girls. As a specimen of them, on September 21, 1839, he would petition Thomas Robert, Earl of Kinnoul, etc., Lord Lyon King of Arms, to revise the Stewart arms so that Sir William could show on them a Drummond quartering. The result would be satisfying: Or, a fess chequé azure and argent between three buckles in chief of the second, and a galley, her oars in action, in base sable: for Stewart. Or, three barrs within a bordure all waved gules: for Drummond. This with a Mackenzie quartering that included fleur-de-lis, and a fourth quartering even more resplendent, with three thighs flexed in triangle and a buck's head cabossed. Above the shield a helmet, gules, doubled argent, and on the liveries two bees countervolant, a motto 'Provyd' on the dexter side, and a motto 'Nil Timeo' on the sinister. The shield encircled with an orange tawny ribbon, and pendant from it the badge of Nova Scotia. . . . There should have been another quartering, say a pipe-hatchet, a possible bag, and a Blackfoot scalp all gules.

Miller's pictures, the consul wrote to Stewart, were in his old studio on Chartres Street and Miller, absent somewhere, would probably be back by the time Stewart reached New Orleans. Crawford did not know how much progress Miller had made but feared not much — 'he seems rather lazy.' Now that the baronet was going home and now that Murthly was really his, those pictures were more important than ever. That was business to settle in New Orleans and so was the partnership with Crawford and the mysterious Vernufft. The latter enterprise was probably a flyer in imports and it had lost 'ten thousand' — possibly pounds, more likely dollars. Stewart went to New Orleans to deal with these and other matters. There on December 17 he wrote to his friend Cut Face, the Left Hand, William Sublette, the prosperous merchant of St. Louis and veteran of the West.

The Indians no less than white men speculated about the stars, why man was born, what wisdom is, and, like white men, they filled the West with myths and formulated symbols of them. There are many springs welling up from crevices in the rocks, Manitou the Fontaine Qui Bouille is only one of them, and many creeks arching spray across a backdrop of gray stone — there are many Western waters on which the supernaturals have put a spell. Drink them once and some day you must come back to drink again. And Stewart had spent five years in that country going 'always a little further,' an old army man with the restlessness of ended battles upon him, urged 'beyond that last blue mountain barred with snow.' Men, the poet quoted says, men are unwise and curiously planned.

Sir William has sent Bill Sublette a cask of wine, which he must bottle at once lest it fall off. He hopes, in a sentence one could wish expanded, that Bill is 'getting on better with your other boy than Silas who is not a fairy.' He may have to draw on Bill for seven hundred dollars till his new estates are cleared. Then, 'I trust you can procure me some tame deer' — American deer, from the country of enchantment. And 'I wish you'd be good enough to send for Antoine and tell him I wish him to get me some gourds of the best form for dippers, also some red birds and keep them in cages as I wish to take them to Eng. and that I expect he will be ready in March.' The waters of Manitou have begun to exert their spell on Stewart. There will be gourds as well as golden goblets at Murthly and mule deer as well as stag and roebuck in its park, and birds such as the Stewart has seen in the cottonwoods on the shore of New Fork Lake. More, the Antoine thus shown to be in St. Louis and waiting for a summons is Antoine Clement, that great hunter, the halfbreed, the companion of the traveler — and he is going to Murthly.

Stewart took the breed with him when he sailed in May of 1839. And when Alfred Jacob Miller followed a year later, he found that Antoine 'has been metamorphosed into a Scotch valet and waits on the table in full suit of black and this is everything he does.'[6] Stewart had lately given him a proper suit of kilts — Miller says it cost fifty pounds, which is unlikely — so that he could mingle with the peasantry at their frolics. So there would always be at Murthly another speaking the gutturals Stewart had learned to speak, and the pidgin English of the West, and the wordless language of signs. In the evenings the two could sit in a room hung with heads of bighorn and buffalo, skins of bear and cougars on the floor, medicine pipes and warbonnets, beaded moccasins, the horn bows of the Nez Perces, an assortment of mementoes whose virtue was that they recalled great deeds. Probably Antoine could not discriminate among ports but the whiskey of the country was far better than any he had ever gulped at trading booths. They would recall the Crows on the warpath or the thunder of stampeding bulls. Or they could stroll among the relics of a warfare not much more advanced than the age of polished stone: pikes, halberds, casques, gauntlets, arquebuses, dirks, sabers, jeweled daggers. Among paintings a touch more important than Miller's; the hall (Miller says) held a Caravaggio Christ, a Correggio Cupid and Psyche, two Poussins, Brunelleschi's 'Judith and Holofernes,' a Raphael, a da Vinci. Together with a lot of Florentine and Roman and Venetian bric-à-brac from the family's diplomatic past and as varied as the seventh baronet's mementoes of the high place. Among the claymores, the lapis lazuli, and the Poussins they could stroll at leisure, their hands rapid in a narrative of the Little Chief urging his Snake braves to annihilate an ambushed party of Sioux.

Six months after Stewart sailed for home he was in London, his inheritance in order and his arms revised. Restlessness would not down and London was just a stopover on his way to Constantinople and Egypt — presumably Antoine was with him. But he felt that he was moving in the wrong direction. His heart failed when he remembered Zion. He thought of Cut Face, old Bill. They had heard the chimes at midnight, many a time they had lain all night in the windmill in St. George's field, there would not be two such swingebucklers in all the inns o' court again. This was the waters of Manitou and so on November 26, 1839, Sir William wrote to Sublette.[7]

He is sending two pedigreed calves to improve the herd at Bill's suburban farm. In April or May, when the colts are sold after the London horse shows, he will send him a fine horse, too. But the point is, 'I must . . . inform you that I have not yet done with the U. S. — and if it pleases God shall be in N. Y. in the Fall of 1840 with a view of going to the Mts. in spring following, if I can get a party to join me sufficiently strong.' Let Bill remember him to Andrew Drips, let him 'or any of my friends in Mts. know that if I am in life and health I shall be on the Susquadee in July '41.'

The 'Susquadee,' Green River, the upper valley where New Fork empties into it, the upthrust of the great Wind River range to the east, or seen from Fort Bonneville across the flat to the as yet unnamed Fremont Peak, lesser mountains north and west, the music of those waters, and over all the tremendous sun. November fog in London and Sir William is remembering the shriek of cart wheels with shrunken hubs and felloes, the complaint of saddle leather, the bellowing of musty buffalo, the scream of a cougar, the ululation of some Indian at the kill. In that reek of coal smoke he can smell buffalo chips burning, sagebrush dew-dampened at sunrise, the alkali that burns your nostrils no less than your cheeks, a shower wetting the shoulder of a peak while your tongue swells in the dust below, the river-smell when you come upon it suddenly in midafternoon and your mules squeal and your horse has to be held from bolting toward it, the stale sourness of an Indian with an arm round you telling you of his love for the white chief which though already great can be doubled by a mouthful of alcohol. Outside Sir William's hotel the carts rattle on cobblestones but they are not his carts miring in the Platte quicksands or hauled and shouted and cursed across the Sweetwater.

Something moves in the willows and the Manton is cocked and Sir William stands up in his stirrups — Ephraim is there, Old Caleb, the white bear of the mountains, so terrible that to kill one is a coup as glorious as striking with your bare hand an enemy in his own tipi. For half a mile mules and wagons are stretched out in flat light, dust above the caravan like an opening umbrella, emptiness everywhere, the earth flowing like water at its edges, a false lake hung with groves that have no reality. Here are the braves riding in from the hunt; their faces are like a sorcerer's mask, they are naked to a g-string, the blood of buffalo has soaked their moccasins and dyed their forearms and calves, the squaws wait for them with basins of clear cold water from the Siskadee. At night the campfire will be carmine and Black Harris describing the landscape of fable and Old Gabe continuing his dictations on the Blackfoot wars. Tom Fitzpatrick, Andy Drips, Henry Fraeb, Joe Meek, Doc Newell, Kit Carson, Bill Williams, Joe Walker. And Lucien Fontenelle dead? — Jesu! Jesu! a' drew a good bow; and dead! a' shot a fine shoot! A Snake girl with a look in her eyes, the young breasts, the fine thighs — a glance toward the willows and a hand flung up meaning when the seven stars line up with the peak. Waking on a mountainside just when the sky turns gray, the horses cropping grass at the end of lariats, a level smoke above the dead fire, a wind cutting to the bone, and below you the earth falling away and the dark shrinking into pools at the foot of distant rocks. Then was Jack Falstaff, now Sir John, a boy and page to Thomas Mowbray, Duke of Norfolk.

The owner of Birnam Wood dips his pen. He hopes that Bill Sublette 'can so arrange it that Ande's equipment may go up and meet a party at Larame's Fork.' Bill's younger brother Andrew, another Sublette in the mountain trade, operating on the smaller scale of the new era. There are Indians to be told, too: let Andrew give 'notice to Bracelet de fer and the Little Chief to meet us at the rendezvous.' (Iron Bracelet was probably a Snake, too, though various tribes had warriors of that name — and how was a baronet in London to know that there would be no rendezvous in 'forty-one or ever again?) The waters of Manitou, in short, are tugging exceeding hard in this November fog and we must bring back the past and smoke and drink and hunt buffalo again. Stewart is 'sorry to hear so bad an account of poor Bill Clark' — what misfortune had overtaken him is not mentioned but he shot a good shoot too. Sublette must go west again, of course, though he grows older and wealthy and portly and is involved in politics. He will have to make the arrangements — try and pick up some tall, strong mules to be ready. 'I am very anxious to be well equipped if I can make it out, so do what you can for me by buying young animals and I think I shall take carts instead of a wagon.' Reverie and dream, the fantasy of going to the mountains again in 1841, and it may sustain a man through a winter in the Near East and after that for another year of Murthly, a castle of dignified tradition but by no means Fort Laramie. But meanwhile, 'pray get me some young deer and buffaloe and send them over.'

Delayed. It was not till 1842 that Sir William got to New York and not till the following summer that he could set out for the never-never country. Before he left Scotland he sold Logiealmond, the Drummond estate which was not entailed, for something over a million dollars and so could shoot the moon. As Western sportsman he had been first in a good many ways and this was the West's first dude expedition, with staggering luxuries, a handful of rich American bloods as paying guests, full newspaper publicity — the grand style ornate. But as it was a new kind of Western trip, so it was made in a changed West, and though the baronet met many of his old companions, the great days ran ahead of him just out of reach, a false lake on the horizon.

In the meantime, though, Bill Sublette had fulfilled his commission. On the south bank of the Tay, on the slope of Birnam Hill where Macduff's men plucked the branches of the augury, shaggy brown-black cattle with humps and evil eyes cropped the Scottish grass. Antoine and Sir William could come down from the pile of Murthly and stand pondering the buffalo. If the halfbreed in kilts felt his trigger-finger twitch, it was as vain as the twitch in the baronet's daydream, for the Tay was not the Siskadee, there was no main herd on the far side of the hill, and the cottagers spoke of these beasts as bison.[8]

In the meantime, too, Stewart had brought his artist to Grandtully. Alfred Jacob Miller had finished some of the big oils that were based on his sketches by May of 1839. Before Stewart sailed for home they were exhibited in the Apollo Gallery of New York, and some of the original water-color sketches with them. The *Mirror* briefly praised them on May 25, and the *Weekly Herald* on May 18, describing eighteen of them, had more to say and yet not enough to differentiate sketches from canvases. After the show they went to Scotland and Miller followed them there in the summer of 1840. Sir William was a lordly host and the artist's letters are a young provincial's report on the high life — the new castle (Rohallion) which Stewart was building near Murthly in the worst approved taste of the period, the ceremonies of the house, the mementoes of a globetrotter's tours, the paintings and the bric-à-brac and the heirlooms and the library, the French chef and the coachman who had been in Stewart's company at Waterloo, lords and sirs and marchionesses and ladies, the grouse season. It was the period's fashionable fiction lived out before his eyes, even to a hint that the baronet was discreetly managing an amour. Miller had a Western memento of his own, rheumatism, and Stewart dosed him with bottled waters from Europe's spas and put him through the physics and exercises of Harley Street. He paraded his fellow veteran of the West among the county families and the servants were obsequious to him, for he presided at table when Stewart was away. They talked about Samarkand.

In, presumably, the lodge. Stewart slept there, Miller says, on a 'cushioned divan of damask cloth . . . over which is spread some magnificent buffalo robes.' There were Persian prayer rugs on the floor and crimson cloth on the walls — and Indian pipes and Stewart's old tomahawk. Here, at least temporarily, the big canvases from the Apollo Gallery were hung, 'in beautiful frames.' Miller names 'The Death of the Panther,' 'Return from Hunting,' 'Indian Belle Reclining,' 'Auguste,' 'Roasting the Hump Rib,' and 'Porte d'Enfer.' He got to work on others, in the grandest style. 'Attack by Crows' was the biggest of them all; the winter ran out and he was still working on its thirty figures in ominous attitudes when spring came. At nearly the same size was 'Cavalcade,' which was the parade of the Snakes as it might be by Cornwallis' army when the world turned upside down. Also the first and biggest 'Trapper's Bride,' which the art-lovers of Baltimore kept him copying for years. These are the lifeless formalities with the brown sauce on them that hung at Murthly till

Sir William died.[9] They hung there perfectly expressing a bad style in painting, while the water-color sketches that were the real thing were kept in drawers in the Baltimore studio, research notes to be used when a fellowtownsman wanted to hang a canvas by Mr. Miller, who had a reputation as a painter of Indians. They hung there till they were sold and scattered, but meanwhile they were the West to Stewart.[10]

Miller worked on his oils, living the county life, for well over a year. Finishing in 1841, he went to London. There he studied the masterpieces in the National Gallery, painted some portraits and a classical Magdalen washing the feet of Christ, saw Catlin's exhibition without quite approving of it, and observed the spectacle of semi-artistic, semi-literary life through a winter of chill and fog that did his rheumatism no good. In April, 1842, he sailed for America to begin a career as a provincial painter. He followed it for the rest of his life, a life not too exigent since money he invested in his brothers' business multiplied. Stewart had shaped his career: he did the odd-job painting any provincial artist had to do but mostly he was Mr. Miller who had been west and had a feeling, an increasingly sentimental one, for Indians.

And in the autumn of 1842 Stewart at last returned to what he had called in a letter to Sublette 'the land of the free, the friendly, and the brave.' He spent the winter at New Orleans, his old resort and always a good town for a man with money, a taste for wines, and a talent for the sporting life. But the importance of winter was that spring would follow it. When it came Stewart went to St. Louis, Bill Sublette, Robert Campbell, such strayed revelers as might have come down from the mountains, and the details of the trip to come. That trip must be the theme of some other book than this: here it is testimony that what the Indians said about the enchanted waters was true.

* * *

In Mary Walker's journal of the trip from the rendezvous of 1838 to Waiilatpu two consecutive sentences put the necessities of travel and the mood of the trail as well as any ever written. It is August 23, the third day beyond Fort Boisé. Ermatinger and the missionaries have been traveling for five weeks — through South Pass, into the mountains between the Green and the Snake, Fort Hall, and then the desert of lava, sun, dust, thirst, canyons, and knife-edge arroyos along the Snake. When the emigration came, the whole trail from Fort Hall to the far side of the Blues, in fact, to the Willamette, would be a crescendo of strain, but this particular stretch was always the one where it first seemed intolerable. There had been a respite at Fort Boisé and Mary had asked its bourgeois, Francis Payette, to tea and had broadened the invitation to include Captain John A. Sutter of the Swiss Guards, though he was one of the damned. Then the trail again and on Tuesday they saw some choke-cherries and elderberries, a noteworthy experience, and the first sumac which this downeaster had seen in all the West. On Wednesday Conner's squaw got sick. (Gray had hired him at rendezvous, to help out at Lapwai.) She was sicker the next morning. That morning also some of the horses were found to have strayed or perhaps been stolen. And in the pause while they were being looked for Mary Walker took up her journal and with no sense of incongruity wrote down the spirit of western travel:

'Conner's squaw just about to give birth. Can't move camp on account of the horses.'

Mary, herself five months pregnant, added a sentence which anticipated the forebodings of thousands of pregnant wives crossing the desert, wives who in August of 1838 had no prescience of dust and wagon wheels along the Snake: 'Feel anxious to reach the end of this journey.'

But Mary belonged to that sisterhood to come and need not have been fearful for the sisterhood they were displacing. The squaw's hour was not yet at hand. The horses were rounded up, the train got started, and the squaw rode twelve hours in comfort though Mary thought her lot cruel. She rode twenty-five miles the next day. On Saturday, the twenty-fifth, they came down into the Grande Ronde and 'She followed camp about 30 miles. At noon she collected fuel and prepared dinner; gave birth to a daughter before sunset.' And the next day, 'The squaw came into camp about ten with the child in her arms, smart as could be.'

This was instructive for the wife of an Oregon missionary. She knew that Alice Clarissa Whitman had been born in March, 1837, the incantations and empirical medicine of Pierre Pambrun's squaw assisting Marcus Whitman. (In June, 1839, the child wandered from the mission garden to the Walla Walla River and when they went to look for her they could not find her till a Nez Perce waded in and lifted the little body from the submerged snag that held it.) She knew that Eliza Spalding had been born at Lapwai in November, 1837, Whitman riding there from Waiilatpu and taking the eight-months-old Alice Clarissa with him so that the Reverend Mr. Spalding could baptize her too when he washed Adam's sin from his own child. The knowledge could not much ameliorate Mary's dread: the mountains that loomed over you, the cliffs up whose face you had to crawl, the distance from your familiar place, the crudities of the roof you would be lucky to have over you when your hour came. The dread was the greater because of what had happened a month before at Fort Hall. Just as the missionaries reached it from the east some Nez Perces got there from the west, sent from Waiilatpu by Marcus Whitman to see if they could overtake Jason Lee, who was by now far down the Platte trail. Word had come up the Columbia from the Methodist mission on the Willamette: Anna Maria Pittman, whom Lee had married a year ago, had died in childbirth and her child was dead, too. (The missionaries sent their hunter, Richardson, to take the news after him but he did not overtake Lee till September, at the Shawnee mission just outside Westport.) While Mary's child stirred in her womb against the high pommel of the sidesaddle that constricted her, she could remember Anna Lee and contrast that tragedy in a new country with an Indian woman who could ride thirty miles and cook dinner before going into the bushes to bear her child.

Mary's foreboding was unjustified. When little Cyrus Hamlin Walker was born (after so long a labor that Mary 'almost wished I had never been married') it was at Waiilatpu, no twentieth-century hospital but clean and quiet and proof against the weather, with boiling water and all the equipment Doctor Whitman ever needed, and with not only Doctor Whitman's skill but the capable hands of Narcissa helping him. Whitman could not save her from the pioneer mother's trial of inflamed breasts, however, and after many attempts to make 'artificial nipples' and the use of 'a mare's tit' Mary lost her milk and had to endure the pioneer mother's heaviest shame and put Cyrus on the bottle.

The squaw's child was born beyond — west of — Fort Boisé. The Hudson's Bay Company's Ermatinger and its Tom McKay at Fort Hall and Francis Payette at Fort Boisé kept the missionaries safe if not comfortable, treated them with the courtesy of the Company's tradition, corrected their tenderfoot errors — and must have gaped at the spectacle they made. The contention never lifted from them, from this little band of selfless people given over to an ideal, whose dread and fatigue only added to their mutual dislike till they hated one another's guts — quarreling out of cussedness that was felt as abhorrence of a companion's lapse from righteousness, beating one another with pious reproach, then kneeling to ask divine Providence to give them Christian fellowship, of which the first requisite was that you must admit your contemner was right when he called you wrong.

Joe Meek lacked the British forbearance. Joe was having wife trouble. The Mountain Lamb having been killed during a brawl with some Bannocks two years before, Joe had married a Nez Perce. The Nez Perce women were skilled, tireless, and trained in the appreciation of husbands. ('Handsom women and verry dressey in their way,' William Clark wrote in 1805, and added that they were 'more particular than any other nation which I have passed in secreting the parts,' though their men were not.) She had borne Joe a daughter whom he named Helen Mar — tribute to the literature courses at the Rocky Mountain College. But at the Popo Agie rendezvous Mrs. Meek failed somewhat in subordination and got sore at Joe. Exercising her prerogative under Indian marriage laws, she packed her parfleches, roped her horses, and started home for her father's lodge. Connubial rage boiled up in Joe. Hanging what he describes as a kettle of alcohol from his saddle-horn, he lit out after her. He cursed his pack mules to the Sweetwater and into South Pass, camped, and woke with a head four times lifesize. The specific for that was in his kettle and he rode into the sagebrush plain singing and envisioning the consolation of lodgepoling his Nez Perce girl. It was a July day, burning-glass sun and your skin sandpaper. Joe needed water but, quartering northwest from the Sandy, he would get none till he reached the Green. Alcohol parched his throat and he treated it with more alcohol, which parched it some more. Hell of a fix to be in over a squaw.

Then he saw a couple of horses ahead of him and when he came up to them a man was stretched out on the ground and a distracted woman was watching his agonies. The Reverend Asa Bowen Smith had given up here and was, so he reported, dying of thirst. His wife Sarah recognized Joe as the agent of Providence and mastered her sobs long enough to plead for water. The angel of the trail had no water but would share his liquor with the reverend. No sale; Smith resigned himself to death. The mountain ethics did not recognize holy dying; they held that you fought back against this country. Joe loosed his vocabulary on the missionary. We may be confident that what he said exceeded Mrs. Victor's report of it.

> You're a —— pretty fellow to be lying on the ground here, lolling your tongue out of your mouth and trying to die. Die if you want to, you're of no account and will never be missed. Here's your wife, who you are keeping standing here in the hot

> sun: why don't *she* die? She's got more pluck than a white-livered chap like you. But I'm not going to leave her waiting here for you to die. Thar's a band of Indians behind me on the trail and I've been riding like —— to keep out of their way. If you want to stay here and be scalped, you can stay; Mrs. Smith is going with me. Come, Madam, let me help you to mount for we must get out of this cursed country as fast as possible.

He shouted down Sarah's protests and got her on the horse. To the dying Christian he must have been a demoniac figure — thick beard, cheeks caked with dust, red-eyed from alkali and hangover, bass voice shouting blasphemies. 'Mrs. Smith can find plenty of better men than you,' he said, quirted her horse, swore at his mules, and was off. Sarah wept, pleading to die with her beloved. Not with Joe Meek on the job. A mile farther into the sagebrush he looked back and it had worked — the Reverend Asa was sitting up, one scalp the Indians whom Joe had extemporized would not get. He brought Sarah into Ermatinger's camp that evening, Asa tooled in after a while, and Joe Meek, the boys said, had kidnaped another woman.

But no go with his Nez Perce wife. She would not come back. Joe went on with the missionaries to Fort Hall, where he signed on with Joe Walker. Presently he turned Helen Mar over to Narcissa Whitman.

As he was to do for many wagon trains disintegrating on this leg of the trail, Marcus Whitman sent food and fresh horses to meet his reinforcements. They reached Waiilatpu at the end of August. Marcus and Narcissa welcomed them and Spalding rode over from Lapwai. Praise services and prayer meetings celebrated the end of the trail and the newcomers, besides the release of a general quarrel among themselves, had the additional bliss of splitting up to take sides in the fundamental disagreement between Whitman and Spalding. At once the ladies formed a Maternal Association.

'Mrs. Whitman plenty jaw at me,' Mary Walker wrote toward the end of December. This may be anyone's impatience with Mary's whining about her sore breasts (which spills self-pity down the pages of her diary) or with her talent for perceiving sinfulness in her companions. Or it may be the erosion of Narcissa Whitman. That had begun. Waiilatpu was reducing the gay, beautiful blonde to a type-specimen of the frontier wife broken in service. Waiilatpu, a pinpoint, was a wilderness station — and what that implies. There was never an end to labor. Or to anxiety, disappointment, heartbreak. Their teeth got bad, their shoulders grew humped and stooped, their knuckles thickened, their cheeks and necks grew hollow, the spectacles received from the States two years after they were sent for never properly corrected eyes that peered at blurring print by candlelight. The voices raised in hymns came to have an undertone of sadness that broke your heart, and the gallantry and eagerness of young womanhood fell away till a visit from the halfbreed woman a few miles upcountry could make a whole week memorable. Till worn and shabby women grew tremulous at the prospect of leaving home for a visit downriver. Till they clung to the familiar hideousness of home as safer than the unfamiliar and were afraid to meet the gaze of women in small frontier villages that were nevertheless the world outside. And they were forever picturing the kitchens of Maine or Ohio or Illinois, and the known fields, and the waterbrooks of childhood, and two thousand miles away the unforgotten folk crowded in laughing groups to speak the beloved trivialities which no tongue of friend or family would ever speak in Oregon.

This is not the story of the Oregon Mission. American history composed that story with a regard for tragedy which eventually extinguishes the vexations and the silliness and the farce. Back at Lapwai, among the Nez Perces who had first conceived this beneficence and had conceived something that neither their supernaturals nor the white men could supply, the Reverend Henry Harmon Spalding, just as the missionaries reached trail's end, received into the Oregon church an old chief named Joseph. He was a good man and a true convert. He learned the stories of Jesus and raised his voice in the mission hymns. He meditated on the instruction he had received, grace and sin, virtue and magnanimity. He is an earnest that the Nez Perces tried hard — tried as hard as the white men and women who lived and died to give them Christ and the culture of the industrial order. He had a son whose lot it was, after the Nez Perces had paid forty years of loyalty for the privilege of losing earth and gaining heaven, to say that there had been enough. The son's name was Thunder Coming from the Water up Over the Land but he is Chief Joseph in the history books. When he led his people on the war trail at last and when that other Christian soldier, General Oliver Otis Howard, took repeated lickings from him, butchering many Nez Perce women and children meanwhile, doubtless the soul of William Walker was going on before.

No one will ever state the labor, suffering, and self-sacrifice of the Mission. It was all nobility, it was in part farce, but essentially it was tragedy, as history writes tragedy in the grand manner, the lives of human beings in pawn to the foredestined. These were, as Jason Lee said, Indians. These others were, as the Indians learned, white men. Perhaps the Indians might have been adapted to the nineteenth-century order and might have saved enough roots from their own order to grow in dignity and health in a changed world — if there had been time. There was no time at all. The missionaries were vortices of force thrown out in advance by the force to the eastward that was making west. They thought that they came to bring Christ but in thinking so they were deceived. They were agents of a historical energy and what they brought was the United States. The Indians had no chance. If it looked like religion it was nevertheless Manifest Destiny.

We may recollect that the first white man known to have been wrong about the Indians' religion was Christopher Columbus. On Tuesday, October 16, 1492, he wrote in the journal he was keeping for the King of Spain: 'They do not know any religion and I believe they could easily be converted to Christianity.'

* * *

By the end of 1847 the Cayuses knew that the followers of the tortured god were sorcerers. William Gray had lately given them an additional demonstration: since the Indians would not abstain out of holiness from stealing the mission vegetables, he devised a punishment for sin. He injected a violent physic in the melons and it worked. Too bad that amoebic dysentery, which has the same symptoms as Gray's physic, crossed with the emigration of '47. The emigrants brought measles, too. All told nearly half the Cayuses died. And as the Nez Perces had told Marcus Whitman when he founded Waiilatpu in 1836, the Cayuses were not Nez Perces.

Whitman was just back from a journey with Spalding — who had set out on the first journey with him nearly twelve years before. There were sick and dying Indians at the mission in the last week of November, 1847. Most of the whites were sick too. The oldest in service among them knew that bad trouble was at hand.

November 29. In the morning Whitman held a burial service for three children of a Cayuse chief who had died of the epidemic. Who, that is, had been killed by sorcery. After lunch an Indian came asking for medicine; he had friends with him. The mission women heard quarreling — and then Marcus Whitman had been struck three times in the head with a pipe-tomahawk. He died slowly while the mission people screamed and milled round him. Narcissa was bending over him when she was shot under the left arm. The women took her upstairs, then downstairs again, while yelling Cayuses chased the white and halfbreed employees. Her husband was not yet dead when she was shot again, twice, and died.

Some of them got away and reached the Hudson's Bay people at Fort Walla Walla. Eleven men, two children, and Narcissa did not. (Joe Meek's daughter Helen Mar, whom Narcissa had been nursing, died when there was no one to nurse her. The daughter of her father's friend, Mary Ann Bridger, survived the massacre but died next spring.) The Cayuses hacked them with axes and blew out their brains at close range; then they carved up some of the bodies. They did not kill everyone, however, but gathered up the women and children and took them to their own camp. They would be handy when the white posse came, for there were lots of white men in Oregon now.

They tried to get Spalding, too, but failed. He had started for Waiilatpu but heard the news in time and got back to the Nez Perces, who would kill no white men for another thirty years.

The first-comers found Narcissa's red gold hair matted with blood and her face welted from the blows of a quirt. They buried the victims in the cemetery which the mission had established for its Christian Indians. But they had to rebury Narcissa for the wolves dug up her body and ate the flesh of one of her legs.

* * *

We saw Joe Meek, after failing to reclaim his wife by his ride from the rendezvous of 1838, signing on with Joe Walker at Fort Hall. Walker had some connection with the American Fur Company but it was slight, for he was acting on his own, too, was running California horses, and was on good terms with the Hudson's Bay Company. Joe Meek took some furs to Bridger in the fall and got cursed out for dealing with the British. But there was nothing much that Bridger or the Company could do: the mountain trade was about washed up.

In this same year, 1838, the Company transformed itself from Pratte, Chouteau and Company to Pierre Chouteau, Jr., and Company, though it would always be the American Fur Company in the mind of anyone who had been to the mountains. It sent two more annual caravans to the mountains, each time holding a rendezvous in the upper valley of Green River, the first one sizable, the second so slight that some writers have assumed it never occurred. In 1839 Doctor Wislizenus was along and in 1840 Andrew Drips at last took to the Flatheads the right kind of missionary. He was the famous Jesuit Pierre-Jean de Smet; he did not ask much of the Flatheads except that they should assign his supernaturals a more powerful medicine than their own, and beyond that he loved them. The last counted most: no Protestant missionary had ever tried liking his Indians.

That ended the rendezvous system. It is doubtful if the Company had ever made money at it. The Company came to the mountain field too late to dominate it and never had the managerial success on the spot that the great rival which it destroyed, the Rocky Mountain Fur Company, had developed. Nor was it able to develop in its mountain employees the *esprit de corps* of the RMF Company, even though it hired the same trappers and the same partisans. There is no suggestion that it ever tried to develop such *esprit de corps.* West of the mountains it lost out to the Hudson's Bay Company, with its lower costs and more convenient base. In the mountains it destroyed the RMF Company but could not destroy the new kind of Opposition that developed in its place. So it abandoned the rendezvous system altogether, concentrating on its fixed posts. At the posts it traded with Indians and such white trappers as it could subsidize or attract. Increasingly it came to base its business on the trade in buffalo robes.

The mountains, then, were left to the British, to small American companies, and to little groups of trappers who banded together. The history of the mountain fur trade from here on is the history of such small companies and smaller groups.

We have already seen an opposition post established almost within gunshot of Fort Laramie and there would be another one there almost at once. There were similar small posts on the South Platte and at the Pueblo. Most of them were short-lived, and others like them briefly appeared in many places — in Brown's Hole, near the Three Forks, in the heart of the Company's private preserve along the Yellowstone, on the Gunnison, in the Medicine Bow, on the Chugwater, on La Bonte's Creek. Meanwhile the Bents and St. Vrain at their great establishment on the Arkansas (La Junta, Colorado) attracted more veteran mountain men than all the others put together and probably made more money. The Bents were the fairest manipulators of Indians in the history of the mountain trade and maintained an elsewhere unheard-of standard of honor in dealing with them.

They cornered the business of the southern Cheyennes, almost cornered that of the Arapahos, and contrived something like a permanent prairie truce in their vicinity. They also had a sounder economic base, since their fur business was combined with their function as factors and entrepreneurs and carriers in the Santa Fe trade. But their great prosperity — centered well out of the mountains — was just beginning as this narrative ends.

The small companies that came into the mountains, built their little posts and advertised for white and red customers were the new Opposition. The Company met it head on, which is to say with spring floods of alcohol, loudly protesting this debauch of the Indian. But with the narrower profit margin of these days the ability of small companies to operate with a smaller overhead counted enormously, which meant still greater floods of alcohol. The mountain Indians had never dreamed of such big drunks or such frequent repetitions of them. Among these Indians must now be numbered the Oglala Sioux and some of the Brules and a few of the Miniconjous, and at the mouth of Laramie Fork where the Company and the Opposition looked down into each other's quadrangles, liquor became the currency of the trade. The Richard brothers, Lieutenant Lupton, and the Company had the Sioux drunk, vomiting, and murdering one another and all comers whenever they had robes to sell. All earlier debaucheries seem sweet by comparison.[11] The Company fell back on an expedient it had used before and had its Andrew Drips made Indian Agent for the Upper Missouri, with jurisdiction throughout the West. He was directed by the Commissioner of Indian Affairs to stamp out the liquor traffic some more, and the Company supplied him with deputies and interpreters from its payroll. Stamping out the liquor traffic meant confiscating Opposition liquor, and Drips worked hard at it, carrying out other commissions for the Company at the same time.[12] He had the usual success: he raised the price. Company and Opposition, with newcomers from as far away as Taos, were still getting the Sioux murderously drunk, and the Company was still weeping over the shame of it all, when Francis Parkman got to Fort Laramie in 1846.

* * *

Following 1838 we must see our veterans in the light of these conditions. Kit Carson, on his way to national celebrity, the safeguarding of Frémont, and an eventual brigadier-generalship in the United States Army, formed a connection with the Bents.

He signed on as a hunter at their fort but also he married a New Mexican heiress and became a landowner. He maintained a group of veterans for miscellaneous purposes, hunting, trading, trailing, guard duty, but also trapping. The Carson men went into the mountains for beaver and sometimes Kit went with them. They were a specialist and expert group and Kit was bright, he kept them equipped with the newest armament and possibles and he learned business as few mountain men ever did.

The Carson men went mostly into the Colorado Rockies, which now became the most important field in the trade. The trapped-out country to the north and northwest did come back somewhat, beaver increased, but only slowly. The importance of Brown's Hole is of this period; some veterans spoke of it mellowly, others abominated it. There was no difference of opinion about South Park; it was a paradise, the last place in the mountains where the old life could be lived to the full. Many of those who have appeared in these pages were associated with it at one time or another but it is primarily the Bill Williams country, thanks to Lieutenant Ruxton. Antoine Robidou had a post on the Gunnison for a while and another one on the Duchesne. Henry Fraeb with John Sarpy and in some relationship with the Company had a post on St. Vrain's Fork (Boulder County, Colorado) for a while. Then on Battle Creek, a tributary of the Little Snake, in August 1841 he died as a mountain man should, in an all-out battle with the Sioux, taking enough of them to hell with him to pay his toll.

Fraeb and Bridger had larger companies than was common in these days. Mostly they were small bands, half a dozen or a dozen co-equals with a couple of horses and a couple of mules apiece, functionally equipped, carrying their own traps and curing their own pelts without pork-eater assistance, carrying also a small pack of awls and bells and cottons and tobacco for the Indians, enough powder, a little coffee. They had the skill of their kind, never more tested than in this period of small hunts. They sold their plews at the posts, stocked up on necessaries, and rode off into the canyons, divining the places where beaver might be taken and the equally critical places where Indians might be met in quantity. In quantity, Indians now had to be avoided since they could no longer be fought. For ten years after 1838 such groups of free companions combed the old stamping grounds over and over: the Humboldt, the Snake and Salmon, Cache Valley, the Big Hole and Deer Lodge Prairie, Picrre's Hole and Ogden's Hole and Jackson's Hole and Gardner's Hole and Ross's Hole, the upper Green, the Medicine Bow, Wind River, Powder River, the Three Forks, the Clearwater — all the great names. They worked minutely, more precariously than ever and more skillfully too, and, in fact, such a reputation as Bill Hamilton's could be won wholly in these years. Yet they were already vestigial and though ghostly mountain men lingered in the farthest gulches well after the country belonged to the settlers, just as ghostly prospectors linger now in the places where the metal was, they were historical curiosities.

They kept on because they had no other trade and could seldom adjust to other ways of living. Some gave it up — Joe Meek and Doc Newell, for example, going off to be respectable citizens in the Oregon settlements. Some kept it up because they scorned softness and did not care to ask anything of anyone. These supplied the emigrant trains and military expeditions with guides, counselors, and wet-nurses. In fact, this was the last proper function of a mountain man except for one other that fell to a considerable number of the best, to Andrew Drips, for instance, and with greater honesty and honor to Carson and Fitzpatrick. As officials in the Bureau of Indian Affairs, which needed many kinds of officials, they were the best representatives the Indians ever had and did their futile best to protect them against the corruption and stupidity of a government which was committed to exploiting them on behalf of the emigration.

In theory the United States had a policy toward the Indians which was at least noble and in a way just. The theory was never consulted by the reality. In practice such men as these provided just about all the intelligence and fairness the Indians got until our own time.

Some veterans added their tipis to the villages of their wives and became Indians in fact, moving about with them in the contracting, increasingly precarious existence of the Plains tribes. These are the ones whom the settlers hated most, alleging against them every villainy that could be alleged against Indians with the further one that they incited their companions to make trouble. They were supposed to live by preying on emigrants and settlers, raiding their herds, stealing the equipment of their farms, terrorizing them in the hope of driving them out of the country, murdering them on raids or up dry gulches. Some part of the allegation was sometimes true but most of it was the anger of men in a hostile country assigning a personal agency to acts of nature.

As the new phase of the West developed, new varieties of hardworking, hard-living men came to symbolize the violence of life in a violent country — stage-drivers, for instance, express-messengers, pony-express riders, bullwhackers. Few veteran mountain men, though many were young, entered these specialties. Gradually a new species developed, called scouts. All told there were a good many of them, though nowhere near so many as got themselves hired and photographed in costume. They were scouts because part of their trade was to read sign, find water, and explain Indians for army detachments, and at this job they were frequently expert, having learned it in the field, though they were sometimes bunglers and fools. But in part also they were vermin-exterminators, like those now hired by government agencies or cattle associations to shoot pumas and poison coyotes: they applied their skill to tracking down solitary Indians or small groups of them and murdering them. Presently they found still another function: to advertise the violent life by means of the nation's developing publicity. In this function The Scout became an image, as The Cowboy has become within this last generation long after the end of the Cattle Kingdom. This function required him to wear costumes which he had tailored for him by tamed squaws, buckskins with fringes longer than a medicine man's and covered with the beaded symbols of antithetical tribes or ceremonies — to weigh himself down with hardware, to grow hair, to look bellicose, and to be photographed. He thus reached an audience which would pay to see him parody his skills and pantomime his press agents' lies under canvas. The West has been fecund in the production of phonies: the Scout was one of the earliest and just about the most noisome. The type lingered on well into this century and men no more than middle-aged today can remember it, all over the West, elder vice with a loud voice, repulsive not because of the lies but because the lies were cheap. Scouts invariably claimed to have been mountain men. Few ever were.

The later years of the veteran summed up as peace-officer in the settlements like Joe Meek, or the fully converted citizen like Jim Clyman, or the elder adviser like Jim Bridger. As the West grew there was always a use for such men as these three — and there was always a use for Old Gabe till he grew so old indeed that he could be robbed in safety. Jim guided emigrant trains. He shepherded captains and colonels and generals and led their detachments by the hand. He ministered to settlers and explorers and surveyors and Mormons and railroad builders. He was an atlas of the West and a compendium of information to whoever needed geography or skill. He is the truest embodiment of the way of life that lingered on after its time.

After his partner Fraeb was killed Jim took another one, the Louis Vasquez of our first chapter, a man qualified in lore and experience to be his partner, of aristocratic birth like Fontenelle — and bits of aristocratic elegance clung to him in the mountains like cottonwood fluff. Bridger and Vasquez hired a band of their peers and, like other partisans, tried to live on the picked bones of the trade. The living was thin indeed. But they saw a way to adapt to the new era. How well along that era was can be seen in the wagon trains that were bigger every year — but more revealing is the coming of John Charles Frémont. The Pathfinder, the West's Greatest Adventurer, traveled the trackless wilderness to Fort Laramie, through South Pass, and on to Captain Stewart's Wind River lakes no more than thirty-two years after Andrew Henry and thirty-one years after Wilson Hunt, a mere decade after Bonneville, and such men as Kit Carson, Tom Fitzpatrick, and Basil Lajeunesse, who had the privilege of witnessing his discoveries, had had only a generation to learn the country which he was showing to them. The presence of an Army officer on assignment beyond South Pass was an even clearer indication than the wagon trains.

Bridger and Vasquez acted on the indications. In the valley of Black's Fork, Uinta County, the southwestern corner of Wyoming, a day's ride from the sites of many rendezvous, on the natural route from the Sandy, a route which they foresaw would prove a better one for wagons coming out of South Pass than the routes by which they had taken pack trains westward — in the valley of Black's Fork they built a new post, Fort Bridger. They established it not as a headquarters for beaver hunters and not as a depot for the trade with Indians, but as a supply station for emigrant trains. It was built (apparently in the summer of 1842) in time to serve the first really big wave, the one which the texts call the Great Migration, the emigration of 1843, and the history of the West through the next fifteen years could be intelligently written along radii that center here. With the establishment of Fort Bridger, General Chittenden is content to say, the era of the mountain man ended.

* * *

But 1839. It was autumn when Jason Lee sailed with 'the Great Reinforcement,' fifty-one additional colonists for the Methodist mission on the Willamette. Far too many of them were parsons to satisfy Lee's sense of what was needed to save Oregon. (He had a new wife among them.) But the movement that makes this the first year of the new era had got under way in the spring.

We have seen various new types of Western venturers arise. One of these repeated itself with distinction as Doctor Frederick Adolphus Wislizenus, a physician of St. Louis who had been driven out of Germany as a student-revolutionist and was now an amateur botanist, mineralogist, and geographer. Also he had an itching foot and a curiosity about the far side of the hill. They were taking him to the Great American Desert, to a blank space which he wanted to fill in — and in 1846 they would again take him west and into the fantastic.[13] In 1839 he is Bradbury, Townsend, Nuttall, Audubon. Another type was somewhat overblown as the Reverend J. S. Griffin. A Yankee exiled in Ohio, he had known Henry Harmon Spalding there and a longing to take up his friend's vocation had grown on him. The American Board would not send him to the Indians, no one would send him though he got the commendation of a village church in faraway Connecticut. Since he could not get commissioned to the service, he determined to follow his own light. He started from Ohio for the Oregon Mission. On the way to the frontier he picked up two items of standard equipment for the Oregon missionary, a wife (she had been christened Desire) and a lay assistant.

These were established types and, true to type, Doctor Wislizenus and the missionaries sought the escort of the Company. Its caravan of carts and pack animals, smaller than usual, was commanded this year by Black Harris. But a wholly new type, this year's creation (and Jason Lee's), also joined Harris. A line of ink was written at the top of a fresh, blank page. Some of these, even, were whispering a word which meant nothing to any of them except what it had meant to their solitary predecessor, John A. Sutter, that is, pure emotion. The word was 'California.'

In these people and in another group traveling west by a different route but carrying the same charge, the new type at its first appearance exhibits all the characters of the emigrant: total ignorance, anxious stupidity, above all the inability to get along with one another that was to make the wagon trains split into halves, quarters, eights, tending always to reduce the society to the family.

They quarreled and blundered from the beginning but Harris kept enough control over their vagaries to get them to Horse

Creek. Here within sight of the crumbling ruins of Bonneville's Fort Nonsense, the last true rendezvous (for next year's would be only a scout) staged a parody of the great days. It is enough that Doctor Wislizenus could write, 'Diminution in the beaver catch made itself noticeable . . . in the quieter behavior of the trappers. There was little drinking of spirits and almost no gambling.'

Francis Ermatinger, whose principals had briefly won a losing fight, shepherded Wislizenus and the pilgrims to Fort Hall, and here the new type fixed another character by completely atomizing. The pilgrims had fought one another to the crumbling point: a party of only twelve, including the missionaries, now became three parties. The missionaries struggled on toward Waiilatpu. So, separately, did five of the pilgrims. Two other pilgrims established another permanent variation by turning back. They hired as guide Paul Richardson, who had chaperoned last year's missionaries and then hurried after Jason Lee with word of his wife's death. This year Richardson had come back to Horse Creek with Harris and on to Fort Hall with Ermatinger. Now he took his new employers quartering past the Bear River Valley in the direction of Brown's Hole. They met and for a while traveled with one of the new era's little groups of trappers described above. (One trapper had a Ute wife he wanted to get rid of; he offered her to Wislizenus as 'young, gentle, and in first-rate order.') In the melodramatic scenery of Brown's Hole they reached a new trading post, Fort Davy Crockett. It was a holding of the Bill Craig for whose squaw Mary Walker had made a dress last year and William Sinclair, whose brother Alexander we saw wounded long ago in Pierre's Hole.

And here at Fort Davy Crockett Wislizenus and the two ex-pilgrims cut the trail of the other group of innocents who had started to settle Oregon this year and were helping the first group fix the type. The Oregon Dragoons.

In fact, the new type had expressed itself even more completely with the Oregon Dragoons, achieving full luxuriance on first appearance. On May 21, 1839, seventeen citizens of Peoria, Illinois, arrived at Independence. Two others of like mind joined them there. The historian of these greenhorn-pilgrims is Thomas Jefferson Farnham, under whose leadership they had traveled from Peoria. Their authors, however, were the Reverend Jason Lee and the Chinook boy whom he had named William Brooks. The Chinook, 'a true Flathead,' had spent the winter at Peoria and had spent it talking about his country, Oregon, as the earthly

Paradise. So seventeen Peorians, ranging in age from the early twenties to an astonishing fifty-six, had formed an Oregon emigrating society — and the mad dream of Hall J. Kelley was not so crazy after all.

It was Farnham who christened them the Oregon Dragoons and they carried a guidon inscribed 'Oregon or the Grave.' None of them made the grave, whereas at least nine and perhaps ten made Oregon. The new type, the saltation, was equipped with nervous system and instincts on first appearance. Instinct, fidelity to the thousands who were to come, made these first specimens organize themselves as both a society and a joint-stock company. The society held a town meeting and reaffirmed Farnham as captain. At Independence they bought a little wagon and a gorgeous big tent and wasted their money on greenhorn stuff. But May 21 made it late for the Platte route (Harris had jumped off more than a month earlier) and Andrew Sublette, who had already reached Independence on the return trip from his holdings, advised them to travel by the Santa Fe Trail — to make better time perhaps and to detour so small a party round the Sioux and the Cheyennes, who were on the prod this year. They attached themselves to a Santa Fe freight caravan and started out.

They had already been quarreling and they kept it up. They were further establishing the type — denying the authority of their elected officers, questioning decisions, disputing routes, rejecting all trail-discipline, bellyaching about alleged fraud and alleged tyranny and alleged or real stupidity, asserting with fists and endless oratory the freeborn American's right to cleave unto his own property in all circumstances and to commit any damned idiocy his whim might suggest. Type-character: already at the Osage River three had had enough and turned back to the now greatly magnified comforts of Peoria. Another: at the crossing of the Arkansas three others would travel no farther with such fools and grumblers as their companions, would not even travel toward Oregon, but slanted off toward New Mexico. (In return, however, the vision was vouchsafed to a member of the Santa Fe wagon train and he joined up for Oregon.) Another: at Bent's Fort they deposed Farnham from his captaincy for incompetence and fraud and wastefulness and strong drink and all the other grievances with which captains were to be charged from now on, then excommunicated him and four of his supporters and broke up.

The larger party, the eight who fired the five, struck north from Bent's Fort east of the mountains to St. Vrain's Fort on the

South Platte. There one of them stayed for the winter. The others made their way thence with a group of trappers through the most formidable Colorado mountains to Brown's Hole. They got to it after Wislizenus had left on his way home, and there all but one of them spent the winter. Of these one seems eventually to have got back to the States but four made Oregon in 1840. But among the trappers at Fort Davy Crockett when they arrived was Doc Newell. Joe Meek's current squaw was there, too, and so was his outfit, a meager one. Presently Joe himself arrived and he and Doc Newell packed up for Fort Hall and eventually the Nez Perces. So one of the original Oregon Dragoons, Robert Shortress, traveled with them to Fort Hall and there found trapper and halfbreed escort to Fort Boisé and on to Waiilatpu. One of the eight thus made Oregon in 1839.

The rump outfit, those with Farnham, did a little better. At Bent's Fort they hired a mountain man named Kelly to hold their hands and he took them crosslots to Fort Davy Crockett. On the way there they kept meeting little groups of trappers, the new era outfits, and others were at the fort when they reached it — among them Newell, the Robinson who was going to be 'Uncle Jim' to many wagon trains, and Sinclair and Bill Craig. The proprietors offered the by now soul-weary pilgrims the post's hospitality for the winter — mild weather, unsurpassed scenery, plenty of game, fabulous trapper talk. But here came Paul Richardson from the north, with Doctor Wislizenus and the fainthearts who had fallen away from the other great dream. Richardson's talk scared off two of the remnant Dragoons but Farnham and the other two would stick, would not even accept Sinclair's snug winter. A Snake at the post was going home and the three who were left hired him to guide them to Fort Hall. The country in between was as safe from hostile Indians as any part of the West could be, but no part of the mountains was safe for so small a party. Farnham was fixing some further characters of the type.

They called their guide Jim. He took them through a wasteland empty alike of Indians and trappers. To the middle Green, to Ham's Fork, to Bear River. Here on Bear River, August 28, 1839, at the meridian of the West, occurred a splendid transit of past and future.

That morning Jim suddenly shouted 'Hoss!' and pointed up the valley. The greenhorns had learned enough to fort up and renew their priming. Three anxious men behind logs, they remembered with sudden poignancy all they had ever heard about the Blackfeet, about all Indians. They waited while Jim rode out making the peace sign. But the single horseman made the same sign and presently was shaking Jim's hand and pounding his shoulder. Friends meeting on the trail. It was all right.

The stranger came in with Jim and when he told his name Farnham recognized the original of a wax statue he had seen at the St. Louis Museum on his way west, a trapper locked in mortal combat with a grizzly. This was the famous bear-killer, Joe Meek.

Joe was on his way to Fort Davy Crockett and his wife and outfit and his partner Newell. He had a shoulder of antelope and in the mountain code offered them breakfast. They had eaten, however, and what they wanted was instruction — the type held true at this meeting. Joe said there was a village of Nez Perces only a day's ride beyond Fort Hall. He himself was going to winter with them when he could get his wife. (A Nez Perce whom he called Virginia; she was to bear him eight children.) He advised the greenhorns to join the village, too, and travel with it to the Nez Perce country where there was a mission, Spalding's Lapwai. The lava and the peaks, the rivers and the gulches, the sagebrush and the thirst — the country between Bear River and trail's end was in Joe's mind and he thought, gently, that they would need the Nez Perces.

Farnham thought him much like an Indian: 'the same wild, unsettled, watchful expression of the eye, the same unnatural gesticulation in conversation, the same unwillingness to use words when a sign, a contortion of the face or body, or movement of the hand will manifest thought [but this was only because he was talking to people who couldn't speak the language]; in standing, walking, reading, in all but complexion, he was an Indian.'

He cursed the American Fur Company for them. It had used his skill, risked his life, paid him little, and now cast him off. Every trapper whom Farnham had met — a good many — had said the same. And he looked poor: it was starvin' times for Joe Meek. He had so sparse and worn an outfit that the wind, which can be cold of an August morning in Bear River Valley, 'made him shake like an aspen leaf.'

The equinoctial had intersected the ecliptic. Thus the old West and the new West passed each other.

Let them watch out for Blackfeet, Joe said. There were some near Soda Springs, which they would presently reach. Farther along they would find Joe's white horse. It had given out and he had had to cache its pack. Take it along with them and leave it for him at Fort Hall. Welcome to use it if they could.

Joe Meek, the bear-killer, a Carson man, a Bridger man, an RMF Company man, a Company man — Joe Meek, free trapper, raised his hand and rode off toward Fort Davy Crockett. And the three greenhorns, authentic settlers, and their Snake guide took to the trail again, toward the Columbia.

# APPENDICES:

## 1. CHRONOLOGY OF THE MOUNTAIN FUR TRADE

### Before the Narrative Begins

1804–1806. Lewis and Clark expedition to the mouth of the Columbia and return. By way of the Missouri, the Clearwater, and the Snake.

1806. John Colter, a member of the Lewis and Clark expedition, returns to (probably) the valley of the Yellowstone with a small group of trappers and winters there.

1807. Manuel Lisa, employing Colter and another member of the Lewis and Clark party as guides, builds a fort at the mouth of the Big Horn River, in the Crow country — the first post for the mountain trade.

1807–1808. Colter travels through Jackson's Hole, Yellowstone Park, Pierre's Hole, and adjacent country.

1809. Lisa forms the Missouri Fur Company for upriver trading; among his partners are William Clark, Pierre Chouteau, Sr., and Andrew Henry. Several parties are sent up the Missouri, the main one going up the Yellowstone to winter at the Big Horn post.

1810. Under Andrew Henry, this party ascends the Missouri to the Three Forks, in the Blackfoot country, and builds a post there. Forced out by the hostility of the Blackfeet, Henry takes his party over the Continental Divide to winter on the north fork of the Snake, thenceforth called Henry's Fork. Some of his men enter Green River Valley and Jackson's Hole from the west.

1811. Under Wilson Price Hunt, the overland portion of John Jacob Astor's Pacific Fur Company crosses to the mouth of the Columbia, leaving some members of the party in the interior West. The other half of Astor's Company reaches the Columbia by sea. Astoria founded. The Missouri Fur Company abandons the Big Horn post.

1812–1813. Robert Stuart, one of the Astorians, goes east overland, perhaps making the first traverse of South Pass by a white man. (Both Henry's men and the Astorians who stayed in the interior may have heard of or traveled it before him.)

1813. Astoria is surrendered to the Northwest Company.

In the next ten years much trading and trapping on the upper Missouri and its tributaries and a number of ventures toward the mountains but no penetration of the interior West.

1821. After hostilities amounting to civil war and at the command of Parliament, the Hudson's Bay Company and the Northwest Company merge.

1822. General William H. Ashley forms a partnership with Andrew Henry. Their first expedition builds a post at the mouth of the Yellowstone and sends a detachment to the Musselshell.

1823. Ashley's second expedition is stopped by the Arikaras. Colonel Leavenworth's punitive expedition against the Arikaras peters out. The Missouri is temporarily closed. Henry abandons the Yellowstone Post and moves his party to the Big Horn. Thence some of his men reach the Wind River Mountains.

1824. Ashley-Henry men cross the Wind River Mountains to Green River Valley, one party by South Pass, another just south of it. Thence they spread out over much of the interior West. Jedediah Smith explores the Snake River and Clark's Fork and looks over Hudson's Bay Company operations. Henry retires from the partnership. A rich harvest of furs is sent from the mountains to Ashley in St. Louis. Jim Bridger and Jed Smith visit Great Salt Lake — just before or just after Etienne Provost does the same.

1825. Ashley, with Tom Fitzpatrick who had earlier traveled part of the trail in reverse, pioneers the Platte route to the mountains. He crosses the Uinta Mountains and quarters across northern Utah. First mountain rendezvous on Henry's Fork of Green River (not of the Snake). His partisans buy a large catch of furs from Hudson's Bay Company deserters.

1826. Ashley's last rendezvous — held either in Cache Valley or Willow (Weber) Valley, Utah. He sells out to Smith, Jackson, and Sublette, for whom he thereafter acts as purveyor and banker. Jedediah Smith crosses to California by the Virgin River and the southern deserts.

1827. Parties of the new firm trap both sides of the Continental Divide and invade the Blackfoot country. Rendezvous at Bear Lake (Utah). Jedediah Smith returns from California, crossing the Salt Desert, then goes back by a variant of the southern route. Pratte, Chouteau, and Company is allied with the American Fur Company as the operating branch of the Western Department. The Columbia Fur Company also is incorporated in the trust as the Upper Missouri Outfit, under Kenneth McKenzie. McKenzie sends Samuel Tulloch into the mountains to look over the Opposition.

1828. Jedediah Smith moves north to Oregon, most of his men being killed by Indians en route; the survivors are protected and their furs recovered by McLoughlin of the Hudson's Bay Company. The American Fur Company sends various agents through the mountains to buy Indians and trappers away from the Opposition. Rendezvous at Great

Salt Lake, most of the year's trapping having been done west of the Divide.

1829. The partners trap the Yellowstone Park country, Snake River, the Wind River Mountains, the Tetons and adjacent territory, the Yellowstone and its principal tributaries, and well into the Blackfoot country. Jackson's Hole receives its name. Rendezvous in Pierre's Hole. The American Fur Company builds Fort Union (originally named Fort Floyd), which is to become its most important post, at the mouth of the Yellowstone.

1830. Smith, Jackson, and Sublette, having made a killing in virgin territory, sell out to their leading partisans, who name the new firm the Rocky Mountain Fur Company. Jacob Berger opens the Blackfoot trade for the American Fur Company, which also sends brigades into the mountains. Rendezvous near the Wind River Mountains, probably on the Popo Agie.

1831. Plans of both trust and Opposition for a summer rendezvous fail to work out. Jedediah Smith, entering the Santa Fe trade with his partners, is killed on the Cimarron Crossing. The American Fur Company builds Fort Piegan at the mouth of the Marias River, deep in the Blackfoot country, and intensifies its on-the-spot competition with the RMF Company, sending brigades under Fraeb, Drips, and Vanderburgh into the mountains. The Nez Perces and Flatheads send their mission to St. Louis.

## Covered by the Narrative

1832. (In the text, the events of this year are narrated following some of those of 1833.) The American Fur Company abandons Fort Piegan and builds Fort McKenzie a few miles away. It also builds Fort Cass in the Crow country, thus completing a chain of fixed posts for the mountain trade. Its brigades go on learning the mountain craft the hard way, consistently losing out to the RMF Company. Wyeth and Bonneville go west. Bonneville builds his fort. Rendezvous at Pierre's Hole, followed by the Battle of Pierre's Hole George Catlin goes up the Missouri.

1833. Captain Stewart goes west with Robert Campbell. Maximilian goes up the Missouri. Rendezvous on the Green, at Fort Bonneville and Horse Creek. Wyeth returns from the Columbia to the Snake. Joe Walker goes to California.

1834. Wyeth goes west again, taking the Methodist mission (Jason Lee) with him. William Sublette builds Fort Laramie and induces the RMF Company to doublecross Wyeth, who goes on to the Snake and builds Fort Hall. Rendezvous on Ham's Fork. The RMF Company dissolves, being succeeded by a partnership of Fitzpatrick, Bridger, and Milton Sublette. The partnership gives up the old alliance with Sublette & Campbell and makes a contract with the American Fur Company and is presently absorbed.

1835. Samuel Parker and Marcus Whitman, representing the American Board of Commissioners for Foreign Missions, go west. Fontenelle's party attacked by cholera. Rendezvous near Fort Bonneville. Whitman and Captain Stewart return to the States.

1836. Whitman and Spalding and their wives go west. Missions established at Waillatpu and Lapwai. The Liberator of the Indian Nations, Montezuma II, begins the conquest of New Mexico and California. Rendezvous on Horse Creek.

1837. Smallpox epidemic on the upper Missouri. Stewart takes his artist, Miller, west. Rendezvous on the Green, between Horse Creek and New Fork.

1838. Stewart's last Western trip. Final reinforcement of the Oregon Mission. Rendezvous at the mouth of the Popo Agie.

# 2. THE FIRST ILLUSTRATORS OF THE WEST

## 1

### The Image and the Fantasy

In the spring of 1837, Alfred Jacob Miller, the young painter whose sketches are reproduced in this book, started for the Far West with his patron, Captain William Drummond Stewart. Historians have always given that same year, 1837, as the one in which George Catlin opened his Indian Gallery, his famous exhibition of Western paintings. The evidence is clear, however, that he exhibited it in both Buffalo and Pittsburgh, if nowhere else, in 1836. There is no reason to suppose that Miller had seen it before he went West but he had probably read descriptions of it. Catlin's first Western trip had occurred in 1832. Since then he had had abundant publicity at his own and other hands.

In 1837, however, Catlin's Indian Gallery did open in New York, and the year may be taken as the beginning of its celebrity. His catalogue of that year runs to thirty-six pages and lists 494 paintings, which he had made during the preceding five years, and a number of 'Indian curiosities.' Up to the fall of 1839 the Gallery was exhibited in various American cities; then Catlin took it to London. There, as the first Wild West Show, it proved to be a sellout success. The nobility, scientists, travelers, and the general public thronged Egyptian Hall and Catlin became a social lion and an important figure in the world of learning. Later he toured the provinces with his show and eventually took it to the Continent, where his success was repeated. It remained abroad till it passed out of Catlin's hands in 1852. His creditors brought most of it back to the United States and the paintings eventually found a permanent home in the National Museum.

Meanwhile it had been renamed 'Catlin's Indian Collection' and had been considerably enlarged. Catlin says that he took eight tons of freight with him when he sailed for England in 1839 (he is not given to understatement) and this was by no means all of his collection, though it did include two live grizzly bears 'from the Rocky Mountains' which he was not able to show in Egyptian Hall. There were more than six hundred paintings and Catlin went on adding to them through the years. (He also made many copies, some of which hang in English town and country houses today.) A visitor who remained unsatiated after looking at six hundred canvases could go on to two dozen dummies dressed in genuine Indian costumes and a sizable museum of medicine bundles, shields, amulets, baskets, robes, travois, moccasins, weapons, pipes, and other artifacts. There were learned, dramatic lectures by the proprietor and *tableaux vivants* posed by local supernumeraries in Indian dress. Presently genuine Indians replaced the supernumeraries. Catlin appears not to have imported them himself but to have engaged various parties brought over by other showmen who tried to cash in on his success. He had them present pantomimes of hunting, skulking, and scalping and the war dances and other ceremonies of various tribes. He was particularly interested in the Indians we deal with in this book, the Plains tribes, from whom in fact his celebrity derived. But since his first actors were Chippewas he probably had to instruct them in the Plains ceremonies. Later some Iowas joined him and doubtless they knew as much about the dances of their Western neighbors as Catlin did.

Meanwhile in 1841 Catlin had published a book, *Letters and Notes on the Manners, Customs, and Condition of the North American Indians.* It was copiously illustrated with crude outline drawings from his paintings and was to be reprinted many times. In 1844 came *Catlin's North American Indian Portfolio*, an album of twenty-five prints in which the lithographer sometimes considerably improved on the originals. (Later editions had thirty-one plates. Note that some of the lithography was by Catlin himself.) These two publications supplemented the Indian Gallery in establishing the first set of conventions of Western painting. Catlin published other books as well and after losing his Gallery painted hundreds of other Indian pictures, but these are not germane to our present purpose.

Catlin's understanding, accuracy, and reliability were attacked during his own time and echoes of the attacks have been repeated down to ours. It is true that he was an enthusiast and even a monomaniac, that he misunderstood much of what he saw, as anyone in his place must have done, that he held some wildly untenable theories, that he never lost his Rousseauian prepossessions about savages in a state of nature, that he made many mistakes, and even that he falsified or invented some details. Nevertheless, he is in the main reliable and both his books and paintings have been immensely important to American ethnology ever since 1837. So far as the Plains tribes are concerned, in fact, and despite all the observations of earlier travelers among them, American ethnology may be said to begin with Catlin. (And with Maximilian of Wied, who will be discussed presently.)

In view of this great and permanent importance it is hard to understand why historians and art critics have disregarded Catlin. There has been no extended attempt to write authoritatively about him since Thomas Donaldson's uncritical and sometimes inaccurate 'The George Catlin Indian Gallery,' which was published as an appendix to the Smithsonian *Annual Report* for 1885. The few brief papers about him since then are superficial, or repeat Donaldson's errors, or are devoted to limited aspects of Catlin's work. The most scholarly of them all is almost useless, since what it says about the paintings is based not on the originals but on the later Cartoons, which differ from them in important ways. In fact it is hard to make dependable statements about Catlin on the basis of what has been written so far. And this is a pity, for he was an extraordinary man, a man with a certain greatness in him; his work is notable and his life was picturesque. Purely as an adventure story his biography would be fascinating and historians, whether of our society or of our art, would find him richly significant. His importance to this book, however, stems from the Indian Gallery. Among the 494 paintings which it contained in 1837 were the first portraits of Plains Indians ever made in their own country and the first pictorial representation of the Far West. Catlin was the first painter of the West.

That last statement must stand, though to be strictly accurate it should read: Catlin was the first painter of the West who had any effect. One painter, Samuel Seymour, had actually gone to the foot of the Front Range in Colorado in 1820, seventeen years before any other got so far west. Another, Peter Rindisbacher, had lived at Lord Selkirk's Red River colony from 1821 to 1826 (he was twenty in the latter year) and had done some painting there, on the edge of the high plains. A third, Joshua Shaw, may have gone up the Missouri in 1820 but if he did he has left no trace.

Of these only Samuel Seymour counts at all. An Englishman by birth, he was an engraver and painter established in Philadelphia and he went West with Stephen H. Long's expedition up the South Platte in 1819–1820. Six of his pictures, crude but authentic, appear as illustrations in Edwin James's account of the expedition, and three others in the London edition. The book itself says that he made a hundred and fifty views, of which sixty were finished by the time of publication. Some of his canvases were displayed at Peale's Museum, where Maximilian saw them in 1832, and presumably were sold at auction in 1854. They seem to have entirely disappeared. James's book was published in so small an edition that it has become extremely rare and the influence of Seymour's canvases, if any, was purely local. He may fairly be said to have been without issue, yet he did draw western buffalo (though not in herds) and four of his illustrations actually depict the Rocky Mountains. (They appear in a separate *Atlas*; they are steel engravings. But in the London edition one has become a woodcut and is run in the text. Seymour's Indians were Otos and Kansas.)

Rindisbacher was born in Switzerland and both the Indians and the whites in his pictures are usually dressed in vaguely Swiss costumes.

He has almost entirely vanished from human knowledge and the sixty-odd paintings of his that remain are difficult to get at. They are also exceedingly crude: his buffalo, for instance, have a strong resemblance to llamas, though they must have been done from the life near Pembina. A water color of his called 'Inside of a Skin Tent' and dated 1824 may be the first actual illustration of a Plains tipi — and yet it looks like no tipi known to ethnology. Doctor Grace Lee Nute says that sixty-four of his pictures are known still to exist and some of them were lithographed during his lifetime and therefore circulated. Two of the illustrations in McKenney and Hall's *Indian Tribes* are attributed to him (one incorrectly, perhaps) and the *American Turf Register and Sporting Magazine* published at least ten lithographs and engravings of his work. Yet he, too, must be dismissed. His Indians were sometimes of the marginal Plains tribes, and he did paint buffalo, but none of his landscape is truly Western, the crudity of his work could hardly be overstated, and he appears to have had no effect at all.[1]

Though the judgment has to be made with certain reservations, it is nevertheless true that Catlin was not a good painter. He appears to have been best at miniatures — at least one of his mother, Polly Sutton Catlin, now in the National Museum, is charming and competent. He was entirely self-taught and devoted himself to miniatures and portraits until the ambition of picturing the Indians for posterity seized him, but examples of this period are hard to find. The tradition that he painted Dolly Madison suggests that he was a good journeyman portrait painter, and the suggestion is supported by the fact that his portraits of Indians are almost incomparably better than his other canvases. They vary in quality — we must remember that he had to paint hastily, in unfavorable circumstances, and occasionally at some risk — but the best of them are better than the portraits of James Otto Lewis if not so good as those of Charles Bird King, artists who had been painting Indians for a good many years when Catlin's first work appeared. In fact, one who has not seen Catlin's portraits will seriously underestimate him on the basis of the much more widely circulated landscapes and *genre* scenes. They have the modeling, expression, and individuality that are usually lacking in his other work and the drawing is much better. As soon as he turns to the full figure, however, the quality of his work falls off.

When in 1943 the Museum of Modern Art assembled an exhibition called 'Romantic Painting in America,' it called Catlin a romantic. It appears to have done so on the basis not of his painting but of his prose. The Museum may yet change its mind and present him as a modern primitive like any Brooklyn street car conductor who takes to painting when he is pensioned. For he has the childlike ignorance of perspective and proportion, the naïve generalization of line, and the disregard of technical correctness that pass as primitive among esthetic sophisticates. His landscapes, which are his poorest work, leave the sky almost out of account and generalize hills and rivers in a way to delight teachers of drawing at progressive grade schools. His prairies are so uniform and unreal a green that the duns and yellows of his badlands come as a distinct relief. He had little skill at composition (a remark which also applies to certain later and better painters of the West, notably Seth Eastman), and when he needed figures in a scene was frequently content with stick-men. Apart from his portraits, his Indians tend to resemble one another and their faces are usually expressionless and without relief.

Nevertheless, Catlin had vigor, drama, and an enthusiastic sympathy. In his pictures of dances, for instance, the movement is admirably rendered. He drew animals better than he customarily drew human figures and he drew buffalo best of all, as well as anyone was to draw them for another generation. He painted buffalo in a great variety of circumstances. Wounded, at bay, charging, galloping, dying on the prairie or in the snow, they established a durable convention, and from Catlin on every artist who painted the West, including Alfred Jacob Miller, did at least one 'Buffalo chase' in exactly Catlin's terms. Moreover, though he habitually generalized most things, he could paint detail when he wanted to and many of his pictures are invaluable to ethnology. Apart from his portraits he is at his best, perhaps, in the paintings of the Mandan ceremonies of the medicine-lodge. Painted with unusual care, doubtless because of his horror and absorption, these are penetrating and dramatic, besides being invaluable illustrations of the most important religious rite common to the Plains tribes.[2]

All this is to say that, though Catlin may fairly be called a romantic on the basis of his book, the impact of his painting was realistic and even literal. The point has to be made emphatically for it defines Catlin's importance in history. For a generation the foremost obligation of Western painting would remain what Catlin understood it to be: illustration. In 1832 photography still struggled to be born in the workroom of Daguerre and Niepce — and the American people were preparing to possess their West. Their imagination had acted on the printed word to create a multiform and fantastic West: somehow images must be formed for their avid eyes. On the tablet of their mind must be drawn figures that would truly represent the reality. Catlin had no predecessors of any influence or effect at all. He began the long job and to this day something of the images he made remains; he has never been entirely erased from the West seen by our eyes and by our imagination.

This was not quite the first time the Plains Indians had been painted but it was the first time that they had been painted as tribes, the first time they had been painted in their own country, and the first time they had been painted at their customary occupations. Granted that ethnological detail is frequently generalized or suppressed, nevertheless Catlin's Indians wear the garments and decorations, live in the huts or tipis, perform the ceremonies, and engage in the labors specific to their tribes. A Catlin Crow is a Crow, a Catlin Mandan is a Mandan, and the differentiation is important. For popular American art had achieved an Indian stereotype, a conventionalized, usually ennobled redskin dressed in the costume of a Mohawk (which two centuries had made familiar) and posed in either a Cherokee cornfield or an Ojibwa canoe.[3] True, the detail is by no means so minute or so exact as that in the paintings of Charles Bodmer, who went up the Missouri a year after Catlin's first visit there and whose pictures were first published in 1839, two years after Catlin's New York exhibition. True, besides sometimes suppressing detail he also sometimes faked it, so that he cannot be accepted without critical scrutiny. Nevertheless, he could be as precise as anyone — see the paintings of the medicine lodge or of Mah-toh-to-pa's robe — and critical scrutiny usually reveals that he was right. In general he is reliable. Rather, in general he can hardly be praised too much. He gave the Plains Indian to the American eye for the first time.

Moreover, he gave that eye much else for the first time. These are the first paintings of the buffalo herds which travelers and explorers had described so vividly, and, as I have said, the individual Catlin buffalo becomes the buffalo of American iconography for a generation. These are the first villages of Mandan or Minnetaree domed huts, the first villages of tipis, the first Plains dances and other ceremonies. Catlin was the first artist, and for a long time the only one, who pictured the ordeals and rituals of the sun dance. In short, he was the first painter of the Plains culture. More important still, his landscapes are the first pictures of the upper Missouri country, of any part of the Far West. (With the exception noted above, Seymour's illustrations of Long's expedition.) In his pictures Americans could see for the first time portions of the country which, by 1837, was exercising an exceedingly powerful influence on the national imagination.

Yet a lag must be noted. Though Catlin established pictorial conventions which many artists were to elaborate, it took time for his influence to make itself felt. Not till about 1850 did 'after Catlin,' as a printed caption or merely as a knowing glint in the artist's eye, strongly affect the lithographs which our ancestors bought in such quantity. The 1850's are the decade when the West first became a popular interest in American graphic art. Even in that decade, despite Catlin and a few other artists who had painted it, the greater part of the West which the public visualized was still out of fantasy. The American people as a whole were not to know what their Happy Isles actually looked like till the end of the decade, when photography and photomechanical processes of reproduction were passing out of the experimental stage — and even then strains of fantasy were to linger on.

Take for instance Currier & Ives (N. Currier until 1857), who published more prints than anyone else but were by no means the only large publishers of prints. They and other publishers issued prints made directly from Catlin and others directly influenced by him — and also they published Western prints in which the West is still Never-Never Land. Thus our western wayfaring, our most cherished folk symbol, got its most universal representation in what has to be called a mythological picture, Fannie Palmer's 'The Rocky Mountains, Emgrants Crossing the Plains,' which collectors call 'The Covered Wagon Print.' It is entitled to respect as a sacred painting but it is neither the plains, the mountains, the covered wagon, nor the emigrants. One is most awed by the mountains, which rise so happily straight out of plains that are lush meadows somewhere in the vicinity of Cooperstown. They are not the Rockies; they are in part the Alps and in part the mountains on the far side of the moon. In the prints of Arthur Fitzwilliam Tait, Louis Maurer, and less celebrated Currier & Ives artists, the Rockies are sometimes the Adirondacks but more often the Catskills of the Hudson River School. (After his Currier & Ives days, Maurer did go west.)

These prints show a curious mixture of truth and fantasy. The artists studied Catlin carefully. They learned from Bodmer and from the by then available canvases of Seth Eastman and John Mix Stanley. They pored over the prose descriptions of the travelers and explorers. And to what they got from their sources they added a willing imagination. Tait's 'The Prairie Hunter — One Rubbed Out,' for instance, is admirable. A few details of the horseman's equipment are surprising but he is a genuine mountain man, the Indians are right, and the landscape is authentic. The picture is so true as illustration, in fact, that I suspect Tait got it from Stanley. But Tait's 'Fire Fight Fire,' another 'Life on the Prairie' print, is false, both landscape and figure in 'Pursuit' are absurd, and though the Indian in 'The Last War Whoop' is right the rest of the picture is tolerably comic. This is the more surprising in that by the time these prints were made there was abundant material for so conscientious a realist as Tait to draw on. As early as 1850 William Ranney, who, to be sure, had visited Texas, had been able to utilize it in a number of authoritative pictures, including the absolutely correct 'Trapper's Last Shot.' [4]

I make a point of this because its significance has usually been disregarded. The great vogue of the lithograph belongs to the eighteen-fifties. During the eighteen-forties, many thousands of people saw Catlin paintings and prints and those of the few other artists who followed him, but the total was comparatively small. Moreover, though technological progress in wood-engraving and steel-engraving and the rise of a highly competent school of artists revolutionized American bookmaking during the eighteen-forties, the revolution did not extend to books about the West. If in the winter of 1848–1849 you had been preparing to start overland for the gold fields as soon as the spring grass came, you would have had at hand as much reliable information about the country ahead of you as you might care to amass, but there were only four or five books that pictured it accurately and only two of these showed country you were likely to travel. Through the decade of our climactic expansion, that is, the westward-making Americans had no instructed image of the land they were bent on possessing. Manifest Destiny was blindfolded.

Neither the exploration of the West nor the Great Migration had been pictured, except by New York hacks drawing curbside cartoons for the weeklies. (Or by better artists whose romantic imagination substituted for experience — the best of all being Felix O. C. Darley.) Most of the early narratives by travelers and explorers were not illustrated at all. Mackenzie, Lewis and Clark, Alexander Henry, and Pike either had no illustrations or at best had a few bad woodcuts of Indian chiefs. Brackenridge's *Views of Louisiana*, 1814, was not illustrated; neither was Bradbury's *Travels in the Interior of America*, 1817; neither was Franchere's *Relation d'un voyage à la côte du nord-ouest de l'Amérique Septentrionale*, 1820. Ross Cox's *Adventures on the Columbia River* (1831), John B. Wyeth's *Oregon* (1833), Samuel Parker's *Journal of an Exploring Tour beyond the Rocky Mountains* (1838),[5] John Kirk Townsend's *Narrative* (1839), and Thomas J. Farnham's *Travels in the Great Western Prairies* (1841) were all without illustrations in the first editions. Irving's popular *Astoria*, 1836, and *The Rocky Mountains*, 1837, were not illustrated. When a book about the West did carry a few illustrations they were almost indescribably bad. Thus Pattie's *Personal Narrative*, published in 1831, includes a few line drawings. The Rocky Mountains they show are copied from the pyramid of Cheops. The Indians are from Cooper — or rather, they are little Rollo Indians. The travelers and trappers wear stovepipe hats, and a horse carries an English racing saddle. Later editions of Irving, Franchere, and others, and certain books published during the 1840's, such as Rufus Sage's *Scenes in the Rocky Mountains* have woodcuts equally crude and inaccurate.

The reason was simple enough: even if artists had been available who knew the West, books about it could not be counted upon to sell widely enough to cover the high cost of reproducing pictures. Nuttall, Townsend, and other trained scientists beautifully sketched the flora and fauna of the West, and nearly every Western expedition included someone capable of making accurate sketches of the scenery. But before 1850 a publisher of Western books was limited to woodcuts if he wanted to show a profit, for steel-engraving (which by now had almost replaced copperplate) was beyond his means, and he could not afford good woodcuts. True, there was lithography, but before 1850 only the national government was willing to pay for it. Of the four or five books which I have said could have visually instructed a Forty-Niner, three were government reports, Frémont's, Albert's, and Emory's. They were all splendidly illustrated with lithographs, those in Emory beautifully drawn by John Mix Stanley, so beautifully drawn that some of them remain unsurpassed today.

The superiority of government illustration was maintained down to the Civil War (and even beyond it, for the superb reports of the geological surveys are post-war). It is not too much to say that the West as a whole was first adequately pictured in the surveys for the Pacific Railroad, published in 1855. Excellent artists accompanied each survey and by that time photography was available to extend and amplify their labors. John Mix Stanley doubled as a photographer with Isaac Stevens' survey of the northern route, in 1853, and in the same year S. N. Carvalho took a camera to the Sangre de Cristo Mountains with Frémont's last expedition, which of course was not government-supported.

## 2

### Catlin in the West

A few individual Plains Indians had been painted before Catlin. As early as 1821, under the auspices of the War Department, an 'Indian Gallery' was established in Washington. Indian chiefs were constantly visiting the capital to consult their Father on tribal business and to be cozened into signing away their lands. It occurred to Thomas L. McKenney, when he was in charge of Indian Affairs under Calhoun as Secretary of War, that their likenesses ought to be preserved. A great many portraits of these chiefs were painted, a majority of them by Charles Bird King, who was a skillful artist. King's originals formed the basis of the Indian Gallery and included a few Plains chiefs. King also copied and added to the Gallery about forty-five similar portraits by an inferior artist, J. O. Lewis, who painted them at Detroit and elsewhere, at assemblies of tribes called for the negotiation of treaties.

Accessions to the Indian Gallery practically ceased in 1837, the year of Catlin's grand opening. When the Office of Indian Affairs was transferred from the War Department to the Department of the Interior in 1849, the Gallery was turned over to the Patent Office. In 1858 it went to the Smithsonian and was added to John Mix Stanley's canvases, which eventually numbered about two hundred — and was burned with them in 1865. About thirty of King's Indian paintings survive. W. Vernon Kinietz's check-list records forty-one surviving Indian pictures by Stanley (two of them landscapes) but only five of these belonged to the original great collection.

Meanwhile, in 1835 J. O. Lewis had published his *Aboriginal Portfolio*, a set of crude portraits badly reproduced by lithography on unsuitable paper and colored by hand. He was doubtless moved to do so by McKenney's preparations to publish a similar collection of portraits based on the Indian Gallery. These preparations had been under way since about 1830. They resulted in the famous McKenney and Hall *Indian Tribes of North America*. The folio edition of this great work was published in Philadelphia, Volume I in 1836, Volume II in 1838, Volume III in 1844. The plates were lithographed by Edward C. Biddle of Philadelphia and his successor, Frederick W. Greenough. There was a London edition. A royal octavo edition was published in 1842 and 1844.[6]

There is no reason to discuss the McKenney and Hall work here. It is a monument of American culture, solely because of the portraits. As

I have said, nearly all of these were copied from the Indian Gallery. The portraits are excellent and the lithography and color are superb. We are interested in it here, however, only because it contains certain portraits of Plains Indians, four Sioux, one Pawnee, one Omaha, one Mandan, two Otos, and nine Iowas. These are formal portraits and they were not painted in the West.[7]

It is interesting that Catlin was offered a partnership in McKenney and Hall's enterprise on the specific ground that he had paintings of the Plains Indians in quantity whereas the Indian Gallery did not. James Hall met him in Cincinnati in the winter of 1835–1836 and in February wrote to him from Philadelphia, proposing that he contribute from thirty to fifty of his portraits with notes on the lives of his subjects. Hall pointed out that the three proprietors would have a monopoly on Indian portraits (he rightly disregarded Lewis's *Aboriginal Portfolio*) and that Catlin's proposed exhibition would get invaluable publicity from the publication. Catlin did not accept the offer and in a letter of 1836 to the *Evening Star*, which will be discussed later on, he expressed a considerable annoyance at the McKenney and Hall publication and its accompanying exhibition. He seems to have believed that hard work entitled him to a monopoly.

Catlin first went West in 1832, traveling up the Missouri on the famous *Yellowstone*, which in the preceding year had made the first steamboat voyage to the upper river. On the way up, difficulties of navigation delayed the boat and enabled him to paint some Sioux at Fort Pierre. (Pierre, South Dakota.) He went on to Fort Union, the American Fur Company's largest post, at the mouth of the Yellowstone River. (Western North Dakota, just east of the Montana line.) Here he painted Crows and Blackfeet, various costumes and weapons, medicines, and some buffalo. He stayed at Fort Union about a month, then with two hired companions descended the Missouri in a dugout to the Mandan villages and Fort Clark. (Sixty miles north of Bismarck, North Dakota.) Here and among the neighboring Minnetarees (Hidatsa) he made his most fruitful visit of all, painting many of his best canvases and recording observations that were among his permanent services to ethnology, notably his account of the medicine lodge ceremonies. He went on downstream to Fort Pierre, where he had painted the Sioux on his upriver journey.[8] He stayed there for a while and made portraits of them. He went on to St. Louis, where he painted the famous Black Hawk only a few weeks after he had been sent a prisoner to Jefferson Barracks, following the end of the Black Hawk War.[9]

As I shall show, Catlin's movements in 1833 cannot be followed. In 1834 he went to Fort Gibson on the southwestern frontier (eastern Oklahoma) and from there accompanied the First Dragoons on a peace mission among the southwestern Indians, getting as far as the village of the Wichitas or Pawnee Picts, then located between the Wichita Mountains and the Red River. His paintings of Osages,

Wichitas, Kaws, Otos, and Wacos belong to this year, and probably also those of the Pawnees, Omahas, Iowas, and Poncas. The following winter he spent along the Gulf coast. Donaldson says he painted Indians at that time, and if there were Indians within reach we may be sure he did so, but I cannot identify them. In 1835 he went to the upper Mississsippi, primarily to paint the Eastern Sioux. He painted some of his Chippewas, Winnebagos, Menominees, and Potawatomies in 1835 also, and made the first of two visits to the Sauks and Foxes. In 1836 he was back on the upper Mississippi but also he went to the upper Great Lakes. This was the year in which he made his famous trip to the pipestone quarries in Minnesota. He was the first white man known to have visited them and wrote the first description of the handsome red claystone which was a favorite material for Indian pipes, especially ceremonial pipes. It is called catlinite after him.

In December of 1837 and the following January, he was at Fort Moultrie, South Carolina, painting captured Seminoles. (The frequently incorrect *Catalogue* of 1871 says that he went to Florida to paint them, but the statement is ambiguous and perhaps unfounded.) From then on till well past the period we are concerned with he was engaged in exhibiting his collection abroad. Later he made other journeys — to Texas, South America, and the Pacific Northwest — and painted many other pictures, but they are all outside our interest.

## 3

## Charles Bodmer

I have remarked that we cannot be sure of Catlin's whereabouts in 1833. In April of that year the German princeling who was an accomplished naturalist, Maximilian of Wied-Neuwied, started up the Missouri from St. Louis aboard the same *Yellowstone* that had taken Catlin upriver in 1832.[10] Like Catlin he went to Fort Pierre, whence a newer and better boat, the *Assiniboin*, took him to Fort Clark, at the Mandan villages where Catlin had stayed, and on to Fort Union, which marked Catlin's farthest penetration of the West. From Fort Union Maximilian went by keelboat far up the Missouri, to the American Fur Company's post among the Blackfeet, Fort McKenzie near the mouth of Marias River. Here, so far as usage and realities of the fur trade are concerned, he was 'in the mountains,' though not so far West as the Rockies nor even actually among mountains. After two months at Fort McKenzie he went down the river by barge to Fort Clark. There he spent the winter studying the Mandans and Minnetarees. In the spring of 1834 he returned to St. Louis and presently went home.

Maximilian's Western experiences are discussed in our text. Here we are concerned with the artist he took with him. This was Charles or Karl Bodmer (he used both names), a twenty-seven-year-old Swiss who had studied painting in Paris and who later became a distinguished member of the Barbizon school. (Biographical accounts of Bodmer are irreconcilable. He may have been only twenty-three when he came to the United States.)

Maximilian was a scientist and his purpose in employing a painter was exclusively scientific. His book, *Reise in das innere Nord-Amerika in den Jahren 1832 bis 1834*, was published in 1839; an English translation followed in 1843. It is a permanent landmark in the study of America. It contributed as much as any other book, perhaps more than any other, to our understanding of the Plains Indians in a state of nature. A very great deal of American ethnology, in fact, rests solidly on it — and a large part of that importance derives from Bodmer's illustrations, which form a separate folio volume called an *Atlas*. That defines Bodmer's place in the painting of the West.[11]

Most of Bodmer's pictures were intended to be illustrations, they were to record scientific information. He was a superb draughtsman; his detail is sharp, minute, exquisite, and laborious. As documents his figure studies are superior to Catlin's and artistically they have an equal superiority. Bodmer's Plates 13 and 14 present 'Mato-Tope,' Four Bears, the Mandan chief whom Catlin had painted the preceding summer as 'Mah-to-toh-pa' in his Gallery, numbers 128 and 131.[12] They have a characterization and vitality which Catlin's have not and which come from Bodmer's superior portraiture. But they were painted in order to portray costume and ornamentation, and here they are incomparably better than Catlin. The cut and tie of the moccasins, leggings, and shirt; the quill work on these and on the collar and fringe; the fringe itself and the painting on it and the sleeves and the shirt-bosoms; the rawhide thongs with fur and hair dangling from them; the head-dress with its fur, horns, feathers, and leaves; the warbonnet; the ceremonial lance with flint blade, feathers, and scalp; the medicine bag; the face and body painting; the ornamentation of the tomahawk — all these and even smaller details are presented with photographic exactness. In fact, they are presented better than photography could present them. These paintings have the focus and selectivity of medical art, the illustration of anatomy or surgical technique by drawing, which permits a clarity, emphasis, and separation of parts and planes beyond the capacity of the camera lens.

Bodmer's Plate 13 is reproduced as our Plate LXX and I have also reproduced his Plate 23, our Plate LXXI, as a further example of his costume studies, though both the black and white medium and the reduction in size impair the detail. A full half of his Plates, as distinguished from the smaller Vignettes, are of this kind. Plate 23, which in some editions is erroneously numbered 28, 'Pehriska-Ruhpa. Moennitarre Warrior in the costume of the Dog Danse [*sic*],' has the same exactness and has as well a compelling suggestion of savage emotion. In Plate 17, Bodmer paints the same chief in full ceremonial dress.[13] Sioux, Crows, Assiniboins, Snakes, and Mandans, some of them squaws, are pictured with equally minute fidelity. There are also paintings of tipis, with their construction and ornamentation carefully documented, and *genre* scenes made with exactly the same purpose. As I have said, American ethnology rests some of its fundamental conclusions about the Plains Indians on these pictures.

The same may be said of another category of Bodmer's work, where his superiority to Catlin is quite as apparent. I have reproduced herein his Plate 18, 'Mandan Buffalo Dance,' our Plate XXVI. Catlin also pictured this ceremony and his version of it was reproduced by lithography as Plate 8 of the *North American Indian Portfolio*. His rendition seems stiff, expressionless, and formal when compared with Bodmer's. All the superb detail of his static studies is repeated here, so that the masks, staffs, and ceremonial equipment are unquestionably presented exactly as they were used. But in addition Bodmer has given the picture an ecstatic violence that is beyond praise. It is a memorable study of savagery. If we were to be limited to a single picture for imaginative insight into the life of the Plains Indians, this one would serve better than any other ever made.

It is, however, only a climax of qualities present in other pictures of this category. Plate 27, 'Scalp Dance of the Minatarres,' is only less dynamic and is quite as exact. Plate 42, 'Fort Mackenzie, August 28, 1833,' which portrays an actual battle between some Blackfeet and a band of Assiniboins, narrated in my text, has a splendid savagery and has never been surpassed as an illustration of Indian war. Plate 38, 'Camp of the Gros Ventres of the Prairies on the upper Missouri'; Plate 43, 'Encampment of the Piekann Indians' (the one reproduced in McKenney and Hall); and similar studies, though more static, have the same representational value. Sometimes fidelity of representation and scientific exactness combine perfectly with Bodmer's esthetic imagination, which is necessarily under restraint most of the time. The happiest example is his Plate 19, 'Interior of the Hut of a Mandan Chief' (in some editions, 'Interior of a Mandan Hut'), which is reproduced among our color plates. This is precisely what Maximilian's text called for and one is not able to appreciate how good an illustration it is till he has studied the careful monographs on the earth lodge by ethnologists. But quite apart from its illustrative value, it is a superb picture.

This is not to say that Bodmer did not have his defects. His buffalo are no better than Catlin's, in fact, not usually so good, and his treatment of the herds is purely formal. He did a running horse no better than his contemporaries. A stiffness enforced by his scientific purpose is extended to some subjects that would have profited from informality. The dynamic action of his buffalo dance and his Indian fight at Fort McKenzie is lacking in several other studies which it would have enhanced. Thus Vignette 29, 'Dog Sledges of the Mandan Indians,' and Plate 26, 'Winter Village of the Minatarres,' are posterlike illustrations, suave but without animation. Vignette 20, 'Horse Racing of Sioux Indians,' must be praised for its horses, which are Indian ponies, not the Arabian chargers of most Indian paintings for the next quarter-century, but the total effect of the picture is sentimental. Plate 25, 'Offering [in some editions, Idols] of the Mandan Indians,' with its distressed figure, stormy sky, galloping horses, and dim village background, is sentimental to an extreme; it is a study in pure corn.

Worse still, Bodmer could be indifferent and even negligent. Take Plate 36, 'Hunting of the Grizzly Bear.' The bear is by no means a grizzly, is in fact so crude a bear as to suggest that Bodmer made it up. The costumes of the hunters are open to doubt and their attitudes are phony. Their arms do not inspire confidence and the sailboat with its square stern never navigated the Missouri. (The same boat — it is the American Fur Company's keelboat — is more attentively drawn in Plate 38.) Again, in Vignettes 23 and 24, the costumes of the travelers put a strain on one's belief and both pictures are perfunctory. Nothing has been lost to art or history, but it is clear that Bodmer sometimes worked carelessly and was sometimes willing to invent what chanced not to be conveniently at hand.

So far I have discussed Bodmer as an illustrator, a painter whose job was to express visual realities. There remains another group of subjects which, though he had to treat them illustratively also, permitted him a greater latitude. These are his landscapes and history has to take note of them. It is true that Catlin preceded him in painting the Western country. It is also true that the small, expensive editions of Bodmer's work circulated only meagerly as compared with Catlin's, whose pictures were seen by large audiences over a period of years in both the United States and Europe. But Catlin was at his worst in landscape.[14] The narrowness of his palette (not more than ten or twelve colors all told, of which usually only four or five appear in a landscape), the extreme generalization not only of color but of land shapes and contours as well, the crudity and monotony of his effects, the absence of imagination — all these seriously diminish his impact. Nevertheless, the Americans, who were hungering for a delineation of their fabulous province, fed gratefully on his landscapes. In the early eighteen-forties they can be found translated into prose in popular literature and by another ten years they are everywhere in popular lithography. Since the greater part of them show the badlands of the upper Missouri, they are strange and wild enough to answer if not to satisfy the demand for the romantic which the public brought to the West even more urgently when it was unknown than today. And yet, for all his scores of renditions, Catlin did far less well by that landscape — considering what a people asked of any artist who came early to the West — than Bodmer did with hardly a dozen.

Apparently not too much interested in the job assigned him, whereas Catlin was a flaming enthusiast, and forced by the conditions of that job to make sure of a literal representation, Bodmer nevertheless had the talent, the technique, and above all the imagination to interpret nobly the new, strange country he had come to. If Catlin has the priority of having first painted the West, Bodmer was the first artist who did it justice. It took time for him to be widely known among a people who wanted just what he had given them, and the reputation he eventually had among them has long since lapsed to obscurity again. But he has an important place in our culture. In a few paintings he created the first sensitive and instructed symbols of the West. In the work of later painters and of literary men, in a feeling of recognition which many people who were neither painters nor writers came to have because of him, those paintings have permanently influenced our national emotions.

One observation must be made at once. The problems of space and light define a large part of any landscape painter's labor, but when artists reached the Far West, they had to deal with vaster spaces and greater intensity of light than American painters had been accustomed to work with before. Vast space and intensity of light are the primary characteristics of the Western landscape, even when they are not all there is to paint in it. In the eighteen-thirties, Bodmer could not use light as younger men were using it a quarter of a century later. Between him and the modern eye there is an emptiness which the Impressionists first began to fill, though it was not till the twentieth century that the effect of desert light was adequately secured on canvas. Bodmer's distances are effects of scale, of the color of his sky, and of cloud shadows. But they are distances and noble ones.

His landscape is that of the upper Missouri, its badlands, and its prairies. It is the aching desolation of Plate 15, 'Fort Clark. On the Missouri,' with the human figures pointlike in vastness and the barrenness made more oppressive by snow, ice, and a winter sky. Or it is Plate 29, 'Junction of the Yellowstone River with the Missouri,' where though the composition is that of a poster there is an overwhelming sense of the land stretching out forever and the waters are weary with the distance they have come down. It is the small rampart of the trading post in Plate 26 (numbered otherwise in various editions), 'Fort Union on the Missouri,' reared in an infinity of land and sky. Most of all it is the badlands of Plate 40, 'Herd of Bisons'; Plate 41, 'View of the Stone Walls'; Plate 44, 'View of the Rocky Mountains,' where the mountains are only the Little Rockies after all; and Plate 37, 'The White Castels.' All these give the warped and writhen bluffs of the badlands with the architecture of water and the sculpture of wind, the inconceivable shapes and the unimaginable colors which made this country both nightmarish and dreamlike. Bodmer has rendered it forthrightly as always, but these paintings have a subtlety of color beyond all his others and they have also a quality of awe and wonder that means an inner response which may well have been against his will.

This was only a small part of the West and only one of its innumerable landscapes but here it is — and at the level of art for the first time. I have seen these pictures even today catch and hold the imagination alike of people who know the West as natives of it and people who have never been there — in so much that they repeatedly take the considerable trouble required of anyone not a millionaire to see them, and pore over them with the intentness of inner recognition. If after more than a century they can still appeal so powerfully to the American imagination, which meanwhile has been instructed by every visual and literary means, consider the charge they carried in the early eighteen-forties, when the nation had never seen its ultimate West but was already quick with Manifest Destiny. (Though we must remember how few saw them.) From the early sixteenth century, when it began at Chesapeake and Delaware Bays and the mouths of the James, the Hudson, and the St. Lawrence, the West had been strangeness, mystery, and the tug of the unknown — nor had strangeness or romance failed in the least as people came up with the realities. Of all the strange landscapes of America, the most powerfully mysterious, the Far West, had been a compelling force on the imagination for as long as there had been rumor of it. And here at last it was realized in paint.[15]

## 4

### Alfred Jacob Miller

Here it becomes necessary to establish another priority.

I have said that Catlin's whereabouts during 1833 cannot be determined. Late in life he claimed to have gone to the interior Far West in that year. If, as seems certain, he did not go in 1833, then he did not see the Far West until long after the period we are concerned with and never saw the interior West at all. If he did not go to the interior West in 1833, then Alfred Jacob Miller was (with the exception of Seymour) the first artist who ever painted the Rocky Mountains, the Indians who lived in them, and the scenery on the way to them.

Catlin's statement was first made in the *Catalogue, Descriptive and Instructive, of Catlin's Indian Cartoons*, published in 1871. Thomas Donaldson, the authority on Catlin so far as there is any, repeats the statement and says, 'Of Mr. Catlin's movements in 1833 no journal was printed.' The statement runs as follows: 'In the summer of 1833 I ascended the Platte to Fort Laramie, visiting the two principal villages of the Pawnees, and also the Omahas and Ottoes [Otos], and at the fort saw a great number of Arapahos and Cheyennes, and rode to the shores of the Great Salt Lake, when the Mormons were yet building their temple at Nauvoo on the Mississippi thirty-eight years ago.'

Quite apart from the matter at issue, the *Catalogue* of 1871 is unreliable, being demonstrably wrong in a number of passages. This statement contains two misapprehensions. In 1833 the Mormons were still several years short of reaching Illinois, founding Nauvoo, or building the Temple. This was the year when the Saints in Missouri were driven from Jackson to Clay County, but the prophet, with the bulk and headquarters of his Church, was still in Ohio. Moreover, in 1833 there was no Fort Laramie and no trading post had yet been erected on its site. As my text shows, Fort Laramie was built in 1834.

But perhaps Catlin did travel the well-worn trail past the mouth of Laramie Creek and thirty-eight years later committed the natural error of remembering that the fort had already been built? I am afraid not. The negative evidence is overwhelming. As Dr. Washington Matthews once pointed out,[16] nowhere in *Letters and Notes* does Catlin actually claim to have been to the Rockies, though in an account of his river journey with 'Batiste' he has his companion intimate that he had been. Doctor Matthews also remarked that Catlin never painted the Rockies — and that we cannot believe he would have refrained from painting them if he had seen them. This argument can be carried still further, for nowhere in *Letters and Notes* or his catalogues does Catlin claim to have painted any Indians of the mountain tribes except at the Missouri trading posts and in St. Louis, and in Letter 48 he admits that the statements he makes about them in the text are based on hearsay. His Flatheads and Nez Perces, whom he does not differentiate, were painted at Fort Pierre, his Crows at Fort Clark, and his Blackfeet at Fort Union. His two Chinooks appear to have been done to printed specifications and at any rate were painted in 1832 at St. Louis, which had never seen any Chinooks. His Gallery contains no Arapahos (though he claims to have seen some at Fort Laramie), no Snakes, no Utes, no Bannocks — tribes which he must certainly have encountered if he had made the trip he claims — and no representatives of other tribes which he would probably have met. It does contain two Cheyennes but these were painted among the Sioux. Donaldson ascribes them to 1834 but Catlin is not known to have visited the Sioux in that year and his book indicates that they were painted in 1832. The absence of mountain Indians is even more conclusive than his failure to paint the mountains. Equally conclusive is the fact that Catlin is not mentioned in any contemporary account of the Rockies in 1833. He could hardly have got to the mouth of the Laramie unless he traveled with a fur company caravan, as Captain Stewart did that very year; it is quite impossible that he could have got to Great Salt Lake without first going to the summer rendezvous and there joining a brigade of trappers. If he had appeared at the rendezvous he would certainly have painted the spectacle, as Miller did four years later, and so great a novelty as a painter at work there would surely have been noted by one or another of the diarists discussed in our text.

I am able, however, to support my contention positively. In the spring of 1836, three years after the supposed trip to the mountains, Catlin wrote a letter to 'the editor of the *Evening Star*.' I have not found the original paper (almost certainly the New York *Star*) but the *American Turf Register and Sporting Magazine* reprinted the letter in its issue of August, 1836. It is a long letter and some of the information it contains has not, I believe, been brought to the study of Catlin. (With customary thrift, Catlin reprinted it in his book — but left out the vital opening paragraphs.) What concerns us is a sentence in one of those paragraphs where Catlin is replying to someone who reproached him for not having opened his exhibition in New York City. In the spring of this year, 1836, 'I had been travelling at great expense and risk of my life for six years,' he says, 'and undergoing privations of an extraordinary kind living and eating with almost every tribe east of the Rocky Mountains, painting my portraits by their own firesides, and studying (for the world) their true manners and customs, and having my arrangements made [i.e., having them made now, in the spring of 1836, when, as we know, he did not go West] for crossing the Rocky Mountains to the Pacific and Gulf of California. . . .' Here is a flat statement that up to 1836 all the Indians he knew lived east of the mountains (though it is not true that he knew almost all the tribes that did) and that he had not crossed the Rockies up to then, as he would have had to do if he had gone West in 1833. I consider that this settles the matter. So the sketches published in this book are, except for the lost canvases of Samuel Seymour, the first paintings ever made of the interior West.

In discussing them we must bear in mind the purpose for which they were made and also the training of the painter. As a boy in Baltimore, Alfred Jacob Miller showed a talent for painting which led to his taking some instructions from Thomas Sully. Eventually he attracted the attention of Robert Gilmore, the rich Baltimorean who was one of the earliest patrons of Doughty and Cole and sent Cole and a sizable number of other painters to Europe. In 1833 he sponsored a European tour for Miller.[17] Miller studied at the École des Beaux Arts and made copies in the Louvre. Later he went to Rome, where he studied at the English Life School. He returned to Baltimore in 1834.[18]

This is the typical experience of the young American of the eighteen-thirties who went abroad to study painting and acquire correct esthetic ideas. Miller, of course, met a number of artists who were devoted to the new and vigorous French romantic movement, notably Horace Vernet. He learned to see and paint like a Romantic, and doubtless to dress, talk, and think like one as well. It was not whimsically that Mr. Macgill James was led to speak of Delacroix. Moods and methods of Delacroix, of the whole school, are evident in our sketches. There is, for instance, the grouping and postures of the Indians — splendid savages to the school — in even the hastiest drawings. The Romantics had a trick, almost an idiom, of rendering distant mountains a pale blue above firm reds and browns in the foreground, and Miller brought it to the Wind Rivers. The lakes and peaks of that great range agreeably composed for him just such vistas as his companions of the Café Greco, freed from laborious composition in the studio, had found delightful in the Alps and Appenines. He probably acquired from them, too, his unpatronizing interest in *genre* subjects, though American painting at home was independently learning the same interest in the eighteen-thirties.

Distance, strangeness, and alien ways of life were favorite preoccupations of the Romantics, who were following them to the Moroccan desert at just about the time when Miller went West. He had been back in the United States something over two years and had taken a studio in New Orleans when, early in 1837, Captain William Drummond Stewart, on half-pay from the British Army, called on him and inspected his work. 'He then told me,' Miller's notebook says, 'that he was making preparation for another journey to the Rocky Mountains . . . and wished to have a competent artist to sketch the remarkable scenery and incidents of the journey.' It may be that Stewart knew he was soon to succeed to the baronetcy then held by his brother, for he was going West this year with a considerably larger outfit than ever before (he had spent the last four summers and one winter there) and he wanted to take an artist along so that he could have Murthly Castle embellished with pictures of the West.

On that Western journey Miller made the sketches reproduced here and more than a hundred known others. A few of them are sufficiently worked up to be considered finished pictures but all were made as sketches, any painter's jottings in his notebook, and they must be thought of as sketches. The end in view determined the choice of subject. Miller was going to paint a number of large canvases to hang in his patron's castle and hunting lodge, they were to remind a hunter and traveler of the country he had enjoyed, and it would be best to have memoranda of all the aspects of life there. In Baltimore after his return from the West and in Scotland whither Stewart took him in 1840, he painted the large canvases that had been commissioned. They seem to have abundantly pleased the baronet but they have much less merit than the sketches. The conspicuous virtues of the sketches are freshness, spontaneity, and vigor but the large oils are massive, conventional, and literary. They are dull in color, reminding Mr. James of 'the fatal brown sauce of the old Masters,' and the fidelity of the sketches to what Miller actually saw in the West is absent from them.[19]

Miller spent nearly two years abroad, painting portraits — and doubtless Indian scenes — in Scotland and London. A family tradition holds that he painted the Queen, but though she made a visit to Stewart's neighbor, the Marquis of Breadalbane, soon after Miller had been his guest, there is no record of a portrait by him. He did, however, meet Catlin in London. On February 10, 1842, he wrote to his brother: 'Catlin is here and visits me sometimes. He had lately had the honor of exhibiting his model of Niagara to the Queen. There is in truth, however, a great deal of humbug about Mr. George Catlin. He has published a book containing some extraordinary stories and luckily for him there are but few persons who have travelled the same ground.' Endemic, doubtless: Miller's notes show that he had swallowed and retold some pretty extraordinary yarns himself.

Miller returned to the United States in June, 1842. (The Academy show was on. 'Chapman is advancing backward, Elliott is about the best portrait painter in Gotham, between Durand and Cole in landscape it is "nip and tuck," to quote a Texan writer, Edmonds is promising finely. There is a "screw loose" in Cropsey, Mount has nothing this season, Rothermel ditto, Weir ditto.') He settled down to a long, active career in Baltimore. He painted portraits and local scenes, made household copies of famous paintings, was a typical journeyman artist of the time. But his Western trip had given him a local celebrity as a painter of Indians. His account book shows that every year he painted a number of Indian scenes for the Maryland trade. Sometime they were enlarged copies of these sketches, sometimes they were studio compositions, and sometimes they were inspired by popular literature of the West. Most of them were done in oil; the quality of those that survive varies a great deal. As time went on Miller took increasing liberties with Western subjects, conventionalizing them entirely out of agreement with his observations. The process of deterioration may be seen clearly in a large portrait of a man in buckskin now owned by Mr. Alfred Miller of Baltimore. The costume is rendered in exact detail and has clearly been referred to the early sketches but the face is stereotyped and sentimentalized; it is a trapper from any illustrator's stockpile. A family tradition holds that the subject was Jim Bridger but the portrait is not in the least a likeness.[20]

It was only his Indian paintings that gave Miller any celebrity outside of Maryland. He showed some of the large oils painted for Stewart in the Apollo Gallery, New York, as early as May, 1839, and they typed him in the public mind. A number of what appear to be illustrations among his effects suggest that he sometimes worked for magazines or publishers, though nothing in his account book identifies them as commissioned and I have been able to find only two books in which his work appears. One of these, C. W. Webber's *The Hunter-Naturalist*, published in Philadelphia in 1851, contains five chromolithographs from paintings by Miller.[21] Four of them are based directly on the original sketches made in the West, two being exact copies, but they have lost much in either the copying or the lithography. Three years later, Putnams published Webber's *Wild Scenes and Songbirds*, which contains five quite different Western scenes by Miller. Again four of them are based on the sketches, one being identical with the original, but they are cruder and less faithful to the originals than those of 1851. On the other hand, Tuckerman, *Book of the Artists* (1867), speaks of him primarily as a water colorist and singles out his buffalo for praise. Clement and Hutton, *Artists of the Nineteenth Century* (1879), appear to have seen only the water-color copies which are now in the Walters Gallery.[22]

These copies, the only Miller paintings publicly known before the researches of Mr. Macgill James, were made more than twenty years after the originals. An entry in Miller's studio account-book dated July 15, 1858, says, 'I commenced [word illegible, probably 'duplicating'] Indian Sketches for Wm. T. Walters. $12 each. Also to furnish small notes.' This was, of course, William Thompson Walters, who with his son Henry came to be known as 'America's nearest approximation of the magnificent Medicis.' Their fabulous collection, unrivaled in some of its aspects and as a whole one of the greatest ever made by any one, is now the Walters Gallery. The account-book shows that ninety of the copies were delivered to Walters in 1859.[23] The commission was completed in 1860. Walters was collecting so furiously at the time that he had to give Miller a four-months note for part of the final payment.

Since only 166 sketches are listed in the notebook called 'Rough Draughts for Notes to Indian Sketches,' which Miller kept in the West, or which he later compiled from notes made on the spot, thirty-four of the Walters copies have no originals. In general the copies are much more finished pictures than the original sketches but also they sometimes show the same process of alteration that I have noted in Miller's other copies. Some of them have become frank studio pictures, with the composition formalized and many decorative details added. They also show the increasing literary content of all American painting of the time. The one called 'The Trapper's Bride,' for instance, which Miller copied and sold to a good many purchasers besides Walters, has lost its authenticity altogether; it is lushly romantic, half-way between Emerson Bennett and Longfellow, and today would inevitably end on an insurance calendar. 'War Path' is wholly synthetic; various stages of it which have been preserved show Miller struggling with the composition and determined to make the color as vivid as possible. (Our Plate LXVI is reproduced not from the Walters copy but from an even more studied one.) Yet even this last has retained some value as an illustration: the hairdress of the Kansas, his position on the horse, the bridle and the war necklace which the horse wears are authentic. In 'The Devil's Gate' the mountains have been set back in order to make room for a foreground and figures not present in the original. In general the copies lack the authority of the originals. They sometimes lack as well the spontaneity that is the outstanding merit of the originals. Yet this is not always true and the copy is sometimes the better picture by far, especially in its colors. In fact, Miller's color-work is most delightful in the Walters copies. It is bright, gay, high in key, wholly different from the drab palette shown in the oil copies. Probably a collector who was not interested in authenticity or historical priority would prefer the Walters landscapes to their originals. Several of our plates have been made from these copies.

About thirty-four of the Walters copies, I have pointed out, appear to have had no originals made in the West.[24] Presumably the manuscript 'Rough Draughts for Notes to Indian Sketches,' now in the possession of Mr. L. Vernon Miller of Baltimore, was intended to include all the originals and no others. But it is clear that not all the pictures it lists were actually made in the West. Thus Number 21, 'Fur Trappers in Trouble,' which under a slightly different title is

Walters Number 163, could not have been made before late 1848 or 1849.[25] There is no way of being sure how many others are studio pictures. The most imaginative, most romantic, and most finished views of the Wind River Mountains, which closely approximate their Walters counterparts, are under some suspicion of having been worked up in the studio from more rudimentary sketches now lost. Yet in no case can we be quite certain about these and among the most finished of the sketches are some which quite surely were painted on the spot. I do not mean to suggest that any considerable number of the sketches that correspond to Miller's notes were not painted in the West, but only that a few of them certainly were and others must be suspected. Most are self-evidently originals painted on the spot.

Miller's notes contain surprisingly few references to his methods and the circumstances in which he had to work. Once Stewart creeps up on him, surprises him, and then rebukes him for being so absorbed in painting that Indians might have killed him. Once Stewart complains that he is not producing enough sketches of a particularly active and interesting scene — to which Miller replies that he has only one pair of hands, not half a dozen. And once he parenthetically explains that Antoine Clement, the halfbreed who was Stewart's chief hunter, was detailed to help him when he was sketching buffalo. 'He did this effectually but after his own peculiar fashion,' Miller's note reads. For this purpose he would wound the animal in the flank, bringing him to a standstill. This was our opportunity. Going as near him as was prudent, holding the sketch book in one hand and the pencil in the other, it often happened that while absorbed in drawing a ludicrous scene would ensue. The brute would make a charge. Of course, sketch and pencil would be thrown down, the bridle seized and a retreat made at double-quick time. This would convulse our Indian "fidus achates" with merriment, in which state he could not have aided us if he had wished.' The chance of being gored and trampled was an ordinary risk for the painter of buffalo; Catlin frequently comments on it.

That is about all Miller says, but the sketches themselves add more. In the note just quoted Miller was sketching with a pencil in a notebook. Unquestionably he made many such brief notes, though only a few have survived, and these notes were the basis of more developed sketches. A few of our sketches are in pencil, a few more in ink. The next stage is represented by a number of wash drawings made with diluted black or sepia ink. (The remarkable 'Snake Indians Migrating,' our Plate XXXVIII, is perhaps the best of these.) Some of the color sketches were certainly made on the spot and in haste — the color has been flowed on, though there was time to pencil in the outlines of mountains, trees, and figures. Most of the color sketches, however, appear to have been done at leisure, doubtless from pencil notes and probably at camp, when Miller got back from the incident portrayed. Some of these show considerable labor. A few are touched up with Chinese white, which he also used as an accent in some of the monochromes, and others have been gone over in part with gouache and then varnished with gum arabic. The 'views' — those which deal with lakes and peaks of the Wind River Mountains, buttes of the badlands, and the formal spectacles of the rendezvous — are naturally the most developed. He had as much time as he might care to use and it is in these pictures that his training and the tradition with which he was allied show most clearly. Even these, however, can hardly be called water-color paintings in a contemporary sense, though a few of them and many of the Walters copies might perhaps be so described. Typically they are color drawings.

Our plates fairly represent Miller's whole range. I am not an art critic and must leave the reader to judge the pictures as he will. Their unique historical value, however, is almost independent of their artistic merits. The shortest way to it is to think of them in relation to what has been said in the first three parts of this Introduction. When Captain Stewart took an artist to the Far West he was, so to speak, assigning a news photographer to cover an area and a way of life that had never been pictured by anyone. Our illustrations might be an issue of *Life* sealed up a hundred and ten years ago and now distributed for the first time. Practically every sketch Miller made in 1837 was spot news. He made the first pictures of Scotts Bluff, Chimney Rock, Independence Rock, Devil's Gate, the Wind River Mountains, and the Tetons — of the upper Platte, the Sweetwater, Green River, Horse Creek, the Big Sandy, the lakes along the upper course of New Fork. Most of these have been abundantly sketched, painted, and photographed since his time — emigration, railroad, and real-estate booms, the tourist industry, and conservation have come in between — but some of the scenes sealed up in his time capsule remain unique. Thus our three views of Fort Laramie are the only ones that survive. For the Fort Laramie of Frémont, Francis Parkman, the Donner Party, the Mormons, all other emigrants, the gold rush, and the Mounted Riflemen and the Sixth Infantry — the Fort Laramie which other artists picture — was later than ours, built of adobe, some distance upstream, in 1841. But ours is the original hewn-log trading post which Sublette & Campbell built in 1834. (A footnote of Elliott Coues' says that he had seen a sketch: it cannot be identified.)

The timber decayed, that is, and presently there was a new fort — and a similar extinction came upon everything else that Miller painted except the countryside. By the time another artist came this way there were no fur company caravans, no annual rendezvous, no bull-boat laden with furs, and no mountain men at the summit of their pride — only a handful of veterans who in small groups were taking a few skins in remote valleys, scouting and interpreting for the Army, or holing up with Indians to prey on the settlers. Innumerable buffalo and large herds of antelope remained, but the elk seldom ran in herds any more and the sheep and goats so accessible to Miller were withdrawing to the cliffs. Rot had come upon the Indians, too; they were more corrupt, more hostile, and nearer their doom than those Miller painted. By that time the durably romantic West had forged new symbols for the American imagination, the emigrant wagon, the pony express, the stagecoach, and in a moment or two there would be the railroad and the cowboy. Captain Stewart had seen the mountain fur trade at its climax and it was already crumbling away when he brought his artist west. A few years later would have been too late. It was already too late in 1843 when, having lately sold one of his estates for £203,000, Stewart went West for the last time and made one of the most luxurious vacation trips ever made in a country that has always attracted millionaire sportsmen. But Miller got there in time — and he was the only artist who did.

With history's hindsight it is easy to wish that he had kept his mind on what seems to us his proper business, that instead of preparing himself to cover an eventual half-acre of canvas with mementoes he had systematically set down every detail of a way of life which was already beginning to disappear. History could have used less spectacle or decoration and more everyday routine. Nevertheless, an astonishing amount of trade detail got set down on the way to Miller's main objective. At its humblest it is a pack saddle or a stirrup, a bag of possibles, the curve of an Indian cradle or pommel or arrow case, buffalo ribs roasting at a fire, a powder horn on a sling — small authentic matters recorded for our use, whose very commonplaceness makes them the more valuable. Above this level are such typical scenes as the carts laboring out of a gully, a horse mired in quicksand, a bull-boat on the Platte, the setting of a beaver trap, a man afoot condemned to walk all day because he was derelict on guard, the buffalo carcass propped on knees and belly for butchering, the moment when the packs are taken off and the horses roll on the ground. I rate above these the glimpses of camp routine that constitute a visual verification of one's imaginative understanding of mountain life — the hour of nooning, breakfast and dinner, the firelight on the faces of the most notable liars in American history, the rush of Blackfeet trying to stampede the horses. Though in general Miller's Indian scenes are less noteworthy, some of them have this same power of verification — the horseman using his shield, the bow-testing, above all the village on the move. Finally, at the highest level there are the scenes of the caravan on the march and of the summer rendezvous. These certainly are of permanent historical importance and they happen also to be among the best of Miller's paintings. There is nothing like them in American art, for Miller was the only painter who ever saw a fur caravan or a summer rendezvous, and till now there have been no such illustrations in American history. It is as if any of the great symbols of our past, the Puritan, the Continental soldier, the cabin in the clearing, the timber raft, the covered wagon, the buffalo herd, the Long Trail — had had only one painter and his work had come to light only today.

All told, then, Miller contrived to set down a good deal of the mountain fur trade, whose era was so short that no other painter ever got round to it. As the first painter of the upper Rocky Mountains and the only painter of a vivid aspect of our history he is entitled to a permanent if necessarily modest fame. It has been postponed too long.

# 3. NOTES

## CHAPTER I: THE PRAIRIE TRAVELER (1833)

1. Though the tribal name is officially written Nez Percé and though the accent mark is preserved in place names, Westerners spoke of them from the beginning as Nez Perces — pronounced exactly as spelled. For the Flathead spellings and meanings of the word here rendered Shahaptan, see Teit, *The Salishan Tribes*, p. 300.

2. Fontenelle and Drips met about fifty lodges of Flatheads and Nez Perces on Beaver Creek (Montana) 'two or three days' after May 28, 1831. Fontenelle started for St. Louis on June 19, but had to make a long southwestern detour to Cache Valley (Utah). W. A. Ferris, *Life in the Rocky Mountains*, Paul Phillips editor, pp. 87, 96. Ferris, who in this very passage praises the decency and religious impulses of these tribes at great length, says nothing about the mission.

3. Catlin's portraits are numbered 145, Rabbit-Skin Leggings, and 146, No Horns on His Head. The corresponding drawings in *Letters and Notes* are Plates 207 and 208.

4. This account of the Nez Perce and Flathead mission rests on a study of all known sources, but in the second half conforms to the latest and best authority, Francis Haines, whose book and articles are listed in my bibliography. See also T. C. Elliott, 'Religion Among the Flatheads,' *Oregon Historical Quarterly*, Vol. 37, No. 1.

5. In his introduction to *Altowan*, Stewart's first novel, James Watson Webb says that Stewart was decorated for bravery but no such decoration is mentioned in the Army Lists or in Wylly's history of the 15th Hussars. His son, William George Stewart, who died before him, received the Indian Medal and the Victoria Cross during the Indian Mutiny. Stewart did hold the Italian Order of Christ. Since his mother's family, the Drummonds, had a long history of diplomatic service in Italy and Sicily, his possession of this order suggests that he may have spent some part of the missing twelve years in that service.

Stewart married a distant relative, Christina or Christian Stewart, two years before he came to the United States, and their only child was born in 1831. (His wife's name is given as Christina in Debrett and similar manuals. But in *The Red Book of Grandtully*, which was prepared at Stewart's direction and under his supervision, it is Christian.) Stewart did not go home between 1833 and 1839.

Some historians of the West have been bothered by the various spellings of his name and because of the variations have professed doubt about his authorship of *Altowan*. He is carried on the Army List as Stewart. The baronetcy had been created in the name of Steuart and all armorial documents use that spelling. The spelling Stuart, which he also used at times, denotes a blood-relationship to the royal house.

6. There is nothing on the known record to suggest that Stewart was in any way a British agent. Wartime conditions have made it impossible to have a search made of War Office files, where perhaps the question might be settled. But I cannot believe that any half-pay Army officer would spend six years in the Oregon country at this period without making occasional reports to authority, or that authority would have failed to request and even order such reports. It has turned out that George Frederick Ruxton was acting as a British agent in 1846 and 1847, when he went hunting in the West, though fifteen years ago I was soundly rebuked by historical scholars for saying he was.

7. References to Webster's indebtedness to the Company run through several years of the American Fur Company Papers. (Library of the New York Historical Society.) See, with many others, documents numbers 3227, 3288, 3330, 3353, 3408, 3519, 3695, etc.

8. Throughout the book Council Bluffs designates the entire region here described, and specifically the site originally so named by Lewis and Clark. This was on the Nebraska side of the river, twenty-odd miles above Omaha, and must not be confused with the Iowa city directly across the river from Omaha.

9. I use *Forty Years a Fur Trader*, the book which Elliott Coues made out of Larpenteur's eccentrically spelled reminiscences. Dr. Coues was one of the great editors and a very large part of Western history rests solidly on his labors. But he permitted himself a latitude that is unforgivable by present standards: he selected and rearranged and rewrote contexts to suit his judgment. In such portions of my text as rest on Larpenteur, therefore, I have — by the kindness of the Minnesota Historical Society and Mrs. Ilse Levi — also used photostats of the original manuscript of Larpenteur's reminiscences and the journal that preceded it.

10. I am indebted to Mrs. Brenda Gieseker of the Missouri Historical Society for a photostat of the invoice and to the Society for permission to use it.

11. Miller's paintings of Scott's Bluff and Chimney Rock are reproduced in our plates. The convention of Western books requires me to remind the reader that the former were named for a Smith, Jackson &

Sublette man who fell ill at Laramie Creek, more than fifty miles to the west, was abandoned by the trappers left to care for him, and in his delirium wandered and crawled this far toward home before dying. His bones were found at the foot of the bluffs the next year by the same party on its way back to the mountains. The story was first told by Irving. Some distance west of Ash Hollow, where the trail usually reached the North Platte, was Brady's Island, supposed to have taken its name from a similar incident. Two trappers of a party who were taking furs down the Platte by boat quarreled and one of them, Brady, was killed by the other while the two were alone in camp. The murderer reported that Brady's own gun had been accidentally discharged and killed him. Farther along the trail he accidentally shot himself and confessed his crime before dying. Rufus Sage says that the deaths took place 'some eight years ago,' which would make the date 1833, Stewart's first year in the West. In 1838, Myra Eells, spelling the name 'Brada,' makes the date 1827.

12. *Adventures in Mexico*, 268–269. Ruxton's dying buffalo is a standard description: the sight of so large an animal in the total ferocity of its last defiance deeply impressed the beholder. Everyone speaks of blood gushing from mouth and nostrils; nearly everyone says that the eyes reddened and glared. A buffalo that was not vitally wounded, however, was extremely dangerous, for it would charge every horse or hunter within sight. In close quarters, experienced hunters came up behind such a one and hamstrung it, then dispatched it with a careful shot.

The quotation shows that Ruxton used a rifle somewhat heavier than was usual among the mountain men, whose 'half-ounce of Galena' supplied a proverbial phrase. A half-ounce round lead ball, 218 grains, meant a caliber of .53 (when the rifle was new — in the circumstances, caliber increased with long use). The mountain rifle had a shorter and usually a considerably heavier barrel than the 'Kentucky rifle,' which had won the trans-Allegheny wilderness. It was stocked either half or full length and usually weighed from ten to twelve pounds. Preferably the bullet was used patched. The powder charge, of course, varied according to circumstances, from about 60 to about 200 grains: the rule of thumb that is traditional among riflemen would make the standard load for a half-ounce ball 93 grains. Dependable ballistic information hardly exists, but the available powder probably gave it, at most, a muzzle velocity no greater than 1600 foot-seconds, probably less than that. This would produce good shocking power but, relatively to modern arms, little penetration. Penetration was also cut down, relatively, by the fact that the ball was round and that it was made of lead without alloy. Though the half-ounce ball may be called standard, weights of 36, 48, and even 52 to the pound (.50, .47, and .45 caliber) are recorded, though the last must have been very uncommon. The most celebrated of mountain rifles were those made in St. Louis by Jacob and Samuel Hawken, whose name is sometimes misspelled Hawkin or Hawkins.

Captain Stewart was using a much more powerful gun. A footnote in *Edward Warren*, his second novel, says 'Captain Stewart, who had first brought up an ounce-balled rifle in 1833, that season went to rendezvous with Campbell's party, and there was more meat killed by that rifle in his hands and in those of that wonderful hunter, Antoine Clement, than by any other gun in camp.' This priority, no less than the marksmanship, seems to have been a favorite boast of Stewart's, but I am by no means sure it is established. Double-barrelled rifles were no novelty in America in 1833, as any collection will make clear, though the first example I have noted in mountain literature belongs to 1834. In that year the naturalist Townsend used one which shot twenty balls to the pound to test the belief that the buffalo's skull was impenetrable. He found it impenetrable to that weight of bullet: the ball flattened against the skull and the bone was not fractured. Since this was after the rendezvous, the gun he used may have been Stewart's, but N. J. Wyeth, who was in command of Townsend's party, appears to have had a similar one.

Stewart's rifles were made by either John or Joseph Manton, the leading English gunsmiths, and might have cost him up to three hundred guineas each. (A Hawken might cost $40, St. Louis.) British rifles of the time were precision instruments and their makers were concentrating on the effort to improve the shooting quality of the arm for wealthy sportsmen. American inventive genius concentrated on the effort to produce rifles by mass manufacture and to develop a repeating rifle — neither end had been satisfactorily achieved by 1833. Meanwhile gunsmiths went on making the individual rifle in the traditional way, and its qualities remained those that had astonished the world half a century before.

In the East the percussion cap had displaced the flintlock. The Western trapper, however, tended to be skeptical of the newfangled innovation. Though caps were reliable in bad weather, whereas rain might put the flintlock out of operation when it was needed most, and though they obviated the humiliating and dangerous possibility of losing your priming, they had in the trapper's estimation one nullifying disadvantage. If you lost your caps you were entirely out of luck, whereas if you lost your gunflint you could always improvise something that would work, even if there were no spares in your possible sack.

Effective ranges are discussed later in the text.

13. If the Indians butchered in this way, it meant that the robe which was made from the hide had to be sewed down the middle. When they intended to make a one-piece robe or to use the hide in a bullboat, they rolled the carcass over on one side, which made the desirable cuts of meat harder to get at. It will be understood that there was no way of stringing up a carcass for butchering and that you could not turn an animal which had a hump over on its back.

14. The hunting and skinning knife, the all-purpose knife of the trapper, was a common butcher knife with more or less heavy blade according to preference. So was the common scalping knife of the

Indian, though red preference selected the heaviest ones that could be afforded at the time of purchase. (The trade 'scalper' was worth from twenty to forty cents, St. Louis. Indians might also have a blacksmith make a blade from any convenient piece of scrap, say part of a cavalry sword or a worn-out rasp, and then seat it in a handle of bone, wood, or horn. Their liking for heavy blades may be observed at any museum. One at the National Museum which is supposed to have belonged to Sitting Bull is nearly a half inch thick along the back.) The best knives were British, of course, and much earlier than our time they had been stamped 'G R' for export. The letters, meaning 'George Rex,' had to be retained down to Victoria, in order to convince the Indians that they were getting the standard article, and as a matter of course they were stamped on American-made knives to meet the competition. But to the trapper 'G R' meant 'Green River.' Hence, 'up to Green River,' up to the hilt, all the way, as far and hard as possible.

15. *Wah-To-Yah and the Taos Trail* by Lewis H. Garrard, one of the best books ever written about the West. It deals with a period ten years later than ours and a country south of that frequented by the men we chiefly deal with, and so is not often mentioned in our text. It is, however, a classic, truer to the West and more understanding of Indians and mountain men than Parkman's *Oregon Trail*. *Wah-To-Yah* and Ruxton's *Life in the Far West* supply the best descriptions ever written of mountain life.

16. Parts of Killbuck's reminiscence are embroidery. There is no proof that Stewart was ever on Pawnee Fork (of the Arkansas). His movements during the spring of 1834, the only time when he could possibly have gone there, cannot be followed, but it is too far east to be likely. There is no evidence whatever that he ever saw the Chippewa country (roughly Minnesota) and the known facts make it all but certain that he did not. He certainly saw many wandering bands of Cheyennes and may possibly have spent some time in a Cheyenne village, but his amatory exploit, if it in fact happened, was more likely at the expense of a Snake 'chief.'

## Chapter II: The Brass Knuckles (1832)

1. No roster of Wyeth's company appears to have survived. John Wyeth says the party numbered twenty-one, *Niles' Register* says twenty-two, Wyeth himself in his 'Statement of Facts' written in 1847 says that he left Boston with twenty and four more joined him at Baltimore. Of these twenty-four, he says, six deserted before the party reached the Platte, leaving eighteen. Seven turned back from Pierre's Hole and eleven went on with Wyeth, one dying on the way. Eight resigned on learning of the shipwreck, of whom five returned to the United States; one died; two stayed in Oregon. Two started east with Wyeth in 1833.

One of these left him at the Yellowstone and the other went on to the States. These figures are sometimes at variance with his journals.

2. On their eastward journey in 1806 Lewis and Clark split their party into several divisions when they reached the mountains. Putting a non-com in charge of the group who were to return to the mouth of the Yellowstone by the route they had all traveled last year, each of the captains embarked on a new exploration, Clark to the south, Lewis to the north. For well over a year the expedition had been hearing dreadful stories of the belligerence of the Blackfeet, and now, near the end of July, Lewis met some on a fork of the Marias River. They were Gros Ventres (Atsina), of the tribe already mentioned in text, allies but not blood or linguistic relatives of the Blackfeet proper (the Siksika). They were in their usual mood and presently one of Lewis's men had to kill one of them and Lewis himself another. (These were the only Indians killed on the entire expedition.) Historians have frequently attributed the implacable anti-Americanism of the Blackfeet to this incident. Others, following Chittenden, attribute their hostility to an occasion when John Colter, a veteran of the Lewis and Clark expedition and the first mountain man, helped a band of Crows with whom he was traveling defeat a band of Blackfeet. Still a third incident involves Wilson Hunt. It seems to me that the importance of these incidents has been overstated. The true continuity is not offenses of the Americans but the character of the Blackfeet, who were an extreme specialization of savage life. Of the Plains tribes only the Comanches had a comparable ferocity and only these two tribes practiced prolonged torture. The Blackfeet refused to observe even the mild conventions of formal, temporary truce that most tribes felt bound by. Their allies and their enemies alike called them treacherous. As tough Indians, who knew and told everyone that they were tough, they not only found murder the cheapest form of trade relations but enjoyed it beyond most Indians. They were no more hostile to Americans than they were to the Flatheads, the Snakes, the Crows, and nearly everyone else.

3. The gory, exciting events of these years can be best followed in W. A. Ferris, *Life in the Rocky Mountains*, one of the most valuable of the mountain narratives. It was brilliantly edited by Paul C. Phillips in 1940.

4. Bannock is a guess. Mrs. Victor rendered it 'Rockway' and everyone who has told the story since her has repeated it. I cannot find any Rockway Indians and they are unknown to my ethnological consultants. Meek says that the Rockway was named Gray, which suggests either a halfbreed or half an Indian name. Stewart, who works a stabbing into the plot of *Edward Warren*, says in a footnote that he is taking over a fact and adds, 'John Gray stabbed Milton Sublette in the back, in a similar scene got up on purpose, the blow happily was not fatal.' (P. 249.) There were Iroquois and Snake halfbreeds named John Gray, and apparently others.

5. William Sublette's figures. When Wyeth was back in Cambridge

analyzing prices before starting on his second venture, he said that the RMF Company had taken $60,000 worth of furs all told in 1831, 1832, and 1833. This was a heroic underestimate.

6. No one has ever determined the exact site of the rendezvous or, so far as I know, of the famous battle that followed it. No contemporary description is detailed enough to be helpful, as I found some years ago when I went to Teton Basin to locate the battle. Local residents believed that the battle occurred to the southeast, near the mouth of a gulch in the Tetons, well to the north of the road to Teton Pass. I believe that it must have been in the other direction, southwestward, and may have been well out of the Basin. My guess is that the rendezvous camps were toward the southern end of Pierre's Hole, west or possibly even southwest of Victor, possibly along Trail Creek. The brigades would be a mile or so apart and the Company camps a somewhat greater distance from the RMF camps.

7. *The Narrative of Zenas Leonard*, W. F. Wagner, ed., p. 102; abbreviated edition by Milo M. Quaife, p. 57. Leonard is a useful witness to many things and very illuminating about craft details and the mountain life, but he must be used with care. This passage is typical: he is a month off in his dates and his version of incidents differs radically from the unanimous statements of other eyewitnesses.

8. On foot certainly, but whether alone, or brought in by two Iroquois halfbreeds who were with one of the searching parties, or accidentally encountered by George Nidever and another trapper named Poe, who were hunting, not for him but for game, is anybody's guess. The numerous eyewitness accounts of Fitzpatrick's arrival cannot be reconciled. Irving uses the Iroquois story. Nidever claims to have found him, Ferris says that he came in alone, Leonard says that 'he was found.' Leonard's account of his wanderings purports to be in his own words but contains too many unacceptable details, among them the incredible statement that an overcast sun had caused this master of trails to lose his way on a stretch west of South Pass which he had traveled on an average twice a year since 1824. Modern books about the trade, even the excellent biography of Fitzpatrick by Hafen and Ghent, says that his hair had turned white during his escape. I have found no contemporary statement to this effect.

9. Modern treatments say that Fitzpatrick lost his outfit crossing Pierre's Creek, which is clearly wrong. He probably would not have had to ferry his stuff across so shallow a stream (though there had lately been much rain and some snow) and certainly if he had had a rifle as far as Pierre's Creek, he would not have been starving when found.

## Chapter III: Massacre: Sport and Business (1832)

1. Exactly how large the party of trappers was and exactly how many Gros Ventres there were are beyond determination. But that the latter

kept coming is proof that they considerably outnumbered the whites. Otherwise they would have turned back and scattered. In their calculation (they knew nothing about the forces back in Pierre's Hole) they were strong enough to make a cleanup.

2. There is equal warrant in the eyewitness accounts for reversing the rôles and having Godin do the shooting, but it would be better plotting to let him offer to shake hands, since the Blackfeet would consider the Flathead an inferior. Some witnesses do not mention the incident and some modern students have therefore concluded that it did not occur. There can be no question that it did, as Townsend's experience will make clear later on.

3. These are Chittenden's figures, include those who died later as the result of wounds, and represent a canvass of all sources known when he wrote. Additional ones discovered since his time would justify raising the numbers somewhat, but William Sublette's letter written two months after the battle and published in the Missouri *Republican* makes the losses lower than Chittenden.

There are more eyewitness accounts of 'the battle of Pierre's Hole' than of any other episode in the mountain fur trade. They differ in both fundamentals and details so much that any modern account must be to some extent arbitrary and even conjectural. Sublette's letter, N. J. Wyeth's journal, and Irving's narrative in *Bonneville* (which was based on both and on personal interviews with several participants) are clearly the most dependable. But John Wyeth, Leonard, and Ferris wrote from notes made on the spot and Ferris has a second account a year later, after the affair had been thoroughly talked out. George Nidever's journal is also on the spot but makes obvious errors. Mrs. Victor's source, Joe Meek, was a participant. The account that varies most from the norm is in the autobiography of John Ball, one of Wyeth's men.

4. Irving says that two of Daniel Boone's grandsons were with this party. But a grandson of Daniel Boone was by now standard equipment for any adventure story.

## Chapter IV: Paul Bunyan's Fair (1833)

1. Ferris says one hundred and fifty. Irving, who also tells the story, does not make an estimate. A hundred and fifty would be a very large war party indeed for the time and tribes, much larger than was customary. On the other hand, the Blackfeet were out for glory this winter and may have mounted an expedition of that size. In general it is safe to scale down most war statistics in the literature. An Indian whose band had either licked an enemy party or been licked by it had good reasons for exaggerating its size. The mountain men were usually reported by eastern journalists and did not shrink from impressing them; the journalists in turn magnified their glory.

2. Here Joe Meek, the first-hand authority for the RMF Company at this period, mentions an Antoine Claymore as a companion of his in several escapades. This may be the halfbreed Antoine Clement who was to become Stewart's hunter and companion.

3. Not the small stream in southern Idaho now called the Malad but the one shown on maps as Big Wood River, in Blaine and Lincoln Counties, Idaho. This is the Malade, Maladi, Sick, and Sickly River of the literature, so named because a party of trappers were made violently sick there by a meal of spoiled beaver meat.

4. Prices current in the St. Louis newspapers for 1833 show beaver at $4.50 a pound in March and $3.50 in October.

5. Probably, however, Wyeth is again considerably underestimating the RMF Company business.

6. The rare dates in *Edward Warren* are always given with a blank, as 183–. The action of the novel begins in the year of the first outbreak of Asiatic cholera, which was 1832, and the hero goes west the next year. Moreover, though Stewart attended six annual rendezvous and events from some of the others are worked into his story, the one portrayed is basically that of 1833 and a number of incidents supposed to be fictional can be recognized as historical.

7. I have elsewhere noted the impression they made on Edwin Bryant, bound west in 1846. *The Year of Decision*, p. 308.

8. None of this is to deny the occurrence of romantic love between the races or to impugn the dignity of many mixed marriages. American history is full of permanent unions of unimpeachable worthiness, Western history no less so than that of New York or the Province of Quebec. But in the nature of things there could be few permanent unions in the mountains. They were common enough at the fixed posts of both the American Fur Company and the Hudson's Bay Company. Francis Chardon's journal at Fort Clark has some amusing episodes of wife-buying, wife-stealing among the partners, and the cuckolding of even the most exalted Company factors when young men came piping in the spring.

9. These locations are clearly stated by Ferris, who is usually reliable, and Wyeth who is nearly always so. Coues, who challenges them, is misreading Irving, who in turn appears to have misunderstood Bonneville's notes. There is independent confirmation of Wyeth and Ferris in the footnotes (and the text) of *Edward Warren*, which Coues had not read.

10. In a long career on the frontier Richard Irving Dodge saw so many tall tales shattered on the hard rocks of fact that he came to doubt practically everything. He says that he had heard a lot about mad wolves in his time but mostly from Indians, who in his considered judgment did not know how to tell the truth anyhow. He says firmly that he had never seen any evidence that anyone had ever died of a wolf bite. But there can be no doubt about this incident: it is too well attested.

In answer to my question, Doctor Ira N. Gabrielson, Director of the Fish and Wildlife Service, Department of the Interior, says that rabies has appeared in many species, domestic and wild. 'Our men happen to know of the reports of these in the cat, cow, horse, mule, sheep, goat, hog, wolf, fox, coyote, hyena, skunk, monkey, deer, antelope, camel, bear, elk, polecat, bat, squirrel, hare, rabbit, rat, mouse, jackal, badger, marmot, woodchuck, porcupine, weasel, hedgehog, gopher, raccoon, owl, hawk, chicken, pigeon, and stork.'

11. An allusion to the piratical attack on Fitzpatrick which is described in the next chapter.

## Chapter V: Absaroka (1833)

1. He was not a traveling companion of Stewart's, as some writers have assumed. Stewart was unaccompanied. At the rendezvous he hired Antoine Clement and perhaps a humbler roustabout or two.

2. As an earlier note shows, Townsend says that someone in Wyeth's 1834 party had a double-barreled rifle. It could hardly have been anyone but Wyeth and he is not likely to have had a Manton rifle. Nor in August, 1833, would Stewart, the newcomer, have been entitled to speak of Wyeth as a greenhorn — he wasn't one.

3. Horses used to whites disliked the smell of Indians. One of many reasons why the mountain men liked mules was that they had this dislike to a higher degree and so made excellent auxiliary sentinels.

4. But it is Lewis to whom an American legend that will not down attributes a child of Sacajawea's. Working desultorily on Lewis and Clark for some years, I have encountered that legend in odd places and have corresponded with a man who claims to belong to the line so founded. This sort of thing can never be proved or disproved. I have never seen any evidence whatever of any kind, nor have I found the rumor in the legendry that has copiously gathered round Meriwether Lewis, following his mysterious death. This child belongs with the innumerable bastards whom a mythmaking people have believed that Talleyrand begot on the gentility and the peasantry of the eastern seaboard from Maine to Maryland. There are those who can convince themselves that Aaron Burr was the father of Martin Van Buren, and the idiotic rumor that made the St. Regis halfbreed Eleazar Williams into Louis XVII of France still persuades that type of mind.

5. Always provided that the tenuous line of scholarly identifications is right throughout.

6. Take your choice of several spellings. This is Beckwourth's.

7. This paragraph mostly from Chittenden.

8. Curtis, Vol. iv.

9. The most remarkable thing in the two novels that Stewart wrote is the appearance in *Altowan* of a berdash. Stewart makes the invert a leading character, describes his dress and behavior at length, shows a

considerable understanding of his emotions, and makes quite clear just what he was. I know of no English or American novel of that time (1846) or for many years later that is half so frank about homosexuality.

10. Alfred Jacob Miller heard the story on his way west with Stewart in 1837 and sketched the scene in water colors. It is No. 149 in 'Rough Draughts for Notes to Indian Sketches' and No. 179 of the Walters Gallery copies. Later he made an enormous oil for Murthly Castle, best described in the Walters Gallery notes.

'*Attack by Crow Indians.* The incident here illustrated happened on a previous journey to our company and is drawn from a narrative furnished by one of the parties. An oil picture painted from this sketch furnishes Cardinal Wiseman an illustration to one of his lectures in London, and as he describes it more happily than we can, we give his relation. After some preliminaries he proceeds as follows: "He (Captain Stewart) is at the head of his tribe, a small insignificant body of men, threatened by one far more powerful and numerous, which is bent on its destruction. He has himself become the chief of his tribe; but as the enemy is coming to battle, they have been told by their soothsayer that they will not succeed, unless the other side strike the first blow. The picture represents this gentleman at the head of his little body of men, surrounded by yelling and irritated savages, provoking him to strife, and for this purpose thrusting their fists into his face, shaking their tomahawks over his head, using the most insulting gestures and uttering the most offensive words: but he stands calm and composed in the midst of them, knowing that the safety, not only of himself, but of all who trust in him depends entirely upon his complete command of self. I consider that really an attitude and a position worthy of a hero. But you will ask how am I going to apply this? Let me present you with another picture of a mental contest. One comes up who is determined to pick a quarrel with you, as we say, and insults you in the presence of others. He provokes you. He even calumniates and says the most opprobrious and unjust things of you. He threatens. He reproaches. Now remember, that so long as you can keep silent, so long as you can command your tongue, your adversary is powerless, the victory is yours. In a short time his store of vituperations is exhausted; by degrees he gets to the end of his vocabulary of abuse; like a man fencing with the air and meeting no resistance, his anger is expended on himself; he languishes; retires discomfited, abashed and ashamed of playing that solitary part; you all the time are calm, unruffled, satisfied, in peace. But speak one angry word in retort, and your adversary has gained his point; Victory is no longer yours. It belongs now to the strong. You have let loose the dogs of war and they will fight it out. You have unlocked the pent-up ocean in your own heart. You have awakened a tempest; Flash will succeed flash, thunder, thunder; and it is only he who can dart the sharpest or roar the loudest, that will carry the day." '

11. In the main my account follows Irving. This is a good place to remark on Irving's usual trustworthiness and on the curious decline in

reputation which *Astoria* and *Bonneville* have suffered. They are little used by modern writers and yet both are original sources, in some contexts the only sources, and both have remarkable accuracy. Their literary quality is superb.

Irving's greatest weakness is that he had never seen the country he was writing about. His distances are sometimes wrong, his ideas about the fundamental geography of the region are discordant and naïve, and he was unable to translate into prose what his informants told him about climate and the necessities of travel. But he had Bonneville's papers, including a daily journal that has disappeared. He had Wyeth's papers (more of them, apparently, than have survived) and sometimes quotes them verbatim. He had other contemporary manuscript material which cannot be identified now and he read the Missouri newspapers conscientiously. Writing *Astoria*, traveling on the prairies, and his intimate acquaintance with the New York Astorians and their business gave him an excellent background for *Bonneville*. Besides this he conferred with Bonneville himself and with other leading characters in his narrative and a miscellany of mountain men. The Sublettes and Robert Campbell supplied him with information and interpretation which he could have got from no one else and which must be treated with the utmost respect. It is clear that much of *Bonneville* rests on the unsurpassed knowledge of Campbell.

Irving is franker about the American Fur Company and more critical of it than would be expected of a writer so dependent on its material. But he is not critical enough and the modern reader must bear that fact in mind.

Bonneville needs the attention of a qualified modern scholar: he needs to be studied in relation to the vast material that has come to light since Irving wrote. In particular, Walker's journey to California needs investigation. It would be easy enough to correct Irving's geographical misconceptions and to reduce his generalizations of routes (all fundamentally correct, since they were based on on-the-spot journals) to specific details.

12. Following the robbery, Stewart wrote in protest to McKenzie at Fort Union. In the letter first quoted in this paragraph (to Mitchell at Fort McKenzie) McKenzie refers to 'my friend Captain Stewart.' This can only mean that Stewart had met him at St. Louis the previous spring. He also mentions Stewart in a letter to Pierre Chouteau, Jr. (Fort Union Letter Book, December 16, 1833.)

13. The first edition of *The Life and Adventures of James P. Beckwourth*, published in 1856, is now a rarity. So is the 1892 reprint edited by Charles Godfrey Leland. Leland's introduction and notes are altogether worthless. I edited a third edition in 1931 and this, though also out of print, is much easier to come by than its predecessors and has a more readable format. My introduction is sound enough but many of my notes are either misconceived or flatly wrong — I should have waited some years before writing them.

In his introduction Leland tells a good story which shows Jim's reputation among his peers. Some of them had turned to mining in the California gold fields. Hearing the astonishing news that Jim had written a book, they determined to procure a copy the next time one of them went to town for supplies. Their agent was not used to the literary life and returned with a copy of the Bible. That night when the boys gathered to listen he opened the book at the story of Samson. By the time he reached the passage where the hero ties firebrands to the tails of three hundred foxes and turns them loose in the Philistine cornfields, one of the auditors had had enough. He stood up and protested. 'Thar,' he said, 'I'd know that for one of Jim Beckwourth's lies anywhere.'

14. We shall see later that Stewart made such an offer in jest and was taken seriously.

Twenty pages before this passage Jim says he was present at the burning of the Arikaras described earlier, as he was not. In this instance he is trying to explain an attack on one of Bonneville's parties and ascribes it to the villainy of a mulatto who had come wandering into the Crow country. The net effect is to suggest that Jim had been present at one of the robberies of Bonneville's men and, as in the present context, is explaining it away.

The mention of the unnamed mulatto is interesting. Jim was a mulatto and so was Edward Rose, whose heroisms he frequently appropriates. Rose, a pre-Ashley mountain man, lived for some years among the Crows and may even have been among them during the first year or so of Beckwourth's stay. He was a ferocious character with steel nerves and nine lives. He had a reputation for treachery that appears not to have been deserved. Obviously Beckwourth resented the glory attached to his deeds but there is no reason to try to establish which were Jim's and which Rose's. The most debated of them, a leap into a Blackfoot fort, was probably Jim's.

15. In a later chapter dealing with a visit to St. Louis which he can be shown to have made in 1836, Beckwourth says that he met Fitzpatrick and four other 'bullies' in a saloon and that Fitzpatrick alluded to the robbery and went after him with a knife. Of course Jim backed him down (which would require considerable believing) and the other four as well. Later, in the presence of Bill Sublette, he forced Fitzpatrick to admit that he did not believe Jim was responsible for the attack and will never spread the rumor again. Jim was a good man with a yarn.

## Chapter VI: The Theme of Wonder (1833–1834)

1. No one sees Stewart anywhere from his letter to McKenzie in early September, 1833, to the rendezvous of 1834. None of his few surviving letters and no passage in either of his novels alludes to any aspect of winter life. (On the other hand, none of those letters goes back as far as that winter and no one sees him in the States.)

The negative evidence for his having wintered in the mountains is stronger. It is of some importance that no states-bound caravan of 1833 is known to have included him. It is more important that no mountain-bound party of 1834 has any mention of him — and they are all documented. (He would almost certainly have been with Bill Sublette, whose trips can be followed in detail.) But every known account of the rendezvous of 1834 mentions him and this justifies the conclusion that he came to it with a party that had made a spring hunt.

That conclusion is heavily supported by a footnote in *Edward Warren*, pp. 288–289. As I have pointed out the footnotes are in Stewart's own person and many of them can be proved historically accurate. In this one Stewart is dating an incident that is described in my chapter VIII. He says: 'It was in the spring of 1834, I was with Jem [*sic*; a misprint, not a mistake: the text of *Edward Warren* contains many typographical errors] Bridger and one of the bravest and most dashing hunters of the day, Captain Lee of the U.S. Army, in a range of mountains whose western slopes give birth to the waters of California and near the city of Taos.' This would be Stephen Louis Lee, one of Kit Carson's early partisans. Taos was by no means a city and the geography is crude for a mountain man, even one who was remembering it in Scotland twenty years later for no 'waters of California' originate in New Mexico. Both the San Juan and the Little Colorado flow into the Colorado River from New Mexico, however, and a long stretch of the lower Colorado was indeed California. Regardless of the geography, here is an unequivocal statement that Stewart was in the vicinity of Taos in the spring of 1834. It is almost inconceivable that he could have got there from the settlements. It is especially unlikely that a Santa Fe caravan from Independence could have got him there that early.

The note suggests that Bridger's brigade may have traveled for a time with those of Fraeb and Gervais, which Meek met on Bill Williams Fork on his way back from California. (Victor, 152.) Finally a reader who is willing to fill with speculation the gaps in Meek's narrative and to make a series of unsupported hypotheses may find here some support for the statement about Stewart made by Ruxton that is questioned at the end of Chapter I, the statement that he once fought on Pawnee Fork. For Meek goes on (p. 154 *et seq.*) to tell an exciting story of fighting the Comanches in a vague geography 'between the Arkansas and the Cimarron.' An eager hypothesis could bring that near enough Pawnee Fork to justify Ruxton. The argument, however, is much too ethereal for my taste.

2. The Sioux of French narratives earlier than the Verendryes are the eastern or river Sioux.

3. Fort Union was 1782 miles from St. Louis according to the U.S. Engineers survey of 1890, which I use for all Missouri distances herein. Precisians will remember that the river is always shortening its course and therefore in 1833 the distances were a little longer than those I give.

Between 1890 and 1932, according to the surveys, the Missouri from the Three Forks to the mouth lost seventy-eight miles.

4. A journal of Culbertson's, sometimes apparently reproduced verbatim or but little changed, is the basis of this part of Lieutenant James H. Bradley's journal printed in Volume III of *Contributions to the Historical Society of Montana.* Other parts of Bradley's Journal in later volumes are excellent on this aspect and period of the trade.

5. Of late years ethnologists have called the Blackfeet proper the North Blackfeet (or rather, the North Blackfoot) and have differentiated the North Piegan(s) and the South Piegan(s) who were one tribe to the mountain men, the latter being the ones usually encountered. Linguistically the Blackfeet belonged to the Algonkin family, which included most of the Indians you learned about in Parkman and Cooper except the Iroquois and most of the famous Great Lakes and upper Middle West Indians, among them Black Hawk and Longfellow's Hiawatha. The Arapahos and Cheyennes were also Algonkin; so were the Plains Crees. So were the Blackfeet's confederates, the Gros Ventres (Atsina).

In their Canadian reaches, the Blackfeet had another small group of confederates, a tough and intelligent Déné-speaking tribe, the Sarsis, who acquired all the belligerence of their allies. They play a memorable part in the history of the Canadian fur trade. Their artifacts are usually well represented in museums.

The origin of the name Blackfeet is uncertain. Folklore ascribes it to the blackening of someone's moccasins by the ashes of a prairie fire. No one would want to depreciate the atrocity record of the Blackfeet but some part of it is undeserved. Some soldiers, explorers, travelers, and even historians confused with them the Sihasapa subdivisions of the Teton Sioux, who wore black moccasins, were called Blackfeet, and did a lot of murdering that went down in the books as the work of the true Blackfeet.

6. He was Lieutenant-Colonel of Sterling Price's Second Missouri. When that regiment reached Santa Fe he was given command of a detachment that was transferred to Doniphan's First Missouri and made the great campaign with it. I have briefly noted some of his prodigies in *The Year of Decision.*

7. The leading authority on the Blackfeet is Clark Wissler. See a series of his studies in *Anthropological Papers of the American Museum of Natural History*, listed in my bibliography.

8. Needless to say it is Culbertson, not Maximilian, who supplies this detail. *Loc. cit.*, p. 108.

9. This of course takes no account of variables or the terrain and simplifies the matter to its essentials. A Hawken rifle was accurate well beyond a hundred yards when new and kept in condition and when aimed by a man in no hurry; it was more or less effective up to two hundred yards; it would kill beyond that. So for that matter could a good bow. My distances are those at which a trapper or an Indian

could count on a kill. Various authorities claim that a muzzle-loading flintlock could be loaded, aimed, and fired five times in sixty seconds. I do not believe it. Experts cannot do so well now with better designed equipment and I doubt if anyone ever could. Making all allowance for the desperate efficiency of cool men in danger of death, it took about twenty seconds to load a trapper's rifle. (Accuracy required the bullet to be patched; the more accurate the rifle was, the longer it took to seat the ball; the pan had to be primed.) It took about ten seconds to aim and fire the rifle — if the shot was going to be made good. The marksman was firing from one knee, supporting the barrel on his left fist clasped round his wiping stick, or prone, or sometimes on his back. If he could load and fire in twelve seconds, then the ball was so loose that it would not shoot straight and his aim was so sloppy that looseness didn't matter. In thirty seconds an Indian could shoot eight or ten aimed arrows.

This danger period, the period of reloading while the Indian closed to his effective range or even to close quarters, is what repeating arms put an end to. The revolution worked by the Colt revolver was first that it gave the white man five shots (not six in the early models), whereas the Indian expectation had always been that he would have only one, and second that it could be used on horseback with the same rapidity and at almost as great ranges as the bow, whereas a rifle was cumbersome in the saddle. After our period the development of rifles and ammunition that greatly increased the effective range, most notably the Sharps, gave the white man another advantage. Finally carbines, or short-barreled rifles, were developed for use on horseback.

10. I cite these distances, the eighty-six paces measured and the three hundred yards estimated by a military man who had to estimate ranges correctly, in support of the immediately preceding note. Eighty-six paces is less than seventy-five yards, and this is accepted as good shooting. At three hundred yards the Assiniboins considered themselves safe from the fort's fire.

11. Especially their shields. The war shield is a good example of the mingling of empiricism and magic in Indian thought. It was effective: made of heat-treated parfleche, it could stop an arrow or a smoothbore ball at mid-range. But to the Indian mind not the properties of the material gave it its protective value but the incantations and rituals used to sensitize it and especially to sensitize its cover of deerskin or some other fine material. Shields and covers had to be made by shield-makers, a guild who were both artisans and priests. Their medicines notified them in dreams or visions that they had the magical power required and revealed the ceremonies they must use, purifications, prayers, songs, sacrifices, and rituals with specific symbolisms. Devices burned and painted on the shields and painted and beaded or quilled on the covers, as well as feathers, tassels, and many other ornaments hung from both were all talismanic: they were part of the magic. It was this magic which the brave trusted to preserve him from harm when he carried the shield into battle.

12. Culbertson, p. 210.

13. Most of Maximilian's precious collection was lost the following summer, 1834, when the *Assiniboin* on which it was sent downriver was wrecked and burned. Maximilian corresponded with various of his western friends for some years and Kenneth McKenzie once paid him a visit at Wied.

14. Fifty-eight by Zenas Leonard's count.

15. A guess but a dictated one. No one has ever been able to pick them up before they reach the Humboldt. Zenas Leonard says that they made their meat on 'the west side' of Great Salt Lake but is certainly wrong. There were no buffalo there and they could not have gone west from there, as Leonard says they did, without crossing the Salt Desert. It is impossible to believe that Leonard, whose narrative is minutely detailed, would have failed to describe that exceedingly difficult and equally picturesque country if he had ever seen it. (Authorities on Western exploration are unanimous that the Salt Desert was not crossed between Jed Smith and the Bartleson Party.) The descriptions which Leonard gives from Great Salt Lake to the Humboldt are unidentifiable; they apply to all the country from about Kelton, Utah, to about Wells, Nevada, and points north as well.

16. He bought it for 'two awls and one fish hook' and says it was worth thirty or forty dollars. It would have been worth more than that in Canada when the French and British were working virgin fields. It would have been *castor gras*, beaver that had been worn for a year or more and so had been converted into the best of all fur for felting.

17. 'Digger' is a term of contempt, not a tribal designation, and in the literature of the West is sometimes confused with another loose term, 'Root-digger,' which describes all the tribes, most of them superior tribes, that lived in localities where there were staple crops of edible roots and bulbs. Some of these were very important sources of food, notably the camas (*quamasia quamash* and related species), the bitterroot (*lewisia rediviva* and related species), the breadroot or prairie turnip (*psoralea esculenta* and related species), the biscuitroot (*cogswellia triternata* and related species), the yampa (*carum gairdneri*, *c. kelloggi*, *c. organum*), and many species of lilies.

But the mountain men meant by 'Diggers' just such economic rejects as Walker encountered here. They lived in the barren deserts of Nevada, Utah, southern Idaho, and southwestern Colorado. Probably all of them belonged to what the ethnologists call the Uto-Aztecan family, which made them kin not only to such tribes as the Snakes, Comanches, Utes, Pimas, and Hopis but to the Mayas and Aztecs too. They had been reduced to Okies, however, and were now sub-marginal. Somewhat better off than most of them were various California tribes west of the Sierra; some of these had been missionized and therefore peonized but therefore also raised above the status of Diggers. These California tribes are the only ones who have had much study; ethnologists lump most of the others together (and loosely) as Gosiutes (in

Utah) and Paiutes (in Nevada, the 'Piutes' of early scarehead stories). Powell separates out those whom Walker met as the Paviotso.

On the evidence they were tolerably disgusting but once they experienced an equal or greater disgust. Some of them crept up to stare into the snowbound hovels of the Donner Party and saw white men feeding not on grubs and beetles but on their dead.

18. Note that this is well to the south of the route by Truckee River and Donner Pass that later became the standard crossing for emigrants. Walker was to pioneer in establishing this route too.

19. Though it is usually Walker, other celebrated mountain men have acquired it by attraction. Note, however, that a story of eating human flesh passed off as other meat is common in folklore and primitive literatures. Most Indian tribes had such a legend. Psychoanalysts deal with an identical phantasy in their daily practice. The oral literature of the American frontier softens cannibalism to the eating of some tabooed animal such as skunk or raccoon (which the pioneers hated totemistically, though some gourmets approved it) and immediate vomiting when the cook reveals his little joke. In this form the yarn appears on all our frontiers.

20. Ruxton's delightful chapter owes something to Ewing Young's California visits, as my text shows, and something also to later raids by Joe Walker, who took to trading in California horses when the fur trade petered out. (He may be seen at Fort Bridger returning from one such business trip in *The Year of Decision.*) But so many details are exactly reproduced from Walker's 1833 visit that I suspect other details, now unrecognizable, may also be historical. It will make an amusing problem for the next historian of Bonneville, who will have to bear in mind that Ruxton talked with more mountain men of the great age than anyone else who ever wrote about them.

21. Bonneville's own statement of Walker's route is given in a letter of his to S. K. Warren in 1857. See the Pacific Railroad Report (full title in my bibliography), Vol. XI, 32–33.

## Chapter VII: The Winter Lodge

1. In Indian stories the logic of fiction is the logic of dream. Red Water did not need to account for the change of scene. I use the version given in *The Oregon Trail.* In the notebook which Parkman kept on the trail and in which he jotted down Red Water's story, there are two men as well as two women, and Red Water takes them all.

2. In 1846 Frederick Ruxton traveled up from Mexico by way of Taos and spent part of the winter at the Pueblo. His account of the Pueblo and his own camps — in *Adventures in Mexico*, not *Life in the Far West* which is quoted so often in my text — is the best description ever written of wintering in the mountains. Of the various journals that exhibit life at a trading post, the most illuminating are those of Larpenteur (mostly at Fort Union) and Chardon (Fort Clark).

3. Ethnologists try hard to limit the word 'parfleche' to the big, flat rawhide envelope whose face and flaps were painted or embroidered and which was used chiefly as a container for dried meat. In a museum 'parfleche' always means this Indian saratoga trunk, but the synecdoche cannot be binding on the historian. To the trapper 'parfleche' meant 'rawhide,' the stuff itself, not objects made of it.

4. Catlin, Letter 27, has an illuminating passage about the agony of walking in moccasins. After a couple of days he 'felt like giving up the journey and throwing myself on the ground in hopeless despair.' A halfbreed taught him to toe in, which promptly relieved him.

5. Women's work and extremely hard work. A fresh buffalo hide might weigh up to eighty pounds and all the processes of tanning were done manually. How did a squaw make a robe of a fresh hide? First she pegged it out on the ground, hair side down, and scraped off the flesh, sinew, and integument with a 'graining' tool of curved bone in which an iron blade had been seated. Then she rubbed the flesh side with warm water and some greasy substance, the brains plus such other fats as her tutor or her medicine had prescribed. This had to be worked into the hide with a smooth stone or something similar, a laborious process, after which the hide lay in the sun, shrinking a good deal, while the grease penetrated. The next step was to soften the hide in water and then bring it back to natural size and make it flexible by twisting and wringing and pulling it — a two-squaw job that lasted many hours. This is as much treatment as the trade robe received and for trade robes it was done as roughly and hastily as possible.

If the skin was to be dehaired an intervening step took place here: it was soaked in a stream and possibly treated with ashes till the hair loosened and could easily be scraped off. In any event it was worked with the hands and the flesh side was scraped with a rough stone or toothed iron blade to make it flexible. As it dried it bleached gray-white. The final step was the hardest. A rawhide rope was stretched at an angle and the hide was sawed back and forth across it endlessly. The squaw used her whole weight and preferably got a friend to trade work with her.

All skins received approximately the same treatment though with certain specific differences. Most of those used for clothing and nearly all the finer ones, for whatever use they might be destined, were given a thorough smoking over slow fires. A well-smoked skin was water-resistant and would dry soft. The beautiful cream-colored and white garments seen in museums had not been smoked; they were bleached by various means and had been whitened with various earths.

6. The Indians packed it in bundles or 'packages' about two and a half feet thick and perhaps eighteen inches long, conveniently sized for use by war parties. These bundles were a standard article of trade; so were pemmican and the fats.

7. Mr. Stefansson's definitive treatise on pemmican has not been published as this is written. Chapters of it have appeared in *Harper's*

and the *Atlantic* and, besides earlier monographs, he published an illuminating summary in *The Military Surgeon*, August, 1944. Space limitations forbid my touching on the vast traffic in pemmican and tallow conducted by the métis of the Red River Settlement in Canada, whose famous carts were coming to the upper plains in great number during our period.

8. There is a large specialist literature, anesthetically dull, on Indian use of plants for medicine. Discussions of the use of plants for food as distinct from agriculture are less common. An exhaustive list, no more than a list but of great service to the student, is Elias Yanovsky's *Food Plants of the North American Indian.* There is little literature on Indian use of meats and I have been unable to find any treatise on the fascinating subject of Indian cookery.

9. Letter to me from Doctor Ira N. Gabrielson.

10. I say that Miller 'claims' because part of his note (No. 48 in 'Rough Draughts') exactly reproduces the language of a passage in Ruxton's *Adventures in Mexico.*

11. Ferris, wintering in a Flathead village, records another Christmas menu: 'buffalo tongues, dry buffalo meat, fresh venison, wheat flour cakes, buffalo marrow (for butter), sugar, coffee, and *rum*, with which we drank a variety of appropriate toasts suited to the occasion, and our enlarged and elevated sentiments respecting universal benevolence and prosperity, while our hearts were warmed, our prejudices banished and our affections refined.' *Life in the Rocky Mountains*, p. 238.

12. After telling this last story Meek says that Stewart and Miller, who were with the brigade, came up just after the bear was killed and took the skin. Miller, he goes on, not only sketched a portrait of Meek on the spot but later made an action picture of the fight. This painting, he adds, 'was copied in wax for a museum in St. Louis, where it probably remains to this day [about 1868?], a monument of Meek's best fight.' (*The River of the West*, 223.)

In 1839, on an occasion described in our final chapter, Thomas Jefferson Farnham met Meek on Bear River. Farnham says that Meek 'figures in the St. Louis Museum, with the paws of an immense grisly [*sic*] bear on his shoulders in front, the fingers and thumb of his left hand bitten off, while with his right hand he holds the hunter's knife, plunged deeply in the animal's jugular vein.' This does not say that Farnham had seen the wax statue or, quite, that he knew about it, though it is so written as to indicate at least the latter. Farther on he quotes Meek as saying 'I think the boys at the museum in St. Louis might have done me up as it really was. [Notice that he does not mention Miller.] The beast only jumped on my back and stripped off my blanket, scratched some but didn't pull my shoulder blade off. Well, after he had robbed me of my blanket, I shoved my rifle against him and blew out his heart. That's all — no fingers bitten off, no knifing: I merely drove a little lead into his palpitator.'

Farnham's book, first published in 1841 (a few copies; title page dated 1843 in most) appears in this passage to be based on notes made on the spot. Mrs. Victor's *River of the West*, which is a biography of Meek based on his own memories, is thirty years later and was written before its author got her long training in research in the history-factory of Hubert Howe Bancroft. Checking it with other accounts show that Meek's memory was remarkably good for action but extremely unreliable for dates. He dates this story 1836, which was the year before Miller came to the mountains. In other passages he confuses Miller with John Mix Stanley — see, for instance, my note on 'The Trapper's Last Shot.' Meek certainly met both painters and Miller may have sketched him, though he is not identified by name in any of Miller's notes and it was Bridger whom he painted in armor, not Meek, as Meek says.

The passages in Farnham and Victor fairly establish that there was a Madame Tussaud grizzly fight in a St. Louis museum and that Meek believed it memorialized one of his exploits. They do not establish Miller's authorship of a painting on which the statue was based. The time element is also against Meek. He would have had to hear about it in the mountains only a little more than a year after the earliest time when it could have been exhibited.

The statue was probably at Koch's Museum, on Market Street, between Second and Third. It is described to me as 'devoted mainly to natural history, Indian relics, etc.,' and its proprietor as 'a very intelligent person and a good business man.' Koch sold some Indian material to the British Museum for 'an annuity sufficient to subsist on for many years.' All the exhibits have been dispersed beyond trace and there is no record of such a wax statue as Meek describes. I am indebted here to Mr. Charles Nagel, Jr., formerly of the City Art Museum of St. Louis, whose letter to me I quote; to Mr. John Bryan, a historian of the National Park Service, who supplied some of the information which Mr. Nagel turned up for me; and to Mrs. Brenda Gieseker.

13. And therefore clearly not 'Pelican Creek near the present well-known camp at Fishing Bridge' as Archer Butler Hulbert makes it in *Where Rolls the Oregon*.

14. So I am willing to guess and so Mr. Hulbert says positively. But Russell's account is so sketchy just here that the route could be read to the west branch of Lewis Fork and on to Lewis Lake. (All in Yellowstone Park.) Mr. Hulbert doubts Russell's statement that they crossed the Tetons, saying they must have circled them to the north. I see no reason why they should not have crossed the range by way of either Moran Canyon or Cascade Canyon. The former is more likely, but neither would have been much of an ordeal to experienced mountain men.

15. This adventure occurred in 1839 and of course is out of chronological sequence here. Fort Hall was not built till the late summer of 1834 and did not become Hudson's Bay property till 1837.

16. It was a Minnetaree who asked Brackenridge if there were no

white women. He had been led to wonder because white men were so avid of squaws.

17. I retell the story from Gilbert Livingston Wilson's 'Hidatsa Eagle Trapping.' The Hidatsa are the Minnetarees, village Indians, neighbors of the Mandans but relatives of the Crows. Mr. Wilson's three papers about them are among the most useful of modern Indian studies.

## Chapter VIII: To Men Benighted (1834)

1. *Narrative of a Journey Across the Rocky Mountains.* The 1839 edition is very rare, the London edition of 1840 somewhat less so. Townsend's *Narrative* is reprinted with John Wyeth's *Oregon* as Volume XXI of Thwaites' *Early Western Travels.*

2. The date of Sublette's jump-off cannot be determined. Anderson says he started ten days later than Wyeth, which is impossible. It could have been at most three days and two is more likely — he passed Wyeth on the thirteenth day out.

3. According to Albert J. Partoll, Anderson's journal was published in a Circleville, Ohio, newspaper, the *Democrat and Watchman*, in two installments, September 29 and October 13, 1871. I have been unable to inspect a file of this paper. In *Frontier and Midland* for Autumn, 1938 (Vol. 19, No. 1) Mr. Partoll published what appears to be a selection from the journal and accompanied it with editorial notes not too informed about the fur trade and the West. When this selection opens, the Sublette party has already got as far west as Chimney Rock. The date is not given but it was probably May 28, for they are at Scott's Bluff on May 29. They are, that is, maintaining a one-day lead on Wyeth.

Years before publishing his journal Anderson had published three short articles on his Western trip, in the *American Turf Register and Sporting Magazine* of 1837. A check of dates and allusions and other internal evidence make it certain that he was the author of 'Adventures in the Rocky Mountains,' in the May issue, signed 'Marshall'; 'Scenes in the West — the Platte &c.,' July, signed 'W. Marshall'; and 'Scenes and Things in the West,' November, signed 'W. M. A.' (The conventions of sporting and humorous journalism of the period made a pseudonym almost obligatory.) They are unimportant and add only a few small facts to our knowledge of the summer. Their principal interest is an early and eloquent protest against the attempt to call Great Salt Lake 'Lake Bonneville.' The protest probably reflects Bill Sublette's and other veterans' animus against Bonneville — and contains some violently hashed misinformation. However unimportant, the articles form an 'overland' and are, I believe, noticed here for the first time and duly called to the attention of collectors.

4. This is what most of the slight indications in the literature suggest. Kit Carson, however, says that Bridger's winter camp was on the Snake

near the place where he had spent the preceding winter. Like Meek, Carson tended to get his dates wrong.

5. The legend in the trade that Milton Sublette had amputated his own foot in the mountains is clearly unfounded. He is supposed to have done so following a bad injury to it in an undated and probably unidentifiable skirmish with Blackfeet, but as my text shows he still had a foot, if an injured one, this spring and the legend is probably a radiation from the apparently historical story of Peg-leg Smith. Returning to St. Louis, Milton was treated as early as May 27 by a Dr. Farrar, who amputated the leg — it was the left leg — in February, 1835. Robert Campbell's brother Hugh later presented him with a specially made cork leg. See *Glimpses of the Past*, Missouri Historical Society, 1941.

6. Sabin, *Kit Carson Days*, rejects the chronology given in Carson's autobiography and accepted here in default of a cross-check, which dates these events early in 1834. He does so because Carson says that this was the year he rejoined the RMF Company, whereas at the rendezvous Fontenelle of the American Fur Company gave him a draft on Pratte, Chouteau & Company, the operating company, to be charged against the 1834 expedition. There is no discrepancy. Carson certainly did not sign up as a 'skin' or contract trapper with Fitzpatrick or any other brigade: he had climbed too high for that and unquestionably went along as a free trapper. It was up to him to sell his furs where he chose. He may well have traded with both companies at rendezvous and may have had a surplus of $70, which Fontenelle's draft covered.

7. Anderson identifies him as 'the celebrated Arapooish,' Rotten Belly. But Rotten Belly was a Crow and there had been no Crows at the battle of Pierre's Hole and there were none at this rendezvous. Rotten Belly, in fact, was off on the foray against the Blackfeet from which he decided not to go home.

8. It is not clear where this left Edmund Christy who had put seven thousand dollars into the RMF Company's 1833 trade and for whose return Fitzpatrick had been waiting last November. He was present at this rendezvous and must have got some share of the division, but the record is silent. He stayed in the trade for several years and his name flickers through the literature but never with any specific information accruing to it.

9. There was a Snake war-chief also named Little Chief and various diarists confuse the two. It was an easy name to bestow on anyone, in fact, and Kit Carson, a small man, was called Little Chief by many Indians.

10. I am not sure that anyone knows exactly where the original Fort Hall stood. Determinations of both latitude and longitude by various hands are irreconcilable. It was probably the Portneuf near its mouth. It was a good many miles from the present agency town of the same name.

## Chapter IX: Parable of the Samaritan (1835)

1. J. S. Chambers, *The Conquest of Cholera*, p. 19.

2. This summary is from Doctor Chambers's *Conquest of Cholera*, a graphic and exhaustive study. No other medical aspect of American history has had so illuminating a treatment.

3. Chiefly a letter of the preceding fall from Fontenelle to Pierre Chouteau, which expresses a suspicion rather than a certainty. See also George E. Hyde's *Red Cloud's Folk*.

4. Carson's autobiography says nothing about the second, conclusive shot and Parker, who may not have witnessed the brawl, says that Shunar pleaded for his life while Kit was getting his other gun and was spared. Both Sabin, who also says that there was rivalry over an Arapaho girl, and Vestal tell the story as I give it here, and the tradition in the fur trade was that Carson did indeed kill Shunar. It must nevertheless be pointed out that no eyewitness speaks of an Arapaho camp at the rendezvous of 1835 and that Vestal has worked into his account of that rendezvous details from the one of 1834.

5. *Edward Warren*, p. 266. Stewart is alluded to in the short autobiography which Carson dictated to Jesse B. Turley, but in connection with the rendezvous of 1837 (the one which Miller saw). He 'will be forever remembered,' Carson says, 'for his liberality and his many good qualities by the mountaineers who had the honor of his acquaintance.' Lakeside Classics edition, p. 52.

6. It is inference, but inescapable inference, that Stewart traveled with Whitman and Fitzpatrick. Whitman's diary shows that the caravan arrived at 'Mr. Cabanny's near Council Bluff' on October 10. Cabanne's old trading post, lately abandoned by the Company in favor of Bellevue several miles downriver, was perhaps twenty miles below the true Council Bluff of Lewis and Clark. Whitman went on to Bellevue October 12 and stayed there till the twentieth, when he started down the river on one of the Company boats under Cabanne himself. On October 16 Stewart wrote to William Sublette one of the few letters that have survived. It is dated at 'Council Bluffs' but since that term applied to this whole vicinity he may have been at Cabanne's or even at Bellevue. He is, he says, sending this letter with 'some boats going down,' certainly Company boats and presumably those captained by Cabanne. Presumably Stewart was going on to St.Louis with Fitzpatrick overland. At any rate, there was no one but Fitzpatrick for Stewart to travel with from the mountains and he had come to rendezvous without even a small party of his own.

## Chapter X: The Meridian Passage (1836)

1. Sillem, the German gentleman in Stewart's spelling, is Narcissa Whitman's 'Mr. Celam,' who becomes 'Celan' in some of the accounts that are derived from hers. He is also William H. Gray's 'young

English blood.' It is a satisfaction to arrive at a few solid facts concerning Stewart in a year during which almost all that can be said about him must be inference. These facts, including the guns and the horses, are from a letter of Stewart's to William Sublette dated at Charleston, South Carolina, February 28, 1836, and now at the Missouri Historical Society. Stewart says he has just arrived from Cuba, will come to St. Louis by way of Washington, Philadelphia, and 'C' (Cincinnati), intends to go west in April but has not yet decided just where or how, and will learn in Washington whether the government may not be sending a survey party west. He reminds Sublette of his 'promise of the black horse,' which may indicate that it was one he had seen and admired at Sublette's farm near St. Louis. He directs him 'to get me one other as fast horse as you can get' and to buy three good horses and four mules as well as saddle and pack saddle for Sillem. William Gray says that Stewart and his companions had 'four extra fine horses,' two dogs, and three servants. The last item corresponds with Mrs. Whitman's letters.

One student has supposed that one of the 'servants' alluded to by Gray was Antoine Clement and that Clement had accompanied Stewart to Cuba. I do not believe that Clement came out of the mountains with him in 1835. Stewart appears to have first employed him at the rendezvous of 1833. Whether or not he remained with Stewart during the winter of 1833–1834 cannot be established, but he did not go to Vancouver in the late summer of 1834. It seems clear that they were together again for a while in 1835, probably from the rendezvous to Fort Laramie and on to the Missouri but no farther. Two sentences in Stewart's brief letter to Sublette from Council Bluffs, dated October 16, 1835, do nothing to clarify the speculation. 'I also wish to mention,' Stewart says, 'that your bill to Antoine Clement will be sent down and that I see it is incorrect as no bill of mine dated July 16 — 34 will be paid. I beg of you therefore not to pay it for reasons I shall explain.'

2. The journals of Mrs. Whitman and Mrs. Spalding establish that the meeting did take place west of the Divide, not on the Sweetwater as Meek says in *The River of the West*. Meek and Gray describe the scene and agree in the larger outline. There is a large literature about Whitman, his companions, his mission at Waiilatpu, and Spalding's at Lapwai. Clifford M. Drury's *Marcus Whitman, M.D.* is the best biography. His *Henry Harmon Spalding* is also invaluable. Narcissa Whitman's letters and journals were published in *Transactions* of the Oregon Pioneer Association for 1891 and 1893 and the *Oregon Historical Quarterly*, 1936–1937, and separately reprinted from the latter as *The Coming of the White Women*. Eliza Spalding's diary is in Eliza Spalding Warren, *Memoirs of the West*.

3. Drury, *Marcus Whitman, M.D.*, pp. 122–124.

4. When Doctor Drury wrote his life of Spalding he denied the long-established legend that Spalding was a rejected suitor of Narcissa

Prentiss, having found no documentary evidence. While he was working on his life of Whitman, however, he found such evidence and my account rests on his later demonstration. See *Marcus Whitman, M.D.*, p. 84 and elsewhere.

5. Samuel Allis and John Dunbar were the two young missionaries who had started for the Flatheads with Parker in 1834 and, failing to reach the caravan in time, had stayed on with the Pawnees.

6. By the time the story reached Ruxton he was able to have Harris show a treasured piece of his putrefaction to 'old Captain Stewart (a clever man was that, even though he was an Englishman).' Ruxton has Harris tell the story in his own person and Harris dates it 'the next spring' after the meteor shower. Actually Stewart's first trip west, 1833, was the next spring and here is a further suggestion that Lieutenant Ruxton had met Captain Stewart somewhere — certainly in England and later than 1843. In Ruxton's story 'A Dutch doctor chap' was with Stewart, and this could be a half-factual reference to the mysterious Sillem. More likely, however, it is factual to an even greater degree and a reference to Doctor Frederick Adolphus Wislizenus, though Stewart knew him, if at all, not in the West but as a physician in St. Louis.

7. Harris's 'cognomen, "Black" must have arisen from an appearance as if gunpowder had been blown in his face, which seemed composed of whipcord & tanned leather, lighted up with a lively & restless eye.' Alfred Jacob Miller, 'Rough Draughts for Notes to Indian Sketches,' No. 23. Also from the later notes written to accompany the copies of Miller's sketches now at the Walters Gallery, No. 67:

'He was of wiry form, made of bone and muscle, with a face apparently composed of tan leather and whipcord, finished off with a peculiar blue black tint, as if gunpowder had been burnt in his face.' So far as I know this is the only personal description of Harris which we can be fully sure is authentic. Harris is supposed to be the Black George of Emerson Bennett's *The Prairie Flower*, which seems to have been based on a manuscript (of disputed authorship) by someone who knew him.

'Naturally dark, his skin had become almost black from long exposure to the weather,' the author says. 'In height he was fully six feet, gaunt and raw-boned, with great breadth of shoulders, ponderous limbs and powerful muscles, which gave him a very formidable appearance. . . . His face was thin and long, with high cheek bones, pointed nose, hollow cheeks, large mouth, and cold, gray eyes.' P. 29. (On the authorship of *The Prairie Flower*, see Charles L. Camp, *James Clyman* and Henry Nash Smith, *American Emotional and Imaginative Attitudes Toward the Great Plains and the Rocky Mountains*.)

8. Letter to me from Perry W. Jenkins. I have been unable to trace the quotation.

9. Whether or not Bridger had given Stewart this memento, he is certainly wrong about Whitman's having operated with a common scalper. There were surgical instruments in the kit he took west.

10. The building of Fort Laramie and its purchase by the Company permitted a modification of the system. The storage of goods there enabled trapping brigades to make shorter and also faster expeditions. Furthermore, the fort maintained permanent herds of mules and horses. A caravan coming back from west of the Divide could profitably lie over here for a space and was under no urgency to start back to the States.

This summer, because of a favorable season and Fitzpatrick's superbly expeditious trip west, the rendezvous was over earlier than usual. Fitzpatrick took his caravan back to Fort Laramie and eventually to Bellevue. The inference is, however, that he stayed at the Fort for a space — and that Stewart, after accompanying Bridger for a while, returned and made the trip with him. Fontenelle was now the bourgeois of Fort Laramie and he took a brigade out from it on a fall hunt. This is the only Company brigade besides Bridger's known to have made a hunt in the fall of 1836, though we must assume that others did.

The Sublette Papers, a closed collection at the Missouri Historical Society, will probably cast some light on this question eventually. The Company records are probably in one of the Chouteau collections but so far as I have been able to learn by correspondence they contain little information about this fall. I have used letters from Pratte, Chouteau and Company to the American Fur Company, at the New York Historical Society, but they say little about 1836.

11. Neither does my geographical authority on the Green River Valley, Mr. Perry W. Jenkins. It is on his authority that I identify New Fork Lake. Note that Matt Field, the journalist who accompanied Stewart's 1843 expedition, says that its outlet was called Piney Fork. (There are several Piney Forks in the vicinity.)

12. I have made an exhaustive search for an authoritative statement about Fontenelle's suicide and have had the formidable help of Mrs. Brenda Gieseker. Items relating to the settlement of his estate can be found but nothing concerning his death. He may have killed himself, and Meek seems to be repeating a story common in the mountains, but if he did so there appears to be no supporting evidence beyond Meek's statement, which dates it wrong.

13. My account is based on Grace Lee Nute, 'James Dickson: A Filibuster in Minnesota,' *Mississippi Valley Historical Review*, September, 1923, and 'The Diary of Martin McLeod,' *Minnesota History Bulletin*, August-November, 1922, Chardon's diary, some scattering items cited by Doctor Nute, and a discussion of Dickson with his discoverer, Professor Frederick Merk.

## Chapter XI: The Conqueror (1837)

1. The records are curiously silent about the disease on the *St. Peter's*. The only explanation offered is by Culbertson, who says that 'Bill May' secreted infected articles of clothing on the boat at St.

Louis because he was denied passage on her. This might explain the long delay in the appearance of the disease, if, in fact, the infection was acquired at St. Louis. Unfortunately, though May is recorded as having started for St. Louis from Fort Clark in April of 1836 and might be presumed to have spent the winter there, Chardon's journal shows that he came to Fort Clark from the Little Missouri, that is, from upriver, on July 20, 1837, bringing 'No News in that quarter except the Small Pox.' He could hardly have got to the Little Missouri not quite two weeks after the steamboat did. (This is the May whose murder by Arapahos in 1846 Francis Parkman records while he is at Fort Laramie.) A reasonable guess would be that the infection was acquired at some stop farther down the river.

2. McKenzie wrote to Catlin that between forty and fifty were left. Mitchell told Schoolcraft there were about 145, then made it 125, mostly women and children. Schoolcraft made it 125. These statistics are more reliable than those for the other tribes.

3. Larpenteur in his book (p. 133), which I use interchangeably with his journal.

4. Thus the book. The journal says '. . . on the 4 day of august my Squaw expired having two days previous [been] attackted by what [those] worms which is said to prey on human boddy after Death but to occur [confer?] more Disagreable feelings on me this was to occur before her death.'

5. Halsey's letter to Pratte, Chouteau and Company of November 2, 1837, says that there were four fatalities at Fort Union, of whom three were squaws. (He is obviously disregarding the death of his wife, which occurred on the steamboat.) He gives the name of the single engagé who died as 'Bte. [Baptiste] Compton.' This must be the 'B. Contois' of Larpenteur's journal. Larpenteur is ambiguous but the best reading of his journal is that three of those who were inoculated died. Chittenden misreads Larpenteur, failing to distinguish between the cases at the fort itself, among the engagés and their wives, and those among the Indians who were camped near by.

6. Perhaps the statement should read that only a few Crows died of it. Mitchell says that none died and most contemporary sources say the same. There is no account of smallpox among the Crows in the literature of the fur trade. Schoolcraft says in one place that they lost a third of the tribe and in another place that 'great numbers' of them died, both statements obviously and even grotesquely untrue.

7. Clark Wissler's account of Petalasharo is in *Indians of the United States*, 135–136. There is a fuller and more circumstantial account by John B. Dunbar in *The Magazine of American History*. John B. Dunbar also describes human sacrifice among the Pawnees and its reappearance following the smallpox; he is my authority for suggesting that perhaps only the Skidis practiced it. Whether or not he was related to the Reverend John Dunbar, one of the original missionaries to the Pawnees, I do not know, but obviously he had access to his papers.

The principal source of my account of the sacrifice is John Dunbar's letter to the *Missionary Herald*, Vol. 34 (1838), p. 383. This letter also describes the epidemic.

## Chapter XII: A Painter on the Trail (1837)

1. A small affluent of the Yellowstone in Carbon County, Montana; not to be confused with Clark's Fork of the Columbia. Meek presently has the smallpox reaching the Blackfoot country, early in the spring of 1837. Obviously the meeting with the Blackfeet which he here describes occurred a year later.

2. These stories are from Russell and Meek. Since Meek has mixed events of three years into his account of one, some of the skirmishes may have occurred the year before or the year following.

3. Audubon also used Townsend's and Nuttall's notes in completing the last two volumes of the *Ornithological Biographies*.

4. Russell says that Fitzpatrick brought 'forty-five men and twenty carts' to the rendezvous. Forty-five men would be little more than enough to take care of twenty carts, not to mention the pack train and the requisite hunting and scouting; also it would be recklessly small escort for so rich a prize in the Indian Country. Russell is certainly in error. (There is the unlikely possibility that more than half of the company had been left at Fort Laramie.) Miller says in his fifth note that the combined parties numbered 150 all told, then in his twenty-third note makes it 120. The latter figure would be close to the annual average.

5. Miller's note No. 72 says that William Sublette 'in an encounter with the Blackfeet . . . received a poison ball from which he never recovered.' This seems to combine Bill's wound at the Battle of Pierre's Hole with Milton's bad leg. I have seen no other suggestion that Bill was partially disabled.

6. The Caravan that crosses the Kansas River in Miller's sketches Nos. 73 and 152 and is described in the accompanying notes is obviously the whole party. If it had started from the vicinity of Bellevue it would not have come anywhere near the Kansas.

7. Miller's note No. 56 speaks of 'Monsieur Prov [rest of word illegible], sub-leader.' This note corresponds to No. 76 of those accompanying the Walters Gallery copies, which reads, 'Monsieur Proveau, sub-leader.' He is a hard man to follow during these years; he is almost unmentioned in the annals.

8. In *The Year of Decision* I assert that Jedediah Smith's party, of which Jim Clyman was a member, made the true 'discovery' of South Pass. This was the best judgment possible when my book was written and was the position of Charles L. Camp. In the *Proceedings* of the American Antiquarian Society for 1944 (published, January, 1946) Mr. Donald McKay Frost's 'General Ashley and the Overland Trail' establishes that Smith's party crossed the Divide south of the

Antelope Hills, that is south of the true pass, and accepts the earlier tradition that the Ashley party which did go through the pass at about the same time was led by Provost. He adds that Fitzpatrick's and Clyman's later journey in 1824 was indispensable to the 'discovery,' since it established for the first time that the Sweetwater was a tributary of the Platte. Mr. Frost's paper, a brilliant contribution to the history of the West, corrects many previously accepted ideas about the Ashley parties and fills in many spaces that had previously been blank. I am indebted to him for the privilege of reading it in manuscript and for many other kindnesses, including access to his splendid collection of Western Americana.

9. Miller's note No. 63 says that they later met Markhead at the rendezvous and that he had little or no hair. There is no way of verifying either this meeting or the description of Markhead. I must note that Miller nowhere alludes to Markhead's having earned Stewart's reward for lifting the horse thief's scalp.

10. The last sentence is clearly a later addition. It is from Ruxton and is quoted from him at the end of our Chapter I.

11. Eugene Manlove Rhodes in *The Trusty Knaves.* Francis Parkman quoted a folk saying: half white, half red, and half devil.

12. George E. Hyde, *Red Cloud's Folk*, p. 53. This is one of the best studies of the Plains Indians and is indispensable for the period beginning with the coming of the army. It must be noted, however, that in Chapter III, quoted here, Mr. Hyde makes a number of erroneous statements about the fur trade in these parts.

13. The note goes on to describe the murder of Bull Bear as recounted by 'a subsequent traveler to the Rocky Mountains,' another instance of revision in Baltimore. His account of the brawl is accurate, so the traveler was probably Parkman.

14. How much farther is far from clear and the indefiniteness of Messrs. Hafen and Ghent, the post's historians, will be adopted here. I am not sure that anyone today knows exactly where the original fort was. In 1940 government engineers who were restoring the old army post as part of the development of a national historical monument could identify the site of the second fort but refused to be certain of the first. In *The Year of Decision* I adopted distances which I worked out at the time of my visit and was then confident of. I now believe that I moved the later post too far from the first one, that it was perhaps less than a mile away. The distances given in the literature simply cannot be reconciled. They are estimates and vary with the estimator and a further confusion is added as soon as emigrant diaries appear and Fort Bernard gets confused with Fort Platte and sometimes, even, Fort Platte with Fort Laramie. The best possible judgment is that of Mr. Merrill J. Mattes, Historian of the National Park Service, in a memorandum forwarded to me by Messrs. Howard W. Baker and Herbert E. Kahler. Mr. Mattes says that the later Fort Laramie was 'approximately two miles upstream' from the mouth of the Laramie and Fort

Platte 'approximately three fourths of a mile' up the Platte from the mouth of the Laramie and on the right bank. This leaves the original site of Fort Laramie undetermined.

15. The full text of the two notes follows.

> *Number 14.* FORT LARAMIE
>
> This fort built for the American Fur Company, situated about 800 miles west of St. Louis, is of a quadrangular form with block houses at diagonal corners to sweep the fronts in case of attack.
>
> Over the front entrance is a large block house in which is placed a cannon, the interior of the fort is about 150 feet square surrounded by small cabins whose roofs reach within 3 feet of the top of the palisades against which they abut. The Indians encamp in great numbers here 3 or 4 times a year, bringing peltries to be exchanged for dry goods, tobacco, beads, and alcohol.
>
> The Indians have a mortal horror of the 'big gun' which rests in the block house as they have had experience of its prowess and witnessed the havoc produced by its loud 'talk.' They conceive it to be only asleep and have a wholesome dread of its being waked up.
>
> On entering the principal room of the fort we noticed 5 or 6 first class engravings, one of which was Richard and Saladin battling in the Holyland and from these immediately surmised that the Commander of the fort was a refined gentleman. When he came in we found our surmise correct. His name was Fontenelle already famous in Indian history. He tendered at once the hospitalities of the place and attendants and gave orders for crocks of milk to be brought to us, a luxury we had been deprived of for a length of time and to which we did ample justice; and while we rested here seemed never tired of extending to us every comfort and aid that he could command.

As Miller makes clear in the next note, the fort was not built by the American Fur Company. He should have reckoned its distance from Independence. This varied according to the route taken to the Platte and through the Nebraska badlands but seldom varied more than about twenty miles either way from the 667 miles that Chittenden gives. By the commonest route of the emigrant days it was 51 miles west of Scott's Bluff, 135 miles east of the Red Buttes, 171 miles east of Independence Rock. The altitude is about 4500 feet.

> *Number 72.* INTERIOR OF FORT LARAMIE.
>
> The view is from the great entrance looking west and embraces more than half the court or area. When this space is filled with Indians and traders as it is at stated periods the scene is lively and interesting. They gather here from all quarters; from the Gila at the south, the Red River at the north, and the Columbia River west, each has its quota and representatives, Sioux, Bannocks, , [The Walters Gallery notes show that the illegible word is 'Mandans.'] Crows, Snakes, Pend-Oreilles, Nez Perces, Cheyennes and Delawares, all except Black Feet who are 'betes noirs' and considered 'de trop.' As a contrast there are Canadian trappers, free and otherwise, half breeds, Kentuckians, Missourians and Down-Easters. A saturnalia is held the first day and some excesses committed. But after this trading goes briskly forward.
>
> There was a cannon or two sleeping in the towers over the two main en-

trances, the Indians having an aversion to their being wakened, entertaining a superstitious reverence for them. They are intended to 'keep the peace.'

This fort was built by Robert Campbell who named it Fort William in honor of his friend and partner William Sublette. These gentlemen were the earliest pioneers after Messrs. Lewis and Clarke and had many battles with the Indians. Once in an encounter with the Black-feet they made their wills in true soldier fashion as they went along, appointing each the executor of the other. We had almost daily intercourse with Messrs. Sublette and Campbell, and Governor Clarke in St. Louis before we started. Captain Lewis had at that time deceased. In an encounter with the Black-feet Mr. Sublette received a poison ball from which he never recovered.

16. Russell says that the caravan reached rendezvous on July 5 but the more detailed journal of the returning missionary William H. Gray shows that the date is thirteen days too early. Gray caught up with McLeod's party on June 27 and the party reached an old camp a few miles from last year's rendezvous on June 28. On that day Doc Newell rode over from the main encampment, about fifteen miles. On June 30 Gray learned that an express from Fitzpatrick — Black Harris and perhaps others — had arrived at the main camp and reported the caravan fifteen days to the east. McLeod moved twice, reaching the vicinity of the main camp on July 11. On July 14 the caravan is judged to be sufficiently near so that Gray can send out a man to inquire if Stewart is carrying letters for him. On July 17 he reports that the caravan has not arrived and on July 18 that it has.

17. Naturally Joe Meek played knight with the others. He ascribes it to the wrong rendezvous, having blended 1837 with 1838. Victor, 237–238.

18. Miller quotes the alcohol at $64 a gallon, Russell at half that. Russell notes some other 1837 prices: sugar $2 a pint, tobacco $2 a pound, blankets $20, 'common cotton shirts' $5. His '$4 or $5 per pound for beaver,' if specific, means that the mountain price had risen somewhat in spite of the prostration of trade at St. Louis.

19. Gray also mentions an 'L. Phillipson,' a name given to a minor villain in Stewart's *Edward Warren*, and a Mr. Ewing. The last may be identified from Jason Lee's letters as F. Y. Ewing of Missouri. Lee says he made the trip for his health; if so, here is another first.

20. Well, you find one that is earlier and American: I can't.

21. Miller also painted Little Chief's son, who at twenty was already a war chief and could count among his coups one of the most honorable, killing a grizzly, which entitled him to wear its claws round his neck.

22. James A. Teit distinguishes as 'the Flathead group' of the Salishan people four tribes, the Flatheads, the Pend d'Oreilles, the Kalispels, and the Spokanes. The other groups of the Salish are the Coeur d'Alenes and the Okanagans.

23. Victor, *The River of the West*, p. 233.

24. Gray says five in his *History of Oregon* and Victor repeats the

number. Gray's account is brief and as deliberately vague as he could make it — and he had a fine gift for the indefinite. His diary does not list the party by name. Whether there were five or six Indians depends on the identity of the one called Big Eneas. He seems to be a Flathead when he is first mentioned; five pages later he is spoken of as 'our guide'; four pages after that Gray counts five Indians and speaks of 'our guide an Iroquois.' (The guide is an Iroquois in *The History of Oregon.*) If Eneas was a Flathead, five; if he was an Iroquois, six.

25. Papin? This was a Company trader and a J. Papin was in the Company's employ in 1833. He must not be confused with Pierre Didier Papin, the bourgeois of Fort Laramie whom Parkman met hereabout in 1846.

26. This entry also says that Gray delivered Ermatinger's son at Buffalo. The boy has not been mentioned in the diary since June 15, when Gray started for the Salmon. To suppose that he traveled east from the rendezvous with Gray would be to bring all the enumerations in the diary into question. Presumably Gray took him to the rendezvous and left him there, and he traveled with the Company caravan to St. Louis, where Gray could have picked him up again when he went to lodge a complaint against the Sioux with the Superintendent of Indian Affairs.

It must also be pointed out that between the Sioux village and Council Bluffs Gray's diary speaks of someone named Lawrence, unidentified, mentioned nowhere else, presumably traveling with him.

All of which shows that Gray doctored his diary.

27. This instrument is preserved at the Missouri Historical Society.

28. I have not seen the original of this. Copy and translation by a friend.

## Chapter XIII: Away, You Rolling River (1838)

1. I assume that the two or three hundred horses which Walker had this summer could not have come from anywhere but California, though this is rather earlier than he is supposed to have set up in the business.

2. Of Walker: 'diffident and unassuming, always afraid to say *Amen* at the end of his prayers. . . . No positive traits of mind.' Of Eells: 'superabundance of self-esteem. . . . great pretensions . . . no soul to laud and admire nature, no ambition to lift his thoughts beyond the sphere of his own ideas of right.' Of Smith: 'his prejudices were so strong that he could not be reasonable with himself . . . failed for want of Christian forbearance and confidence in his associates.' But Gray liked young Rogers.

3. The last two paragraphs practically stolen from the only good biography, James P. Zollinger, *Sutter, the Man and His Empire.*

4. Walker's diary, unpublished but liberally quoted in Drury, *Elkanah and Mary Walker*, has only occasional brief entries east of Oregon. Mary Walker's diary from the lower Platte to the Columbia was published in *The Frontier* for March, 1931, but with most of her acerbities

about her companions deleted. The originals of both are in the Huntington Library and I quote from microfilms of them. Myra Eells' journal was published in *Transactions* of the Oregon Pioneer Association, 1889. It has been touched up for grammar but I have not inquired whether the editing extends to personalities.

5. Crawford acknowledges receipt of this letter in the letter to Stewart at St. Louis dated October 11, which is referred to in the next paragraph. Crawford's letter is at the Missouri Historical Society.

6. Unpublished letter to D. H. Miller, dated at Murthly, October 31, 1840.

7. Letter at the Missouri Historical Society.

8. Fraser, *The Red Book of Grandtully*, xl-xli.

9. Of the canvases mentioned in this paragraph 'Cavalcade' is now at the Oklahoma Historical Society and 'Roasting the Hump Rib' is owned by Mr. Everett D. Graff of Chicago. Mr. Graff owns seven of these original oils, including at least one that is listed by the *Weekly Herald* (N.Y.) as being in the Apollo show and two later ones. I am indebted here to Mrs. Mae Reed Porter.

10. Stewart died at Murthly, April 21, 1871, in his seventy-seventh year. His son and heir William George Stewart, had died in 1868. Sir William's younger brother, Archibald Douglas Stewart, succeeded to the title and estates, but within a month of Sir William's death a series of suits and counter-suits involving the succession broke out. They concerned Sir William's adopted son, known as Francis Nichols Stewart and also as Francis Rice Nichols. He was an American and may have been Stewart's illegitimate son. Twice Stewart had tried and failed to have the entail of Murthly and Grandtully broken on his behalf. In the end he was adjudged to have inherited by will personal property to the value of £40,000, including the pictures (and it was in his name that they were sold) but Sir Archibald was confirmed in the title and estates.

I am much indebted here to Mrs. Mae Reed Porter. I know nothing about this adopted son or the American romance of which he may have been the issue. Since they obviously have no bearing on the fur trade or Stewart's experiences in the mountains, I have not seriously tried to find out about either, gladly relinquishing the job to Mrs. Porter, who is preparing to write a book about Stewart's 1843 journey to the West and his later life.

11. The most trustworthy account of mountain life at this period and the most vivid pictures of getting the customer drunk are in *Rocky Mountain Life*, by one of Lupton's employees, Rufus Sage. Its almost intolerably jocose style has tended to obscure its importance. The great works of Ruxton and Garrard come at the very end of the period.

12. See his correspondence, *South Dakota Historical Collections*, Vol. IX, 1918.

13. See *The Year of Decision*, 120, 415, etc.

## Appendix: The First Illustrators of the Far West

1. The third painter mentioned, Joshua Shaw, was much better known than either Seymour or Rindisbacher and Sartain once called him the ablest landscape painter in the country. Doctor Robert Taft, of the University of Kansas, to whom I am indebted not only for help with Rindisbacher but for calling Seymour and Shaw to my attention and supplying me with almost all that is said of them herein, writes me in regard to Shaw's rumored trip up the Missouri: 'I have never been able to verify and extend this statement but in 1935 the Newhouse Galleries in New York City had a Shaw painting on exhibit, "Indians Hunting Buffalo." I have several other notes on Shaw which suggest Western incidents but my information as yet is so indefinite that I can make no positive statement. It is quite obvious, however, that he had but little influence on Western art (save perhaps locally) if he really did go west.' I have been unable to find that Shaw accompanied any upriver party in 1820 — or any other year.

I have not seen the forty Rindisbacher paintings at Ottawa or the eighteen at West Point. What I say of him rests on the six paintings at Peabody Museum (once the property of David I. Bushnell, Jr.) and a few reproductions. In his reprint of McKenney and Hall Frederick W. Hodge identifies the frontispiece of Volume II, 'Hunting the Buffaloe,' as by Rindisbacher. Not only is it signed 'A. H.' but it is in both drawing and color unlike anything by Rindisbacher I have seen; Hodge's identification is open to doubt. The frontispiece to Volume I is unquestionably Rindisbacher — and the caption is by his publisher.

2. Strictly speaking, the Mandan ceremony which Catlin called O-ka-pee is not the medicine-lodge or sun dance of the Plains tribes. It is closely related to it, however, and need be distinguished from it only by specialists. Schoolcraft's famous denunciation of Catlin as a faker rested largely on these paintings and the accompanying text, but Catlin has been abundantly verified.

3. Catlin painted many Indians who did not belong to the Plains tribes — the tribes of the Middle West, the Great Lakes country, and the old Southwest, as well as scattering Seminoles, Delawares, Iroquois; and other individuals. But more than half his paintings are of the Plains tribes or the tribes of the upper Missouri whose culture cannot be separated from theirs. These paintings are his most important work. Not only was he the first to paint them but they were closer to the natural state than any other Indians he saw.

4. Historians of the West have usually ascribed 'The Trapper's Last Shot' to John Mix Stanley. (No artist is named on the Currier & Ives print which is the best-known version of the picture.) They have done so because Joe Meek told Mrs. Victor that he was the trapper portrayed in it and that Stanley had painted the picture in 1837 to commemorate one of Meek's hair's-breadth escapes. (Victor, *The River of the West*, 230.) He also said that our artist, Alfred Jacob Miller, painted him twice, a

remark which is discussed in the text. Meek met both Stanley and Miller, but Stanley did not go West at all till 1842, did not reach the Far West till 1845, and did not meet Meek until 1847.

The Currier & Ives chromolithograph, 'The Trapper's Last Shot,' H. T. Peters Check List No. 1575, is undated. It could not have been published before 1857 and is probably later than the quite dissimilar print called 'The Last Shot,' Peters No. 1552, which was published in 1858, probably from a painting by Louis Maurer. Note that a 'Last Shot' by Charles Deas, a painter who actually had been west, was listed by the American Art Union in 1857. But the Currier & Ives 'Trapper's Last Shot' is a faithful reproduction of a painting by William T. Ranney. The picture was painted in 1849 or 1850, apparently as 'The Last Shot.' It was bought by the American Art Union before April 1, 1850 and under that title appears in the catalogue published in various issues of the *Bulletin* up to and including that of December 1. In the December issue of the *Bulletin*, however, which announces the Union's annual lottery, the title has become 'The Trapper's Last Shot.'

Meanwhile a steel engraving of Ranney's picture had been made as 'The Trapper's Last Shot.' The engraving was made by T. D. Booth of Cincinnati and the print, which was hand-colored, was distributed to the members of the Western Art Union. As early as the May issue of the American Art Union *Bulletin*, which lists the picture as 'The Last Shot' in its own catalogue, describes the print by the Western Art Union under the longer title. This is a larger and much better print than the later Currier & Ives version.

Note that Stanley did paint two pictures of Meek whom he met, presumably when he went to Oregon from California in 1847. Stanley himself dates these canvases 1851, which means that he painted them after he returned to the East and can hardly have regarded them as portraits. His notes on them and on Meek can be found in Smithsonian *Publications*, No. 53, 1852. (Also *Smithsonian Miscellaneous Collections*, Volume II, 1862, and elsewhere.) These are the Stanley pictures which I suspect Tait studied most carefully. Stanley's descriptions of them exactly describe two of Tait's pictures which became Currier & Ives prints, 'A Check. Keep Your Distance,' Peters No. 1521, and 'The Prairie Hunter — One Rubbed Out,' Peters No. 1565. They were burned with the rest of Stanley's great collection in the Smithsonian fire of 1865.

5. Parker's book did carry a single drawing of a geological formation along the Columbia River.

6. Dates from Frederick W. Hodge's invaluable introduction to the 1933 reprint. Many of the copies made from the Indian Gallery for reproduction in the McKenney and Hall work were made by Henry Inman.

7. All but three of the 123 plates in McKenney and Hall are portraits. (One of them is Pocohontas!) See my note No. 1 in regard to

two of the frontispieces. The frontispiece to Volume III is 'Encampment of Piekann Indians. Near Fort McKenzie on the Mussleshell River.' This is an inferior copy of Bodmer's Plate 43. Curiously, in his reprint Hodge did not correct the error in the caption. Fort McKenzie was not on the Musselshell but near the mouth of Marias River. Maximilian's book describes the painting of this picture.

8. Catlin is an exceedingly confused and confusing writer. His chapters are in the form of 'Letters,' and their dates sometimes have no reference to the times when they were written. They are without external or internal sequence and disregard chronology almost altogether, seldom giving any dates at all and sometimes scrambling the events of several years. In Volume I (1902) of the *South Dakota Historical Collections*, p. 347, Charles E. DeLand works out a minimum of sixteen days for Catlin's two stays at Fort Pierre. Mr. DeLand adds, as is obviously true, that he may have stayed there longer.

9. It is worth examining this statement to illustrate the difficulties of dating Catlin. After the most exhaustive study that Catlin's work has so far received, Thomas Donaldson (*op. cit.*, p. 25) says that he painted Black Hawk at Jefferson Barracks in October, 1832. In the 1933 reprint of McKenney and Hall (Vol. II, p. 95) Hodge says that the painting was made before Black Hawk was taken to Washington but suggests that it was not long before, that is, in 1833. Catlin's *Letters and Notes* suggests that the famous portrait may have been made at a time when Catlin was visiting the Sauk and Fox reservation. He made two visits there, in 1835 and 1836.

10. Curiously enough Catlin's No. 311 is a more accurate picture of the Yellowstone than either of Bodmer's.

11. I have found no bibliographical study of Maximilian. There is no dependable study of Bodmer. There is, in fact, no such thing as systematic scholarship in the history of American painting. Apart from a small handful of books dealing with individual artists there is no scholarship at all; the disregard and contempt of fact, the singular ignorance of what facts are, that characterize the average writer on nineteenth-century art in the United States appall everyone who approaches the field from outside. In the field which this book tangentially approaches, the early painting and illustration of the Far West, there has been no scholarly study whatever until now. At this moment Doctor Robert Taft, the author of the exceedingly valuable *Photography and the American Scene*, a chemist at the University of Kansas, has published in *The Kansas Historical Quarterly* the first two of a series of articles called 'The Pictorial Record of the Old West.' They are superb and invaluable but the amazing thing is that they are literally the first treatments of the subject that have been based on investigation, examination and verification of fact, and decent regard for historical realities. Doctor Taft writes me that he has had some difficulty interesting certain art museums in his studies. Well, I have convulsed certain museum directors by simply asking what resources their institutions possessed that would

assist my study — and it was my fortune to discover that one of the greatest of American art museums has not so much as a single Western print earlier than Frederic Remington. The average writer on nineteenth-century American art comes to his job from such a background and with such a state of mind.

Wagner and Camp say that there are pirated editions of Bodmer's *Atlas* and that they are markedly inferior. That would seem to be true, though the variation among copies of what appear to be legitimate editions is also extreme. No one has yet tried to differentiate the various editions, and much of what has been written about them is clearly wrong. I have seen three states of the *Atlas*, black and white, three color, and full color. Wagner and Camp list another state, costumes only in color. All statements made in my text refer to editions in full color. Among these printings of various years can be made out and, contrary to what has usually been said, of various places also. Within the edition there is a wide variation in quality. Between editions the number of plates varies somewhat and the numbering is not always uniform. The difference between the best and the poorest specimens is very great indeed, and certain printed criticisms of Bodmer which express dissatisfaction with his color seem to me to be based on inferior copies. The New York Public Library has several copies of the *Atlas* and keeps two of them in its Rare Book Room. One of these is an unbound portfolio and this is the best copy of some twenty-five I have examined, though a copy (probably bound after purchase) at the Boston Athenaeum is almost as good. All esthetic judgments in my text are based on this portfolio.

12. Also later and from his own portraits, not from the life, No. 611. Numbers by Donaldson, taken from Catlin's catalogues. All those I refer to are also reproduced as drawings in *Letters and Notes*, where the plates have different numbers. In each case I have examined the original painting at the National Museum.

13. Maximilian describes Pehriska-Ruhpa, whose name he translates as Two Ravens, as a Minnetaree and cannot possibly have been mistaken. Catlin's No. 164, 'Pa-ris-ka-roo-pa, the Two Crows' is probably the same Indian, and if he is then Catlin is wrong in describing him as a Crow. (The Crows and Minnetarees were closely related and Catlin met and painted him at the Minnetaree village.) The trouble with this identification, however, is that there was a fairly celebrated Crow war-chief named Two Crows at this time.

14. But not so bad as exhibitors seem determined to make him out. Three out of the four canvases shown by the Museum of Modern Art in 1943 were distinctly below his average. And while this Appendix remained in manuscript a very interesting exhibition by the Art Institute of Chicago moved to the Whitney Museum of Modern Art in New York. Called 'The Hudson River School,' it was intended to illustrate 'the early American landscape tradition.' It contained three Catlins and, fresh from laborious hours studying some seven hundred

Catlin canvases, I wondered whether selection had not arrived at the worst three of all. In both exhibitions the Catlins had been chosen at random; he had to be represented, he was represented, and there was no further obligation. But anyone who arrived at an opinion about Catlin on the basis of either exhibition was seriously wrong about him. Is not an artist entitled to be judged by his best work rather than by his worst?

15. An amusing incident in Bodmer's career briefly made an Indian painter out of an artist who would hardly have become one on his own account, Jean François Millet. In 1850, asked by an American print-publisher to prepare a series of Indian lithographs, Bodmer turned over the commission to his young friend Millet. There were to have been a hundred in the series but only five had been completed when the publisher learned that an unknown was doing them, not the great Indian painter Bodmer, and so cancelled the order. These five were signed by Bodmer, though his contribution to them seems to have been slight. Four of these were printed in 1852 in, apparently, a small edition as 'Annals of the United States Illustrated — The Pioneers.' They are exceedingly literary. Two deal with the capture of Daniel Boone's daughters by Indians (though one of these appears to have been based on *The Last of the Mohicans*), one with the legendary 'McCullough's Leap,' and the fourth with another incident celebrated in Revolutionary literature. Though the content is literary and the Indians mythological, the drawing and lithography are superb. I am indebted to Goodspeed's Book Shop of Boston for the privilege of examining a set. See *The Month at Goodspeed's* for March-April, 1945, and references there given.

16. 'The Catlin Collection of Indian Paintings' by Washington Matthews, *Report* of the National Museum for 1890. Also as a Government Printing Office separate, 1892.

17. Statement made under date of February 17, 1854, in the unpublished notebook of Frank Blackwell Mayer, which is in the library of the Minnesota Historical Society. Mayer, also a native of Baltimore, was a pupil of Miller's in the late eighteen-forties. Doubtless influenced by his instructor, he went to the Minnesota frontier in 1851 and drew and painted Indians there. Bertha L. Heilbron has edited his journal of that year and published it under the title of *With Pen and Pencil on the Frontier in 1851*. (St. Paul, 1932.) Text and introduction contain scattered references to Miller.

18. Unpublished manuscript by Macgill James, the Assistant Director of the National Gallery of Art. Mr. James is the rediscoverer of Miller. A biographical sketch which he wrote for his Miller exhibition at the Baltimore Municipal Museum some years ago is the source of all the notes about Miller that have appeared in various art journals.

19. I can speak only on the basis of photographs for I have not seen the originals. What I say, however, embodies the judgment of Doctor J. Hall Pleasants, the historian of Maryland art, of Macgill James whose

father once owned several of the large canvases, and of Mrs. Clyde Porter, who owns one and has studied others. Some of the landscapes in the large oils have a markedly Barbizon appearance, and in one of them Independence Rock has moved square into the Wind River range. Miller's letters identify some of them by title, 'The Death of the Panther' (he sold smaller copies of this one several times), 'Return from Hunting,' 'Indian Belle Reclining,' 'Auguste,' 'Roasting the Hump Rib,' 'Porte d'Enfer' (doubtless Devil's Gate), 'Threat by Crows,' and 'The Trapper's Bride' (on a canvas 8 by 10 feet). To these may certainly be added a vast rendition of a buffalo surround, two buffalo chases, several views of the Wind River mountains (which have come to have an Alplike and exceedingly romantic appearance), and at least one version of the great parade of Snake Indians at the rendezvous of 1837.

20. Miller's true vocation was portrait painting. Among the portraits in the possession of the Miller family today several, especially those of his parents and his sister-in-law, compare favorably with the best American work of the time.

21. The subtitle of the book is 'Romance of Sporting: or Wild Scenes and Wild Hunting.' The catalogue of a recent auction sale called this 'the earliest book with colored lithographs [i.e., chromolithographs] published in America,' but the statement is untrue. It is presented as the first of seven projected volumes, each of which is to contain at least five plates, 'devoted to the illustration of the Wild Scenes of our Indian Life, which will be furnished from the novel and unequalled pencil of Alfred J. Miller of Baltimore. . . .' I cannot find that any of the remaining six contemplated volumes was ever published.

22. The student must be warned that both Tuckerman and Clement and Hutton are extremely inaccurate in their discussions of Miller.

23. In the same year Miller made twenty-two 'colored Indian scenes' at twelve dollars each and 'one oil Picture, Indian Scene, $35' and 'One oil Picture. Shooting Elk' for William C. West, besides 'Two oil Pictures (Italy).' He also sold to a Doctor S. A. Harrison a large oil of the Wind River Mountains for $150.

24. The reader must understand that this Introduction does not purport to be more than a tentative account of Miller's Indian paintings. My esthetic opinions have no authority, and much work remains to be done before anyone can write critically about Miller. There is not even a dependable list of the original sketches, still less a census of all his work.

25. It illustrates a scene in Ruxton's *Life in the Far West*, which was serialized in *Blackwood's Magazine* toward the end of 1848 and published as a book in 1849. *Life in the Far West*, which is abundantly discussed in my text, was based on Ruxton's own experiences in the West in 1846 and 1847 (and earlier) and, though fictional in form, is mostly factual and historical. Ruxton attributes the incident which Miller's picture illustrates to 'a Scotch sportsman' who is unmistakably Stewart. (Elsewhere in the book he mentions Stewart by name.) Though Ruxton

seems to have known Stewart personally and as his text shows unquestionably knew a good deal about Stewart's 1843 expedition, I am by no means sure that this particular incident is historical — in fact, there are strong reasons for believing it fictional. (For instance, Matt Field does not mention it in his letters to the *Picayune*, and I cannot believe he would have failed to if it had happened.) If it ever happened to Stewart, however, Ruxton makes clear that it must have happened in 1843. But Miller's notes, though they actually quote the language of Ruxton's book of 1849, imply that it happened in 1837 and that Miller was an eyewitness. His note on the Walters copy, though shorter, makes the same implication. There are similar anachronisms in certain other passages of the 'Rough Draughts' which in so far must have been revised long after they were written. This does not necessarily mean that the pictures the notes relate to were painted as late as the anachronisms suggest; it may mean only that the notes are being brought up to date. But obviously it introduces further confusion into the effort to date the pictures and decreases one's assurance. (The Huntington Library has a copy of *Life in the Far West* for which some unidentified artist has supplied illustrations, among them one of this same scene drawn quite differently. Even photographs — all I have seen — show conclusively that this was not Miller.)

# 4. BIBLIOGRAPHY

Five hundred and six canvases from George Catlin's original Indian Collection and a few other Catlin paintings are in the National Museum, Washington, D.C. So far as I know, all the surviving paintings which Catlin actually made in the West during the eighteen-thirties are in this collection, though it may be hard to tell whether a given canvas is an original or a later copy. A good many of these canvases, mainly portraits, are hung in the Museum but the bulk are stored; they may be viewed on request. Upwards of two hundred of the later Cartoons are at the American Museum of Natural History, some hung in the exhibition halls, most of them stored; these also may be viewed on request. The New York Historical Society has a collection of two hundred and twenty pencil and ink drawings by Catlin. The Heye Foundation has eleven Catlin water colors, noteworthy only because they are water colors. The Peabody Museum, Cambridge, Massachusetts, has several ink drawings and four paintings. The Ayer Collection, at the Newberry Library, Chicago, has an exceedingly interesting set of two hundred and seventeen drawings bound in two volumes, with manuscript notes facing each drawing and a short preface by Catlin which says that they were made from the original paintings in 1852. A few Catlin canvases are scattered elsewhere, usually singly; none I have seen are important.

The Ayer Collection has fifty unpublished Bodmers: two lithographs, eleven water colors, the rest pencil sketches, all of them working notes for the *Atlas*. Sixteen were later worked up into plates that appear in the *Atlas*; the rest were not used. They are of the utmost interest to the student and several of them are superb as drawings. So far as my researches and the much more extensive ones of Doctor Robert Taft have been able to reveal, these are the only surviving remnants of Bodmer's Western work. Some of his material was supposed to be at an ethnographic museum at Stuttgart but is not. Other parts of it are supposed to have been sold to a New York museum in 1868 but so far I have been unable to locate them.

All but a few of the surviving Western water colors of Alfred J. Miller are owned by Mrs. Mae Reed Porter of Kansas City, L. Vernon Miller, Lloyd O. Miller, Alfred J. Miller, and Mrs. Joseph Whyte of Baltimore, and Mrs. Hugh P. King of Hewlett, Long Island. My text tells the present whereabouts of all the Murthly oils known to survive. The Johns Hopkins Hospital and the Baltimore Municipal Museum have later Western oils by Miller. A good many similar ones and various portraits are in the possession of the Miller family and in other private hands in Baltimore and the vicinity. No one who is interested in Miller can afford to miss the two hundred Western water colors, over a hundred and sixty of them copies of the original sketches, at the Walters Gallery, Baltimore. They lack the historical importance of the original sketches but as painting they are Miller's best work.

I have used transcripts of Miller's studio account-books, his letters from Scotland and England, certain fragments of autobiography, 'Rough Draughts for Notes to Indian Sketches,' and the notes accompanying the Walters copies. Stewart's letters are at the Missouri Historical Society. So is most of the other manuscript material I have used: the Fort Union Letter books, the various Chouteau collections, etc. Charles Larpenteur's original journal and Frank B. Mayer's notebook are at the Minnesota Historical Society. There is an enormous collection of American Fur Company papers at the New York Historical Society.

It seems idle to list the scores of newspapers I have consulted, since everything I found in them of importance to my text is cited by footnote. It does seem worth pointing out that certain confusions in earlier books would have been prevented if some of those who have referred to William Walker's letter had observed that when it was published *The Christian Advocate and Journal* was temporarily combined with *Zion's Herald.* I have used both *Niles' Register* and *The National Intelligencer* as a running index to the times and prefer the latter. St. Louis prices current cited in my text are always from St. Louis newspapers, always of the season and usually of the month under discussion.

The bibliography that follows is by no means complete. I believe that it is enough to substantiate every statement of fact made in the book. I suggest, however, that any patient mind which exhausts the bibliography and finds some such statement uncovered communicate with me by letter before denouncing me in the trade-journals of historians, for I have a couple of thousand bibliographical cards not transferred to this list.

*Alfred Jacob Miller*, [Macgill James ?], Municipal Museum, Baltimore, Md., n.d.

Allen, Miss A. J., compiler, 'Travels and Adventures of Doctor E. White and Lady,' *Ten Years in Oregon*, Ithaca, N.Y., 1850.

Alter, J. Cecil, *James Bridger*, Salt Lake City, 1925.

Anderson, William Marshall, 'Adventures in the Rocky Mountains,' (signed 'Marshall'), *American Turf Register*, Vol. 8, No. 9, May, 1837.

———, 'A Horseback Ride to the Rocky Mountains in 1834,' edited by Albert J. Partoll, *Frontier and Midland*, Vol. 19, No. 1, Autumn, 1938.

———, 'Scenes & Things in the West,' (signed 'W.M.A.'), *American Turf Register*, Vol. 8, No. 12, November, 1837.

———, 'Scenes in the West — The Platte & C.,' (signed 'W. Marshall'), *Ibid.*, Vol. 8, No. 10, July, 1837.

Atwood, Wallace W., *The Rocky Mountains*, New York, 1945.

Bancroft, Hubert Howe, *History of California*, San Francisco, 1886.

———, *History of Oregon*, San Francisco, 1886.

———, *History of the Pacific States of North America*, San Francisco, 1885.

———, *The Native Races*, San Francisco, 1886.

Beers, Henry Putney, 'The Army and the Oregon Trail to 1846,' *Pacific Northwest Quarterly*, Vol. 28, 1937.

Bennett, Emerson, *Leni–Leoti*, Cincinnati, 1849.

———, *The Prairie Flower*, Cincinnati, 1849.

Benton, Thomas Hart, *Thirty Years' View*, New York, 1856.

Bieber, Ralph P., editor, *Journal of a Santa Fe Trader*, Glendale, 1931.

Bonner, T. D., editor, *The Life and Adventures of James P. Beckwourth*, New York, 1856. Reprint edited by Bernard De Voto, New York, 1931.

Brackenridge, Henry Marie, *Views of Louisiana*, Pittsburgh, 1814.

Bradbury, John, *Travels in the Interior of America*, Liverpool, 1817. Second edition, London, 1819.

Bradley, James H., Journal, *Contributions to the Historical Society of Montana*, Vols. 2, 3, 8, 9.

Brinckman, Rowland, *Historical Record of the Eighty-Ninth Princess Victoria's Regiment*, Chatham, 1888.

Brosnan, Cornelius J., *Jason Lee, Prophet of the New Oregon*, New York, 1932.

*Bulletin of the American Art Union*, 1850.

Burlingame, Roger, *March of the Iron Men*, New York, 1938.

Bushnell, David I., Jr., 'John Mix Stanley, Artist-Explorer,' *Annual Report of the Smithsonian Institute*, 1924.

———, *Seth Eastman: The Master Painter of the North American Indian*, The Smithsonian Institution, Publication 3136, Washington, 1932. Also in *Smithsonian Miscellaneous Collections*, Vol. 87, No. 3, April 11, 1932.

Camp, Charles L., *James Clyman American Frontiersman 1792–1881*, San Francisco, 1928.

Carey, Charles H., editor, *The Journals of Theodore Talbot, 1843 and 1849–52*, Portland, 1931.

Carvalho, S. N., *Incidents of Travel and Adventure in the Far West*, New York, 1856.

Case, Robert and Victoria, *Last Mountains*, New York, 1945.

Catlin, George, *Letters and Notes on the Manners, Customs, and Condition of the North American Indians*, second edition, New York, 1842. The same as *North American Indians*, Philadelphia, 1913.

Chambers, J. S., *The Conquest of Cholera*, New York, 1938.

Chittenden, Hiram M., *The American Fur Trade of the Far West*, new edition, New York, 1935.

———, *The History of Early Steamboat Navigation on the Missouri River*, New York, 1903.

———, *Life, Letters and Travels of Father Pierre-Jean DeSmet, S.J.*, New York, 1905.

Clark, W. P., *The Indian Sign Language*, Philadelphia, 1885.

Clement, Clara Erskine, and Hutton, Laurence, *Artists of the Nineteenth Century and Their Works*, Boston, 1885.

Coues, Elliott, editor, *Audubon and His Journals* by Maria R. Audubon, New York, 1897.

———, *Forty Years a Fur Trader on the Upper Missouri*, New York, 1898.

———, *New Light on the Early History of the Greater Northwest*, New York, 1897.

Cox, Ross, *Adventures on the Columbia River*, London, 1831.

Cullom, George W., *Biographical Register of the Officers and Graduates of the U.S. Military Academy*, Cambridge, 1891.

Curtis, Edward S., *The North American Indian*, Vols. IV, V, Cambridge, 1909. Vol. VI, Norwood, Mass., 1911.

Dale, Harrison C., *The Ashley-Smith Explorations and the Discovery of a Central Route to the Pacific*, revised edition, Glendale, 1941.

*Debrett's Illustrated Baronetage*, 1868.

*Debrett's Illustrated Peerage*, 1868.

Decatur, Stephen, 'Alfred Jacob Miller: His Early Indian Scenes and Portraits,' *American Collector*, December, 1939.

DeLand, Charles E., 'The Aborigines of South Dakota, Part II, the Mandan Indians,' *South Dakota Historical Collections*, Vol. IV, 1908.

Dillen, John G. W., *The Kentucky Rifle*, Washington, 1924.

Dodge, Richard Irving, *The Plains of the Great West*, New York, 1877.

Dorsey, George A., *The Arapaho Sun Dance*, Field Columbian Museum, Publication 75, June, 1903.

Dorsey, James Owen, *A Study of Siouan Cults*, U.S. Bureau of American

Ethnology, Eleventh Annual Report, 1889–90, Washington, 1894.

*Dragoon Campaigns to the Rocky Mountains*, by a Dragoon, [James Hildreth], New York, 1836.

Drumm, Stella M., editor, *Journal of a Fur-Trading Expedition on the Upper Missouri 1812–1813* (Journal of John C. Luttig), St. Louis, 1920.

Drury, Clifford M., *Elkanah and Mary Walker*, Caldwell, Idaho, 1940.

————, *Francis Harmon Spalding*, Caldwell, Idaho, 1936.

————, 'Gray's Journal of 1838,' *Pacific Northwest Quarterly*, Vol. 29, 1938.

————, *Marcus Whitman, M.D.*, Caldwell, Idaho, 1937.

Dunbar, John, Letter in *Missionary Herald*, Vol. 34, 1838.

Dunbar, John B., 'The Pawnee Indians, Their Habits and Customs,' *Magazine of American History*, Vol. V, 1880.

————, 'The Pawnee Indians, Their History and Ethnology,' *Ibid.*, Vol. IV, 1880.

Eells, Myra F., Journal, *Transactions of the Oregon Pioneer Association*, 1889.

Eells, Rev. Myron, D.D., *Marcus Whitman: Pathfinder and Patriot*, Seattle, 1909.

Elliott, T. C., *The Coming of the White Women, 1836*, Portland, 1937.

————, editor, 'The Coming of the White Women, 1838,' *Oregon Historical Quarterly*, Vol. 38, 1837.

————, 'Religion Among the Flatheads,' *Ibid.*, Vol. 37, 1936.

Ellison, William Henry, editor, *The Life and Adventures of George Nidever*, Berkeley, 1937.

Emory, William Helmsley, *Notes of a Military Reconnaissance, from Fort Leavenworth, in Missouri, to San Diego, in California*, Washington, 1848. Also House Executive Document, No. 41, 30th Congress, 1st Session, 1848.

Farnham, Thomas Jefferson, *Travels in the Great Western Prairies*, Poughkeepsie, 1841.

Fletcher, Alice C., *Indian Ceremonies*, Salem, Mass., 1884.

Foreman, Grant, *Pioneer Days in the Early Southwest*, Cleveland, 1926.

Franchere, Gabriel, *Relation d'un voyage à la côte du nord-ouest de l'Amérique Septentrionale*, Montreal, 1820.

Frémont, John Charles, *A Report on an Exploration of the Country lying between the Missouri River and the Rocky Mountains, on the line of the Kansas and Great Platte Rivers*, Senate Document, No. 243, 27th Congress, 3rd Session, 1843.

————, *Report of the Exploring Expedition to the Rocky Mountains in the Year 1842, and to Oregon and North California in the Years 1843–44*, Washington, 1845.

Frost, Donald McKay, 'General Ashley and the Overland Trail,' *Proceedings of the American Antiquarian Society, 1944*, Worcester, 1945.

Fulton, Maurice Garland, *Diary and Letters of Josiah Gregg*, Norman, Okla., 1941.

Garrard, Lewis Hector, *Wah-To-Yah, and the Taos Trail*, New York, 1850. Reprint edited by Ralph B. Bieber, Glendale, 1938.

Gay, Theressa, *Life and Letters of Mrs. Jason Lee*, Portland, 1936.

Ghent, W. J., *The Road to Oregon*, New York, 1929.

Goddard, Pliny Earle, *Indians of the Northwest Coast*, second edition, New York, 1934.

Goodwin, Cardinal, *The Trans-Mississippi West*, New York, 1930.

Gray, William H., Journal from December, 1836 to October, 1837, *Whitman College Quarterly*, June, 1943.

Gregg, Josiah, *Commerce of the Prairies*, New York, 1844.

Grinnell, George Bird, *The Cheyenne Indians*, New Haven, 1923.

Hafen, LeRoy R., and Ghent, W. J., *Broken Hand*, Denver, 1931.

Haines, Francis, 'The Nez Perce Delegation to St. Louis in 1831,' *The Pacific Historical Review*, Vol. VI, 1937.

———, 'The Northward Spread of Horses Among the Plains Indians,' *American Anthropologist*, July-September, 1938.

———, *Red Eagles of the Northwest*, Portland, 1939.

———, 'Where Did the Plains Indians Get Their Horses?' *American Anthropologist*, January-March, 1938.

Hall, Courtney Robert, *A Scientist in the Early Republic: Samuel Latham Mitchill*, New York, 1934.

Hamilton, W. T., *My Sixty Years on the Plains*, New York, 1909.

Harmon, Daniel Williams, *A Journal of Voyages and Travels in the Interiour of North America*, Andover, 1820.

Hart, H. G., *The New Annual Army List for 1841*, London, 1841.

———, *The New Annual Army List for 1842*, London, 1842.

Haven, Charles T., and Belden, Frank A., *A History of the Colt Revolver*, New York, 1940.

Hebard, Grace Raymond, *Sacajawea*, Glendale, 1933.

Heilbron, Bertha L., editor, *With Pen and Pencil on the Frontier in 1851: The Diary and Sketches of Frank Blackwell Mayer*, The Minnesota Historical Society, St. Paul, 1932.

Herrick, Francis Hobart, *Audubon the Naturalist*, revised edition, New York, 1938.

Hewitt, J. N. B., editor, *Journal of Rudolph Friederich Kurz*, Bureau of American Ethnology, Bulletin 115, Washington, 1937.

Hicks, James, *Notes on United States Ordnance*, second edition, Mt. Vernon, N.Y., n.d.

*Historical Register and Dictionary of the U.S. Army, 1789–1903.*

Hodder, Frank H., *Audubon's Western Journal*, Cleveland, 1906.

Hodge, Frederick Webb, *Handbook of American Indians*, Bureau of American Ethnology, Bulletin 30, Washington, 1907.

———, 'The Origin and Destruction of a National Indian Portrait Gallery,' *Holmes Anniversary Volume*, Washington, 1916.

———, 'A Proposed Indian Portfolio by John Mix Stanley,' *Indian Notes* (Heye Foundation), Vol. VI, No. 4, 1929.

Hornaday, William T., 'The Extermination of the American Bison,' *Report of the United States National Museum, 1887.*

Howay, Frederick W., editor, *Voyages of the 'Columbia,'* Boston, 1941.

'Hugh Evans' Journal of a Dragoon Campaign of 1835,' *Mississippi Valley Historical Review*, Vol. 14, 1927–28.

Hunter. Thomas, *Woods, Forests and Estates of Perthshire*, Edinburgh, 1883.

Hyde, George E., *Red Cloud's Folk*, Norman, Okla., 1937.

Innis, H. A., *The Fur Trade in Canada*, New Haven, 1930.

————, *The Fur Trade of Canada*, Toronto, 1927.

Irving, Washington, *Astoria*, Philadelphia, 1836.

————, *The Rocky Mountains*, Philadelphia, 1837.

Jaeger, Ellsworth, *Wildwood Wisdom*, New York, 1945.

'John McLoughlin Letters, 1827–49,' *Oregon Historical Quarterly*, Vol. 37, 1936.

Johnson, C. T., 'Did Webster Ever Say This?' *Washington Historical Quarterly*, Vol. IV, 1913.

Johnson, Overton, and Winter, Wm. H., *Route Across the Rocky Mountains*, Lafayette, 1846.

*Journal of Colonel Dodge's Expedition from Fort Gibson to the Pawnee Pict Village*, Senate Executive Document, No. 1, 23rd Congress, 2nd Session, 1834.

*Journal of the Royal Geographical Society*, 1845, 1846, 1847, 1848, 1849.

Kane, Paul, *Wanderings of an Artist Among the Indians of North America*, London, 1859.

Kelly, Charles, and Howe, Maurice L., *Miles Goodyear*, Salt Lake City, 1937.

Kephart, Horace, *Camping and Woodcraft*, New York, 1921.

Kroeber, Alfred L., 'The Arapaho,' *Bulletin of the American Museum of Natural History*, Vol. XVIII, Parts I and II, New York, 1902.

————, 'Ethnology of the Gros Ventre,' *Anthropological Papers of the American Museum of Natural History*, Vol. I, Part IV, 1908.

Laut, Agnes C., *The Fur Trade of America*, New York, 1921.

Lee, Daniel, and Frost, Joseph H., *Ten Years in Oregon*, New York, 1844.

Lee, Rev. Jason, Diary of, *Oregon Historical Quarterly*, Vol. 17, 1916.

Leonard, Zenas, *Narrative of the Adventures of Zenas Leonard*, Clearfield, Pa., 1839.

Lewis, William S., 'Some notes . . . on the . . . name of Oregon. . . .,' *Washington Historical Quarterly*, Vol. XVII, 1926.

Libby, O. G., 'Typical Villages of the Mandans, Arikara and Hidatsa in the Missouri Valley, North Dakota,' *Collections of the State Historical Society of North Dakota*, Vol. II, 1908.

*A List of the Officers of the Army and Royal Marines on Full and Half Pay*, London, 1819.

*A List of the Officers of the Army and Royal Marines on Full, Retired, and Half Pay*, London, 1832, 1838, 1840.

Lowie, Robert H., 'The Assiniboin,' *Anthropological Papers of the American Museum of Natural History*, Vol. IV, Part I, 1909.

———, 'Crow Indian Art,' *Ibid.*, Vol. XXI, Part IV, 1922.

———, *The Crow Indians*, New York, 1935.

———, 'Dances and Societies of the Plains Shoshone,' *Anthropological Papers of the American Museum of Natural History*, Vol. XI, Part X, 1915.

———, 'The Material Culture of the Crow Indians,' *Ibid.*, Vol. XXI, Part III, 1922.

———, 'Minor Ceremonies of the Crow Indians,' *Ibid.*, Vol. XXI, Part V, 1924.

———, 'Myths and Traditions of the Crow Indians,' *Ibid.*, Vol. XXV, Part I, 1918.

———, 'Notes on the Social Organization and Customs of the Mandan, Hidatsa, and Crow Indians,' *Ibid.*, Vol. XXI, Part I, 1917.

———, 'The Northern Shoshone,' *Ibid.*, Vol. II, Part II, 1909.

———, 'Plains Indian Age-Societies: Historical and Comparative Summary,' *Ibid.*, Vol. XI, Part XIII, 1916.

———, 'The Religion of the Crow Indians,' *Ibid.*, Vol. XXV, Part II, 1922.

———, 'Social Life of the Crow Indians,' *Ibid.*, Vol. IX, Part II, 1912.

———, 'Societies of the Crow, Hidatsa and Mandan Indians,' *Ibid.*, Vol. XI, Part III, 1913.

Maloney, Alice Bay, editor, *Fur Brigade to the Bonaventura* (John Work's California Journal, 1832–1833), San Francisco, 1945.

Mandelbaum, David G., 'The Plains Cree,' *Anthropological Papers of the American Museum of Natural History*, Vol. XXXVIII, Part II, 1940.

Marcy, Randolph Barnes, *The Prairie Traveller*, New York, 1849. Second edition, edited with notes by Richard F. Burton, London, 1863.

Maximilian, Prinz zu Wied, *Reise in das innere Nord-Amerika in den Jahren 1832 bis 1834*, Coblenz, 1839. Translated as *Travels in the Interior of North America*, Reuben Gold Thwaites, editor, Cleveland, 1905.

McCoy, Isaac, *History of Baptist Indian Missions*, Washington, 1840.

McDermott, John Francis, editor, *The Western Journals of Washington Irving*, Norman, Okla., 1944.

McKenney, Thomas H., and Hall, James, *The Indian Tribes of North America*, Folio: Philadelphia, 1836–1844. Octavo: Philadelphia, 1842–1844. Reprint, F. W. Hodge, editor, Edinburgh, 1933.

Merk, Frederick, *Fur Trade and Empire* (George Simpson's Journal), Cambridge, 1931.

*Mission Record Book of the Methodist Episcopal Church, Willamette Station.*

*The Missionary Herald*, 1837 and 1838.

Mooney, James, and Olbrechts, Frans M., *Cherokee Sacred Formulas and Medicinal Prescriptions*, Bureau of American Ethnology, Bulletin 99, 1932.

Moreland, J. C., 'Address,' *Transactions of the Oregon Pioneer Association*, 1899.

Morison, Samuel E., *The Maritime History of Massachusetts*, Boston, 1921.

———, 'New England and the Opening of the Columbia River Salmon Trade, 1830,' *Oregon Historical Quarterly*, Vol. 28, 1927.

———, 'Nova Albion and New England,' *Ibid.*, Vol. 28, 1927.

Morris, Ralph C., 'The Notion of a Great American Desert East of the Rockies,' *Mississippi Valley Historical Review*, Vol. XIII, 1926–27.

Murray, Charles Augustus, *The Prairie Bird*, London, 1844.

———, *Travels in North America*, London, 1839.

Nininger, H. H., *Our Stone-Pelted Planet*, Cambridge, 1933.

Nute, Grace Lee, 'The Diary of Martin McLeod,' *Minnesota History Bulletin*, Vol. IV, 1922.

———, 'James Dickson, A Filibuster in Minnesota in 1836,' *Mississippi Valley Historical Review*, Vol. X, 1923.

———, 'James McLoughlin, Jr., and the Dickson Filibuster,' *Minnesota History*, Vol. 17, 1936.

———, *The Voyageur*, New York, 1931.

*Official report of expedition of squadron of Dragoons under command of Col. Henry Dodge*, House Document, No. 181, 24th Congress, 1st Session, 1836.

Ogden, Adele, *The California Sea Otter*, 1784–1848, Berkeley, 1941.

Paden, Irene D., *The Wake of the Prairie Schooner*, New York, 1943.

Parker, Samuel, *Journal of an Exploring Tour Beyond the Rocky Mountains*, Ithaca, 1838.

Parkman, Francis, Jr., *California and Oregon Trail*, New York, 1849. Also Centenary Edition, Boston, 1937, and an edition edited by Mason Wade, New York, 1943.

Parrish, Philip H., *Before the Covered Wagon*, fourth edition, Portland, 1931.

Pattie, James Ohio, *The Personal Narrative of James O. Pattie*, Cincinnati, 1831.

Pelzer, Louis, editor, 'Captain Ford's Journal of an Expedition to the Rocky Mountains,' *Mississippi Valley Historical Review*, Vol. 12, 1926.

———, *The Prairie Logbooks*, Chicago, 1943.

Pike, Albert, 'Narrative of a Journey in the Prairie,' *Publications of the Arkansas Historical Association*, Vol. IV, 1917.

———, *Prose Sketches and Poems written in the Western Country*, Boston, 1834.

'Portraits of North American Indians with Sketches of Scenery, etc. Painted by J. M. Stanley,' *Smithsonian Miscellaneous Collections*, Volume II, Washington, 1852.

Powell, Fred Wilbur, *Hall Jackson Kelley, Prophet of Oregon*, Portland, 1917.

Powers, Kate Ball; Hopkins, Flora Ball; Ball, Lucy, compilers, *Autobiography of John Ball*, Grand Rapids, 1925.

Rasmussen, Louise, 'Artists of the Explorations Overland, 1840–1860,' *Oregon Historical Quarterly*, Vol. XLIII, 1942.

*Report from the Office of Indian Affairs*, Senate Executive Document No. 1, 23rd Congress, 1st Session, 1833; Senate Executive Document No. 1, 23rd Congress, 2nd Session, 1834.

*Report of Joshua Pilcher, Agent for the Upper Missouri River*, Senate, Executive Document No. 1, 25th Congress, 3rd Session, 1838.

*Report of the Commissioner of Indian Affairs*, Senate Executive Document No. 1, 24th Congress, 1st Session, 1835; Senate Executive Document No. 1, 24th Congress, 2nd Session, 1836; Senate Executive Document No. 1, 25th Congress, 2nd Session, 1837; Senate Executive Document No. 1, 25th Congress, 3rd Session, 1838.

'Report on the Expedition of Dragoons under Colonel Henry Dodge, To the Rocky Mountains in 1835,' *American State Papers*, Military Affairs, Vol. VI, No. 624, 24th Congress, 1st Session, 1835.

*Report of the Secretary of War*, Senate Executive Document No. 1, 25th Congress, 3rd Session, 1838.

*Reports of Explorations and Surveys to ascertain the most Practicable and Economical Route for a Railroad from the Mississippi River to the Pacific Ocean*, Washington, 1855.

Roberts, Ned H., *The Muzzle-Loading Cap Lock Rifle*, second edition, Manchester, N.H., 1944.

Robertson, Doane, 'A Comprehensive History of the Dakota or Sioux Indians,' *South Dakota Historical Collections*, Vol. II, 1904.

Rollins, Philip Ashton, *The Discovery of the Oregon Trail*, New York, 1935.

Russell, Osborne, *Journal of a Trapper*, Boise, 1921.

Ruxton, George Frederick, *Adventures in Mexico and the Rocky Mountains*, London, 1847.

———, *Life in the Far West*, London, 1849.

———, 'Life in the Far West,' *Blackwood's Magazine*, June-November, 1848.

Sabin, Edwin L., *Kit Carson Days*, revised edition, New York, 1935.

Sage, Rufus B., *Scenes in the Rocky Mountains*, Philadelphia, 1846.

Sawyer, Charles Winthrop, *Our Rifles*, Boston, 1944.

Schoolcraft, Henry, *Information Reflecting the History, Condition, and Prospects of the Indian Tribes of the United States*, Philadelphia, 1847.

Scott, Leslie M., 'Indian Diseases as an Aid to Pacific Northwest Settlement,' *Oregon Historical Quarterly*, Vol. 29, 1928.

Sharpe, Philip B., *The Rifle in America*, New York, 1938.

Shortess, Robert, 'First Emigrants to Oregon,' *Transactions of the Oregon Pioneer Association*, 1896.

Skinner, Constance Lindsay, *Beaver Kings and Cabins*, New York, 1933.

Smith, Arthur D. Howden, *John Jacob Astor*, Philadelphia, 1929.

Smith, Henry Nash, *American Emotional and Imaginative Attitudes toward the Great Plains and the Rocky Mountains, 1803–1850*, Ph.D. thesis, Harvard College Library, 1940.

Smith, Winston O., *The Sharps Rifle*, New York, 1943.

Spier, Leslie, 'The Sun Dance of the Plains Indians: Its Development and Diffusion,' *Anthropological Papers of the American Museum of Natural History*, Vol. XVI, Part VII, 1921.

Stansbury, Howard, *An Expedition to the Valley of the Great Salt Lake of Utah*, Philadelphia, 1852. Also Senate Executive Document No. 2, 32nd Congress, Special Session and Executive Document No. 3, 1853.

Stewart, Sir William Drummond, *Altowan*, New York, 1846.

———, *Edward Warren*, London, 1854.

Teit, James A., *The Salishan Tribes of the Western Plateaus*, Forty-fifth Annual Report of the Bureau of American Ethnology, 1930.

Townsend, John Kirk, *Narrative of a Journey across the Rocky Mountains*, Philadelphia, 1839.

Tuckerman, Henry Theodore, *Book of the Artists*, New York, 1867.

Vestal, Stanley, *Kit Carson*, Boston, 1928.

———, *Mountain Men*, Boston, 1937.

Victor, Frances Fuller, *The River of the West*, Hartford, 1871.

Walford, Edward, *County Families of the United Kingdom*, third edition, London, 1865

Warre, Henry James, *Sketches of North America and the Oregon Territory*, London, 1848.

Warren, Eliza Spalding, *Memoirs of the West* (Journal of Eliza Spalding), Portland, n.d.

Webb, Walter Prescott, *The Great Plains*, Boston, 1931.

Webber, C. W., *The Hunter-Naturalist*, Philadelphia, 1851.

———, *Wild Scenes and Songbirds*, New York, 1854.

Wedel, Waldo Rudolph, *An Introduction to Pawnee Archeology*, Bureau of American Ethnology, Bulletin 112, 1936.

Weitenkampf, F., *American Graphic Art*, New York, 1924.

Wheat, Carl I., editor, *The Shirley Letters*, San Francisco, 1933.

Wheeler, Olin D., *The Trail of Lewis and Clark*, New York, 1904.

Whelen, Townsend, *The American Rifle*, New York, 1918.

Whitman, Narcissa, Journal, *Transactions of the Oregon Pioneer Association*, 1890.

———, Letters, *Ibid.*, 1893.

Wilson, Gilbert L., 'Hidatsa Eagle Trapping,' *Anthropological Papers of the American Museum of Natural History*, Vol. XXXIII, Part IV, 1928.

———, 'The Horse and the Dog in Hidatsa Culture,' *Ibid.*, Vol. XV, Part II, 1924.

———, and Weitzner, Bella, 'The Hidatsa Earthlodge,' *Ibid.*, Vol. XXXIII, Part V, 1934.

Wislizenus, Frederick Adolphus, *Ein Ausflug nach den Felsen-Gebirgen im Jahre 1839*, St. Louis, 1840. English translation, St. Louis, 1912.

Wissler, Clark, *The American Indian*, second edition, 1931.

———, 'Ceremonial Bundles of the Blackfoot Indians,' *Anthropological Papers of the American Museum of Natural History*, Vol. VII, Part II, 1912.

———, 'Costumes of the Plains Indians,' *Ibid.*, Vol. XVII, Part II, 1915.

———, 'General Discussion of the Shamanistic and Dancing Societies,' *Ibid.*, Vol. XI, Part XII, 1916.

———, *Indian Beadwork*, New York, 1931.

———, *The Indians of the United States*, New York, 1940.

———, 'Material Culture of the Blackfoot Indians,' *Anthropological Papers of the American Museum of Natural History*, Vol. V, Part I, 1910.

———, *The Relation of Nature to Man in Aboriginal America*, New York, 1926.

———, 'Riding Gear of the North American Indians,' *Anthropological Papers of the American Museum of Natural History*, Vol. XVII, Part I, 1915.

———, 'The Social Life of the Blackfoot Indian,' *Ibid.*, Vol. VII, Part I, 1911.

———, 'Societies and Ceremonial Associations in the Oglala Division of the Teton-Dakota,' *Ibid.*, Vol. XI, Part I, 1912.

———, 'The Sun Dance of the Blackfoot Indians,' *Ibid.*, Vol. XVI, Part III, 1918.

———, and Duvall, D. C., 'Mythology of the Blackfoot Indians,' *Ibid.*, Vol. II, Part I, 1908.

Wolverton, Charles E., 'Address,' *Transactions of the Oregon Pioneer Association*, 1899.

Wraxall, Sir C. F. Lacelles, *The Backwoodsman*, Boston, 1866.

Wyeth, John B., *Oregon*, Cambridge, 1833.

Wyeth, N. J., 'The Indian Tribes of the South Pass of the Rocky Mountains; the Salt Lake Basin; the Valley of the Great Saaptin; or Lewis' River, and the Pacific Coasts of Oregon,' *History of the Indian Tribes of the United States*, Vol. I, by Henry Schoolcraft, Philadelphia, 1857.

Wylly, H. C., *XVth (The King's) Hussars, 1759 to 1913*, London, 1914.

Yanovsky, Elias, *Food Plants of the North American Indians*, Department of Agriculture Miscellaneous Publication No. 237, Washington, 1936.

Young, F. G., editor, 'The Correspondence and Journals of Captain Nathaniel J. Wyeth,' *Sources of the History of Oregon*, Vol. I, Eugene, 1899.

———, 'Journal and Report by Doctor Marcus Whitman,' *Oregon Historical Quarterly*, Vol. 27, 1926.

Young, Stanley P., and Goldman, Edward A., *The Wolves of North America*, Washington, 1944.

Zollinger, James Peter, *Sutter, The Man and His Empire*, New York, 1939.